JERUSALEM AND ATHENS

The critical essays in this book are dedicated to Cornelius Van Til on the occasion of his 75th birthday and 40th anniversary as professor of apologetics at Westminster Theological Seminary, in recognition of his tireless efforts in the statement and defense of the Christian faith.

As author of such books as *The New Modernism, The Defense of the Faith, Christianity and Barthianism,* and *A Christian Theory of Knowledge,* his influence has been both strategic and controversial. The extensive impact of this original and penetrating Christian apologist has been aided by the private distribution of numerous "unpublished" class syllabi. His lectures, whether given in Roman Catholic, Jewish, fundamental, liberal, or Calvinistic institutions are equally challenging and demanding. Yet for all this prodigious activity, the influence of Cornelius Van Til has been spread mostly by his students with whom in the course of his forty years at Westminster he shared his convictions and concerns.

Van Til is not only a philosopher and theologian. A born teacher, he is an outstanding and persuasive lecturer and preacher, possessing, in his lecturing, the gift of simplicity. A warm-hearted and humble man, he draws love and loyalty to himself and gives it with equal readiness.

Cornelius Van Til was Born into a large family on May 3, 1895, in The Netherlands. His family migrated to the United States in 1905, when he was ten years old, settling in Indiana. They farmed near the borderline of Indiana and Illinois, close to Chicago, at Highland.

The family faith was Reformed, and church membership Christian Reformed. Van Til's great love and abiding interest in Kuyper and his works are a notable aspect of the man and date back to his youth. Dr. Van Til is a graduate of Calvin College (A.B.), of Princeton Theological Seminary (Th.M.), and Princeton University (Ph.D.). In 1925 while still a student he married a long-time home-town friend, Miss Rena Klooster.

After a year in the pastorate he spent one year (1928-1929) as Instructor of Apologetics at Princeton Theological Seminary. After the reorganization of that institution he was asked to remain by the new Board of Control but chose rather to accept the position of Professor of Apologetics in the newly formed Westminster Theological Seminary. He continues to hold this position to the present time.

This symposium is composed of essays which deal, more or less directly, with the problems and issues raised and discussed in the apologetics of Cornelius Van Til. A basic, non-philosophical introduction to his own thought is embodied in a preliminary essay from his own pen, entitled "My Credo." The impact of the book is sharpened by Van Til's response to those essays which he felt necessitated a reply.

E. R. Geehan, editor of this volume, is a graduate of the University of Illinois (B.A.), and Westminster Theological Seminary (B.D.). He is presently a Ph.D. candidate at the University of Utrecht, The Netherlands.

Jerusalem and Athens

**Critical Discussions on the Theology and Apologetics of
CORNELIUS VAN TIL**

CORNELIUS VAN TIL

Jerusalem and Athens

Critical Discussions on the Theology and Apologetics of
CORNELIUS VAN TIL

Edited by

E. R. GEEHAN

PRESBYTERIAN AND REFORMED PUBLISHING CO.
Phillipsburg, New Jersey
1980

Distributed by
Westminster Discount Book Service
P.O. Box 125-H
Scarsdale, New York 10583

Photolithoprinted in Korea

CONTENTS

CONTENTS

What indeed has Athens to do with Jerusalem? What concord is there between the Academy and the Church? What between heretics and Christians? Our instructions come from "the porch of Solomon," who had himself taught that "the Lord should be sought in simplicity of heart." Away with all attempts to produce a mottled Christianity of Stoic, Platonic, and dialectic composition! We want no curious disputation after possessing Christ Jesus, no inquisition after enjoying the gospel! With our faith, we desire no further belief. For this is our palmary faith, that there is nothing which we ought to believe besides.

—Tertullian, *The Prescription*
Against Heretics, VII

DEDICATION

These critical essays are dedicated to Cornelius Van Til on the occasions of his 75th birthday and 40th anniversary as professor of apologetics at Westminster Theological Seminary, in recognition of his tireless effort in the statement and defense of the Christian Faith. As the author of *Common Grace, The New Modernism, The Defense of the Faith, Christianity and Barthianism,* and *A Christian Theory of Knowledge,* his influence has been both strategic and controversial. The extensive impact of this original and penetrating Christian apologist has been aided by the private circulation of such "unpublished" class syllabi as *Apologetics, Christian Theistic Ethics, Christian Theistic Evidences, New Evangelicalism,* and *Christianity in Conflict* (3 vols.) which have found their way far outside the confines of the classes for which they were written.

Prof. Van Til's writings, with their depth and logical rigor as well as prophetic urgency, have not won him many allies. In this ecumenical age he is disturbingly but intentionally out of place. To maintain that the Christian must continue, and that the non-Christian must begin, to bring every thought into obedience to the biblical Christ is, in this pluralistic age, *déclassé.* His warnings against the church's parasitic existence on the wisdom of the world divide his readers into equally adamant friends and foes. His writings drive "hard bargains" in the day of the "wheeler-dealer" and the precedence of a pragmatic theory of action over any and all theories of truth.

Dr. Van Til's lectures, whether given in Roman Catholic, Jewish, fundamentalist, liberal, or Calvinist institutions, are equally demanding. Concern for the souls of men, the life of the church, and the glory of God comes across with a passion and love not so evident on the printed page. His disarming personal warmth and humble manner, his pre-eminent devotion to Christ and his church, and his clear and homespun exposition have afforded him favorable reception among the many who would not have been reached with the complex and philosophically oriented arguments of his books and syllabi.

Yet for all this prodigious activity, the influence of Cornelius Van Til has been spread mostly by his students. In his 40 years at Westminster Theological Seminary he has shared his convictions and concerns with thousands of students from dozens of denominations from around the world. It is these men who now write and preach, not as disciples of Van Til, but as those men who, with his help, have seen the necessity of a Christian life and world view. They have learned from him that a full-fledged Christian perspective, whether in culture, in the sciences, in politics, or in business, is not something which now exists, but is a goal always to be pursued. Along with Herman Dooyeweerd in the Netherlands and H. G. Stoker in South Africa, Cornelius Van Til has worked to establish the foundations of a Christian world and life view in the United States. A *Festschrift* to Dooyeweerd has appeared in Europe; one is shortly to appear in Africa to Stoker. This "American version" is now published as a tribute to Cornelius Van Til with the prayer that it too will be a significant step toward the goal which he so earnestly has sought: a consistently Christian apologetic.

E.R.G.

E. R. Geehan

INTRODUCTION

This symposium is composed of essays which deal, more or less directly, with the problems and issues raised and discussed in the apologetics of Cornelius Van Til. Nevertheless, it is precisely these issues—the authority of the Scriptures, the noetic effects of the Fall, the existence of "common ground" between believer and unbeliever—which have been at the forefront of theological discussion in the twentieth century, especially in evangelical circles. The essays contained herein are, in this regard, significant continuations of these discussions and therefore become of interest to all concerned with such problems and not only to those who seek to honor Cornelius Van Til in this way.

In order to increase the usefulness of this symposium within this wider context of interest, especially for those either new to the issues themselves or unfamiliar with the work of Prof. Van Til, three alterations have been introduced into this work which thereby distinguish it from its European counterpart, the *Festschrift*. First, Dr. Van Til was prevailed upon to write a basic, non-philosophical introduction to his own thought. This is found in the first essay, "My Credo." Second, he was asked to respond to each essay which he felt necessitated, in some way, a reply. Third, it was decided to provide this introduction to the work as a whole, thereby providing the reader with a "road map" to the logical structure of the book.

* * * * *

In Parts I and II are essays which serve to acquaint the reader with the position of Cornelius Van Til, giving him a fairly secure "point of reference" from which to evaluate the discussions in Parts III and IV. Nevertheless, Part II takes the reader into the complex philosophical structure of Van Til's thought and therefore should be read *last* by those who are new to the field of theoretical apologetics. They will profit most greatly by reading Parts I, III, IV, and II in that order.

In Part I, "My Credo," Prof. Van Till sets himself to explaining in non-philosophical terms precisely what he proposes as a consistently Christian apologetic. He especially wants to show that the Christian's commitment to the "self-attesting Christ of Scripture" implies a theological and apologetic method which *excludes* the use of inter-subjective criteria or methods common to both Christians and non-Christians either to settle religious disputes or to answer religious questions.

Part II, "Letters from Three Continents," is composed of the two major essays by Hendrik G. Stoker and Herman Dooyeweerd and the responses by Dr. Van Til. Stoker, in his "Reconnoitering the Theory of Knowledge of Prof. Dr. Cornelius Van Til," develops *philosophically* the point of view expressed in Van Till's "Credo." He compares Van Til's Calvinistic epistemology to that of Dooyeweerd (whose *A New Critique of Theoretical Thought* is itself an attempt at developing such a Calvinistic life and world view) and finds in Van Til's theory of knowledge a more profound and biblical understanding of the *condition humaine*. Herman Dooyeweerd, "Cornelius Van Til and the Transcendental Critique of Theoretical Thought," responds to Van Til's criticism of his "transcendental" method. He maintains that Van Til misunderstands him and does so because of vestiges of scholastic and rationalistic elements in his thinking.

In Prof. Van Til's responses he finds basic agreement with Stoker's interpretation of his thought, while he spends considerable effort in a detailed critique of Dooyeweerd's "transcendental" method, finding in it a pervasive inconsistency and a virtual denial of Reformed theology In so doing Van Til clarifies his own position, differentiating it from the Dutch school of Calvinistic philosophy.

*   *   *   *   *

Parts III and IV are concerned, respectively, with what might be called the "theologic question" (What do I believe?) and the "apologetic question" (Why ought I to believe what you believe?). The theological question, "What do I believe?," is not only of interest to theologians. While theologians *answer* the question, apologists concern themselves with (a) the meaning of the question; (b) devising an acceptable method to use as a tool in answering the question, and (c) drawing out the implications of such beliefs for the construction of an acceptable method of defending them.

Part III, "Essays in Theology and Theological Method," approaches the "theological question" from the perspective of the apologist. The first five essays deal with the implications of the Christian's faith for apologetics.

Philip Edgcumbe Hughes begins by affirming that a Christian apologetic must "be founded on the testimony of Scripture to the nature of reality in its divine, its human, and its cosmic aspects." He then undertakes a survey of scriptural teaching in these areas.

J. I. Packer attempts to show "the link" between the Christian's belief in biblical authority on the one hand and his theological and apologetic method on the other. In addition he asks whether biblical authority can be maintained without a corresponding doctrine of biblical inerrancy.

Jack B. Rogers asks whether the current orthodox understanding of biblical authority, as derived uncritically from B. B. Warfield, is not a severe departure from the intent of the Westminster divines whom Warfield claimed to follow. Is not Van Til especially tempted to defend a scientific view of the origin and content of Scripture when such was never intended by the Westminster Confession?

C. Trimp, noting the fondness of such theologians as Berkouwer, Kähler, and Barth for the term "witness," inquires into its biblical meaning. He concludes that it is primarily used to refer to God's testimony on behalf of his Son, the aim of such testimony being the closing of the knowledge-gap between God and man.

John A. Witmer picks up a theme of Trimp regarding Christ's own self-witness and asks whether such theologies as those of J. A. T. Robinson, D. M. Baillie, R. Bultmann, and O. Dibelius can be called "Christian" when they include the rejection of Jesus' own self-consciousness and therewith his self-identification.

The next four essays in Part III deal with questions of theological method.

G. C. Berkouwer questions in his essay whether one may ever *assume* the correctness of the confessions of his church. He argues strongly for the primacy of exegesis over all man-made theological structures.

S. U. Zuidema finds in Rudolph Bultmann's theology a hermeneutic which rests on the existential philosophy of Martin Heidegger. Such a hermeneutic leads to a theology in which the traditional "theological question," "What do you believe?," is rejected in favor of the existential-theological question, "Whom do you believe in?" In this manner existential theology empties Christianity of all knowledge-content and reduces it to an ineffable encounter between the unknowable God and man. Zuidema argues that such a view actually hinders rather than promotes "the existential encounter between God's kerygmatic revelation and the existential man and his *Gottesfrage.*"

Paul K. Jewett, in a critical review of Van Til's *Christ and the Jews*, a monograph on the philosophically informed hermeneutics of Philo Judaeus, the Pharisees, and Martin Buber, poses several questions to Van Til regarding anti-Semetism, revelation, and history, maintaining that if Van Til had dealt with them in that monograph, the value of the work would have been greatly increased.

Richard B. Gaffin, Jr., studies the debate between G. Vos and A. Kuyper over the "theological" character of the writings of the apostle Paul. He comes down heavily on the side of Vos, maintaining that Paul was indeed a theologian. He then attempts to draw implications from this for theological method.

The final two essays in this third section are by *Herman Ridderbos* and *William Lane*. Both attempt, in different ways, to handle historical problems: Ridderbos, the synoptic problem; Lane, the speeches of Paul recorded in the Book of Acts. They undertake this effort in such a way as to spell out at what points the Christian belief in biblical authority has implications for such historical studies.

Part IV, "Essays in Philosophy and Apologetics," contains papers on the "apologetic question," "Why ought I to believe what you believe?"

Traditionally, the question has been regarded as legitimate and answerable. From Justin Martyr to Thomas Aquinas to Bishop Butler, attempts have been made to satisfy the non-Christian's request for reasons, acceptable to him on his grounds, which indicate both the reasonableness and validity of the Christian's knowledge claims. Apologists who use this method in defending the Christian faith maintain that there are inter-subjectively ascertainable rational (logical and evidential) grounds which demonstrate, either conclusively or very probably, the truth of the Christian's assertions.

There have been some, however, who have challenged the propriety of the "apologetic question." They observe that the question itself assumes the existence of "common notions" in terms of which religious issues can be resolved. They maintain that there are no such "common notions." All such epistemological methods and criteria of truth, they say, only function as tools in the service of the religious presuppositions of the user. Therefore, there can be no such methods as can be used "neutrally" with respect to religion. In view of this, the only form of "argument" possible is "argument by presupposition." The Christian presents his faith as a totally coherent, world and life view which is identified and authenticated by God and God alone. Cornelius Van Til is generally regarded as the "father of presuppositionalism" in the United States.

The first five essays in Part IV deal with the implications of the presuppositionalist position for philosophy.

Robert D. Knudsen, Prof. Van Til's associate at Westminster Seminary, provides a clear introduction to the whole subject of evangelical apologetics, showing the inter-relations between various schools of thought. He then closes by suggesting that Van Til's method itself suffers from several internal difficulties as well as clear incompatibilities with the Christian philosophy which has been developed by Herman Dooyeweerd.

J. P. A. Mekkes in a study of "knowing" maintains that in so far as the Christian world view is a total conception it involves a reconstruction, along biblical lines, of the whole idea of "knowing" which, he says, is completely dominated by Western philosophical constructions wholly foreign to Christian faith.

Gilbert B. Weaver compares Van Til's view of analogy with that of Thomas Aquinas, seeking to find out whether Gordon Clark's charge that they are the same is well founded.

C. Gregg Singer finds in Van Til's philosophy of history a re-statement of some of the basic themes of Augustine. He notes that Van Til draws conclusions consistent with presuppositionalism when he rejects all attempts at reading the "meaning" of history from history itself, but rather finds the interpretation of history given to us only in special revelation.

Rousas John Rushdoony analyzes the one - many problem of classical philosophy and says that only in Van Til's working out of this problem in terms of the many-in-one of the Trinity does one find an answer to it.

The final seven essays of the symposium deal with problems associated with the debate between those who adhere to the traditional method of apologetics and the presuppositionalists. The first four are in pairs: Lewis and Horne; Montgomery and Reid.

Gordon H. Lewis defends the traditional approach as it is found in the writings of Edward John Carnell. He finds a fundamental agreement between Van Til and Carnell in that both affirm, he says, a "logical starting point" common to Christians and non-Christians. Both also deny, he continues, the existence of any theoretically "metaphysical" common ground. He accuses Van Til, however, of

begging the "apologetic question" when he assumes that the Bible is
self-authenticating.

Charles M. Horne, contrasting Van Til and Carnell, says that Van
Til's apologetic method assumes that all men have everything in
common metaphysically and nothing in common conceptually. He
concludes that Carnell and Van Til hold radically different positions.
He ends his paper with a chart of the various apologetic-theological
positions.

John Warwick Montgomery argues that if the traditional approach
is rejected because of lack of common ground, then all argument for
Christian faith ceases. He proposes that all men will accept the
weight of historical evidence, for "all men can compare alternative
interpretations of fact and determine on the basis of the facts themselves which interpretation best fits reality."

W. Stanford Reid asks whether Montgomery's "probabilitistic
objectivism" is tenable. He argues that Montgomery's optimistic view
of man in religious matters is unscriptural and that Montgomery
cannot really account theoretically for the biblical emphasis on the
necessity of the work of the Holy Spirit.

The fifth essay, by *Clark H. Pinnock*, is an attempt to show that
in rejecting the "apologetic question" Van Til commits himself to a
"curious epistemology derived from a modern Calvinistic school in
Holland" which has led him "to align his orthodoxy with a form of
irrational fideism." He proposes, in opposition, an "inductive method
applied to the cosmic and historical stuff of revelation."

The sixth and seventh papers seek for a further understanding of
Van Til's position.

Arthur F. Holmes wants to find out whether he and Van Til have
basic agreements or disagreements. He accomplishes this by asking
Van Til if he will follow him as he attempts to deal with such modern
problems as "subjectivity," "informal logic," and the "meaning of
religious discourse."

Frederic R. Howe questions whether Van Til has not made an
exegetical and systematic mistake in correlating "witnessing for"
and "defending" one's faith. Looking at Van Til's essay, "Mr. Black,
Mr. White, Mr. Grey," he says that at numerous points *kerygma* is
viewed as inseparable from *didache*.

*   *   *   *   *

The reader must now go to the essays themselves and apply himself to the issues involved. Many will want to pursue the issues

further in works outside this volume. In this connection the very thorough bibliography of the works of Prof. Van Til which appears at the end of the volume will be helpful. I wish to thank Arthur Kuschke, the librarian of Westminster Theological Seminary, and his staff for preparing it.

E.R.G.

PART ONE

MY CREDO

By

CORNELIUS VAN TIL

Cornelius Van Til

MY CREDO

How can I express my appreciation adequately for the honor you have conferred on me by your contributions to this *Festschrift?*
   I shall try to do so first by setting forth in this, my "Credo," a general statement of my main beliefs as I hold them today. Then I shall deal separately with the problems and objections some of you have raised in respect to my views in separate response to the essays themselves. I hope that by doing this we may be of help to one another as together we present the name of Jesus as the only name given under heaven by which men must be saved.

I.   The Self-Attesting Christ of Scripture

The self-attesting Christ of Scripture has always been my starting-point for everything I have said. What this implies for various problems will appear more clearly, I hope, as I go along. Allow me in this section to illustrate what I mean by recalling the incident of Jesus' healing of the man who had the palsy. When Jesus said to this man, "Son, thy sins be forgiven thee," certain of the scribes reasoned in their hearts, "Why does this man thus speak blasphemies? Who can forgive sins but God only?" (Mark 2:5, 6). Over and over "the Jews" charged Jesus with blasphemy. For it they nailed him to the cross.
   These "Jews," call them "Pharisees," were very "orthodox." They swore by Moses and the prophets. Abraham was their father, and the God of Abraham was their God. "We thank thee, God, that we are not polytheists as other nations are." There is and there can be only one God. "Hear; O Israel; the Lord our God is one Lord" (Deut. 6:4).
   When Jesus, therefore, claimed to be one with the Father they were certain that he blasphemed. What an outrage for Jesus, a mere man, to claim that he was the Son of God. Away with him from the face of the earth!
   What zeal this was for the one God, the only true God, the God of Moses! Of course, they did not like to put any man to the torture

of crucifixion. But the God of Moses wills it; we must save the people from their sentimental love for this man. Soon it appeared that they had indeed "saved" the people. "Then cried they all again, saying, Not this man, but Barabbas. Now Barabbas was a robber" (John 18:40).

The irony of it all—the leaders of the Jews did not love and serve the God of Abraham at all! Like the nations about them, and especially the Greeks, they had become worshipers of the creature rather than the Creator! They made their own apostate moral consciousness the standard of right and wrong. With their notion of a "living Torah" they were able, so they thought, to do justice to the changelessness of the law and, at the same time, to live according to the principles of the "new morality."

It is in the face of this Pharisaic opposition that Jesus' assertion of his identity as Son of God and Son of man stands out in its significance. Every fact in dispute between the Pharisees and Jesus involved the ultimate claim that Jesus was the Son of God, and, as such, the promised Messiah. Jesus told the Pharisees, in effect, that they had twisted beyond recognition the meaning of every word of the Old Testament.

It was natural, therefore, that they should think of Jesus as a blasphemer. Not that the idea of blasphemy could have any meaning on their view of things. If Jesus' claim to be the promised Messiah, the Son of God, were true, then they, the Pharisees, were reactionaries, revolutionaries, apostates. They were intellectually, morally, and spiritually wrong in everything they said and did. Could they admit that Jesus was right when he said that they were of their father the devil? Could Jesus be right when he said that though they were lineal descendants of Abraham yet, spiritually, Abraham was not their father at all? Could Jesus be right when he said: "But I know you, that ye have not the love of God in you" (John 15:42)?

As Christians we are not, of ourselves, better or wiser than were the Pharisees. Christ has, by his word and by his Spirit, identified himself with us and thereby, at the same time, told us who and what we are. As a Christian I believe first of all in the testimony that Jesus gives of himself and his work. He says he was sent into the world to save his people from their sins. Jesus asks me to do what he asked the Pharisees to do, namely, read the Scriptures in light of this testimony about himself. He has sent his Spirit to dwell in my heart so that I might believe and therefore understand all things to be what he says they are. I have by his Spirit learned to understand something of what Jesus meant when he said: *I am the Way, the Truth and the Life.* I have learned something of what it means to make my every thought captive to the obedience of Christ, being converted anew every day to the realization that I understand no fact aright unless I see it in its proper relation to Christ as Creator-Redeemer of me and my world. I seek his kingdom and its righteousness above all things else. I now know by the testimony of his Spirit with my spirit that my labor is not in vain in the Lord. "I know whom I have believed and am convinced that he is able to guard what I have entrusted to him until that day" (II Tim. 1:12, NASB). All of my life, my life in my family, my life in my church, my life in society, and my life in my vocation as a minister of the gospel and a teacher of Christian apologetics is unified under the banner *Pro Rege!* I am not a hero, but in Christ I am not afraid of what man may do to me. The gates of hell cannot prevail against the ongoing march of victory of the Christ to whom all power in heaven and on earth is given.

II.   Christ Writes Me a Letter

I have never met Christ in the flesh. No matter, he has written me a letter. Not he, himself. He chose helpers. By his Spirit, the Spirit of truth, these helpers wrote what he wanted me to know. From heaven my Lord then sent his Holy Spirit on Pentecost to dwell in the hearts of all those whom he came into the world to redeem. I am, by his grace, one of them. Together we form the church, his people. In us and through us he establishes his kingdom. As a soldier of the cross, strengthened by his power in the inward man, I fight daily against Satan, who seeks at every point to establish his own kingdom in the hearts and to the hurt of men.

In his letter Jesus tells me that all men are made of one blood because all are created by God. As such all men are God's children; they all bear his image. But the first pair, from whom all later generations of men came "by ordinary generation," sinned against God. God set before them the ideal of joy which he would give them if they led their lives in the direction he indicated to them. That direction was to be marked by love and obedience to their Maker and benefactor. But our first parents had a person-to-person confrontation with Satan. Satan told them how free he had become since declaring his independence of God. To be self-determining man must surely be able to decide the "nature of the good"—regardless of what God says about it.

Adam saw Satan's point. "You are right, Satan, I must first decide whether such a God as often speaks to us (1) knows what the 'good' for us is, (2) controls history so that he can determine what will happen if we disobey him, and (3) has the right to demand obedience from us. After I decide these issues, and if the answer is 'yes,' then I shall obey him. Certainly not before."

But by taking to himself the right to decide these issues, Adam had already decided them—in the negative. If God is such a one as knows the "good" for us, controls whatsoever comes to pass, and has the right of unquestioned obedience, then man obeys his word because it is *his* word. Adam, in disobedience, became a "free" man.

But Satan miscalculated. Refusing to believe that God controls the course of history, Satan began his attempt to take over the whole of mankind to himself. Having succeeded with the first Adam, he tried his trick on the Second Adam. But the Second Adam replied to Satan's scheme, "Get thee behind me, Satan," and, "It is written"! The Second Adam both knew and received the Word of God, for he was God, the Word. He lived his life according to what he, in his program, had written down in advance. Even the words, "I thirst," spoken on the cross, were spoken in accord with what was written.

Now what was written consisted chiefly in his promise to his people that he would, in the face of Satan and his hosts, redeem them from their sin. He would be their *Great High Priest* by giving himself as their substitute. "Cursed is everyone that hangeth on a tree." He would be their *Prophet*, like unto Moses, proclaiming the final word of deliverance to his people, establishing them in the truth in the face of Satan's effort to make them believe the lie. He would be their *King*, establishing his elect nation of "holy ones" against the effort of Satan to establish a kingdom based upon the self-righteousness of the Pharisees.

He came, he saw, he conquered: there was a transition from wrath to grace in history. The new age had come, the age of grace and glory. In his letter Jesus tells us of this new age. Much of this letter comes to us through his servant Paul. Much of the early growth of Christ's kingdom came through the work of his servant Paul. How did Paul tell the story of the Christ?

In Romans Paul tells us of the wayward path of mankind. Both Jews and Greeks, being from the beginning of the world confronted with the truth of God, have nevertheless exchanged the truth of God for a lie and worshiped and served the creature rather than the Creator. Since they chose not to have God in their knowledge, the wrath of God is revealed from heaven against these men who hold back the revelation of God as if it were some awful, destructive flood. Such a flood it will be for men who refuse to turn back to God through his Son.

As children of Adam they have always made and continue to make the effort required to cover-up the truth about themselves and God. They see every fact as other than it really is. By means of their literature—drama, poetry, and philosophy—they try to prove to themselves that the world is not the estate of God and that they are not made in his image. Both Jew and Gentile have blinded themselves to the true state of affairs about themselves and their world—about their past, their present and their future. Not being creatures of God, they could not have sinned against such a one. They do not need, therefore, the atoning death of Christ for the remission of their sins. As Stephen said of the Jews, so also it must be said of the Gentiles, that they have always resisted the Holy Spirit—to their own damnation.

In his address on the Areopagus Paul proclaims the name of the resurrected Christ to the Gentile covenant-breakers, would-be fugitives from divine judgment. Paul does not place himself on their level in order with them to investigate the nature of being and knowledge in general, to discover *whether* the God of Abraham, Isaac, and Jacob might possibly exist. He tells them straight out that what they claim not to know, he knows. He tells them that their so-called ignorance is culpable, for God is as near to them as their own selves. He tells them, therefore, to repent of their worship of idols, to turn to the living God, lest they stand without the robes of righteousness before the resurrected Lord Christ on the day of judgment.

Paul's preaching to the Greeks was similar to Noah's preaching to the men of his time. When at first Noah claimed that God had given him a word of warning which men reject only to their own peril, they were nevertheless sure that they could dispose of such claims in terms of their own wisdom. There were, they said, no "facts" or "valid reasons" to support Noah's claim, unless one accept the "fact" that God spoke to Noah. But there was only Noah's word for this and who was Noah? But when the last men were drowning they saw themselves and their wisdom for what they really were, namely, foolishness. It was then too late. Even so at the end of time, in the face of the wrath of the Lamb, men will again see themselves and their wisdom for what it is and will call upon the hills to cover them lest they fall into the hands of an angry God.

Paul knew that the Greeks could not identify themselves truly in terms of their philosophy. "Chaos" and "Old Night" were their only substitutes for what Paul told them of the origin and destiny of the world. They tried various combinations of ultimate rationality (unity) and ultimate chance (diversity) in terms such as "form" and "matter" to take the place of creation and providence, but to no satisfaction. Even so, Paul could not prove to the Greeks in their sense of the word "prove," that what they believed was foolishness and what he believed was "good sense." Paul could not adopt the principles of the "free" first Adam to "prove" the principles of the Second Adam. Paul recognized, as did his Greek audience, that his ideas were, all of them, foolishness to the non-Christian mind. The Greeks would not believe any single one of them, much less all of them in their proper relation to each other, unless by the regeneration of the Holy Spirit they were given eyes with which to see the whole truth of God in Christ. Paul knew that the natural man, like Xantippe who is said to have kept on clipping her fingers even though these fingers were all that was left of her above the water, will keep on saying that Christ is wrong and that Satan is right so long as he has breath except the Spirit in mercy give him light and life.

This, then, is the message of the letter written to me and to the whole Church by Christ himself. Ever since I can remember it was of this letter of Christ which my father read to me and to the family. It was also this letter which I heard in church, spoken by the minister of Christ. Every minister in those days had a V.D.M. degree: *Verbum Dei Minister*. When, therefore, I became a teacher of apologetics it was natural for me to think, not only of my Th.M. and my Ph.D., but above all of my V.D.M. The former degrees were but means whereby I might be true to the latter degree.

How else, I thought, can anyone be a follower of the Reformation? Calvin and Luther: they expounded the Scriptures for the edification of the church of Christ. They rescued the Bible as the Word of God for the people of God from the apostate church of Rome. When they insisted on the necessity, authority, sufficiency, and the perspicuity of the Scriptures, they rejected in principle the entire Roman theological structure as it was largely based upon the very Greek thought against which Paul so vigorously preached.

Wanting to follow the Reformers, it was natural that I read and appreciated the works of those who before me likewise attempted to do so. I first used the works of Abraham Kuyper and Herman Bavinck. How basic and how broad was their view! The *idea* of Scripture, they said, must never be separated from its *message*.

The Roman Catholics, for example, in separating the two, distort the biblical views of sin and salvation. According to the position of Rome, the transition from sinner to saint is a metaphysical process of elevation on the "scale of being." This Greek-Christian metaphysics of salvation brings with it a false view of the nature of Scripture. Scripture, on this view, cannot be "sufficient." The Roman church adds itself as the continuing organ of revelation to written revelation, therewith achieving the sufficiency which Scripture, of itself, lacks. As Bavinck truly said, the nature of the message of salvation and the nature of Scripture are always involved in one another.

Just so, from the Reformed point of view, all so-called "evangelical" non-Reformed theologies (all those which, although non-Reformed, hold to what J. I. Packer calls the "evangelical equation" of Scripture with the Word of God, such as orthodox Lutheranism, traditional Arminian-Wesleyanism, and synergistic fundamentalism), which have an inadequate view of sovereign grace, have also an inadequate view of Scripture. A God who cannot control history because of countless men with wills not fully dependent on his own can only make salvation a bare "possibility." Christ might have died in vain. Being "free," all men might refuse to exercise their supposedly "God-given-freedom" to "draw their check for 'eternal life' put in the Bank of Heaven for all men." God's plan, to call out a people for himself, might never have been realized. Needless to say, every major teaching of Scripture excludes such a "scheme." God *is* God. Christ finished the work of salvation for his own. Only those "in Christ" from the foundation of the world died with Christ on the cross. Christ saved his sheep; he did not just make their salvation "possible." The emphasis, therefore, on human autonomy in non-Reformed evangelical theology not only plays havoc with the scriptural message of salvation by grace alone, but distorts the doctrine of Scripture itself by finding the ultimate exegetical tool in the subjective experience of human freedom and by denying to Scripture and the Holy Spirit the power, authority, and necessity of invading the souls of men. The Holy Spirit and the Word of God do not change men, men first *agree* to be changed! For this reason no non-Reformed theology can properly be called a "theology of the Holy Spirit." A theology which loses the right to be called a "theology of the Holy Spirit" loses also the right to be called "a theology of the Word of God." It is no wonder, therefore, that G. C. Berkouwer speaks of the "isolation of the Reformed view of Scripture."[1]

This point receives even stronger confirmation in the case of existential theology.

If non-Reformed evangelical theologies *tend* toward subjectivism, modern non-evangelical theology stands on it flat-footed! Take the theology of Karl Barth, for example. The free grace of God, Barth maintained, could not be communicated through a stabilized, objectivized revelation. Orthodox theology, he argues, has reduced the living, active revelation of God to that of a lifeless form. When Barth spoke agreeably, therefore, of verbal inspiration he "actualized" it and therewith fitted it "into his system."[2] In bringing down the Bible to the dimension of "causal relations," orthodoxy brings down the entire religious relation between God and man to the level of impersonal concepts and ideas. Orthodoxy is the theology of the "blessed possessors," the theology of those who control the freedom of God. The God of orthodoxy, indeed the God of Calvinism, is not sovereign! The God of Calvin is not the God of sovereign, universal grace.

We may say, therefore, that the Barthian soteriology of "sovereign, free grace" which comes to us only in our *subjectivity* entails a radically new view of Scripture itself. The Bible may now be called the Word of God only in so far as it brings this message of subjectivity to us. To say "the Bible *is* the Word of God," for Barth, does not imply a directly discernible revelation of God in history as we know it.

From these examples of Roman Catholic, Arminian-Wesleyan-Lutheran, and finally modern theology, it is clear (1) that the idea of Scripture can never be separated from the message of Scripture, and (2) that none of these non-Reformed evangelical and modern theologies have a view of Scripture such that the Lord Christ speaks to man with an absolute authority. The self-attesting Christ of Scripture is not absolutely central to these theologies. Just so, he will not be central in any apologetic form to defend them.

III.   Toward a Christ-Centered Apologetic

Deciding, therefore, to follow the Reformers in theology, it was natural that I attempt also to do so in apologetics. I turned to such Reformed apologists as Warfield, Greene, and others. What did I find? I found the theologians of the "self-attesting Christ," defending their faith with a method which denied precisely that point! That this was the case may be shown by a brief survey of what I call the "traditional" method of Christian apologetics.

The traditional method, offered first in detail by Thomas Aquinas in its Catholic form and by Joseph Butler in its Protestant form (but being in principle that offered by the very earliest of apologists), is based upon the assumption that man has some measure of autonomy, that the space-time world is in some measure "contingent" and that man must create for himself his own epistemology in an ultimate sense.

The traditional method was concessive on these basic points on which it should have demanded surrender! As such, it was always self-frustrating. The traditional method had explicitly built into it the right and ability of the natural man, apart from the work of the Spirit of God, to be the judge of the claim of the authoritative Word of God. It is man who, by means of his self-established intellectual tools, puts his "stamp of approval" on the Word of God and then, only after that grand act, does he listen to it. God's Word must first pass man's tests of good and evil, truth and falsity. But once you tell a non-Christian this, why should he be worried by anything else that you say. You have already told him he is quite all right just the way he is! Then the Scripture is not correct when it talks of "darkened minds," "wilful ignorance," "dead men," and "blind people"! With this method the correctness of the natural man's problematics is endorsed. That is all he needs to reject the Christian faith.

Seeing, therefore, the failure of even Reformed theologians and apologists in their efforts to defend consistently the self-attesting Christ of Scripture, it became clear to me that new ground work needed to be done. I did not, however, undertake this task *de novo*. I learned much from other men, just as I did in theology from Kuyper and Bavinck. Since I conceived of Christian apologetics as focusing on the self-attesting Christ of Scripture, it was natural that I should learn most of the development and defense of the doctrine of the person of Christ in the historical, theological development of the church. There are three eras in history in which Christian apologetics was helped forward in the right direction.

The Council of Nicea.—Here, in A.D. 325, the church concluded that the only adequate expression of the teaching of Christ concerning himself and of the apostles concerning God, was in a formulation such that all three persons of the Trinity were equally ultimate. The church rejected the subordination of the Son to the Father in any "ontological" sense. Herman Bavinck points out that herewith was rejected any attempt to unite God with man in terms of some change wherein God ceased to be himself as God.

The Chalcedon Creed.—This formulation of the church deals particularly with the difficult question of the relation of the divine to the human "natures" of Christ. Adopted in A.D. 451, it says that the divine and human "nature" of Christ are related unconfusedly, unchangeably, indivisibly, and inseparably. The first two adjective were directed against the Eutychians, the second two against the Nestorians.

This effort of the church to understand the Christ was theological and therefore apologetically crucial. The work of Christ remains cloudy until the biblical teaching with respect to his person is clearly understood. Yet the true significance of his person becomes clear only as we understand what he has accomplished for his people. For this latter insight we must turn to the Reformed confessions. They give more exact expression to the work of the Spirit of Christ, the Holy Spirit, as part of the continuing historical work of Christ as he is now with us.

The Reformed Confessions.—We take the Belgic Confession as illustrative: "We receive these books, and these only, as holy and canonical, for the regulation, foundation, and confirmation of our faith, believing, without any doubt, all things contained in them, not so much because the church receives and approves them as such, but more especially because the Holy Spirit witnesseth in our hearts that they are from God, whereof they carry the evidence in themselves. For the very blind are able to perceive that the things foretold in them are fulfilling" (Art. V).

It appears, then, that not until the time of the Reformers do we find the church, as the *church*, confessing before the world anything like an adequate view of the Holy Spirit as the one who ministers to us, as he did to the disciples and apostles, the very Word of Christ. Only in the Reformed creeds do we find the Spirit of Christ to be an essential part of the work of Christ in saving his sheep.

In these three areas we see the church's increasing understanding of the person and work of Christ. Individual theologians, too, helped the cause forward. One such was Tertullian. Another was Augustine. Both men had very "high" views of Christ and his work. Both saw the centrality of the Holy Spirit to the redemptive work of Christ. They attempted to be consistent with these views in their arguments with non-believers. Tertullian was, in this respect, more successful in this attempt than Augustine.

In the case of Tertullian, we have, says Warfield, a remarkable instance of the right man for the right place and time: "the real father of the Christian doctrine of the Trinity."[3] With a very high view of Christ, Tertullian could say, "After Jesus Christ we have no need of speculation, after the gospel no need of research. When we come to believe, we have no desire to believe anything else; for we begin by believing there is nothing else which we have to believe."[4] This statement is not for Tertullian a mere *formal* submission to Scripture. For Tertullian it is *Christ* who, in the Scriptures, gives us the "system" of truth which men must believe. "What you must seek is what Christ taught. . . ." For Tertullian all search for truth is meaningless unless it is in the light of the basic truth which is before men in the Scriptures, the word through which Christs speaks to us from heaven. But Tertullian was no obscurantist or literalist. "Provided the essence of Truth is not disturbed, you may seek and discuss as much as you like."[5] Having set forth this "system" of truth which confronts men in the Christ of Scripture, Tertullian concludes: "From this point onwards I shall contest the ground of my opponents' appeal."[6] Men are not to determine in advance of meeting Christ what his nature must be, for "our Lord himself declared, while he lived on earth, what he was, what he had been, how he was fulfilling the Father's will, what he was laying down as man's duty."[7]

It is clear that I learned from Tertullian. But Tertullian was nevertheless, like us all, a son of his times. He never succeeded of ridding himself of the stranglehold which the Logos-speculation of his predecessors had on him. "The Logos was in principle God conceived in relation to things of time and space: God, therefore, not as absolute, but as relative. In its very essence, therefore, the Logos conception likewise involved the strongest subordinationism. . . . The Logos was therefore necessarily conceived as reduced divinity—divinity, so to speak, at the periphery rather than at the center of its conception."[8] So observes Warfield.

Here, then, we see a truly great Christian theologian who, while developing the idea of the self-attesting Christ of Scripture, falls into the ditch of Greek speculation calculated to deny this Christ *in toto*. In his argument with the Gnostics he adopts not a mere "form" but the very content of their own emanation theories, hoping to convince them that he but wishes to add "Christ" to their already adequate ideas of the origin of man and the world. He does not even attempt to "contest the ground of his opponents" as he set out himself to do. He failed, therefore, to be consistent with a method which he himself proposed. It fell to Calvin to *follow* the method of Tertullian, cleansing it of its Logos theology.

I have said that the development of the church's doctrine of Christ took place in three basic steps and that these three steps were necessary prerequisites for a truly biblical apologetics. Further I observed that Tertullian was a man ahead of his time, both in Christology and in apologetic method. The third step, the Reformed creeds, was basically an expression of the theology of John Calvin. We shall understand the third step more fully, therefore, if we look in detail at the Christology of Calvin. In doing so we shall also see a development and application of the method of Tertullian and therewith the beginnings of a Christ-centered apologetics.

For Calvin speculation about God, independently of Scripture, is excluded. Natural theology, therefore, is also excluded. Natural theology starts with man as autonomous and with the world as "given." Natural theologians assume that "reason" and "logic" and "fact" are "religiously neutral." They are but "tools" by which man may and must determine what is and what is not possible.

Now if there is anything which is basic to the ideas of the Reformation it is that which Calvin expresses at the very outset of his *Institutes*: man is what God in Christ through Scripture says he is. This God is triune. "The tripersonality of God is conceived by Calvin, . . . not as something added to the complete idea of God, or as something into which God develops in the process of his existing, but as something which enters into the very idea of God, without which he cannot be conceived in the truth of his being."[9] For Calvin the doctrine of the Trinity was involved in his experience of salvation "in the Christian's certainty that the Redeeming Christ and Sanctifying Spirit are each Divine Persons."[10] "The main thing was, he insisted, that men should heartily believe that there is but one God, whom only they should serve; but also that Jesus Christ our Redeemer and the Holy Spirit the Sanctifier is each no less this one God than God the Father to whom we owe our being; while yet these three are distinct personal objects of our love and adoration."[11] It was because of his deep religious interest in making the triune God of Scripture the starting point of all his theology that Calvin found it necessary to exclude every last vestige of subordinationism which might even be said to be sanctioned by the language of Nicea. He therefore used the word αὐτόθεος with respect to the Son of God.

The significance of this for Christian apologetics should be clear at once. "All those who were for any reason or in any degree unable or unwilling to allow Christ a deity in every respect equal to that of the Father were necessarily offended by the vindication to him of the ultimate divine quality of self-existence."[12] Calvin explicated the person of Christ solely in scriptural terms, i.e., his method is exegetical rather than speculative. As such his method is simple: who Christ is depends on Christ's self-identification. If Christ is who he says he is, then all speculation is excluded, for God can swear only by himself. To find out what man is and who God is, one can only go to Scripture. Faith in the self-attesting Christ of the Scriptures is the beginning, not the conclusion, of wisdom! It was, therefore, not until the fully developed trinitarian theology of Calvin, which says that Christ is authoritative because αὐτόθεος, that there was therewith developed a truly Christian *methodology* of theology and of apologetics. The method by which a Christian develops the content of his faith must not be denied by the method he uses to defend that content. Calvin, seeing this, denied all speculation and natural theology as "avenues" to faith. Rather, faith and understanding are pure gifts of free grace.

The apologetic method thus far outlined will be made clearer if we consider an objection, indeed the "stock" objection, to such an approach as Calvin's. It comes from Stuart Cornelius Hackett in his *The Resurrection of Theism*. We must, says Hackett, have "a rational justification for the metaphysical ultimate" which we believe in. Calvinism denies this. The Calvinists say that God has "created rational men as mere puppets of his sovereignty. But if it seems to be the case that man is under *obligation* to believe the gospel and that he must accept Christ as Savior *before* the Spirit of God regenerates the heart—if, I say, man is a moral and rational agent confronted with a revelation for the acceptance of which he is morally and rationally responsible—then let the presuppositionalist framework be consigned to the irrationalism that is written so plainly through its structure. . . . With her opponents thus languishing in defeat, reason pushes on to consider experience itself to determine whether God is real."[13]

With these words Hackett sums up the issue between himself as an Arminian and myself as a Calvinist very well. It goes without saying that we two have radically different beliefs as to what the Bible says about man and his sinfulness and about the Holy Spirit and his sovereignty. Indeed, the issues between us are total. There are no "fundamentals" in common between us: we will necessarily understand creation-providence, the fall of man, the atonement of Christ, his sinlessness and his resurrection, his second coming and his ultimate triumph, the doctrine of Scripture, the nature of saving faith—we will necessarily understand, I say, these doctrines in different ways. Hackett's Christian faith and my Christian faith, which we both desire non-Christians to accept, are radically different. They are different not only in their *content* but also in the very *method* of their construction.

I make two broad points in reference to this. First, any non-Christian epistemology, i.e., any theory of knowledge based upon principles acceptable *per se* to the "mind of the flesh," (and therefore those of Hackett's own method) is doomed to utter failure; not only failure as an avenue to Christian faith, but as an avenue to any form of knowledge whatsoever. This I think can be, and has been repeatedly, shown by myself and many others. Second, Hackett's basic charge that Calvinism is determinist and irrational is simply not true. First, as to the charge that it is determinist and that men are but "puppets," one need only read Calvin himself to be persuaded that such an understanding of Calvinism is false. The Calvinist notion of divine sovereignty has nothing to do with the philosopher's notion of physical, causal determinism. I have developed at length in other places the covenantal, exhaustively personalist view of providence which is clearly part of Calvin's thought.

As to the charge that the Calvinist position is "irrational," I assume that Hackett cannot mean that it is inconsistent. After all, one of the so-called "sins" of Calvin was that he was too deductive, too logical, in drawing implications from this and that in Scripture, that in "logicizing" theology he destroyed its heart. I assume that what Hackett means is that on the Calvinist position man is called upon to repent of his sins and accept Christ *without having reasons* for doing so. The Calvinist cannot give reasons because he has no *point of contact* with the non-Christian. There are, for the Calvinist, no *reasons* to which he might appeal in an effort to get his friend to accept Christ.

In response to this I observe that this also is not the case. Hackett assumes that unless one finds a point of contact with the natural man by way of agreeing with him on his false views of man and the world then one has no point of contact with him at all. Against this position, I maintain, with Calvin following Paul, that my point of contact lies in the *actual state of affairs between men* as the Bible tells us of it. It is Hackett who has no *real* point of contact, for his lies in what men *imagine* (and, to be sure, "agree") to be the case. The Calvinist's point of contact is rooted in the *actual* state of affairs. All things are what they are because of their relation to the work of the triune God as reported in Scripture. Hackett's "point of contact" as an evangelical Arminian is an essentially Kantian epistemology, an epistemology in terms of which men stand utterly unrelated to one another and are, at the same time, reduced to relations of one another.

To look for a point of contact with the unbeliever in the unbeliever's notions of himself and his world is to encourage him in his wicked rebellion and to establish him in his self-frustration. We have already seen that the natural man is under the self-imposed delusion that he is "free," i.e., independent of the control and counsel of God, and that the "facts" about him are also "free" in this way. He may pretend to be "open-minded" and ready to consider *whether* God exists. But in being so "neutral" he commits the same sin as Adam and Eve.

Why seek truth where only a lie is to be found? Can the non-Christian tell *us* and therefore the Christ himself *what* the facts are and how they are related to each other, in what way they cohere, while yet excluding creation and providence? If he can, and if he can tell us truly, then the Christian story simply is not true! Because the natural man cannot do this, because the Christian message is true, I have sought and still seek to reap the benefit of a theology in which the triune God of Scripture has the initiative in salvation.

The Calvinist's idea of an *actual* as opposed to an *imagined* point of contact is not just some useless notion. It is the only intelligible point of contact possible. The non-Christian holds that pure chance and absolute fate are equally ultimate and mutually correlative limiting concepts or heuristic principles which man uses to explain the fact that we have learned much about the world, that there is order in the world, a uniformity, while there is also continual change and development. But the non-Christian's "explanation" is no explanation at all. To say "it just happens" as an explanation of an event is really to say, "There is no explanation that I know of."

The Calvinist, therefore, using his point of contact, observes to the non-Christian that if the world were not what Scripture says it is, if the natural man's knowledge were not actually rooted in the creation and providence of God, then there could be no knowledge whatsoever. The Christian claims that non-Christians have made and now make many discoveries about the true state of affairs of the universe simply because the universe is what Christ says it is. The unbelieving scientist borrows or steals the Christian principles of creation and providence every time he says that an "explanation" is possible, for he knows he cannot account for "explanation" on his own. As the image-bearer of God, operating in a universe controlled by God, the unbeliever contributes indirectly and adventitiously to the development of human knowledge and culture.

When Hackett maintains that the Calvinist position is irrational because it cannot give "reasons" for believing, he must mean that on a position such as mine the Christian does not accept the non-Christian scheme wherein the non-Christian determines what are "good reasons" and "valid proofs." This is perfectly true, but this is not irrational. Rather the Christian offers the self-attesting Christ to the world as the only foundation upon which a man must stand in order to give any "reasons" for anything at all. The whole notion of "giving reasons" is completely destroyed by any ontology other than the Christian one. The Christian claims that only after accepting the biblical scheme of things will any man be able to understand and account for his own rationality.

But I have said enough so that readers should have a clear picture of the drift of my thought. Nevertheless, I think it might be helpful if in a final section I put, in only outline form, the total picture. This will make it easier for the contributors and the general reader, as they go on to the rest of this *Festschrift*, to refer back and see at a glance what my position is.

IV.   The Total Picture

A.   My problems with the "traditional method."
1. This method compromises God himself by maintaining that his existence is only "possible" albeit "highly probable," rather than ontologically and "rationally" necessary.
2. It compromises the counsel of God by not understanding it as the only all-inclusive, ultimate "cause" of whatsoever comes to pass.
3. It compromises the revelation of God by:
   a. Compromising its *necessity*. It does so by not recognizing that even in Paradise man had to interpret the general (natural) revelation of God in terms of the covenantal obligations placed upon him by God through special revelation. Natural revelation, on the traditional view, can be understood "on its own."
   b. Compromising its *clarity*. Both the general and special revelation of God are said to be unclear to the point that man may say only that God's existence is "probable."
   c. Compromising its *sufficiency*. It does this by allowing

for an ultimate realm of "chance" out of which might come "facts" such as are wholly new for God and for man. Such "facts" would be uninterpreted and unexplainable in terms of the general or special revelation of God.

d. Compromising its *authority*. On the traditional position the Word of God's self-attesting characteristic, and therewith its authority, is secondary to the authority of reason and experience. The Scriptures do not identify themselves, man identifies them and recognizes their "authority" only in terms of his own authority.

4. It compromises man's creation as the image of God by thinking of man's creation and knowledge as independent of the Being and knowledge of God. On the traditional approach man need not "think God's thoughts after him."

5. It compromises man's covenantal relationship with God by not understanding Adam's representative action as absolutely determinative of the future.

6. It compromises the sinfulness of mankind resulting from the sin of Adam by not understanding man's ethical depravity as extending to the whole of his life, even to his thoughts and attitudes.

7. It compromises the grace of God by not understanding it as the necessary prerequisite for "renewal unto knowledge." On the traditional view man can and must renew himself unto knowledge by the "right use of reason."

B. My understanding of the relationship between Christian and non-Christian, philosophically speaking.

1. Both have presuppositions about the nature of reality:
   a. The Christian presupposes the triune God and his redemptive plan for the universe as set forth once for all in Scripture.
   b. The non-Christian presupposes a dialectic between "chance" and "regularity," the former accounting for the origin of matter and life, the latter accounting for the current success of the scientific enterprise.

2. Neither can, as finite beings, by means of *logic* as such, say what reality *must* be or *cannot* be.
   a. The Christian, therefore, attempts to understand his world through the observation and logical ordering of facts in self-conscious subjection to the plan of the self-attesting Christ of Scripture.

    b. The non-Christian, while attempting an enterprise similar to the Christian's, attempts nevertheless to use "logic" to destroy the Christian position. On the one hand, appealing to the *non-rationality* of "matter," he says that the chance-character of "facts" is conclusive evidence against the Christian position. Then, on the other hand, he maintains like Parmenides that the Christian story cannot possibly be true. Man must be autonomous, "logic" must be legislative as to the field of "possibility" and possibility must be above God.

3. Both claim that their position is "in accordance with the facts."

    a. The Christian claims this because he interprets the facts and his experience in the light of the revelation of the self-attesting Christ in Scripture. Both the uniformity and the diversity of facts have at their foundation the all-embracing plan of God.

    b. The non-Christian claims this because he interprets the facts and his experience in the light of the autonomy of human personality, the ultimate "givenness" of the world and the amenability of matter to mind. There can be no fact that denies man's autonomy or attests to the world's and man's divine origin.

4. Both claim that their position is "rational."

    a. The Christian does so by claiming not only that his position is self-consistent but that he can explain both the seemingly "inexplicable" amenability of fact to logic and the necessity and usefulness of rationality itself in terms of Scripture.

    b. The non-Christian may or may not make this same claim. If he does, the Christian maintains that he cannot make it good. If the non-Christian attempts to account for the amenability of fact to logic in terms of the ultimate rationality of the cosmos, then he will be crippled when it comes to explaining the "evolution" of men and things. If he attempts to do so in terms of pure "chance" and ultimate "irrationality" as being the well out of which both rational man and a rationally amenable world sprang, then we shall point out that such an explanation is in fact no explanation at all and that it destroys predication.

C. My proposal, therefore, for a consistently Christian methodology of apologetics is this:

1. That we use the same principle in apologetics that we use in theology: the self-attesting, self-explanatory Christ of Scripture.

2. That we no longer make an appeal to "common notions" which Christian and non-Christian agree on, but to the "common ground" which they actually have because man and his world are what Scripture says they are.

3. That we appeal to man as man, God's image. We do so only if we set the non-Christian principle of the rational autonomy of man against the Christian principle of the dependence of man's knowledge on God's knowledge as revealed in the person and by the Spirit of Christ.

4. That we claim, therefore, that Christianity alone is reasonable for men to hold. It is wholly irrational to hold any other position than that of Christianity. Christianity alone does not slay reason on the altar of "chance."

5. That we argue, therefore, by "presupposition." The Christian, as did Tertullian, must contest the very principles of his opponent's position. The only "proof" of the Christian position is that unless its truth is presupposed there is no possibility of "proving" anything at all. The actual state of affairs as preached by Christianity is the necessary foundation of "proof" itself.

6. That we preach with the understanding that the acceptance of the Christ of Scripture by sinners who, being alienated from God, seek to flee his face, comes about when the Holy Spirit, in the presence of inescapably clear evidence, opens their eyes so that they see things as they truly are.

7. That we present the message and evidence for the Christian position as clearly as possible, knowing that because man is what the Christian says he is, the non-Christian will be able to understand in an intellectual sense the issues involved. In so doing, we shall, to a large extent, be telling him what he "already knows" but seeks to suppress. This "reminding" process provides a fertile ground for the Holy Spirit, who in sovereign grace may grant the non-Christian repentance so that he may know him who is life eternal.

I hope that by this, "My Credo," I have been able in a small way sincerely to thank all those who took the time to write for this birthday-book.

—C.V.T.

PART TWO

LETTERS FROM
THREE CONTINENTS

Hendrik G. Stoker

I. RECONNOITERING THE THEORY OF KNOWLEDGE OF PROF. DR. CORNELIUS VAN TIL

M y dear friend and highly esteemed colleague,
This letter makes me remember with a sense of nostalgia those very pleasant days I spent with you, when I was a guest at your home with your happy family. It was during the days of our first Ecumenical Synod of Reformed Churches in 1946. Although there is truth in the saying "tempora mutantur et nos in illis"—how much the world has changed since then!—I was glad, in my recent reading of many of your works, to find that you have not only remained true to the fundamental principles of your theory of knowledge, but also have developed your unique theory on these principles so extensively as well as intensively. It is important to say this today, because lately so much uncertainty about fundamental matters has arisen—even and especially in leading Reformed circles—a state of affairs that causes much concern in my country.

I consider this opportunity to converse with you in this open letter a great honor. A penetrating discussion of your remarkable theory of knowledge would require a rather extensive treatise and this is accordingly not the occasion to go into all the significant problems your theory poses. Therefore this letter is limited to a mere reconnoitering of some of the main points of your theory, proceeding from my views on knowledge—for what these views may be worth; and you must consider this discourse as a heart to heart talk.

Your approach is primarily apologetical, i.e., theological, notwithstanding your penetrating criticism of theories concerning philosophy and empirical science. My approach—presupposing the validity of your approach—is primarily philosophical. The main point I wish to make is that a primarily philosophical pursuit of the problem of knowledge may contribute a necessary supplement to your theory and I will refer to such a pursuit as *my special problem*. I am anxious to know whether and to what extent you will agree with my exposition. My own views on knowledge I shall state as concisely as possible.[1]

I shall pass over your criticisms of Roman Catholicism, Arminianism, evangelicism, and less consistent Calvinism, however significant they may be. When I use the term "Christian" to distinguish our theories from those of non-Christians, I take "Christian" to mean "Reformed Christian," or (as you term it) "Theistic Christian" or "Calvinist Christian," without implying that, for instance, Roman Catholics or other Reformed Christians are not Christians; I use the term "Christian" in this limited sense only for the sake of achieving economy of expression.

A. On Contexts of Knowledge

You are primarily concerned about the ultimate dependence of man's knowledge on our triune God and his knowledge. I mainly am concerned about the problem of man's knowledge, presupposing this ultimate dependence. I speak intentionally of man's knowledge and not of "human" knowledge, in order to state the relevant problems as concretely as possible. We both accept the presuppositions (1) that God is the absolute origin of all "things"—also of man's knowledge—and that accordingly one's *view of God* (or an "absolute" in other theories) determines in an ultimate sense one's view of man's knowledge; (2) that man (created as[2] the image of God) belongs to our created universe and, accordingly, his knowledge belongs to the universe as, for instance, an atom, a cell, and animal instinct do, and that thus one's *view of the universe* co-determines, in a basic sense, one's view of man's knowledge; and (3) that it is man that knows and, accordingly, that one's *view of man* basically co-determines one's view of his knowledge. Also, we both admit the necessity of seeing all problems of knowledge in the light of the fundamental truths of Holy Writ.

B. On Knowledge

B.1. I agree with Vollenhoven that when we investigate man's knowledge, we should distinguish and find the relations between man as *knower*, his acts of *knowing*, the *knowable*, and *knowledge*.

B.1.1. We need not dwell here on man as *knower*, created as the image of God, appointed by God as *mandator Dei* of the created universe, entrusted with a responsible divine calling, subjected to the love, will, and law of God, who has fallen into sin and is essentially in need of God's redemptive grace and the atonement of Jesus Christ.

B.1.2.1. The act of *knowing* is *unique*. It is irreducible to anything else in our created universe or cosmos. Accordingly, it cannot be defined. Every description of knowing presupposes knowing and is given either in terms of knowing or in analogical terms that presuppose knowing. We primarily know what knowing is by knowing.[3]

B.1.2.2. The act of *knowing* is a *unit*. This is important. "Perceiving" and "thinking" are part-acts of knowing. ("Perceiving" I take, in a wide sense, to be aware of the knowable; it includes, for instance, perceiving by means of the senses, psycho-introspection, psycho-extrospection,[4] dynamic awareness of resistance,[5] evaluation [*waardekeuring*], intuition [in its diverse meanings], and religious faith[6].) By thinking man forms a theoretical realm of, for instance, concepts, judgments, conclusions, models, theories, and systems. Concrete and genuine perceiving is a *knowing* perceiving, and a concrete and genuine thinking is a *knowing* thinking. Both are led by knowing. Furthermore, knowing uses thinking as a means; thinking is but an instrument in the hands of knowing. In this case too the tenet holds good that the whole (*in casu*: knowing) is more than the sum of its parts (*in casu*, for instance: perceiving and thinking[7]).

B.1.3.1. To the *knowable* belongs the *revelation* of *God* to man concerning *himself* and his *relation* to *all things* in his Word and in his creation (usually called "natural revelation").

B.1.3.2. *Knowable* is also *heaven* (with its *angels*) as revealed in the Scriptures.

B.1.3.3. *Knowable* is furthermore the cosmos (our created universe comprised, for instance, of material "things," the vegetable and animal kingdoms as well as man; nature, culture, and religion;[8] facts, principles, values, and so on). It is not man that makes the cosmos knowable or gives the cosmos its meaning; God has (as you rightly insist) created the universe according to his plan; he gives the cosmos (as a whole and in all its "parts" and relations) its meaning; he created the cosmos knowable. The cosmos itself is meaningful. In this sense knowability is an ontic ("ontological") characteristic of created reality itself. This is a significant point concerning *my special problem*, a point that you definitely allow for and remark upon, but—as far as I can see— on account of your primarily apologetic approach— do not investigate as such.

B.1.4. *Knowledge* may be described as the *result* of a knowing exploration and exploitation of the knowable by man, the knower; and belonging to knowing man, it is not separable from knowing and is accordingly not merely a result.

B.1.5. You rightly stress the *creaturely* or *derivative* "nature" of man's knowledge; and this holds good for man the knower, his knowing acts, the knowable and knowledge. Even God's revelation as knowable—as it is present in our universe or cosmos—is creaturely in "kind," although it has in God its trans-cosmic origin—a truth that is sometimes expressed in the words that God's revelation is *pro forma humana.* This holds good for his revelation in his Word as well as in creation (or "nature").⁹ As you put it, man's knowledge is in consequence *limited*; man does not know comprehensively as God knows, yet he may know truly.

B.2.   After the distinction between man as knower, his acts of knowing, the knowable, and knowledge, the problems of the relations between them have to be raised. Man's acts (and functions) of *knowing* and the *knowable* presuppose one another; they are in a principial sense *correlated*; the one without the other is, in principle, meaningless. Human knowledge—belonging to our universe—is enstatically bound up with the knowable. Firstly, we attend to the following relation between them.

B.2.1.1.   By *perceiving* (cf. B.1.2.2, taken in a wide sense) man knowingly comes into *contact* with the knowable.

B.2.1.2.   Man, however, *meets* knowingly the knowable by *trusting* it. In order to know, *faith* in the knowable (as met by knowing perceiving) is an indispensable necessity. ("Faith" is taken here in a wide sense, as, for instance, is also done by Bavinck.) Faith, too, is an act of knowing, without which man, the knower, does not really meet the knowable. Faith is, in a specific sense, a surrender;¹⁰ only by surrendering himself to the knowable, i.e., by accepting it, can man responsibly fulfil his task of knowing.

B.2.2.1.   On the basis of the perceived knowable, man forms his theoretic realm (cf. B.1.2.2) by *thinking*. Knowing uses thinking as a means to answer the tasks set by the knowable. Thinking has no purpose in itself. To think in order just to think is meaningless. *Thinking* finds its purpose (which transcends thinking) in knowing. The task and purpose of knowing gives thinking its meaning. But thinking also requires *faith* (taken in a wide sense); for instance, faith in the validity of its processes, as Bavinck has pointed out.

B.2.2.2.   *Thinking* has a remarkable control over its theoretical constructions. Left by itself, it can abritrarily break up, take apart, separate, tear asunder, as well as combine, join together, connect, and unite its theoretical constructions, can analyze and synthesize, deduct and induct (generalize and extrapolate), and so forth. This striking control has contributed much to the illusion that human reason is autonomous. But we should never forget that thinking is essentially *bound by* the perceived knowable and the task of knowing.

B.2.3.   *Knowing* does not stop at thinking. It *requires*—with the use of the constructions of thinking—a *renewed meeting,* a renewed involvement, with the *knowable.* This renewed meeting is more than a mere verification (taken in a wide sense). Even more so, it establishes a unison between the knower and the knowable—comparable (to borrow a term of Blondel's) to a *symbiosis* of man (as the knower) and the knowable, whereby the renewed meeting ever and anon yields a deeper as well as a more extensive penetration into the knowable[11] and at the same time ever and again a discovery of new tasks. Here too faith (taken in a wide sense) has to play its role.

B.2.4.   Of fundamental significance is the *act* of *religious faith* directed as it is towards the revelation of God (or to a supposed higher being or an absolute).[12] To be able to observe and know creaturely "things" in their finitude and limitedness presupposes, in a principial sense, the ability to know God, the absolute, by the act of religious faith. The finite and the relative are what they are because of the absolute. This means that had man no possibility of religious faith, knowledge of finite "things" as finite and of relative "things" as relative would not have been possible.[13] This assertion is akin to your contention that without a revelatory consciousness of God, self-consciousness (and I may add: consciousness of "things"[14]) would, in a principial sense, not be possible.

Man's knowledge is basically founded on faith (in a wide sense as well as in its specific religious sense). Faith is the opposite of all supposed human autonomy. It is virtually a surrender, an acceptance.

B.2.5.   By means of language knowledge is *"objectified"* and *communicated.* This concerns, however, not only an "objectification" and communication of thoughts but of knowledge, whereby man as the knower also expresses his emotions, desires, will, and so forth, as the tonality and structure of language clearly show. After all, it is man that knows and communicates.

B.2.6.   This leads us to the *human* as well as the *personal factor* in knowledge. The human factor concerns the creaturely, derived, incomprehensive "nature" of knowledge as well as the part man (with all his acts and functions) plays in forming knowledge. The personal factor[15] concerns the specifically or individually personal character of knowledge as it differs from man to man.

B.3.1.   But we have not yet reached the *fundamental "nature"* of man's knowledge-situation. A *mystery* lies at the root of man's knowing by meeting with the knowable.

How are we to understand the principial connectedness of the act of knowing (for instance, a rose) and the knowable (for instance, the rose itself), whereas both—the act of knowing and the knowable—are radically different, the one not being reducible to the other? How the radically different can yet be connected, is basically a hyperdox,[16] something that surpasses human understanding. We are, however, in the knowledge-transaction, faced by the *mystery* of *revelation* that lies at the root of all man's knowledge. Rightly Bavinck, as well as you, takes revelation to be the key to man's knowledge.

The *unity of revelation* requires one who reveals, something that is revealed, and someone to whom it is revealed. The unity of revelation at the base of man's knowledge discloses the principial connectedness of knowing and the knowable, thereby at the same time leaving the radical difference between them intact.[17] This is apparent when we consider that God reveals himself in his Word and works (our created universe); that he has created our universe or cosmos knowable; that he has endowed man with the acts and functions to know; and that he sets man his calling to know and to act upon it. Here again it becomes clear how enstatically man's knowledge of the revelation of God (in his Word and his creation), as well as of the created universe itself, is interwoven with created reality itself.

B.3.2. H. Bavinck and V. Hepp distinguish between

a. the revelation of *God* himself *to himself* within his trinity;

b. the revelation of *God* himself *to himself* through his works;

c. the revelation of *God* himself and of *his relation* to all "things" *to man* in his Word and in his creation; and

d. the revelation of the *created universe* (including *man*) to *man* in an ultimate sense by *God*.

Your theory concerning *God's knowledge* of *himself* of his counsel, creation, providence, grace, and so forth appears to be on the same level with the first two types of revelation.

Your theory of God's revelation of *himself* (in his Word and creation) *to man* coincides with the third type of revelation.

But it is the *fourth type* of revelation that concerns *my special problem*. The concern of your theory of man's knowledge of created reality is, primarily, that the created universe (as a whole and in all its "parts," e.g., "facts") is revelational of God and his counsel; and this concern falls under the third type of revelation. (This assertion will be amended later on.) But you do allow for the fourth type of revelation and make significant comments upon it, although—probably due to your primarily apologetic approach to man's knowledge—you do not develop it as such—at least not as far as I know. *It is exactly this fourth type of revelation (presupposing the other types) that I require for a philosophical (as well as for a particular scientific) approach to man's knowledge.*

B.3.3.1. Objections may be raised against calling this *fourth type* also a *type of revelation,* because revelation is here used in an uncommon sense. For it is not a revelation of God himself to man, but a revelation of created reality (in an ultimate sense by God) to man. But to state the case as simply as possible (although I am somewhat apprehensive of using the term "conscious"): why should man's being conscious of (i.e., his perceiving), for instance, a rose not to be taken to be equivalent to the revelation of a rose to (perceiving) man[18]—a revelation that has ultimately its origin in God, who created the universe knowable and endowed man with the acts and functions of knowing? Especially when we keep in mind the principial correlative interdependence of knowing and the knowable?

Stated in a more general way: on the one hand God reveals himself in our created universe; in your words: God has created the universe according to his plan and every fact and every relation between facts therein is revelational of God. But on the other hand—*and* this is the point I wish to stress—this plan, however revelational of God, *belongs to and is present in our universe itself;* every man, the sinner too, is virtually *confronted with this plan;* all his knowings and all his doings presuppose and show this; man simply cannot escape this plan; it forces itself upon man everywhere ever and again. Man can know this plan truly, though not comprehensively; but by knowing it man, as sinner, falsifies it in one or other significant respect. Of course, when this falsification is seen in the light of the third type of revelation, it is seen as a radical or ultimate falsification—the point you rightly stress very strongly. In other words, the approach to man's knowledge, according to the fourth type of revelation (that I suggest as a supplement to your theory of knowledge) is not an ultimate approach as your approach is, but a derivative approach in the sense of an approach to knowledge of the universe (including man) in its creatureliness, its derivativeness. But as such this approach is not reducible to your approach and yet it is a truly significant approach too. Such is *my special problem.*

B.3.3.2. But revelation to man is not in vain; man is not endowed with acts and functions of knowing in vain; God has not created the universe knowable in vain. Whatever is revealed to man sets to man his tasks, his calling, namely, to know and to act upon it. The knowable, as such ontically (you would say: "metaphysically"), requires to be known by man and to be acted upon. It is not only revealed to man, but, in a mute but clear way, it addresses him, comes to man as a *request* that has its origin in God's counsel, will, creation, providence, and grace. To know and to act upon the knowable is man's *answer*, his *response*. By answering—responding—man fulfils his calling set by God. Primarily and principially man is in every-thing he knows and does an answerer, a responder, one who is called—duty-bound to fulfil his calling. This is the exact opposite of human autonomy. Re-sponsibly responding to his call, man—as a responsible means in the hands of God—contributes in a creaturely way to the realization of God's plan and has to do so to the honor and glory of God.

B.3.3.3.   As an answer to the question put by the plan of God together with the question itself forms an *asymmetrical mutually com-plementary unity*, likewise, by realizing the task set by the creaturely knowable, knowing and the knowable (man—as *mandator Dei* of the cosmos—and the cosmos) are bound together. Here, too, it appears how knowledge, as the fulfilment of the call of revelation, is enstati-cally embedded in created reality as a whole.

B.3.4.   But this *fourth type* of revelation presupposes the *third*. The latter gives to the former the ultimate ground for knowing as an answer, a response to the knowable as a setting of a task, a request, as a call to man. Ultimately man's knowledge answers (responds to) God's call (revelational of himself) and the *unity* established in this case between call and answer is that of the *covenant* which God has made with man—as you so profoundly and penetratingly stress. This means that man's answer to the fourth type of revelation falls, fundamentally, under this covenant as well.

B.4.   I only mention the *order of law* (*wetsorde*) that God has determined for created reality as a whole (and all its "parts" and relations)—a truth which the "Cosmonomic Philosophy" (*Wijsbegeerte der Wetsidee*) rightly stressed so definitely. Man's knowledge, as well as created reality, is radically subject to the laws concerned.

B.5.   The intricate problem of *truth*, and especially of the truth of man's knowledge, I shall pass over. I shall say only that the *truth* of man's *knowledge* lies in its *answering* to the *knowable*,[19] and that this is more than mere correspondence.

B.6.1.   This exposition of man's knowledge, given in outline thus far, falls under (what Calvin calls) the "order of creation."

We now have to turn to (what Calvin calls) the "order of the fall and redemption" and to its significance for the knowledge-situation of man. You rightly also start with the order of creation, when you so penetratingly investigate and differentiate between what you call the adamic consciousness—the consciousness of fallen man—and the consciousness of regenerate man. With all this you have given us a very signficant contribution to a Christian theory of knowledge. I do not intend to go into this matter now, but will limit myself to a few remarks.

B.6.2. The *sequence* of *these orders* is significant, not only for a Christian (or Calvinist) theory of knowledge, but also for Calvinist philosophy in general. In my investigation of (what I have called) the cosmic dimension of events (*kosmiese dimensie van gebeurtenisse*),[20] and thereby, for instance, of causality, teleology, labor, education, human freedom, and history, I found it necessary to start with the order of creation and, after that, to investigate these and other problems according to the order of the fall and redemption. But there is a difference between our conceptions of the order of creation. You take as the "order of creation" (*in casu* with reference to the adamic consciousness) creation (or consciousness) before the fall of man. By the "order of creation" I mean *creation as it exists even today*, but *disregarding* the facts, workings, and effects of sin and evil. To do this is possible, on the one hand, because God's created universe essentially remained the same universe notwithstanding the fall into sin and evil; for instance, man is yet man and knowledge yet knowledge. On the other hand, it can rightly be done only if created reality, man and his knowledge, be seen in the light of God's Word-revelation.

B.6.3. Notwithstanding his fall into sin, man still has *contact* with the knowable, *in casu* with the knowable universe. (Your contention that man—the sinner—yet knows God but represses it, I will discuss later.) God created the universe according to his plan, and this plan, as revealed in created reality (including man himself), confronts man, the knower (*my special problem*). The sinner yet has *contact* with this plan itself; but he does *not* fully *meet* it (i.e., the creaturely knowable) in a truly answering fashion; his presuppositions are wrong; he perceives (taking this in a wide sense) the knowable in wrong perspectives; he directs his faith wrongly; he "derails" his thinking by forming wrong concepts, judgments, theories, and so forth; he thus perceives the knowable in accordance with wrong theoretical constructions;[21] and so forth. All this implies that he draws a *veil* between himself as knower and the knowable. His knowledge no longer answers fully the knowable, but falsifies it. The genuine connection between knowing and the knowable is disrupted. I have used the metaphorical "veil" because (in so far as a veil is transparent) man as sinner, is *not blind* to the knowable (*in casu*: to the plan of creation). Ever and anon the knowable (although being wrongly perceived, wrongly thought of and therefore wrongly known) may pierce the veil; and man accordingly ever and again finds himself obliged to change his theories (his knowledge) in the concerned respects, as the history of science so abundantly shows. *This is because of common grace.* But the above concerns the *fourth type* of revelation. With regard to the *third type* of revelation, however, the unbeliever is (as Calvin puts it) as blind as a bat; in other words, the veil is opaque; and its removal requires special grace, in other words, regeneration and the Word-revelation of God. The above again implies, with regard to the *fourth type* of revelation, that on the one hand the believer, still being a sinner in our dispensation, may yet be enveloped in veils with regard to his knowledge of some knowable or other, whereas on the other hand the theories of unregenerate man have moments of truth, that the believer should acknowledge. All this concerns *my special problem* that will be treated more fully later.

At any rate, your own apologetic approach of adamic, unregenerate, and regenerate knowledge forms, rightly, a major theme and a very significant, as well as original, contribution to a Christian theory of knowledge.

C.   On Science

C.1.   The believer knows God; a mother knows that she loves her child; a farmer knows his cattle. What should I call this kind of knowledge as distinct from scientific knowledge (or science in a wide sense—including theology, philosophy, particular and inter-sciences)? "Naive," "natural," "usual," "primal," "primary" knowledge or what else? I suggest we call it "pre-scientific" knowledge, but thereby keeping in mind that pre-scientific knowledge is basic and that science has historically, as well as principially, its origin in pre-scientific knowledge. Of special significance for us is that man's life and world view (including his religious faith) essentially belongs to pre-scientific knowledge and forms its comprehensive content.

In this significant sense the basic presuppositions of science belong to man's pre-scientific life and world view; science obtains its own meaning from these pre-scientific convictions. Accordingly, science can never prove its presuppositions scientifically.

For instance, evolutionism confronts us with a host of facts concerning accidental— genetic and mutational as well as ontogenetic and phylogenetic—variations, phenotypes and genotypes, analogies, sequences of strata, fossils, and so on, but yet it presupposes, for instance, autonomy of thought, a positivistic (even if neo-positivistic) conception of facts, a universal dynamic continuity of causes, a right to universal generalization and extrapolation and that nature must be wholly explicable by nature alone. These presuppositions cannot be proved scientifically, but without them evolutionism falls to pieces; and evolutionism must appear to him who does not accept these presuppositions to be a grand speculation virtually comparable to the speculative system of Hegel. These presuppositions exclude, from the start, our (biblically founded) Christian presuppositions; they are not neutral and form what you would call a "negative universal."

C.2. All science starts with pre-scientific presuppositions and should responsibly account for them. This also holds good especially for our Christian (you call it "Christian Theistic") pursuit of science.

It is elucidating, as regards exposing pre-scientific presuppositions, to compare your and Dooyeweerd's criticism of knowledge (including thought and science). Before doing so, a few distinctions have to be made. Criticism may be either positive or negative. Criticism may (a). be applied to knowledge (the concrete acts, facts, and data of knowing) or (b). to some scientific theory (or system). Significant also is the distinction between the terms (i). "transcendent" (and "transcendently") and (ii). "transcendental" (and "transcendentally").

(i). *Transcendent criticism* of knowledge *proceeds from one's own presuppositions* (or *standpoint*) and (a). demonstrates the implication of these presuppositions for the understanding of knowledge or (b). criticizes some theory of knowledge (or of science) or other. This method is necessary; it may in a certain sense be called dogmatic; but it need not be dogmatistic in so far as one is willing to *responsibly account for one's presuppositions*. (ii). *Transcendental criticism* of knowledge (a). starting from acts of functions of knowing proceeds to its basic presuppositions or (b). investigates some theory of knowledge (or of science) and exposes the presuppositions on which it is based. The transcendent and transcendental methods of criticism follow opposite directions, respectively proceeding from or proceeding towards the basic presuppositions concerned. Through the use of the (ii). *transcendental criticism* of human thought *Dooye-weerd* (a). starts from the distinction between the analytical and non-analytical aspects of cosmic reality, proceeds to man's selfhood (or heart) that brings about a synthesis between the analytical and non-analytical aspects, and he thence demonstrates that the human heart is directed either towards our triune God or loses itself apos-statically in the diversity of created reality, and he (b). critically investigates philosophic theories (or systems), exposes the presup-positions on which they are based, proceeding to the religious ground-motives that function as the ultimate motives of the systems concerned; he furthermore demonstrates how systems, motivated by non-Christian "ground-motives," fall into antinomies and dialec-tical tensions, whereas this is not the case with Christian philosophy on account of its religious "ground-motive" of creation, the fall, and redemption. *Your* criticism of knowledge, however, is (i). a *transcendent* criticism, starting with God and his knowledge of him-self and of his counsel; but it is (ii). *transcendental* in your criticism of opposing philosophical and empirical scientific theories by ex-posing their ultimate presuppositions of brute fact, chance, and hu-man autonomy; and it again becomes (i). a *transcendent* criticism when criticizing the presuppositions concerned.

Both methods of criticism, the *transcendent* and the *transcendental,* are necessary and complement one another. But *Dooyeweerd's* ap-plication of the transcendental method of human thought is *primarily philosophic* and *your* application of the method of transcendent criti-cism is, on account of your apologetic approach, *primarily theologi-cal. Dooyeweerd* with the use of the transcendental method stops (a). at the directedness of the human heart towards God or apostatically towards a theoretic idol and (b). at his exposition of the religious ground-motives (and their implications). Should he proceed any further, namely to an exposition of God and his counsel (something that he can hardly do with his transcendental method), his theory of knowledge would become theological. But, as a Christian phi-losopher, when he uses the transcendental method, he must and implicitly does presuppose all the ultimate biblical truths concerning our triune God and his relation to all things, from which you explicitly start. *You,* on the other hand, by using your transcendent method, investigate the very ultimate conditions of human knowledge as they concern God and his counsel and so forth, and criticize chance and brute facts as the ultimate conditions of the non-Christian phi-losophies and empirical sciences concerned. In this respect your theory of knowledge has attained a depth (or should I say, a height) that the transcendental theory of Dooyeweerd—from the nature of his procedure—does not attain. In this respect especially your theory of knowledge is in our Calvinist community definitely original and of unique significance; even Bavinck and Hepp—as far as I know— did not penetrate so fully into the ultimate conditions of man's knowledge as you have done.

C.3.   Distinguishing between science and pre-scientific knowledge, *pre-scientific knowledge* is firstly, theoretically and practically, without a special stress, interwoven with the whole of man's experience; *science* (taken in a wide sense) *intentionally* pursues knowledge as such; and this special stress is, in the pursuit of science, significant.

Secondly, *pre-scientific knowledge* (*in casu* life and world view, including religious faith) may be, on account of its own accord (and thus not intentionally), systematic. But *science* seeks answers to the "what?," the "why?," the "wherefore?," the "through what?," the "how?," *et cetera*, of the knowable in order to grasp, understand, describe, explain, and evaluate the knowable; to do so it has to discover the relations and the coherence between the knowable, and by doing this it *intentionally* forms systematic knowledge, i.e., knowledge that lays bare the relations and coherence of the knowable. *Science* is in this sense *intentionally* systematic (i.e., coherence manifesting) knowledge.

Thirdly, *pre-scientific knowledge* may, in the cases concerned, require verification (taken in a wide sense), as a rule it is not (and need not be) intentionally verified knowledge; tradition and accepted authority generally suffice. But *science* has *intentionally* to make sure that its observations and conclusions are valid. *Science* is *intentionally verified* (founded and proven) knowledge.[22]

Fourthly, although the forming of pre-scientific knowledge does not require methods, science *intentionally and responsibly* has to use, in its pursuit of systematized and verified knowledge, technical methods.[23]

Accordingly *science* (including theology, philosophy, the particular, inter-and intermediate sciences) is knowledge which is, by means of technical methods, intentionally, *as far as possible* systematic (laying bare relations and coherence) and *as far as possible* verified (founded and proven) knowledge as such of the knowable.

I have intentionally inserted the phrase "as far as possible." The given description of science appears to me to hold good for all concepts of science, whether formed in the past or the present and

whether Christian or non-Christian.[24] It may be called a "formal"
description of science. The differences between the diverse concepts of science, however, become manifest, when scientists determine
what precisely they mean by "as far as possible" with regard to,
for instance, presuppositions, principles, sources or data, limitations,
purpose or aims, verifiability, methods, and so forth, of science. In
our case, for instance, we, *inter alia*, stress the necessity and significance of the fundamental truths of the Scriptures for the pursuit of
science and acknowledge the limitations caused not only by man's
creaturely and derivative, but also by his sinful "nature," essentially
requiring regeneration and grace. At any rate, according to our
concept of science, theology, the particular, inter- and intermediary
sciences all are genuine sciences.[25]

D.   On the Division and Unity of Science

D.1.   You distinguish between theology, philosophy, and science.
Sometimes you use the term "philosophy" in the pre-scientific sense
of a "world and life view," but mostly in a technical (I would say,
"scientific") sense. By "science" you mean what I would call "empirical science" (including, for instance, physics, chemistry, biology,
psychology, and sociology). In order to understand the scope of your
theory of knowledge (taken in a wide sense) correctly, a more detailed division of science appears to me to be necessary. (With
reference to my arguments in the later sections of this letter it is important to keep my following descriptions of *theology* and *philosophy*
in mind.)

D.2.   *Science* I take in a wide sense. It includes the following
special sciences.

(A)   The *individual sciences* or *sciences proper*.

My first principle of division corresponds with the division of the
knowable according to the distinctions between God and his creation;
regarding creation, that between heaven (with its angels) and "earth"
(i.e., the cosmos or cosmically created reality); and regarding the
cosmos, that between the cosmos as totality and the diversity within
this totality. The special sciences I call *individual sciences* to contrast them with the *inter-sciences* and I call them *sciences proper* to
contrast them with *intermediary sciences*.

(1)   I will first consider the *individual sciences*.

(a.i).   *Theology* is the science of the revelation of God in his
Word and in creation (or "nature") concerning himself and his

relation to all "things." In the case of non-Christian theology, theology is the science of that which is taken instead of God as the absolute, for instance, the "absolute" as in the case of the "god" of Aristotle or of Spinoza, and its relation to all "things."

(a.ii). *Ouranology* (including *angelology*) as the science of heaven (with its angels) is to be intrusted to the guardianship of theology, because the data concerned are to be found in the Scriptures only.

(b). *Philosophy* is the science of the totality as well as of the coherence of the radical diversity of the cosmos (or our created universe).

(c). A *particular science (Fachwissenschaft)* is the science of a particular group of "things" belonging together on account of common characteristics or of a particular aspect of our created universe (or cosmos). Particular sciences are, for instance,

(i). the *natural sciences;*
(ii). the *cultural sciences;* and
(iii). the *social sciences.*

(d). *Note.* The distinction between *theology* and *philosophy* does not, according to my opinion, coincide with that between the revelation of God in his *Word* on the one hand and the *cosmos* (or created universe) on the other. This is the case, because on the one hand theology also deals with God's revelation in *creation,* the *cosmos,* viewed in the light of his Word-revelation, whereas the Scriptures on the other hand disclose not only who God is and what his relation to all "things" is, but also matters concerning the created universe (or the *cosmos*) as such. (God's Word even makes assertions on matters relating to the field of some particular science or other, for instance that the labor*er* [note: not "labor"] is worthy of his [not of its] reward.) Because to the field of theology belong the ultimate problems, it may be called the "*scientia prima inter pares.*"[26]

(B) The *intersciences.*

(1) I would stress, especially in order to grasp the scope of your theory of knowledge and to do it justice, that epistemology (or the theory of knowledge) be taken in a wide sense; it includes (a). the theory of science (*Wissenschaftslehre*); (b). the theory of knowledge (gnoseology); and (c). the theory of knowing or epistemology (in a narrow or specific sense).

Theory of knowledge (in a wide sense as inclusive of the other sciences mentioned) concerns the individual sciences mentioned above too.

This is the case because *each* of the individual sciences has not only its specific field of research (as described above) but is also—each in its own way—faced by and concerned with the problem of knowledge (including that of method) and because *each* of the individual sciences does contribute—each in its own way—to the theory of knowledge. Accordingly, it is wrong to assign (panphilosophically) the theory of knowledge as a whole to philosophy only, however intensive as well as extensive philosophy's contribution to the theory of knowledge may be. A few observations may elucidate these assertions.

(a.i). Firstly there are the *contributions of theology* to the theory of knowledge. Theological doctrines concerning, for instance, the dependence of man's knowledge (and science—taken in a wide sense) on the knowledge that God has of himself and of his relation to all "things," of his counsel, creation, and grace; concerning the effect of the fall of man as well as of regeneration on man's knowledge; God's revelation and grace; the authority of God's Word; the nature of faith and the testimony of the Holy Spirit in man's heart that the Word of God truly is his Word, and so forth; all have a definite, as well as supremely significant, bearing on the problems of man's knowledge (and science). How fundamental and significant these bearings are, your theory of knowledge has eminently demonstrated. Furthermore, although there are methods common to all or to many of the individual sciences, theology has also to use specific methods of its own. To this must be added that theology has not only the divisions of its disciplines as a task, but is also concerned with its relation to the other special sciences from a theological point of view. Moreover, special stress should be laid on your unique presentation of a theory—not of man's but—of God's knowledge of himself, of his counsel, and so forth. We may not ignore theology's significant contribution to the theory of knowledge nor assign the whole field of research of knowledge (including science) to philosophy only.

(a.ii). The intensive as well as extensive *contribution* of *philosophy* to the theory of knowledge I need only mention here. I may add: your theory of knowledge also plays in this respect a significant role, especially in its criticism of opposing views.

(a.iii). Thirdly, particular sciences make their respective *contributions* to the theory of knowledge too. I limit myself in this respect to psychology. A psychology of knowledge (as, for instance, elaborated by the Külpe Denkschule) yet belongs to the special field of psychology and is not relevant here. Relevant here are the technical epistemological-psychological approaches to its field of research, the specifically psychological methods to be used (for instance, whether the retrospective method yields more trustworthy results than the introspective method); the subdivision of psychological disciplines and the relation of psychology to other special sciences, seen from a psychological point of view. Your criticism of various empirical sciences falls in many respects under the contributions particular sciences make to a theory of knowledge.

(b.i). Delimitation of the respective fields of research of the special sciences is not only a philosophical concern; the delimitation of its own fields of research is the concern of every other special science as well. When a question of determining boundary lines arises, both neighbors have a say. The distinction between, for instance, the fields of research of theology and philosophy concerns the theologian as much as the philosopher. The same holds good respectively for a distinction between either theology or philosophy and a particular science, and also between particular sciences themselves. As knowledge (or science) develops, boundary lines between the special sciences may even be shifted, as, for instance, the history of the distinction between philosophy and psychology so abundantly displays.

(b.ii). Moreover—and this is of paramount significance—the theory of knowledge does not consist of unrelated epistemological contributions of the various special sciences. It should form a unity. We should distinguish here between the unity of the theory of God's knowledge and the unity of the theory of man's knowledge. In the latter case the ultimate basis of its unity will be manifest in its radical dependence on the truths of the theory of God and his knowledge. The unity of the theory of man's knowledge can be attained only by a full co-operation of the special sciences of theology, philosophy, and the particular sciences. The field of research of the theory of knowledge as a unity intersects—as it were at right angles—the respective fields of research of the individual sciences. That is the reason why I call it an *interscience*. For an illustration I limit myself to methodology (an interscientific discipline of theory of knowledge taken in a wide sense): methodology investigates problems concerning methods as such, methods common to all special sciences (as, for instance, analysis and synthesis, deduction and induction), specific methods belonging to one or more special sciences only and the interrelatedness as well as the interdependence of all methods. Moreover it investigates the respective principles that the use of methods presupposes, the respective purposes for which the methods are used, the norms to which they are respectively subject, and the validity of the respective results that methods yield (i.e., their respective epistemological truths; and so forth[27]). It may especially be stressed that methods and their uses are interrelated, interdependent, and mutually complementary; this is a methodological problem in its own way contributing to the question of the unity of science.

(b.iii).   Because a theory of knowledge (taken in a wide sense) is an *interscience*, you, as an apologist (and thus primarily a theologian), have a full right to discuss critically philosophical as well as empirical-scientific contributions to the theory of knowledge and to demand that philosophers and empirical scientists should not only acknowledge theology's contribution to a theory of knowledge, but should also presuppose and fully take it into account in their own researches. Your penetrating criticisms of non-Christian philosophical and empirical scientific theories of knowledge are not external interference, but an intrinsically interscientific concern; rightly your theory functions fullfledgedly interscientifically. (As an apologist you, of course, hardly treat the converse of this problem: namely, how and to what extent a theological approach to knowledge should fully take into account the respective relevant contributions of philosophical and particular scientific theories of knowledge.) Of special significance is your interscientific-theological foundation of philosophical and empirical scientific theories of knowledge.

(2)   The interscience *theory of knowledge* or *epistemology* (taken in a wide sense) comprises of the *intersciences* of

(a)   the *theory of science* (*Wissenschaftslehre*—sometimes also called "encyclopedia of science" or "scientology"—including methodology);

(b)   the *theory of knowledge* (or gnoseology); and

(c)   the *theory of knowing* (or *epistemology*)—in a specific sense.

(C)   The *intermediary sciences*.

Yet another distinction is necessary to rightly understand your theory of knowledge.

If we compare the following special sciences: 1. physics, 2. chemical physics, 3. physical chemistry, and 4. chemistry; 1. chemistry, 2. bio-chemistry, 3. chemical biology, and 4. biology; 1. psychology, 2. socio-psychology, 3. psycho-sociology, and 4. sociology; 1. psychology, 2. educational psychology, 3. psychology of education, and 4. education; 1. education, 2. philosophy of education, 3. educational philosophy, and 4. philosophy; 1. history, 2. philosophy of history, 3. history of philosophy, and 4. philosophy; and 1. politics, 2. philosophy of politics, 3. political philosophy, and 4. philosophy—we may call the first and the fourth of these special sciences "*sciences proper*" (e.g., physics-proper, biology-proper) and the second and third of these special sciences *intermediate sciences*. Intermediate sciences are possible and necessary, because the respective fields of research of the special sciences proper cannot be isolated from one another; they of necessity cohere and are related in indefinite ways.

Of paramount significance is the question—and this question especially concerns your theory of knowledge—whether we should recognize next to a theology-proper and a philosophy-proper also the *intermediate special sciences* of a *philosophical theology* and a *theological philosophy*.

The answer to this question co-depends upon one's delimitation of theology-proper and of philosophy-proper [cf. my distinction given at D.2.(A).(1).(a). and (b).]. To my mind, for instance, Aristotle's theory of "god," Spinoza's theory of *deus sive substantia sive natura* and of the *natura naturans* and the Thomistic "natural theology" are illustrations of a philosophical theology, whereas the main themes of A. E. Loen's *De Vaste Grond* appear to belong to a theological philosophy. If I remember rightly, William Young made, in his doctoral dissertation, a plea for Calvinist metaphysics on the lines of J. Woltjer's contribution to philosophy; and would such an undertaking not lead to a theological philosophy?[28] Could basic points of Dooyeweerd's Christology (for instance, that Christ is—according to his human nature—the religious concentration-point of the meaning totality of the created cosmos) and Bavinck's view of God's revelation as ground of cosmic reality not also be illustrations of a theological philosophy? But why should we look any further? Your own theory of knowledge does give us a clear answer to the problem concerned. Your theory of *God's knowledge* of himself and of his counsel, creation, providence, grace, and so forth belongs to *theology-proper;* and so do some aspects of your theory of *man's knowledge* (fundamentally of his religious faith) of God, of his counsel, and so forth. But your confrontation of *God's knowledge* as well as of certain fundamental aspects of *man's knowledge* of God and of his revelation in his Word and creation with the contentions of non-Christian philosophers and of empirical scientists takes the form of either a *philosophical-theological* or of a *theological-philosophical* theory of knowledge—according to the respective arguments concerned. Why should all this not be feasible, considering that not only is theory of knowledge an interscience, but also that the fields of research of theology-proper and philosophy-proper (i.e., between the Word-revelation of God and our created universe) are related in many ways? Why should all this not be fully acknowledged? After all, these fields of research are inseparable. According to my opinion the theological-philosophical as well as the philosophical-theological aspects of your theory of knowledge constitute a unique contribution to a Christian theory of knowledge.

But there still remains *my special problem*, namely a philosophy-proper theory of knowledge, a problem to which you refer and allow, but that you—probably on account of your primarily apologetic approach—do not especially elaborate, as far as I know, although you do touch upon it in your defense of criticisms of your theory.

D.3.   Unity[29] may concern (a). the *absolute transcosmic ground* of unity, namely God, of and to and through whom are all things; (b). the *formal unity* of "things" belonging together on account of common characteristics (for instance, the vegetable kingdom); (c). the diverse types of *material unity* (of, for instance, mechanic, holistic, organic, teleïc, or teleological unities, the unities of a piece of art, of a historic process, etc.); and (d). the *unity of repair* (for instance, of recovery, restoration, cure, rehabilitation, peacemaking, reconciliation, and so forth). Each of these four types of unity has a bearing upon science. We may also speak of *unity* of science as *determined by* the unity of *man* as the knower, by the *unity* of the *knowable*, by the *unity* of scientific *presuppositions* (amongst which by faith in the absolute, by faith in God's revelation, and by, what Dooyeweerd calls, religious groundmotives) and by *mutual co-operation* as well as by *interaction* of the diverse special sciences (*wisselwerking*). I only mention all this; but the *unity* secured *by* what I call "*perspective* or *contextual* meaning moments" deserves, with reference to your theory of knowledge,[30] special attention.

E.   On the Analytical and Perspective (or Contextual) Meaning Moments

E.1.   In our created universe we find (a). a diversity of "things"[31] and (b). their coherence or relations. No "thing" is separable from other "things." The meaning of a "thing" is essentially constituted not only by (a). what it specifically is (its analytical meaning moment), but also by (b). its position in a (higher) perspective or context. Because cosmic diversity essentially coheres, (a). the analytical meaning moments and (b). the perspective or contextual meaning moments of a "thing" are inseparable. This truth you have pointed out by, for instance, stressing that the meaning of any "fact" essentially depends upon the position it occupies in God's plan for the created universe. The number "2" could not have a meaning of its own, unless its position in the realm of numbers and all their relations be taken into consideration. Or again, if we visualize two paintings, each with a blue color patch of the same quality, intensity, form, and size, these patches may analytically be taken to be identical; but when each of these patches is seen in the perspective of its aesthetic functional relations to the whole of the painting concerned, they appear to differ; each concrete patch accordingly has inseparably and simultaneously analytical as well as perspective or contextual moments of meaning. This holds good *mutatis mutandis* for every "thing" in our created universe.

The methods of analysis (including synthesis and generalization) and of (higher) perspective (or contextual arrangement) follow diametrically opposed directions, are in a fundamental sense of equal value, are both necessary in the pursuit of science, and their use should go hand in hand. A scientist should not only analyze according to the principle *principia non sunt multiplicanda praeter necessitatem*, but also should follow the higher and highest perspectives according to the principle *principia non sunt diminuenda praeter necessitatem*. The general and excessive preference for the analytical method in secularistic modern times is a kind of favoritism; it is— notwithstanding the remarkable achievements attained by this method —a main reason of the present day disintegration of (especially empirical) science.[32] Only (higher and especially the highest) perspectives or contexts can guarantee the unity of science.[33]

The point at issue, however, is that every "thing" has inseparably analytical and perspective (or contextual) meaning moments at once.

E.2. The illustrations I referred to above were intra-cosmical. But of paramount significance is what you have elaborated so intensively as well as extensively, namely that (in my words) the whole of creation and every "thing" within it, as well as every relation between "things," has not only analytical (intra-cosmical) meaning moments but revelational meaning moments as well; they are revelational of God and his plan, ultimately depending on God and on God's knowledge of himself and of his counsel. Here we have arrived at the *ultimate* meaning moment of everything created. The rose in my garden is, of course, a rose; but it is at once also a creature revelational of its origin, God and his counsel (and plan). This rose has at once and inseparably its specific cosmic and its ultimate creational and revelational meaning moments; fundamentally it is God's work. If its ultimate (revelational) meaning moment (and herewith its position in the plan according to which God created the universe) is denied, this rose can no longer be taken for what it virtually is; it is then, according to your view, a mere brute fact. Leaving aside the problem of brute facts (which we will touch later), your contention that only if we accept any fact for what it revelationally really is, can we know it truly (although not comprehensively), is of basic significance.

Of interest is to note that you—as an apologist—primarily stress the ultimate meaning moment of anything in our created universe, whereas its cosmically specific or analytical meaning moment needs a stress too (of course, presupposing its ultimate meaning moment), which you allow for, but do not especially elaborate. Here again I touch upon *my special problem*. A rose is not only a revelation of God (and has its position in the plan of God), it is also a rose and, for instance, not a lily or a butterfly. Modern particular (especially empirical) scientists wrongly disregard the ultimate meaning moments of their fields of research and thus ultimately falsify them (as you rightly contend) and thereby science is disintegrated; but we may not fall into the opposite error of not giving the specific or analytical meaning moments of created reality their full due too.

F.   Outlines of Your Theory of Knowledge

F.1.   In the reconnoitering of your theory of knowledge I have thus far made very concisely a number of important preliminary distinctions. In this section I limit my survey of your theory of knowledge to mere outlines. At the same time I intend to pave the way to an elucidation of *my special problem* as a supplement to your theory. Furthermore I limit myself to distinctions between and relations of theology and philosophy and pass over those between theology and philosophy on the one hand and the empirical sciences on the other. This passing over need not be a serious omission in so far as your criticism of the empirical sciences mostly takes the form of a (theological) philosophy of science.

F.2.   The disciplines of your theory of knowledge (if I am not mistaken) may be divided as follows.

(A)   The theory of *God's knowledge*

(1)(a)   of *himself* and
(1)(b)   of *his counsel*.

These disciplines belong to a *theology-proper* theory of knowledge.

(2)   The theory of *God's knowledge* of his *creation* (including man), created according to *his plan*; of his *providence, revelation, grace,* and so forth.

According to your different approaches these disciplines fall under a theology-proper, a philosophical-theology, and theological-philosophy respectively. This is not only manifest in your own constructive theory, but especially, too, in the way you criticize opposing theories of knowledge, more particularly those of non-Christian philosophers and empirical scientists.

(B)   The theory of *man's knowledge*

(1)   of *God* (including his knowledge of God's counsel, creation, providence, revelation, grace, and so forth).

According to your different approaches, this discipline falls under a theology-proper, a philosophical-theology, a theological-philosophy respectively, and (in a limited sense, presupposing all the former) under a philosophy-proper (as is the case, for instance, of a philosophy of religion). It may even fall (in a limited sense, again presupposing all the aforesaid) under a particular science (as is the case, for instance, of a psychology of religion). This too is apparent not only from your own contributions to the subject itself, but especially too from your criticism of opposing theories.

(2)(a)   of *man's knowledge* of the *created universe* (including man himself and his knowledge) *viewed* in its *dependence* on *God* (and on God's knowledge and his counsel) and thus *seen* as revelational of *God*.

According to your different approaches this discipline belongs to a theology-proper, a philosophical-theology, and a theological-philosophy respectively but not to a philosophy-proper—*my special problem*. This too is apparent from your own contributions to this subject, but also from your criticism of other, and especially of opposing philosophical and empirical scientific theories of knowledge.

(2)(b)   concerning problems to which you repeatedly refer, the theory of knowledge that you allow for and give significant comments upon, but do not especially elaborate as such. It is the theory of *man's knowledge* of the (created) *universe* or *cosmos* (including man himself and his knowledge) according to its special or specific meaning (thereby presupposing its ultimate meaning, presupposing that it is revelational of God, that it is created according to the plan of God, and that God guides and rules it according to his providence). This theory of knowledge belongs to *philosophy*-proper and is that to which I have referred as *my special problem* as distinct from your theory of knowledge. As an apologist you have no direct need to develop this theory. Had you done so, however, you could still hold your fundamental contentions—as far as I can see—as well as your ultimate criticism of opposing theories of non-Christian philosophers and particular scientists (and even your relevant and striking criticisms of Roman Catholicism, Arminianism, evangelicism, and less consistent Calvinism), but you would probably have rephrased several of your criticisms here. In any case, your theological, philosophical-theological, and theological-philosophical contributions to our (i.e., to a Calvinist, or as you call it, to a Reformed or Christian Theistic) theory of knowledge, are supremely important and should be fully and gratefully acknowledged, especially by Christian theologians, philosophers, and particular scientists pursuing a theory of knowledge. They may differ from you on some relative viewpoints or other, but should accept the main issues of your contributions.

My own special problem I will elucidate in the section on *points of contact*. It is, in this connection, of interest, however, to note that the disciplines mentioned in F.2. under (A)(2), (B)(1), and (B)(2)(a) approach the problems of knowledge in another direction than the discipline mentioned under (B)(2)(b) does. These directions may be said to intersect one another at right angles; the former may be called a vertical and the latter a horizontal approach (the vertical being fundamental and to be presupposed by the horizontal).

F.3.   Essential to your theory of knowledge is the order of precedence and of dependence of the respective problems of your epistemological disciplines (F.2). The problems of (B)(2)(a) presuppose those of (B)(1); the latter presuppose those of (A)(2); and again the latter presuppose those of (A)(1). To this should be added that the problems of (B)(2)(b) presuppose all the former. This essential sequence of dependence you have elaborated extensively as well as intensively in detail. It forms a main theme of your theory of knowledge and is of supreme significance. I particularly wish I could go into this aspect of your theory of knowledge in greater detail, but I must limit myself to the following remarks.

According to this order of dependence you rightly contend that if there were no God, if there were no knowledge of God of himself and of his counsel, if God had not created our universe according to his plan and did not guide and rule it according to his providence, there would have been no real and true facts in our universe and no relation between them. You also contend (and this point I will have to enter into later) that whoever—as sinner—rejects these presuppositions must ultimately fall back upon brute facts and mere chance, and in whatever order he may relate these facts, he does so on a (falsely) assumed autonomy of man's reason.

F.4. Another essential point in your theory of knowledge is that of the *relation* between *being* and *knowledge*, contending that God's being coincides with his knowledge, but that man's being precedes his knowledge. You raise, in this respect, very important problems, but I, unfortunately, have to pass them over as well.

F.5. Lastly, I mention your very significant and penetrating theory concerning man's knowledge before the Fall (the adamic consciousness), the knowledge of the fallen man (the unregenerate consciousness), and the knowledge of the regenerate man (the regenerate consciousness). However important, I must limit myself to only mention this theory.

G. The Point of Contact

G.1. A Christian and a non-Christian pursuit of science (taken in a wide sense) differ in fundamental respects. Yet there is much agreement in the results of their respective pursuits. Moreover, God calls mankind to the pursuit of science. Notwithstanding the difference in principle, co-operation between a Christian and a non-Christian pursuit of science (without disregarding fundamental differences—admitting conflict because of the fundamental differences—yet not neglecting opportunities for co-operating), is, according to my view, unavoidable and a necessity. You too admit all this in one way or other. Christian scientists (theologians, philosophers, and particular as well as inter-scientists) may never be untrue to their fundamental biblical presuppositions, and yet they necessarily require contact with non-Christian scientists. You especially stress this. Regarding the calling of a pursuit of science, Christians should not only reform science wherever and whenever it goes astray, but should primarily play their full part in forming science and should in both cases endeavor to convince non-Christian scientists of the truth of their presuppositions and scientific results based on these presuppositions, and to point out that they accordingly can "better" understand and give "better" explanations of the knowable than non-Christians on their presuppositions can do; and they should do all this to the honor and glory of God.

Of this *general problem* of *point of contact* between Christian and non-Christian scientists the *contact* sought by the *apologist* is a *special case*, because he has to vindicate the gospel and thereby the fundamental truths of God's Word-revelation and has not only to defend them in the face of scientific (theological, philosophical, particular— and inter-scientific) criticism but also to attack non-Christian scientific presuppositions and results in their own domain. In this sense you have intensively entered upon the question of the point of contact between Christians and non-Christians—especially concerning the problems of knowledge (including science). The necessity of points of contact according to your theory of knowledge need not be expounded here.

G.2.   *Common notions as a point of contact.*—As a first problem of a point of contact between believers and unbelievers we may treat of *common notions* between men concerning, for instance, the belief in a *supreme* or *higher* being or power and other relevant *central truths.* You rightly affirm that there are in some sense or other such so-called common notions, but before mentioning why you reject them as a point of contact, it may be worthwhile to pose the question of the origin of such notions.

I pass over the possibility held by some that the belief in a supreme or higher being (however much falsified during the passage of time) has traditionally its origin in the Word-revelation of God to man before man fell into sin.

Firstly, there is ontically (or ontologically; you call it "metaphysically") a revelation of God in his creation (commonly called "natural revelation"). As you phrase it: our created universe and every fact within it as well as every relation between these facts are "objectively" and perspicuously revelational of God and of his majesty, power, and glory; no man can escape from it. *Secondly*, God has created man as his image and has endowed man with a sense of deity.[34] Man can, by virtue of his creaturely "nature," know God's revelation in creation. Without these two conditions man would not have been able to form what is called "common notions" of a supreme or higher being or power. But in order to understand why these common notions cannot be accepted as a real point of contact between believers and unbelievers, the following expositions may be of value.

There is the case of the *sun-worshipers.* They *have* a sense of deity and the sun *is* revelational of God. Because of man's sinful "nature" and through the lack of God's Word-revelation as well as by virtue of their sense of deity, sun-worshipers do not distinguish between the sun as a creaturely (merely physical) body and God's revelation of himself in the sun. They accordingly identify both and become sun-worshipers. (I may add that the personification of their deities—so apparent, for instance, in Greek mythology—is a result of man himself being a person, and man's sense of deity as such requires the deity concerned to be a person too.)

As a second illustration we may take the revelation of God in man. By this I do not refer to man created as the image of God, but to the fact that man also (in all his being, acts, and functions) is as creature revelational of God's majesty, glory, and power. Does not, for instance, man's *thinking* reveal in a unique way the majesty, glory, and power of God? But on account of the sinner's sense of deity and God's revelation of himself in "nature"—*in casu*: in man's thinking and by lack of belief in God's Word-revelation, the sinner identifies man's creaturely thinking and God's revelation of himself in man's thinking. This is a significant reason for the unbeliever's faith in the autonomy of human reason and for the jubilation of the Dutch poet Kloos: "I am a god in the depths of my thoughts."

As a third illustration we refer to all the *isms* in theology, philosophy, particular, and inter-sciences, which absolutize something that appertains to the self-insufficient created universe (including man). If man did not have a sense of deity and had God not revealed himself in his creation, such *absolutizations* would have been impossible; they all identify, somehow, something creaturely or appertaining to self-insufficient creation with God's revelation of himself in creation. The materialist, for instance, may rightly contend that matter exists and that all "things" are somehow related to matter, but how precisely does he know that matter is absolute, that of and through and to matter all things are? The absoluteness of matter he cannot observe or infer from his observations; only his religious faith, his sense of deity (with which he is creationally endowed) and God's revelation in matter makes this absolutization possible.

In all these cases I may refer to Romans 1:23: "and they changed the glory of the uncorruptible God into an image made like to corruptible man, and to birds and fourfooted beasts, and creeping things" (to which we may add) and to the sun as a physical body, to the (supposed) autonomy of human reason and to the (supposed) absoluteness of matter. We may phrase the same fact conversely: they extrapolate something creaturely (or appertaining to self-insufficient creation) to a (supposed) god or absolute, thereby making the supposed "god" or absolute a lengthening-piece of self-insufficient created reality, virtually identical with created reality.

Thus, also, common notions or central religious truths are formed. You rightly reject this as a point of contact between Christians and non-Christians, because, as you contend, they are sinful and although they may refer to *a* god, they do not concern our living triune God and do not contain the elemental truths of creation and providence. These man-made notions, for sure, are false and are somehow apostatically directed by man's faith (or his sense of deity) to something appertaining to created reality, thereby somehow identifying it with God's revelation of himself in created reality.

G.3. *The fundamental point of contact.*—But back of these common notions there is, as you rightly contend, the ontic (or, ontological, you call it the "metaphysical") real knowledge situation: God *does* exist; he *does* reveal himself; there *is* an "objective," perspicuous and inescapable revelation of God in creation; man *is* created as the image of God; he *has* a sense of deity; man *does* know God; *even* the *sinner* knows God deep in his heart but suppresses this knowledge; he knows that he is a creature of God, that creation is revelational of God; that his assumed idea of autonomy is false; but he rejects all this, serving the creature rather- than God. You contend that all this is implied in Romans 1:19-20. Ethically and epistemologically there is no common area or common ground between believers and unbelievers; but at the back of this there is the real ontic (or "metaphysic") point of contact between them. Ontically, believers and unbelievers have *all reality, all* its *revelation of God* in common; they they are alike image-bearers of God; together they operate in the God-created and Christ-redeemed world—as you formulate it. That is why the truths of God's Word-revelation can and must be presented without dilution to unbelievers and absolute surrender to these truths be demanded of them. The Christian should not seek contact with the sinful common notions of natural man, but with the ontic ("metaphysical") or ultimate fact that he cannot escape God, and the Christian should do it by antithetically opposing all the unbeliever's common notions or so-called central truths as well as all other apostatic convictions. I trust I have given your views on this point of contact correctly. This view, which you have elaborated so intensively and extensively, is right and it presupposes your contentions that man's knowledge ultimately and essentially depends on God and on God's knowledge of himself as well as on God's creation, providence, revelation, and grace. It is a unique and fundamental as well as very significant contribution to our Christian theory of knowledge.

G.4. *Contact by language.*—You have been criticized because you borrowed several distinctively technical terms, especially from absolute idealism. You meet your critics in this respect by contending, for instance, that this point of contact is possible and necessary, that even the apostles borrowed the term *logos* from non-Christian sources and that you yourself attach to these terms genuinely and thoroughly biblical meanings. For, as you contend, a Christian can speak to non-Christians by translating Christian truths into their language.

I limit myself to the following terms. By calling God a *concrete universal* you mean nothing but our living triune God; and when you speak of the *rational* relations between God and us, the absolute *rationality* of God and of Christianity being in the last instance *absolute rationalism* or of the *rational* being *real* and the *real* being *rational*, you want these expressions to be understood in a genuine and thoroughly biblical sense. *To do you full justice we, of course, have to do so; we may not misunderstand what you really intend to convey.* Your theory is, notwithstanding the terms you borrow from non-Christian philosophy, essentially neither humanistic, rationalistic, nor idealistic, but genuinely Calvinistic. Yet, this point of language contact with unbelievers poses some very interesting problems.

G.4.1.   There are times when one should give new meanings to distinctive old terms as well as times when distinctive new words should be coined (as, for instance, in our times Dooyeweerd and Heidegger do). For this contingent question (cf. Eccl. 3:1-8) there are no hard and fast rules; ultimately it is a question of wisdom. Different circumstances, intentions, and approaches influence the issue. Whatever a scientist (theologian, philosopher, particular as well as inter-scientist) may do, the danger of misunderstanding is always present,[35] and real contact insecure. Even the non-Christians you address in their language may yet misunderstand you. But no one may deny you the right of giving new meanings to distinctive old terms as long as you clearly define them. And that you do.

G.4.2.   But there is a deeper issue at stake. The distinctive old terms concerned may have been formed in answer to (and they thus may presuppose in someway or other) *false problems*. For instance, the interesting and complicated history of the term *universal* (from Socrates up to the modern absolute idealists) presupposes the (according to my view, false) problem, whether and to what extent reality can or may be grasped in terms of general concepts of thought, *thereby implying* (in some way or other) that reality should conform to the "nature" of general concepts of human thought; and the terms "rational," "rationality," and "rationalism" presuppose a (according to my views, wrong) special stress on reason (*Vernunft*) as distinct from understanding (*Verstand*). To what extent is it possible, by giving Christian meanings to such distinctive technical old terms used in non-Christian philosophy, based as they may be on non-Christian and accordingly false problems, wholly to avoid the predilective or preferential slant which the false problems gave these terms?

G.4.3. Our problem should be viewed in an even wider context.

As history proceeds man is again and anon confronted by *new* developments, circumstances, situations, discoveries, problems, tasks, and what have you. No one can escape or try to avoid it. God's dynamic and providential realization of his counsel manifests itself in this process. Every juncture sets man in his divine calling anew.

In this march of time we Calvinists theologians, philosophers, particular and inter-scientists neither can nor may try to avoid what Dooyeweerd calls the "western community of thought" (*Westerse denkgemeenschap*). We are influenced by it; we co-operate with it; we contradict and oppose it and take part in its battle of minds. Our opposition to non-Christian attitudes and contentions may be reactionary or reformative. Reactions are in a negative way yet bound to the preceding adversary actions (attitudes and contentions), whereas reformations are (scripturally led) *de novo* orientations.

Calvinists agree upon basic biblical (and confessional) truths as well as upon the significance of the light cast by basic biblical truths upon created reality. But in the elaboration and precision of their contentions they differ amongst themselves too. It would be artificial and "unnatural" if it were otherwise. The differences may be a result of the functioning of dissimilarities of personal factors, of dispositions, talents, education, experience, situations, tasks, interests, or what have you—in general: to difference between personal callings as well as shortcomings. These differences testify to the dynamic character of Calvinism as well as to the fact that Calvinists too are sinners.

These differences amongst Calvinists may be mutually complementary (because of the differences between personal callings) or may be mutually contradictory. Differences may be a result of the state of mental development at every new juncture, time being needed for discovering the right responses to the new problems; and the responses concerned would accordingly be virtually of a provisional nature, although not always seen and propounded as such. In these latter cases, following generations are generally in a better position to judge the shortcomings of former generations; for instance, today we can see better in what respects Bavinck and his contemporaries erred as they did. But the mutually contradictory differences may also be a result of our sinful nature, for instance, by adapting ourselves to faulty notions in our "community of western thought" or by being reactionary towards such faulty notions rather than reformative.

The point I wish to make is that you have been criticized by co-Christians (including Christian theists, as you prefer to call them) and in your turn you have criticized them. Moreover—to limit myself to this point only—in your apologetics the notions of "universals" and "rationality" play a larger role than in theologies and philosophies of other Christians.[36] Your predilection for using these terms (giving them genuinely biblical meanings) is probably a result of your intensive and extensive knowledge of the philosophy of the absolute idealists and of of your conviction of the necessity to criticize them. Your use of the terms expresses accordingly a fundamentally reformative (i.e., genuinely biblical) criticism of this philosophy. But by doing this you, at the same time, have contributed your unique contribution to our theory of knowledge stressing the necessity that we should start with the ultimate condition of human thought, namely the existence, self-knowledge and counsel of God—the absolute—and that, consequently, every fact and every relation between facts of our created universe is what it is but only on account of God and his plan; and that whoever rejects this must ultimately fall back upon pure chance, brute facts, and human autonomy. You have thus excellently demonstrated the necessity of a theological contribution to our theory of knowledge and its fundamental significance for all our philosophical and empirical scientific approaches to the problems of knowledge and also in what fundamental respects such theories held by non-Christian philosophers and empirical scientists err.[37] Would you have attained all these and other unique insights of your Christian theory of knowledge had you not been so thoroughly versed in the conceptions of absolute idealism, being thereby obliged to criticize them from your strictly Calvinist stand?[38] Is what you thus have so magnificently achieved not a very essential, moreover a fundamental, complement to what other Calvinist theories of knowledge present? What you have given us (some of us probably would like to rephrase in some respects) should be gratefully acknowledged by us all, be elaborated further and never be lost sight of.

G.5. *Facts as a point of contact between believers and unbelievers:*
G.5.1. *Dualities*
G.5.1.1. You rightly hold a two-layer theory of reality: (i). the

absolute, all-sufficient, self-contained triune *God* and (ii). his created, derivative, self-insufficient *universe*; the latter presupposing and being in every respect absolutely dependent on the former.

G.5.1.2.   You rightly hold a dual-level theory of thought: (i). the all-comprehensive absolute *thought of God* and (ii). the creaturely, derivative *thought of man*; man having receptively creatively to think God's thoughts after him.

G.5.1.3.   You rightly hold two levels of interpreters of our created universe: (i). *God*, who interprets absolutely, and (ii). *man*, who must be a reinterpreter of God's interpretation. God's interpretation preceding the created universe and its facts.

G.5.2.   Your theory of knowledge—as I understand it—implicitly and in several instants explicitly agrees with what I call a reflection of this duality in created reality as well as in man's knowledge of created reality. This is meant in an ontological ("metaphysical") sense.

G.5.2.1.   There is (i). a revelation of *God* in his creation, all things being revelational of him (cf. section B.3.2.c.) and, as I see it, (ii). the revelation of the *created universe itself*, including man [cf. sections B.3.2.d., B.3.3.1., F.2.(B)(2)(a) and (b)]. Though distinguishable, these revelations are not separable, the latter presupposing in a fundamental sense the former.

G.5.2.2.   Every fact (keeping myself to your term "fact") thus (i). has an *ultimate* meaning moment (cf. section E.2.) revelational of God's majesty, wisdom, power, and glory, and at the same time, (ii). a creaturely *specific* meaning moment; for instance, a rose being revelational of God and at the same time being a rose and not a lily or a butterfly. These meaning moments, though distinguishable, are not separable.

G.5.2.3.   God created the universe according (i). to *his* plan, all facts and their relations displaying its order, presupposing and being revelational of God and, as I see it, (ii). this plan itself being present in our self-insufficient universe and knowable in a creaturely and derivative way; but man should in his investigation thereof always presuppose that it has its origin in God and his counsel, in other words, that God determined every fact and its place in this plan and accordingly every fact for what it is.

G.5.2.4.   All this implies a twofold approach of created reality in man's pursuit of knowledge, including science taken in a wide sense, namely, (i). according to your *apologetic* (theological, philosophical-theological and theological-philosophic) approach and (ii). a derivative (*philosophy-proper*) approach, as, for instance, Dooyeweerd has presented us and as I have ventured to give in the introductory parts of this letter. If you would not misunderstand me, I could call your approach dimensionally a *vertical* and the other a *horizontal* (or intra-cosmical) approach. But, and this is essentially significant, the latter approach must ever and anon presuppose the former approach. You allow for this latter approach (*my special problem*) and give important comments upon it, but do not especially elaborate it as such. It seems to me worthwhile to elucidate the distinction between the two approaches at some length.

G.5.3. *The two approaches.*—A friend, pointing to a building on our university campus, says to me: "Is it not marvellous that the foundation, the roof, every room, every passage, every stairs, every window, every door, all their functions and all the relations between them, in other words the plan (*P*) of this building as a whole and every part thereof has its origin in the mind of its architect (*A*)?" I agree. I call this the *P-A* context, view, or approach. But then I ask my friend to turn right and to tell me how many rooms, passages, stairs, windows, doors there are, what their functions and purposes are, where they are situated, and thus to explain to me the contents (*C*) of the plan (*P*) according to which this building was built. I call this the *P-C* context, view, or approach. The difference of directions of *P-A* and *P-C* could be illustrated by the two lines *P-A* and *P-C* drawn at right angles; in other words, and I wish to stress this point, the two approaches differ, and the directions of these approaches are not reducible to one another; the one yields knowledge the other does not yield. But the *P-C* approach presupposes the *P-A* approach.

My friend hands me a novel and says: "Is it not wonderful that every word, every sentence, every paragraph, every chapter and their sequences, and that every man, every woman, every child, every occurrence, and every deed and their sequences, in other words, the plan (*P*) of the book as a whole and every part of it has its origin in the mind of its author (*A*)?" Again I concur. But again I ask my friend to turn to the right and to tell me what each sentence, paragraph, chapter says, who the different persons are and what they do and what the story is about; in other words, what are the contents (*C*) of the plan (*P*) that is developed in this novel. Again the *P-A* and *P-C* contexts, views, or approaches differ; their directions are not reducible to one another; and although the *P-C* approach yields other knowledge than the *P-A* approach, the former presupposes the latter.

These illustrations concern intra-cosmical examples meant to
elucidate your theory of knowledge by contrasting it with *my special
problem*. Your *P-A* approach (and according to your argument it
may as well be an *A-P* approach) is, however, a cosmically transcendent or an ultimate (or vertical) approach. You rightly contend
that every fact in our created universe and every relation between
facts, in other words, the whole plan (*P*) of our universe absolutely
depends upon, presupposes, and reveals God and his counsel, his
majesty, glory, and power (*A*). I concur. But now I ask you to make
a right turn and tell me precisely what material things, plants, animals, human beings, causes and ends, principles, facts and values,
nature, culture and religion, logic, language and art, economics,
rights and morality, individuals, communities and societies, mar-
riages, families, nations, states and churches, hospitals, industries,
schools, education, sports, labor, techniques, history, and so forth
are and how they are related; in other words, what the content (*C*)
of the plan (*P*) of our created universe is, the plan present everywhere in and around us. Of course my (horizontal) *P-C* approach
fundamentally and essentially presupposes your *P-A* (or *A-P*) approach, but it yields knowledge different from the knowledge your
approach yields; the directions of approach differ and are not reducible
to one another.

Intentionally I have stated the problems in a simplified way. Your
theory of knowledge is much more complicated. This is apparent
when we take God's Word into consideration. The Scripture gives
us very clearly the *P-A* (or *A-P*) context or approach: God is the
ultimate ground of all things; he created everything according to his
plan; the whole creation and everything thereof, every fact and
every relation and every occurrence and every deed reveal God, his
plan, his majesty, power, and glory. But the *P-C* content of the
Scripture is complicated. *On the one hand* the Holy Writ speaks
of matter, plants, animals, and men; of nature and culture, of farms
and buildings, of countries, mountains, and rivers, of peoples and
wars, and so forth. Let us call it the *mere P-C content*. *On the other
hand*, the Scripture relates of God's doings with man; he speaks
to men; he sends his angels to them; relates of his probationary command and of the fall of man into sin; relates of his covenant with
man; of the deluge he sent, and so forth; of the virgin birth, crucifixion, resurrection, and ascension of Jesus Christ; of his providence
and grace, of the last things, and so forth. Let us call this the *sal-
vational* content of the Scriptures and indicate it as the *P-C/A* (or

P-A/C) content. With this distinction of contents no Roman Catholic or Protestant scholastic dualism is intended at all. The *mere P-C* approach presupposes the *P-C/A* (or *P-A/C*) approach, and this presupposes the *P-A* (or *A-P*) approach, and moreover all these approaches form together an indivisible unity. However, to elucidate *my special problem* I limit my exposition to contrasting your *P-A* (or *A-P*) and my *mere P-C* approaches.

G.5.4. *Facts are not a contact point between believers and unbelievers:*

G.5.4.1. This tenet concerns your *A-P* or *P-A* approach. Our self-contained God is the final reference point of everything created. On account of his counsel, creation, control, governance, and providence as well as his interpretation, every fact as well as the plan of the universe is precisely what it is. Every fact, the relations between facts, the plan of created reality, all display this and are, in other words, revelational of God. To be a fact at all it must be a revelational fact. Without the presupposition of God, the whole creation and every fact is meaningless and its interpretation and explanation futile. Every fact that faces man through his constitution as well as through his environment puts man face to face with God; man's understanding of any fact is an understanding of something of the ways of God. Every knowledge transaction is a reference to our God. No area, no fact can be objectively, correctly, and truly interpreted unless it be seen in its absolute dependence upon God. To interpret one fact without God, as unbelievers do, is to maintain brute fact; it is to fall back on mere chance; it is to make man the final reference point of reality and to have recourse to the supposed autonomy of human reason. Between believers and unbelievers the "factness" of fact is at issue. Facts do not constitute a common area, a point of contact, between Christians and non-Christians.

G.5.4.2. Notwithstanding all this, you also rightly stress again and anon that we should appreciate the accomplishments and contributions of empirical scientists who are not Christians; they know much about the universe; discover many truths by the methods they employ; and have made marvellous technological advances.

G.5.4.3. They could (according to your contention) make all these contributions not because of *but in spite of* their unbiblical assumptions, their misconceptions of ultimate relations, their being alienated from God. They may be blind to the truths about God, but are not blind in every sense to the true state of affairs in the phenomenal world.[30] Empirical science is a technique; and (ethically seen) counting, measuring, weighing, logical reasoning, and so forth are equal to both the Christian and the non-Christian; they have an equal use of such gifts and non-Christians may in cases be even more skillful than Christians in using them; but non-Christians assume that the facts they count, measure, weigh, and reason are not created and controlled by God. Non-Christians have brought to light many details we should gladly recognize and which indeed are true when considered apart from their false ultimate postulates. It must be remembered that, metaphysically seen, man cannot efface his sense of deity, being created as the image of God; and, that sin did not destroy the powers that God gave men at the beginning when he endowed them with his image. Moreover, the cultural productions (including the results of the pursuit of science) of non-Christians should be ascribed to common grace that God works in them. God's grace curbs in some measure the hostilities of sinful men and restrains them. Except for the common grace of God, there could be no discoveries of truth. By God's common grace creative forces implanted in man are to some extent released and unbelievers are enabled to make contributions to the edifice of human knowledge in spite of their ultimate principles. Non-Christian scientists could be seen as the Phoenician laborers of Solomon; they are not the architects, but make tributary service in the area of the works of God. The discoveries of non-Christian scientists virtually belong to the edifice of the Christian theistic scientists, at least to them who pursue science as covenant-keepers.

G.5.4.4. But notwithstanding all this (as you contend), non-Christian scientists do not see facts as God-made facts. All depends upon the ultimate nature of facts. *Epistemologically*—I stress this word—facts do not represent a common area, a point of contact between Christian and non-Christian scientists. In this respect a head-on collision between them is unavoidable. And, you maintain, this fundamental conflict can finally be won only by means of the work of *special grace* and regeneration of the unbeliever.

G.5.5. *Facts are a point of contact between Christians and non-Christians.*—I trust that I have given in the former section (G.5.4) your *P-A* or *A-P* approach correctly. The following is given according to a *P-C* approach as a supplement to your approach. This does not mean that you did not make several significant comments on the latter approach, but only that you did not especially elaborate it as such; and this specific approach is what I have called *my special problem* several times.

The plan of our university building (or respectively of the novel) in the mind of the architect (or in that of the author respectively) precedes the plan as it is realized and *as it thus is itself present* in the building (novel). Likewise, the plan conceived by God and according to which God created and providentially governs and guides our universe, is realized in and *is itself present* in created reality. This plan confronts us everywhere, in and around ourselves; it forces itself upon us; we cannot avoid or escape it; all our knowings and doings presuppose it; without the actual and virtual presence of this plan, man could not know and act. It includes every fact and every relation between facts. This *P-C* content is meant ontologically ("metaphysically"). You yourself hold that all men (and therefore Christians as well as non-Christians) have "metaphysically" all reality in common; but you still see it in a *P-A* perspective: all men together operate in a God-created and Christ-redeemed world. Although this is undoubtedly the case, my point is that according to the *mere P-C* approach (at right angles to your P-A approach), non-Christians too are faced by the plan itself as it is realized and present in our universe, notwithstanding the fact that they do not believe in our triune God as he has revealed himself in his Word; this plan confronts them and forces itself upon them too, nor can they too escape it. In other words, I distinguish between (a). the plan as it is revelational of God (*P-A*) and (b). (turning right) the plan as it is itself actually present in created reality (*P-C*); between (in your terms) (a). the fact that God is our environment (*P-A*) and (b). that we have a derivative, self-insufficient environment (*P-C*); between (a). the ultimate meaning moments of created reality (*P-A*) and (b). its specific meaning moments (*P-C*): thereby fully admitting that these distinctions respectively cannot be separated, but contending that they are yet distinguishable and again admitting that respectively the latter (b). essentially presupposes the former (a). You too speak about the latter, when you (to give just one example) contend that in creation the lower universes of discourse anticipate the higher and the higher look back upon the lower.

According to Romans, as you rightly observe, "metaphysically" all men know *God*, but the sinner represses this knowledge. To this I should like to add the observation that ontologically (or "metaphysically") all men know the *plan* of the universe (including facts and their relations), but that unbelievers *falsify it in some fundamental respect* or other; and that this falsification ultimately is due not only to their *repression* of their knowledge of God, but also to their *substitution* of non-Christian ultimate presuppositions for the ultimate Christian truths. The unbeliever can do this because man is created as the image of God, has a sense of deity, and identifies something creaturely with God's revelation therein. But by doing so a veil is formed between him and the knowable universe, i.e., between him and the plan present in the universe; he accordingly sees reality in false perspectives.[40] But yet he has contact with this plan and, again and anon (not by special, but) by common grace this plan pierces in some way or other this veil, effecting a change of vision. Of this the history of science richly testifies. But being yet an unbeliever, the new visions become veiled again in a new way.[41] To gain the true *P-A* perspective, however, the work of special grace is the final condition.

With reference to your reasons for the contributions of non-Christian scientists (I still use the term "scientist" in a wide sense), I am inclined to go further than you (see section G.5.4.3). Empirical sciences appear to me to be more than mere techniques; their aim is pursuit of knowledge. The contributions of non-Christians cover a larger area than mere details. I admit all you assert about the significance of common grace for the contribution to the edifice of knowledge by non-Christian scientists; but to this I would add that these contributions are (according to the *P-C* approach) in a positive sense a result of the fact that common grace maintains the contact of man with the plan present in created reality itself, however much man as a sinner may veil and accordingly falsify it.

The fact of the inescapable contact of man *with the plan* of our created universe *itself*, is the positive explanation why there is, in respect of the *P-C* context, so much agreement between believers and unbelievers. To this should be added, however, that the points of agreement differ when they are seen in the light of the respective opposing fundamental presuppositions (*P-A*), from which they may be distinguished, but cannot be separated. In other words, the agreement between Christian and non-Christian scientists holds good only in a restricted sense and only when they are seen separate from their respective fundamental presuppositions.

Admitting that the *plan itself* of created reality confronts man everywhere, the non-Christian scientist may, according to his experience, appeal to it for his conception of the order of the universe or for what is called the uniformity of nature. From the *P-C* approach this order need not be seen as a chance allocation of facts, except in the cases where a philosopher or a particular scientist admit-

tedly starts from chance and pure facts and falls back upon the supposed
autonomy of human reason that brings order into assumed brute facts.

You have penetratingly demonstrated that the systems of philosophers and of empirical scientists that you have criticized ultimately
presuppose pure chance, brute factuality, and the autonomy of human reason. But according to what I have expounded above, this
need not always be the case, at least seen from the *P-C* approach.
Let us take, for instance, a consistent materialist. He explicitly
rejects the autonomy of reason by explaining it, for instance, as a
function or epiphenomen of material brain-processes. For the order
of his system he may appeal to the plan of creation that confronts
him (however much he may falsify it). He, according to his own
system, does not fall back upon chance, brute facts, and a contingent
allocation of brute facts. Your disjunction that man makes either God
or himself the ultimate point of reference appears in this case, according to the *P-C* approach, to be too narrow, because for the
materialist, matter and not man is explicitly his ultimate point of
reference. From the *P-C* point of view the first choice is that either
God or something belonging to the (created) universe is taken as the
ultimate point of reference and in the latter case either man or something else of the universe may be taken to be the ultimate point of
reference.[42] This argument holds good for other "isms" as well as,
for instance, for energeticism, vitalism, psycho-monism, naturalism,
evolutionism, and so forth.

G.5.6. *No contradiction between the two approaches implied.*—
The *P-A* (or *A-P*) and the *P-C* approaches differ and yield different
insights, the latter yet presupposing the former.

In the case of the non-Christian philosophers and empirical scientists (as, for instance, those you have criticized so penetratingly),
who explicitly fall back upon and fundamentally keep to chance,
brute facts, a contingent allocation of brute facts, and an autonomy
of human reason, there is no contradiction between the tenets of the
two approaches.

But in the case of non-Christian philosophers and empirical scientists (as in the case, for instance, of the materialist), whose systems
explicitly hold to an objective order (or uniformity of nature) and
do not accept the autonomy of reason, the contentions of your *P-A*
(or *A-P*) and of my *P-C* approach seem to contradict one another.
To point out in reply that the materialist's system could have been
formed only on account of a covert belief in or assumed use of the
autonomy of reason, does not hold good and confuses the two ap-

proaches. The materialist's absolutization of matter (identifying matter with God's revelation in the matter) is, however, due to his *faith* (his sense of deity) and in this respect an autonomy of apostatic faith functions. As such the disjunctions of your approach, namely the choice between either God or man as ultimate reference points does hold good and does not contradict the fact that the materialist explicitly makes matter his ultimate point of reference. Furthermore, if you, according to your *A-P* (or *P-A*) approach (i.e., according to your contention that our self-contained triune God and his counsel is back of everything) would ask, for instance, the materialist about the origin of matter, he could only appeal to its "just-thereness"; and this admittance implies that his *A-P* (or *P-A*) presuppositions are (in contrast to your presuppositions) fundamentally contingent, i.e., nothing but chance. Seen in this perspective or context, the order the materialist observes between facts, ultimately, can be nothing but contingent as well, and this order (still in contrast to your presuppositions) could hardly be anything else than a contingent connection of brute facts. (Advisedly I speak of a "contingent *connection*" and not of an "*allocation*" of brute facts by the materialist, because epistemologically his appeal is to the order (or plan) of nature that he observes and cannot escape, however much he may falsify it.) All this means that you may still keep your ultimate criticism that whoever rejects (or does not acknowledge) the existence of God and his counsel, ultimately must fall back upon chance and brute facts, notwithstanding that according to the *P-C* approach non-Christian philosophers and particular scientists (in the cases concerned as, for instance, that of the materialist) may explicitly appeal to the order, or plan, of nature with which they are confronted and (according to their systems) may explicitly deny chance, brute facts, and even the autonomy of human reason.

In other words, by and large, there is no *neutral* area common to Christian and non-Christian scientists ("scientists" still taken in a wide sense) and accordingly there is no *neutral* science, because so far as—because of common grace—facts are a point of contact between them, i.e., so far as there is agreement (upon facts and their relations, i.e., on the plan itself of the created reality) between them, they agree upon what virtually belongs to God and because whatever they agree upon is inseparably seen either in the light of the fundamental biblical or of fundamental unbiblical presuppositions.[43] In this sense you rightly hold that the battle between them is of a totalitarian nature.

H.   On Method

H.1.   With respect to your theory of knowledge you rightly distinguish between the starting points and methods of Christian and non-Christian pursuits of science (taking "science" in a wide sense). We have already considered the question of starting point and I restrict my exposition of method[44] to a few remarks relevant to your view of the problem of method.

H.2.1.   You rightly stress that a Christian pursuit of science is presuppositional. To this I would add that a non-Christian pursuit of science is presuppositional as well. After all, science has historically and principially its origin in pre-scientific life and world view (including religious convictions), and this fact holds good for non-Christian science as well. In section C.1. I have mentioned pre-scientific assumptions of, for instance, the theory of universal evolution. To this may be added your demonstrations of the presuppositions of chance and of the autonomy of human reason in the cases of the philosophical and empirical scientific theories, which you have penetratingly criticized. The differences between a Christian and a non-Christian pursuit of science are in this context, among others, that in a Christian pursuit of science the ultimate presuppositions are (a). obtained from God's Word-revelation, (b). in submission to the authority of God's Word, and (c). are explicitly stated and answered for, whereas in a non-Christian pursuit of science (a). the ultimate presuppositions are unbiblical, (b). the authority of the Holy Writ is radically rejected, and (c). the presuppositions are more often than not covertly, i.e., only implicitly, present and not accounted for. At any rate, both pursuits are necessarily presuppositional. But the difference of the presuppositions implies that there is basically no neutral pursuit of science. The issues concerning ultimate presuppositions cannot be settled by a direct appeal to facts, insofar as their interpretations presuppose the presuppositions concerned. The ultimate reference points determine the stand taken. What you contend concerning a Christian pursuit of science, namely that a circular reasoning is implied in the mutual involvement of starting point, method, and conclusions, holds good for a non-Christian pursuit of science as well.

H.2.2.   However, the radical difference between the two pursuits of science—as you rightly contend—is that Christian knowledge *is* and non-Christian knowledge *is not* analogical. Christian knowledge is analogical because of the dualities it presupposes (see section

G.5.1). God and his creation differ radically; God's knowledge is original, whereas man's knowledge is derivative; man's knowledge is not identical with but analogous to God's knowledge; man must creaturely and receptively constructively think God's thoughts after him. As opposed to this, non-Christian pursuit of knowledge (and science) is not analogical, because its basic presuppositions are but absolutizations of something created; they thus cannot appeal to a revelation of a personal reality that is radically different from their experience. That is why they, in a circular fashion, can generalize and extrapolate something of created reality to a universal or absolute principle, thereby making it a lengthening-piece of created reality, as so many *isms* in philosophy and particular sciences do.[45] As you formulate it in another context, the god of the non-Christians is but a projection or a limit; the possibility of this projection or conception of a god or a limit goes back to the pre-scientific presuppositions concerned. All this too implies, as you contend, that in a basic sense there is no neutral pursuit of science and that there can be no compromise on ultimate issues.

H.3.   Also in the case of hypotheses and the inductive method I would suggest a distinction between the *P-A* (or *A-P*) and the *P-C* approaches.

Concerning the *P-C* approach, there are firstly the *mere* and restricted *empirical hypotheses*. Let us take a very simple example. X has been murdered by either A, B, C, or D. Four *equally relevant* hypotheses accordingly may be held (of course, until it is proved who really murdered X); but it cannot be determined in advance to what conclusions a hypothesis may lead. In the pursuit of empirical sciences such like hypotheses are abundant; and they hold good for a Christian as well as a non-Christian pursuit of science. In this limited sense co-operation between Christians and non-Christians is feasible. This is the case, because the (God-given) plan of the created universe forces itself upon man. But to restrict science to such like hypotheses would mean to disintegrate science and to let it fall apart into pieces, because the necessary higher and ultimate perspectives or contexts are wanting.[46] The significance of such hypotheses (especially when proved) depends on the role attributed to them within higher and especially ultimate perspectives or contexts; and on such issues Christians and non-Christians differ in principle.

Secondly (again according to the *P-C* approach) there are what could be called *principial hypotheses*. They concern the radical (and therefore mutually irreducible) diversity of created reality; a diversity that has its origin in God's creative will. The point at issue here is that one hypothesis may respect but another may reject this radical diversity in some instance or other (for instance, between inorganic matter and a living organism; between human and animal being; between the ethical on the one hand and, for instance, the psychical, the logical, the economical, the juridical, the religious, and so forth on the other), thus theoretically reducing the one or explaining the one in the terms of the other. This is theoretically possible, because all radical diversity of created reality coheres and some instance of coherence being used as a means of leveling. Hypotheses acknowledging and those rejecting radical diversity are not equally relevant, because only those that from the outset acknowledge the real radical diversity concerned are true. However, hypotheses acknowledging, as well as those rejecting, radical diversity can be neither proved nor disproved by an appeal to mere empirical facts, because these facts are from the outset interpreted in terms (viewed in the light of) one or the other of these principial hypotheses. With regard to acknowledging radical diversity, Christians and non-Christians may in some cases agree. But ultimately the choice between such hypotheses is co-determined by the choice of ultimate (P-A) presuppositions, and in this respect Christians and non-Christians necessarily disagree in principle.

But you, as an apologist, are mainly concerned with hypotheses according to the P-A or A-P approach, i.e., to what may be called *ultimate hypotheses*. I call them hypo-theses, although they are fundamental presuppositions, because empirical scientists often refer to them as hypotheses. The critical question is what the ultimate reference point of such a hypothesis is. You rightly contend that hypotheses must be consistent with the fundamental truths concerning God and his counsel as the ultimate explanation of all things. In other words, the test for the relevancy of any hypothesis is—as you state it—its correspondence with God's interpretation; hypotheses that *exclude* the existence of God must from the outset be considered irrelevant; no hypothesis that does not interpret facts in the light of the fundamental Christian (i.e., biblical) truths can be relevant to any group of facts. This is, for instance, the case when an evolutionist starts with the ultimate hypothesis that nature must be wholly explicable by nature alone. Ultimate hypotheses of Christians as well as of non-Christians can be neither proved nor disproved by an appeal to empirical facts, because these facts from the outset presuppose in a fundamental sense the ultimate hypotheses (or pre-suppositions) concerned.

A non-Christian (empirical scientific and philosophic) methodology that acknowledges neither *ultimate* nor *principial* hypotheses but only *mere empirical* hypotheses (thereby implicitly reducing the former to the latter) and that accordingly maintains that any sort of hypothesis is as relevant as any other, and likewise claims that it cannot be determined in advance to what conclusions any hypothesis must lead, excludes from the outset not only the radically diversity of created reality, but moreover (as a "negative universal") God and his counsel, his creation, providence, and grace. But this means that it reduces the *ultimate hypothesis* as such to the status of a *mere empirical* hypothesis, thus falling prey to pure empiricism. You rightly hold that any such methodology should be radically challenged by a Christian methodology and that whoever follows the non-Christian methodology must give up his Christian faith. Christian methodology cannot allow the legitimacy of assumptions that underlie non-Christian methodology. There is no neutral methodology in theory as well as in practice. Every method is bound by its presuppositions.[57]

Notwithstanding all this you rightly hold that Christians can yet co-operate with non-Christians (and I would suggest that it is especially the case in the *P-C* approach) in seeking truth in science, but that Christians, wherever co-operating, cannot excuse themselves from the task of witness-bearing, of being fully true to their ultimate presuppositions (the *P-A* approach).

H.3.   In conclusion I may stress that in your criticism of, for instance, Arminian apologetics, you rightly hold that an appeal to facts of created reality (i.e., to what I have called the *P-C* approach) as a common area between Christians and non-Christians is untenable, because non-Christians view these facts from the outset in the light of their non-Christian presuppositions.

I.   My Special Problem

This I will state as concisely as possible, referring to the accompanying (rather oversimplified) diagram of your theory of knowledge.

If I may call the sides of the triangle vertical lines and its base a horizontal line, then your apologetic theory of *man's knowledge of the created universe* (*M-U*) relates every fact and every relation between facts of the universe, as well as man's knowledge of it, *vertically* to its dependence on God's knowledge of himself and of

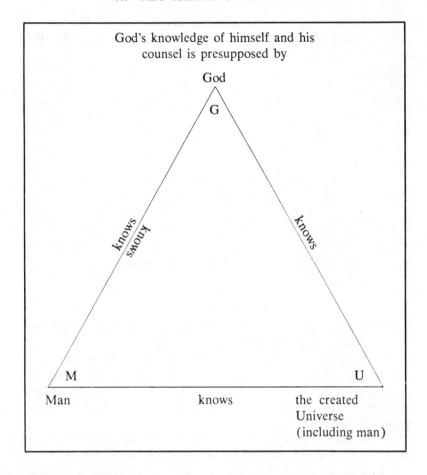

God's knowledge of himself and his
counsel is presupposed by

God

G

knows

knows

knows

M   U

Man   knows   the created
                                    Universe
                                    (including man)

his counsel (*G-M; G-U*), according to what I have called your *P-A*
(or *A-P*) approach.

With *my special problem* I suggest as a supplement to your
theory that a Christian theory of man's knowledge (although necessarily presupposing the truths of your vertical view of man's knowledge of created reality, *M-G; U-G*), also has the task to turn to
the right and to investigate *man's knowledge of created reality* in a
horizontal way (*M-U*), according to what I have called the *P-C*
approach, as it should be done (and has been done) by philosophy-
proper and by particular science-proper theories of knowledge. This
approach yields specific contributions to a Christian theory of knowledge in addition to what your approach yields.[48]

Your criticism of non-Christian theories also follows the vertical lines and exposes their ultimate unbiblical presuppositions and the implications thereof.

A criticism of non-Christian theories according to *my special problem* follows the horizontal line. It can accordingly explain in a specific way the agreement between Christian and non-Christian scientists as well as the possibility of a co-operation between them, but will also expose the differences and the necessity of conflict between them on account of mutually contradictory presuppositions. The horizontal criticism will furthermore always have to fall back upon the vertical criticism, because it is not ultimate and it unseparably presupposes the truths of the vertical criticism.

Should you accept my suggestion of a supplement to your theory, you will probably have to re-phrase several of your observations, especially in the cases of some of your criticisms on non-Christian theories; but in substance you will not have any need to change your views.

J.   In Conclusion

Of the many merits of your profound, rich, and highly significant theory of knowledge I mention only the following:

You have convincingly demonstrated the necessity of and have penetratingly elaborated a theological, philosophical-theological, and theological-philosophical theory of knowledge. Its truths should serve as presuppositions of a philosophy-proper and particular science-proper theory of knowledge.

Of special significance is the ultimacy of your approach. You have penetrated to the ultimate conditions of man's knowledge, namely the existence of our triune God and his counsel, and have demonstrated the fundamental significance of these conditions for all of man's pursuit of science, and from this ultimate stand you have radically criticized apostatic pursuit of science as well. In these fundamental respects your theory is unique and I am thankful for what you have given us.

The corollary of the ultimacy of your approach is that of antithesis. You confront scientists (taken in a wide sense) with the words of of God: "I am the first and I am the last; and besides me there is no God." Admitting co-operation between Christian and non-Christian scientists in the derivative respects concerned, with regard to our Christian principles you definitely reject every compromise. The honor and glory of God demands a radical antithesis to every theory founded on unbelief. This resolute testimony is wholesome in our current times of leveling fundamental differences and of tendencies to compromise.

Lastly, I wish to stress the significance of your theory of knowledge as regards to what you call the adamic, the sinner's, and the regenerate consciousness.

———

My friend, I am concerned about the length of this letter. I have by far exceeded the bounds of hospitality that I could expect for this *Festschrift*, yet I am grateful for being allowed to do so. My only excuse is my intensive interest in and desire of a personal engagement with the main tenets of your theory of knowledge in so far as they have a bearing upon my view of man's knowledge; and this called for a general survey of your rich and comprehensive theory.

My study of your theory has been an intellectual feast, and I am grateful for your unique and significant contribution to our Christian theory of knowledge and for what it means to me personally.

May God bless you and all your work!

With Christian greetings,
Hendrik G. Stoker

———

Response by C. Van Til

Dear Mr. Stoker:

I am deeply grateful to you for your analysis and evaluation of my work. You have taken great pains to write your article. It is a very long article. It is not too long. You have dealt with my views in greater detail than I would ever have dared to expect you would.

Quite rightly you say: "You are primarily concerned about the ultimate dependence of man's knowledge on our triune God and his knowledge." As for your self you add: "I mainly am concerned about the problem of man's knowledge, presupposing this ultimate dependence." For you "the act of *knowing* is a *unit*. This is important. 'Perceiving' and 'thinking' are part-acts of knowing" (B.1.2.2). With what you say in this sentence and with everything you say in the paragraph of which the sentence is a part, I am in hearty agreement.

I quote again: "On the basis of the perceived knowable man forms his theoretic realm (cf. B.1.2.2) by *thinking* (B.2.2.1. You agree that "without a revelatory consciousness of God, self-consciousness (and I may add: consciousness of 'things') would, in a principial sense, not be possible" (B.2.4).

Of course "a mystery lies at the root of man's knowing by meeting with the knowable." "We are, however, in the knowledge-transaction, faced by the *mystery* of *revelation* that lies at the root of all man's knowledge" (B.3.1).

You are concerned with "the revelation of the *created universe* (including man) in an ultimate sense by God" (B.3.2). This is your special interest as a philosopher and as a philosopher of science.

On the basis of this revelation of the created universe you propose a "supplement" to my "theory of knowledge" (B.3.3.1). In this connection you speak of your "special problem." You want "the revelation of the created universe" included with the other three forms of revelation of which you speak in one comprehensive covenantal relationship between God and man. Nothing could suit me better.

You continue by saying that fallen man does not react properly to God's revelation to him. "The genuine connection between knowing and the knowable is disrupted." The knowable is "wrongly perceived, wrongly thought of, and therefore wrongly known" (B.6.3). Of course, there is common grace, but we need not remark on that here. You want to speak of science and then of your *special problem*.

"All science starts with pre-scientific presuppositions and should responsibly account for them" (C.1). Here you describe Dooyeweerd's method of *transcendental*, as over against *transcendent*, criticism and then you add: "Your criticism of knowledge, however, is (a). a transcendent criticism; but it is (b). transcendental in your criticism of opposing philosophical and empirical theories by exposing their ultimate presuppositions of brute fact, chance, and human autonomy; and it becomes (a). a transcendent criticism when criticizing the presuppositions concerned" (C.1). On this point may I refer you to my response to Dr. Dooyeweerd? I must hasten on to your *special problem*, which you offer as a "supplement" to my theory. I wish I could do it better justice than I can.

You deal with your *special problem* in your section on "The Point of Contact."

"*Firstly* there is ontically (or ontologically; you call it: 'metaphysically') a revelation of God in his creation (commonly called 'natural revelation')" (G.2). "*Secondly*, God has created man in his image and has endowed man with a sense of deity" (G.2). "Without these two man would not have been able to form what is called 'common notions' of a supreme or higher being or power" (G.2). But these "common notions" cannot serve as a point of contact (G.2). Men have in and by them "changed the glory of the uncorruptible God into an image made like to corruptible man . . ." (G.2). "But back of these common notions there are, as you rightly contend, the ontic (ontological, you call it the 'metaphysical') real knowledge situation: God *does* exist; he *does* reveal himself; there *is* an 'objective' perspicuous and inescapable revelation of God in creation; man *is* created as the image of God; *even* the *sinner* knows God deep in his heart but suppresses this knowledge; he knows that he is a creature of God, that creation is revelational of God; that his assumed idea of autonomy is false—but he rejects all this, serving the creature rather than God" (G.3). You agree with this. You call my stress on the necessity of always relating dependent human knowledge to the self-knowledge of the triune God the P-A context. This P-A context always comes back to the fact that every item of a building was planned by the architect. But there is also the P-C context. This P-C context discusses the details of the building. "But the *P-C* approach presupposes the *P-A* approach" (G.5.3). You say I stress the P-A approach. Then you ask me to turn right and explain the detailed relations of the facts of the universe operating on God's plan. Well Dr. Stoker, I leave that to you. I have tried to learn from you as you have discussed these details in your various writings. But I cannot do what you have done. You have made a great contribution in developing a truly great Calvinist and therefore Christian philosophy and philosophy of science. I wish your works were all translated into English. In that case their full significance for science and philosophy would get a much better hearing in the English-speaking world than it now does. I again marvel at your willingness to go to such pains in setting forth my views. *Ons kan dat nie begrijp nie.*

—C.V.T.

Herman Dooyeweerd

II. CORNELIUS VAN TIL AND THE TRANSCENDENTAL CRITIQUE OF THEORETICAL THOUGHT

My good friend,

You have from the beginning expressed your sympathy with the reformatory tendency of the Philosophy of the Cosmonomic Idea. It is no wonder that, as a professor of apologetics, you are especially interested in the transcendental critique of theoretical thought, which this philosophy has laid at the foundation of every further philosophical investigation. No wonder, indeed, since this critique has been presented as the only critical way of communication between a really reformatory Christian philosophy and philosophical schools holding in one sense or another to the supposed autonomy of theoretical thought. It is this very method of communication which could be also of fundamental import for a reformatory apologetics that seeks to avoid any compromise with the traditional scholastic conception of the relative autonomy of human reason with respect to so-called "natural knowledge." You have tried to develop such an apologetics in a consistent way in your book, *The Defense of the Faith.* In your class syllabus on "Biblical Dimensionalism,"[1] which was kindly placed at my disposal, you have dwelled at length on the question about whether my transcendental critique can indeed clear the way for a real communication with philosophical trends that hold to the autonomy of theoretical thought.

From your critical comment on this discussion it appears that you are not satisfied with the way in which I have applied this critique in the dialogue with neo-thomistic and and other philosophers. Your main objection is that, in your opinion, I do not carry through my reformatory biblical starting point in such a dialogue in a consistent manner. This failure would already appear from my distinction between a transcendental and a transcentent criticism of philosophical views.

I am afraid that you have misunderstood what I mean by this distinction. You think that by transcendental critique I understand a critique that *starts from* the (transcendent) "fulness and unity of truth accepted on the authority of Scripture."[2] By my opposing such a transcendent critique to the transcendental one, as the "dogmatical" to the "critical" method of communication, I am supposed to forget "that the whole point of transcendental criticism is lost unless it is based upon transcendent criticism."

In the syllabus this latter statement is wrongly ascribed to Berkouwer. I suppose it is, in fact, your own as appears from your explanatory addition: "That is to say, the entire transcendental method hangs in the air except for the fact that it rests upon the fullness and unity of truth accepted on the authority of Scripture."

But by a transcendent criticism, as opposed to the transcendental critique of theoretic thought, I understood something quite different from what you suppose. I meant by transcendent criticism, the dogmatic manner of criticizing philosophical theories from a theological or from a different philosophical viewpoint without a critical distinction between *theoretical propositions* and the *supra-theoretical presuppositions lying at their foundation.*

In *A New Critique of Theoretical Thought*, I have explained in detail why I *reject* such a *transcendent* critique, which in scholastic theology has been repeatedly applied to condemn scientific and philosophical ideas that did not agree with traditional scholastic views. In view of this state of affairs I remarked: "Besides, there is another ever present danger" (viz. in transcendent criticism). "What is actually a complex of philosophical ideas dominated by unbiblical motives, may be accepted by dogmatic theology and accommodated to the doctrine of the church. The danger is that this complex of ideas will be passed off as an article of Christian faith, if it has influenced the terminology of some confessions of faith."[3] Among the Reformed confessions I am reminded of that of Westminster, which renders the Christian belief concerning human nature in terms of the dualistic Thomistic-Aristotelian conception, just as the Council of Vienne had done before. To clear the way for a reformatory philosophy it was necessary to subject this traditional scholastic view, inclusive of its whole Greek metaphysical background, to a transcendental critique from the radical biblical standpoint.

This criticism laid bare the unbiblical ground-motive lying at the foundation of this metaphysics. Valentine Hepp, the late professor of dogmatic theology at the Free University of Amsterdam, was of the opinion that rejection of the traditional scholastic view of human nature was a deviation from the Reformed confession; and the theological faculty of that time shared this opinion. We are confronted here with a transcendent critique in *optima forma.*

I guess that you will gladly agree that this kind of criticism is rejectable. But the point at issue is whether, and if so, *how*, the transcendental critique meant in the sense of the Philosophy of the Cosmonomic Idea is able to join issue with philosophical trends which do not share its radical biblical starting point, but rather in one sense or another hold to the autonomy of theoretical human thought.

*   *   *   *   *

To understand the true meaning and purport of this transcendental critique, it is necessary to realize that its primary purpose was to institute a radically transcendental inquiry into the inner nature and structure of the theoretical attitude of thought and experience, and into the real nature of the presuppositions lying at the foundation of every possible philosophical reflection.

This inquiry was necessary to answer the question whether the traditional dogma concerning the autonomy of theoretical thought may in some way or another be based upon the inner nature and structure of the latter. This critical investigation was concerned with philosophical problems of a primordial transcendental character, for these problems arise from the inner nature and structure of the theoretical attitude of thought and experience itself.

The task of a transcendental critique, which makes this theoretical attitude as such a critical problem, is quite different from that of a theological apologetics. It does not aim at a "defense of the Christian faith" but at laying bare the central influence of the different religious, basic motives upon the philosophical trends of thought. For that purpose it was necessary to show the *inner point of contact* between theoretical thought and its supra-theoretical presuppositions which relate to the central religious sphere of human existence. This is why this transcendental critique is obliged to *begin* with an inquiry into the inner nature and structure of the theoretical attitude of thought and experience *as such* and *not* with a confession of faith. In this first phase of the critical investigation such a confession would be out of place. Not because the first question raised by our transcendental critique might be answered apart from the central religious starting-point of those who take part in the philosophical dialogue, but because the necessity of such a starting-point has not yet come up for discussion. For, so long as the dogma concerning the autonomy of theoretical thought has not been subjected to a transcendental critique, adherents of this dogma who enter into a dialogue with the Philosophy of the Cosmonomic Idea might rightly confine themselves to the simple statement that theoretical philosophy has nothing to do with questions of faith and religion. In other words, the dialogue would be cut off before it could start.

The confrontation of the biblical and the non-biblical ground-motives of theoretical thought belongs to the third and last phase of the transcendental critique. Only in this phase the transcendental problem crops up concerning the possibility of a concentric direction of theoretical thinking to the human ego, as its central reference point, and concerning the inner nature of the latter.

This problem, too, arose from the inner nature and structure of the theoretical attitude of thought and experience itself. For, this attitude turned out to be characterized by an intentional antithetical relation between the logical or analytical mode of theoretical thinking and the non-logical modal aspects of human experience within the horizon of cosmic time. Both this theoretical antithesis and the inter-modal theoretical synthesis, necessary to gain a conceptual insight into the modal structures of the non-logical aspects of our temporal horizon of experience, bind theoretical thought to a divergent direction. Nevertheless both of them presuppose the human ego as the central reference point of our consciousness which as such must transcend the modal diversity of the temporal horizon of human experience.

This means that the third problem of the transcendental critique, though it be evoked by the transcendental critical turn of theoretical thought to the thinking ego, cannot be solved within the boundaries of theoretical thought and experience.

*　*　*　*　*

Self-knowledge is here at issue and true self-knowledge is, as you so rightly remark, completely dependent upon true knowledge of God, which is to be obtained only from his Word-revelation fulfilled in Jesus Christ. This central knowledge is, however, certainly not of a theoretical conceptual character. In his high priestly prayer Jesus says that this *knowledge is eternal life in the love-communion with the Father and the Son.* In his earthly life in which the Christian is still subject to the consequences of sin, he can have only a principle of this religious knowledge. The latter presupposes the opening up of his "heart," i.e., the religious center of his existence, by the Holy Ghost to the moving power of the Word-revelation. Since man has been created in the image of God, the religious impulse, as Calvin rightly observes, is an innate impulse of the human heart. He calls it

"semen religionis." It is a natural disposition which in itself is unable
to lead man to true self-knowledge and knowledge of God. But it
brings about the restless longing for communion with the absolute
upon which he may concentrate all the relative, primarily his own
self as the creaturely religious concentration-point of his existence.
The religious impulse was, from the beginning, thrown on the central
motive power of God's general Word-revelation, which alone could
give it true content and a right direction.

By the fall into sin it got an apostate trend. Turning away from
the Word of God and lending ear to the temptation to be like God
in his self-sufficiency, man directed his innate religious impulse
towards idols originating from an absolutization of creaturely meaning-structures of the temporal world.

Hence the necessary ambiguity of the term "religious" in the
Philosophy of the Cosmonomic Idea. It always refers here to the
central sphere of human existence and consciousness in its active
relation to God, and to the central motive power operating in it.
But Holy Scripture teaches us that this central *dynamis* may be that
of the Word-revelation leading us into the Truth, as well as that of
the spirit of apostasy who leads the innate religious impulse of the
human heart in a false direction.

Naturally it is possible to eliminate this ambiguity of the terms
"religious" and "religion" by ascribing to them only an idolatrous or
a Christian sense respectively. Karl Barth did so in the former sense
and consequently opposed all religion, including the Christian, as a
supposed product of the apostate human nature, to the Word of God
and the life out of grace alone. But this arbitrary restriction of the
meaning of the term, which is in line with Barth's antithetical conception of the scholastic basic motive of nature and grace, is unacceptable.

The innate religious impulse of the human heart does not result
from man's apostate nature, but, as we observed above, from his
creation in the image of God.

I was therefore really surprised by your comment on the ambiguous
use of the term "religious" in my transcendental critique.[4] "The basic
trouble," you said, "is that the term religious is used by both Dooyeweerd and Berkouwer first in one way and then in another. Basically
it means for them the biblical scheme of things. . . . But then they
also use the term religious in a general sense of any position that
recognizes the need of religious presuppositions in addition to logical
thought or theoretical reason." You apparently view this general use

of the term (that for the rest of this form is not to be found with me) in close connection with (1) the contradistinction between a transcendent and a transcendental critique and my rejection of the former; (2) my supposed idea that the "states of affairs" "have an objectivity" apart from the biblical presuppositions; and, (3) in particular, my supposed view "that irrationalism and subjectivism can be answered without reference to biblical content."

*   *   *   *   *

The first point can now be considered settled as resting on a misunderstanding. As to the third point I must remark that I have rejected both rationalism and irrationalism, both subjectivism and objectivism from the biblical view concerning the correlation and mutual irreducibility of law and subject. As to the second point, I wonder how you could ascribe to me the opinion that the "states of affairs" would have an objectivity which gives them a neutral position over against the biblical presuppositions of my transcendental critique. You have apparently deduced this opinion from my explanation of my standpoint with respect to the "states of affairs" in the controversy with van Peursen in the year 1960 of *Philosophia Reformata*. You seem to to have been particularly impressed by van Peursen's question if there does not exist a dialectical tension between my statement that there are undeniable states of affairs which can be discovered by both Christian and non-Christian scholars, and my thesis according to which, for instance, the statement $2 \times 2 = 4$ has no truth in itself, but can function only within the total dynamical meaning-context of our experiential horizon. You understood van Peursen's question as follows: "On the one hand, . . . Dooyeweerd tells us that the truths of arithmetics must be seen as a part of the whole cosmic structure as this in turn is seen in the light of Christian truth, and then again he speaks of it as though it were a truth independent of this Christian scheme."[5]

This was not exactly the point in van Peursen's question. Van Peursen started from the erroneous opinion that I would have conceived the "states of affairs" in the sense of "brute facts" apart from their meaning. If this were true there would naturally exist a striking antinomy between my conception of the "states of affairs" and my fundamental view concerning the meaning-character of creaturely reality. In my reply I gave therefore, once more, an ample exposition of my conception concerning this point. In this exposition I stressed the fact that the "states of affairs" have never been conceived by me as "brute facts" in the sense of a positivistic empiricism.

The "states of affairs" presenting themselves within the temporal order of our experience are, in my opinion, of a dynamic meaning-character, i.e., they refer outside and above themselves to the universal meaning-context in time, to the creaturely unity of root and to the absolute Origin of all meaning. This was the religious presupposition resulting from the biblical ground-motive of my philosophical thought. But it would naturally be a serious error to suppose that this religious presupposition as such would provide us with a philosophical insight into the transcendental meaning-structures of our temporal world.

To acquire such an insight we need, in the first place, a careful investigation of a great number of "states of affairs" which appear to be helpful to a theoretical analysis of these meaning-structures, but which, as such, must be considered independent of our subjective philosophical interpretation. Van Peursen wrongly considered my insistence on this latter point as an indication of an objectivistic view of the "states of affairs."

In fact it was nothing but a result of my biblical conviction that the "states of affairs" in which the transcendental meaning-structures of our temporal horizon of experience reveal themselves are not founded in our subjective consciousness, but in the divine order of creation to which our subjective experience is subject. For this very reason they also cannot be dependent upon the religious conviction of the investigator, so that they may be discovered in a particular context by both Christian and non-Christian thinkers.

It is not so that the discovery of "states of affairs" which turn out to be of great importance for our insight into the modal meaning-structure of a transcendental aspect, is seen by everybody in that way. It may be that they are immediately given a philosophical interpretation which is incompatible with the modal meaning-structure of the aspect concerned.[6] The "states of affairs" may also be too hastily interpreted in terms of a particular conception of the modal meaning-structure concerned which turns out to be liable to justified criticism. This is why I consider it a critical requirement to suspend our philosophical interpretation of the "states of affairs" at issue until we have so many of them at our disposal, relating to all the modal aspects of our temporal experiential world which until now we have learned to distinguish, that we can try to conceive them in a philosophical total view. In this whole explanation to van Peursen of my standpoint with respect to the "states of affairs" there is not a trace to be found of the ambiguity which you think to have discovered in it.

Nowhere have I said that the "states of affairs," lying at the foundation of my philosophical theory of the modal spheres, have an "objectivity" apart from the "biblical presuppositions." On the contrary, I have stressed the fact that they are founded in the divine order of creation. Nowhere have I claimed "to use a transcendental method that is not directly(?) dependent upon the truths of Scripture," nor have I appealed "to supposedly objective states of affairs that have an objectivity not depending upon the truths of Scripture."[7]

* * * * *

Asking myself what may have induced you to ascribe to the Philosophy of the Cosmonomic Idea such a dialectical dualism, I find myself confronted with, what I fear to be, a typical rationalistic scholastic tendency in your theological thought. This tendency reveals itself first in your objections against my distinction between theoretical conceptual knowledge, and the central religious self-knowledge and knowledge of God. On this point you appear to agree with the neo-scholastic thinkers, Robbers and Mrs. Conradie, and in some degree also with van Peursen. I fear your rationalism may go even further than that of the neo-scholastic thinkers mentioned, for the latter have never claimed that philosophical ideas are to be *derived* from the supra-natural truths of divine revelation, and that is exactly what you seem to defend. In "Biblical Dimensionalism" you mention my rectification of van Peursen's erroneous assertion that according to vol. II, p. 54 of *A New Critique of Theoretical Thought* my transcendental idea of cosmic time has been borrowed from revelation.[8] The passage to which van Peursen refers reads in fact as follows: "It is only the biblical religious basic motive that gives the view of time the ultimate direction to the true fulness of meaning intended by our cosmonomic Idea."

In this context I observed that none of the three transcendental ground-ideas of the Philosophy of the Cosmonomic Idea is to be derived from the biblical basic motive which controls the ultimate direction of its theoretical reflection, since this basic motive is of a supra-theoretical character. Upon this statement you comment as follows: "We would ask Dooyeweerd, however, how he can put an intelligible content into the phrase 'Christian thinking' in terms of control (*beheersen*) rather than in terms of derivation (*afleiding*). If we are to avoid mysticism, then we must do something with the actual revelational content of Scripture. Dooyeweerd needs to borrow nothing from any theologian. But revelation is expressed in thought-content. And it is this thought-content, unmixed with any interpretation of any man, which controls his own thinking. This being the case, what difference remains between the idea of his thinking being controlled (by) or being derived from Scripture. Control without derivation is an empty mystical phrase." In reply to this comment I can only ask the counter question, how it would be possible to *derive* from the biblical revelation a philosophical idea of cosmic time with its diversity of modal aspects, of which it does not speak in any way.

The Bible does not provide us with philosophical ideas, no more than it gives us natural scientific knowledge or an economic or legal theory. But theoretical thought needs a central starting-point which transcends the modal diversity of our temporal horizon of experience and must consequently be of a supra-theoretical character. It is only by virtue of its supra-theoretical character that this starting-point can give central lead to our theoretical thought. This has been shown by the radical transcendental critique of the theoretical attitude of thought and experience which I have laid at the foundation of all my further philosophical investigations. This critique could be truly radical only because in the three phases of its critical investigation it had its supra-theoretical starting-point in the central ground-motive of the Word-revelation, viz., that of creation, fall into sin, and redemption by Jesus Christ, as the incarnate divine Word, in the communion of the Holy Ghost.

In my various explanations of the transcendental critique both within and outside my work, *A New Critique of Theoretical Thought,* I have always emphasized its biblical starting-point. What, then, so I ask myself again, may have made you think that this critique would be not "directly" dependent upon the transcendent "biblical truths"? It seems to me that it is again a certain rationalistic view of the divine Word-revelation that hinders you from seeing the fundamental difference and the true relation between the central religious and the theoretical-conceptual sphere of knowledge. The difference you apparently deny, and this is why the question concerning their true relation does in fact not come up for discussion in your train of thought."

This appears, in my opinion, from your objections to what I have observed with respect to true self-knowledge and true knowledge of God in their unbreakable coherence, and especially with respect to the central ground-motive of the biblical revelation as moving power or *dunamis* addressing itself primarily to the heart or the religious center of our existence.[10] As to the first point you ask me (1) how I may avoid falling into the trap of Kant's idea of the primacy of practical reason,[11] and (2) how I can avoid placing the self in a vacuum over against all the conceptual knowledge that we have of anything.

"Why not rather say that since a true knowledge of self and the world depends upon a true knowledge of God and since the knowledge of God about himself, about man, and about the world was mediated to man from the beginning through ordinary language, including conceptual terms, we now, as sinners saved by Christ, subordinate all our thinking to the truths of Scripture. . . . Listening to Scripture, obeying the voice of God speaking through Christ in Scripture, means making every human thought subject to divine thought.

"In Christ, says Dooyeweerd, our hearts are enlightened. But who then is Christ? He is what the Bible says he is in thoughts expressed in words, in concepts. Dooyeweerd speaks of the 'central *dunamis*' of the Divine 'Word' as taking hold of us in the depth of our being. If this idea of *dunamis* is not to lead us into a Kantian sort of noumenal, then it must be based upon the spoken Word, full of thought-content. . . . Dooyeweerd's discussion of the *dunamis* of the divine revelation as over against the simple thought-content of Scripture adds still further to the ambiguity contained in what he says about the transcendental method. . . . Why did not Dooyeweerd tell van Peursen that his basic view of objectivity is the normativity of the Scriptural concepts of creation, of sin and of redemption? . . . It is *concepts* that need interpretation, yes, by human concepts based on revealed concepts. The whole attempt at reforming philosophical thought in terms of the modalities of thought as set forth by Dooyeweerd breaks down unless he reforms the concept of *dunamis*."

I guess this ample quotation sheds a clear light on the rationalist tendency in your thought in consequence of which you are unable to escape dilemmas which the Philosophy of the Cosmonomic Idea has unmasked as polarly opposite absolutizations.

Rationalism as absolutization of conceptual thought evokes necessarily irrationalism as its alternative.[12] The objectivism implied in traditional scholastic rationalism evokes as its alternative subjectivism, etc. It is consequently quite understandable that from your standpoint you consider my distinction between conceptual knowledge and central religious knowledge a result of an irrationalist mystical view of the latter. In line with Robbers and van Peursen you interpret this distinction as a *separation*, so that the central supra-conceptual sphere and the conceptual sphere of knowledge are conceived of as opposite to, and independent of, each other. In this way the distinction is naturally transformed into a dialectical tension, testifying to a dualistic trend in my thought. In my discussion with van Peursen I have dwelled at length on this radical misrepresentation of my view and I have given an ample rectification. You do not go into this rectification, and I fear that so long as you stick to this rationalist standpoint you will not be able to understand what I have written in this context.

In your train of thought the matter seems to be quite simple. The Word-revelation results from divine *thought*. It is mediated to man through ordinary language. Its content is *thought*-content expressed in words (wrongly identified with concepts).[13] Consequently, listening to Scripture, obeying the voice of God speaking through Christ in Scripture, means making every human *thought* subject to divine *thought* expressed in scriptural *concepts*, so that man has to "think God's thoughts after him."

Is this really a biblical view? I am afraid not. Nowhere does the Bible speak of obeying the voice of God in terms of subjecting every human thought to divine thought. The New Testament understanding of obedience is doing the Father's will revealed in the gospel of Jesus Christ, by believing with all our heart that we belong to him. There is no real obedience to the will of God that does not result from the heart, in the pregnant biblical sense, as the religious center of our existence, which must be regenerated and opened up by the divine moving power of the Holy Ghost. It is exactly this central biblical condition that is lacking in your circumscription of obedience. You do not, of course, at all deny the necessity of rebirth. But I fear that the biblical conception of the religious center of human existence does not fit in with your view of the human nature.[14]

That the Word-revelation was from the beginning mediated to man through human language is naturally unquestionable. But that verbal language would necessarily signify conceptual thought-contents is a rationalist prejudice that runs counter to the real states of affairs. By means of language we can signify symbolically not only conceptual thought contents, but all sorts of contents of our consciousness, such as subjective moods and emotional feelings, volitional decisions in a concrete situation, our faith in Jesus Christ, pre-theoretical aesthetical and moral experiences, often expressed in short exclamations such as "How wonderful!" or "Shame on you!"

etc., which certainly do not give expression to conceptual knowledge of the experiential modes concerned.

The transcendental critique of theoretical thought has shown why true self-knowledge in its biblical sense, i.e., in its dependence upon true knowledge of God, cannot be itself of a conceptual character. The reason is that all conceptual knowledge in its analytical and inter-modal synthetical character *presupposes* the human ego as its central reference-point, which consequently must be of a supra-modal nature and is not capable of logical analysis. This does not mean, as you suppose, that the human self is placed in a vacuum over against all the conceptual knowledge that we have of everything. The human ego cannot be theoretically opposed to conceptual knowledge since, as the central reference-point of the latter, it transcends every theoretical antithesis.

It would be placed in a vacuum only if we would try to conceive it apart from the three central (and consequently supra-logical) relations without which it loses all meaning and content. I mean its relation to our multi-modal existence and experience in the temporal world, the I-thou relation to our fellow-men, and the religious I-Thou relation to God, in whose image man has been created. Since the last mentioned relation encompasses the two others, we may say that, according to its positive meaning, the human ego is the religious concentration point or center of man's existence. This is what the Bible, in a pregnant sense, calls the "heart," from which are the issues of life, from which proceed all sins and in which takes place rebirth out of the Holy Ghost.

The Bible does not speak of this religious center in conceptual terms, no more than Jesus in his night conversation with Nicodemus gave a conceptual circumscription of rebirth as the necessary condition of seeing the kingdom of God. The same holds good with respect to the biblical revelation of creation, man's fall into sin, and redemption through Jesus Christ. You often speak of the "scriptural concepts of creation, of sin, and of redemption," as revealed concepts, whose normativity ought to be our basic view of objectivity. But the Word-revelation does not reveal *concepts* of creation, sin, and redemption.

You do not seem to have seen that words and concepts cannot be identical. "Now, to be sure," you say, "when we speak of creation, we use concepts. There is no other way of speaking of God and of his relation to man." What, in my opinion, you *should* have said is that when we speak of creation, we use human *words* varying with the language of which we avail ourselves, and multivocal in common parlance. But in biblical usage they have got an identical revelational meaning in so far as they relate to God in his self-revelation as the absolute Origin of all that through his Word has been called into being. This revelational meaning transcends every human concept[15] since it is of a supra-rational character. *Supra-rational* should by no means be confused with *irrational*. It is not, like the latter, the opposite, but the presupposition of the rational, just like the human self-hood is presupposed in every human thought and every human concept. God's *self-revelation* in Holy Scripture as Creator and Redeemer concerns the central religious relation of man to his absolute Origin. Its true meaning is therefore to be understood by man only if his *heart* has been opened up to it through the moving power of the Holy Ghost, which is the *dunamis* of the biblical Word-revelation. What is said here about the *dunamis* of the Word-revelation and the central role of the heart in the understanding of its meaning is in complete accordance with the biblical testimony (cf. Isa. 6:10-13; Acts 16:14) and with the opinion of Calvin (cf. the citations from the *Institutes* in *New Critique*, I/516,7). But you place it "over against the simple thought-content of Scripture" and are of the opinion that it adds still further to the ambiguity of my transcendental critique. You think so, however, not on biblical ground, but in consequence of a rationalistic view of the Word-revelation and of the religious relation of man to God, which, you feel, is of a rational-ethical character. This rationalism implies also a relapse into a metaphysical theory of the intrinsical divine being and its attributes, which Calvin called a "vacua et meteorica speculatio."[16] That this theological metaphysics is necessarily involved in antinomies is, in your opinion, not a consequence of its vain attempt to exceed the boundaries of conceptual thought. It is only because of the necessary incompleteness of our theoretical knowledge about God and the created universe. The antinomies exist therefore only seemingly, but are nevertheless inevitable.[17]

But now you will ask me if I myself am not obliged to use *concepts* of God and the human ego in the threefold transcendental ground-idea whose necessity the transcendental critique has shown. It is true that I used the term limiting idea in this context and you appear to be willing to conceive of the "concept of creation" as a limiting idea. I guess that then the same must hold good with respect to what you call the other revealed concepts. But what is meant by the term "limiting idea" in the transcendental critique of theoretical thought as developed by the Philosophy of the Cosmonomic Idea? Nothing else is meant but the concentric religious turn of our theoretic conceptual thought, which is bound to the modal diversity of our temporal existence and experience to its supra-conceptual presupposita. This means that the genuine *conceptual* contents of these transcendental limiting ideas do not transcend the modal dimension of our temporal horizon of experience. The same applies to the theological limiting concepts relating to the so-called attributes of God. In *The Defense of the Faith* you deal with these attributes within the traditional framework of a metaphysical theory of being. They are, you say, not to be thought of otherwise than as aspects of the one simple original being;[18] whereas in fact, they are taken from the modal dimension of our temporal horizon of experience and existence in its central relation to God as its absolute Origin. But since they are ascribed to God, such as he has revealed himself to man in Holy Scripture, i.e., within the human horizon of experience and existence, they are to be understood only in the analogical sense of belief as analogies of faith (*analogiae fidei*) whose material content is exclusively determined by God's Word-revelation. For, in their sense-proper, the modal aspects of our temporal horizon cannot be ascribed to God's being as its properties, since they are of a creaturely character. But the analogies of belief, insofar as they relate to God's self-revelation, are preëminently fit to give expression both to God's presence in the temporal world and to his absolute transcendence; to his presence, since they imply the whole temporal order of the modal aspects; to his transcendence, since they refer to God's absoluteness, which transcends every creaturely determination. In any case, they cannot be given a metaphysical interpretation as if they would be determinations of God's absolute being, for they too belong to the modal dimension of the human horizon of experience. Because they refer to God's absoluteness, they are unbreakably bound to the central religious dimension of this horizon. For it is only in the religious center of his consciousness that man is confronted with the absolute, so that even the absolutizations in apostate philosophical views originate in the central religious impulse of the human heart, which has been led in an erroneous direction. Since the analogical moments in the modal structure of the different aspects of our experiential horizon are arranged in an unbreakable order and meaning-context, their meaning is bound to this context. As to the analogies of belief relating to what metaphysical theology called the "attributes of God's being," this implies that they should not be separately called absolute, or be identified with God's absolute being. This is why I cannot agree with your statement that God's being is exhaustively rational.[19] My objections concern your whole view of God's self-revelation in Holy Scripture according to which it would contain a metaphysical *theory* of the divine being. It is true that it was not your intention to make deductions on the basis of one attribute by itself[20] and that, in line with Calvin, you say that no knowledge of God's nature is available to man except such as is voluntarily revealed to him by God. But by interpreting God's self-revelation in Holy Scripture in terms of a metaphysical theory of God's being, you could not stick to this biblical standpoint. Nowhere can you find in the Bible support for your statement[21] that "logic and reality meet first of all in the mind and being of God," so that God's being would be "exhaustively rational." We are, indeed, confronted here with a metaphysical absolutization of the logical analogy of belief in what the Bible reveals about God's omniscience. This appears from what you observe with respect to Leibniz's distinction between *truths of fact* and *truths of reason*.[22] According to you, the Reformed apologist should hold to the truths of fact presented in Scripture only because to him they are truths of reason. It is true that you yourself, as a creaturely human being, are not able to show "the exhaustive logical relationships between the facts of history and nature which are in debate as between believers and unbelievers in Christian theism," but in the plan of God they function, you say, within an absolute system of logical relations which does not detract anything from their individuality. We should, however, realize what Leibniz meant by his distinction between *truths of reason* and *truths of fact*. The former are, according to him, those whose opposite is excluded by the logical principle of contradiction. The latter are those whose opposite is not impossible in a logical sense, because they are of a contingent, i.e., not necessary, character. This does, however, not mean that in Leibniz's opinion the facts would happen by blind chance or that they would lack logical coherence. They happen according to God's will and are subject to the logical *principium rationis sufficientis*, which in Leibniz' logistic view embraces all kinds of causal relationships. Leibniz maintains the distinction between truths of fact and truths of reason even with respect to God's mind: the former depend upon God's will, the latter upon God's reason. I am afraid that you have not realized that a theological reduction of the truths of fact to Leibniz' truths of reason would make even the central facts of creation, fall into sin, and redemption a consequence of logical necessity in virtue of the principle of contradiction. This would result in an extreme logicistic view of "God's world-plan" which would leave no room for the sovereign freedom of God's will. For God's will can, in your view only *carry out* the plan of God, not *determine* it.[23] I am sure that in fact the author of *The Defense of the Faith* will never accept this consequence.

*   *   *   *   *

In the above I have tried to answer the questions which you have asked me with respect to the transcendental critique. I could not do so without going into the background of the objections you have alleged against my standpoint. This has doubtless brought to light important differences between your view of a Christian philosophy and that of the Philosophy of the Cosmonomic Idea. At least if I have not misunderstood you on essential points, which might occur because, at times, your terminology is not always clear to me. In this case I shall be happy to be corrected by you, if you should wish to do so in your response.

Sincerely,
Herman Dooyeweerd

Response by C. Van Til

Dear Dr. Dooyeweerd:

You have written an enormous amount of material. All of it is profound and penetrating. Much of it I have read and re-read, especially your *De Wysbegeerte der Wetsidee* (1935). Perhaps this accounts for the fact that I have not fully appreciated what you later, in your *A New Critique of Theoretical Thought* (1953), speak of as a "second way" by which "to subject philosophic thought to a transcendental criticism."[1]

By a truly transcendental criticism of the theoretical attitude of thought, you say, "we understand a critical inquiry into the *universally valid conditions which alone make theoretical thought possible, and which are required by the immanent structure of this thought itself.* In this latter restriction lies the difference in principle between a *transcendent* and a *transcendental* criticism of science and philosophy.

"The former does not really touch the inner character and the immanent structure of the theoretical attitude of thought, but confronts, for instance Christian faith with the results of modern science and with the various philosophical systems, and thus ascertains, whether or not factual conflict exists."[2] "Transcendent criticism, in other words, is valueless to science and philosophy, because it confronts with each other two different spheres, whose *inner point of contact is left completely in the dark*. One can then just as well proceed to exercise criticism of science from the standpoint of art or of politics!

"In order to guarantee from the outset a really critical attitude in philosophy, transcendental criticism of theoretical thought should come *at the very beginning* of philosophical reflection."[3]

You speak of your own earlier approach as "The First Way of a Transcendental Critique of Philosophic Thought."[4] This first way you speak of as "the way from above" and then add: "But in this line of thought, we had to start from a supposition about the character of philosophy, which is not at all universally accepted in philosophical circles. Besides, it might seem, that a due account of the transition from the theoretical basic problem of philosophy to the central religious sphere was lacking."[5] Accordingly you have in *The New Critique* directed all your attention to "a sharpening of the method of transcendental criticism, whereby the objection, mentioned above, might be met."[6] This "sharpening of the method of transcendental thought" is accomplished by dropping all merely transcendent or "dogmatic" criticism and turning to an exclusive analysis of "the theoretical attitude of thought as such."[7] Only by dropping the left-overs of a dogmatic approach can we face squarely "the primary question, whether the theoretical attitude of thought itself, with reference to its inner structure, can be independent of supra-theoretical prejudices."[8]

You will understand, Dr. Dooyeweerd, that, with my interest in developing a Christian apologetic, I was much interested in your description of your *second way*. I had for many years rejected the Thomistic-Butler type of approach to apologetics. I had done so because of the unbiblical view of man and the cosmos which underlay this apologetic. I had over and over pointed out that non-Christian schemes of thought, whether ancient or modern, presupposed a view of man as autonomous, of human thought or logic as legislative of what can or cannot exist in reality, and of pure contingency as correlative to such legislative thought. I had for years pointed out that for a Christian to adopt these non-Christian presuppositions about man, together with the dialectical interdependence of legislative logic and brute contingency, and then to join the natural man in asking *whether*

God exists and *whether* Christianity is true would be fatal for his enterprise. If we allow that one intelligent word can be spoken about *being* or *knowing* or *acting* as such, without first introducing the Creator-creature distinction, we are sunk. As Christians we must not allow that even such a thing as enumeration or counting can be *accounted for* except upon the presupposition of the truth of what we are told in Scripture about the triune God as the Creator and Redeemer of the world. As a Christian believer I must therefore place myself, for the sake of the argument, upon the position of the non-Christian and show him that on his view of man and the cosmos he and the whole culture is based upon, and will sink into, quicksand. If the unbeliever then points to the fact that non-Christian scientists and philosophers have discovered many actual "states of affairs," I heartily agree with this but I must tell him that they have done so with borrowed capital. They have done so *adventitiously.* The actual state of affairs about the entire cosmos is what the Bible says it is.

In its response to what the Bible says is the actual state of affairs, the Christian church has written its creeds. In these creeds we have a response on the part of redeemed people of God to his revelation of sovereign grace to them and of his calling all apostate men to repent and submit themselves to Christ. In the creeds men who are made in the image of God, who have fallen into sin and who have been redeemed in principle by the death and resurrection of Christ in their place and subsequently born again by the Holy Spirit, think God's thoughts of mercy after him. The Reformed creeds have been more faithful in giving a proper response to the mercy of God to men in Christ than have other creeds. Roman Catholics, Lutherans, and Arminians have, to some extent, reduced the offer of the sovereign grace of God in Christ by means of a schematism of thought borrowed from the natural man. "We are, all of us, in the same boat," they say. "Let us see *whether* we can together stop the leaks and get to shore." "Let us together row harder and harder, till we reach the shore. Let us not despair. Let us keep telling each other that in all probability some great one, very likely Christ, will meet us and help us. In all probability there is a Father God who will send us food and drinking water on our way." Meanwhile, except for the grace of God, who in Christ forgives men such God-dishonoring tactics, lost men keep dying only to appear before the judgment of Christ whom they rejected by not taking him at his word.

One more thing I must mention here. I had criticized Warfield, the great Reformed theologian of Princeton, for taking over the traditional Butler type of apologetics and attaching it artificially to his own Reformed view of the relation of God and man. I agreed with Kuyper as over against Warfield on this point. Still further, when I saw that Kuyper, though opposing Warfield, yet retained elements of a scholastic methodology in his thinking, I proposed that we must *go beyond* Kuyper (cf. *Common Grace*).

I was criticized by the Calvinistic followers of the Butler-Warfield type of apologetics. How could I, with my method of starting from above, find a point of contact for the gospel with unbelievers? Had not Warfield shown that the unity of science cannot be maintained on Kuyper's view? I was also criticized by the followers of Kuyper. Did not Kuyper show that in the field of counting, of weighing and measuring, in the somatic aspects of the spiritual sciences, and in the field of formal logic the principle of the antithesis between Christians and non-Christians did not apply? How could I maintain communication with unbelievers if I maintained the idea of an "absolute antithesis" between believers and unbelievers? Did I not with Hoeksema, in effect, if not in words, deny common grace? Was I not a follower of that revolutionary group in the Netherlands, centering around Vollenhoven and Dooyeweerd, some of whom even denied the immortality of the soul?

Well, I was a great admirer of this group. I knew that they rejected the Greek notion of man as consisting of an intellect that made it participate in an abstract impersonal principle of thought. I knew that this "revolutionary" group was seeking in the face of much false criticism on the part of some Reformed theologians (cf. Steen, *Philosophia Deformata*, and Hepp, *Dreigende Deformatie*) to cleanse Reformed theology from the Greek notion of the "primacy of the intellect." This notion would, they pointed out, kill the Christian story.

In agreement with this group I sought to work "in Kuyper's line," not forgetting that Kuyper had at crucial points failed to carry out his own deepest religious convictions with respect to the all-inclusive view on the sovereignty of God. Calvin was right. We must not, like the Greeks and the scholastics after them, engage in vain speculation about the essence of God. We must not, like Descartes, start from man as a final point of reference in predication. We must listen to what God has told us about himself, and about ourselves, and our relation to him throught Christ in Scripture as our Creator-Redeemer.

How I rejoiced when I found that men of great erudition and of deep penetration were pointing out that "logic" and "fact" can have no intelligible relation to one another unless it be upon the presupposition of the truth of the "story" Christ has told us in the Scriptures.

Or am I reading some of my own apologetic views into the writings of this "revolutionary" group? Perhaps I am. I know that they are "doing" Christian philosophy, not apologetics. Even so I thought of their Christian philosophy as supporting my apologetic methodology. Did not their philosophy trace the intricacies of the entire history of "immanentist" thinking of apostate man and show that it was self-frustrative and destructive of intelligent predication?

Is it a wonder then that I gave a number of copies of *The New Critique* to, among others, a Roman Catholic Seminary and to a neo-orthodox theologian? Is it a wonder then that in the minds of many my views on apologetics were "bad" because they were so much like those of Dooyeweerd?

As recently as August 26, 1969, I received a letter from one of my long-standing Butler-Analogy critics in which he said: "I have had the impression that you adhere to the school of the *Wysbegeerte der Wetsidee.* Have you published anything to which I can refer the students on this question? Or does Dooyeweerd's four volume *New Critique of Theoretical Thought* fairly represent your views?"

Is it a wonder then, Dr. Dooyeweerd, that when I re-read some of your shorter writings since W.d.W. (1935), such as your article on "De Transcendentale Critiek van het Wysgeerig Denken en de Grondslagen van de Wysgeerige Denkgemeenschap van het Avondland,"[9] "De Verhouding tussen Wijsbegeerte en Theologie en de Strijd der Faculteiten,"[10] "Het Wijsgeerig Tweegesprek tusschen de Thomistische philosophie en de Wysbegeerte der Wetsidee,"[11] your small book, *Transcendental Problems of Philosophic Thought*,[12] your great four-volume work, *A New Critique of Theoretical Thought.* and your smaller book, *In the Twilight of Western Thought*,[13] that I concentrated my attention on your *second way* and its possible implication for my work in apologetics?

I asked myself what can Dr. Dooyeweerd mean when he says that a truly transcendental criticism of theoretical thought must look into "the immanent structure of this thought itself," and that "in this latter restriction lies the difference in principle between *transcendent* and a *transcendental* criticism of science and philosophy."[14]

What will this "restriction" accomplish? It will, you contend, furnish the foundation for a community of thought between truly philosophic minded people. You ask those who in the past have assumed that theoretical thought is self-sufficient now afresh to reconsider the presupposition of their position. Will they not see their assumption of the autonomy of theoretical reason is really dogmatic? You for your part will give up any dogmatic criticism of their position. "Equally dogmatic would be an authoritative dictum from the side of the 'Philosophy of the Idea of Law,' that the synthesis cannot start from the theoretic thought itself because this 'autonomy' would contradict the revelation concerning the religious root of human existence."[15]

If there is to be a restoration of a true philosophical community of thinking (*wijsgerige denkgemeenschap*) then every form of dogmatism must be uprooted.[16] This uprooting can be accomplished, you add, only by means of the "restriction" discussed above.

With the community of thought (*denkgemeenschap*) restored we can expect to have intelligent dialogue between those who in their religious convictions may hold to opposing views. "This is due to the fact that this criticism," i.e., that of the Philosophy of Law, "rests upon what is indeed the *universally valid ontic structure* of philosophic thought and not on a *merely subjective* prejudice."[17]

Even the various schools of immanentistic thought can now afford to give up their mutually exclusive attitudes toward one another. They may cooperate with one another on the same level. Similarly the Philosophy of the Cosmonomic Idea has constantly enriched itself with the philosophical insights attained by immanentistic "thinkers."[18] Surely then what has often been a monological form of criticism should become dialogical in nature. If Christian philosophers use the truly transcendental method, they will be humbly self-critical first of all.

Finally, philosophers should realize that it is not a merely "subjective, merely epistemological, apriori, but an *ontic,* structural apriori" that underlies this community of thought; they will understand why a community of thought has been present between the past and the present.[19]

You think you can book some gains by the use of your *second way*. For a long time Roman Catholic writers merely reacted in dogmatic fashion to your devastating criticism of their nature-grace scheme. But in 1948 Dr. H. Robbers, S.J., published a book under the title *Wysbegeerte en Openbaring*. In this book Robbers is still self-defensive. But in the April, 1948, issue of *Studia Catholica* he speaks quite differently. Apparently he has sensed the fact that the philosophy of the cosmonomic ideas was not requiring that, as a condition for dialogue, he must give up his basic religious commitment. But now he realizes that your criticism is truly transcendental and not transcendent at all.[20] That is to say, Robbers has apparently understood the significance of your *second way*.

You express delight at this change on the part of an able protagonist of the nature-grace scheme of Roman Catholic thought. "It may indeed be a source of happy satisfaction to us that our pressing call to critical self-examination has been understood and appreciated at its true value."[21] Again: "In Prof. R.'s treatise Thomism has come to the point of self-criticism and has acknowledged, that its conception of autonomy is in its essence controlled by a religious ground-attitude and a transcendental ground-idea, which has roots that go deeper than theoretical thought."[22]

You call upon your followers to respond in kind. They must not think that what they have worked out in the philosophy of the cosmonomic idea must appear as obviously true to anyone who is able to think straight. They must rather continually remind themselves "that the real key to this philosophy consists of a transcendental criticism which cuts off every form of philosophical dogmatism and compels a thinker to approach his principial opponents from their own ground-motif."[23]

You express great surprise, Dr. Dooyeweerd, at what you say is my misunderstanding of the difference between your use of a transcendent and a transcendental method of criticism. So you patiently explain the difference between them once more as you did so plainly in *A New Critique*. You want to make a critical inquiry "into the *universally valid conditions which alone make theoretical thought possible, and which are required by the immanent structure of this thought itself*." I thought I had understood, at least the main thrust of this *restriction*, when I read your explanation of its significance the first time. I at once, however, had difficulty with it. I asked myself, "Can this mean an *Umkehr* in my friend Dooyeweerd's thought? He speaks of a *first way* that he formerly employed and of a *second way* that he now employs." "In the 'Introduction' we chose the way from above."[24] That *first way*, used in the W.d.W. (1935) is now, apparently, *replaced* by the *second way* with its "restriction" to an analysis of the "immanent structure of this thought itself." "Does Dooyeweerd really want to make such a sharp contrast between his two ways?" I asked. Was he not, even in the W.d.W., again and again speaking of the very structure of theoretical thought itself as requiring a religious starting-point in the human self and then beyond the human self in an absolute Origin? Is not this the reason why he says in the *New Critique* that he has directed all his attention to "a sharpening of the method of transcendental criticism" whereby the objection to his *first way*—effect that it was "not at all universally in philosophical circles"—might be met?[25]

It seems then that I must think of the *second way* as a *sharpening* of the first way, but not as a radical change. The result of this *sharpening* is negatively that it definitely excludes every form of *transcendent* criticism. Transcendent criticism does not make "the theoretical as such a critical problem." Transcendent criticism therefore cannot show the inner structure of the critical thought nor the inner connection between theoretical thought and experience.

Scholastic thinkers often used the transcendent method in order by means of it to introduce their nature-grace scheme of thought surreptitiously into the minds of men. They often succeeded. As you say in your letter, even the late Professor Valentine Hepp and the theological faculty at the Free University of Amsterdam in his day were of the opinion that to reject the "traditional scholasic view of human nature was a deviation from the Reformed confession."

Then too, your letter continues, "the task of a transcendental critique, which makes this theoretical attitude as such a critical problem, is quite different from that of a theological apologetics. It does not aim at a 'defense of the Christian faith' but at laying bare the central influence of the different religious motives upon the philosophical trends of thought."

May I, in passing, Dr. Dooyeweerd, express surprise at what you say about "theological apologetics"? Do you really think a Reformed theological apologetics seeks merely to indicate that as a matter of fact there is a difference between Christian faith and unbelief? As indicated above, I think of it quite otherwise.

I do set the Christian faith, most consistently set forth in the Reformed confessions, sharply over against the non-Christian faith. The non-Christian faith may express itself in many forms. No one has traced these various forms better than you have. They are all man-centered. I do not speak, as you sometimes do, of "fundamentally different conceptions" and of "a fundamental difference in presuppositions" between various immanentistic philosophers.[26] It is not the differences between them but that fact that all of them, whatever their differences, have in common the assumption of human autonomy that is basic to an understanding even of their internal differences. I do not speak of the *autonomy of theoretical thought* but of the *pretended* autonomy of apostate *man*. It is this and, as it appears to me, basically *only* this which all schools of apostate thought have in common. Assuming this autonomy apostate man gives a rebellious covenant-breaking response to the revelational challenge that he meets at every turn. The face of the triune God of Scripture confronts him everywhere and all the time. He spends the entire energy of his whole personality in order to escape seeing this face of God. When Parmenides insisted on the identity of thought and being he was basically, unknown to himself in his surface consciousness, engaged in trying to escape the face of his Creator. When Heraclitus said that all is flux he was basically in agreement with Parmenides in *their common ethical hostility* to their Creator.

When I try to win someone for Christ I therefore first make the difference between the Christian and the non-Christian positions as clear as I can. The two positions are mutually exclusive. Mr. Jones and I have opposing views of man, of fact, and of the function of logic. For me the presupposition of the possibility of theoretical thought and experience is the truth of Christ's words when he said *I am the Way, the Truth and the Life.* Committed as he is by his virtual confession of faith in human autonomy, apostate man is also committed to the idea of pure contingency. Accordingly he cannot distinguish one "fact" from another "fact." To distinguish one "fact" from another "fact" he must do so by means of his principle of logic or continuity. To distinguish between "facts" is to bring them into intelligent or inner relation to one another. But to do so by the only means he has at his disposal, Jones must, like Parmenides, reduce these "facts" to identity.

It is this that I tell my friend Jones. I tell him that I do not claim to be able to show the *inner* relationships between "logic" and "fact" any better than he can, but that I have been told by Christ in Scripture what I am as his image-bearer, and that as such I undertake my cultural task in reinterpreting his revelation to me to his praise. Can you not see, Mr. Jones, that you must repent and believe, lest you and your philosophy, your science, your art, in short your culture, go to ruin? You have nothing on which to stand in order to remove the Creator-Redeemer God from your sight. By his light alone you can see light. By his light alone can you distinguish between truth and falsehood. You are trying to remove the sun by taking out your own eyes.

You see, Dr. Dooyeweerd, unless I have again failed to make myself clear, why I cannot be happy about your *restriction*, by your *sharpening* of your transcendental method. If I must take your restriction at face value—as from your repeated insistence on its indispensable character for a truly transcendental method of criticism it seems that I must—then I cannot follow you. I believe that whether we are Christian philosophers or Christian theologians we must tell all fallen covenant-breaking mankind everywhere that what they have in their hostility to the Creator-Redeemer of men sought in vain, is found in him who before Pontius Pilate witnessed the good confession. When any man searches for truth, without searching for it in terms of the answer that everywhere confronts him in the self-authenticating Christ, then he is, in effect, doing what Pilate did when he said, "What is Truth?" and then gave Jesus over to the "Jews" who had already repeatedly charged him with blaspheming because he made himself out to be the Son of God.

You see then, Dr. Dooyeweerd, that I hold two points about Christian apologetics which apparently you do not hold. In the first place I believe that Christian apologetics, and in particular Reformed apologetics, is not really *transcendental* in its method unless it says *at the outset* of its dialogue with non-believers that the Christian position must be accepted on the authority of the self-identifying Christ of Scripture as the presupposition of human predication in any field.

Then secondly, I believe that a Christian apologist must place himself for argument's sake upon the position of the non-believer and point out to him that he has to presuppose the truth of the Christian position even to oppose it. I saw a little girl one day on a train sitting on the lap of her "daddy" slapping him in the face. If the "daddy" had not held her on his lap she would not have been able to slap him. In his day Hitler wanted to shoot across the channel into London; to do so he needed emplacement for his guns. A man swimming next to an iceberg in water may try to push the iceberg because it's in his way from nowhere to no place but it is he, not the iceberg, that will move. When you are now, with your *restriction,* insisting on a co-operative analysis of the nature of theoretical thought, you seem to be granting that such an operation can and should be performed *first* before the question of the claim of Christ comes into the picture.

I know very well, of course, that you constantly speak of creation, fall, and redemption in your book. But what you say on the subjects seems to come into the picture too late and in the way of a *Deus ex machina* into your main argument. You seem to me not to have given them their proper place at the outset of the argument, and you have *not presented them as the presupposition of the possi-*

bility of analyzing the structure of theoretical thought and experience.
You have, it appears, by your restriction, definitely excluded the
contents of biblical teaching as having the basically determinative
significance for your method of transcendental criticism.

The Three Steps

However, I find great difficulty in believing that you want to do
this. Recently a student argued with me to the effect that you were
doing the same sort of thing that I was doing. You were, he said,
placing yourself for the sake of the argument upon your "opponent's"
position in order to show him that his view of "men and things"
would lead him to the destruction of significant predication. I hoped
desperately that this student, Mr. Grey, might be right.

But then I reread what you say about the three steps in your
transcendental criticism. These three steps, you say, must be taken
one at a time if we are to have a really transcendental criticism.
"In order to guarantee from the outset a really critical attitude in
philosophy, transcendental criticism of theoretical thought should
come *at the very beginning* of philosophical reflection."[27] But for
this very reason you do not want Christian truth brought into the
picture at this point. A truly transcendental critique is, you say,
obliged to *begin* with an inquiry into the inner nature and structure of
the theoretical attitude of thought and experience *as such* and *not*
with a confession of faith. In this first phase of the critical investigation such a confession would be out of place. As you observe in
your letter, the question of "the central religious starting point of
those who take part in the philosophical dialogue . . . has not yet
come up for discussion. The confrontation of the biblical and the
non-biblical ground-motives of theoretical thought belongs to the
third and last phase of the transcendental critique."

How then are we to take our first step? We must show to the pro-
ponents of the autonomy of theoretical thought that its structure
cannot come into view except it be seen to be operative in relation
to naive, pre-theoretical experience. "The real inner structure of
theoretical attitude of thought can be discovered only by confronting
together the theoretic attitude and the pre-theoretic or pre-scientific
attitude of common experience."[28] If we do not, from the outset, set
theoretical thought in relation to pre-theoretical experience we absolutize the *"gegenstand relation."* We would then absolutize the
logical modality as though it could function in a vacuum. We must
then hold that the *gegenstand relation* corresponds to reality. We

would then create a great gulf "between the logical aspect of our thought and the non-logical aspect of its *Gegenstand*. There would be no possibility of throwing a bridge across this abyss. The possibility of knowledge would be lost."[29] Theoretical thought can begin and can be seen as beginning only when it sees itself as operating in relation to naive experience.[30]

On the other hand, "as soon as we have realized . . . that the theoretical attitude of thought arises only in a theoretical abstraction, we can no longer consider theoretical reason as an *unproblematic datum*."[31] We can then see that the "first basic problem of our transcendental critique of theoretical thought may be . . . formulated as follows: What is the continuous bond between the logical aspect and the non-logical aspects of our experience from which these aspects are abstracted in the theoretical attitude? And, how is the mutual relationship between these aspects to be conceived?"[32]

When I now look at this first of your three steps, Dr. Dooyeweerd, I fear that you are not doing justice to your own biblical convictions with respect to the nature of man, the nature of the logical modality, and the nature of man's experience of himself and his temporal experience.

As a Christian you believe that man and his world are what Christ tells us they are. The nature of theoretical thought is, therefore, what it is, as it appears in the light of the framework of truth given you in Scripture. One who does not see both the "logical" and the non-logical modalities of created reality in the light of this framework misinterprets them in radical fashion.

When the would-be autonomous man seeks to structure the multitude of his temporal experiences he seeks to do so by reducing them to blank identity by means of his legislative logic. The method of Parmenides is typical of all forms of non-Christian thinking. Even Kant's supposedly transcendental method was basically similar to that of Parmenides. In both cases it was the would-be-autonomous man who insisted that the world of change has no structure in it unless man himself, as ultimate, brings this structure to it.

Step One: Time

Suppose now you were to ask Parmenides and Kant to realize that if they are to understand the nature and structure of theoretical thought they must see that this structure is what it is as an abstraction from time. You give each one of them a copy of your *New Critique*. You read to each of them one sentence: "The idea of time constitutes the basis of the philosophical theory of reality in this book. By virtue of its integral character it may be called new."[33] Then you explain to them just what you mean by cosmic time, as you have set it forth so fully and ably in your various works. What will they answer you?

Parmenides would, I imagine, tell you that you still have the disfiguring detritus of the seaweeds of ultimate contingency upon you even as you are, in vain, struggling to emerge from it. You will not get even a glimpse of the nature and structure of theoretical thought, he answers you, unless you see that theoretical thought and being are one.

Kant would, I imagine, say that he agrees with you as over against Parmenides. "You have, Mr. Parmenides, to be sure attained to *pure* structure. But that is your trouble. Your structure is not structure of reality as we know it, i.e., of temporal reality, at all. It is a structure that destroys all temporal reality, by means of absorption of all temporal diversity into an abstract logical principle of identity."

"We must," adds Kant, "therefore assume the ultimacy of time or contingency. When by means of my categories of causality, substance, and modality I seek to structure reality I realize that the result of my effort at this point is like an island of ice *somehow* produced by and floating upon a shoreless and boiling cauldron of pure contingency."

What would you, Dr. Dooyeweerd, say in reply to Parmenides and Kant? In your major works you have shown at length that the form-matter scheme of the Greeks and the nature-freedom scheme of the moderns are together based upon the assumption of human autonomy. It does not help to supplement Parmenides with Kant. It does not help to set the *pure* static rationalist determinism of Parmenides in dialectical, mutually determinative, relationship with the *pure* "dynamic" irrationalist indeterminism of Kant and his followers. You have shown over and over again that the rationalist-irrationalist, and the nominalist-realist contrasts spring from the immanentistic presupposition of man as autonomous. The Christian, you have repeatedly urged, must never state and defend his position in terms of the problematics constructed by immanentistic thinkers.

What then can you now, on the basis of your *restriction*, say after listening to Parmenides and to Kant? Can you say that you agree *more* with Kant than with Parmenides because Kant as over against Parmenides agrees that theoretical thought has no knowable structure unless it is related to time? No, you cannot say this because what Kant means by time is something radically different from what you, as a Christian, mean by time. For Kant time involves *pure contingency*. For you it is what it is in relation to the Christian story of creation-fall and redemption.

The significance of this fact is that on your view as a Christian one cannot understand the nature and structure of theoretical thought unless it is integrally related to the Christian story. The nature of theoretical thought is what it is as a means by which those who are what they are because of their relation to their Creator-Redeemer God can in some measure understand the *magnalia dei*, and challenge all men to repent. You have, it seems to me, virtually told Parmenides and Kant that in much of your work.

Yet you are at the same time insisting that you can analyze the nature and structure of theoretical thought without any reference to that Christian story. You are seeking to show that you can analyze theoretical thought *as such* and show that it points to the Christian story. On this basis theoretical thought is not itself a part of that story. I cannot follow you at this point. I would say that the structure of theoretical thought cannot be seen for what it is in terms of the scheme of the natural man. In his dialogue with the natural man the Christian must show that theoretical thought as such is a non-entity. Theoretical thought is what it is only as it is seen to be operating as revelatory of the Christian story. The natural man must then be shown that in all his theoretical thinking he is seeking to repress the truth of the Christian story. Even if we are Christian philosophers, rather than theological apologists, our dialogue with our non-Christian friends must still partake of the argument between the city of God and the city of man. You have told us that a Christian, a Calvinist philosopher, must be ready to take upon himself the scandal of the cross of Christ, as the Savior of believers and of their culture. It is because by the grace of God in Christ and by the regeneration of the Holy Spirit our eyes have been opened that we now see the nature and structure of ourselves and our world about us.

Step Two: the Self

We proceed to watch you as you take the second step of your transcendental method. You speak of it as "a second transcendental problem." "*From what standpoint can we reunite synthetically the logical and the non-logical aspects of experience which were set apart in opposition to each other in the theoretical synthesis.*"[34]

We can discover the answer to this question only after we have found the answer to our first question. We must stand on the first step in order to see the necessity of taking the second step. The insufficiency of theoretical thought pointed to the need of relating it to cosmic time. Now the insufficiency of the inter-relation of theoretical thought with cosmic time points to the need of the idea of a self which transcends time. After a while, when we stand on the second step, we shall see that there must be a third step. But we cannot see the need of taking a third step so long as we stand on the first step. Whatever may be possible because of our faith we are now reasoning transcendentally. We must therefore not bring in Christian Truth at the first and second steps.

We took the first step because we saw that theoretical reasoning presupposes a cosmic world order. We now take the second step because we see that theoretical thought, even when operating in relation to a world-order, presupposes an Archimedean point beyond time.

The Archimedean point must "transcend the *coherence* in the diversity of the modal aspects."[35] An immanent coherence among the modal aspects of meaning of the cosmos is not sufficient. It is only in the self as "elevated above the modal diversity of meaning" that we have the concentration point that we need for philosophic thought as it seeks a totality view of life.[36] We therefore maintain "that no philosophical thought is possible without a transcendent starting point."[37] This transcendent starting point must needs be supra-temporal.

We took our first step because we say that cosmic time was the presupposition of theoretical thought. To think at all we had to take the first step. Having taken the first step we see that in order to keep thinking we must take the second step. We need a "veritable notion of time. Beings that are entirely *lost* in time lack that notion."[38]

Here the shades of Kant and Parmenides again appear to us. For Kant time is ultimate. According to Kant, Parmenides was quite wrong when he made it his ambition to rationalize time. Parmenides thought that if you were to have any awareness of self you must have a veritable concept of yourself as being *above* time. You must think of yourself as non-temporal. So also to have any awareness of time, you must deny its ultimacy. You must think of reality as supra-temporal. To have veritable self-awareness the self must know itself exhaustively in relation to eternal changeless being *as such*. The self must penetrate logically to the *inner* connection between itself and absolute, timeless being. But there is no way for Parmenides c.s. to attain to this *inner* logical connection between itself and timeless being unless all temporal reality be seen to be not only participant in but identical with one block of eternal being. Thus there is for Parmenides no individual self-awareness unless by means of its total absorption in abstract logical identity. Parmenides thinks that self-awareness and time-awareness presuppose the idea of abstract thought thinking itself. Abstract thought thinking itself is for Parmenides, as exemplar of Greek thinking, the presupposition of the possibility of predication.

"You are right, Dr. Dooyeweerd," says Parmenides, "in saying that 'no philosophic thought is possible without a transcendent starting point.' You are right in saying that this starting point must be supra-temporal. But I do not think that you really have a supra-temporal starting point unless you find it with us Greeks in pure form. I know that this pure form must be attained by negation. If your human self in which you seek a supra-temporal starting-point has any dynamic in it, then this starting-point is not really supra-temporal. Every bit of dynamic has its origin in non-being. And of non-being or nothing, nothing can be said. There is at this point, I realize, a 'difficulty' in my view. I must think of myself as nothing. If I were to think of myself as *anything* in myself I would have to do so in terms of the dynamics that springs from non-being or contingency, call it time. But I cannot think time. Therefore it is nothing. How can it then even be a principle of individuation for me? Yet I would have to use time as a principle of individuation in order to escape being swallowed up by pure form. I can therefore find no structure of any sort in my individual self. I know that if there is to be any structure in *myself* as engaged in theoretical thought I must immerse myself and be lost in time. You are quite right, Dr. Dooyeweerd, in saying that to account transcendentally for theoretical thought I must, as you say, relate it to cosmic time. But for me to *relate* theoretical thought to time is to immerse in it and be lost in it. Because of this difference between Kant and me on the meaning of time I was unable to take the first step with you on *your* transcendental criticism. You slipped in *your* view of cosmic time as derived from your Scriptures. You brought in dogmatic considerations prematurely.

"Now you are again doing the same thing as you are asking me to take your second step. I quote your words: 'If we say, that we transcend cosmic time in the root of our existence, we must guard against metaphysical Greek or Humanistic conceptions of the "supra-temporal."' Are you not, in saying this, excluding *my* view of the supra-temporal in advance? But let me read further from your *New Critique*, p. 32. 'We shall later on see, that the central sphere of human existence is in the full sense of the word a *dynamic* one. Out of it the dramatic conflict between the civitas Dei (City of God) and the civitas terrena (earthly city) takes its *issue* in the history of the world. We can even call it the central sphere of *occurrence*, for *that which occurs* cannot be distinguished too sharply from the *historical aspect* of cosmic time, which is only one of its temporal *modalities of meaning.*'

"In saying this you seem to me to be untrue to your *second way,* the way of showing us the presuppositions of the possibility of genuine philosophic thought without any reference to your dogmatic convictions about God and man. And here at your second step, the step pertaining to the necessity of having a supra-temporal self as an Archimedean point, you bring in your offensive tale about the *civitas Dei* and the *civitas terrena,* and for good measure introduce your *temporalities of meaning.* But I shall not take offense. I shall only ask you, with Socrates, what the nature of the holy is regardless of what gods or men say about it. I cannot listen to your extraneous descriptions about the structure of thought and experience. Under cover of a purely transcendental method you are seeking to have me submit my rightful claims as a free man to your supposedly divine human Christ.

"But let all this pass for the moment. I submit that a really transcendental inquiry demands a self which is *nothing* in itself, nothing in itself because it is only a sign pointing toward the principle of a pure form which is always beyond the possibility of having anything said about it. But I've talked too much. Let us hear what friend Kant says."

"Well, both of you know my position," said Kant. Especially you, Dr. Dooyeweerd, know my position very well. You have argued in very great detail at various places, that my transcendental method is not really transcendental or critical at all. But my basic agreement is with Parmenides. Both of us believe in freedom. From your biblical or Christian point of view you call this our freedom *autonomy.* You say that this autonomy came into the world when your first man Adam refused to obey his Creator in whose image he had been made. You say that true freedom comes to men only if by the regenerating power of your Holy Spirit they believe in Christ, who said: 'I am the Way, the Truth and the Life.' You have, accordingly, argued that the structure of theoretical thought is what it is in terms of your temporal *modalities of meaning* and in terms of your self which you think of in terms of creation-fall and redemption through your Christ. I submit that you have therefore determined the structure of theoretical thought and experience in subordination to the assumed truthfulness of your Christian story. You cannot rightly call such a method transcendental. How could any of us on the presupposition of our freedom have any knowledge of your Creator-Redeemer God? How could any of us experience real *thinking*, thinking that is *our* thinking, if thinking is first defined in terms that are beyond all thinking?

"To be sure, I have my differences with Parmenides. We have opposite priorities; he stresses the priority of thought and I stress the priority of time. But we agree on the nature of the self, of thought, and of time as over against your view on these three points.

"Holding to human freedom we naturally hold, with Socrates, that we must, by concepts, by thought, determine what can or cannot exist. Because of my stress on time as ultimate I no longer think that thought can, in any given period of time, actually legislate with respect to the nature of what can or cannot happen. But I retain the *ideal* of exhaustive penetration of all being by thought. In practice this means for me, as well as for Parmenides, your story *cannot* be true. In this point I am as adamant as is Parmenides, witness my book on *Religion Within the Limits of Reason Alone."* At this climax Kant stopped speaking.

Now I am of the opinion that what Parmenides and Kant said to you, Dr. Dooyeweerd, is true. Of course there are many other views put forth by immanentistic philosophers besides those of Parmenides and Kant. Yet, as you have proved to us so well, the nature-freedom scheme of modern thinkers is composed of the same elements as is the form-matter scheme of the Greeks.

It is their deepest conviction of all non-Christian thinkers that no man can think, i.e., use the process of rationalization properly in relation to himself and his environment except in terms of the framework of man as the final point of reference. Every immanentist philosopher assumes that it makes no sense even to ask any questions, let alone to expect to get intelligible answers, except on the presupposition of human autonomy and its implicates with respect to logic and time.

In direct opposition to this we as Christians believe that it makes no sense to ask questions, let alone expect to get answers to questions, except on the presupposition of the self-identifying Christ of Scripture. This conviction underlies, as it seems to me, all properly developed Christian theology, all properly developed Christian philosophy and science. I hold that your Christian philosophy and my Christian apologetics are valid to the extent that they are true to this principle.

However, it is not clear to me that, with your *second way*, i.e., with your *sharpening* of the purely transcendental method, with your *stricture* by which you want to analyze the structure of theoretical thought *as such*, and with your insistence that it is not till the *third step* in your transcendental analysis that Christian truth may be brought into the picture, that you are fully true to your own Christian convictions.

Step Three: the *Archy*

In the third step of a truly transcendental knowledge we must point out that the self is empty in itself except in relation to its Origin. The Archimedean point points toward the Archy. To quote: "The self seeks, by an original innate tendency—that is, the law of religious concentration—its divine origin, and cannot know itself except in this original relation."[39] As the inter-relations between the various modalities point beyond themselves to the supra-temporal self, so this self in turn points beyond itself to its Origin. "The mystery of the central human ego is that it is nothing in itself, i.e., viewed apart from the central relations wherein alone it presents itself." But the "first of these relations, namely that of the selfhood to the temporal horizon of our experience cannot determine the inner character of the ego, except in a negative sense." In other words, the self cannot discover its inner character in the relation to "modal diversity of the temporal order."[40] But neither can the self find its inner character even in relation to other human selves. "The reason is that the ego of our fellow-men confronts us with the same mystery as our own selfhood."[41] Well, "it may be that there exists a central love-relation which is capable of determining the inner meaning of my ego in its essential communal relation to that of my fellowmen. But as long as this love-relation is only viewed as a temporal relation between me and my fellowmen, we must posit that we do not know what is really meant by it." "Both the central relations which we have considered up to this point, are empty in themselves, just like the human ego that functions in them.[42]

Still further, "For it is only in its central religious relation to its divine origin that the thinking ego can direct itself and the modal diversity of its temporal world upon the absolute. The inner tendency to do so is an innate religious impulsion of the ego. For as the concentration point of all meaning, which it finds dispersed in the modal diversity of its temporal horizon of experience, the human ego points above itself to the Origin of all meaning, whose absoluteness reflects itself in the human ego as the central seat of the image of God. This ego, which is empty in itself, is only determined in a positive sense by its concentric relation to its divine origin. And it is also from this central relation that the relation of our ego to its temporal horizon and its central communal relation to the ego of our fellow-man can take a positive content."[43]

The "real starting-point of philosophical thought cannot be the ego in itself, which is an empty notion. It can only be the religious basic motive in the ego as the center of our temporal horizon of experience. This alone gives the ego its positive dynamic character also in its central interpersonal relation to the other egos and to its temporal world."[44]

In all this you are, Dr. Dooyeweerd, carrying forth your second way of transcendental method of criticism. We have now taken the *third* step of which this method is composed. Standing on the first step we saw that theoretical thought can operate only in relation to the temporal world order. Standing on the second step we saw that theoretical thought operating in relation to the temporal world order needs a supra-temporal self as an Archimedean point. Now, standing on the third step we see that having taken two steps we are compelled to take the third step if we are to attain the totality vision we crave. We have to go upward to "an idea of the Origin, whether or not it is called God, relating all that is relative to the absolute."[45]

We have herewith reached the "third and last phase of the transcendental critique." The "confrontation of the biblical and the non-biblical ground-motives" must *now* be taken up. Such a confrontation would be out of place during the first two steps or phases of the argument. My contention over against this is, Dr. Dooyeweerd, that this confrontation must be brought in at the first step, and that if it is not brought in at the first step it cannot be brought in properly at the third step. *But to say this amounts to saying that there is only one step or rather that there are no steps at all.*

I am of the opinion that your procedure corroborates my view on this point. I have pointed out that you did bring the Christian view of the created order at the level of the first step and the Christian view of man at the level of the second step, as you now bring in the Christian view of God in the third step. How could you escape doing so? You are convinced as a Christian that the Christian framework of truth as revealed by the triune God in Scripture is the transcendental presupposition of the possibility of intelligent predication in any field. If there is not to be a basic dualism between your religious convictions on this point and your process of rationalization you should proceed differently than you do in your *Critique*. To avoid dualism you should not start from the structure of theoretical thought *as such*. There is no such thing. There is no autonomy of theoretical thought *as such*. There is a would-be-autonomous *man*, who thinks about his entire environment in terms of his thought as legislative and as determinative of the structure of the temporal world. With all due respect for your very great learning and penetration I cannot help but say that to me it is ambiguous to speak of theoretical thought as needing to be placed in relation to the temporal cosmic order or to naive experience as a *primary datum*. There is no naive experience as a primary datum any more than there is anything like theoretical thought as such. Every item that man meets in his temporal horizon *is already interpreted by God*. It is the interpretation of the triune Creator-Redeemer God that every man meets in his every experience of anything. This is the "state of affairs" as it actually exists. The universe in which man lives is God's estate. The ownership of God is indelibly imprinted on every "thing" man meets. He cannot think of theoretic thought *as such*. I know not what else Calvin means by saying that at every turn man, the creature, faces his Creator. Man cannot have any "naive experience" in which he is not either a covenant-breaker or a covenant-keeper.

Of course, I know, Dr. Dooyeweerd, that by theoretical thought, by the temporal world-order, and by naive experience you mean what these mean in the Christian framework. But in your transcendental method you insist not only that they *may* but that they *must* be used *without* reference to the Christian framework.

Similarly, now that you take the third step in your argument, you, as a Christian, mean that man as created in the image of God must be the organizing center of his temporal experience. However, your argument for the need of a supra-temporal self not only may but *must* exclude such a view of man. To maintain the "community of thought" you are willing to go so far as to say that the supra-temporal self needs an Origin "whether or not this is called God."

It is such a featureless "God" that is the ultimate presupposition in terms of which you are now seeking to maintain a community of thought between covenant-keepers and covenant-breakers. But the idea of thought as such and the idea of time *as such* added to thought as such are inventions of the would-be-autonomous man in order by them to repress the truth. Modern autonomous man constructs his concrete universal as a replacement for the abstract universal of ancient thought. To add the idea of *an* Origin, *an* Absolute, is an invention of autonomous man. By means of it he thinks he does justice to the religious impulses that he finds operative within himself. By means of these "impulses" he represses the sense of deity created within him.

In the form-matter scheme of the Greeks the would-be-autonomous man said that naive time-experience was nothing in itself. It needed to be interpreted by man as supra-temporal. This supra-temporal man, still clinging sluggishly to temporal reality because of his body, is nothing in itself. It has no *dunamis* in itself. It is only a personi- fied and reified abstraction. This abstraction needs to be "inter- preted" by an all-comprehensive abstraction, again personified and reified. But how could this reified logical abstraction be said to be the absolute Origin of man, as a logically subordinate abstraction? If there was to be any *dunamis* in man it must spring from a source above and beyond all that can be logically said about anything. It was Diotema the inspired, who pointed to the vision of a unity beyond all logical distinctions made by man.

Surely this being beyond all knowable being, so the argument goes, must be *good*. Let us call it *Good*. Then let us add that all Good is diffusive; are we not all the offspring of God as *the Good*? Plotinus brought it all together in his idea of the scale of being. Dionysius the Areopagite and John Scotus Erigena "interpreted" the Christian story in terms of this scale of being.

It is thus that would-be-autonomous man, starting from himself as the final reference point of predication, followed upward and upward by the way of pure negation, dropping all content in the process, until pure form was attained. Man, with all his temporal experience be- came, as Plato says, incorporate with being. The freedom-nature scheme of modern thought follows essentially the same method as did the Greeks. Kant's transcendental method obviously rests on man as autonomous. It is not that Kant merely absolutizes *one* function of human experience, the moral modality, and not the others. To believe in man as autonomous is virtually to have him take the place of his Creator. This is to absolutize man in all his functions. The differences between the various schools of immanentistic philosophy are not that one of them absolutizes one modality and another of them absolutizes another modality. In absolutizing man himself they are all of them absolutizing *man's* operation in *every* modality. Kant would quite agree with me if I said that theoretical thought operating apart from time is like a meat-grinder without any meat in it. But the meat Kant offers his meat-grinder is that of pure contingency. How else could he maintain his position of human autonomy? How else can he repress the revelation of God within himself and his world? Kant would, finally, quite agree if I said that the whole of human experience points beyond itself to *a* God. Modern dimensionalist philosophers of various schools show that man cannot interpret himself and his world adequately in terms of the I-it dimension. One needs the I-thou dimension really to interpret even the I-it dimension properly. Then, beyond that, we need an I-Thou dimension in order to properly interpret the I-it and the I-thou dimension. Such is the argument of modern post-Kantian dimension philosophy.

A truly reformational philosophy should therefore, as it seems to me, Dr. Dooyeweerd, challenge this ancient-modern-dimensionalism based on the idea of human autonomy from the beginning. It should show to these various immanentistic philosophers of dimensionalism that on their view they cannot get started on the process of knowing and that adding *their* type of religious dimension to their intellectual dimension is of no avail to them. Their God is unknowable because made in the image of man who is in the first place unknowable.

Beyond this a reformational philosophy should, it seems to me, following Calvin, insist that God's face is clearly present in the facts of the world and in man as the image-bearer of God. Following the Apostle Paul Calvin portrayed the true state of affairs about man and his environment in his *Institutes*. Men have the requirements of their covenant-God clearly before them. It is not their "temporality" that should lead them to *conclude* by a process of reasoning that they need themselves to be supra-temporal and that they need an eternal God as *an* Origin beyond their supra-temporal selves. It was not Adam's temporality that made it imperative for him to *reason toward* an eternal God. It was the eternal triune Creator-God who was clearly present to him in every item of the universe about him as well as in himself. This Creator-God *spoke* to Adam and by *speaking* to him set the whole of every bit of contact between himself and his creature in a covenantal configuration. Even fallen man is responsible for this original *speech* of God to Adam the covenant-head of mankind.

Calvin says that when men do not see wickedness being punished as soon as it is perpetrated, they should conclude that God is merely postponing punishment, to the judgment day. They must not think that no punishment will be administered. Paul tells the Athenians that the resurrection of Christ in the temporal world is evidence of the coming judgment day. If men do not regard it as such they are seeking in vain to escape the wrath of the Lamb.

Now Dr. Dooyeweerd, I know that you believe all this. But you do not present it as the presupposition of that which makes *all* human experience intelligible. You believe that "history" is the struggle between the *civitas dei* and the *civitas terrena*. When Pontius Pilate asked, "What is *Truth?*" he was *insulting* him who said he was *the Way, the Truth, and the Life.* All men are in a similar position. They are all "without excuse" when they do not worship the triune God whose face appears to them in every fact of the world.

I feel constrained to say, Dr. Dooyeweerd, that your transcendental method, based on your restriction, is *not reformational either in its conception or in its consequences.*

That such is actually the case becomes particularly apparent from the way you seek to relate your own religious convictions to your transcendental method when in your third step you undertake to connect them.

Right after you say that your transcendental method leads man to "an idea of the Origin, whether or not it is called God, relating all that is relative to the absolute" you add that "Though such a transcendental basic idea is a general and necessary condition of philosophical thought the positive content given to it is dependent upon the central basic motive which rules the thinking ego."[46]

To discover the "general and necessary condition of philosophical thought" it appears from what you say we need a truly transcendental argument. This truly transcendental argument shows that to understand the nature and structure of theoretical thought we need to see that such thought has *a* religious basis and that this religious basis finds its central point of reference in the idea of an absolute origin *whether or not we call the Origin God.*

Up to this point all is clear. Our transcendental basic idea must *not* have *positive content. If it had positive content it would not be the universally acceptable presupposition of philosophical thought.*

But now it also appears that such a contentless transcendental basic idea is not adequate for its task. Our transcendental basic idea *needs* content. It must have content in order to be the source of the *dunamis* that the human ego needs in order to perform its unifying function. Here then at this third step is where at last you bring Christianity into the picture. You say to those who have followed you to the point where they may well agree that theoretical thought needs *an* absolute origin, that this Origin *must* be the God of the Christian framework.

You seem to sense that those who, among the immanentistic philosophers, have followed you to this point will refuse to take this *jump* with you. They will gladly accept the idea of the indispensability of belief in *an* origin, but they will not believe that this Origin must be the Creator-Redeemer-God of the Bible. To them the absolute origin must be an *apeiron,* an indefinite, a featureless source of power. It must not, they are sure, it *cannot* be the God of Paul, of Luther, of Calvin. Out of pure contingency any sort of God may spring forth *except* the God of Christianity. If the God of the Bible were to be thought of as the presupposition of the intelligibility of human experience then the idea of pure contingency and human autonomy would first have to be abandoned. What Christian thinker has more carefully traced the development of immanentistic thought in all its nuances than have you?

Yet at this juncture you seem to expect your immanentistic friends to follow you as you add the *positive content* of your Christian faith to their admittedly contentless transcendental basic idea of a featureless unknowable deity. You seem to be suspicious as to whether these immanentist thinkers will follow you. When you ask them to accept the new transcendental basic idea that is controlled by the *positive content* given it on the authority of the self-attesting Christ to the contentless absolute so far attained you say: "This gives rise to two critical questions which you will doubtless ask me at the conclusion of my explanation. First: How can this criticism have any conclusive force for those who do not accept your religious starting-point? And second: What may be the common basis for a philosophical discussion between those who lack a common starting-point?"[47]

Apologetics

You will realize, Dr. Dooyeweerd, that because of my interest in a reformational apologetics I am much interested in your answers to these two questions.

In replying to the first question you say that you "had no other aim primarily, than to lay bare the structural data of our temporal horizon of experience and of the theoretical attitude of thinking, both of which are of a general validity."[48] Who could object to that?

But suppose you now start your dialogue with immanentistic philosophers. You say: "When I told you that theoretical thought is
based on a religious foundation, you had no occasion to look askance
at me. I made plain that my description of religion was done in a
'formal-transcendental' way. In such a formal-way, I pointed out,
we seek a 'theoretical approximation' of the general notion of religion
and this can be done only by means of a 'transcendental *idea,* a limiting concept, the content of which must remain abstract, as long as it
is to comprehend all possible forms in which religion is manifested
(even the apostate ones). Such an idea invariably has the function
of relating the theoretical diversity of the modal aspects to a central
and radical unity and to an Origin."[49]

"I also pointed out that I adopted my‹*second way*, my 'sharpening
of the method of transcendental criticism' for the very purpose of embracing 'every possible conception of the philosophic task.' I said in
my book that no veritable philosophy whatever can refuse to listen
to me if I do not speak 'from above' and thereby bring *content* into
the heart of my critique."[50]

Well then, your immanentistic critics will say, why do you now
bring your "biblical basic motive" into the argument? You are, we
accept it, in all seriousness, introducing this biblical motive as an
aspect of your sharpened transcendental method. Does this sharpening of your transcendental method now require the addition of
content to your formal argument? We thought that you sharpened
your transcendental argument for the very purpose of excluding every
form of dogmatic content.

In answer to such objections on the part of immanentist philosophers you reply that in your third step you introduce your "radical
biblical motive" because it "unmasks any absolutization of the relative, and may free philosophical thought from dogmatic prejudices,
which impede an integral view of the real structures of human
experience. This effect is verifiable since it manifests itself within the
temporal experiential horizon, whose structural data have a general
validity for every thinker."[51] If you are worried that my introduction
of the biblical motive prejudices the truly transcendental character of
my analysis of philosophic thought, let me say again that "Structural
data, founded in the temporal order of human experience . . . are
facts of a transcendental significance, which should be acknowledged,
irrespective of their philosophical interpretation."[52]

You need not worry then, my friends, that I am forsaking the path
of truly transcendental criticism. On the contrary, by my introduction

of the biblical motive I am seeking to unmask still remaining pockets of dogmatism, and thereby enabling all of you to join me in testing our various dogmatisms by the standard of the "structural data, founded in the temporal order of human experience."[53]

I may now tell you, Dr. Dooyeweerd, about what I overheard recently when another couple of imaginary immanentistic philosopher friends were speaking together about your philosophy.

Said Mr. Godot: "I was happy when I read in Dooyeweerd's *New Critique* that he was no longer going to 'start from a supposition of the character of philosophy, which is not at all universally accepted in philosophical circles.'[54] But now he is introducing his 'radical biblical motive' again. The fact that he does not introduce it till he comes to his third step does not change things for me.

"Does Dooyeweerd now mean to say that, after all, we need his *true*, his biblical view of the Origin and Absolute, his Creator-Redeemer God received on authority, in order to discover the really transcendental presuppositions of the intelligibility of the temporal horizon of our experience? Did he not, especially since 1941, insist that his transcendental religious root consists of *an* Origin, of *an* Absolute which has *no* content? Does he now want us to follow him when he says the ultimate Origin must be the Creator-Redeemer God of the Bible?

"I can understand those who say that the whole of their biblical teaching with the self-attesting Christ at its center must be taken as the presupposition of the intelligibility of human predication. They would say that the structural data founded in the temporal horizon of our experience, are ultimately what they are because of the spot they occupy in the plan their God has for them in relation to the whole course of history from Adam to the day of judgment. Recently I dipped into John Calvin's *Institutes* again. It's all there. It's all there too in the Reformed confessions. I also read Abraham Kuyper's *Encyclopedia*. Only the elect, only the redeemed by the blood of Jesus, only the born-again by the Holy Spirit can see these 'structural data' for what they are. How then could we, poor blind reprobates, use these structural data as tests for the truth about statements made by elect men about them? In their view we are reprobate, we are covenant-breakers, we are non-regenerate and therefore cannot see these 'structural data' for what they are. Oh yes, because the world is what it is, and only because we and all men were created in the image of God, and because of their 'common grace,' we can 'adventitiously,' i.e., in spite of our false principles, discover certain 'true states of affairs.' We can even contribute to the one goal, to the fulfilment of the 'common philosophical task,' the 'cultural mandate' assigned to their Adam, the first man for all mankind, but all this, mind you, *in spite of our principles.* Our principles as immanentistic thinkers are based on man as 'falsely' (according to these Calvinists) thinking of himself as ultimate. We hold that creation out of nothing *cannot* be the ultimate source of temporal reality. We hold that our categories of logic are legislative for what can and what cannot exist. Our whole interpretation of ourselves and of the temporal horizon of our experience involves the dialectical relationship of an abstract all-absorbing impersonal being and an equally abstract all-absorbing womb of chance. These extreme Calvinists do not think of telling us that we can, on an equal footing with themselves, judge of the truth of their faith about man and his environment. They tell us, rather, that the sun is plainly visible in the heavens. Christ is, for these people, the Sun in whose light all things are seen for what they really are. Blind men do not see the sun. They do not see the facts of the world lit up by the sun. Only if we as blind men are given spiritual sight can we even judge of material things truly. And, these extreme Calvinists won't give us any hand in regenerating ourselves so that we may believe. They tell us that we are responsible for not being thankful to the Creator, the true Origin of all things, even as they assert that without regeneration we cannot relate things to this true Origin.

"Now I know that Dooyeweerd comes from a line of sturdy Dutch Calvinists. When his first major work, *De Wysbegeerte der Wetsidee,* appeared, I was stupified. Here was a man still very young, producing a comprehensive work on *philosophy,* a philosophy which, he said, 'seeks its resting point in Christ, who is the Way, the Truth, and the Life.' Those who would follow him in this new philosophy must be prepared, he said in his foreword, to forsake the 'traditional view of reality and of knowledge.' Here was to be a Christian, a biblical, a Calvinistic philosophy. I was interested. I was impressed by the enormous erudition and philosophical penetration of the man. But, of course, I thought of his whole enterprise as fantastic and self-delusive. So I 'forgot about it.' I forgot about it till an enthusiastic admirer of Dooyeweerd presented me with a copy of his *New Critique.* He told me it was different from the W.d.W. From this point he went on for an hour about the *purely transcendental* method that Dooyeweerd was now developing, and how it differed from the method of those extremist Calvinists who claimed that a man cannot account for counting except on Christian presuppositions.

"I promised my friend I would read about the new approach. I was encouraged when I saw that Dooyeweerd did not to bring in his Christian position into the picture at all at what he calls his first and second stages of transcendental criticism. But now at his third step he does bring it in and bring it in openly. I thought we had gotten past that stage. Oh yes, he tones down the significance of his 'radical biblical motive.' He does *not* say that it, and it *alone* must be taken as the presupposition of human predication. But how else can any Christian, particularly, how can any Calvinist bring in his radical biblical motive in any other way than as the foundation for the meaning of human life and history? And how can any Christian, particularly any Calvinist, do other than ask, even require of us apostate men in the name of their Christ to forsake our own view of reality and knowledge and accept theirs in its place lest we lose ourselves and our thinking fall into a dialectical pendulum swing of antinomies? I think that Dooyeweerd is not true to his own basic position when he now tries to incorporate *his* true Origin in Christ into a transcendental method that must lead to, himself being witness, *an* Origin such as we immanentistic thinkers can *on* our principles, not in spite of them, accept. Besides, I am sure it is his loyalty to his Christ that is of first importance to him. He says that in the third problem of the transcendental critique self-knowledge is at issue. He adds that self-knowledge is a religious, not a theoretical matter. 'In his high priestly prayer Jesus says that this knowledge is eternal life in the love-communion with the Father and the Son.' Self-knowledge 'presupposes the opening up of his "heart," i.e., the religious center of his existence, by the Holy Ghost to the moving power of Word-revelation.' You see this leaves us out. All three persons of the triune God must act for us and within us or we cannot exist or act at all. This is, I feel certain, Dooyeweerd's chief interest.

"Dooyeweerd no doubt thinks that it is his Christian religious beliefs which must be accepted if we are to understand the structural data of this world. But I wish he had said this plainly instead of seeking to weave *his private convictions* into his transcendental method which is *supposed to be acceptable to us as well as to himself.*"

It was Mr. Heim who listened to this speech of Mr. Godot. In reply to Godot, Heim said: "You know I am a modern dimensionalist philosopher. You know that my dimensionalist philosophy has been very influential in the circles of the *Intervarsity Christian Fellowship,* especially in Great Britain. This was no doubt because of the fact that I worked out the idea that the realm of science, the I-it dimension, is not sufficient to itself and that it needs to be supplemented by religion. I have shown that the I-it dimension points beyond itself to the dimension of person-to-person confrontation, to the I-thou dimension. Then finally, I have shown that this I-thou dimension is empty in itself unless it is seen as pointing to the I-Thou dimension.

"I found that this I-it-I-thou—I-Thou dimensionalism shows the *inner relation* between religion and modern philosophy. Of course this would not be the case if you meant by *religion* the traditional type of thing.

"Now when I noted that Dooyeweerd was also talking about the insufficiency of theoretical thought, the need for a supra-temporal self, and that this was the kind of self that points beyond itself to *an* Origin, then I thought the lines of communication between old style Calvinists and post-Kantian dimensionalists had actually been reopened. I was particularly happy when, in employing his *sharpened* transcendental method, Dooyeweerd argued as though the insufficiency of the I-it dimension was a result of its *temporal* character as such. Such men as Luther and Calvin did not seem to think that man's temporality *as such* indicated any insufficiency. What they stressed was the idea that when man was first created as a temporal being he was perfect. Man's heart was not restless because he was temporal. It was not till he became a sinner by breaking the ordinance or law of God that he, in consequence, became restless. Someone told me that a Dutch theologian named Herman Bavinck kept repeating that the Reformation, in stressing the ideas of sin and grace, was therewith, over against Romanism, stressing the heart of the Christian religion. I was so glad when Dooyeweerd seemed to soft-pedal this 'ethical' question and spoke instead of the inherent insufficiency of man's time experience as such. I thought that this would make him open to the idea of the I-it dimension as pointing to the I-thou dimension and the I-thou dimension as pointing to the I-Thou dimension. I was even happier when Dooyeweerd offered the idea that human self-consciousness comes to rest when it relates itself to consciousness of an Origin 'however conceived.' 'It is only when it relates itself to a Source that theoretical thinking finds rest for itself, because there is no meaning to the idea of asking questions theoretical beyond the Source.'[55] If then to presuppose *a* Source, a Source *indefinite* in character as the final and sufficient point of reference for predication, why then are we now asked to make the triune God of the Bible our final point of reference after all?

"Dooyeweerd no doubt seeks communication with us 'immanentistic' philosophers. This communication is welcome to us in terms of an I-it-I-thou—I-Thou dimensionalism. We ourselves want to add religion to theoretical thought as much as he does. We know that we cannot speak conceptually of the God we worship. We as well as he therefore speak of approaching this God with limiting concepts. It seemed to me that on the basis of his *sharpened* transcendental method we had reached the place where we could communicate on equal terms. But now that he is introducing his traditional views derived from Calvin, Kuyper, and such men we must go our separate ways again. He is apparently now trying to splice his radical Christian motive consisting of a God whose presence in the person and work of Christ is supposed to give us an absolute criterion of truth and life in the I-it dimension, into our view of the I-it-I-thou—I-Thou relation as based on the total absence of any absolute truth criterion in the phenomenal world.

"I had hoped that as the result of the application of his transcendental method we might together, in one ecumenical church, confine religion to a realm above the I-it dimension. But now my hopes are shattered. Dooyeweerd will continue, it appears after all, to absolutize the phenomenal and therewith cut himself and his followers off from communication with those who worship a really transcendent God, a God beyond all conceptual expression."

It appears, Dr. Dooyeweerd, that Mr. Godot and Mr. Heim have touched upon the same three points that I took up in the syllabus you discuss in your letter to me. There is the question of your transcendental method; it leads, say these gentlemen, if carried through, in the end to the idea of human self that is nothing but a transition point between abstract logic and abstract contingency and to the idea of man's temporal horizon as nothing but a point of intersection between abstract form imposed upon abstract contingent, "stuff," and at last, back of everything as the presupposition of human predication to the idea of a featureless God.

There is, secondly, the idea of "states of affairs" which, when interpreted by the transcendental method, enable the immanentistic thinker to verify the truth of the transcendental method as leading to *an* Origin, again to a featureless God.

There is, thirdly, the idea of a sharp distinction between the realm of man's conceptual activity in the world of his temporal horizon and the realm of man's religious activity in the world of his supra-temporal existence. These three points imply one another.

A further word needs to be said about the third point. When using your transcendental method you no longer work from above. Working from the bottom up you cannot adequately distinguish your Christian view of man, of the world, and of God from the non-Christian view of these subjects. Working from the bottom up you attain a view of man as having no content. Your view of man is that of a supra-temporal self consisting as a pure form. Though nothing but an empty form this "self" must, of itself, recognize its emptiness and point toward an absolute Origin. This absolute Origin, attained by further negation, and therefore also empty of content, must, by "a strange inversion of logic," be postulated as the Source of supra-temporal man's *dunamis*. This supra-temporal man, in turn, conveys this *dunamis* to his temporal horizon.

It is thus that you join the would-be-autonomous man on his way upward from himself as the ultimate starting point toward a God of pure negation and indetermination and on his way downward from the God nobody knows back to the man nobody knows.

When you work with this method then you are carried back and forth in the dialectical pendulum swing between pure rationalism and pure irrationalism, between pure nominalism and pure realism.

Of course, your religious convictions go counter to all this. No one has shown more fully than you have that the assumption of human autonomy leads to the destruction of predication. But you do not furnish us with an adequate basis for this. In fact, your second way leads toward the opposite conclusion. The only adequate basis for this is to insist that as Christians we start from above. This is no doubt what you believe. But in your reasoning about Scripture and its teaching you do not succeed in showing how *starting from above* implies a reversal of approach at every point of the method of immanentistic philosophers who start from below. Both Mr. Godot and Mr. Heim complained that you were seeking to inject your own religious convictions as a foreign element into your transcendental method, and that in doing so these religious convictions do not come to their own and are artificially connected with your transcendental method.

Biblical Teaching

We now look at what you say about the Bible and its teachings. Of course you believe the Christian story. You believe that man and his world clearly reveal the presence and activity of the triune God of Scripture. You have told us that often enough.

Yet even while telling us this you try to weave these religious convictions into a dimensionalistic scheme that would destroy what you believe.

Your sharpened transcendental method is destructive of the Christian story. This method has its focal point in the human self which as supra-temporal points beyond itself to *an* Origin as the source of its *dunamis*.

It is this man, a contentless intersection between pure irrationalistic indeterminism and pure rationalistic determinism, that you speak of as the "central sphere of occurrence." The entire struggle between the *civitas dei* and the *civitas terrena* takes place in this supra-temporal sphere of occurence. We must even say that "*that which occurs* cannot be distinguished too sharply from the *historical aspect* of cosmic time, which is only one of its temporal *modalities of meaning.*"[56] If we may speak of any occurrence as taking place in man's temporal horizon it is only as a pointer toward the supra-temporal self. And the "mystery" of this "central human ego is that it is nothing in itself. . . ." This self as *nothing* in itself in turn points beyond itself. All *dunamis* must therefore come from God. But then this God *must not be*, according to your transcendental argument, the Creator-Redeemer God of Scripture. If this God were the Creator-Redeemer God of Scripture then man would *ab initio* be placed in covenantal relation with God. Then the "religious" relation would not be expressed in some supra-temporal realm contrasted with man's temporal horizon. God's face would be directly present to man in every spot of the temporal world. Then man would be acting either as a covenant-keeper or as a covenant-breaker in the I-it dimension as well as in the I-thou dimension. Except upon the presupposition of the truth of the Christian story the human self would have to act in a vacuum.

I fear, Dr. Dooyeweerd, that the view of man as a supra-temporal sphere of occurence undercuts the entire Christian view as to the struggle between the *civitas dei* and the *civitas terrena*. There is no occurrence of any sort in this contentless self, except *dunamis* be poured into it from a featureless God. This *dunamis* then filters down into the temporal world.

It is on some such purely nominalist view that Karl Barth founded his idea of the sovereignty of God's election. Grace is sovereign; there need not be and there cannot be, on this view, any transition from wrath to grace accomplished through the death and resurrection of Christ as the electing God. Election would not be sovereign over "history" if any such thing as the death and resurrection were needed for man's salvation.

But then, correlative to Barth's nominalist view of the sovereignty of God's grace is his realist view of the universality of this grace. The recipients of God's grace need not in any sense have any cognition of what happened through the death or resurrection of Christ in history.

In short, the realm of ordinary temporal occurrence is not the sphere of the drama of creation, fall, and redemption. The *real* occurrence takes place in the sphere of the supra-temporal. The temporal is only a pointer toward this supra-temporal sphere of occurrence.

Now I am not in the least bringing in this matter of modern dimensionalism and of Barth's sovereign-universal grace, Dr. Dooyeweerd, if I did not seriously fear that your sharpened transcendental method with its supra-temporal self as the central sphere of occurrence really opens the door for an entrance into historic Reformed thinking for a form of the nominalist-realist dialecticism which is surrounding Christian believers at every turn.

It remains for me to make a few remarks on the second part of your paper. In it you conclude that I have misconstrued the nature of your transcendental method because I, myself, am of a metaphysical and rationalistic turn of mind. This being the case I do not even realize that "a theological reduction of the truths of fact to Leibniz's truths of reason would make even the central facts of creation, fall into sin and redemption a consequence of logical necessity in virtue of the principle of contradiction."

Such *must* be true because I have used the expression "truths of reason." The Apostle Paul says that he has become all things to all men so that *he might save some.* Does this prove that Paul thought that *he,* not Christ, was saving man? But that I mean by that expression nothing like what Leibniz means by it is evident from the fact that on the very page from which you quote (p. 134, *The Defense of the Faith*) I am rejecting the entire position of Leibniz. "Leibniz was not less a rationalist in his hopes and ambitions than was Parmenides." The metaphysics and epistemology of the rationalist would kill the Christian story. The same would be true of the irrationalist. Therefore "in contradistinction from the rationalist and the irrationalist, and in contradistinction from the forms of thought that seek some sort of combination between these two, the Reformed apologist must hold to the idea of absolute system and to that of genuine historic fact and individuality."

This "absolute system" is not the sort that idealist philosophers have in mind. In direct opposition to such a "system" the Christian maintains that the truths of fact presented in Scripture must be what Scripture says they are or else they are irrational and meaningless altogether. The Christian apologist has his principle of discontinuity; it is expressed in his appeal to the mind of God as all-comprehensive in knowledge because all-controlling in power. He holds his principle of discontinuity then, not at the expense of all logical relationship between facts, but because of the recognition of his creaturehood. His principle of discontinuity is therefore the opposite of that of irrationalism without being that of rationalism. The Christian also has his principle of continuity. It is that of the self-contained God and his plan for history. His principle of continuity is therefore the opposite of rationalism without being that of irrationalism. Conjoining the Christian principle of continuity and the Christian principle of discontinuity we obtain the Christian principle of reasoning by presupposition. It is the actual existence of the God of Christian theism and the infallible authority of Scripture—which speaks to sinners— of this God that must be taken as the presupposition of the intelligibility of any fact in the world. The Christian "must maintain that the 'fact' under discussion with his opponent must be what Scripture says it is, if it is to be intelligible as a fact at all. He must maintain that there can be no facts in any realm but such as actually do exhibit the truth of the system of which they are a part. It is only as manifestations of that system that they are what they are."[57]

At a later point in this same volume I have contrasted the Christian and the non-Christian positions schematically.[58] It amounts to saying that the Christian accepts the Christian story on the authority of the self-attesting Christ, on the authority of the triune God of Scripture. His philosophy of "logic" and of "fact" is what is in terms of this Christian story. On the other hand the non-Christian accepts his story on the authority of the "autonomous" man. His philosophy of "logic" and of "fact" is what it is in terms of his own story.

How then can there be communication between the Christian and the non-Christian? Because the Christian story is true and the non-Christian story is false. The Christian knows the "true state of affairs" from what he learned of Scripture teaching.

According to the Christian story man is made in the image of

God. His own consciousness is revelatory of God. Consciousness of God, the true God, is *given* with the consciousness of self. Consciousness of all the facts of the universe as revealing God is *given* together with consciousness of self and of God.

However, it is only because of the redeeming activity of the triune God of Scripture with respect to myself as a member of the people of God that I accept such to be true. With the dawning of daylight in my heart I run to tell others of it. I seek by the power of the Holy Spirit to be steadfast and unmovable, always abounding in the work of the Lord. I know that my labor will not be in vain in the Lord.

How could it be? I have no worry about a point of contact for the truth as it is in Jesus in the heart and mind of the natural man. I know that he is not what he thinks he is, and that the universe is not what he thinks it is. If he were anything like what he assumes he is and if the world were anything like what he assumes it is, I could find no point of contact with him. In that case man would be an intersecting-point between an abstract formal principle of thought or being, and an abstract formal principle of abstract, formal principle of irrationality or contingency. Still further, if the world were anything like the non-Christian assumes it to be then no one *would* have, because no one *could* have, approached me or any other human being with the gospel; I too would be a meaningless intersection point between pure logic and pure contingency. Finally, if the world were anything like the non-Christian assumes it to be there would have been no gospel to bring unto men. There *would* not have been, because there *could* not have been, a Jewish rabbi, named Jesus of Nazareth, who was the Son of God and son of man, who died on the cross to bear the wrath of God for the sins of other men and who was raised from the dead for their justification.

Yet, my non-Reformed evangelical friends seek for a point of contact with unbelieving men in terms of principles of interpretation which would destroy the meaning of human experience altogether. Seeking for a point of contact in terms of man as autonomous, my evangelical friends naturally also seek for a method of reasoning in terms of principles that would destroy the very meaning of reasoning. They would have to add purely contingent *newness* to stark changeless identity.

It is, of course, because of the nature of their theology that non-Reformed evangelical apologists can and must use such an unbiblical type of apologetical methodology. Roman Catholics and Arminians attribute some measure of autonomy to man. They start from their naive experience of freedom as an ultimate. Doing this they at the same time conclude that it is logically impossible to hold that man is both free and determined by the plan of God.

Thus they exegete away the teachings of Scripture with respect to God's relation to man by means of a "system" of "reality" and "knowledge" based on human autonomy. They *add* the Scripture teachings to their already constructed interpretation of man and the world.

Of course Roman Catholics and Arminians are often much better than their systems indicate, but we are speaking of theologies, not of men.

However, it is the responsibility of Reformed apologists to be first of all loyal to the self-attesting Christ of Scripture. To the extent that they are loyal to Christ and Scripture they will come to men and urge them to forsake the path of futility and judgment and take refuge in Christ. If they come to Christ, and only if they do, their philosophy, their science, and their theology will be saved with them. Then too they will no longer be galley slaves who must, even in their frequent discoveries of the true states of affairs in the universe, contribute willy nilly to their own and Satan's defeat and thus indirectly to the victory of Christ.

From the beginning of my work as a teacher in 1928, Dr. Dooyeweerd, I told my students essentially the same thing that I have said just now. The first paragraph of chapter I of a syllabus I wrote when I had not yet read any of the major works of the *Wysbegeerte der Wetsidee* reads: "According to Scripture, God has created the 'universe,' God has created time and space. God has created all the 'facts' of science. God has created the human mind. In this human mind God has laid the laws of thought according to which it is to operate. In the facts of science God has laid the laws of being according to which they function. In other words, the impress of God's plan is upon the whole creation."[59]

In the University at Princeton I had familiarized myself with the terminology and thinking of the history of philosophy, ancient and modern. What was I to do in order to set the biblical and more especially the Reformed points of view of reality, of knowledge, and of ethics as a challenge over against the man-centered view of men like Plato, Aristotle, Descartes, Locke, Leibniz, Kant, etc.? Should I devise a new terminology in order by means of it to express biblical truth, and thus make clear the differences between it and the thinking of man-centered philosophies? I could not if I had wanted to do such a thing. I had not the genius that you have. I decided to approach my non-Christian friends with the content of Scripture teaching by means of an *Umdeutung*. I put Christian meanings into their words. I would tell them that my view of reality and knowledge—call it metaphysics and epistemology if you wish—is taken from Scripture. To do otherwise would be for me to engage in vain speculation with the result that I would have an otiose deity dangling before my mind as my own projection into the void. Moreover, this is the terminology current in the English-speaking world in which I labor. I say, therefore, to those who ask about the Christian system somewhat as follows: "You, my friends, state and defend or reject what you call *systems* of reality and knowledge. Well, I too have a 'system,' but it is a different kind of system. It is neither a deductive nor an inductive system, in your sense of the term. Nor is it a combination of these two. My 'system' is not that of empiricism, of rationalism, of criticism, or of any of the other 'systems' you may read about in the ordinary texts on philosophy. Nor is my 'system' a synthesis between one of your systems with that of the Bible. My 'system' is attained by thinking upon all the aspects of reality in the light of the Christ of Scripture. I try to think God's thoughts after him. That is to say, I try as a redeemed covenant-creature of the triune God to attain as much coherence as I, being finite and sinful, can between the facts of the universe. God's revelation is clear, but it is clear just because it is *God's* revelation and God is self-contained light. My 'system' is therefore an analogical reinterpretation of the truth that God has revealed about himself and his relation to man through Christ in Scripture. I construct my 'system' by means of a variety of gifts that God has created within me. Among these gifts is that of concept-formation. But my 'concepts' are not, as they are in your case, instruments by which man destroys the Christian story even as he explains it. My concepts work subject to the truth of the story. My concepts with respect to the story limit and supplement one another. Since my concepts are *ab initio* limiting concepts in the Christian, not the Kantian, sense of the term, they enable me to 'understand' and by understanding appropriate for myself, for my fellow-believers, and for all men the significance of the story."

But I must stop. I hope that by what I have said in this article, Dr. Dooyeweerd, I am enabling you to have a somewhat more satisfactory insight into my view; as I have, I think, by reading your letter and by rereading a good deal of your writing elsewhere, attained to a more satisfactory insight into your view. I hope too that this interchange of ideas between us may help others, after us, to listen more humbly to the words of the self-attesting Christ of Scripture in order that they may better bring the word of truth to all men everywhere—all to the praise of our triune God. Soon we shall meet at Jesus' feet.

—C.V.T.

PART THREE

ESSAYS IN THEOLOGY
AND
THEOLOGICAL METHOD

Philip Edgcumbe Hughes

III. CRUCIAL BIBLICAL PASSAGES
FOR CHRISTIAN APOLOGETICS[1]

The construction of a system of apologetics that is distinctively Christian should be founded on the testimony of Scripture to the nature of reality in its divine, its human, and its cosmic aspects. It should, moreover, be founded on the biblical testimony in its entirety, for the teaching concerning God, man, and the universe is plain and consistent throughout the whole of Scripture and is not dependent on the selection of a few isolated proof texts. But, as with all biblical doctrines, there are certain passages which bring a subject into a sharply defined focus and which therefore merit careful and detailed consideration. The purpose of this chapter is to examine a number of passages which are of particular importance for the theme of Christian apologetics, though, because of limitations of space, the attention it is possible to give them will be much less full than they deserve.

I. Genesis 1:1-31

Of absolutely radical importance for the development of Christian apologetics is the biblical doctrine of creation. Indeed, so much is this the root of the matter that apart from it no effective apologetic is possible; for the doctrine of creation is the indispensable foundation of our understanding of all existence. This doctrine affirms, first of all, the absolute primacy or priority of Almighty God, and thus the eternity and total independence of his existence. "In the beginning God. . . .": these words with which Holy Scripture opens sound a theme which is dominant throughout the whole of the biblical revelation. God is *at* the beginning, and therefore he is *before* the beginning, and he *is* the beginning of all things. The scope of his work of creation is comprehensive: heaven and earth, the universe in its totality; and the bringing of all things into existence was effected by the utterance of his dynamic word: "God said, Let there be . . . and it was so" (cf. John 1:1ff.). The Word of God is the expression of the mind and will of God and consequently the whole created order bears the imprint of the mind and will of God. The biblical doctrine of creation means unambiguously that the being of God is the ground and principle of all other being, and thus that all other being is, unlike God, not self-subsistent but is completely dependent on God both for the origin and for the continuance of its existence.

The biblical doctrine of creation means, moreover, that the knowledge of God is the ground and principle of all other knowledge, both because it is eternally prior to all other knowledge and also because it is comprehensively exhaustive, whereas all other knowledge, being that of finite creatures, is at best partial and fragmentary. There is, in other words, only one authentic knowledge of reality, and that is God's knowledge. God's knowledge, which is absolute and uncaused, is the sole source of the knowledge which is available to man. Man's knowledge, which is an aspect of his being (no being, no knowledge!), is derived and can only be derived from the knowledge of the Creator to the extent that it is revealed in his works and words.

The knowledge accessible to man from God's works (general or natural revelation) and words (special revelation) comes, so to speak, from without—though the fact must not be overlooked that man too belongs to the works of God and therefore may not adopt an attitude of independence or superiority. There is, however, a third center of knowledge which is *within* man and belongs to the essence of his constitution as man. This becomes apparent in the account of creation when it is said that God created man "in his own image." The wealth of meaning implicit in this phrase cannot be discussed here, highly important though the subject undoubtedly is, especially with regard to man's inherent faculties of personality, rationality, morality, sovereignty, and creativity, which contribute to the uniqueness of his humanity and place him apart from all other creatures. All that can be said now is that man, constituted in the image of God, cannot possibly isolate himself from God; he cannot possibly be ignorant of God; he cannot possibly usurp the place of God. The image of God is the most intimate and distinctive feature of man's constitution as man, and he cannot possibly cease to be what he is. The image of God is stamped upon his creature man, at the very heart of his being.

This means not only that no man can divorce himself from the knowledge of God but also that every man is answerable to God. Man's responsibility is an important aspect of man's dignity, of the uniqueness of his humanity. Man is answerable to God for the life that has been given to him. He cannot contract out of this answerability, simply because he is what he is, namely, man. The Creator-creature relationship is essential to his existence and the image of God is constitutive of his humanity. The fulfilment of his being is dependent on these two fundamental factors. To deny them is to cut the life line which alone gives meaning and purpose to his being; in doing so he inevitably cuts himself adrift and experiences alienation and disintegration at the very heart of his being.

II.   Genesis 3:1-24

If the doctrine of creation is indispensable to our understanding of the constitution of man, the doctrine of the fall is no less indispensable to a proper understanding of the realities of the human situation. All the elements of the human predicament are present in the account of the fall given in Genesis 3, and the combination of the biblical doctrine of creation with biblical doctrine of the fall makes it absolutely plain that it is not in his finiteness but in his fallenness that the critical problem of man resides. In the garden, man freely realized the fulfilment of his being by living in accordance with the Word of his gracious Creator and thus gratefully glorifying God and honoring the relationship which alone could give meaning and purpose to his existence. The satanic strategem which effected man's fall involved an assault on the Word and thus on the authority of the Creator. This took place in two stages: firstly, by calling in question the Word of God ("Yeah, hath God said . . .?"), and, secondly, by actually contradicting the Word of God ("Ye shall not surely die!"). The explanation is then added that God is threatened by man's existence and is concerned to protect his own selfish interests; a unilateral declaration of independence therefore, through the rejection of the Creator's Word, will result in man being as God and lord of all he surveys. This is the essence of the fallen state of man, that in rebellion against the sovereign authority of the Creator he madly attempts to make God in the image of man and at the same time to overthrow the Word and the will of God. Of course, the ontological situation is not altered by one iota: God is still God, supreme over all as Creator and now also as Judge; man is still man, totally subject and dependent in his creaturely being. But the epistemological situation becomes one of disastrous upheaval, for sinful man, by making himself instead of God the center and key to the understanding of the reality both of himself and of the universe, severs the life line of the Creator-creature relationship so essential to the right knowledge of things and drifts off in to the ocean of alienation, where the fulfilment he desperately seeks will always elude him.

III. Romans 1:18-32

Nowhere is the gravity of the human predicament more incisively
described than in this passage written by the Apostle Paul. All men
know the truth about the existence of the divine Creator, but in their
unrighteousness they hold it down, they suppress it (vs. 18). It is
futile, however, to imagine that they can do away with the knowledge
of God and, by the same token, with their answerability to him who
is their Creator, "since what can be known about God (τὸ γνωστὸν
τοῦ θεοῦ) is plain (φανερόν) within them (ἐν αὐτοῖς) because God
made it plain to them (αὐτοῖς ἐφανέρωσεν)." There is no question,
in other words, of men having to grope about tentatively for the truth
about God or of their having somehow and in innocence missed the
message; for the knowledge is there *within* them. The inwardness of
this knowledge may be understood in two respects; firstly, in a general sense, inasmuch as all knowing and knowledge, even when
derived from external data, is internal to man; secondly, in the
specific sense that this knowledge of God is within men because, as
creatures made in the image of God, it is stamped upon their inmost
being, and, as we have observed, no man can separate himself from
the reality of his own constitution.

But equally inescapable is the testimony to the existence of God by
which man is surrounded on all sides. The invisibility of God and his
attributes provides no excuse for ignorance concerning his being; "for
his invisible nature (τὰ ἀόρατα αὐτοῦ), in particular his eternal power
and deity, is clearly perceived (καθορᾶται) from the created order of
the universe (ἀπὸ κτίσεως κόσμου), being intellectually apprehended
from the things that have been made (τοῖς ποιήμασιν νοούμενα)." The
whole cosmic system points incontestably to the truth that there exists
a Creator of all who is unique in the eternity of his sovereign divinity.
This knowledge is obvious to man as a rational creature. The rationality of the whole, itself a witness to the rationality of the Creator,
is a truth from which man cannot rationally dissociate himself; he can
only irrationally seek to suppress it; but in doing so he is "without excuse" (ἀναπολόγητος); he has no defense to offer; he is acting contrary to the integrity and dignity of his own being.

Furthermore, while man has the faculty, denied to non-rational
creatures, of viewing the cosmos as it were from a position of de-
tachment, yet he cannot possibly disengage himself from the universe
which he contemplates as though it were something entirely separate
from himself; for he too belongs to this same universe; he himself is

an integral component of the cosmic whole which points so unmistakably to the truth about God. He *belongs* and, once again, he cannot escape from himself; he cannot contract out of the environment which is the setting of his whole existence. Indeed, of all the wonders of the created order none is more to be marvelled at than man himself, the crown of God's creative work. Hence the adoration of the psalmist: "O Lord, our Lord, how majestic is thy name in all the earth!" (Ps. 8:1, 9); "Wonderful are thy works!" (Ps. 139:14); and the recognition that, of all that exists, it is man who has been crowned with glory and honor and who has been given dominion over all the works of God's hands (Ps. 8:5ff.). Especially dramatic is the opening paragraph (vss. 1-4) of Psalm 19:

> The heavens are telling the glory of God;
>   and the firmament proclaims his handiwork.
> Day to day pours forth speech,
>   and night to night declares knowledge.

In other words, the message comes through loud and clear, that all things are created and sustained by God. It cannot be missed. This is genuine knowledge, and essential knowledge, and it "shouts at us" whichever way we turn. At the same time, however:

> There is no speech, nor are there words;
>   their voice is not heard;
> Yet their voice goes out through all the earth,
>   and their words to the end of the world.

This loud testimony is also a silent testimony. It is inescapable because it is universal; and the testimony is all the more eloquent because of its majestic silence.

The life of man is, in fact, based on the presupposition (instinctive and subconscious though it may be) that the whole of reality is a coherent unity, that it makes sense, that it is a universe and not a jumble, a cosmos and not a chaos. The scientist, for example, takes it for granted, by a right instinct, that all facts are interrelated, and therefore that every fact has meaning and one fact leads on to another, and, further, that there can be no such thing as a bare or unrelated fact, which in itself would be meaningless and, indeed, unimaginable. If the consistency of the universe were not a datum of reality, not only would scientific research and discovery be impossible but the whole of existence would be stultified by a chaotic lack of meaning. Nothing would make sense. The logical faculties of thought and speech would be unknown and unattainable. The making and execution of plans would be inconceivable, as would conceivability itself. As things are, however, the logic of reality is such that rational thought, communication, planning, and investigation belong to the normal pattern of human existence. We live, instinctively, as rational beings in a rational world. The whole, which includes ourselves, bears the stamp of the rationality of him who designed it and brought it into existence.

This truth about God, known to each man by the testimony both of the created order and of his own constitution in the image of God, and therefore at the same time this truth about man, is the truth that must constantly be affirmed in Christian apologetics. The seat of all sin lies in the denial or suppression of this truth in man's arrogant claim to autonomy in defiance of the sovereign authority of his Creator.

The Christian apologete must insist on the *certainty* of the existence and the sovereignty of Almighty God. He should never take his stand, even with the best of intentions, on the same ground as that occupied by the unregenerate mind; for that ground, as we have said, involves the denial of the Creator and accordingly the denial by the unbeliever of his own creaturehood, that is, the denial of the very essence of his being and the disruption of his Creator-creature relationship which alone can give meaning to his existence. This is a position of untruth and unreason, and as such it cannot be adopted or condoned, even temporarily, by the Christian. God is the great fundamental and dynamic fact behind and above all other facts. There can be no uncertainty about God.

Nothing is more destructive of the dignity and integrity of man than to know the truth about God and yet to suppress it, and it is important that the Christian apologete should have a clear understanding of the evil consequences of the suppression of this fundamental truth. These are unequivocally described in the passage we are considering. But, before we enumerate them, it must be emphasized that it is not just a question of the *mental* rejection of the truth, for what is involved is nothing less than the rebellion of the whole man, man in the totality of his being, mind, emotion, and will, against God. It is the refusal to give God the glory which is his due. It is the grossest ingratitude. "Although they knew God," says the Apostle, "they did not honor him as God or give thanks to him." This is the root of the plight of man which has produced the tragic harvest of human fallenness and alienation. The dire consequences of man's suppression of the truth about God may be summarized under the following heads:

(1) *Intellectual futility*: "all their thinking has ended in futility" (NEB); "they made nonsense out of logic" (Jerusalem Bible).

(2) *Spiritual darkness*: "their senseless minds were darkened" (RSV); "their misguided minds are plunged in darkness" (NEB).

(3) *Incredible stupidity*: "claiming to be wise, they became fools" (RSV); "the more they called themselves philosophers, the more stupid they grew" (Jerusalem Bible). Yet what else could be expected in those who have "exchanged the truth of God for a lie"?

(4) *False religion*: This is seen in the proliferation of idolatry in all its manifestations, whether crass (they "exchanged the glory of the immortal God for images resembling mortal man or birds or animals or reptiles") or sophisticated (they "worshipped and served the creature rather than the Creator") as displayed in the perspectives of egocentrism, humanism, hedonism, materialism, intellectualism, and so on.

(5) *Gross immorality*: The degrading effects of man's mutiny against God involve not only his mind and spirit but also his body. Indeed, nothing could be more eloquent of the depth of man's fallenness than the substitution of the lust of flesh for flesh in place of the love of the creature for his Creator. This depravity is exhibited in the pursuit not simply of fornication and adultery but also of all kinds of perversion and unnatural vice. Thus our passage asserts that "God gave them up to the lusts of their hearts to impurity, to the dishonoring of their bodies among themselves. . . ."

(6) *Social depravity*: This rottenness inevitably infects human society in general and is destructive of those standards and structures which are essential to the maintenance of the decency and dignity of civilized existence. This, again, is graphically depicted by the Apostle:

> Since they did not see fit to acknowledge God, God gave them up to a base mind and to improper conduct. They were filled with all manner of wickedness, evil, covetousness, malice. Full of envy, murder, strife, deceit, malignity, they are gossips, slanderers, haters of God, insolent, haughty, boastful, inventors of evil, disobedient to parents, foolish, faithless, heartless, ruthless. Though they know God's decree that those who do such things deserve to die, they not only do them but approve those who practice them (Rom. 1:28-32).

So far is all this from being out of date and irrelevant that its applicability to our much-vaunted Western civilization (which, despite the brilliance of a multitude of technical achievements, is now face to face with disintegration from within) is so alarmingly obvious as to need no elaboration. This is true of our unhappy world as a whole: in our mutual nearness and awareness experienced through the wonders of modern means of transport and communication, the truth of the human situation as described in this passage is more starkly obvious than ever.

IV.   1 Corinthians 2:14

The plight of fallen man is further complicated, however, by the fact that he is incapacitated from seeing things as they really are. He is unable to discern the reality of the human situation, which also, of course, includes his own situation. But this incapacity is not an incapacity of constitution; it is an incapacity of choice. He has chosen a lie instead of the truth, darkness instead of light, death instead of life. Unlike a blind man who longs to see the sun but cannot because of his affliction, he is unable to see because he has wilfully closed his eyes to the source of life and light. He knows the truth about his Creator and therefore about himself, as we have already explained, but he does not *want* to know it and so he suppresses it; he shuts his eyes to it; he cuts the life line of his relationship to God and in consequence finds himself adrift in an ocean of unreality and alienation. It is he who has incapacitated himself. This is the tragedy of the "natural" man of this passage. It would be more appropriate to call him the unnatural man, and it is good that the rendering of the King James Version, despite its long currency as a virtually technical term of theology, has been abandoned by modern versions in favor of the expression "the unspiritual man"; for the adjective ψυχικός, admittedly difficult to translate here, describes man as fallen, degenerate, unregenerate, because he has preferred ψυχή, animal existence, to πνεῦμα, the Spirit of God, as the principle of his being.

Accordingly, the unregenerate man finds "the things of the Spirit of God" unacceptable; he dismisses them as foolishness because they do not fit into his chosen frame of reference. "He is not able to understand them because they are spiritually discerned." His spirit is the spirit of the world, but these great realities are known only to the Spirit of God and to those to whom he reveals them (vss. 10-13). Sin has rendered man degenerate and incapable of responding and returning to the light of the truth about God and himself; his great need is the experience of regeneration; his only hope is a transforming work of the Holy Spirit of God at the very center of his being.

V.   Ephesians 2:1-10

The incapacitation of man through sin is not just a matter of degree. It is total and ultimate. The effects of sin are lethal. The human predicament could not be more serious than it is. That is why this passage describes man in his fallenness as being "dead in trespasses and sins" (cf. Rom. 6:23). The dead man is totally incapacitated; there is absolutely nothing that he can do. So also the unregenerate man is dead towards God; there is nothing at all that he can do to bring about his regeneration. This is the proper background of the Gospel. Apart from it the incarnation and the cross of Christ make no sense. The incapacity of the sinner is overcome by the omnipotent love of God. In Christ the new birth is triumphant reality; the new man in Christ owes everything to grace, the free, undeserved, sovereign grace of God. Accordingly, the Apostle Paul reminds his Ephesian converts that, prior to their response to the Gospel they "had lived in the passions of the flesh, following the desires of body and mind," and "were by nature children of wrath, like the rest of mankind," but that God, rich in mercy and moved by the greatness of his love for them, had made them, dead as they were through their sins, alive together with Christ. No wonder he speaks of "the immeasurable riches of God's grace in kindness towards us in Christ Jesus." The glory belongs entirely to God.

From first to last salvation is by grace through faith: "and this is not your own doing, it is the gift of God—not because of works, lest any man should boast." The Christian believer, accordingly, is God's workmanship, "created in Christ Jesus"; and in this new creation we see the restoration and fulfilment of all God's purposes in the original creation.

VI.   Revelation 21:1-4

In responding to the task of Christian apologetics it is important to see things in the full sweep of the biblical perspective. We must start with Genesis and we must end with Revelation. The doctrine of creation is essential if we are to understand the creaturehood of man and all that it implies. We must understand also the fallenness of man and the fatal consequences of his sin, and thus his desperate need for the regenerating grace of God in Christ Jesus. This understanding of the human situation must be related to the symptoms of man's sickness unto death as they manifest themselves in the world of our day. While at root the disease remains the same throughout the ages, its outward expression varies in accordance with the temper of the times, the shifting moods of society, and the prevalent fashions and factions of thought and philosophy. If we are to speak effectively to our age we must be sensitive to these things, and the announcement of our diagnosis should be marked by the compassion that befits those who are ambassadors entrusted with the message of the grace of God in Christ Jesus. But we must not stop with man as he is; we must go beyond this and see him as he will be. For each man is a man of destiny, and his destiny is either judgment or glory.

Apologetics is incomplete and inadequate without eschatology, and this dimension of eschatology, while it is present throughout the Scriptures, is brought into special focus in the book of Revelation. The majestic scope of God's everlasting purposes extends from creation to consummation. It covers the whole of human history and provides a comprehensive perspective, past, present, and future, of the human situation.

This passage, from the concluding section of the Apocalypse, affords a preview of the consummation of all things. Satan and his followers have been judged and destroyed (20:10ff.) and the scene is that of "a new heaven and a new earth" in which righteousness prevails everlastingly (cf. 2 Pet. 3:13) and God dwells in the midst of his people. All the evil consequences of sin—sorrow, pain, death—are unknown, "for the former things have passed away." Thus the promises of God's covenant of grace receive their full fruition and God's creation, pronounced "very good" at the start, is, as the new or renewed creation, very good at the end. The indefectibility of his will, his Word, and his work is gloriously demonstrated and all his purposes are brought to fulfilment. Man, redeemed and glorified, is man at last as he was always intended to be: without interruption enjoying harmonious fellowship with his Creator. joyfully governed by the Word of God, at peace with God and man and the whole of creation, ceaselessly serving and praising the triune God—Father, Son, and Holy Spirit—who has freely blessed him with life and truth and grace in a universe of inexhaustible wonder and beauty.

What a perspective this is! What an incentive to confident and full-ranging apologetics! To know God in Christ Jesus through the gracious operation of the Holy Spirit within, to be brought into the midstream of God's eternal purposes, to see man in his true perspective as he was, as he is, and as, by God's grace or by God's judgment, he will be—truly we have the key that unlocks the secret of the universe! We know and are sure, and in the field of apologetics, as in all other areas of experience and encounter, if we are true to what we have received, our knowledge and our assurance will never waver as we join battle with the forces of scorn and unbelief.

J. I. Packer

IV. BIBLICAL AUTHORITY, HERMENEUTICS AND INERRANCY[1]

The importance of reflecting on the relation between biblical authority and hermeneutics appears from the single consideration that biblical authority is an empty notion unless we know how to determine what the Bible means. It appears also from the fact that every hermeneutic implies a theology, just as every theology involves a hermeneutic, so that where a false hermeneutic operates the Bible will not in fact have authority, whatever is claimed to the contrary. The importance of reflecting on the question of biblical inerrancy in relation to these two subjects is that the evangelical view of both assumes it, and that any denial of it afflicts both with unsteadiness, inducing collapse. To show the link between these three matters is the main aim of the present essay.

I. Biblical Authority

The first step is to set out the meaning of biblical authority, as historically (and, in my judgment, rightly) understood by evangelicals. The principle is a complex dogmatic construction made up of seven elements, as follows.

Inspiration

The first view of *inspiration* as an activity whereby God, who in his providence overrules all human utterance, caused certain particular men to speak and write in such a way that their utterance was, and remains, his utterance through them, establishing norms of faith and practice. In the case of those written utterances which make up the canonical Scripture the effect of inspiration was to constitute them as norms, not merely for that limited group of people to whom God's messengers directly addressed their writings, but for all men at all times. This, I judge, is the precise notion expressed by Paul in II Timothy 3: 15, where he describes "all scripture" as *theopneustos* (literally "God-breathed"), and therefore "profitable" as a standard of intellectual and moral perfection for anyone who would be a "man of God."

The theological basis of biblical inspiration is the gracious condescension of God, who, having made men capable of receiving, and responding to, communications from other rational beings, now deigns to send him verbal messages, and to address and instruct him in human language. The paradigm of biblical inspiration (not from the standpoint of its literary types or of its psychological modes, which were manifold, but simply from the standpoint of the identity which it effected between God's word and man's) is the prophetic sermon, with its introductory formula, "Thus saith the Lord." The significance of biblical inspiration lies in the fact that the inspired material stands for all time as the definitive expression of God's mind and will, his knowledge of reality, and his thoughts, wishes, and intentions regarding it. Inspiration thus produces the state of affairs which Warfield (echoing Augustine) summed up in the phrase: What Scripture says, God says. Whatever Scripture is found to teach must be received as divine instruction. This is what is primarily meant by calling it the Word of God.

It is hardly possible to deny that what God says is true, any more than it is possible to deny that what he commands is binding. Scripture is thus authoritative as a standard of belief no less than of behavior, and its authority in both realms, that of fact as well as that of obligation, is divine. By virtue of its inspiration the authority of Scripture resolves into, not the historical, ethical, or religious expertise of its human authors, however great this may be thought to have been, but the truthfulness and the moral claim of the speaking, preaching, teaching God himself.

Canonicity

The second element in the historic evangelical account of biblical authority is a view of the principle of *canonicity*, as being objectively the fact, and subjectively the recognition of inspiration. This follows from what has just been said. All Scripture was given to be the profitable rule of faith and practice. It is not suggested that all the inspired writings that God ever gave were for the church's canon; the Scriptures themselves show that some books of prophetic oracles, and some church epistles of Paul (to look no further) have, in God's providence, perished. What is suggested is not that all inspired writings are canonical, but that all canonical writings are inspired, and that God causes his people to recognize them as such. Not that the church created the New Testament canon by recognizing and isolating it, any more than Newton created the law of gravity by recognizing it and catching it in a formula; nor did the early church, which over four centuries achieved the recognition, ever suppose itself to be creating anything. What it understood itself to be doing, rather, was implementing its perpetual obligation to order its faith and life by the teaching of the Jewish Scriptures, as supplemented and interpreted by the further teaching that came from the first century circle of inspiration which was part of the total Messianic fact, and which had the apostles at its center. Accounts of canonicity which distort, or discount, the reality of inspiration and rest the claims of Scripture on some other footing than the fact that God spoke and speaks through them, misrepresent both the true theological situation and the actual experience of Christians. This leads to our next point.

The Witness of the Spirit

The third element in the evangelical position is a belief that the Scriptures *authenticate themeselves* to Christian believers through the convincing work of the Holy Spirit, who enables us to recognize, and bow before, divine realities. It is he who enlightens us to receive the man Jesus as God's incarnate Son, and our Saviour; similarly, it is he who enlightens us to receive sixty-six pieces of human writing as God's inscripturated Word, given to make us "wise unto salvation through faith which is in Christ Jesus" (2 Tim. 3:15). In both cases, this enlightening is not a private revelation of something that has not been made public, but the opening of minds sinfully closed so that they receive evidence to which they were previously impervious. The evidence of divinity is there before us, in the words and works of Jesus in the one case and the words and qualities of Scripture in the other. It consists not of clues offered as a basis for discursive inference to those who are clever enough, as in a detective story, but in the unique force which, through the Spirit, the story of Jesus, and the knowledge of Scripture, always carry with them to strike everyone to whom they come. In neither case, however, do our sinful minds receive this evidence apart from the illumination of the Spirit. The church bears witness, but the Spirit produces conviction, and so, as against Rome, evangelicals insist that it is the witness of the Spirit, not that of the church, which authenticates the canon to us. So the fourth answer of the Westminster Larger Catechism declares: "The Scriptures manifest themselves to be the Word of God, by their majesty and purity; . . . by their light and power to convince and convert sinners, to comfort and build up believers unto salvation: but the Spirit of God bearing witness by and with the Scriptures in the heart of man, is alone able fully to persuade it that they are the very Word of God."

Sufficiency and Clarity

Fourthly, evangelicals maintain that the Scriptures are *sufficient* for the Christian and the church as a lamp for our feet and a light for our path—a guide, that is, as to what steps we should take at any time in the realms of belief and behavior. It is not suggested that they tell us all that we would like to know about God and his ways, let alone about other matters, nor that they answer all the questions that it may occur to us to ask. The point of the affirmation is simply that, in the words of Article VI of the Church of England, "Holy Scripture containeth all things necessary to salvation," and does not need to be supplemented from any other source (reason, experience, tradition, or other faiths, for example), but is itself a complete organism of truth for its own stated purpose. The grounds on which this position rests are, first, the sufficiency of Jesus Christ as Saviour; second, the demonstrable internal completeness of the biblical account of salvation in him; third, the impossibility of validating any non-scriptural tradition or speculation relating to Christ by appeal to an inspired source.

Fifthly, evangelicals affirm that the Scriptures are *clear,* and interpret themselves from within, and consequently, in their character as "God's Word written" (Article XX), are able to stand above both the church and the Christian in corrective judgment and health-giving instruction. With this goes the conviction that the ministry of the Spirit as the church's teacher is precisely to cause the Scriptures to fulfil this ministry toward the church, and so to reform it, and its traditions, according to the biblical pattern. It is also held that the ministry of the Spirit as interpreter guarantees that no Christian who uses the appointed means of grace for understanding the Bible (including worship and instruction, both formal and informal, in the church—there is no atomic individualism here) can fail to learn all that he needs to know for his spiritual welfare. Not that the Christian, or the church, will ever know everything that Scripture contains, or solve all biblical problems, while here on earth; the point is simply that God's people will always know enough to lead them to heaven, starting from where they are.

The Mystery of Scripture

Sixthly, evangelicals stress that Scripture is a *mystery* in a sense parallel to that in which the incarnation is a *mystery*—that is, that the identifying of the human and the divine words in the one case, like the taking of manhood into God in the other, was a unique creative divine act of which we cannot fully grasp either the nature or the mode or the dynamic implications. Scripture is as genuinely and fully human as it is divine. It is more than Jewish-Christian religious literature, but not less, just as Jesus was more than a Jewish rabbi, but not less. There is a true analogy between the written Word and the incarnate Word. In both cases, the divine coincides with the form of the human, and the absolute appears in the form of the relative. In both cases, as we said above, the divine in the human manifests and evidences itself by the light and power that it puts forth, yet is missed and overlooked by all save those whom the Holy Ghost enlightens. In both cases, it is no discredit to the believer, nor reason for rejecting his faith, when he has to confess that there are problems about this unique divine-human reality that he cannot solve, questions about it that he cannot answer, and aspects of it (phenomena) which do not seem to fit comfortably with other aspects, or with basic categories in terms of which it asks to be explained as a whole (sinlessness, for instance, in the case of Jesus; truthfulness, for instance, in the case of Scripture). When you are dealing with divine mysteries you must be prepared for this sort of thing; and when it happens, you must be quick to recognize that the cause lies in the weakness of your own understanding, not in any failure on God's part to conform to his own specifications.

Seventhly, evangelicals hold that the obedience of both the Christian individually, and the church corporately, consists precisely in *conscious submission,* both intellectual and ethical, to the teaching of Holy Scripture, as interpreted by itself and applied by the Spirit according to the principles stated above. Subjection to the rule of Christ involves—indeed, from one standpoint, consists in—subjection to the rule of Scripture. His authority is its, not its is his.

II. Hermeneutics

Such is biblical authority; what, now, is hermeneutics? Hermeneutics, as commonly understood, is the theory of biblical interpretation. Interpretation has been defined as the way of reading an old book that brings out its relevance for modern man. Biblical hermeneutics is the study of the theoretical principles involved in bringing out to this and every age the relevance of the Bible and its message. Evangelical practice over the centuries has reflected a view of the process of interpretation as involving three stages: exegesis, synthesis, and application.

Exegesis means bringing out of the text all that it contains of the thoughts, attitudes, assumptions, and so forth—in short, the whole expressed mind—of the human writer. This is the "literal" sense, in the name of which the Reformers rejected the allegorical senses beloved of medieval exegetes. We would call it the "natural" sense, the writer's "intended meaning." The so-called "grammatico-historical method," whereby the exegete seeks to put himself in the writer's linguistic, cultural, historical, and religious shoes, has been the historic evangelical method of exegesis, followed with more or less consistency and success since the Reformers' time. This exegetical process assumes the full humanity of the inspired writings.

Synthesis means here the process of gathering up, and surveying in historically integrated form, the fruits of exegesis—a process which is sometimes, from one standpoint, and at one level, called "biblical theology" in the classroom, and at other times from another standpoint, and at another level, called "exposition" in the pulpit. This synthetic process assumes the organic character of Scripture.

Application means seeking to answer the question: "If God said and did what the text tells us he did in the circumstances recorded, what would he say and do to us in our circumstances?" This applicatory process assumes the consistency of God from one age to another, and the fact that "Jesus Christ is the same yesterday, and today, yea and forever" (Heb. 13:8, R.V.).

Hermeneutics Controlled by One's Doctrine of Scripture

Now, it is already clear from what has been said that the principle of biblical authority underlies and controls evangelical hermeneutics. The nature of this control can conveniently be shown by adapting Bultmann's concept of the "exegetical circle"—a concept springing from recognition of the truth (for truth it is) that exegesis presupposes a hermeneutic which in its turn is drawn from an overall theology, which theology in its turn rests on exegesis. This circle is not, of course, logically vicious; it is not the circle of presupposing what you ought to prove, but the circle, or rather the ascending spiral, of successive approximation, a basic method of every science. Without concerning ourselves with Bultmann's use of this concept of the "exegetical circle" we may at once adapt it to make plain the evangelical theologian's method of attaining his hermeneutic. First, he goes to the text of Scripture to learn from it the doctrine of Scripture. At this stage, he takes with him what Bultmann would call a "pre-understanding"—not like Bultmann, a Heideggerian anthropology, but a general view of Christian truth, and of the way to approach the Bible, which he has gained from the creeds, confessions, preaching, and corporate life of the church, and from his own earlier experiments in exegesis and theology. So he goes to Scripture, and by the light of this pre-understanding discerns in it material for constructing an integrated doctrine of the nature, place, and use of the Bible. From this doctrine of the Bible and its authority he next derives, by strict theological analysis, a set of hermeneutical principles; and then, armed with this hermeneutic, he returns to the text of Scripture itself, to expound it more scientifically than he could before. Thus he travels round the exegetical circle, or up the exegetical spiral. If his exegetical procedure is challenged, he defends it from his hermeneutic; if his hermeneutic is challenged, he defends it from his doctrine of biblical authority; and if his doctrine of biblical authority is challenged, he defends it from the texts. The circle thus appears as a one-way system: from texts to doctrine, from doctrine to hermeneutic, from hermeneutic to texts again.

Exegesis Controlled by Evangelical Hermeneutics

What controls does the hermeneutic which derives from the evangelical doctrine of Scripture place upon one's exegesis? First, it binds us to continue using the grammatico-historical method; second, it obliges us to observe the principle of harmony. A word must be said about each of these, though brief formal discussions of them (which is all that space allows) can scarcely give an idea of how far-reaching they really are.

The grammatico-historical method of approaching texts is dictated, not merely by common sense, but by the doctrine of inspiration, which tells us that God has put his words into the mouths, and caused them to be written in the writings, of men whose individuality, as men of their time, was in no way lessened by the fact of their inspiration, and who spoke and wrote to be understood by their contemporaries. Since God has effected an identity between their words and his, the way for us to get into his mind, if we may thus phrase it, is via theirs. Their thoughts and speech about God constitute God's own self-testimony. If, as in one sense is invariably the case, God's meaning and message through each passage, when set in its total biblical context, exceeds what the human writer had in mind, that further meaning is only an extension and development of his, a drawing out of implications and an establishing of relationships between his words and other, perhaps later, biblical declarations in a way that the writer himself, in the nature of the case, could not do. Think, for example, how Messianic prophecy is declared to have been fulfilled in the New Testament, or how the sacrificial system of Leviticus is explained as typical in Hebrews. The point here is that the *sensus plenior* which texts acquire in their wider biblical context remains an extrapolation on the grammatico-historical plane, not a new projection on to the plane of allegory. And, though God may have more to say to us from each text than its human writer had in mind, God's meaning is never less than his. What he means, God means. So the first responsibility of the exegete is to seek the human writer's mind, by grammatico-historical exegesis of the most thorough-going and disciplined kind—always remembering, as Calvin so wisely did, that the biblical writer cannot be assumed to have had before his mind the exegete's own theological system!

The Analogy of Scripture (the Principle of Harmony)

As for the principle of harmony, this also is dictated by the doctrine of inspiration, which tells us that the Scriptures are the products of a single divine mind. There are really three principles involved here. The first is that Scripture should be interpreted by Scripture, just as one part of a human teacher's message may and should be interpreted by appeal to the rest. *Scriptura scripturae interpres!* This does not, of course, imply that the meaning of all texts can be ascertained simply by comparing them with other texts, without regard for their own literary, cultural, and historical background, or for our extra-biblical knowledge bearing on the matter with which they deal. For instance, one cannot get the full point of "Thou shalt not seethe a kid in its mother's milk" (Ex. 23:19; 34:26; Deut. 14:21) till one knows that this practice was part of a Canaanitish fertility rite, and this one learns, not from comparison with other texts, but from archaeology. Similarly, this principle gives no warrant for reading the Bible "in the flat" without any sense of the historical advance of both revelation and religion, and the differences of background and outlook between one biblical author and another. Such lapses would show failure to grasp what grammatico-historical exegesis really involves. But the principle that Scripture interprets Scripture does require us to treat the Bible organically and to look always for its internal links—which are there in profusion, if only we have eyes to see them.

The second principle is that Scripture should not be set against Scripture. The church, says Article XX of the Church of England, may not "so expound one place of Scripture, that it be repugnant to another"—nor should the individual expositor. The basis for this principle is the expectation that the teaching of the God of truth will prove to be consistent with itself.

The third principle is that what appears to be secondary and obscure in the Scripture should be studied in the light of what appears primary and plain. This principle obliges us to echo the main emphases of the New Testament and to develop a Christo-centric, covenantal, and kerygmatic exegesis of both Testaments; also, it obliges us to preserve a studied sense of proportion regarding what are confessedly minutiae, and not to let them overshadow what God has indicated to be the weightier matters.

These three principles together constitute what the Reformers called *analogia Scripturae*, what we have termed the principle of harmony. It is a principle which makes an integrative aim in interpretation mandatory at every point. To have such an aim is, of course, no guarantee that the interpreter will always succeed in achieving what he aims at, but at least it keeps him facing in the right direction and asking some of the right questions.

Here, then, are two hermeneutical axioms which we may call "deductive" principles, though, as we have seen, they derive from an exegetical induction in the first instance. They are presuppositions, gained through exegesis of some texts, which demand to control the exegesis of all texts. They have historically, and in my view rightly, been taken as basic to evangelical interpretation of Scripture.

Arbitrariness in Biblical Interpretation

Indeed, the evangelical thesis is that only as these presuppositions govern interpretation can it be genuinely scientific and objective, in the proper sense of being wholly determined by the object of study— that is, in this case, the self-revelation of God. Otherwise, since nature abhors a vacuum, other presuppositions, brought to Scripture *a priori*, will inevitably operate as an alien frame distorting our apprehension of the realities which the Bible presents. Three examples of how evangelicals see this happening in modern theology may be mentiond.

(i). Karl Barth holds that God communicates with man through the Scriptures by freely deciding to use them to make Jesus Christ, the true Word of God, known. The statement that Scripture is the Word of God means simply that God constantly uses it in this way. Christ is the reality to which all Scripture, when thus used by God, bears witness. Barth's hermeneutical method, therefore, is to apply the "Christological method" of his *Dogmatics* to all texts, asking each the same question—what have you to say of Jesus Christ? Only when we are reading Christ out of the texts, Barth holds, do they tell us anything about either God or man. This sounds promising, as does the discovery that Barth probably quotes more texts in the *Dogmatics* than any other divine has ever done in a single work. But arbitrariness creeps in to spoil the whole picture. Barth's insistence that no man exists out of Christ (a principle which was brought to the Bible, not drawn from it) leads to conceptions of universal election, universal reprobation on the cross, and universal redemption, which systematically distorts his exegesis, while his *a priori* reluctance to define Jesus Christ in terms of history, as the Bible does, makes the ontological status of Christ as hard to be sure of as the final salvation of all men is, on Barth's principles, hard to doubt.[2]

(ii). The "biblical theology" and *heilsgeschichte* movements tell us that God has revealed himself through a sequence of redemptive events which came to its climax in the life, death, and resurrection of Jesus Christ. To this historical sequence Scripture is man's interpretative witness. Scripture is the product of illumination and insight, but not of inspiration as we earlier defined it, and there is no identity of God's Word with man's. It is in this *a priori* denial, despite abundant biblical teaching to the contrary, that the arbitrary element in these movements comes into focus. Their hermeneutical method is to ask the texts what witness they bear to the acts of God, and to integrate their testimony into a complex Christo-centric whole by means of the organizing categories of prospect and fulfilment. ("Prospect" is a better word than "promise" here; the God of "biblical theology" does not speak, and so cannot make promises.) One odd result is that theologians of this type seem a good deal more sure that this pattern as a whole corresponds to the acts of God as a whole than they are about the truth of any single part of it! This is particularly noticeable in such a writer as Alan Richardson. The preaching that springs from this movement is a summons to trust in the God, and the Christ, of this whole story, which is good so far, but since this teaching affords no basis for a direct correlation between faith and Scripture in general, or the biblical promises in particular (since it is not held that God has ever actually used words to talk to man), the total effect is unavoidably lame and inadequate.

(iii). Bultmann holds that God acts in man's consciousness through the myths of the New Testament *kerygma* (which myths, he says, we may now ceremonially debunk, and replace, in order to show modern men that they are nothing more than myths!). The divine action consists of bringing about in experiences a dynamic encounter with the "word of God." This "word of God" is a summons and a decision to live in openness to the future, not bound by the past: which is the whole of Bultmann's understanding of faith. Nothing depends for Bultmann on the fact that the Christ of the myths has no basis in the facts concerning the historical Jesus: "faith" for him is not correlated to particular historical facts, any more than it is to particular divine words. His hermeneutical method is to ask how the texts, read as myths, disclose the human situation according to Heidegger, and how they summon us to the decision of faith, as described above. The arbitrariness of Bultmann's use of the unbiblical category of myth, on which his whole reading of the New Testament depends, is so glaring that comment is superfluous.

III. Inerrancy

How does all this relate to the question of the inerrancy of Scripture? The concept has come under heavy fire in recent years, from professed evangelicals no less than from others. It has been dismissed as speculative, unnecessary, and unprofitable. It has been attacked as viciously rationalistic, in the sense of expressing a concern to show that one "has the answers" to all seeming contradictions and difficulties in the biblical text, and a belief that by showing this one can "prove" that the Bible is the Word of God. It has been accused of betokening the kind of exegetical arbitrariness which we ourselves have been censuring, in such matters as allegorizing, wresting prophetic scriptures unhistorically, and making the Bible teach science in the modern sense and with modern precision. It has been linked in the minds of some critics with the pietistic mistakes of supposing that if one's approach to Scripture is reverent enough, no problem of interpretation will remain, so that he who adoringly proclaims an inerrant Bible will emerge an inerrant interpreter. In face of this array of misunderstandings (for such they all are) it is necessary to begin by stating explicitly what the assertion of inerrancy does and does not mean.

Inerrancy is a word that has been in common use since only the last century, though the idea itself goes back through seventeenth-century orthodoxy, the Reformers and the Schoolmen, to the Fathers, and, behind them, to our Lord's own statements, "the scriptures cannot be broken," "thy word is truth" (John 10:35; 17:17). The word has a negative form and a positive function. It is comparable with the four negative adverbs with which the Chalcedonian definition

fenced the truth of the incarnation. Its function, like theirs, is not
to explain anything in a positive way, but to safeguard a mystery by
excluding current mistakes about it. It, like them, has obvious meaning only in the context of the particular debates that have caused it
to be used; apart from that context, it, like they, may well seem eso-
teric and unhelpful. The idea it expresses—namely, that all Scripture assertions are true and trustworthy in all that they assert—is not
a speculation, but is directly entailed by the fact of inspiration, which,
as we saw, asserts direct identity between man's word and God's.
Logically, the function of the assertion of inerrancy has been to express a double commitment: first, an advance commitment to receive
as truth from God all that Scripture is found on inspection actually
to teach; second, a methodological commitment to interpret Scripture according to the principle of harmony which we analyzed above.
It thus represents not so much a lapse into rationalism as a bulwark
against rationalism—namely, that kind of rationalism which throws
overboard the principle of harmony. What it expresses is not an ir-
religious interest in "proving the Bible" but a retention of reverence
for the sacred text which some were irreverently expounding as if it
were in places self-contradictory and false. To assert biblical inerrancy is not, however, to prejudge any questions about the literary
genre, range, and content of particular biblical passages; these things
must in every case be determined inductively and *a posteriori*, by
grammatico-historical exegesis. The assertion, in other words, does
not function as an exegetical short cut! Nor does it imply a blanket
claim to have up one's sleeve a convincing solution, here and now, of
all puzzling biblical phenomena of detail,[3] or an expectation of not
having to leave any of these problems open as one advances in one's
earthly pilgrimage of Bible study. He who asserts inerrancy with
understanding expects, rather, to have to live with such problems all
his days, perhaps in quite acute form, simply because he will not
settle for anything less than a convincing harmonization, and declines
to cut any knots by saying flatly that the Bible errs.

It has been proposed to limit the confession of inerrancy to biblical
doctrine as distinct from biblical history, or, more precisely, to doc-
trinally significant facts as opposed to other facts. But this is impossible: by what method of enquiry could one hope to determine which
biblical facts have no doctrinal significance? Also, the proposal is
unsound: for as students of history-writing now recognize, all facts
presented by historians are, willy-nilly, *interpreted* facts, and if that
is so, then the doctrine of inspiration, which posits that man's witness

to God in the Bible is identical with God's witness of himself, obliges us to assign to all facts reported in Scripture the status of *God-interpreted* facts. It is true that careful distinctions must be drawn between the form and the content of the biblical revelation (i.e., between concepts used for making an assertion and the assertion itself); also, between the varying strengths of human affirmation (absolute certainty, non-committal reporting of sources, voicing of hopes, guesses, provisional beliefs, etc.). But the sole purpose of these distinctions is to help us discern how much the writers are actually, in the logical sense, asserting, i.e., asking their readers to accept as true. When this has become clear, our part is to accept the assertions as not simply human, but divine instruction, guaranteed to us by the veracity of God.

The significance of the confession of inerrancy in relation to the evangelical understanding of hermeneutics and biblical authority is now plain. By making explicit the identity of man's witness to God and God's witness to himself in the Bible, it undergirds the maxim that a harmonistic synthesis of the fruits of grammatico-historical exegesis is the sure and only way into God's mind; and thus it establishes the further proposition, basic to sound theology in a fallen world, that if biblical teaching and my own thoughts clash, it is my thoughts that are wrong every time! Furthermore, its insistence on the divine authority of all that the biblical writers assert safeguards, first, the identity of the Christ of faith with the Jesus of the gospels, the "Jesus of history," and, second, the covenantal continuity and correspondence of God's saving acts in history under both Testaments—the two foundation-principles apart from which the contents of the Bible cannot exert their due authority at any point. To the weaknesses of its hold on these principles the theological malaise of modern Protestantism is directly due. The fact is that inerrancy, as we have defined it, is not merely a truth, but an essential and fundamental truth. Surrender it, and neither the authority of the Bible nor the knowledge of Jesus Christ, and God's grace in him, can remain intact.

Jack B. Rogers

V. VAN TIL AND WARFIELD ON SCRIPTURE IN THE WESTMINSTER CONFESSION

Van Til's Criticism of Warfield's Apologetics

Much of Van Til's work is devoted to developing a new method of apologetics. Often he does this by contrasing his method with what he terms the traditional method. According to Van Til the traditional method of apologetics begins with the natural man. Such an apologetic works up a natural theology to show that Christianity is more probably true than any other theory of reality. Then it shows that Christianity is more probably true than any other theory of sin and redemption.[1] This traditional method was developed by Thomas Aquinas, who attempted to synthesize the natural theology of Aristotle with the supernatural theology of Christianity.[2] The Roman Catholic lead was followed by the Arminian theologians. Bishop Butler's *Analogy* became a standard Protestant apologetic guide just as Aquinas' *Contra Gentiles* was for Roman Catholics.[3] The apologetics of the "Old Princeton" school, including that of B. B. Warfield, was taken largely from Butler's *Analogy*.[4]

Warfield wished to begin reasoning on neutral ground with the non-believer. He appealed to the natural man's "right reason" to judge of the truth of Christianity.[5] Van Til quotes Warfield regarding the inspiration of Scripture on this point.

> Inspiration is not the most fundamental of Christian doctrine, nor even the first thing we prove about the Scriptures. It is the last and crowning fact as to the Scriptures. These we first prove authentic, historically credible, generally trustworthy, before we prove them inspired.[6]

Warfield felt that his apologetic was necessary if Christianity was to be proved objectively true.[7] Of the theological disciplines, only apologetics does not presuppose God. According to Warfield, the other theological disciplines are dependent on apologetics for the facts of God's existence with which they then work.[8]

Contemporary with Warfield, but developing a different method of apologetics, was Abraham Kuyper. Kuyper's apologetics begins from presuppositions. One either presupposes man's autonomy or God's sovereignty. One either presupposes that the natural man's reason can rightly judge religious truth, or that special revelation from God is needed. For Kuyper, the natural principle (of man's autonomy) and the special principle (of God's revelation) are mutually contradictory. One can hold only one of these as an ultimate principle.[9] Kuyper begins his apologetics from the special principle of the self-revelation of God in Scripture. Van Til plainly states: "I have chosen the position of Abraham Kuyper."[10]

The apologetic method of Warfield cannot be harmonized with the apologetic method of Kuyper and Van Til. The problem is not simply a matter of emphasis. Van Til asserts: "It is impossible to hold with Kuyper that the Christian and non-Christian principles are destructive of one another and to hold with Warfield that they differ only in degree."[11] Van Til even charges Kuyper with inconsistency because "Kuyper too sometimes reasons as though he were on neutral grounds with unbelievers."[12] Kuyper sometimes does apologetics in the same manner as Warfield, and at that point Van Til rejects the work of both men.[13]

Van Til's Agreement with Warfield's Theology

At the same time, Van Til feels himself to be generally in harmony with both Kuyper and Warfield. In an irenic vein, Van Til urges us "to listen to both Warfield and Kuyper and also to Calvin, and then do the best we can as we ask just what the genius of the Reformed Faith requires of us."[14]

On theology in general and on the doctrine of Scripture in particular Van Til is in hearty agreement with Warfield. In Van Til's lengthy (65 pages) "Introduction" to the 1948 edition of Warfield's *The Inspiration and Authority of the Bible* Van Til offers not one word of criticism of Warfield. His attitude is perhaps summarized in the statement: "There can be then no way of avoiding the fact that it is in the theology of Warfield, the Reformed Faith, that we have the most consistent defense of the idea of the infallibility of Scripture."[15] More recently, Van Til has given even more lavish praise to Warfield.

> For many year Dr. Benjamin Breckinridge Warfield taught systematic theology at Princeton Theological seminary. We may compare him to Augustine. Together with his colleagues Warfield, a man of great genius, taught a theology of the sovereign grace of God. Warfield thought of the Westminster standards as giving superb expression to this theology of the sovereign grace of God in Christ.[16]

From the above statement we can conclude that allegiance to a theology of the sovereign grace of God as expressed in the Westminster standards is a basis of agreement between Van Til and Warfield. Van Til and Warfield use the term "particularism" to express the central significance of this common theology. According to Warfield all evangelicals believe that all power exerted in saving the soul is from God. The particularist believes that God exerts this saving power only on particular men, those who are actually saved. Thus the decision as to man's salvation rests solely with God and not with man.[17] This particularism is the hallmark of a truly biblical theology.[18] And particularism is a distinctive mark of Calvinism. "Warfield speaks therefore of Calvinism as being the only form of Protestantism 'uncolored by intruding elements from without.' "[19] For Warfield and Van Til, this particularism is the heart of Calvinism. This agreement in theology apparently means a general agreement in apologetics. Van Til says:

> When Warfield makes the high claim that Calvinism is "nothing more or less the hope of the world," he is speaking of the Reformed system of theology and of the Reformed point of view in general. . . . But then, by precisely the same reasoning, *Reformed apologetics is the hope of the world.*[20]

Van Til can therefore consider himself and Warfield to be in agreement as apologists for a Reformed system of theology even though they differ on the proper style of apologetics.

In addition to this general agreement as Calvinistic particularists, Van Til agrees heartily with Warfield's doctrine of Scripture. After criticizing Warfield's manner of defending the Scriptures, Van Til adds:

> It is not of course, that Warfield himself entertains any doubts about the plenary inspiration of Scripture. He was one of its greatest advocates. Nor is it that he disagrees with Calvin in maintaining the clarity of natural revelation or in holding that all men have the sense of deity. It is only that in apologetics, Warfield wanted to operate in neutral territory with the non-believer.[21]

Van Til holds that the theology of old Princeton Seminary (Warfield) and the theology of Amsterdam (Kuyper) are essentially the same. His principal evidence for this agreement is their common understanding of Scripture and its use.

> The Hodges, Warfield, DeWitt, Greene, and others are insistent as are Kuyper, Bavinck and their followers that the Scriptures are the Word of God and that its system of truth is an analogical

system. All of human experience must therefore be interpreted in terms of it.[22]

Supernatural revelation was necessary to supplement natural revelation even before man sinned. The Holy Spirit convicts man of his sin and in the same act convinces him that the Bible is the Word of God. The evidences of divinity in Scripture are part of this process of the self-attestation of God.[23] According to Van Til, all the facts of the universe attest God. "They are all inter-related in their testimony."[24]

The concept of God and the concept of Scripture which Van Til holds in common with Warfield are themselves intertwined. Van Til asserts that "it is apparent then that the Reformed doctrine of God as by his counsel controlling whatsoever comes to pass and the Reformed doctrine of Scripture as containing an absolute system of truth stand or fall together."[25] Holding to these interrelated principles, Van Til feels that he honors both Warfield and Kuyper in the main thrust of their thought. To thus honor Warfield and Kuyper is, for Van Til, to be "most faithful to Calvin and to St. Paul."[26]

Scripture in Van Til's Apologetics

Van Til outlines his concept of apologetics in his "Introduction" to Warfield's *The Inspiration and Authority of the Bible*. In this context he elaborates a concept of Scripture which he feels is consistent with the doctrine of Scripture of Warfield and the Westminster Confession of Faith.

Presupposition takes precedence over fact for Van Til. This is because a fact is basically unintelligible unless interpreted. Since the only correct interpretation of any fact is God's interpretation, an understanding of God's Word must precede an understanding of any facts.

> In practice, this means that, since sin has come into the world, God's interpretation of the facts must come in finished, written form and be comprehensive in character. God continues to reveal himself in the facts of the created world but the sinner needs to interpret every one of them in the light of Scripture.[27]

Van Til explicates this relationship between presupposition and fact, by calling them both limiting concepts. He says: "In the idea of objective revelation to man the ideas of fact and interpretation of fact are therefore limiting concepts one of the other."[28] Put in another way, natural and supernatural revelation are limiting concepts of one another.[29] Supernatural revelation occurs not only in Scripture, but to some extent presents itself as an innate knowledge of God.

This innate knowledge is "a God given activity within man that needs to feed upon factual material which is itself the manifestation of the self-contained plan of God."[30] Innate knowledge thus becomes a limiting concept which needs over against itself the limiting concept of factual material "that can serve as grist for its mill."[31] In constructing a doctrine of Scripture, Van Til uses the idea of limiting concept as well. He says: "Just as facts and word revelation require one another so the doctrine of inspiration of Scripture is once again the limiting concept that is required as supplementation to the idea of fact revelation given to us in word revelation."[32]

From the idea of Scripture as a limiting concept to fact, Van Til proceeds to the idea that Scripture must necessarily exist as a system. Van Til clearly states that the facts of God's creation reveal God. Natural man, however, refuses rightly to interpret these facts. Van Til contends that "it is not because the evidence is not clear but because man has taken out his spiritual eyes that he does not, and ethically cannot, see any of the facts of the world for what they really are."[33] Therefore, supernatural revelation is necessary to give right interpretation of the facts to sinful man. But Scripture is also necessary for the redeemed man. Christian men are "to an extent under the influence of the old man within them and so would even when redeemed never be able to interpret mere revelational facts correctly and fully."[34] So Scripture is necessary, and it is necessary that it exist as a system.[35]

Scripture is an "existential system." This means that "when the Christian restates the content of Scriptural revelation in the form of a 'system' such a system is based upon and therefore analogous to the 'existential system' that God himself possesses."[36] A Christian systematic theology, based on Scripture, is fully true although at no point identical with the content of God's mind. Rather, our system is analogous to God's system.[37] For such an analogous system to be valid, it must be based on Scripture, which in turn "must come in finished, written form and be comprehensive in character."[38] When our systematic theology is based on the system of doctrine in Scripture itself, then "all human interpretation is regarded as re-interpretative of God's self-conscious interpretation."[39]

The philosophical, and thus apologetic, significance of Scripture as an "existential system" is that Christianity alone is fully rational. Van Til notes: "Such philosophical relevance cannot be established unless it be shown that all human predication is intelligible only on the presupposition of the truth of what the Bible teaches about God, man and the universe."[40] For Van Til the position which works in terms of the self-contained God who has revealed himself in a systematic plan is the only position which can establish any connection between rationality and factuality.[41] There is a mystery here, but that mystery does not exclude logic and rationality. "The non-Christian concept of mystery, as implied in the modern principle, is that which is involved in assuming that all reality is flux and that factuality is more basic than logic or plan."[42] An infallible Bible is necessary, according to Van Til, "if man is to have any knowledge and if his process of learning is to be intelligible."[43] Man does not need to know everything. But he does need to know that "all reality is rationally controlled."[44] Man needs to know that all things are what they are because of the plan of God. "The knowledge of anything is by way of understanding the connection that it has with the plan of God."[45] Reformed thinking is therefore the only consistently Christian thinking and also the only truly rational thinking because it develops a biblically based system. Van Til contends that this is not seeking a system in the way that non-Christian thought does. The contention of Reformed thought "is that a 'system' in the Christian sense of the term rests upon the presupposition that whatever Scripture teaches is true because Scripture teaches it."[46] The Calvinist philosopher or scientist seeks to order the facts of God's creation "in self-conscious subordination to the infallibile authority of Scripture."[47] Reason itself must be interpreted in terms of biblical truth about it. For Van Til, such truth is centered in the fact that "it is unreasonable for a creature of God to set up himself as God requiring a system of interpretation in which man stands as the ultimate point of reference."[48] Roman Catholic and Arminian thought cannot effectively challenge the reason of natural man precisely because they do not have "a *system* of theology and philosophy in which reason itself is interpreted exclusively in terms of biblical principles."[49] Van Til concludes his "Introduction" to Warfield's work by stressing the rational intelligibility of Christianity.

> The presupposition of all intelligible meaning for man in the intellectual, the moral and the aesthetic spheres is the existence of the God of the Bible who, if he speaks at all in grace cannot, without denying himself, but speak in a self-contained infallible fashion. Only in a return to the Bible as infallibly inspired in its autography is there hope for science, for philosophy and for theology.[50]

In this concern for demonstrable rationality, Van Til and Warfield are one.

Scripture in the Westminster Confession

The above material sketches Van Til's conception of the role of
Scripture in apologetics. It indicates both his disagreement with
Warfield's apologetic method and his essential agreement with War-
fields doctrine of Scripture. It is more difficult to compare the views
of Van Til and Warfield with those of the Westminster Divines.
Warfield's interest in the Westminster Assembly was historical as
well as theological. His articles on the subject are collected in
The Westminster Assembly and Its Work.[51] However, Warfield's work
on the Westminster Assembly suffers from the ahistorical bias of
equating the theology of the seventeenth-century Westminster Divines with that of the nineteenth-century Princeton theology.[52] Indeed
the Westminster Divines belong to the mid-seventeenth century, which
was pre-scientific. A new conception of the universe, brought about
by the rising empirical science of Newton and the philosophy of
Locke, did not become prevalent until well after the Westminster
Divines had finished their work.[53] The Westminster Divines had more
ideological continuity with the time of the Reformation than that of
the modern world. They lived and worked at the end of the "Age of
Faith." The "Age of Reason" was still to come. Thus issues such
as higher criticism, evolution, and empirical philosophy, which were
of great moment to Warfield, were unknown to the Westminster
Divines. In response to criticism based on natural science, Warfield
tried to give objective scientific proof for the validity of Scripture.
The Westminster Divines, by contrast, offer no significant illustration
of arguing for the Bible's inspiration from external evidences.[54] Van
Til is correct that Warfield's apologetic method is non-Reformed.
Van Til himself makes few references to the Westminster Confession
and no references to the Westminster Divines. Van Til's allegiance
to the Westminster Confession apparently is not predicated on any
historical interest. He assumes an equation of the theology of the
Westminster Divines with that of Warfield and the old Princeton
Theology and thus commits the same general error as Warfield
himself.

The theological emphases of the Westminster Divines are quite
different from those of Van Til and Warfield which have been examined. Perhaps two examples will illustrate the differences. First,
Van Til and Warfield are both concerned with the objective defense of the Christian faith. Van Til says:

Hence Warfield was quite right in maintaining that Christianity is objectively defensible. And the natural man has the ability to understand intellectually, though not spiritually, the challenge presented to him. And no challenge is presented to him unless it is shown him that on his *principle* he would destroy all truth and meaning.

When explaining why he believes the Bible, Van Til paraphrases words of the Westminster Confession. "I believe in this infallible book, in the last analysis, because 'of the inward work of the Holy Spirit, bearing witness by and with the word in my heart.' "[55] It would seem that Van Til is more in harmony with the emphasis of the Westminster Divines than Warfield, who stressed objective evidences which we could see intellectually by reason but would only come to believe religiously by the Holy Spirit. Yet Van Til rejects a wholly subjective assurance as decisively as does Warfield. For Van Til also, the Holy Spirit enables us to accept reasonable truth. He says: "And then as it is the grace of God that must give man the ability to see the truth in preaching so it is also the Spirit of God that must give man the ability to accept the truth as it is presented to him in apologetical reasoning."[56] Christianity must be rationally defensible and there must be proof. Van Til's method differs from that of Warfield, but their object is the same. In discussion with Warfield, Van Til asserts: *"All the disciplines must presuppose God, but at the same time presupposition is the best proof."*[57]

The emphasis of the Westminster Divines is not on rational proof, but on relation to a person. Men are convinced of the truth of Scripture when they are converted to trust in Jesus Christ, the central figure in Scripture. The Holy Spirit brings men to Christ through the Scripture. For the Westminster Divines, the Holy Spirit does not witness to proofs for the Scripture, but to the content of Scripture, Jesus Christ. The union of the Word and the Spirit is not just a formal principle of knowledge, but the means by which God works saving faith in men's hearts. The Westminster Divines are concerned to hold the Spirit and the Word together against the Roman Catholics and the Antinomians who would separate them. Edward Reynolds affirms: "So the spirit doth not, and the Word cannot alone by itself convince or convert, but the Spirit by the Word as its sword and instrument."[58] Reynolds continually emphasizes that the Spirit is the Spirit of Christ and works in the Word in relation to Christ. He says: "Which should teach us what to look for in the *Ministry of the Word,* namely that which will *convince* us, that which puts an edge upon the Word, and opens the heart and makes it burn, namely, the Spirit *of*

Christ; for by that only we can be brought unto the righteousness of Christ."[59] Most striking of all is the attitude of Samuel Rutherford, who seems at times to be the most rationally oriented of the Westminster Divines. Yet when asked how men know the Scriptures to be the Word of God, Rutherford appeals to no objective proofs but rather answers that in the Scriptures we hear Christ speaking.

> Sheep are docile creatures, *Ioh.* 10.27 *My sheep hear my voyce, I know them, and they follow me.* . . . so the instinct of Grace knoweth the voyce of the Beloved amongst many voyces, Cant. 2.8. and this discerning power is *in the Subject.*[60]

Rutherford goes on to say that there is also power in the Object. He simply means that we recognize Christ from all others, but in a very personal and subject way. "To the new Creature, there is in *Christ's* Word some character, some sound of Heaven, that is in no voyce in the world, but in his only, in *Christ* represented to a beleever's eye of Faith."[61] Not objective defense of Christianity, but subjective drawing of Christ is the emphasis of the Westminster Divines.

A second example can be given of the differing emphases on the one hand of Van Til and Warfield and, on the other hand, of the Westminster Divines. For Van Til and Warfield the emphasis is on Scripture as a system of truth yielding information. For the Westminster Divines the emphasis is on Scripture as a focus on Christ offering salvation.

Van Til specifically states that "theology is primarily God centered rather than Christ centered."[62] He elaborates the significance of that statement as follows:

> It does not follow from this that it is about God alone that we wish to obtain knowledge. It only means that it is primarily of God that we speak. We wish to know all that God wishes us to know about anything. The Bible has much to say about the universe.[63]

In this view, the Bible is used as an encyclopedia of useful information. In addition to information about God, it gives information about the universe. Van Til says of this latter aspect that "it is the business of science and philosophy to deal with this revelation."[64] Van Til further contends that to separate the religious and moral instruction of Scripture from what it says about the physical universe is tantamount to rejecting the Bible as the Word of God.[65] The Scriptures are full of information about our salvation "and about many other things that concern us."[66] But for Van Til, salvation is not the central focus of Scripture. He contends:

> But it will not do to say on this account that man is the center of theology. All that the Scriptures say about man, and particularly all that they say about man's salvation, is after all for the glory of God. Our theology should be God centered because our life should be God centered.[67]

For the Westminster Divines, Scripture is not a book of God-given information on many topics, including the physical universe. For the Westminster Divines, the Bible is a religious book with a central message—salvation through Jesus Christ. Again none other than Samuel Rutherford, conservative Scottish representative to the Westminster Assembly, illustrates the difference of emphasis between the Westminster Divines and Van Til and Warfield. Van Til contends that the Bible is authoritative on everything of which it speaks and that it speaks of everything either directly or indirectly.[68] Rutherford enumerates cases in which Scripture is the rule and other cases in which it is not the rule. Rutherford declares: "The Scripture is our Rule, but 1. Not in miraculous things. 2. Not in things temporarie, as Communitie of Goods. 3. Not in things Literally exponed, as *to cut off our hands and feet.*"[69] In contrast to Van Til's emphasis that the Scripture speaks of the physical universe, Rutherford says that the Scripture is not our rule "in things of Art and Science, as to speake Latine, to *demonstrate conclusions of Astronomie.*"[70] Rutherford goes on to say of Scripture: "But it is our Rule. 1. in fundamentalls of salvation."[71] For the Westminster Divines, Scripture gives the whole counsel of God concerning, not every possible subject, but all things necessary for God's glory, man's salvation, faith, and life. Van Til seems to believe that God is glorified by providing us with an authoritative interpretation about everything relating to our life, including faith and salvation. The Westminster Divines seem rather to believe that God is glorified in man's salvation, and salvation has implications for faith and life. For the Westminster Divines, the Scripture is a mine of knowledge, but they never lose sight of the one central purpose toward which all that knowledge tends. Edward Reynolds says: "The gospel of Christ is honoured in our studying of it, and digging after it in our serious and painful enquiries into the mysteries of it"[72] But he continues his thought saying that if men had more of the spirit of the Apostle Paul they would not waste their time on anything else "but would set more hours apart to look into the patent of their salvation (which is the book of God), and to acquaint themselves with Christ before hand, that when they come into his presence, they may have the entertainment of friends, and not of strangers."[73]

Conclusion

Apologetics old or new is a precarious occupation. When defending the faith one is easily led into recasting the faith to conform with the current questions being asked of it. Warfield felt the Bible to be threatened by science and he tried to make the Bible's validity scientifically provable. In doing so he diverted attention from the pre-scientific, religious purpose of Scripture and raised doubts about its authenticity by asking questions which it was never intended to answer.

Van Til has felt the Scripture to be threatened by interpretations rising out of a Kantian philosophical framework. Kant denied metaphysics and declared that the thing-in-itself could never be known. He shifted the attention of the philosophical world to epistemology and rooted men's attention on the question how is knowledge possible? Van Til according to what has been shown is wholly absorbed by the problem of knowledge. In trying to defend Scripture from Kantian attack, he has conceived it as a book of knowledge intended to give valid information on every subject directly or indirectly. For Van Til, a commitment to an infallible Bible can solve the difficult Kantian problem of knowledge and assure that we have valid rational and objective answers to our life questions. But in trying thus to defend Scripture, Van Til also has diverted attention from its actual form and obscured its central content.

Neither Van Til nor Warfield correctly represents the doctrine of Scripture in the Westminster Confession. They are concerned with questions which the Westminster Divines did not ask. The Westminster Divines were not defenders of the faith. They were not committed to finding in the Bible answers to scientific or philosophical problems. The Westminster Divines were more concerned with expounding the Scriptures through preaching. They understood the Bible to be given for the practical purpose of presenting men with Christ in whom is salvation. They did not rely on objective proofs which would leave men intellectually inexcusable if they did not accept the Scripture. They relied on the Holy Spirit to move men as they had been moved to trust in Jesus Christ and so to rely on his Word.

The Westminster Divines have a pre-scientific understanding of

Scripture. Thus their doctrine of Scripture does not serve Van Til or Warfield's apologetic needs. But then, the Bible is a pre-scientific book. Perhaps the Westminster Divines better understand that Scripture's purpose is to meet man's central human need which pre-dates all science—how to be a new man. Scripture answers this need not by pointing to a new principle, scientific or philosophical. It points rather to a person, Jesus Christ. The Bible offers not proofs, but a person to persuade us.[74]

Van Til has made a genuine contribution to apologetics by emphasizing that we begin from a faith commitment which determines everything else that we think and do. But should not our ultimate commitment be simply to the person of Christ, rather than to a principle of interpretation?

Response by C. Van Til

Dear Dr. Rogers:

I am grateful to you for connecting my view of Scripture with that of B. B. Warfield and, further back, of the Westminster Confession. You speak of my criticism of Warfield's apologetics, but your main interest is, if I understand you correctly, to point out the fact that the "theological emphases of the Westminster Divines are quite different than those of Van Til and Warfield which have been examined."

In the first place, you assert that the interest of Warfield and myself is on "rational proof," while that of the Westminster Divines is "on relation to a person. . . . For the Westminster Divines, the Holy Spirit does not witness to proofs for the Scripture, but to the content of the Scripture, Jesus Christ. The union of the Word and the Spirit is not just a formal principle of knowledge, but the means by which God works saving faith in men's hearts."

In the second place, you say, "for Van Til and Warfield the emphasis is on Scripture as a system of truth yielding information. For the Westminster Divines the emphasis is on Scripture as a focus on Christ offering salvation."

On my view, you add, "the Bible is used as an encyclopedia of useful information. In addition to information about God, it gives information about the universe. Van Til says of this latter aspect that 'it is the business of science and philosophy to deal with this revelation.' " In opposition to such a view in which salvation is not the central focus of Scripture stands the view of the Westminster Divines who held that "the Bible is a religious book with a central message—salvation through Jesus Christ."

Accordingly, "neither Van Til nor Warfield correctly represents the doctrine of Scripture in the Westminster Confession. . . . The Bible offers not proofs, but a person to persuade us."

By putting the matter in this way you are placing before me a challenge to relate my view of God's revelation in Scripture to God's revelation in "nature" more clearly than I have done before. I have tried to state my view on this subject succinctly in the essay "Nature and Scripture" in *The Infallible Word*. I shall summarize the argument of that article and relate it to your problem.

The aim of that essay was to set forth the Reformed view (as I see it) of God's revelation to man over against the Roman Catholic view. I also attempted to contrast the point of view expressed in the Westminster Confession with that of modern post-Kantian theology expressed in neo-orthodoxy.

When the traditional Reformed view speaks of God's revelation, it thinks of this revelation in terms of the covenant which God made with man. Man was originally placed on the earth under the terms of the covenant of works. When man broke the covenant, God was pleased, in his mercy, to make a second covenant with man that he might be saved. This covenant, the covenant of grace, is centered in Christ. But the revelation of God in nature does not speak of grace. Grace must, of necessity, be revealed by "supernatural" word-communication. This revelation of grace speaks with its own authority. It could not be otherwise. Moreover, this revelation is sufficient; nothing beyond it would or could be given. This revelation is clear or perspicuous. Not only the learned, but also the unlearned "in a due use of the ordinary means" may "attain unto a sufficient understanding" of God's covenant of grace as revealed in Scripture.

But how should God's revelation in Scripture be related to his revelation in nature? To be sure, *saving grace* is not manifest in nature; yet it is the *God* of saving grace who is. Can God be revealed apart from saving grace? How can these be harmonized?

The answer must be found in the fact that God is "eternal, incomprehensible, most free, most absolute." Any revelation that God gives of himself is therefore absolutely voluntary. The twofold revelation of God forms one grand scheme of covenant revelation. They presuppose and supplement one another. They are aspects of God's plan as worked out in the works of creation and providence and, as such, basic ingredients in our general philosophy of history.

Every action of every man at every stage of history is therefore covenantal. Every dimension of created existence, even the lowest, was from the beginning part of the exhaustively personal relationship between God and man. The "ateleological," no less than the "teleological"; the "mechanical" no less than the "spiritual," were and are covenantal.

Love of God and obedience to his requirements mark the man who, in Christ and by his Spirit, has learned to be a covenant-keeper. With Calvin he wants to do everything with an eye to his covenant-keeping, triune God. Whether he eats, or drinks, or does *anything else*, he would do all to the glory of God. As a scientist he wants to fulfill his task of searching out the riches of power hidden in the bowels of the earth. He knows that God's covenant wrath is revealed from heaven on the world because of the one decisive act on the part of Adam, covenant head of mankind. But he knows also that through God's covenant with Noah, day and night, winter and summer shall continue to the end of time (Gen. 9:11). He knows that the covenant with Noah serves as the foundation for the covenant of grace in Christ, through whom man will have true fruition of God. This fruition of God will itself be mediated through nature. The prophets, and Christ the Great Prophet, tell us of the future course of nature. It is the whole man, body and soul, that will enter into and live in the new heaven and the new earth in which righteousness shall dwell.

Christ as the Great Prophet foretells the future of all things in heaven and on earth. Christ as the Great High Priest atones for the sin of man so that the curse of God on man and on nature may be lifted and his blessing rest on the labors of man. Christ as the Great King makes every force of nature subservient to the work of redemption accomplished by himself on Calvary as the High Priest.

But those who love not God and who do not do what Christ as the Lord of history tells them to do, have the wrath of God abiding on them. Always and everywhere, in whatever he does and thinks as a scientist, philosopher, or theologian, whether learned or unlearned, man acts either as a covenant-keeper or a covenant-breaker. There is no I-it dimension in which man can, with William James, take a "moral holiday." Christ's words, "he that is not for me is against me and he that gathereth not with me scattereth abroad," ring in every man's ears every day and every night.

In a fashion such as this, I think, Calvin, the Westminster Divines, many Reformed theologians, and, more recently, many Reformed philosophers think of the whole specter of man's relations as being *religious*. To be sure, I go to church on Sunday, and, if I am a scientist, I go to the laboratory on Monday. But my "work" on Monday, as much as my "worship" on Sunday is Christ-centered. Pick up Warfield's sermon on *God's Immeasurable Love* and you will understand what I mean. Not that Warfield was a philosopher. But he knew post-Kantian liberal theology well. He knew the Ritschlian dichotomy which controlled its development. In the world of "nature" one does not, indeed cannot, meet with the promises and threats of the Christ through whom and in whom all things consist. In the world of "morality" and "religion" one cannot be confronted with the covenant promises and threats of the same Creator-Redeemer who confronted him in the world of "nature." Such was the fundamental credo of liberalism.

In other words, Warfield knew that the *phenomena-noumena* distinction of the many Kantian disciples was based on the rejection of the idea that man is inherently a covenant-being and that he must see all things in heaven and on earth and under the earth as united in the Christ of God revealed in Scripture.

With this fact in mind, read any of Warfield's sermons. They *all* center on the immeasurable love of God for man.

Listen only to what he says on John 3:16. "Conceive the world as vastly as you may, it remains ever incommensurable with the immeasurable love of God."[1]

The immeasurable love of God must not be measured by the greatness of the world or of the individual human soul. Do not think of God's love as "merely opening of a way of salvation before each and every man. . . ."[2] God's love is not content with "half-measures." "God did not then only so love the world as to give it a bare hand of salvation: he so loved the world that he saved the world. And surely this is something far better: and provides a much higher standard by which to estimate the greatness of God's love."[3] The love of God does not expend itself in "inoperative manifestations."[4]

Nor must we even limit the "world" of John 3:16 to those who repent and believe. "Its prime intention is to convey some conception of the immeasurable greatness of the love of God. The method it employs to do this is to declare the love of God so great that he gave his son to save it."[5]

Here is "the Lord God almighty whom the heaven of heavens can-

not contain. . . ." "Serene in his unapproachable glory, his will is
the resistless law of all existences to which every motion con-
forms."[6] "Now the text tells us of this God—of *this* God, remember—that he loves."[7] "We do not then speak of God as some philosophical Absolute. Why waste words on this?" "Enough for us that
a God without emotional life would be a God without all that lends
dignity to a personal Spirit whose very being is movement; and that
is to say as much as to say no God at all."[8] "And more than enough
for us that our text assures us that God loves, nay that he is love."[9]
But beyond this, even "what is it that he is declared to love?" "This
is nothing other than 'the world.' "[10] "It is just in this that lies the
mystery of the greatness of his love."[11] For what is this world? Let
John tell us. "The 'world,' he tells us, is just the synonym for all that
is evil and noisome and disgusting."[12] A follower of Christ must not
love the world; he must overcome it. "The whole world lieth in the
'evil one.' "

Of ourselves, as sinners, we are of the world and the flesh and the
devil. Now then we understand what it means that God loves the
world. "The world then was perishing: it was to save it that God
gave his Son. The text is, then, you see, in principle, an account of
the coming of the Son of God into the world." He came not to condemn the world "but that the world through him might be saved."
"Not wrath, then, though wrath were due, but love was the impelling
cause of the coming of the Son of God into this wicked world of
ours."[13] Paul says that "God commendeth his love toward us, in that
while we were yet sinners, Christ died for us." This is what John
meant. The marvel of God's love for the world is that "it is able to
prevail over the Holy God's hatred and abhorrence of sin."[14]

Here is, Dr. Rogers, as I believe, the same theology of history as
that which is found in the Westminster Confession. "The world does
not govern him (God) in a single one of his acts: he governs it and
leads it steadily onward to the end which, from the beginning, . . .
he had determined for it."[15]

"As it was created for his glory, so shall it show forth his praise:
and this human race on which he has impressed his image shall reflect that image in the beauty of the holiness which is its supreme
trait. . . . Through all the years one increasing purpose runs, one
increasing purpose: the kingdoms of the earth become ever more and
more the kingdom of our God and of his Christ. The process may
be slow; the progress may appear to our impatient eyes to lag. But
it is God who is building: and under his hands the structure rises as

steadily as it does slowly and in due time the capstone shall be set into place, and to our astonished eyes shall be revealed nothing less than a saved world."[16]

Now, how does Warfield know all this to be true? Because he believes the Scriptures, which he simply exegetes, assuming them to be true as the Word of God. Jesus' word about the love of God "is a comment upon the discourse of our Lord to Nicodemeus. . . . And what does this discourse teach us except this: that all that is born is of the flesh and only what is reborn of Spirit is Spirit, that no man can enter the Kingdom of God, therefore, except he be born again of God; and that this birth is not at the command of men, but is the gift of a Spirit which is like the wind that bloweth where it listeth, the sound whereof we hear though we know not whence it cometh and whither it goeth— but can say of it only, lo, it is here! Here then is the essential difference in men revealed in the varying receptions they give to the Son of God."[17]

I quote in this connection a passage of an article of Warfield's on "Calvin's Doctrine of the Knowledge of God." The revelation of God in nature and in man's constitution is, according to Calvin, perfectly clear. But what help would natural revelation give a sinner who is spiritually blind? "A clearer and fuller revelation of God must be brought to men than that which is afforded by nature. And the darkened minds of men must be illuminated for its reception. In other words, what is needed, is a special supernatural revelation on the one hand, and a special supernatural illumination on the other."[18]

Thus it is that Warfield, following the Westminster Confession, following Calvin, following Paul, following Christ, asserts that the natural man needs the regeneration of the Holy Spirit if he is to accept what God tells him through Christ in Scripture.

When men are enabled to believe by God's Holy Spirit then what is the *object* of their faith? It is the Gospel men believe, yes indeed. But the Gospel is variously presented. Therefore, "in believing this variously presented Gospel, faith has ever terminated with trustful reliance, not on the Promise but on the Promiser—not on the propositions which declare God's grace and willingness to save, or Christ's divine nature and power, or the reality and perfection of his saving work, but on the Saviour upon whom, because of these past facts, it could securely rest as on One able to save to the uttermost."[19]

It is this Christ, the Christ of Calvin, the Christ of the Westminster Confession and all the other historical Reformed confessions, the Christ of Abraham Kuyper and of Herman Bavink, on whose thinking

I was first nurtured, the Christ of Benjamin Breckinridge Warfield, the Christ of Geerhardus Vos, and the Christ of John Gresham Machen, the Christ whose Word is the Bible. It is this Christ which the composers of *The Confession of 1967* of the United Presbyterian Church of America are, so far as they are able, removing from his rightful place as the Redeemer of men.

I cannot here dwell on this point. I have given, as I think, adequate documentation for the claim that such is the case in a pamphlet on *The Confession of 1967*. The composers of this new Confession are anxious that their theology be in accord with the assertions of modern science and modern philosophy. Yet modern science and modern philosophy are not built upon the biblical view of history. Accordingly they are inherently unable to offer any intelligible foundation for their work. To point out this fact is not to seek a "rational" foundation for the claims of the truth of Christianity. It is only to point out that if the Word of the self-attesting Christ is rejected, men not only labor in vain but abide under the wrath of the lamb in doing so.

Dr. Rogers, you will notice that in other discussions in this volume I have dealt with the nature of scriptural authority. I trust you will look to those for further amplification. However, in response to your essay I wish to indicate the supreme *purpose* of revelation: the gathering of Christ's people unto himself, not through rational arguments as such, but through meeting the Christ of Scripture as the Holy Spirit reveals him to us as we stand in the presence of God's revelation in nature and in Scripture.

—C.V.T.

Cornelius Trimp

VI. THE WITNESS OF THE SCRIPTURES

In the theological terminology of the last several decades, the word "witness" is a preferred term in doctrines concerning the Holy Scriptures. Particularly those who contest, or have large reservations concerning, the orthodox doctrine of the Bible as the inspired and infallible Word of God, show great fondness for this term. However, it is evident that the profuse usage is inversely proportional to exegetical accountability and verification.

I

As early as 1938 this compelled K. Schilder to write of "the ill-used and degraded-to-a-cliché (also in the pulpit) concept of *witnessing*."[1] On account of this theological usage, the term eventually penetrated into the ecclesiastical writings; the *Confession of 1967* of the United Presbyterian Church gives ample proof of this. In it Jesus Christ is called "the one sufficient revelation of God," "the Word of God incarnate, to whom the Holy Spirit bears unique and authoritative witness through the Holy Scriptures" (I:C.2). Subsequently this "witness to God's work of reconciliation in Christ" is presented as a hermeneutical key. At the same time it is resolved that although these Scriptures are clearly given "under the guidance of the Holy Spirit," they are "nevertheless the words of men." Here, apparently, the witness of the Scriptures functions as *human* witness, i.e., the human *form* in which God's Word comes to us. According to the "Preface," the preaching of the church, which confesses its faith "when it bears a present witness to God's grace in Jesus Christ," has the same basis as *the* "witness." Thus, even though, according to the confession, the witness in the Scriptures is "authoritative," "the witness without parallel" (as opposed to the allegation that it is "a witness among others"), this double usage of the word "witness'" was not prevented.

In the Netherlands, G. C. Berkouwer, in his *De Heilige Schrift,* opposed E. P. Clowney's criticism of this usage.[2] Berkouwer also shows a special preference for the term *Schrift-getuigenis* (witness of Scripture). He states that *theopneustos* can be correctly understood only through the perspective of the Scriptures as human witness. For human witness is the *modus* of *theopneustos*. With deference to that we rise above unfruitful debates about the formal relationship of a divine and a human "factor" in the origin of Scripture.[3]

The revelation of the Holy Spirit pertaining to Christ takes place through human witness.[4] For this reason Berkouwer speaks of "the *modus* of human witness which makes decisions for the Scriptures," and finds its "foundation and authorization" in the witness of God.[5,6] *Deus dixit* manifests itself in this human witness, which is called the "human form" of God's witness.[7,8] Berkouwer means by this that human witness is so characteristic (decisive) for the nature of the Holy Scriptures, that with that witness the Scriptures stand and fall.

It is clear that the word "witness" gives Berkouwer conclusive aid in overcoming the many problems which have been thrown up around the character and authority of the Scriptures. However, this now-commonplace confessional and dogmatic usage lacks exegetical accountability in many respects. Without such accountability there is the great danger of the *equalization* of biblical terms.[9] Such equalization prohibits our necessary opposition to the Barthian doctrine of Scripture. The *Confession of 1967* speaks about the Bible as it does on the basis of an elaboration of this equalization. This equative locution is even more remarkable to those who remember the 1938 dissertation in exegesis defended by R. Schippers which was completely devoted to making clear the meaning of the verb "to witness."[10] Schippers pointed out that "to witness" is continually used in the New Testament as the decisive word in courtroom-controversy. The witness does not express his own views and experiences but narrates *the events* which have taken place and of which he is an ear-and-eye witness. In this manner the witness promotes the good course of justice. A witness is, therefore, an advocate for him who has justice on his side and an accuser of the violator of truth and law. Schippers adheres consistently to this juridical meaning as he examines the specific preaching of Scripture. A climate of the courtroom's struggle for justice is continually created: Christ before the tribunal of the Jews; John the Baptist before the forum of the envoys from Jerusalem (John 1:7, 19); the apostles before the Sanhedrin; the church in her struggle against the contradiction of truth by heresy. A witness is one who puts forward the superior factual account of the events which took place: Christ's advent, crucifixion, and resurrection; and, what is more, chooses for Christ and in doing so is a mouth of the Spirit of Pentecost (e.g., Luke 24:44ff.; Acts

1:8, 21, 22; 2:32; 10:39, 41, 42). In this manner the witness testifies in "the case of Christ," the ever actual case of the Messiah, who has title to the life of all peoples ever since Pentecost. The witness is the advocate of this good case and an accuser of unbelief. In these matters he seeks to win the hearts of those who hear him, in order to make them realize the superiority of the produced facts and to persuade them to bow to the truth of the Gospel (e.g., John 15:26, 27; 16:8-11).

With these considerations in mind, John 5:39, a crucial text in this connection, is clarified. We have already determined to what a great degree the definition of "witness" is stipulated as involving the cause of justice. This verse in John deals with the great case concerning the claim of God's Son, who received power to grant life and execute judgment (vss. 25, 27). The witness of the Scriptures means that the Scriptures *testify for Christ*, corner deniers and deprive them of all excuse, making them defendants before God, the highest Judge (cf. vs. 45). It is small wonder that Schippers' dissertation concluded in a rejection of Karl Barth's doctrine of Scripture.

It is typical of the elaborations of Berkouwer, as voiced in his books on Scripture, to negate this conclusion. If he had taken Schippers' study to heart, he would never have arrived at his generalized proposition that human witness is the *modus* of *theopneustos;* he would have been prepared to contest the *Confession of 1967*.

II

We shall now more closely examine the use of "witness" in the doctrines concerning the Holy Scripture. Why is the term "witness" so preferred in modern discussions concerning the Bible? We suggest the following:

First, *aversion to the rationalistic historical criticism of the nineteenth century*. This is found clearly in the thinking of the German theologian Martin Kähler (1835–1912). With great dismay Kähler viewed the destruction which this historical criticism brought forth in the faith of the congregation. For by means of precise historical methods a quest was made to determine the actual course of events which are described in the Bible. This was an attempt to free the story of God's great deeds in Christ from the "Christ-image" of dogmatics. The "historical Jesus" must be brought into the open and freed from the "dogmatic Christ." The biblical image of Christ's life and death was "purified" from all elements which were offensive, unable to be "proved," and unacceptable to an enlightened, civilized people. The result was that every investigator presented, as the only trustworthy and reliable restoration of the actual purport of the New Testament, *his own purified Jesus-image*. It was constantly evident that everyone's Jesus-image conformed to his own ideas concerning God and man. "Jesus" had become a mirror of the aspirations of the scientific man, a product of man's brain and hands.

Kähler was sure that the faith of the congregation must never be dependent on this so-called "historical" scholarship of the Bible. How great, in that case, would be the slavery into which faith was to be delivered! Faith must have a more certain ground; it can and may and does not need to exist on the basis of eventual results of historical learning. For that reason Kähler sought for that sure ground on which faith can build and on which it would be untouched by the problematics and uncertainties of learning. He attempted to find a "storm-free zone."[11] By distinguishing between the "historical Jesus" and the "super-historical Christ" he thought it possible to define this zone. The "historical Jesus" is the object of inquiry for historical research; the "super-historical Christ" is the Christ out of whom faith lives.

The "historical Jesus" is the resultant of study of those who regard the Gospel stories as biographical material, as historical "sources"; the "more-than-historical Christ" presents himself to anyone who reads the Gospel stories and the letters of Paul as the preaching (*kerygma*) of the first congregation of Christ concerning the meaning of Christ in its life. Therein the living Christ manifests himself in actual presence to the church today.

Allow scholarship and learning to criticize and reduce what they will, *this* preaching concerning Christ will not be changed. For we do the Gospel account no justice if we consider its factual material as objective neutral photography, but only as we regard it as the faithful and believing art of portrayal. So we simply must not discuss the historical problems with historical criticism. The evangelists describe for us Christ's course of life on earth as they viewed it through their knowledge of Christ's crucifixion; the glorious end of that course of life enlightened everything that preceded it.

It is right here that learning, with all its biographical and exact historical norms, falls short; it cannot, as such, do justice to the super-historical purport of the biblical account. Where learning sees the end, faith finds the beginning: the cross of Calvary. Kähler calls the faith of the congregation away from the uncertainties of learning. The congregation may not search behind texts for historical facts that may eventually be verified historically, but must base itself on the texts-as-such and the *kerygma* contained therein, the preaching of the first congregation (*Ur-gemeinde*), which lived and spoke from out of the richness of Christ's resurrection and ascension. Kähler uses the word "witness" in this framework. With this word, as with the word *kerygma*, he wishes to voice his opposition to the totalitarian claims of historical learning. "Witness" is used as a qualifier of the factual account of the New Testament as over against "source." *As "faith" stands over against "historical learning," so "witness" stands over against "source."*

In this manner a terminology which neglects the interest for facts and considers them secondary, was introduced into theological usage. For Kähler the primary issues at stake was the "message." However, just as it is impossible to isolate the message from the facts, so it is also impossible to isolate the facts from the message; the facts come to us *in the form of* witness-preaching! Factual account and confession of faith run through each other and intermix thoroughly. It is only in this way that Christ can be understood by the congregation in his "more-than-historical" meaning to her.

This theme of Kähler has become exceedingly popular in the twentieth-century writings of P. Althaus, E. Brunner, and R. Bultmann. The search for a "storm-free zone" for the congregation appears to be largely an escape maneuver or, at least, a withdrawal movement. The historical-critical inquiry, which sought to reconstruct the image of Jesus from the Gospel account by means of the so-called "neutral scientific method" was not "shown the door," but merely told to occupy a separate room in the house of Christianity.[12] Critical inquiry could go its own way as long as it left a private area for faith. It was allowed to exploit the Gospel as "source" as long as "faith" was allowed to read and study the same Gospel as "witness." Kähler in this manner delineated a proper area of endeavor for criticism of the Scriptures and put up a protective wall around the area of faith. He did not oppose the first pretensions of this category of biblical criticism, i.e., that scientific inquiry has its own law and should be recognized in its autonomy. This is the dichotomy present in Kähler's observations. It continues in many modern views of Scripture. It has received new food from recent existentialistic reflections. In all these views we encounter a dualism between historical learning *and* faith, between examination of a mere object *and* the meeting of persons, between the Bible as document *and* as confession. Place has been reserved for biblical criticism, which continues to forward its rights, even in exegesis.[13] Here lie the points of contact with Barth and Bultmann and the *formgeschichtliche* method of hermeneutics. A special pressure is put on the word "witness" whereby it is stretched into a term which asks attention for the prophets' and apostles' subjective expression of faith.[14]

III

Second, *the conviction that we are not able to speak, in the manner of Reformed orthodoxy, of a Holy Scripture which is infallible by godly inspiration.* This tendency, already present in Kähler, received broad elaboration by Brunner and Barth.[15] Restricting ourselves to the latter, we point out the following characteristic points:[16]

a.   Barth, as Kähler, places "witness" over against "source" and attempts to point out and limit a private domain for criticism.[17]

b.   With great emphasis Barth states that Scripture is *merely* witness; witness of remembrance of revelation which has taken place (N.T.) and of expectation of revelation which still must come (O.T.). Barth accuses the orthodox doctrine of inspiration of being a high-handed human attempt to stabilize the revelation of God. God does not, maintains Barth, give his revelation away and does not allow it to be identified with a book. The Bible offers us a number of approach-attempts by people who have met God in his revelation and now *bear witness* in their own language and manner in thankful remembrance and hopeful expectation. But the Bible *per se* is a product of human activity, a fallible document with noticeable errors and a way of thinking now out of date. The Bible is a purely human, "worldly" document. We should be thankful to historical criticism for this clarification of the nature of the Bible.[18]

c.   The Holy Scripture is, as human witness, the (second) form of God's revelation, the mediating authority between Jesus Christ and the preaching of the church. But this "form" is an inadequate one. It is not transparent. It is not clear glass, so that the contents, the quality of the revelation, would be easily visible. On the contrary, the form is a *covering* and *concealment* of the revelation. As human witness the Scriptures are not suitable to relay God's revelation; after all, the Bible has part in all the mortality and sinfulness of things human.[19] Actually, Scripture stands in the path of the light of revelation and provides the component of "mystery" to the event of revelation.

d.   Because of this resistance to the light of revelation, a "direct identity" between the Bible and God's Word is not possible.[20] It is an inexplicable miracle of God's free grace whenever Scripture is actually *witness*, when the revelation of God really *comes through*.[21]

In this way the word "witness" is subject to Barth's desire that the miracle of God's free grace in the origination of the revelation be honored. In spite of themselves, the apostles became witnesses by the virtue of a sovereign disposal of God over their work.[22] By means of that same working of God's grace, we become pupils and associates of the apostles as we learn of their witness.[23] No apostle was suited to deliver the witness, nor is the witness of Scripture of direct assistance in the hand of God. Precisely as human witness it is a matter of vexation and offense to the revelation; it always represents an opposition which can be removed only by God's conquering grace. But when this happens we stand before a repetition of the "great paradox" of John 1:14: the incarnation of the Word. The human witness *becomes* God's Word in fact, and God "raises" the resisting means of human witness "up" to Word of God.[24] Accordingly, Barth also can speak of the *unity of witness and revelation*, an indirect identity on the strength of sovereign identification, a unity which is not a property of witness but a matter of sovereign grace.[25,26] Here Barth's resistance to the orthodox doctrine of inspiration reaches its climax.

e. Barth persistently illustrates the nature of the normative strength of the human witness with the figure of John the Baptist. As he witnessed *of* Christ by pointing *to* Christ, so the Bible incessantly refers us to him who has spoken and shall speak. Consequently the Bible does not wish to reign over us, but exists to serve; it serves us *and* the Word of God. Christ does not come *to* us in the Bible, but the Bible is the standard for *our* request *for* the Word of God; it takes us along in the moving of the apostles. Not that we should simply give up our convictions for those of the apostles, for the Bible is "witness," not "edict." We must allow ourselves to be taken into the dynamic of the Bible and be taught the *demeanor* of the apostles.[27] We shall yet see how, by the of use John the Baptist figure, Barth breaks the brunt of John 5:36, 39.

f. It appears that the Scriptures, in Barth's view, have fallen prey to a dualistic construction. The Bible is a *wholly* human, and, as such, useless book. Bible criticism is, therefore, a useful and legitimate effort.

On the other hand, the Bible is taken up, *again completely*, in the dynamic of God's revelatory works and acquires a certain normative strength.

The connection with Barth's doctrine of *time* and *history* is evident. God's revelation carries its own time with it: the time of Jesus Christ, the highest qualified time, the fulfilled time, the time of grace, God's pure presence.

In opposition to this stands the time of man, our created and lost time, which must be raised to God's time by the revelation. The church, with her preaching, lives in this time. The link between the former and the latter time is formed by the time of the apostles, who fixed their witness in the Bible and delivered it to the church. They bear the witness across the "abyss of time," and in this manner biblical witness becomes the revealed form of the otherwise hidden presence and dominion of Christ in the time between the resurrection and the second coming.[28] In the valley of our time the Bible points out to us God's time in Christ. It is subservient to God as he speaks his revelation in our life. Barth seeks his "third road," against the subjectivism of experimental theology and the objectivism of orthodoxy, in dialectical tension between "Word" and "witness." This dialectic takes the place of a reinstatement of the normative power of the Bible as the Word of God.

IV

In our study we have noted that the popularity of the word "witness" is closely linked with the long-existing bewilderment concerning the nature of the Bible. What is the place and function of biblical criticism? What is the relationship between God's revelation and the Bible? The attempt has been made to intercept and assimilate all kinds of unresolved tension pertaining to these matters in the word "witness." But there has been little serious exegesis of this word. How scanty is the respect for the typical color of this word in the Bible itself! How seldom has the Bible been allowed to speak about itself!

Kähler took no notice of this typical color of "witness" as plea and bill of indictment in the case of God vs. the world concerning his honor, Christ's pretension, and the truth of Christian doctrine. He virtually identifies "witness" with "individual expression of faith," which is proclaimed as the happy "message." "Witness," therefore, is almost a synonym for "confession of faith."

Barth also took little notice of the juridical character of the word. As often as he did use it, he hardly knew *how* to use it.[29] This is partly due to the fact that Barth began expounding his idea of the "objective reconciliation of all mankind" in connection with "witness." As far as a "trial" was still pictured, he saw God litigating within the church with "the" man, and *that* man is, as such, the reconciled child of God.[30]

The conclusion is apparent: respect for the Bible forces us to clean up dogmatic formulations concerning the nature of Holy Scripture.

With respect to Kähler's contribution, our conclusion means, among other things, that we may not contrast "commentary" and "confession" with regard to the witness of the apostles. By virtue of Luke 24:48 and Acts 1:8, the apostles' function as ear-and-eye witness must be emphasized: they were to vouch for the factuality of the salvation which had taken place in Christ. This does not mean that the apostles were unbiased, objective reporters, personally not caring about the "case" or the "person." In their *witness* they simultaneously proclaim the *truth* about Jesus of Nazareth; they pronounce to church and world in the language of faith: this Jesus is the Messiah. Therefore they give a "spiritual" report, a witness of the facts which the Holy Spirit has taught them corresponding to the promise of John 14:26; 16:13, 14. We consequently do not designate this spiritual report by the merely exact term "interpretation," as if this were only a case of the individual faith-perspective of the apostle.[31] For through the Spirit the "truth" of Jesus of Nazareth has been unfolded to the apostles. Only a *non*-faithful "report" is "after the flesh" (cf. II Cor. 5:16).

In many discourses about the nature of Scripture it is possible to note a strong inclination toward considering the Bible as a collection of personal expressions of faith concerning God-placed facts. We must resist this tendency. The Holy Spirit has taught the prophets and apostles that they should speak as Words of God's wisdom (Matt. 10:20; Luke 10:16; John 15:26, 27; I Cor. 2:10, 12, 13). The peculiar nature of the apostles' witness will be spared only if we do not trade it in for "confession," but rather continue to understand it in its characteristic meaning: these witnesses were the servants of God, who had heard the words of God's only begotten Son, had seen his deeds, and had perceived the facts of cross and resurrection.[32] They were subsequently empowered by Christ and his Spirit to proclaim the factual truth and veracity of the salvation which occurred in Jesus Christ and to cast this truth at the lie that reigns over the world, in order to shame unbelief and work conversion. This unique function of the apostles is today exercised by the fixed and written apostolic word. The witness of the apostles is not a reference to, but is taken up into, the revelatory work of God.[33]

With reference to Barth's construction this conclusion is of great importance. For Barth "witness" is *the* word to protect the idea of the indirect identity of revelation and the Bible, and the "reference" is the constitutive element in his circumspection of the significance of the "witnesses."[34] Therefore "witness" is continually understood as a human activity toward God's revelation: as reference, answer, and account.[35] The subordination of preaching to biblical witness is a relative subordination in the light of both their relationships to revelation itself.[36] It is not God's taking up the apostles in his revelatory action which gives the apostolic witness its normative power; rather this normativity is found in their being *primary* witnesses, the first in a long procession, called by Barth the "order of witnesses."[37]

These deliberations are, however, denied by the clear teaching of Scripture itself: that the revelatory work and word of the Spirit come to us from Christ through the mouths of the apostles.[38] Certainly resistance to the Barthian view of Scripture demands precise and careful usage of the word "witness." The continual suggestion of Barth's discourses, that "witness" is the characterization of the *human* speaking of the Bible, deserves to be denied emphatically. It is very regrettable that Berkouwer has not marked this word clearly, but appears to have shifted toward the Barthian suggestion when he proposes that the "human witness" is the specific *modus* of God's revelation and *theopneustos*. Exegesis gives no support to this assertion.

V

The witness points to the issue at stake: the choice for the veracity and right of God's work of salvation in Christ, in the presence of much opposition, untruth, and oppression. Choosing sides is to further the triumph of the claim and justice of God's Christ: *that* is the specific color of the word "witness." This activity is not exclusively human. On the contrary, the decisive witness is always lastly delivered by him who is the Truth, Judge of all the issues at stake on earth. *God himself* is witness to the veracity of his revelation in his Son (I John 5:9, 10).

The Holy Spirit is witness by making the Gospel of truth triumph over the "world," the degenerated community of the Jewish synagogue (John 15:26, 27; 16:8-11). The Paraclete turns his defense into an accusation, makes the judges (Sanhedrin) the accused, the defendants (the apostles) the accusers, and exchanges the forum of man for the judgment seat of the Father of Jesus of Nazareth. The Book of Acts gives a striking affirmation of this work of witness by the Holy Spirit. He is crown-witness in the case of God against un-

belief and heresy (cf. also I John 5:6, 7). Also, God's speaking in
the Old Testament is called the witness of the Holy Spirit (Heb.
10:15; 7:17), while the work of the apostles in the New Testament
and the word of the prophets of old are seen as God's work (I Peter
1:11, 12). It is absolutely impossible to speak of an "individual
expression of faith" of the prophets in the light of these texts.

Likewise, the work of the Son of God, in humiliation and exaltation, is put forward as "witness" (John 3:11; 4:44; 7:7; 18:37; Rev.
in his Son (I John 5:9, 10).

Special notice should be given to John 8:12ff. In the issue of
Christ's exclusive pretension ("I am the Light of the world"), Christ
casts the weight of his descent and future, the miracle of his person
as Son of God, onto the balance of justice. As such he is not subject
to the rules of human legal proceedings: he has the unique right of
self-witness. As Son of God he is also never, as such, *an individual*.
He is always the Son; he always lives in communion with his Father.
The Savior constructs the circle of his claim of verity around this
center: his Word in John 8:12. He who has never found the center
by recognizing Christ as Son of God can likewise never hear or honor
the second Witness (the Father). But whosoever did hear the Son
of the Father in the words of Jesus of Nazareth has no need of the
human law which requires two witnesses. In the Person Jesus Christ
the believer finds all that is necessary for the witness of truth. Standing outside this circle, it is impossible to get in by way of human
deliberation; listening inside the circle one knows himself to be
beneficially bound and freed by the truth of the Son of God.

The self-witness of Jesus Christ leads us directly to his divine nature,
the deep secret of his person, his *oneness* with the Father.

In this connection careful note should be taken of a similar case
involving Christ's pretension: the struggle related in John 5:31ff.

There Christ blazes the trail for man; he unlocks the entrance to
the circle of truth by thinking with man and by traveling the path of
the human administration of justice and the verification of his claim.
For it is here that the Son *does* submit himself to the law of human
legal procedure (John 5:31, 32a). Here the great question is: *"Who
is that 'another' who is the decisive (second) witness?"*

After Christ has referred to John the Baptist, he next casts a
"greater" witness into the balance of justice (vs. 36b). Large parts
of the broad discourses of Barth on "witness" get stranded on this
word "greater." Christ does not confine himself to John. The greater
witness exists in the *works* he performs. For not he himself speaks

therein, but the Father (vs. 36b). In those works Christ proves that he was sent by the Father. In *this* way Christ comes to the climax of verse 37a: "And the Father himself which hath sent me, hath borne witness of me"! The highest classified witness, the God of all truth, the Witness pre-eminent—he backs up the pretension and stands beside Christ!

How is this witness reachable for the forum of Jewish quarrellers? It is not possible to summon God or examine him as was done with John (vs. 37b); nevertheless, this witness is not far away, not unreachable. He is present in the works of Christ; he is present in the words of the Christ sent by the Father (vs. 38). Here, as in John 8, it is a reversion to the great mystery of Christ: that he is Son, the Sent-One, the Word of the Father.

Yet how does Christ lead his audience to *this* holy truth? How can a human heart be reached by this high and unique claim of the Messiah? Is there a witness greater than that of John and yet audible, reachable to man? John 5:39 answers these questions: "You search the Scriptures, because you think that in them you have eternal life; and it is these that bear witness of me." By virtue of the context this well-known text can never be anything but the indication of the finding place of the witness of the Father concerning his Son. That decisive witness lies at hand in the Scriptures, in those same Scriptures which the Jewish scribes research, scrutinize, and examine thoroughly. Do they search for the decisive witness in the Messianic case? They have already possessed the witness of that great "Another" (vs. 32) for many ages. The Scriptures lead the way to Christ and give life to each who lets himself be led. The veracity of the Messiah is guaranteed by the Scriptures. But whosoever does not allow himself to be led to him by this witness shall be accursed and condemned by those same Scriptures on account of his blindness and deafness in the age of the Anointed of God (John 5:45-47).

In this manner Christ himself speaks of the witness of Scripture. It is quite another thing to say that John 5:39 gives material to a theory which reduces "witness" about Christ to the level of a human attempt to appraise the truth or a human reference to the truth. "Witness" is not a word that aims to keep secure a *distance* from Christ, but, on the contrary, a word used to make the distance between unbelief and Christ *disappear!*

The Bible itself puts the witness of the Scriptures on the highest level. It unlocks the deep mystery of godliness: that Jesus is the Son of God. It opens our eyes to recognize the eternal Father of

Jesus Christ in the works of Jesus. Whenever the Scriptures do not open eyes, they, nevertheless, *remain* crown-witness in the great case, for this witness then become the decisive *accuser* before the Father.

The continually valid witness of God comes to us in the Scriptures; in this way the Bible also mentions itself elsewhere.[39] On the basis of all this data we deny that the word "witness" is the characteristic expression for the nature of the relationship of the Scriptures' divinity and humanity. It does not enlighten to us the *modus* of God's revelation; nor does it serve as an indication of the human attempts to approach a revelation which is not at hand; neither is it a last resort against "atheistic" examination of the facts of salvation. In this word God reveals himself as the One who is the present, reachable, and audible witness in the great controversy of all history and every life: whom do men say is the Son of Man? In *that* controversy the Scriptures are effectively active as revelation of the Father, who conquers and subdues "flesh and blood" through the power of his Word and his Spirit.

(Translated by A. J. Van der Jagt)

John A. Witmer

VII. WHAT THINK YE OF CHRIST?

Christianity Is Christ is the title of a handbook by W. H. Griffith Thomas written almost half a century ago on what he called "the central subject of Christianity—the Person and Work of Christ."[1] The affirmation of his title and his statement is true. Whatever else may be involved by way of tenets of faith or canons of conduct, the essence of Christianity is personal union with Jesus Christ, the incarnate Son of God, as Savior and Lord by grace through faith. No matter how strategic may be one's view of the Bible—and strategic it is—the crucial question every human being must face is the one Jesus asked the Pharisees, "What think ye of Christ?" (Matt. 22:42). All who answer worshipfully by faith with Thomas, "My Lord and my God" (John 20:28), are Christians; all others are not.

Confronting his contemporaries with the issue of his identity as the incarnate Son of God, the anointed one whom God the Father had sent into the world, was a part of Jesus' ministry on earth. The rest of his question to the Pharisees was, "Whose son is he?" Their response, based on the accepted Jewish interpretation of the Old Testament (cf. John 7:41-42), was, "The son of David." Jesus then asked, "How then doth David in spirit call him Lord?" (Matt. 22:43). To substantiate his assertion that David does call the Christ Lord he quoted the statement from an acknowledged Messianic psalm (v. 44; Ps. 110:1). Then he summarized the issue in the question, "If David then call him Lord, how is he his son?" (v. 45). Without thrusting himself and his claims into the picture Jesus sought to confront the Pharisees on the basis of their own rabbinic interpretations of their Scriptures with the fact that the promised Messiah is presented as a divine being whom David worshiped as Lord as well as a descendant of David. Among the Pharisees "no man was able to answer him a word" (v. 46). The answer is found in the biblical record of the incarnation of the eternal Son of God as the Holy Spirit conceived son of a virgin daughter of the house of David (Luke 1:30-35; Matt. 1:20-23; Gal. 4:4). The answer is found in the unique theanthropic person of the Lord Jesus Christ. This the Pharisees would not—yes, even could not—see.

In similar fashion Jesus confronted his disciples with basically the same question of his identity. In fact their response to this question marked a turning point in Jesus' teaching and his whole ministry (Matt. 16:21). First Jesus asked, "Whom do men say that I the Son of man am? (Matt. 16:13). In reply the disciples recited the confused welter of erroneous identifications current among the Jews— "John the Baptist . . . Elias . . . Jeremias . . . one of the prophets" (v. 14). Then Jesus faced the disciples personally and directly, "But whom say ye that I am?" (v. 15). Speaking for the group Peter confessed Jesus as "the Christ, the Son of the living God" (v. 16). Jesus' commendation made the point that this conviction (cf. John 6:69) came not from human insight or instruction, but was the gift of divine revelation (v. 17). The enigma the learned Pharisees could not fathom God solved for the uneducated disciples (cf. Acts 4:13). So it ever is (cf. Matt. 11:25).

The parallels between the generation when Jesus walked this earth and today are obvious. When he lived among men, Jesus was largely unknown in his true identity. The same is true today. Although he contributed little to an accurate identification, Bruce Barton correctly called Jesus *The Man Nobody Knows*.[2] Many of the religious leaders today refuse to accept the identity Jesus claimed for himself just as did the Pharisees and chief priests when Jesus ministered on earth. Men today hold as many or more erroneous views of Jesus' identity as they did when Jesus queried his disciples. Yet people today are interested in Jesus just as the crowds gathered around him in Galilee and Judea. Young people today show little interest in the church and Christianity as an established religion, but they are eager to hear about Jesus as a person. As Harrison asserts, "Those who have little or no theological interest in him are nevertheless powerfully affected by the quality of Jesus Christ . . . they stand erect and salute the man."[3] As a result Christians today need to confront this generation with the same questions Jesus asked, "What think ye of Christ?" and "But whom say ye that I am?" But the questions today must be accompanied by the biblical evidence and the Christian witness that Jesus is "the Christ, the Son of the living God" who died to accomplish redemption for sinful men estranged from God. When the questions are asked and the witness is given, God the "Father which is in heaven" will reveal the truth to whom he wills as he did to the disciples.

The Contemporary Problem

The crux of the problem of the identity of Jesus today, as it was when he presented himself to his generation, is the recognition of the reality of his deity—that Jesus is the eternal Son of God, the Second Person of the triune God incarnate. This was what the Jews, with their stress upon God as one (Deut. 6:4), could not fathom and would not accept. As a result Jesus' claims to deity threw the Jews into a frenzy of indignation against him as a blasphemer (cf. John 5:18; 8:59; 10:31, 39). Under this accusation of blasphemy, after eliciting Jesus' confession under oath that he was "the Christ, the Son of God" (Matt. 26:63-64), the Jews condemned him to death (vv. 65-66). Similarly the miracle of incarnation as revealed in Scripture and the absolutely unique theanthropic person of the Lord Jesus Christ portrayed there is what the twentieth century man cannot comprehend and refuses to accept. As a result, in his frenzy of rejection, he restructures the person of Jesus as essentially human, or at least as less than fully God. In so doing he simply repeats in modern form and words the ancient error of Arius, which was condemned as heresy by the ancient Christian church, and its recapitulation in Socinius and others.

The irony of twentieth century Christendom is that such men are in large measure the leaders in the church and the spokesmen for Christianity. Instead of being honored as churchmen and spiritual leaders, they should be branded as heretics, false teachers (cf. II Peter 2:1; I John 4:1-3), and promoters of apostasy. But they are permitted to promote their heresy as the truth to be accepted by the Christian church and they present the historic doctrine of the Scriptures and the church concerning the Lord Jesus Christ as the error to be repented of and to be denied. Ferré, for example, asserts that "from Judaism and Islam Christianity should learn and repent of its central idolatry: its substitution, in effect, of Jesus for God, its making Jesus God."[4] When the historic doctrine of the deity of the Lord Jesus Christ is called "idolatry," Isaiah's prouncement of woe upon "them that call evil good, and good evil" (Isa. 5:20) needs to be invoked.

The latest twist in this topsy-turvy theological world is for liberal theologians to classify the historic Christian doctrine of the person of Christ as a specific heresy, which is docetism. Robinson asserts, "In fact, popular supernaturalistic Christology has always been dominantly docetic. That is to say, Christ only appeared to be a man or looked like a man: 'underneath' he was God."[5] Now docetism was the earliest Christological heresy to be faced and contradicted by the early church, appearing even in apostolic times. Building upon the

dualistic idea of the essential evilness of anything material, including
the human body, it denied the physical reality of Jesus' humanity,
making his body in effect a phantasm. John dealt with this error in
his first epistle, showing it to be wrong by stressing the reality of the
Lord's body in its subjection to sensory perception (I John 1:1-3).
Later he declared that "the Spirit of God" in contrast to the spirit
"of antichrist" is known by the fact that he "confesseth that Jesus
Christ is come in the flesh" (I John 4:1-3) with the emphasis falling
on the phrase "in the flesh." In the light of this New Testament
denial of docetism, it is obviously false to accuse the historic doctrine
of being that.

In his presentation of the historic doctrine as disguised docetism,
which he acknowledges to be "a parody,"[6] Robinson reveals a critical
lack of understanding of the biblical doctrine of incarnation. He declares that "Jesus was not a man born and bred—he was God for a
limited period taking part in a charade."[7] This implies, if not directly
states, that the incarnation of Jesus Christ was a temporary thing
which ended at his death. Nothing could be farther from the truth
of the New Testament teaching and the church doctrine. In the
incarnation God the Son joined himself with human nature in the
theanthropic Lord Jesus Christ once for all.

Furthermore, throughout his discussion of the historic doctrine and
its caricature as docetism, Robinson is careful to note that his picture
is not what the historic doctrine states nor what orthodox theologians
understand by it but only that his description is the way the average
person conceives of the doctrine. He says that the traditional view
"leaves the impression" or "conjures up the idea" or "inevitably suggests"[8] the docetic distortion he graphically portrays. His logic is
that the doctrine should be abandoned and changed because the popular picturing of it—or at least his picturing of it—is wrong. Robinson's basic complaint is not with the historic doctrine of incarnation
but with the biblical revelation of the incarnation and the supernaturalism that undergirds it.

Contemporary Views

After contemporary theologians such as Robinson have expressed
their discontent with the historic doctrine of the person of Christ, it
is fitting to ask how they answer the question, "What think ye of
Christ?" If Jesus queried them, "Whom say ye that I am?" how
would they respond? The answers, of course, are as individual as
the men who make them, but it is valid to say that a common theme

runs through them all. This theme is the essential humanness of Jesus. The biblical emphasis on Jesus' deity is reinterpreted in one way or another so that he becomes the servant of God or the personification of God in a sense that all men can be, but to a degree that only he was. This is nothing more than the immanent spark of divinity of old modernism expressed in new terms.

D. M. Baillie is an illustration. He interprets the mystery of the incarnation as the paradox of grace of the Christian life raised to its fullest measure. He writes: "If the paradox is a reality in our poor imperfect lives at all, so far as there is any good in them, does not the same or a similar paradox, taken at the perfect and absolute pitch, appear as the mystery of the Incarnation?"[9] In the light of such a view, Jay rightly asks, "Is his [Jesus'] divinity, then, simply that his God-consciousness, to use Schleiermacher's phrase, is complete, whereas in the rest of us it is imperfect?"[10] Schultz concludes that Baillie's position—a view he presents as shared by most neo-liberals—holds that "God was in Christ, working through him as he has worked through others, but to an infinitely greater degree."[11]

Robinson presents a different approach but the same end result. He makes it plain that he builds his Christology on Tillich and Bonhoeffer. "Jesus," therefore, "reveals God by being utterly transparent to him, precisely as he is nothing 'in himself.' "[12] He is the one, therefore, "in whom Love has completely taken over, the one who is utterly open to, and united with, the Ground of his being."[13] As a result, "the life of God, the ultimate Word of Love in which all things cohere, is bodied forth completely, unconditionally and without reserve in the life of a man—the man for others and the man for God."[14] Robinson seems to restrict his concept of God to something immanent in man which is perfectly displayed in Jesus. As Jay concludes, "His doctrine of incarnation blurs the distinction between God and man in such a way as to raise the question whether he believes God to have any existence apart from the existence of man."[15]

In their opposition to the historic doctrine of the person of the Lord Jesus Christ many contemporary liberal theologians attempt to create a chasm between the faith of the early Christians that Jesus was "the Christ, the Son of God, which should come into the world" (John 11:27) and the teaching and claims of Jesus concerning himself. This is not to be confused with the old theory of modernism that both the teachings of Jesus and the simple faith of the early church were changed and, in their judgment, perverted by the theological ideas of Paul. Harnack presented this when he wrote, "Paul became the author of the speculative idea that not only was God in Christ, but that Christ himself was possessed of a peculiar nature of a heavenly kind."[16] More recent study has demonstrated that the other apostles and the early church shared Paul's faith in the deity of the Lord Jesus Christ. Ramsey says, "The truth is that it is impossible to penetrate back to a time in the history of the church when the Risen Christ was not looked upon as a Divine Being. . . . From the very beginning he was proclaimed to be the heavenly Son of man in utterly transcendent terms. From the beginning he was assigned attributes heretofore reserved strictly for God."[17] But it is the view that this faith of the early church in Jesus Christ as the Son of God was not claimed by Jesus for himself in his teaching, but was developed by the church after his resurrection and was inserted into the teaching of Jesus in the Gospels.

Bultmann expresses this argument as well as anyone. He writes, "The common opinion is that this belief of the earliest Church rests upon the self-consciousness of Jesus; i.e., that he actually did consider himself to be the Messiah, or the Son of Man. But this opinion is burdened with serious difficulties. It does agree with the evangelists' point of view, but the question is whether they themselves have not superimposed upon the traditional material their own belief in the messiahship of Jesus."[18] Bultmann seems to forget that according to the Gospels Jesus himself solicited from his disciples their confession of his Messiahship and he commended them for it. Furthermore, their confession marked a distinct turning point in the ministry and teaching of Jesus. It does not constitute, therefore, a simple superimposition of an extraneous idea upon "the traditional material," but a crucial fulcrum in the account of Jesus' life and ministry.

Bultmann recognizes the logical force of the argument that it is easier to understand the early church's faith in the Messiahship of Jesus as coming from Jesus' teaching of it rather than their belief being inserted in their records of his teaching. He writes, "Some advance the following reasoning as an argument from history: The Church's belief in the messiahship of Jesus is comprehensible only if Jesus were conscious of being the Messiah and actually represents himself as such—at least to the 'disciples.' But is this argument valid? For it is just as possible that belief in the messiahship of Jesus arose with and out of belief in his resurrection."[19] Bultmann, however, does not accept the historical reality of the physical resurrection of Jesus. Furthermore, the disciples' faith in the resurrection that really did not happen, according to the liberal argument, developed from their hope that Jesus was the Messiah. So now the argument goes in a circle. If the disciples' faith in Jesus' Messiahship actually rested upon their faith in his resurrection, as Bultmann says, then where did their faith in Jesus' resurrection come from except from the event itself. On the other hand, if the disciples' faith in Jesus' resurrection rested upon their faith in his Messiahship, then that faith must have come from Jesus' claims and teaching. In either case Bultmann is caught on the horns of a dilemma.

No one questions the fact that the gospel writers had a purpose in writing their accounts of Jesus' life and ministry. The four Gospels are witnesses to the Lord Jesus Christ; not impersonal, totally objective history. All history is interpretative to a greater or lesser extent. The apostle John plainly stated his purpose (John 20:31). The purposes of the other gospel writers are not stated, but are fairly obvious. But recognizing that John and the others had a purpose in writing does not necessitate the conclusion that they distorted the facts and deliberately made Jesus say things he had not said. At most all that having a purpose implies is that the writer from the total mass of material available records selected events and statements that demonstrate the validity of his purpose. This is exactly what John explained that he did (John 20:30-31; 21:25). Scripture declares that in doing this John and the other gospel writers were sustained and guided by the Holy Spirit (II Peter 1:21).

An examination of the qualifications of the gospel writers to provide a record of the life and ministry of Jesus is revealing. If traditional authorships are accepted—good arguments can be marshalled to support them—then two of the authors belonged to the band of twelve apostles and were eyewitnesses of the events and teaching they report. One of these records the promise of Jesus to his disciples that "the Holy Spirit . . . shall teach you all things, and bring to your remembrance all that I said unto you" (John 14:26). A third, Mark, is generally recognized to have written his Gospel under the supervision of Peter, another of the apostles. Furthermore, his home and his personal experience aided him in his task. The fourth writer makes the point of telling his readers that he has gained "perfect understanding" of what he writes about from "eyewitnesses, and ministers of the word" (Luke 1:1-4). From the human perspective these men were ably qualified to give faithful, accurate records.

If the faith in the Messiahship of Jesus of the early church has been "superimposed upon the traditional material," as Bultmann insists, then these four gospel writers did it. First of all, insufficient time exists between the events themselves and the production of the gospel records for legendary accounts of the events to develop and to be accepted by the church. Furthermore, the eyewitness writers would know the difference between the true incidents and any embellished accounts. In the second place, legendary details could not have been woven into the gospels after their original composition. No literary or textual evidence of such tampering exists. As Dibelius writes, "The doubt as to whether our Gospels have been preserved in their original form turns out to be more and more unwarranted. . . . No book of antiquity has come down to us in such old, such numerous, and such relatively uniform texts as the Gospels and the Pauline Epistles."[20] Therefore, if Bultmann's theory is accepted, the gospel writers must have been responsible for the superimposition. This makes them in effect deliberate deceivers, reporters that Jesus did and said what they in truth knew he did not do and say. Such a conclusion does not jibe with their historical accuracy where it can be checked, with their portrayal throughout Scripture as honest and sincere men, or with their devotion even unto death to the Lord they proclaim and what they proclaim about him.

The Claims of Christ

In more recent years strong reaction to Bultmann's position has set in. Jay discusses Bultmann's arguments at length and then concludes: "This writer holds that the rise of this faith in Jesus was occasioned in the way the New Testament suggests, by what Bultmann and his school sometimes call 'the Christ-event.' . . . The Christ-event included, must have included, Jesus' teaching about himself and his mission. . . . his teaching about himself no doubt was cautiously given, with the intention of drawing the truth out of his disciples. . . . We hold then that Jesus did speak to the disciples of his person and his sense of divine mission. We find it too great a psychological improbability to suppose that the early Church, or any member, or group of members of it, invented a Christology which attributed to Jesus a status of which he had given them no hint and had even denied."[21] Similarly Vincent Taylor entitles one chapter "The Divine Consciousness of Jesus" and explains why he adopts it instead of the more familiar phrase *Messianic Consciousness*. By the phrase *Divine Consciousness*, Vincent writes, "I mean the sense in which he was conscious of being more than a man, of sharing during his earthly existence in the life of Deity itself. This putting of the question has the advantage of raising the central issue."[22]

The central issue to which Vincent refers, as mentioned earlier, is the reality of the Lord Jesus as the eternal Son of God, second person of the Godhead, united with human nature forever as the theanthropic person. Closely tied to this is the question of whether Jesus knew and presented himself as such or not. As Bowman expresses it, "And this after all is the point at issue: *Whom did Jesus know himself to be?* It is interesting to know what Mark or Luke or Peter or Paul thought about Jesus. . . . But they are not after all very important—not, at all events, by comparison with the supreme question of Jesus' own consciousness regarding himself! For obviously, if it could be shown that Jesus failed to agree with those above mentioned on this vital topic, then his view in our judgment would quite outweigh all of theirs combined. *The Church cannot indefinitely continue to believe about Jesus what he did not know to be true about himself!* The question, accordingly, of his Messianic consciousness is the most vital one the Christian faith has to face."[23] Bultmann and his school insist that the faith of the church in Jesus Christ does not rest upon Jesus' consciousness and claims, but common sense as expressed by Bowman does. It is worth mentioning that Bultmann accepts neither the historic doctrine of the person of the Lord Jesus Christ nor the idea that this was the claim of Jesus.

The bulk of the evidence from the four Gospels supporting Jesus' consciousness and claim to be the Son of God incarnate comes from the Gospel of John. This is understandable. John's stated purpose is "that ye might believe that Jesus is the Christ, the Son of God" (John 20:31). It would be surprising if this were not the situation. But as Harrison asserts, "No apology need be made for this. Clearly this gospel has a more sustained christological interest than the others, but to say that it stands completely apart and gives an entirely different picture of Christ's person than the Synoptics is to revive a dogma of the criticism of yesteryear. Today men of various schools of thought are agreed that it is vain to try to establish a lower Christology from the Synoptics than is taught in the Fourth Gospel."[24]

The witness from the Gospel of John can be multiplied almost endlessly. There are direct statements—"I and the Father are one" (10:30), "Before Abraham was, I am" (8:58), "I am in the Father, and the Father in me" (14:11; cf. 10:38; 17:21, 23), "I that speak unto thee am he [Messias]" (4:26; cf. v. 25), "the Son of God . . . is he that talketh with thee" (9:35-37). There are claims that he "came down from heaven" (3:13; 6:38, 51) and was sent from the

Father (3:17; 6:57; 7:29; 8:29). He insists he has authority over his own physical life (10:18) and over the physical and spiritual lives of all men (11:25-26; 4:14; 6:40, 44, 47). He presents himself as "the bread of life" (6:35, 48), "the light of the world" (8:12; 9:5), "the good shepherd" (10:11, 14), "the door" (10:7, 9), "the resurrection, and the life" (11:25), "the way, the truth, and the life" (14:6). In fact, the divine consciousness and claims of Jesus so permeate the discourses which form so much of the Fourth Gospel that it is almost pointless to separate individual statements from the impact of the discourse as a whole.

A significant christological discourse which is frequently passed by is the one with the Jews following the healing of the impotent man at the pool of Bethesda recorded in John 5. Several observations need to be made about this discourse. First, although Jesus usually spoke of himself as the Son objectively in the third person, he changed to the first person at the beginning, middle, and end of the discourse (vv. 17, 24, 30) and made it plain that he was talking about himself. Furthermore, his auditors (the Jews) understood Jesus to be speaking about himself, and they were in a better position to perceive than a twentieth century Bible critic (v. 18). Second, Jesus used the titles "Son of God" (v. 25) and "Son of man" as, for all practical purposes, interchangeable. He used each title where he did with deliberate intent and special significance, and yet they are obviously basically interchangeable titles. Third, Jesus spoke of God as "my Father" in a way which stated a unique personal relationship (v. 17). Jesus never spoke of his filial relationship to God as being on the same level as those to whom he spoke, even his disciples (cf. John 20:17). The only time he used the phrase "Our Father" was when he expressed a model prayer for his disciples in response to their request that he teach them to pray (Luke 11:1-2; cf. Matt. 6:9). Once again confirmation of this meaning of the phrase "my Father" is the fact that the Jews to whom he spoke "sought the more to kill him, because he not only had broken the sabbath, but said also that God was his [own] Father, making himself equal with God" (John 5:18).

The final and most meaningful evidence of Jesus' divine consciousness in this discourse is the emphasis throughout the discourse on the complete and exact parallelism between what the Father does and what the Son does (e.g., vv. 17, 19b, 21, 26). The equality between the Father and the Son is stressed in these verses, because the emphasis is that exactly what the Father does the Son does also in

precisely the same way. The heart of the entire discourse and the purpose of God in all that he commits to the Son is expressed in the
words, "That all men should honour the Son even as they honour
the Father" (v. 23). For added emphasis Jesus then stated the same
truth negatively, "He that honoureth not the Son honoureth not the
Father which hath sent him."

As Bauman summarizes the evidence, "It must be maintained just
as strongly, however, that Jesus knew himself to be the Son of God,
partaking fully of the divine nature. . . . This unique filial consciousness contributed a divine dimension to every word and act of
his life. The author of John built his Gospel on this conviction, but it
is just as obvious in the Synoptics, where Jesus is *the* Son of God."[25]
The Synoptic Gospels are the ones which record the trial of Jesus
before the council of the Jews where the high priest places him under
oath to say whether or not he is "the Christ, the Son of God" (Matt.
26:63). Mark says, "the Christ, the Son of the Blessed" (Mark
14:61), and Luke makes two questions with Jesus answering the
one, "Art thou then the Son of God?" (Luke 22:70). In all three
Gospels Jesus in effect (the wording varies slightly) acknowledges
under oath this identity. To his admission Matthew and Mark add
the statement: "Henceforth ye shall see the Son of man sitting on the
right hand of power, and coming in the clouds of heaven" (Matt.
26:64; Mark 14:62). Instead of accepting Jesus' statement under
oath as the truth and acknowledging him as "the Christ, the Son of
God," the high priest and the council condemn him as guilty of blasphemy by his own words and worthy of death. Their accusation of
Jesus before Pilate was sedition and treason (e.g., Luke 23:2), but
John records their acknowledgment of Jesus' divine consciousness
and claim when the Jews explained to Pilate, "We have a law and by
our law he ought to die, because he made himself the Son of God"
(John 19:7). Many modern churchmen are like the Jewish leaders;
in spite of the evidence they refuse to accept it.

Facing the Alternatives

The incongruity and logical inconsistency of modern theology on
this point is recognized by many. Harrison points this out when he
writes, "Those who exalt Jesus as the great teacher do not always
realize the awkwardness of their position when they go on to refuse
to him the rank of deity. It it logical to accept his teaching on God,
on man, on the ethical life, and then refuse to accept his teaching
about himself?"[26] The logical alternatives to the biblical evidence of

Jesus' divine consciousness and claims are (1) he was indeed the Son of God incarnate; (2) he was a liar and a deceiver; (3) he was insane, suffering from illusions of grandeur. If either of the latter two alternatives is accepted, then Jesus' teaching should no more be extolled and believed than his claims. Harrison writes, "Is it psychologically possible for a person to project such claims, which lie so far outside the realm of human attainment, and be otherwise completely normal; and could the record of these claims as they stand in the Gospels have created such profound reception and faith as it has created, apart from having solid truth behind them"[27]

Hiram Elfenbein carries the logic a step farther. As a Jew he does not accept the New Testament records concerning Jesus of Nazareth. But he does recognize the centrality of the deity of the Lord Jesus Christ to those records and to the Christian faith. He writes, "But 'Christianity-without-Christ' is as sensible as a rice pudding without rice. It just can't be."[28] He insists that modern churchmen who agree with him in the denial of the deity of Jesus are at best playing a great game of make-believe by continuing to call themselves Christians and to remain in the Christian church. He asks, "If Jesus is eliminated from the credo as a God Who once lived in Human Form, how can the church's buildings, personnel and 'services' be justified? How can individuals honestly and intellectually continue to patronize and to belong to that establishment of brick and mortar and ritual and clerics minus the nominal God around Which they worship?"[29] He summarizes as follows, "Obviously, if you delete from the New Testament, the one all-important detail of Jesus' divinity, we see the collapse of the whole story of his prophesied birth and death, his miracles, and his long mistaken and misunderstood expressions, which together in an inseparable union form the foundation of Christianity."[30]

Modern churchmen should face the question, "What think ye of Christ?" in the light of Elfenbein's logic. If they cannot honestly respond with Thomas, "My Lord and my God" (John 20:28), they should resign from their positions and separate themselves from the Christian church. In turn all believers who from the heart answer the question, "Whom say ye that I am?" with Peter's confession, "Thou art the Christ, the Son of the living God" (Matt. 16:16), need to recognize their responsibility to confront this generation with the witness concerning the Lord Jesus Christ as the incarnate Son of God and Savior from sin.

G. C. Berkouwer

VIII.   THE AUTHORITY OF SCRIPTURE
(A RESPONSIBLE CONFESSION)

When congratulating someone on his long productive life, the congratulations can be fully intended, even when there may be far-reaching differences of opinion between them. Such differences need not make any difference to the respect which is implied in the congratulations. Neither is it contradictory to reflect at the same time on the nature and background of these differences in order to find out whether they are incidental or whether they have an important influence on one's view of the truth of God. When our point of departure lies in a common confession of Holy Scripture as the authoritative and reliable Word of God, which requires absolute obedience of all our thoughts to Christ, the question arises as to where our differences originate. This is the situation in which I find myself as a participant in a publication dedicated wholly to the life work of Cornelius Van Til. To me it seems meaningless on this occasion to avoid our differences by flight to some "objective" article calculated to create the impression that the (theological) differences between us are, on the whole, not far-reaching.

*   *   *   *   *

Van Til has been intensely occupied with a number of important problems. He has tirelessly entered into many theological discussions of our time of which I mention his views on apologetics, on "common grace," and on many other theological trends. Among the latter the best-known would be his antipathy towards the so-called "New Modernism" which he considers, in Barth's works in particular, to be a lethal danger which *threatens* the whole life of the church. In this controversy the question is about the deepest intentions of Barth's theology, and it is not surprising that this should lead to many a difference of opinion. Personally, over many years, I have come to a different view of Barth's theology, but I fully understand why Van Til, from *his* point of view, has more appreciation for my first book on Barth in 1936 than for the one of 1954. Van Til has never been able to feel at home in the growing appreciation for the theology of Barth in Reformed circles. He has not seen a single connection between it and Reformed theology. In spite of Barth's controversies with Bultmann and in spite of his fierce defense against the fashionable trends of the "death of God" movement, Van Til saw various apostatic motives underlying Barth's theology which gave the whole an "anti-Christian" character. I do not intend discussing this in more detail here. The search for the deepest dimension in Barth's theology is, after all, a *matter of analysis* of his *Kirchliche Dogmatik* and one can differ in the evaluation and position of this theology in the whole of Christian thought.

However, the differences between us become more significant when the confession of the church, the Christian confession, is discussed. Personally, I consider it of more consequence when Van Til thinks that I misinterpret the confession of divine election and deprive it of its biblical foundation, than when we differ in our interpretation of Barth; although I admit that there could be a correlation between historical interpretation and dogmatic differences. I mention the confession of election because Van Til discusses this in his study, *The Sovereignty of Grace*. No subject—apart from the confession of Scripture—has interested me more than *this* confession. When I visited the USA in 1952 and saw Herman Hoeksema, I returned with the conviction that Hoeksema's view on election was biblically *untenable*. I discussed this fully in my book on *Election* in 1955. Since that time I have been intrigued with this confession. My interest was, of course, immediately stimulated by the new book of Van Til. I do not mean to identify the views of Van Til with those of Hoeksema, but the *issues* which are raised by both are concentrated upon the search for the meaning of the sovereignty of grace. These issues are currently accentuated in the Netherlands by a *gravamen*[1] which was brought in against certain expressions in the Canons of Dordt resulting in a synod ruling that the expressions in question had no foundation in Holy Scripture and that it could not be said of the submitter of the *gravamen*—an elder—that he came into conflict with "the Canons" in respect to the sovereignty of grace. The synod wanted to uphold the point, the real intention, the *skopus* of the Canons (the sovereignty of grace) and was of the opinion that it could not be maintained that reprobation, as it appears in the Canons —reprobation from eternity—is founded in the Scriptures. Thus it is not only my problem—fortunately not—but concerns the reflection of the *church*. To me it has become increasingly clear that the *scriptural* proof of reprobation from eternity does not hold, particu-

larly the reference to Matthew 11:25, 26 (about the εὐδοκία), because *precisely here* the gracious will of God is related to the "wise
and understanding" *and* to children. I consider this development
(ecclesiastical!) to entail a number of problems which are connected with the total exegesis of all scriptural evidence concerning
the election of God, particularly of Romans 9-11. The differences
within Reformed circles come to the fore clearly in the sharp criticism of the *vrijgemaakte* (liberated) wing and from the *verontrusting*
(the concerned group) against the exegesis of Herman Ridderbos
in his commentary on Romans 9-11, whereas there are also those
within the liberated churches who hold to other views—especially
those of Holwerda, Jager, and Veenhof—which are much closer to
the new exegetical studies over election. The main question in this
connection is whether the sovereignty of God is affected by this new
understanding of reprobation or whether it is, at least, relativized.
It is obvious that this question can and must *only* be answered on the
basis of Holy Scripture. Reformed thinkers can obviously not base
their decision on confessional tradition, because this tradition must
itself be judged on the basis of God's Word (Art. 7, Belgic Confession). Thus one can only expect light on these problems after
patient, submissive, and *listening* scriptural investigation. We must
seek this light because the authentic comprehension of the sovereignty of God is at stake. It is of great importance that we should
agree on this matter.

Van Til's objections do not arise from his hallowing the confessional tradition and precisely therefore a fresh discussion about the
meaning of Scripture is possible, especially of Romans 9-11. Here we
enter the field of hermeneutics, the problems concerning the interpretation of Scripture. This is not a twentieth century problem, but
already arises—as a warning!—in the New Testament itself, where
self-originating interpretation is rejected (II Peter 1:20) as being in
conflict with the *origin* of prophecy in the Holy Spirit (II Peter 1:21).
The value and truth of what one thinks, feels, and believes about
God's election depends *totally*, according to the Reformed point of
view, on its conformity to Holy Scripture. Here there is not a single
difference between Van Til and me. This is clear in his emphatic
confession that Holy Scripture is the infallible Word of God, reliable
in all respects, and the one and only rule for our faith.[2] If, as Van
Til says, Scripture is "self-authenticating,"[3] then I would like to say of
it what he says elsewhere: "The significance of this point can scarcely
be over-estimated"[4] because now the decisive significance of the

Reformed maxim *Sacra Scriptura sui ipsius interpres* comes to the fore. In this case no dogmatic tradition can have the "last word" along side the Scriptures (H. Bavinck) and the *Sacra Scriptura est Verbum Dei* gets *concrete* significance. No independent views of the sovereignty of God—again and again an inroad for rationalism, irrationalism, spiritualism, and mysticism—can have the final say, but only the Word of God itself. The implications of the Reformed confession—*sui ipsius interpres*—are limitless since the *opened* Bible repeatedly requires fresh attention for the witness of God.

One can understand, therefore, that I approached Van Til's book on the *Sovereignty of Grace* in the expectation that here *exegesis of Holy Scripture would play a decisive role*. That this was not the case disappointed me theologically. That Van Til is a philosopher and dogmatician and professionally not an exegete does not solve the Reformed problem. Certainly each dogmatician has this problem— he is not an expert in the exegesis of the Old and New Testaments— but this does not diminish his responsibility to be occupied with the *interpretation* of the Scriptures. If he fails to do so, he must certainly be found on the way of an unreformed sanctioning of tradition. Rome accused the Reformation of scorning the traditions and the guidance of the Holy Spirit, but the Reformers examined the tradition of the church on the basis of the Word of God and were, therefore, for their whole lives concerned with the understanding of Scripture. Luther pointed out the necessity of knowing the *Sprachen* which were so closely connected to the way of the Holy Spirit in the θεόπνευστος of Scripture. When Van Til writes that my "pattern of language has changed, this no doubt in the interest of winning modern man to an acceptance of the gospel"[5] and that this pattern seems like neo-orthodoxy, then I think he is mistaken. But of far greater consequence that this misunderstanding is the total lack of biblical reflection and the absence of a *reply* to all the exegetical questions brought forward by Ridderbos, Holwerda, Vaanhof, and even myself. Yet such reflection *cannot* and *must not* be absent if Van Til's "Introduction" to Warfield's bibliology is to be *relevant* and *plausible*. In fact, that Van Til in his *Sovereignty of Grace* includes references to the Bible, but *only* in quotations from *my* publications, has upset me and has once again set me to thinking about the concrete meaning of the Reformation and about the *sui ipsius interpres*. When Ridderbos and I investigate the ἐκλογή in Romans 9:11 as to its evident meaning for Romans 9-11 and for the doxology at the end and for other biblical passages, *then only the interpretation of Scrip-*

ture can be our court of appeal. When the *sui ipsius interpres* does not function concretely then there is, I fear, a severe limitation and weakening of the authority of Scripture.

Van Til acknowledges that I have "never forsaken" my conviction with respect to "the absolute authority of Scripture."[6] I declare the same about Van Til.[7] But obviously this does not solve the problems. It is clear that Van Til sees many dangers particularly concerning the *seriousness* of the "never forsaken conviction." He claims to be able to point out "an activist pattern" in my work and recognizes therein "the principle of the autonomous man, using a Parmenidean-Spinozistic principle of continuity."[8] It is not very important that I do not understand this accusation (may people deal with each other in *this* manner in the church and in theology?). What is more important is the fact that Van Til ends his book on the *Protestant Doctrine of Scripture* by referring to the "faith of the Reformers" and to the subjecting of "every thought to the obedience of Christ."[9] Once again we agree on the point of departure, and yet we part courses. I am not interested in the reference to Parmenides or Spinoza *when the Scriptures have not been consulted anew and have ruled*, if need be, against Ridderbos, Veenhof, Holwerda, and me, but then *not without having given careful attention to the words of the Scriptures in their deepest meaning and authority. Sacra Scriptura sui ipsius interpres!*

* * * * *

In his latest publication, *A Christian Theory of Knowledge*, Van Til deals with the necessity, the authority, the sufficiency, and the perspicuity of Scripture.[10] It must be here decided, I think, whether Van Til is correct when he sees many theologians (*Gereformeerde*) as standing in the corner of "neo-orthodoxy." It appears that he *underestimates* the significance of these "attributes" of Holy Scripture, or at least does not sufficiently recognize their concrete significance (full of responsibility since the Word of God is the sword of the Spirit [Eph. 6:17] not in an "activist" but certainly an "active" way [Heb. 4:12]). Should this be taken into account in the less easy combination of exegesis and dogmatics, then Kant, Parmenides, and Spinoza could remain out of the picture, *at least for the time being*, while all attention is concentrated on the deepest significance of the Word of God. "The Scripture must be interpreted by Scripture."[11] Van Til correctly points out: "No interpretation as such may be said to be infallible. There is an ever deeper insight into the truth of Scripture promised to the church if it submits in efforts at interpretation to the Scripture iself."[12] The discussion always arises over this "if it submits." Is this discusssion—between good friends with sincere mutual respect—senseless and hopeless? In solving this problem one automatically seeks the significance of the common starting-point. In his *Theory of Knowledge* Van Til deals with my warning against the incorrect use of the "attributes" of Scripture. "His point is that unless the *message* of Scripture be taken together with the *idea* of Scripture, we have an empty form. The *what* of Scripture cannot be separated from its *message*, just as the words of Christ cannot be separated from the person of Christ. It is this very point which the present writer has continually stressed."[13]

Is there therefore yet a consensus all along the line? It would be superficial to answer this question affirmatively. But certainly in "this very point" lies, perhaps, a new starting-point for re-reflection on the questions which have arisen not only beween Van Til and myself, but which preoccupy the whole church. To me there is no question about our discussion being between a more *absolute* and a more *relative* view of the authority of Scripture. We should in our discussions concentrate far more on *taking the confession of the authority of Scripture seriously.* This is not easy, since no escape from the *verba* is possible. We could be lazy and fall back on tradition as though it had authority in itself. Had the Reformers done this, there would not have been a Reformation. To understand this in "the obedience of Christ" means to choose a course on which the sword of the Spirit preserves and manifests its power. One would be bound to remind oneself constantly that "no interpretation as such may be said to be infallible" (Van Til). *This has incalculable consequences.* But one should not fear this course since here the promise of the Spirit accompanies us. On the way of "obedience" we shall also become more careful in our judgment of others, not by relativizing the authority of Scripture, but by acknowledging our limited insight, our seeing "in a mirror darkly" (I Cor. 13:12). If we do not temper our judgment in this way, we would further consider ourselves superior to Paul with his dim vision. Such vision did not prevent him, however, from writing the poem of *love* (I Cor. 13), and it need not impede us either, and it *will* not impede us if we do not isolate ourselves, but seek the course together, since all dimensions are involved (breadth, length, height, and depth, Eph. 3:18), and if all our discussions become purified of intentions contrary to those of the Spirit. We will certainly not differ on this point.

But we shall all be judged as to our *concrete* obedience to and confession of the authority of Scripture. This happens by testing whether we understand "the authority of Scripture" in the same way as the Bereans (Acts 17:11), who eagerly received the Word and who *examined the Scriptures daily.* According to Reformed confession these Scriptures are never exhausted in human terms, even in important church confessions. Hence, we have the permanent vocation to listen attentively so that we do not distort the words in the Scriptures (II Peter 3:16) but preserve them in our hearts and lives.

(*Translated by J. Brümmer-Heatie*)

Response by C. Van Til

Dear Dr. Berkouwer:

I appreciate deeply your willingness to contribute to this volume. I have profited much from all your many works.

I agree that my little book on *The Sovereignty of Grace* should have had much more exegesis in it than it has. This is a defect. The lack of detailed scriptural exegesis is a lack in all of my writings. I have no excuse for this. The great works of biblical exegesis in the Bottenberg series of commentaries, as well as others, have been of help to me throughout the years. I have read Dr. Ridderbos on Romans as well as John Murray. I agree basically with Murray. I could have quoted from his extensive and detailed exegesis. I should, perhaps, have compared your own exegesis and that of Ridderbos on Romans with that of Prof. Murray. I wish now that I could have done so. Perhaps the readers will be able to do this for themselves. I hope so.

I realize too that I must watch against the danger of falling into a "new traditionalism." Perhaps you will think that in my response to Prof. Dooyeweerd, in this volume, in addition to other things, I point to the fact that I have fallen back on a traditional position already. Well, I have often enough been called a "reconstructionist" because I wanted to make full use of recent Reformed exegetical and philosophical works for the development of what I think of as a biblical and therefore Reformational apologetic. The traditional view of apologetics was based on some form of empiricist and/or rationalist philosophy. This was true, obviously, in the old Princeton apologetics. It was also true, to a less extent, in the Amsterdam apologetics as found in the writings of Kuyper, Bavinck, and Hepp. I tried to go "beyond" these men, always with great appreciation for the work they had done, by *starting* from the authority of Christ speaking in Scripture as the presupposition of predication on any point, in any field of investigation. I do not see how we can truly evaluate recent theology, philosophy, and science except on this basis. With the greatest respect for your work and that of Dr. Dooyeweerd and, I pray, with proper humility, I must say that the danger of traditionalism is present to all of us. If I now have the temerity of trying to go "beyond" Dooyeweerd and you on the matter of presenting the gospel to modern man, I do so because I think the Christ of the Scriptures compels me to do so. I wish I could have given better exegetical justification for this position than I have, but, of course, every bit of exegesis of Scripture already involves a view of the nature of Scripture. We all see through a glass darkly. We must seek to state the truth in love. But I cannot change what is in print. I can, therefore, only apologize for any unduly harsh judgment I have expressed on the work of those who with me seek to make the Christ of the Scriptures known unto men for the solution of their problems.

—C.V.T.

S. U. Zuidema

IX. EXISTENCE AND THE CONTENT OF REVELATION IN THE THEOLOGICAL HERMENEUTICS OF RUDOLF BULTMANN

I.   The Selbstverständnis[1]

To be a Christian means to live as a Christian and to live as a Christian means to live wholeheartedly by and out of divine revelation. Such a life is a life of faith. If a person no longer believes *in* God, that is, in his God, and—in the midst of the church of Christ—in our God, then he cannot live by and out of divine revelation. He may still be called a "Christian," but he is one in name only. Having ceased to live by and out of divine revelation, he will inevitably live by and out of an idol, which, as Paul writes, is not anything.

This place and source of the Christian life is certainly being recognized in contemporary theology. Today, theologians are well aware of their task to reflect on divine revelation and on the life of faith that finds its place and source in this revelation. There is also a general consensus among them that this reflection is not possible without taking into account the person of Jesus Christ, the Holy Scriptures, and the preaching of the gospel.

As a Christian, I know, therefore, that these theologians also speak about *me*. Indeed, they speak about me in a fundamental manner: as a believer, I may and, in fact, must say to myself, *tua res agitur*. Not only does it concern me, but also every Christian and the church so dear to Christ. Yes, even God's cause is in question here because the theologians are reflecting on his revelation. However, what is written, said, or thought about God not only concerns him as my *God*, but also as *my* God, or—speaking of all believers— as *our* God. Thus also in this indirect manner our interests as believers are involved. We should, therefore, be interested to the extent of our abilities.

This interest should involve a critical reflection, that is, we should not blindly believe and accept as fact everything that is written, said, or thought about us. So much is being written, said, or thought about us that makes no sense at all; and how many misconceptions do we ourselves not entertain about our own person? In theology, however, it is always decisive what is being written, said, or thought, since the theologian, by the very nature of his task, operates near the very center of our lives, as believers in Christ.

However, this reflection of the theologian and every "interested" Christian is, whatever else one may wish to say about it, *thought*, thought *about* the very center of our lives as believers in Christ. Inevitably the question arises whether such reflection is possible, or, if possible, whether it is permissible. It could be maintained that it is impossible, or that it is possible only in the sense that it is thought about the unthinkable. Thus, this center would be thought about in the manner in which the unthinkable would be thought about: *as* unthinkable. A third position could be held, namely. this center existentially witnesses to itself and this self-witness makes reflection possible. In this self-witness man's existentia! *Selbstverständnis* discloses itself and this self-disclosure gives "food for thought." Thus, according to this position, not the *Selbstverständnis* itself, but the witness in which it has disclosed itself can be reached and grasped by this reflection. However, one reflects not only on the self-witness and its content but also on the direction of the *Sache* (the subject-matter itself) about which this witness has testified. The intention of this reflection is to come to an interpretation or understanding of the witness. Even though it be posited that this interpretation must take place within the "existential" circle of this self-witness and must live out of it and be rooted in it, then it still remains true that the understanding attained here is different from the understanding denoted by the term *Selbstverständnis*. As thought *out of* the *Selbstverständnis* the reflection is nothing more than thought *about* the witness of this *Selbstverständnis*, be it in the direction of the original *Selbstverständnis*.

Thus, on the one hand, according to this position, it is possible to existentially witness from out of the individual and original *Selbstverständnis*. This witnessing inevitably results in a wit*ness*, which no longer changes as soon as the umbilical cord with which it originally was united to the *Selbstverständnis* is tied off. It has become a fixed independent entity.

On the other hand, it is also possible to reflect on the structure of the *Selbstverständnis* and on the dynamic act of witness*ing* which flows out of and is determined by the *Selbstverständnis*. Martin Heidegger is of the opinion that such reflection is essentially different from the reflection on everything that does not belong to man's concrete existence. This latter reflection takes place with the help of the so-called categories; the former with the help of *Existentialia*. In Heidegger's *Sein und Zeit* (1926) the *Selbstverständnis* itself appears to be an *Existenzial* of man's concrete existence. The concern of man's concrete existence is concern for itself. According to Heidegger, the *Existenzial* of the *Selbstverständnis* is for this reason a *structural* moment of man's existential *Geschichtlichkeit* (historicness) which is a power phenomenon, a *Können*, a *Selbstmächtigkeit,* a freedom implying an absolute sovereignty, a sovereign *Subjektivität;* in other words, it is a structural moment of the autonomous self-determination, which is inviolable and unassailable and which belongs to man's existential, foundamental freedom. Heidegger's conception is, in form and content, the conception of man's (rational) autonomy. This conception as an autonomously rational conception is distinguished from that about which it is a conception, namely: everything that arises out of the existential autonomy. There is a principial distinction between, on the one hand, the philosophical and rational understanding of man's concrete existence and, on the other hand, the existential *Ereignis* (event) of this existence, thus, also the *Ereignis* of the existential *Selbstverständnis*. This important distinction is not held by Karl Jaspers, who attempts to explain—unsuccessfully, I think—the conception of the *Existentialia* directly in terms of the existential *Ereignis*.

Man's *Selbstverständnis* is, therefore, according to Heidegger, a power phenomenon wherewith man in existential freedom realizes himself as a selfhood and as *en route* to his selfhood. He is the builder of his own future "self," which he allows to come to himself and which comes to him as his own future (advent). This future (advent) is man's origin as man. His *eschaton* is his origin.

The Antipole

But Heidegger cannot let it rest at that. He needs an antipole lest man's freedom and the conception of this freedom hang in mid-air as *absoluta* lacking all concreteness. This antipole is the world of beings (*Seiendes*). It is everything in and outside of man which is *nicht-daseinsmäszig* (non [human-] existential). It is the *Seiendes* into which man as an existentially free and autonomous being is said to be thrown (*geworfen*). In Heidegger's view, there is no inner connection between man and the *Seiendes*. Man is *das Wesen der Ferne* (the being from afar). He remains so even when he finds himself in the midst of the *Seiendes*, in his "thrownness" (*Geworfenheit*). This *Seiendes* is in itself meaningless, but it becomes meaningful as antipole for man's self-realization, also in his *Selbstverständnis*, as a free and autonomous subject, because man's concrete existence at the zero or starting point of its autonomous freedom is always on the level of this *Seiendes*. This *Seiendes* is for it something *zuhanden* (within our reach) and, owing to scientific abstraction, also something *vorhanden* (thinkable, a scientific object), *vorgreiflich* (anticipatory) and objective. It is there so that man can continually trancend it *en route* to his own self. When he situates *himself* in the *Seiendes*, he has also given *himself* the power to transcend it, and to relativize his own self-situation as a provisional and temporary act, and to overcome it in the direction of a new self-situation which again begs to be transcended, leading to another new self-situation which again must be overcome, *ad infinitum*.

Thus, to be truly, existentially man means to be *en route*, by way of a continual transcending of one's own historicalness that is, the contingent situation in which one as sovereign subject has situated himself in a supra- or extra-historical manner, as *Geschichtlichkeit*.

Along with historicism, which teaches that man is totally caught up in his own historicity, existential philosophy maintains that inescapably man is historically situated. This, according to the latter, is the truth to be found in the former. Man can indeed be approached as a relative, finite, historical phenomenon.

But over against historicism, existential philosophy teaches that the knowledge of man attained from his objective history and historicity fails to grasp man in his truly existential character and the actual depth of his humanity. This existential depth and origin of true humanity is not historical but *geschichtlich;* it is not to be approached in an objective and scientific manner, and therefore not to be searched for in the objective, historical time in which man lives and works, thinks and strives. For as a *geschichtlich*, eschatological being, man is not only situated in a given, finite time, but also and in the first place sovereignly situates himself again and again: choosing, deciding, creating, determining, "en-finitizing" himself.

Consequently, according to this anthropology, it is correct to say that man can only choose himself by choosing something, anything; he can only decide for his own sovereign freedom by deciding on something; he can only form himself by giving form to a certain situation; he can only witness to himself and his own *Selbstverständnis* by giving an objective, *vorgreiflich* wit*ness*. Therefore, it follows, according to this position, that there is a legitimate place for a historical, critical science, which is objective, neutral, and universally valid. In this science, the objective, external, historical culture, abstracted from the original living relation from which this culture results and resulted, can be studied. It can be studied as something passed, as the past which will not and cannot ever return.

The Written Document and Its Keys

From what has been said so far it is apparent that existential philosophy definitely allows room for the objective study of a philosophical document, for once such a document is written it is beyond the control of the author. It then belongs to the world of *Seiendes,* and as a historical *datum* is available to everyone. Its content has been totally and unconditionally surrendered to the interpretation of the reader and exegete. The scientific exegete can carry out his exacting task of determining *what* was written, *when* the document first appeared, *what* happened to it in the course of history, and similar questions.

A consistent historicist will remark that "what" was written is "of course" only true and valid for the time in which the document was first published; and, when asked what the message of this writing may be for us, he will answer that whatever it may be, it is at any rate not the same as what it was for the people of that time. Indeed, it is questionable whether we, caught up in our own time as we are, are able to understand "what" this document actually meant to say. Are we able to give an interpretation of this document at all? However, even when the historicist remains faithful to the conviction that a universally valid, scientific interpretation is possible, he will still maintain that if this document is to have any message for us it will have to be first of all purged of everything which we can determine to be time-bound and therefore irrelevant for today. By means of an objective textual analysis and scientific interpretation, the document, as it objectively lies before us, must be "translated" in such a way that it is transformed from a relic of the past into a piece of writing that has "something" to say to the world of today.

The existential philosopher, however, will maintain that this "translation" and interpretation is still not the real hermeneutical task that this document places before us—certainly not if it is a philosophical document. How can it? It is only the preliminary historical-critical treatment. It remains entirely within the sphere of objectivity, within the *vorhanden, vorgreiflich,* not typically human sphere. In fact, he will have to maintain in his philosophical hermeneutics that this pole, which is necessarily contingent, necessarily external, necessarily impersonal, and within which every philosophical document is to be found, threatens to lead us away from the real "meaning" of this document. Its meaning is not, for example, to give expression to the time in which it was first published. Its meaning cannot be grasped, therefore, when we seek to interpret it only in the light of its own time: as an expression of its own time, which throws light on its own time—a typical hermeneutical circle. The real meaning of this document is that the author wanted to give expression to "himself," to his own concrete existence, his own being *en route* to fulfilled selfhood, and his own *Selbstverständnis*. The meaning is that the author witnesses in it and this witness*ing* transcends the wit*ness* and its content. The philosophical reading and interpreting of a philosophical document can take place only when the philosophizing reader or exegete brings about communication between himself and the author. He must, so to speak, conjure the author up from the dead by making the author contemporaneous with the reader. The author's past time is thereby transformed into a unique present time, into the "moment"; while his *Selbstentäuszerung* (self-exteriorization) in the document is read back, as it were, toward the *Er-innerung*, toward the act of his witnessing, toward his *Geschichtlichkeit,* toward his supra- and pre-historical *Selbstverständnis.* Along this way the philosophizing reader and interpreter communicates with the philosophizing Plato or Aristotle.

This existentialistic interpretation of the written document can take place only within the confines of the *Existentialia* and the *Begrifflichkeit* (conceptuality), which is presented to us through the *Existentialia.* The interpretation discloses, reveals to us the *Selbstverständnis* which the author, in his existential humanity, not merely *had* but *was,* and it reveals that he, *en route* to a perfect selfhood, was becoming. The psychological and historical-critical scientific methods of interpretation are the springboard for the philosophical, existentialistic "method." The former is used in order to be transcended by the latter. The written text of the document and its objective interpretation are life behind, and, in a philosophical understanding and an open communication, the exegete enters into a new present with the author and encounters him in a living dialogue. The subject-object relationship, which is constitutive, of the scientific methods, has in this moment been transcended and overcome by a new and totally different one, namely: the relationship of subject to subject, of *Subjektivität* to *Subjektivität.* This relationship, created by the existentialistically philosophizing interpreter, means that the imterpreter gives the author the opportunity, as it were, to reveal himself. The act of giving the author this opportunity to reveal himself, however, is also itself an act of revelation.

Thus, three keys of revelation are operative in the existentialistic interpretation of a philosophical document:

1. The key of the historical-critical, and if you like, the psychological and other scientific interpreters, who make the document, as an impersonal and unchangeable object, understandable, and in this way reveal what the document says.

2. The key of the philosophizing interpreter. He sovereignly makes use of the written document and its objective scientific interpretation in order to translate these back to the act of the writing author, who through this act gives primarily expression to his own *Selbstervständnis*. With the help of the document, which has been handed down from the past, the philosophizing interpreter brings, as it were, the author into the present and gives him the opportunity to reveal "himself."

3. The key of the author, who in a living dialogue made possible by the philosophizing interpreter very relevantly reveals himself in the present, communicates with us, and demands that we listen.

The first two keys serve to make the third possible. The intention of the whole procedure is to get the author to speak, to witness, to reveal his own *Selbstverständnis* and to get the reader to listen attentively to him. The first two keys are in the hands of the reader; the third in the hands of the author himself, who, revived from the dead, is contemporaneous with the reader and speaks to him. The reader becomes his audience who does not interrupt him. Thus the last key opens up the real purpose, the actual "meaning" of the written document.

The Historical-critical Key

According to the claims of existential philosophy it is an *apriori* fact that the existentialistic hermeneutical basic rules and procedures mentioned above are incontestable. The first key is incontestable because it honors science as science, that is, as universally valid, neutral, certain, and trustworthy knowledge. Otto Weber has correctly observed that the quest for certainty is the paramount concern of the historical-critical method in the interpretation of the Bible, and that this method is considered to be the only safe one of this quest. To this observation more could be added. For example: however much existential philosophy may be combating what Jaspers calls the

Wissenschaftsaberglaube (the superstional belief in the sciences), it nevertheless joins its opponent, rationalistic scientism, in cherishing, as a precious heirloom from classical rationalism, the faith in the incontestable validity of the objective sciences in the sphere of the facts and the *data*, the *Vorhandene* and *Vorgreifliche*. Again: along with this scientism, this philosophy maintains that in this sphere the scientific method and its results may be regarded as, and indeed ought to be, universally valid, compelling, neutral, and presuppositionless. Finally: this philosophy teaches that certainty in this sphere can be attained—if indeed it can be attained at all—only by means of scientific research, and that no degree of certainty is attainable which could compete with the degree of certainty attained by science, namely: the degree of probability.

We should not underestimate the important role this first key plays in the hermeneutics of existential philosophy. Its importance, nature, and trustworthiness may be illustrated from Bultmann's conflict with Barth and Weber. In this conflict, Bultmann contends that the faith in the resurrection of Christ on the Easter Sunday after his crucifixion involves nothing less than a *sacrificium intellectus*. When he thinks to have discovered an entirely different conception of the resurrection in the Gospel of John, he is of the opinion that he has found a criterion with which he can discard the credibility of the Gospel of the resurrection as it is expressed in other parts of the New Testament, for example: Paul's preaching in I Corinthians 15. Is this criterion a canon within the canon? Not exactly. According to Bultmann it is rather a scientific proof that the "witness" of the Scriptures is time-bound—a presupposition of the whole historical method. Thus when he by means of the second key gives Paul the opportunity to speak in the "present time," he has already made certain by means of the first key that the preacher Paul does not come on to the pulpit with anything like I Corinthians 15. This passage, this "objective witness," has already been demythologized and when the "contemporary" Paul witnesses he passes this particular passage over in silence. It belongs to the past, doesn't it? Then it ought to stay there.

The Historical-critical Method as Ancilla

Fundamentally, however, the issue here is not that the writings of John are played off against the writings of Paul. Even if it were a fact that these writers were to differ on such a cardinal point as the resurrection of Jesus Christ, that fact could in itself not give us the criterion by which to decide whether Paul or John—or even both—had missed the point. The fact that Bultmann, by using the historical-critical method, has come to choose for John rather than Paul indicates, among other things, that the historical-critical method is itself rooted in a certain world and life view, in certain Western philosophies. Hence, it also indicates the common heritage in classical rationalism that existential philosophy has at this point with neo-rationalism, i.e., positivism. Their common contention that modern man is, and ought to be, no longer receptive to the *mythologoumena* of the ancient world is maintained by existential philosophy not only in the radically relativistic sense that this simply happens to be the case for *our* time, but also in the sense that here modern man is in the right for *all* times. Thus, all the things that Bultmann has classified as *mythologoumena* in the Scriptures were intended, intend, and will intend to serve only as the *Selbstverständnis'* objective media for witnessing to itself, so that they mean something else than what they literally say.

It is clear that the second key, the existential-philosophical one, can be harmoniously used with the first key, the historical-critical one. In fact, the way Bultmann uses the historical-critical key, it must be, and has been, harmonized with the existential-philosophical one. The historical-critical method is *ancilla*, maidservant to existential philosophy and theology. Both in theory and in practice, Bultmann will recognize this method as a universally valid, neutral key of autonomous, scientific rationality only if it does not come in conflict with his use of the second key. In the same way, the use of this existential-philosophical key must serve the use of the third by the author, who reveals his own *Selbstverständnis* in existential sovereignty and power.

Before this last revelation takes place, however, Bultmann has already apriorily applied severe restriction to this sovereign power of the author. There is a very great deal which the author "cannot" reveal and also cannot have "wanted" to reveal, namely: everything that would not make him fit into the existential framework in which man is for all times placed, in Heidegger's philosophy of the *Existentialen*, modified by Bultmann's additions and corrections.

All three keys are therefore existential-philosophically approved keys. The existential philosopher or theologian may think to have adjusted his receiver to the author or speaker and listen to him unbiasedly; he has, in fact, attuned the speaker to his receiver, existential philosophy. Should the speaker not be found on the particular wavelength of the receiver, then he will fail to come through; he may wish to reveal all he likes, but he does not even get the opportunity to say, "He that has ears to hear, let him hear."

The "Dialogue"

Obvious as it may seem, the fact that the hermeneutic of existential philosophy is an existential-philosophical one is all too often ignored. It needs to be emphasized that this hermeneutic has a frame of reference that its adherents cannot allow to be subjected to any serious interrogation. It is presented and evaluated by them as a matter of autonomous rationality, a matter not even to be questioned in a "dialogue." To the contrary, this so-called rational philosophy dominates every dialogue and excommunicates many a person who wishes to communicate with its adherents. The later Heidegger has correctly observed about Jasper's philosophy of *Scheitern* (failure) that the *Scheitern* of philosophy is put beyond discussion. There is no place for it on the agenda. The philosophy of communication allows no room for communication about itself, but it has the prerogative claimed for it to have all communication take place within its own confines and according to its own rules. A typical case of sectarianism. The philosophizing about *Wagnis* (risk), *Scheitern*, communication, dialogue, listening, *Selbstverständnis* and *Selbstvergewisserung*, witness and revelation is withdrawn from every *Wagnis*, dialogue, listening, etc.

However, if we are to have a real philosophical and existential dialogue with the adherents of this philosophy and its hermeneutical rules, then it will have to be a dialogue about this philosophizing and its claim to validity. Without such a confrontation, a real principial philosophical encounter would be impossible. Inescapably we would be imprisoned within the confines of this philosophy and any dialogue would be like a dialogue of slaves in the presence of their master. At most we would be able to modify or perfect some of the basic conceptions of this philosophy.

II.　The Gottesfrage

Up till now I have consciously avoided the typically theological questions of today, which center around the problem of divine revelation, in order to keep the questions and answers dealing with existential anthropology's own peculiar brand of revelation as distinct as possible. In this way it is also easier to localize the sharp differences that Bultmann has with Karl Barth and Otto Weber.

Bultmann, who engages in turn in exegesis, hermeneutics, philosophy, and theology, but whose main concern is the latter, feels that he cannot really theologize without philosophizing. His exegetical and hermeneutical labors bear the mark of this conviction.

For his philosophizing he takes as his starting point the philosophizing of Martin Heidegger in *Sein und Zeit*, and secondarily of Karl Jaspers. He appropriates Heidegger's principial distinction between the *Existenzialia* and the categories, with the result that, in his scientific hermeneutics and exegesis, he regards the historical-critical method as the initial and provisional key for coming to an understanding of the Holy Scriptures, "the man Jesus of Nazareth," and the preaching of the gospel.

Characteristically, however, he will not adopt Heidegger's doctrine of the *Existenzialia*, and therefore also of man's *Selbstverständnis*, except on condition of one important amendment. This amendment is that this *Selbstverständnis* takes place only, and can take place only, in correlation with the *Gottesfrage*, the "God-question" or quest for God. This holds even if man does not realize it. Bultmann will readily admit that it is only from out of divine revelation that one becomes aware of this correlation, but he nevertheless, at the same time, posits that outside this correlation human *Selbstverständnis* is structurally impossible.

Now it is this universal *Gottesfrage* and this *Selbstverständnis* common to all men that turns out to be the target of God's revelation of himself in Jesus Christ. Divine revelation can only be an answer to this question, even though the answer corrects the question. Should it not be an answer to this question, it would miss its target, it would not be *vernehmbar*, audible, for man. When Barth and the Barthian theologians claim that true human *Selbstverständnis* is possible only as a result of the *Vernehmen* of God's Word, then Bultmann responds that the problem is precisely how this *Vernehmen*, this hearing, is possible if it is not picked up by man in his own *Selbstverständnis*. How can man understand this revelation except as an answer to his own *Gottesfrage*? Even though this understanding of revelation is in itself nothing more than a negative theology, a quest for God, a Gottesfrage, still it is indispensable for understanding God's revelation in Christ Jesus.

Thus, on the one hand, the nature of man's *Selbstverständnis* is for Bultmann the same as for Heidegger. It is existential, characterized as something typically human, in which the concern of man's own concrete existence is concern for itself. However, on the other hand, the content of this *Selbstverständnis* has been drastically modified by Bultmann. In Bultmann's thinking it has a pronounced Lutheran twist to it. The *Gottesfrage* is the quest for that God who liberates us from ourselves because he liberates us from all work-righteousness and self-boasting. It is the quest for the gracious, forgiving, absolving God, who liberates us from this burden time and again in the preaching of the Gospel. God solves our *Gottesfrage* by absolving us from our past. In this way he makes us free for the future, for our neighbor and for self-surrender. Divine revelation gives no intellectual solutions but anthropological "absolutions." Jesus Christ, who, once in the past, was present, though hidden; who did not shrink back from his *Hingabe*, his submission to the way of the cross; and who, from out of the past, is objectively, in black and white, presented to us in the Holy Scriptures simply as Jesus—this Jesus is time and again, in the preaching *hic et nunc*, in the *aktuelle* Word of God, made contemporaneous with us as the *Christus praesens*. He did not reconcile on the cross through satisfaction, but reconciled through submission to the cross. In the same way the Christian, crucified with Christ, reconciles through submission to the future of *Schicksal*, fate, and through encountering his neighbor, to whom he also submits himself. Christ's resurrection is the resurrection through the preaching, the *kerygma* in which he is continually made contemporaneous with us. It is not the propositions and statements of the sermon that "liberate" us; they do not even have any revelatory value. It is rather the actuality of the happening of preaching that liberates us from ourselves and from our vain attempts to work out our own righteousness and thus to boast about ourselves. The preaching, as a happening, kerygmatically liberates us for the *Hingabe* to *Schicksal* and neighbor, so that we no longer look back to our past and past self-righteousness in order to add these up as the established worth of our own person.

The Content of Revelation

In Bultmann's theological hermeneutics the content of revelation is therefore so meagre that with the utmost of consistency he can say that outside of all contents of revelation we already know from our own existential *Gottesfrage* what revelation is and can be. Thus revelation is not any revelation-content. It is only God's answer to our *Gottsfrage*. How can it be anything else? The answer must be contingent, therefore, upon this *Gottesfrage*. The result is that the connection of this revelation in and with Jesus of Nazareth, the

Bible, and preaching is completely arbitrary. The revelation of Jesus of Nazareth consisted only of *the fact that* he revealed that revelation takes place in him. Nothing more, nothing else.

The content of revelation, however, must be entirely attuned to our *Gottesfrage*. Thus the content is that through which God, by the indirect means of letting Bible texts become preaching texts and having sermons make Christ contemporaneous with us, gives us an answer to our *Gottesfrage;* this redeems us from the pride of self-righteousness, which is our sinful past; notwithstanding which reconciles himself with us; and frees us for a life of loving self-surrender. This event is kerygmatically existential and existentially kerygmatic.

At the same time, however, the content of revelation is something quite different from the statements we use to describe it. It is eschatological. By this Bultmann means that it transcends the pole of the objective, the given to which also all our statements belong. The content is relevant to us only insofar as we too existentially transcend the "world" of the *Gegenständliche* and insofar as we, being in the "world," are not of the "world." It corresponds with our existential *Entweltlichung* (dis-worlding [a German neo-logism]) in which we have as though not having. As historical beings we have, as *geschichtliche* beings we transcend this having, and, therefore, as *geschichtliche*-historical beings we have as though not having. As-though-not-having is possible only when there is something, anything that we have; and this having is only anthropologically acceptable when we transcend it as not-having. Divine revelation does not in any way alter this basic structure of our humanity. On the contrary, its meaning is precisely that it liberates us from the delusion that we have so much power over ourselves as *geschichtliche*-historical beings that we can resist the temptations of the "world," the despair that results from the fact that we continually do fall into the sin of having as "havers," and again the delusion that we can redeem ourselves from the temptation, and the fall into it, in our own strength. The task, place, and meaning of divine revelation is to liberate us from this delusion and despair, and at the same time to redeem us from the fall into the sin of having as "havers." Nothing more, nothing else.

In agreement with Ernst Käsemann, a disciple of Bultmann, I am of the opinion that Bultmann cannot maintain the contention that divine revelation contains no propositional truth, and I join Käsemann in the question: What would preaching, confession, and even hermeneutics be without propositional truth?[2]

However, we must dig a little deeper. The unbearable, dialectical tension between existential philosophizing and the *philosophoumena* of the *Existenzanalytik* lies at the root of Bultmann's conception of the content of revelation, with the result that he gives precedence to the *fides qua creditur* over the *fides quae creditur*.[3] He evidently ignores the fact that the existence about which he philosophizes does not necessarily warrant the existence of his philosophizing, and that his philosophizing about existence exists only by the grace of his faith in the *Existenz-Analytik*, which is grounded in autonomous Reason. Within the framework of this philosophy there is no room for independent propositions, but the framework itself stands or falls with the propositions of the *Existenz-Analytik* and the correlative propositions of the historical-critical science, however much the latter may be deprecated.

As soon as Bultmann admits that theology is impossible without the recognition that preaching, confession, and even hermeneutics cannot do without propositional truths, then his *whole theology* not only collapses, but his *philosophy* and conception of human *Selbstverständnis* as well. Because he has sought a legitimate place for theology and faith and for divine revelation and the Word of God in terms of this philosophy and within the confines of this philosophy, Bultmann cannot recognize that preaching, confession, and biblical hermeneutics are nonentities without propositional truths.

Bultmann's view of concrete human existence, in its affinity with and close adherence to Heidegger's philosophy, prevents him from ever making room for theological propositional truths which play a valid and indispensable role in the existential encounter between God's kerygmatic revelation and the existential man with his *Gottesfrage*. Only if he breaks with this philosophy, its anthropology and theory of reality, will a principial change of his theology and his conception of the content of revelation be possible. Only if he breaks with this system of thought will the way be open for a radical change in his view of the "man Jesus of Nazareth," the Bible, and the preaching of the gospel.

Christian Philosophy: The Liberating Solution

In conclusion I will make two remarks.

1. Existential philosophers and theologians all teach that—to use the words of Monseigneur Beckers, a popular Dutch bishop—not "solution" (*oplossing*) but "liberation" (*verlossing*) is to be the central concern of reflection on human existence. Solutions belong to scientific analyses, but liberation is the proper response to our

existential problems. Thus, the theologians who show affinity to existential philosophy will add that the concern of church, preaching, Bible, and Jesus Christ is not to solve but to liberate, to redeem. I am of the opinion that this polarization is much too simplistic. A scientific solution to a problem can clear the way to a practical liberation from deeply human problems and burdens. This polarization, as it is used by them, is itself already such a distinct solution aiming at anthropological liberation. This distinction that is made between solution and liberation functions no less than as a liberating solution and a problem-solving liberation. Can faith, for that matter, do without distinguishing? The distinguishing character of faith cannot take place without the analytical function of thought, even though it is certainly not exhausted by it. If I cannot analytically distinguish Jesus Christ from Pontius Pilate, how can I in faith single him out as my Redeemer and the Redeemer of the world? It is crystal clear to me that the Christian faith is the faith that makes the fundamental distinction that Jesus Christ and he alone is the Saviour, who gathers not only others but also me into the assembly of the elect. That this is more than a merely logical distinction is obvious. The reduction of the distinguishing character of faith to merely logical distinguishing can certainly be called the distinctive mark of a false orthodoxy, a false confessionalism, and a false traditionalism. However, such a reduction should not conduce us into the wrong reaction of banning from faith its distinguishing character. Such a reaction still presupposes, in company with dead orthodoxy, that all distinguishing is nothing more than a purely mental, logical activity. The distinction between "believing" and "believing in" can be of help at this point. For example, he who believes *that* God exists does not yet believe *in* God, but he who believes *in* God must obviously believe that he exists. Do we not find this distinction in Hebrews 11:6? There it is written: "For he that comes to God must believe that he is [first instance], and that he is the rewarder of them that seek after him [second instance]."

2. In the conclusion of his dissertation, *Geloof en Openbaring in de Nieuweve Duitsche Theologie* (1932), G. C. Berkouwer presented as a kind of indirect proof for the truth of the Reformed confessions concerning the infallible authority of Scripture, by pointing out the endlessness of the theological problems about faith and revelation in the newer theologies up to the early nineteen thirties. I doubt whether such a proof is valid or convincing. Taking this into account, I shall not give in to the temptation to use as an indirect

proof for the need of a Christian philosophy the basic weakness from which Bultmann's theological hermeneutics suffers. It is, undeniably, the inevitable result of his adherence to a modified existential philosophical anthropology and theory of reality, which is the latest fashion in which the humanistic dialectic of nature and freedom has dressed itself. Nevertheless, I feel compelled to say that Bultmann's theological hermeneutics is but another proof of the fact that theology continually seems to be bound to philosophical presuppositions—at any rate the way theology has been practiced in our Western culture. One cannot therefore grasp in depth the theological views and practices of someone like Bultmann without recognizing these philosophical presuppositions and dealing with them on a philosophical level. The *need* for a Christian philosophy is not proved by this; it has a more integral, Christian root. However, for those who are already convinced of this need for a Christian philosophy and the call to philosophize Christianly, the *desirability* of such a philosophy and way of philosophizing is, I am sure, demonstrated here. For theology and theologizing such Christian philosophizing holds the promise of liberating solutions from out of the redemption in Jesus Christ.

(*Translated by Gerben Groenewoud*)

Paul K. Jewett

X. CONCERNING CHRIST, CHRISTIANS, AND JEWS

The Jewish-Christian polemic is written large on the pages of the New Testament. It was the Jews who stirred up opposition to the apostles in Pisidian Antioch (Acts 13:45, 50), in Iconium (Acts 14:2), and in Lystra (Acts 14:19). In Thessalonica, Jewish agitation created a veritable uproar with the result that Paul and Silas were secreted off by night to Berea (Acts 17:5-10). But even there they could not escape; pursued by hostile Jews from Thessalonica, Paul was hastily sent on his way to Athens. The experience evidently left its mark, for in a subsequent letter to his Thessalonian converts he bitterly castigated the unbelieving Jews as those "who both killed the Lord Jesus and their own prophets, and have persecuted us; and they please not God and are contrary to all men, forbidding us to speak to the Gentiles that they might be saved, to fill up their sins alway. For wrath is come upon them to the uttermost" (I Thess. 2:15-16). Paul was not alone in expressing such deep feeling. Toward the end of the Christian era, John, the "apostle of love," darkly alludes to those "who call themselves Jews" but are really a "synagogue of Satan" (Rev. 2:9; 3:9).

Christian history, unfortunately, has exacerbated this polemic by returning the hatred which *some* Jews evidenced for Jesus in the first century, with an even greater hatred for *all* Jews in the last nineteen centuries. The great heaviness and continual sorrow of heart that Paul felt, when he thought of his brethren, his kinsmen according to the flesh (Rom. 9:1-3), seems to have vanished from Christian consciousness. Gone is the remembrance of the ameliorating circumstances which tempered the judgment of Peter, the great apostle to the circumcision, when he referred to Jewish involvement in the crucifixion. Though Peter accused his fellow countrymen of having killed the "prince of life," he hastily added that they had done it, indeed, through ignorance. Therefore, if they would repent and be converted, their sins would be blotted out and they would receive seasons of refreshing from the Lord (Acts 3:17f.). But through the long centuries of Christian history, DEICIDE, that capital crime in capital letters has generally been laid at the feet of the Jews exclusively, as though they had all the guilt and Christians all the grace stemming from the death of Jesus.

Anti-Semitism, which we associate in our day with the Arab cause, is by no means the peculiar property of Islam.[1] Though Arab fanatics have threatened clamorously to drive Israel into the sea, it was in "Christian" Germany that this "final" solution to the Jewish problem was not simply threatened, but ruthlessly carried out. The Germans didn't *talk* about it, they *did* it. Six million Jews were annihilated.

> The Chronicler of anti-Semitism is beset at every turn with the problem of superlatives. Long before reaching the contemporary scene, he has exhausted his supply and has been forced to re-enlist many for double duty, certainly at the risk of straining the reliance of his reader. The problem is not only verbal but real. From the first literary strictures against Judaism in ancient and early Christian times to almost any major manifestation of anti-Jewish animus in a later epoch, a crescendo in violence has ununfolded. The progression from early riots to the Crusades, to the Black Death, to Chmielnicki, to Czarist pogroms, to World War I has comprised an ascent in horrors, each grade of which promised to be the upper limit but which unfailingly paled before what followed.

> With the coming of Hitler the problem is infinitely aggravated, for suddenly events no longer resemble those of the past and the usual comparisons no longer convey the new realities.[2]

Of course Nazi anti-Semitism was not Christian in its essence; in fact it was anti-Christian. Next to the Jews, there was no one Hitler hated more than the Christians. And what resistance the Nazi did encounter, was largely inspired by the church. But these palliating reminders of Christian suffering and heroism can hardly alleviate the reproaches which the Christian conscience must feel when it views Auschwitz in the light of all the centuries of Christian persecution of the Jews.

As I turned to Van Til's book about the Jews, there was a measure of disappointment that this question of Christianity and anti-Semitism was not touched upon. True, the book *Christ and the Jews* is in a series dealing with philosophy and theology, not ethics. And as the title indicates it is concerned with *Christ* and the Jews, not *Christians* and the Jews. But theology and morality are related as root to flower. Theology is concerned with right thoughts about God and men which move one to right acts before God toward one's fellow-men. And though we may insist that the crux of the "Jewish question" is what the Jews think about Christ, still it is impossible to talk about "Christ and the Jews" in an adequate fashion without talking about *Christians* and the Jews, for all people, including Jews, learn about Christ from Christians whose lives are epistles known and read of all men. I must hasten to say, there is no anti-Semitism in Van Til's study and those who have known him as a teacher and a man of God could never doubt where he stands on these matters. It is just that it seems difficult to see how in 1969 a book on the broad theme of Christ and the Jews could be written from a Christian perspective with no mention of these problems.

Van Til's first chapter is on Philo Judaeus. We generally think of Philo as the father of the allegorical method, with all that it has contributed to the misunderstanding of Scripture and the gospel. Van Til has placed the error of Philonic hermeneutics on the larger canvas of philosophic speculation, by observing that Philo reduced Old Testament revelation to virtual identity with the non-historical thought of Greek philosophy and the Eastern mystery religions.[3] This, it seems to me, is indeed the crux of the matter. By turning the Torch "into a great allegory," Philo sought to alleviate the offense of historical contingency. But so to alleviate the offense of historicity, which theoretical reason cannot tolerate, is to redefine biblical faith in terms of philosophy; and philosophy always finds salvation in the metaphysical, never in the historical. In other words, when the "scandal of particularity" is removed, biblical faith is unnecessary. This scandal, of course, came to its apogee in Jesus Christ. Philo's reading of the Old Testament made it impossible that Jewish Scripture should have its fulfillment in Jesus.

There is one passage in Van Til's treatment of Philo which I am not sure I understand. Speaking of the doctrine of the unknowability of God, "Philo asserts that reason and revelation are in full harmony on this point," says Van Til. He then continues,

> In contradistinction from Philo we would maintain that "reason" and revelation stand in complete opposition to this. "Reason" as understood by Greek philosophy assumes, even if it does not verbally teach, the utter unknowability of God. The "reason" of the Greeks is the reason of apostate man. And apostate man has every reason for teaching the unnamability of God. If God is unnamable then he cannot name anything in the world. Only if God is unknowable can man think of his own knowledge as autonomous.

But God, who at the beginning named all things that he had
created, would not allow his name to be blotted out by the creature who refused to be named by God. He sent his Son, the full
expression of his substance, to speak out his name among sinful
men. This son allowed his name to be blotted out on the cross
in order to rename a people in his own name. He sent his servant
Moses to speak forth his name for him. Having appeared in
grace to Moses, he gave his law to be a teacher of his name.[4]

I am not sure whether "unnamable" is intended to be synonomous
with "unknowable" in this passage or not. Is the thread of the argument this: Reason (i.e., sinful man using his reasoning powers) denies
that God has made himself known by revelation, because apostate
man, having refused to accept this revelation, has no other recourse
but to trust his own reason? If he were to submit to revelation, he
would have to abandon his trust in his own reason and humbly receive the truth which God has revealed? If this is the meaning, how
does the injection of the "name" theme illumine such a thought?

Leaving Philo, Van Til begins Chapter II with a discussion of
Buber's attempt to make a radical distinction between Jesus and
Paul. Whereas Jesus considered the law as capable of fulfillment
(in the Sermon on the Mount), Paul argues it cannot be, according
to Buber. In fact, says Buber, Paul thought of man as unavoidably
frustrated in his attempt to obey the law, and all this is tied up in
the apostle's thinking, with the mystery of divine predestination.
"When I contemplate this God, I no longer recognize the God of
Jesus nor his world in this world of Paul's."[5] Assuming "that the
resurrection of an individual person does not belong to the realm of
ideas of the Jewish world," Buber dismisses the whole Christology
of Paul as based on an untenable apriori. In discussing these points,
Van Til has indeed probed the real issue between Buber and Christian thinkers.

As we all know, however, Buber's *I and Thou* is one of the most
influential books written, so far as contemporary theology is concerned. For this reason one could wish that Van Til had pursued this
aspect of Buber's thinking in more depth. Van Til apparently believes there is merit of a sort in the I - Thou distinction which Buber
makes: "Believers in Christ," he tells us, "should claim that on the
Christian I - Thou scheme is it possible to find meaning in anything
that confronts man."[6] Just what is a "Christian I - Thou scheme"
in Van Til's thinking? A Christian use of I - thou personalistic
thought has been attempted by many thinkers (see E. Brunner's
Divine Human Encounter) whose thought Van Til has consistently

opposed. It would be enlightening to see how he manages these different questions for himself. The desire for a further word is heightened when Van Til concludes, "We cannot think that with such a philosophy Buber, any more than other I - Thou philosophers or any more than other existentialists, has escaped the *Icheinsamkeit* that they rightly found in Idealism."[7] If these thinkers "rightly" found the Achilles' heel in Idealism, where did they go wrong in countering philosophic *Icheinsamkeit* with this affirmation, no *I* without a *thou*?

As Van Til's study of Christ and the Jews progresses, I found it increasingly difficult to interact with the argument, principially because there is little argument with which to interact. Chapter III, for example, on the *Torah*, is largely made up of quotations from another source. Here, in a space of fourteen pages, R. Travers Herford's *Talmud and Apocrypha* is quoted fifty-five times, some of the quotes making up lengthy paragraphs. Van Til's main objective seems to be to show how the Jews, by developing the principle of the Unwritten Torah, lost the Torah as a "once for all, finished revelation of God to man," and reduced it to a "form that would contain any content that respectable men might care to put into it."[8] This, he observes, is the very point on which Jesus clashed with the Pharisees, and the Reformers with the Roman Catholic Church.

Here again the point is well taken; I could only wish that Van Til might have said more about the implications of history for the Christian concept of revelation. Do Christians really believe that the Torah was a "once for all, finished revelation of God to man"? Even if the term Torah be taken in the broad connotation of the whole Old Testament, do we not have to say that revelation is unfinished? As redemptive history has unfolded, the Old Testament has been "finished" by the addition of the New Testament. And whereas it is true that Scripture does not share its revelatory character with tradition, in some sense the Holy Spirit has been actively guiding the church into the truth, bearing witness in and with the Scripture, throughout the centuries of Christian history.

These are some of the provocative questions which a reading of Van Til's study of the Jewish question has aroused in my mind. The prospect of his speaking to them in a *Festschrift* has encouraged me to ask them. We live in a day when the conservative Christian is troubled, both by the increase of anti-Semitism on the one hand and an effort to neutralize it, on the other, with a Jewish - Christian dialogue that soft-steps the basic question which Jesus put to his disciples:

"Whom say ye that I am?" Since God has given Cornelius Van Til to be a teacher and "father in Israel," to covet from him a further word of wisdom and help in these crucial matters is but to express the honor which is due him and the debt which we owe him.

Response by C. Van Til

Dear Dr. Jewett,

I think I can best respond to your generous contribution by trying to answer directly the questions you pose with respect to my pamphlet, *Christ and the Jews*.

I had one main purpose in mind in writing it, namely, to point out that Judaism, the modern child of Pharisaism, makes the religious, ethical consciousness of man the source and standard of truth and morality. Consequently, the God of the Bible is first bound and gagged and then reduced metaphysically to the abstract principle of unity of Greek philosophy.

(1) I did not write about anti-Semitism. In addition to it being very far afield of my purpose, I know I am not qualified to write on it.

(2) My quotations from *Talmud and Apocrypha* by Herford are extensive, perhaps, as you say, far too extensive. My only excuse, however, is that I regard his discussion of the Jewish commitment to the *Unwritten Torah* of first-order of importance for an understanding of both ancient and modern Jewish philosophy. Just as an understanding of the Roman Catholic view of the church as the continuation of the incarnation helps us to understand how Catholic theology may handle Scripture in, what appears to us, such a cavalier way, so also the notion of the *Unwritten Torah* helps us to understand how Judaism may handle the Old Testament the way it does.

(3) My mention of a Christian *I - thou scheme* was more of an "aside" than a point of major importance. However, I think it does deserve spelling out. Christians want an *I - thou scheme*, but not one tied to the pure *inwardness* of modern phenomenology. I view the modern notion of inwardness as a counterfeit of the Old and New Testament revelation of God's covenant, especially that with Abraham. Within this covenant there is true dialogue between God and man, for only upon the basis of it does God truly speak for himself. On the modern view the words which man wishes to hear are put in

God's mouth. In revelation God names, i.e., identifies, himself to the patriarchs and on the basis of this self-identification stipulates the conditions of this covenant.

Throughout the history of philosophy man has carried on a monologue with himself. Attempts have been made at isolating the "objective" element of this dialogue which may stand about the flux of human opinion, thereby aiding man in breaking out of the monotony of speaking to himself. Appeals were directed toward Moses, the Ideals of Reason, the Church, the Categorical Imperative, *et al.* But in all these searches for help "from the outside" man knew that the very existence of this help somehow depended on man the constructor. The price that one pays for rejecting the biblical idea of covenant is eternal silence, or, at best, the sound of one's own voice.

(4) The questions you raise regarding the continuing nature of revelation were not treated in detail, for I have done so elsewhere. In this instance I might point out the three places where I have discussed the nature of revelation in depth: in the class syllabi *Introduction to Systematic Theology*; and *The Doctrine of Scripture* and in *A Christian Theory of Knowledge.* I want to say most briefly at this point that the question of continuing revelation since the time of the apostles through the church falls away when one becomes impressed with the "humanity" of theologizing. In this connection Prof. Dooyeweerd's letter is significant. It is very difficult to construct a theory regarding the Holy Spirit's activity in our theologizing, when the New Testament is almost totally silent on it.

(5) I found the name-motif helpful, for when one thinks of the Old Testament in this respect, one remembers that in naming something, the name reveals something about the thing named. Only God may name himself and in naming himself God *reveals* himself. In addition, in swearing God only swears an oath by his own name, for there is none higher. God could only swear by his own self-revelation. The notion, therefore, of the "Name" of God is, it seems to me, pregnant with apologetic implications.

I am so glad to have had this opportunity to discuss my booklet on Jewish thought with you, for, sad to say, interest in Jewish theology and apologetics is not very large in evangelical circles.

—C.V.T.

Richard B. Gaffin, Jr.

XI. GEERHARDUS VOS AND THE
INTERPRETATION OF PAUL

I. Introduction

On one of the walls in Dr. Van Til's office is an enlarged photograph of Geerhardus Vos. This is an indication of an esteem and admiration which is not purely academic in character, but includes a personal element dating from his student days at Princeton Seminary. On more than one occasion, I have heard him express deep appreciation for Vos both as a scholar and as a man. One of his most cherished memories is the solemn privilege he had in August of 1949 of conducting the funeral of his teacher and friend. The following contribution is a reflection, in the hermeneutically charged atmosphere of contemporary theology, upon an important but so far ignored aspect of the work of this man, who may rightly be called the father of Reformed biblical theology and who has so decisively influenced the one to whom this volume is presented.

Vos's *Pauline Eschatology* is of abiding value not only because it provides a rich and penetrating analysis of the basic elements in the apostle's teaching but also because throughout the work are found a variety of statements which are particularly instructive concerning the *way* in which he approaches Paul. This, what one may call the methodological or hermeneutical significance of the book, appears so far to have been entirely overlooked. It is that aspect, however, to which I will here give careful attention.

II. Paul, the Theologian

Vos's approach to Paul is determined by the fact that he has found in the apostle one who "may justly be called the father of Christian eschatology."[1] Even more striking is his observation that in Paul one is confronted with "the genius of the greatest constructive mind ever at work on the data of Christianity."[2] Statements echoing a similar tone can be multiplied. "No doubt Paul's mind had by nature a certain systematic bent, which made him pursue with great resoluteness the consequences of given premises."[3] His was "a mind highly doctrinal and synthetic."[4] Accordingly, one must think in terms of "the Apostle's theological system,"[5] "the Pauline system of truth," "the Apostle's construction of Christian truth."[6] His "energetic eschatological thinking tended toward consolidation in an orb of compact theological structure."[7] The facile one-sidedness of which all too many of his interpreters have been guilty, has resulted in part "because Paul's mind as a theological thinker was far more exacting than theirs. . . ."[8]

When these statements are read together, the impression they make is unmistakable. In particular, two factors stand out. (1) They reflect a deep appreciation of the distinctiveness and individuality of Paul, specifically in his capacity as a *thinker*. The nature of Paul's mind, it will be observed, is reflected upon in some detail. (2) They evince a definite sense of continuity between the apostle and his interpreter. Both have a common interest: the "data of Christianity." Christian eschatological reflection has Paul as its initiator, its "father." Moreover, the nature of this continuity, its specifically "theological" character, is indicated in a variety of ways. In short, it is not going too far to say that Vos approaches the apostle as one with whom he is involved in a common theological enterprise. It should be noted that this is done without any sense of incompatibility with a conviction of the unity and divine origin and authority of Scripture.

III. Vos and Kuyper

The interests of this discussion may be advanced by setting directly over against this sketch of Vos's approach Abraham Kuyper's rejection of the expression "biblical theology."[9] This is especially in order because the latter's work on theological encyclopaedia has never really been supplanted. It has had a determinative role, second to none, in shaping Reformed theological method and still continues to exert a perhaps indirect but nonetheless definite influence.

At a first glance it may appear that Kuyper's objections are primarily historical in character, based upon reaction to rationalistic theology which masqueraded its thinly veiled attacks on the authority of Scripture under the slogan, "biblical theology." This factor indeed plays an important part,[10] but upon closer examination his rejection is seen to have a much deeper basis. It is the latter aspect which especially concerns us now.

Nothing less than the way in which Kuyper understands Scripture as the *principium theologiae* prohibits his use of the expression "biblical theology." Scripture itself is not theology but underlies it.[11] One must not speak of the biblical writers as theologians.[12] This is so because theology is unthinkable apart from previously formed dogmas, and dogma is a product of the life of the (institutional) church.[13] Thus stress is placed exclusively upon the sharp distinction, the discontinuity in principle, which exists between Scripture and the biblical writers, on the one hand, and the dogmas and theologians of the church, on the other. The Bible itself contains no dogmas but rather the "material" out of which the church "constructs" dogma.[14] The biblical revelation is given in the "stylized, symbolic-aesthetic language of the East"; it is only when the "Western mind" with its penchant for "dialectical clarity" goes to work on it (the biblical material) that theology comes into being.[15]

It is essential to see, then, that in terms of the sequence—Scripture, church, dogma, dogmatics, (theology)[16]—and in view of the manner in which the stress upon discontinuity is distributed, Kuyper rejects biblical theology not only in name but in *concept*. To be sure, he does go on to approve the material interest of biblical theology, namely, its concern with the historical character of the Bible, laments the shortcomings of the *loca probantia* method of dogmatics in this respect and looks for real progress in biblical understanding to result from a study of the *historia revelationis*.[17]

Even from these brief sketches one has little difficulty in recognizing that there exists between Vos and Kuyper a decided difference in emphasis and approach. In fact, the stress of the one is precisely the opposite of the other. (1) Kuyper's construction is characterized by what is perhaps best described as a "levelling" treatment of the biblical authors. At the level of *encyclopaedia* no attempt is made to take into account their respective differences. Indeed, it is fair to say that there is at least an implicit tendency in the opposite direction.[18] Consequently, in marked contrast to Vos, who thinks in terms of the "systematic bent" and the "highly doctrinal and synthetic" quality of Paul's mind,[19] for Kuyper, the apostle, along with the other biblical writers, speaks the "stylized, symbolic-aesthetic language of the East."[20] (2) Again in pointed contrast to Vos, Kuyper stresses exclusively the *discontinuity* between the biblical writers and the theological activity of subsequent Christian generations. Accordingly, Vos's description of Paul as a specifically "theological" thinker and his repeated references to the apostle's "theological system" are modes of expression which are forbidden to Kuyper *in principle*.

It is clear that we are confronted here with two points of view which at least at key points are mutually exclusive. Hence the question naturally arises which, if either, is correct. It may be the case that Kuyper's position represents what has been the characteristically Reformed attitude and still continues to determine thinking, particularly concerning the relationship between the interpretation of Paul and dogmatic formulation. Nevertheless there is a great variety of considerations which point to Vos's approach as the only proper way of dealing with Paul as a biblical writer, that is, as an instrument of revelation. It is to a consideration of the factors which we now turn. In so doing I will have to limit myself for the most part to initiating and sketching lines of argument without fully expanding them. Many related questions, in themselves important, must be by-passed completely.

IV. Scripture as History of Revelation

Biblical revelation has a *historical* interest. The distinguishing character of Scripture is that it is a record of the history of revelation of which its production itself is a part. It is fair to say that an answer to the methodological question which has just been raised is given with this fundamental recognition, especially as certain of its ramifications are developed.

Analysis of the history of special revelation, an analysis which—as noted above—Kuyper himself welcomed, has made it increasingly clear that the phenomena of revelation is a differentiated one. Revelation comes as acts or as words. Or to formulate differently, God discloses himself both in redemption and revelation, in what he does as well as what he says. Moreover, the organic relationship between these two facets has also become more and more evident. Revelation never stands by itself. It is always concerned either explicitly or implicitly with redemptive accomplishment. God's speech is invariably related to his actions. It is not going too far to say that redemption is the *raison d'etre* of revelation.[21] An unbiblical (one could say, quasi-gnostic) notion of revelation inevitably results, when one considers it of and by itself or as providing general truths, self-evident in and of themselves.[22] This means, then, that the character of revelation is such that it is either authentication and description or explanation and interpretation of God's redemptive action. Usually both these aspects can be found in a given biblical writer or instrument of revelation, although in each instance one will be more prominent than the other.[23]

So far as the writings and preaching of Paul are concerned, there can be no doubt which of these aspects is more characteristic. His almost exclusive concern is in expounding, explicating, interpreting, "exegeting" the history of redemption as it has reached its climax in the death and resurrection of Christ. In other words, the apostle's place in the history of revelation, his functioning as an instrument of revelation is conditioned by and is exponential of a specific redemptive-historical context. This is a perspective of fundamental importance for the understanding and study of Paul. Only as it is appreciated together with its implications does the real significance of his revelatory functions become apparent.

V. Paul, the Interpreter

One of these implications especially concerns us at this point. From the perspective of the history of redemption—for the believer there is no perspective more basic—believers today are in the same situation as was Paul.[24] Together with him they look back upon the climactic events of Christ's death, resurrection, and ascension, while together with him they "wait for his Son from heaven" (I Thess. 1:10), the one event in that history which is still outstanding. It is the same tension between "already" and "not yet" which marked Paul's experience that characterizes the life of the believer at present.

Thus it is clear that there is continuity between Paul and his interpreters. Specifically, they are related in terms of a common redemptive-historical index. Moreover, when the correlation between redemptive act and revelatory word is kept in view, that is, the focus of Scripture upon the history of redemption, then the pointedly *theological* nature of this continuity is also apparent. This is so on the assumption that all theological endeavor must be founded upon the text, that as a historical discipline, biblical exegesis is likewise theologically normative. For if the characteristic interest of Paul is interpreting the history of redemption, then the interpretation of Paul necessarily has the same interest, and as—it may be underscored again—it is carried out in a common redemptive-historical setting. Theology, whatever its scope may be and whatever final shape it should take, can have no more basic and distinguishing interest than with Paul, and in his footsteps, to explain and interpret, together with its resolutions, the redemptive-historical tension which characterizes the believer's existence, to expound and elucidate "the mystery which has been kept secret for long ages past, but now is manifested . . ." (Rom. 16:25f.). In a word, the concept of theology is redemptive-historically conditioned. The essence of theology is interpretation of the history of redemption. Consequently, it is not only possible but necessary to speak of a theological continuity between Paul and his interpreters.

With more explicit reference to the role of the interpreter, the point may be put in this way: Generally when one speaks of biblical theology he has in view a survey of the progression of the redemptive-revelatory activity of God in history, which the student of Scripture carries out from a basically (i.e., redemptive-historically) different situation. This, most properly, is a description of Old Testament biblical theology. To be sure, this element of concern with the progress of revelation is not lacking in New Testament biblical theology. The latter, however, has, as a distinguishing characteristic, the fact that, in the manner noted above, the exegete comes to see himself, despite every cultural and temporal dissimilarity, as standing in principle (i.e., in terms of the history of redemption) in the same situation as the writers of the New Testament and, therefore, as involved with Paul (and the other letter writers) in a *common interpretative enterprise.*[25]

Key aspects of the line of thought being developed here may be put somewhat differently by simply observing that Paul's function in the economy of revelation cannot be abstracted or divorced from his office and functioning as ἀπόστολος. In other words, his activity as an instrument of revelation is qualified *ecclesiastically.* This, in turn, means that the inspired, infallible revelation which he gives is at the same time the authoritative teaching and opinion (dogma) of the church, and that, as various dogmas which he teaches display obvious relationships to each other, one may speak of his *theology.*

The point expressed in this last statement needs especially to be emphasized. In the preceding paragraphs certain methodological considerations have been introduced. At least some of these have relevance for the study of the entire New Testament, particularly the epistles. My present concern, however, is to stress their applicability for Pauline studies. They provide the perspective out of which one is to view his writings with their distinctive traits. Specifically, this means that it is in terms of the notions of common redemptive-historical interest and common redemptive-historical situation that one has to deal with the pronouncedly didactic, the pervasively doctrinal nature of the apostle's teaching. That his epistles have this reasoned character hardly needs to be argued, particularly where Reformed scholarship is concerned.[26] But an awareness of the redemptive-historical factors involved is necessary to appreciate the deeper significance of this doctrinal quality and systematic interest. This awareness provides the warrant for speaking of Pauline theology in the proper sense of the word. At least with respect to Paul, then, it is in order to say that the *principium theologiae,* Scripture, itself contains theology or, perhaps better, that the nature of the continuity between our theology and its *principium* (the Bible) is at points distinctly *theological*. Along the lines indicated, Kuyper's sequence is at least subject to supplementation. Recognition of the discontinuity between the New Testament and its subsequent interpretation in the church must always be balanced by a recognition of the (ecclesiastical-theological, redemptive-historical) continuity between them.[27]

VI. Implications

The burden of the foregoing discussion has been to vindicate and develop the approach to Paul adopted by Geerhardus Vos. Hence stress has been placed upon the necessity (1) that Paul's interpreters deal with him as they stand with him in the same redemptive-historical context and so share a common interpretative interest, and (2) that in the light of these factors they do justice to his doctrinal interest, his distinctiveness as a thinker. In a word, the combination of motives involved in this stress upon continuity may be expressed by saying that Paul is to be viewed as a *theologian*. From this fundamental point of departure follow several conclusions which are essential to a comprehensive understanding of the apostle's teaching.

(1) To approach Paul as theologian means that no encyclopaedic structure or set of distinctions may be employed which makes the situation in which he developed the teaching of his epistles incommensurable in principle with the *dogmengeschichtlich* contexts in which the later church has hammered out her doctrines. In terms of the history of redemption, to the extent, for instance, that Paul's soteriological teaching discloses a structure it may be contrasted and compared directly with the structure of Reformed soteriology. In other words, to state what appear to be the broader methodological implications, biblical theology and systematic theology may not be arbitrarily and artificially separated. The proper interest of the former is revelation as a *historical process*. Inevitably, then, it draws attention to the distinguishing characteristics and peculiarities of the respective biblical authors and what they have written. The significant gain, however, is not that the "humanness" of the Bible is thereby underscored. In and of itself this is of no value. Rather, because attention is directed to the human instrumentality in the giving of revelation, the divine procedure is made more specific and so the *structure* of that revelation as *product*, the proper concern of dogmatics, comes into sharper focus.[28]

This mutual interest of biblical theology and systematic theology or, to formulate somewhat rhetorically in view of traditional attitudes, the challenge to the latter by the former becomes especially pronounced when Paul in particular is the object of study.[29] If Paul is a theologian and his letters and preaching disclose a structure of thought, then it follows that the shape an exegetically based theology takes should reflect that structure as explicitly as possible.[30] This applies especially to the locus of soteriology, where Pauline material inevitably figures so prominently. Again, if, in the common enterprise of theologizing, Paul, as apostle and instrument of revelation, is distinguished from his interpreters by the "spirated" and infallible character of what he writes and so provides part of the indispensable foundation, the *principium*, for subsequent theological activity, it follows that the latter should be concerned not only with the material, the particular conceptions, which he provides but also with the *way* in which he himself treats this material and structures the various conceptions.

It is necessary, of course, to avoid a *klankexegese* of Kuyper's statements. However, so long as one continues, with him, to speak of the Bible as providing the "material" out of which the church "constructs" dogmas and develops a dogmatics, it is difficult to see how the *loca probantia* method is really and effectively overcome, despite insistence to the the contrary. As long as one operates with his encyclopaedic distinctions, the structure of revelation, at least at points, is subject to distortion. On such an approach, it is almost inevitable that the synthesizing principles employed by Paul are at best only obscurely perceived and hence either implicitly or explicitly replaced by others foreign to him. To conclude, Scripture must determine not only the content but also the *method* of theology.[31]

(2) To approach Paul as theologian helps to define the *problem* of Pauline interpretation. The church has had its difficulties with Paul's writings from the very beginning. This is verified for us by the apostle Peter himself. He acknowledges that they contain "some things which are hard to understand" and alludes to the disastrous consequences which have resulted from their misuse in certain quarters (I Peter 3:16).[32] This statement should cause the serious student of Paul to pause and reflect. Not only does it attest the antiquity of the problem of Pauline interpretation; it also gives to that problem, one may say, *canonical* proportions.

The history of Pauline interpretation may be written in terms of the defects and shortcomings of his interpreters. In general it has been characterized by an excess of ingenuity and a scarcity of real penetration. Interpretation has tended to take exploratory outings when it should have been digging deeper. Only too seldom has it gone deep enough.[33] My immediate interest, however, is not in the variety of factors on the interpreter's side which has so often closed off and still continues to bar the way to a deepened understanding of the apostle's thought. Rather, what may be called the "proper" problem of Pauline interpretation needs to be underscored.

The real difficulty for interpretation lies in the fact that in his writings one encounters a thinker of constructive genius, with a dogmatic bent, but only as he directs himself to specific situations and questions, only as he expresses himself in "occasional" fashion. In short, the true problem in understanding Paul is given with the circumstance that he is a theologian, a careful and systematic thinker who is accessible only through pastoral letters and records of his sermons. His writings are obviously not doctrinal treatises; but clearly neither do they consist in a variety of unrelated, *ad hoc* formulations or an unsystematic multiplication of conceptions. They reflect a structure of thought. The Pauline epistles may be aptly compared to the visible portion of an iceberg. What juts above the surface is but a small fraction of what remains submerged. The true proportions of the whole lie hidden beneath the surface.[34] The shape and contours of that which can be seen at first glance may also prove deceptive. Stated less pictorially, that conception or line of thought which has relatively little explicit textual support, upon reflection may prove to be of the most basic, constitutive significance.[35] It is this state of affairs which makes the interpretation of Paul, particularly a comprehensive attempt, such an inherently arduous and precarious undertaking.

(3) Consequently, to approach Paul as a theologian helps to pin-point the fundamental *task* of Pauline interpretation. Here one can hardly do better than formulate with Vos: "Our task consists of ascertaining the perspective of thought in the revealed Gospel delivered by the Apostle." "It is the subtle weaving of these threads of perspective into the doctrinal fabric of thought as a whole that we must endeavor, so far as possible, to unravel."[36] The interpretation of Paul is above all a matter of careful attention to underlying structure. In his writings and preaching the interpreter comes upon a mind of unusual constructive energy with an unparalleled capacity for synthetic thinking, in a word (again with Vos!), a "master-mind."[37] To the extent that interpretation fails to appreciate this fact, it narrows Paul's horizons, flattens his perspectives, and so obscures both the

breadth and the depth of his teaching.[38] With a sense of redemptive history, with an understanding of himself as one, together with Paul, "upon whom the ends of the ages have come" (I Cor. 10:11), the immediate task of the interpreter must be to provide an increasingly distinct articulation of the structure of thought which is reflected in his statements, to contribute to an ever-clearer refraction of what Vos has described in such classic fashion as that "luminosity radiating from the core of condensed ideas."[39]

VII. Conclusion

Reflections upon method are inevitably related to the area of investigation in a circular fashion. They presuppose (and require) a high degree of acquaintance with the subject matter to be studied and only the concrete act of application makes apparent their relative validity and appropriateness. The brunt of the foregoing remarks is that as a theologian Paul's governing interest lies in explicating the history of redemption. Only careful exegesis will bear this contention out. However, it should be pointed out that in the Reformed tradition, where there are but two attempts to deal with the teaching of Paul as a distinct unit in anything approaching comprehensive fashion, both Vos[40] and then, later, Herman Ridderbos[41] have arrived at and worked out essentially the same basic conclusion. It is not the doctrine of justification by faith or any other aspect of the *ordo salutis* which is found to be the center of the apostle's teaching. Rather, they both maintain that his primary concern is with the *historia salutis* as that history has attained to its eschatological denouement in the death and especially the resurrection of Christ. With Vos the point is implicit but unmistakable.[42] Ridderbos expresses it deliberately and programmatically.[43] Inasmuch as this conclusion represents a marked shift from the traditional Reformed consensus, it ought to be evaluated carefully and its implications explored fully, especially those which bear upon the relationship between Reformed exegesis and dogmatics and the resultant shape of the latter.[44]

Response by C. Van Til

Dear Dr. Gaffin:

You have done a useful piece of work in calling attention to the difference between Abraham Kuyper and Geerhardus Vos on the nature of theology. Allow me to make a few remarks on the reasons Kuyper gives for holding the view that he does.

In the early days of his career Herman Dooyeweerd wrote an important article on Kuyper's view of the nature of "science." Its title is "Kuyper's Wetenschapsleer."[1] The *Wysbegeerte der Wetsidee* is concerned, Dooyeweerd says in this article, to construct a truly biblical and Reformed philosophy.

In order to do so it had to reject the nature-grace scheme of scholastic theology. In particular it had to reject the scholastic view of man as *anima rationalis*. We must replace the scholastic view of man with the truly Reformational and biblical one. We must take man out of the context of the synthesis philosophy of scholasticism and place him in the context of the biblical story of creation, fall, and redemption through Christ.[2] The same thing holds true, says Dooyeweerd, with respect to the scholastic view of the realism of ideas (*ideen-realisme*). "On a Christian transcendence point of view the dilemma between nominalism and realism is unacceptable."[3] In conjunction with a "metaphysical logos doctrine" and the notion of "analogia entis" this idea of realism led logically to a falsification of scriptural teaching.[4]

It would seem obvious enough then that a Reformational philosophy, to be worthy of its name, must sever all connection with both the scholastic view of man and of the world. How else could a properly biblical philosophy ever get under way?

Dooyeweerd wrote his article because some of Kuyper's followers kept on defending the notion that the scholastic and the biblical views of man and the world could and should be combined. Was not the *Wysbegeerte der Wetsidee* a departure from Kuyper's approach?

No, argues Dooyeweerd, the philosophy of his associates and himself is *not* a departure from Kuyper. On the contrary, it builds on Kuyper. It is "in Kuyper's lyne" as C. Veenhof speaks of it.

However, in order to say this we must distinguish between two aspects of Kuyper's teaching. Kuyper's basic commitment was, of course, Reformational and anti-scholastic. That is to say, Kuyper's "religious ground-conception" was biblical, but he had carried with him something of the traditional scholastic problematics. Kuyper was far ahead of his colleagues, Bavinck and Woltjer, in his Reformational thinking.[5] His religious ground-conception involved the confession of divine sovereignty, the absolute sovereignty of God as Creator, which expresses itself in Calvin's adage, *Deus legibus solutus est, sed non exlex.*[6]

It was in line with this religious ground-concept, says Dooyeweerd, that Kuyper refused to say, as Woltjer did say, that God is the object of theological study. Human reason is limited to the temporal cosmos. For this reason it is not God but the revelation of God "as falling within the cosmos" that can properly be said to be the object of theology.[7]

One more point must be added. Dooyeweerd observes that in the second of his "Stone Lectures" on Calvinism Kuyper developed a truly Reformational concept of the idea of law (wetsidee). "Here the metaphysical logos-doctrine is excluded entirely. The law-idea is thought of in purely religious fashion."[8]

However, in spite of all this it must be pointed out that in his discussion of his *Wetenschapsleer* Kuyper does not escape an internal dualism. On the one hand he seeks to be true to the religious principle to which he is committed. On the other hand there is a line of thinking that springs from the "metaphysical logos doctrine."[9] Here Kuyper betrays the influence of his colleague Woltjer.

When dealing with the problem of the possibility of knowledge Kuyper takes over uncritically the subject-object scheme of traditional non-Christian thought. According to this scheme all our knowledge derives exclusively from two functions, observation and logical thinking. On this basis the question must be asked how the object of knowledge can enter our subjective consciousness. There are "moments" and there are "relations" in the knowledge situation. The latter are of a logical and the former are of a non-logical nature.[10]

But this entire contrast, says Dooyeweerd, between "moments" and "relations" springs from the non-Christian philosophy of John Locke. David Hume worked out the sceptical conclusion inherent in this distinction. Would that Kuyper had built his view of *Wetenschap* on the foundation of his own Calvinistic religious view of man and the world.[11]

We are therefore driven to a rejection of Kuyper's logos-speculation. It is when Kuyper cuts himself loose from the schematism of scholastic philosophy by means of his truly religious ground-conception and on it lays the foundation for Calvinistic thinking that we can follow him. It is in line with his basically religious ground-idea that Kuyper speaks of the necessity of religious pre-conceptions, of the all-controlling idea of antithesis and "the no less important doctrine with respect to the function of the πίστις in the knowing process."[12]

It is this last point, about πίστις, Dr. Gaffin, that I think is of special interest to both of us. It is at this point that I differ with

Dooyeweerd. I can make this difference clear by looking to chapter two of volume two of Kuyper's *Encyclopedie der Helige Godge-leerdheid*. In it he discusses the fact of sin in relation to "science."

There are those who believe and there are those who do not believe in the fact of sin. "Thus the one considers normal that which for the other is utterly abnormal." Each party operates with a different criterion. As a consequence the unity of science disappears.

Scepticism might, therefore, well be considered the acme of wisdom.

However, the course of history protests against this. Throughout history "thinking mankind" has devoted itself to the search for truth with unbroken courage and with unfailing determination.[13]

How shall this fact be explained? Well, in the first place, there is sound common sense and wisdom. In common sense and wisdom there is available to man a way of knowledge that is "totally different" from that attained by discursive thinking. Common sense and wisdom build on an independent starting-point. It gives us "intuitive knowledge which rests on definite awareness that is given with our self-consciousness. Scepticism directs its chief assault on our self-consciousness as the reference point of both the process of observation and the process of reasoning. However, we need not fear this onslaught because in sound sense and wisdom, built into our consciousness as it is, we can escape scepticism."[14]

It is at this point that Kuyper begins his discussion of faith and its significance. In faith we have, says Kuyper, a still stronger tool with which to resist scepticism. But then, naturally, we must take faith *as a formal function*. It is not faith in God or faith in Christ that we must think of as a barrier against scepticism. If faith is to serve as a barrier against scepticism it must be inherent in the general and communal sense of the term. For this reason it must not be a faith that some men have and other men do not have. Faith must serve as an antidote to scepticism for men as men, not for men as Christian believers only.

If faith were to be taken as having content, i.e., in a narrow soteriological sense, then we could do nothing with it in the field of epistemology. It would then appear as though faith had no general character at all.[15] Some might contend that in Hebrews 11:1 Scripture presents faith in a soteriological sense. A sound exegesis, says Kuyper, will prove the opposite.[16] We may therefore safely use the term faith as a function of our soul by which, without any process of discursive reasoning, it attains to certainty, directly and immediately without any process of reasoning.[17]

Finding safety against scepticism is, however, not the only advantage faith offers mankind. Faith in one's self is also "the starting point" for the process of knowledge. "Never can anything other than πίστις give you certainty with respect to the existence of your ego. . . ."[18]

At this juncture of his argument Kuyper stresses once more the formal character of faith. Only if the formal character of faith is maintained can we speak of it as that which is the condition of the possibility, or as we would say, the presupposition of all knowledge.[19]

Having established the certainty of self-existence as the starting point of knowledge Kuyper goes on to build a bridge from the knowledge of self to a knowledge of the world. Without this formal πίστις you can never escape from your self to the not-self. There is no other bridge from the phenomena to the noumena. Without this faith all scientific knowledge based on observation hangs in the air.[20]

Moreover, what holds true with respect to observation also holds true with respect to ratiocination. The πίστις is the mysterious link that binds your ego to axioms of logic.[21]

Still further, the πίστις is the controlling motive for the enterprise of science as a whole. The concept of cause rests on πίστις.[22] The justification for drawing general conclusions from particular observations rests on πίστις.[23]

In 1955 I set forth and criticized Kuyper's view of formal faith by saying that it was out of accord with his basically Christian conception of man and the world.[24] Kuyper's view of formal faith is part and parcel with his view of "moments" and "relations."[25]

Kuyper's basic Reformational principle is based upon the idea that the true state of affairs with respect to man and the world is known only by those who listen obediently to the self-attesting Christ of Scripture. Kuyper's philosophy of science is to a considerable extent based upon the idea that the true state of affairs can be known by all men alike, if only they start from faith in themselves as men. The former position starts "from above," the second position starts "from below." The two positions are mutually exclusive. In dealing with "objects" and "relations" Kuyper works *von unten*. It would have led him into, just as it is was based upon, modern subjectivism. However, suddenly, he "brings in the idea of an original Subject, who has thought the universals and has given them being."[26] The case is similar with Kuyper's view of faith. Here too his basic commitment is to the idea that there is no faith in the proper sense of the word unless its object is God as revealed in Christ. Only that man knows the true state of affairs about himself and his world who, with Calvin, knows all created things, as standing from the outset in the relation of total dependence upon the creative-redemptive work of Christ, the Son of God and Son of Man.

Over against this way of thinking on the question of faith is that which starts from below. We have seen already how this *second way* works. The human self has faith in itself.[27] Kuyper does not criticize the *cogito ergo sum* principle by means of Calvin's idea that knowllege of self involves knowledge of God and of Christ and Creator and Redeemer. All that is wrong with the *cogito* statement is that it includes logical derivation. He argues that faith in ourselves, in our self-consciousness, must precede every act of observation and of thinking.[28]

When man has thus become certain of himself prior to observation and ratiocination Kuyper builds a bridge to the world about him.[29] At last the question of God comes upon. Here faith is of special importance. Here we deal with religion and with worship. In the cosmos you have the support of observation. In the knowledge of other persons you have the support of the "self-consciousness of your ego. But here nothing supports you." "Between you and the object of your devotion there is always the unfathomably deep ravine of the *metabasis eis allo genos*."[30]

It is at this point that Kuyper brings up the question of the nature of theology. What he says in Volume III about the nature of theology seems to presuppose what he says in Volume II about theology in relation to *Wetenschap* as a whole. His idea of *Wetenschap* has been built up *von unten*. It therefore leads to an indeterminate God, a God without whose revelation man already knows himself and his world up to a point, a purely superfluous God. This is not the God of Calvin or of Paul. Paul required the Greeks to reject this sort of God and accept the Creator-Redeemer God of Scripture. Kuyper himself constantly asks men to renounce this false god. Yet in his *Wetenschapsleer* he joins apostate mankind in raising an altar to this unknown God.

Kuyper's *Wetenschapsleer* keeps plaguing him as he builds up his encyclopedic edifice. This is true in particular when he sets revelation diametrically over against theology.[31] By doing so he seeks to safeguard the divine character of revelation. But it is the characterlessness of God that he is thus conserving. He is working with the idea of the unknown God of the Greeks.

The basic difficulty is that neither Kuyper nor Bavinck, nor Woltjer, had worked out a Christian concept of logic as implied in the Christian view of man and of fact. These men assumed that if you were to engage in reasoning with unbelievers you must first agree with their view of man, of fact, and of logic.

It was the Philosophy of the Cosmonomic Idea that helped us forward at this point. The question now is whether this Christian, this Calvinistic philosophy, will work out the implications of its own position. To do so it is of basic importance to realize that for a Christian every interpretative endeavor of man presupposes the absolute interpretation of all things through Christ in Scripture. When man receives the revelation of God given him he must, from the outset, realize that his observational and conceptualizing endeavor is at every point subordinate to the teleology of Scripture. His "concepts" must from the outset "be seen to be limiting concepts" operating in subordination to the verbally revealed body of truth of Scripture. This cannot be done so long as faith is not, from the outset, seen to be what is as either belief in Christ as the Creator-Redeemer of man or belief in man as autonomous. My concern with respect to Dooyeweerd's position lies precisely at this point. He has indeed gone beyond Kuyper. We are appreciative of this. But he has not gone far enough beyond Kuyper. This fact is exemplified in his failure to reject Kuyper's idea of formal faith along with his rejection of "moments" and "relations." Kuyper's idea of formal faith is a "scholastic" idea. His "contact" with unbelievers is based on it. His apologetics tends to slide back into the method of old Princeton because of it. One could wish that Dooyeweerd did not seek to analyze theoretical thought as such or appeal to men to judge of his analysis of theoretical thought in relation to time and to the supra-temporal self pointing to an origin, by the "empirical world" as such. If Christians, non-Calvinists as well as Calvinists, are to receive full benefit from Paul's interpretation of the facts of the death and resurrection of Christ then they must make their own theology, their own process of concept-formation fully subordinate to the "theology of Paul." Calvin has helped us forward; Kuyper has helped us forward; Dooyeweerd has helped us forward.

We may, because of their work, go forward further still. This is what you are earnestly trying to do. You are wise to make good use of the work of Geerhardus Vos in doing so. We who are about to die, salute you!

—C.V.T.

Herman Ridderbos

XII. TRADITION AND EDITORSHIP
IN THE SYNOPTIC GOSPELS

The doctrine concerning the Holy Scriptures is a matter which the believing Scripture-researcher is always encountering anew and which always introduces to him new questions. The more he goes into the contents of the Scriptures, trying to see through the connections of that which is revealed to us in the Scriptures, to uncover the inner unity of that which the apostles and the prophets each by himself and all of them together have set down, the more he is impressed by what the apostle Paul has called "the depth of the riches, both of the wisdom and knowledge of God" and with greater inner conviction shall he confess that which Scripture says of itself, namely, that it is *theopneustos*, God-breathed. He also comes to understand how the divinity of the Scriptures can sometimes be spoken of in such absolute terms, that the word of Scripture is equated with the Word of God himself; even that, in a remarkable variation, at one time it can be said "the Scripture says" and at another "God says" or "the Holy Spirit says." On the other hand he will, just when he goes deeper into the Scriptures, be impressed again and again with the humanity of Scripture; human in its language, human in its images, human in its composition. From the earliest days of exegesis this has been discovered and attempts have been made to analyze and qualify theologically and philosophically this duality, which is at the same time a unity, for it is impossible to come to a point of division here. Within the theological tradition from which I arose (and to which the esteemed person celebrating his jubilee is no stranger!) such men as A. Kuyper and H. Bavinck spoke of organic inspiration. They wanted, with this (certainly not faultless) qualification, to point out that the human authors of the Bible were not stripped by the Spirit of their human idiosyncracies, their talents, and their limitations. Scripture, because it is inspired by the Holy Spirit, is not relieved of its human, that is to say, its historical, character. When the Spirit moved the biblical writers, he did not paralyze their *own* activity in order to make them better instruments and performers, but rather he stimulated them to be in his service in their own way and with their own gifts, powers, and possibilities. It is for this reason that there is, in the result of that which they brought about under the movement and guidance of the Holy Spirit, so much difference—a difference not only in language and style, but also in depth, in command of the subject matter, in aim, and in the use of the material which was at their disposal.

In a former essay I attempted to face the questions which arise out of this in reference to the nature of the authority of Scripture and occupied myself also with the more detailed dogmatic formulations of this authority in such conceptions as infallibility and inerrancy. I know that the one to whom we dedicate this book has a book in his library (by his own courtesy!) in which I treated this theme in Dutch.[1] Rather than occupying myself directly with this theme again, I want at this time to illustrate further the above-mentioned personal character and personal activity of the Bible writers with the help of a clear example. At the close of this exegetical activity there will be opportunity to return to our point of departure, i.e., to the question of the nature of the authority of Scripture, with a brief word.

A subject which is receiving renewed special attention in current New Testament literature is the specific nature and purport of the four Gospels in general and of each Gospel in particular. Especially the three synoptic Gospels are being subjected to an exact investigation from this point of view.

In this respect there is to be asertained a clear reversal in the direction of the investigation. Until a short time ago the study of the Gospels in New Testament literature was dominated by the so-called "*formgeschichliche*" method. The starting point of this method is that the synoptic Gospels must be looked on as secondary formations, as the late closing of a prolonged process of previous transmission. If one wants to come to an insight into the original forms of the gospel tradition and into the significance thereof in the life of the early church, then one must—according to this method—break out the subject matter which is transmitted in the Gospels from the frame of these secondary collections. He must try to distinguish the different *original* species ("genres," "forms") of this tradition and try to trace the function which these different tradition-species had in the life of the original congregation (their "Sitz im Leben"). This investigation would then also yield the criteria for what should be more or less old, original, and historically trustworthy in the synoptic tradition, as well as which transmitted words one may or may not still ascribe to Jesus. The attention of the form-historical method was thus not directed upon the Gospels as such, which are viewed as a secondary framework, but upon the older and younger traditions brought together within that frame.

At the present time the stream runs in reversed direction. One does not deny that the tradition (oral and written) before it became the gospel-narrative already existed and functioned (e.g., in preaching) in another way, but all attention is now directed on the way in which the evangelists forged this tradition into a new unity in their Gospels. Each evangelist does it in his own way, or, as one might say, each evangelist edits the transmitted subject matter according to his own plan and outline. This investigation, which is concerned with the specific editorship of Matthew, Mark, and Luke, one calls, in distinction from the form-historical school, the *"redaktionsgeschichtliche methode,"* the editorship-historical method.

Although this development, which has taken place particularly in the German literature, comes close, in many respects, to the results of the form-historical school and therefore proceeds with a certain understanding of the tradition which is stamped by these results, nevertheless it opens perspectives also for those who acknowledge the synoptic tradition as fundamentally a fruit of the apostolic transmission and not only of "church-theology." The advantage of this method is that the evangelists no longer fill, in preponderant measure, the roles of compiler and funnels through which the stream of tradition is caught, channeled, and bottled, but that they are recognized again as independent authors, each working with his own purpose and plan and with a selective principle in harmony with them. Of this we have a definite right to speak because we have *three* gospels which, more or less, are constructed out of the same tradition materials, each according to a separate pattern, and which therefore allow *mutual comparison.* The result is that there is, again especially in Germany, a certain proliferation of writings which are occupied with what are called the "theologies" of Matthew, Mark, and Luke.

Now even in this area there is nothing absolutely new under the sun. It has always been known, for example, that Matthew wrote more with an eye to Judaism than Luke, who obviously concentrated more on the gentile Christians. The differing form of the genealogical registers in Matthew and Luke, the former descending from Abraham, the latter going back to Adam, is evidence of this. But one may come to more precise and subtle observations, if one does not content himself with these general trends, but rather subjects the specific form and wording of the comparable materials within the three Gospels to a closer investigation. It is then frequently possible to notice in this different editing of the same material definite tendencies within the separate Gospels which might be able to supply an answer to the question why one evangelist has written one way while the others another.

One must undoubtedly exercise great caution here. To what extent is it possible to say that the evangelists could make use of the *same* tradition material for the composition of their gospel narratives? It would certainly be an unjustified hypothesis to maintain that the different forms in which the same stories out of the life of Jesus and the same words of the Lord are told and transmitted is entirely and completely reducible to the way in which each evangelist handled and edited this material. As, for example, when in the story of the Gadarene demoniac(s), one possessed man is spoken of by Mark and Luke and two men are spoken of by Matthew, we cannot simply attribute the second person to the "editing" of Matthew. The same is true for the differences in the transmission of the institution of the Lord's Supper, of the "Lord's Prayer," the beatitudes of the Sermon on the Mount, etc. The evangelists have not only been able to draw out of one common (oral or written) transmission; they each had obviously their own sources. This is especially visible in Matthew and Luke. This fact has led, in the past, to all sorts of (often unconvincing) intricate source theories.

Nevertheless there are still clear indications that the evangelists arranged the same material in different ways and edited differently as to matters of detail. This is most clearly evident from the sequence and the shaping in which the same story appears in Matthew, Mark, and Luke. If one compares the evangelists on this point, then one can see that certain stories appear in all three evangelists in the same order so that one can draw, in a synopsis, specific "blocks," e.g.:

The Healing of the Paralytic	Matt. 9:1-8	Mark 2:1-12	Luke 5:17-26
The Call of Levi	Matt. 9:9-13	Mark 2:13-17	Luke 5:27-32
The Question of Fasting	Matt. 9:14-17	Mark 2:18-22	Luke 5:33-39

Such "blocks" can appear, however, in one Gospel in a completely different place and also in a different sequence from the others. Primarily in Matthew, in the first part of his Gospel, one finds important shiftings in comparison with Mark. Moreover, it has been discovered (in the last century!) that Matthew and Luke only show the same

order in the narrative material when the same "block" is also present
in Mark. Therefore, in this respect, Mark takes a certain key position
in between Matthew and Luke, i.e., the sequence in which Mark
tells the gospel stories seems to offer the explanation for the appearance of these "blocks" in Matthew and Luke. This has led to the
so-called "Marcian-hypothesis," that Mark has priority over Matthew
and Luke and, in some form or other, is used by these evangelists.
At present this theory is accepted by most scholars.

It is not necessary, however, for our purposes, that we enter into
the details of this theory. It is clear in any case that the evangelists
set down specific series of stories in the same order; also that they,
in giving shape to these stories, depart considerably from each other
and manipulate these series of blocks in different ways. It is clear,
however, even without taking notice of these blocks, that they
group and edit the same stories in different ways. It is obvious
also that the individual plan and individual purpose of the evangelist
plays an important role.

I would like to illustrate this with a specific (and limited) example,
i.e., with the "miracle chapters" of Matthew 8 and 9. It has always
attracted attention that Matthew brings together in both these chapters a number of miracles which one finds spread over a much
larger area in the Gospels of Mark and Luke. Here Matthew clearly
edits according to a personal architectural principle, a principle
which can, for that matter, be observed in the whole of his Gospel.
Further analysis of his book enables us to know him as a real
"systematician." This is evident in the total structure. In this structure four almost equal parts can be distinguished, each of about 270
verses: 1:1–9:35 (270 vss.); 9:36–16:12 (270 vss.); 16:13–23:39
(272 vss.); 24:1–28:20 (258 vss.). Furthermore, within this structure he places a number of long addresses of Jesus which end each
time with the same formula and which bear, in reference to their
contents, a different character: The Sermon on the Mount (5-7);
the Commissioning (10); the Parables (13); the Congregation
Address (18), and the Eschatological Address (24-25). Here also
the evangelist clearly proceeds following his own plan of work: sorting, compiling, uniting the equal parts.

If we now return, however, to our "miracle chapters," then we
see that these chapters too are part of a very systematically constructed whole. They belong to the first section of the Gospel, 1:1–
9:35. This section falls into two sub-sections, of which the first part

spans precisely one third (90 vss.). It acts as a general introduction and comprises the so-called "antecedent history" (the genealogical register, the birth, the adventures of the child Jesus), the appearances of John the Baptist, Jesus' baptism and his temptation in the wilderness, and, finally, a general characterization of Jesus' appearances in public. This last passage, 4:12-25, ends with the general characterization that Jesus went about the whole of Galilee, teaching in the synagogues and preaching the gospel of the kingdom and healing all sickness and disease among the people, 4:23.

It is very striking and important for this insight into the structure of the Gospel, that this characterization at the close of the introductory section returns in almost the same wording at the end of the first large division, namely, in 9:35. Chapters 5-9 are, in this way, flanked and qualified by identical utterances. This is entirely in accordance with the contents of these five chapters, because therein is given ample illustration of Jesus' preaching (in the Sermon on the Mount, 5-7) as well as of his miracles (in the miracle chapters, 8-9). These five chapters consist of 180 verses, precisely double that of the number in the introductory part, chapters 1 to 4 (90 vss.). By this analysis the structure of the first large division of the Gospel, 1:1–9:35, as regards the dimension as well as the contents, becomes entirely transparent.

When we look now more closely at the miracle chapters, then it becomes evident that Matthew in this part also proceeds both systematically and according to his own plan. He introduces in these miracles an entirely personal sequence, a different one than that which we find in Mark (and Luke), although he uses, again and again, (Marcian) blocks (see above) as building stones. He places these, however, using his own discretion and without following the over-all structure which we find in Mark. In this respect Luke is much closer to Mark, as will appear from the chart (see next page). One can ascertain from this overview:

a) that Matthew and Luke exhibit a common order in the narrative materials *only* when this sequence is present in Mark also. This demonstrates that Mark, somehow or other, forms the link between Matthew and Luke;

b) that, if Luke includes certain story material which we also find in Mark, then he also retains the order of Mark (even if he inserts his "own" material);

c) that Matthew handles, on the contrary, the order of Mark with great liberty in chapters 8 and 9. Certainly he has various Mar-

Cleansing of the Leper	Matt. 8:1-4	Mark 1:40-45	Luke 5:12-16
The Centurion of Capernaum	Matt. 8:5-13	—	Luke 7:1-10
Mother-in-law of Peter Healed	Matt. 8:14-15	Mark 1:29-31	Luke 4:38,39
The Sick Healed at Evening	Matt. 8:16-17	Mark 1:32-34	Luke 4:40,41
On Following Jesus	Matt. 8:18-22	—	Luke 9:57-62
Stilling the Storm	Matt. 8:23-27	Mark 4:35-41	Luke 8:22-25
The Gadarene Demoniacs	Matt. 8:28-34	Mark 5:1-20	Luke 8:26-39
The Healing of the Paralytic	Matt. 9:1-8	Mark 2:1-12	Luke 5:17-26
The Call of Levi	Matt. 9:9-13	Mark 2:13-17	Luke 5:27-32
The Question about Fasting	Matt. 9:14-17	Mark 2:18-22	Luke 5:33-39
Jairus' Daughter and the Woman with a Hemorrhage	Matt. 9:18-26	Mark 5:21-43	Luke 8:40-56
Two Blind Men	Matt. 9:27-31		
The Dumb Demoniac	Matt. 9:32-34		

cian blocks, but these blocks do not appear in the same sequence as they do in Mark (and Luke).

When we concentrate more particularly on the miracle chapters of Matthew themselves, we come across within them also a very systematic construction. In closer analysis it becomes obvious that these chapters break into four precisely alike parts, each of 17 verses: 8:1-17; 8:18-34; 9:1-17, and 9:18:34. Together they give examples of all the kinds of miracles Jesus performed, a series which is again recalled in 11:1-5. To this "kinds" aspect is added a thematic aspect which might also be called a "Christological" aspect because it brings the meaning of Jesus' messianic work to the fore in more than one way. We want to attempt to demonstrate this successively for the aforementioned sub-sections.

a) 8:1-17. The first sub-section begins with the story of the cleansing of the leper, 8:1-4. Immediately Matthew departs here from Mark and Luke, who both relate, as the first miracle, the healing of the possessed man in the synagogue of Capernaum, Mark 1:21-28; Luke 4:31-37. One can suppose that the evangelist, who clearly makes a choice, did not include the narrative of the possessed man because further on in these chapters he tells of such healings of possessed people, 8:28ff. and 9:32ff., which have partly the same features which are contained in the story of the possessed man in Capernaum in Mark and Luke (comp. Mark 1:23, 24 with Matt. 8:29ff.). However, of no less importance is the positive aspect. When we look at the story of the healing of the leper more closely, then it appears that the evangelist had good reasons to place especially this narrative in the beginning.

The first thing that should attract our attention is that the narrative is so particularly short (much shorter than the parallel verses in Mark and Luke). Through this shortness everything becomes concentrated on two main motifs. The first is that of Jesus' *authority*. This authority is confessed by the leper very tersely ("if you will, you can. . . .") and this is confirmed and realized by Jesus in the same words ("I will, be. . . ."). All this is closely related, by the transitional verse 8:1, to the closing of chapter 7, where the real reason for the amazement of the crowd is mentioned: Jesus taught as one having *authority* and not as their scribes. This same authority is now pointed out by the evangelist in the *deeds* of Jesus. It was that authority which formed the (messianic) background to Jesus' words and deeds.

To this is added now, as a second main motif, again Jesus' relationship to the scribes on the one hand and the law of Moses on the other. There is, in the miracle, a threefold reference to "purifying." Although the occurrence of this word, in this connection, refers to the healing of the leper, nevertheless it bears a cultic and legal connotation: in general, in such matters the priest played a role. The leper appeals to Jesus alone for his cleansing, and Jesus stretches out his hand, touches him and says, "Be cleansed!" One might then ask if something should or could be added to this purification if Jesus' authority is so great and incontrovertible. Against such a misunderstanding or charge to the effect that Jesus might wish to make superfluous or undo the command of Moses, he arms himself beforehand by ordering the leper to show himself to the priest "for a testimony to them." Obviously we find here the same motif as at the beginning of Jesus' authoritative words in the Sermon on the Mount: "Think not that I have come to undo the law and the prophets." For the evangelist everything hinges on this command to the leper; he does not narrate the end of the story as we find it in Mark and Luke.

In this way all the stress comes to be laid on what Jesus does. He proceeds in absolute authority, but with full respect to the law; indeed, he fulfills the law. "For a testimony to them" has here an antithetic point, namely, against those who would charge him with undoing the law. But this also is positive. Jesus is not a charismatic who sets himself outside the law. He comes in order to fulfill the law and the prophets as the Messiah in his miracles as well as in his commandments (comp. vs. 17).

After the story of the healing of the leper follows that of the centurion and his servant, 8:5-13. This passage does not appear in Mark, while in Luke it appears in a completely different context (see Luke 7:1-10). The insertion of the narrative into this place (after that of the leper) and the incorporation of verses 11 and 12— the parallel verses in Luke 13:28, 29 are not connected with the story about this centurion—is very characteristic of Matthew's construction. To begin with, Jesus' *authority* is again brought to the front with special emphasis in this story. It is expressed in a highly characteristic manner by the centurion using military terms: just as he, in his service, so Jesus in a divine way, has the command. However, in addition to the former, a completely different motif is found. Whereas the cleansing of the leper is executed entirely within the limits of the law of Moses, Jesus here meets the gentile leader without any reservations and declares himself—at least according to the most obvious translation, "I will come and heal him"—prepared to go under the roof of this non-Israelite. When the centurion declares himself unworthy of it and desires only a word from Jesus (from a distance), then Jesus praises his faith above all that he has found in Israel. Thereby the utterances of verses 12 and 13 fit in: on the one hand, full of expectation for the gentiles; on the other hand, full of judgment for Israel. Already here, in the beginning of the gospel, the case of Israel appears to be decided in a negative sense. One sees here the reason why one might suppose that these words which, as has been said, are used by Luke in a completely different context, were put here by Matthew from thematic motives. In any case it is clear how much the evangelist, both in the construction of the miracle chapters and in the combination of these first two miracles, reveals a specific plan. He is guided by motives which are especially typical of *his* editing of the gospel materials.

The last verses of this section, vss. 14-17, narrate the healing of Peter's mother-in-law and the "evening healings," parallel to Mark 1:29-34 and Luke 4:38-41. For the evangelist this traditional block forms an appropriate transition to one of his known "formula quotations," 8:17: "in order that what was spoken through the prophet Isaiah might be fulfilled, saying, 'he himself took our infirmities, and carried away our diseases.' " This fulfillment-motif is the first main point of view under which the evangelist wants to have the miracles of Jesus viewed. It has a universal meaning, embracing Jews and gentiles, Jesus' special relatives, and all those who ever turn to him. But it is the prophetic, salvation-historical prediction to Israel that is fulfilled in Jesus' salvation-bringing miracle power which, in this fulfilling, places first of all Israel in front of the great and definitive decision.

b) The second section, 8:18-34, does not begin with a new miracle, but with a number of sayings which relate to following Jesus. Frequently one has troubled himself over the question why Matthew interrupts his miracle stories by these sayings—which stand in Luke in a completely different context—and why he places *these* particular sayings precisely here. All sorts of explanations are given for this. The best known, coming from the German professor, Bornkamm, is that the evangelist wants, in this way, to bring the next miracle (that of the stilling of the storm) under a special viewpoint: that of following Jesus. The point of the narrative would then be found, not so much in the miracle itself as in the faith which Jesus requires of those who follow him. Therefore the small boat becomes the "Schifflein der Kirche." The most important argument for this interpretation is that the narrative of the stilling of the storm begins with the words, "and when he got into the boat, the disciples *followed* him." The explanation, therefore, for the insertion of the foregoing sayings would be found especially in the word "follow." In particular, the narrative would be then intended to focus attention on the risk, on the little faith, and on the preservation of Jesus' followers; and, in this way, notably, to delineate especially the position of the later congregation for whom Matthew writes.

There might be, to be sure, some truth in this idea. Not only the way of Jesus, but also that of his disciples, all those who in earlier times and in later times shall want to follow him, become visible here. Nevertheless, it seems to me that the evangelist, by inserting these sayings here, wanted to bring under a specific viewpoint in the first place, not the picture of the later congregation but of the historical Jesus himself. We see Jesus here in the restlessness of his existence. When he, seeing the crowd, drew aside for a moment with his disciples, the storm as a hostile power found him under way. Therefore just here: "the foxes have holes, and the birds of the air have nests, but the Son of Man has nowhere to lay his head." This is then combined certainly also with the warning to those who want to follow him not to allow themselves to be held up or hindered by anything or anyone: "let the dead bury their dead." However, the real attention remains directed toward Jesus himself as he goes forth from there, while he is in the ship, where he seeks rest but is awakened through the anxiety of his disciples, whom he then rebukes for their fear and unbelief and whose dangers he exorcises. Yet hardly have they come to the other side, when those unfortunate men possessed by the devil meet him, men whose fate concerns him. When the demons take their retreat into the herd of swine—for there is still time before their torture!—the inhabitants of the city turn against him. Once again he goes off into the boat and returns to the place from which he left.

Therefore, in this second part appears also a picture of Jesus' miracles. But the viewpoint is changed. Here also certainly is the motif of power and of the willingness of Jesus to take the diseases of the people unto himself; but here this motif is still clearly connected with the other motif of the struggle against the powers which are hostile to him and which he exorcises, but whose power is not yet at an end. The saying about the Son of Man is characteristic of the whole. It is one of Jesus' titles, an indication of his authority. But the way of the Son of Man is that of unrest, conflict, and confrontation with enmity. This aspect of Jesus' existence becomes visible also in Matthew's design of his miracle power, and certainly also in its meaning for those who want to follow him.

c) The third section, 9:1-17, consists of three passages which are present in another context in these same blocks in Mark and Luke: the healing of the paralytic, the call of Levi, and the question about fasting (comp. Mark 2:1-22; Luke 5:17-19). For Matthew this combination is important, because therein Jesus' miracle power is visible in another way, in connection with his *authority to forgive sins*. Healing means also forgiving and Jesus' authority to heal is founded upon his authority to forgive. This new element dominates the narrative of the healing of the paralytic, gives it a special imprint and "revelation meaning" and brings Jesus, because of this, into conflict with the scribes. After this story follows the calling of Levi and the dinner with the sinners. These two narratives interrupt, in a certain sense, the on-going description of Jesus' miracle power. It has been said that Matthew here apparently retains the traditional sequence of narrative material. However, that he does not break with this order here, as elsewhere, is not unintentional. In any case he edits this passage according to his own style and construction. He formulates more tightly and better than Mark (e.g., comp. Matt. 9:10 with Mark 2:15, 16). He inserts, once again, an appeal to the Scriptures in vs. 13, which is again characteristic of all his editing activity. The main point, however, is that these narratives of Levi's calling and of Jesus' dinner together with the publicans stand in clear connection with the main motif of the preceding miracle narrative: Jesus' miracle power and his power to forgive sins are one. One cannot separate these two powers. The miracle does not only have a relation to bodily or mental suffering: it has to do with man in the whole of his lost existence. Therefore, Jesus also calls the sinners and sits with them at the table and the recovery of the whole of life is celebrated at the messianic dinner.

d) Finally, a word about the last or fourth part of these miracle chapters, 9:18-34, which contains the narrative of Jairus' daughter and a woman with a hemmorhage, the two blind men, and the dumb demoniac. According to some, particularly these three narratives in 9:18-31 should be brought together, because in them the *theme of faith* comes into prominence, 9:22 and 9:29. This would then be evidence that this section has received this form and been edited especially with an eye on the "congregation of Matthew." Not the miracles themselves, but the role which *faith* must play in the life of the congregation should receive the major emphasis here.

Such a characterizing of the three miracles in 9:18-31 appears to us to be at least one-sided. To be sure, the motif of faith in Jesus' miracle power is, in an important way, under discussion. But this is not the specific point of these three miracles nor even their main perspective. With respect to *faith*, this plays already a role clearly in the narrative of the centurion too, 8:10, of the stilling of the storm, 8:26, and of the paralytic, 9:2. The main motif of the dual narrative of the woman with the hemmorhage and the daughter of Jairus appears to us to lie in this: that Jesus' miracle power shows its culminating point in the conquering of death. That the narrative of the hemmorhaging woman had been connected with this traditionally is apparent from Mark. In order to understand the editing of Matthew one will have to keep looking for the guiding thought of the construction of the miracle chapters in the delineating of Jesus' miracle power itself in its different aspects.

The closing of this section with the story of the two blind men and
the dumb demoniac is no less typical of Matthew's compositional
gift. Both of these narratives are important because of the *reactions*
mentioned in them which were elicited by Jesus' miracle power. They
form, therefore, the transition to the continuation of the gospel narrative wherein these reactions will appear to form the key to the further
development of the history of Jesus (see esp. chapters 11 and 12).

The narrative of the two blind men, 9:27-31, is very striking in
this location. It has no parallels in Mark and Luke, but it certainly
reminds one very strongly of the story (which is also present in
Matthew) of the blind men (man) from Jericho which comes at the
end of the Gospel. The characteristic feature of the editing of the
narrative in Matt. 9 is that, as the blind men call after Jesus as the
"Son of David," he goes into the house, and after he had granted them
healing on the basis of their faith, impresses upon them, with stern
words, that they must not make him known. On the one hand it
appears that Jesus' miracle power awakened Messianic sentiments
in the multitude; on the other hand, that Jesus did not want to be
made known in this way. Just as one, so is the other, typical of Jesus'
miracle power, as the evangelist in the following chapter will intentionally make clear: the Messianic meaning of Jesus' miracles in
11:4ff. in confrontation with John the Baptist; the intentional covering and keeping secret of his glory by Jesus himself in 12:15ff., with
an appeal (by the evangelist) to Isaiah 42:1f., the prophecy concerning the Servant of the Lord. Therefore is this seemingly superfluous narrative—after what has already been related—of the healing
of the two blind men, a hinge on which the door on that which follows
turns. The same holds for the short and inconspicuous narrative of
the dumb demoniac. Here also the concern is with the reaction of
the crowd. On the one hand there is the amazement, the consciousness, that something like this had never been seen in Israel; on the
other hand, the slander of the Pharisees is revealed: "He casts out
the demons by the ruler of the demons." This last motif returns
later on in great emphasis in 12:22ff. It even seems that the story in
9:32 reappears in 12:22ff. but with some amplification. Be that as
it may, the function of the last two miracles in chapters 8 and 9 is
clear: behind Jesus' miracles stands the entire secret of his person.
This secret beams out through his deeds and cannot remain concealed.
Yet Jesus' messianic glory comes to the fore only indirectly in his
miracles. He did not want to be called after as the Son of David.
The Pharisees could then interpret it in *their* hostile and slanderous

way. That is all characteristic of Jesus' appearances. This will especially come up for detailed discussion and be explained in chapters 11, 12, and 13 (in chapter 10 a continuation of chapters 5-9 can be seen).

As we survey the whole of the miracle chapters we see how the evangelist deliberately orders, groups, edits, and thereby interprets the materials to place Jesus' miracle power in the light of a variety of perspectives. In 4 x 17 vss. he handles four different themes:

1) 8:1-17; *in his miracle power Jesus fulfils the prophecy of the Servant of the Lord*, who took the sicknesses of the people unto himself. He acts not only on behalf of Jews but also on behalf of gentiles, on the basis of the faith of all those who turn to him. He sets Israel before the great decision by his, miracles and from the beginning with his appearance the division becomes visible.

2) 8:18-34; *in his miracle power Jesus has to wage a restless and continuous war against the power of the enemy.* He had no place to lay his head; he had to ask of his disciples absolute preparedness; he had to battle against powers and demons without finding rest or quiet.

3) 9:1-17; *in his miracle power he not only cured sickness and disease but also attacked the power of sin* by proclaiming forgiveness to the suffering, by calling publicans to follow him, and by fellowshiping with sinners and by celebrating with them the deliverance of life.

4) 9:18-34; *in his miracle power wherein he also conquered death he became both recognized and contended with as the Messiah.* Revelation and concealment went therein together and made his appearance ambiguous because of the way which he still must travel in order to fully complete his work.

If I now return to the beginning of my paper, we can see that the above analysis of a small section of the Gospel of Matthew undertaken from a specific viewpoint can clear up our insight into the manner in which the Scriptures were brought about and the nature of their authority. We see how the evangelists handled what is most often called the "synoptic tradition," but which we, following Luke 1:1-4, may call also the "apostolic tradition." They have composed, edited, and in this way also interpreted the tradition, each in his own way. By analyzing the Gospel of Matthew this becomes especially clear; nevertheless, similar observations can be made in the other evangelists. On the one hand, from this appears the freedom with which they handled the transmitted subject matter. Matthew has incorporated all sorts of alterations into the sequence of the materials which we find in Mark and Luke. Although the connections between the different narratives suggest that they form a continuous tale (sometimes with a temporal sequence—"then he spoke these things to them"—or a spacial connection—"then he went further from there"), nevertheless it is still not possible to draw positive conclusions from this. The evangelist arranges his narrative under thematic, not under temporal, viewpoints and does not hesitate elsewhere—when we compare him with his fellow evangelists—to break the connections. This thematic design also implies that he gives the narrative the form which is most appropriate for his design. All sorts of details which appear in Mark are either left out by Matthew or shortened; conversations are summarized, and differently stylized; sometimes they are also amplified or changed. Matthew does this clearly not for historical reasons, as if he were better and more accurately informed; he does it rather from thematic considerations: according to the picture that he wants to draw of Jesus as the Christ. Therefore he gives to it a form such as most agrees with the design that he himself has composed.

This is not to say—on this we must lay no less emphasis—that the history, that which *really happened*, was less interesting to him and that he was only interested in preaching, in kerygma, in the "essence" of what happened. The evangelists want to make Jesus Christ known through history. The kerygma has not produced the history, but history has produced the kerygma. There are serious reasons to caution against the reversal of this order such as is evident in current New Testament literature. If we can establish, therefore, that the evangelists made a real impact on the form and sequence of the gospel stories, this does not mean that they were history-*makers* or that they have created a historical form to that which they wanted to proclaim concerning Christ or the faith of the later congregation. Undoubtedly they have in the narratives not only wanted to give witness of the historical Jesus but through the witness wanted to summon all men to faith in the resurrected and living Lord whom the congregation confessed as the Christ. This is so because the "historical" and the exalted Lord are one and the same. But it may not be deduced from this that those who set down the apostolic tradition concerning Jesus of Nazareth were no longer conscious of the border between the life of the historical Jesus and that of the exalted Lord. In the Gospels they proclaim the living and not the dead Lord. But they proclaim him as he once became knowable in his coming to men, in his fellowship with them. Who he *is* is preached in the Gospels on the ground of who he *was*. Just precisely so and not otherwise the Gospels present themselves and only in this way can they be understood truly.

Nevertheless it is their intention to call for faith in Jesus as the Christ, the Son of God, who controls everything. If they had told fanciful stories for that purpose, then they would have served their purpose badly and would have been found to be false witnesses (see I Cor. 15:15). Nevertheless their purpose was not only to increase our historical knowledge, but to evoke faith. Of this, also, their books give ample illustration. This design explains the construction, selection, and forming of the materials; it also explains the freedom with which they used their available material. They are carried along by the Spirit to that purpose and their work takes from that purpose its divine authority: to be the infallible testimony that *that* Jesus of Nazareth, in his words and works, in his death and resurrection, was the Christ whom the congregation confesses as its Lord in heaven.

(Translated by E. R. Geehan)

William L. Lane

XIII.   THE SPEECHES OF THE BOOK OF ACTS[1]

The book of Acts remains in focus in critical debate, for it is the one biblical document which purports to rescue from oblivion the crucial period between the resurrection of Jesus and the conversion of the apostle Paul. Apart from the first chapters of Acts the sources for the thought and practice of the early Jerusalem community are meager and problematical. Only if the tradition incorporated in Acts 1-7 is historically reliable and authentically primitive can something certain be known of the self-consciousness of the primitive Christian community.

Since Luke's primary vehicle for advancing the narrative is the speech-form, a crucial question concerns the relative primitiveness of statements within the speeches of Acts and the essential reliability of the tradition embodied. If these speeches represent the free literary composition of Luke, they cannot be regarded as reliable historical sources for reconstructing the thinking of the primitive church. They reflect not primitive theology, but rather Luke's conception of what primitive theology may have been.[1a] On such an understanding there can be little or no confidence that distinctive formulations are genuinely native to the early Jerusalem community.

I.   The Reliability of the Tradition

The critical rejection of the essential historicity of the speeches in Acts rests upon several grounds. Luke's use of stylistic devices indicates that he was sensitive to the practices of Hellenistic historiography.[2] It has been presumed, therefore, that he conformed to the common practice of the Hellenistic historians in composing appropriate speeches for his narrative.[3] The brevity of the speeches recorded in Acts underscores the improbability that they are a record of what was actually expressed on any given occasion.[4] For none of the speeches does there seem to be a suggestion of written notes or records. Even if a report of what was said was transmitted orally by the hearers or repeated by the speaker himself in subsequent narration of the event, probability is against any extensive verbal agreement of the ultimate record with the original.[5] A careful study of the vocabulary, idom, and style of the several speeches indicates that responsibility for the language must rest with the author of Acts.[6] The speeches in Acts are not entirely independent of each other. Their similarity to each other extends beyond vocabulary and style to subject matter and interdependence of thought, so that an argument fully developed in one speech is merely referred to in a second address.[7] These considerations, it has been asserted, argue for the common origin of the speeches in the mind of the editor of the narrative.

Each of these considerations, however, must be carefully evaluated before any weight can be attached to this critical assessment. While it is clear that Luke was sensitive to the conventions of Hellenistic historiography, facets of his work indicate that he was not bound by them. It is also necessary to define more carefully than has been customary those conventions which dominated Hellenistic historiography at that time when Luke was writing.

It is commonly assumed that Luke's approach to speech material may be estimated from Thucydides' statement of his practice in this matter.[8] Thucydides attempted to produce at all events the main ideas of genuine speeches, even if he gave them the content and form which he himself considered appropriate.[9] In the main the historian Polybius (c. 200–118 B.C.) followed this tradition, although his work contains fewer speeches, and he tends to be stricter about their veracity.[10] But Polybius writes with a consciousness that Hellenistic historiography was setting for itself another ideal. His statement that historians should not parade their oratorical skill before their readers, but merely present what was actually said,[11] reproducing the most essential features as far as possible, is directed at the newer historians who viewed history as an art and an occasion for display of rhetorical brilliance.[12] During the last century before the Christian era and up to the time when Luke was writing, under strong rhetorical influence Helenistic historiography moved increasingly further from the ideals which dominated Polybius. A typical exponent of this new development was Dionysius of Halicarnassus (c. 60 B.C.– ?) who thoroughly subordinated his historical material to the rhetorical ideal.[13]

A comparison of Luke and the Greek historians must be made in the light of the historiographical ideals which dominated the first century A.D., and not those of an earlier period.[14] In contrast to the ideals of Luke's day, the speeches of Acts do not exhibit the Lucan style in its most polished form. On the contrary, the literary style of many of the speeches is inferior to that of the narrative,[15] in spite of indisputable evidence that Luke could compose elegant Greek. In the light of contemporary rhetorical taste and the artistic license shown in the composition of speeches, the Acts is a work which differs considerably from the style then most in favor.

A second characteristic which distinguishes Acts from contemporary works of history is its kerygmatic purpose. Luke is an evangelist not only in the Gospel, but in the Acts as well; a kerygmatic intention controls the use of speeches in both halves of his work. In a careful analysis of the speeches of Acts, M. Dibelius attempted to show that Luke's work should be understood in the light of Hellenistic historiographical practice.[16] He recognized, however, two essential differences between Luke's work and that of the classical historians. The fundamental assessment of the meaning of the speeches is different, since Luke writes a history which he believes has happened according to the will of God. Stylistically, Luke's speeches are much shorter, lacking two prominent elements common to the historians: (i) the deliberative element, the debating of the "for" and "against" and (ii) the epideictic element, the rhetorical elaboration of the ideas concerned.[17] With respect to the missionary sermons, Dibelius cautioned, "the analogy of historical writing fails, for here the kerygmatic aim of the book, i.e., not only to narrate, but also to proclaim, comes into evidence."[18]

This is an important observation, for it permits a consideration of Acts in the light of Jewish, rather than Hellenistic, historiography. It has frequently been observed that in the Gospel Luke used his sources in a way that parallels the Jewish tradition of writing history.[19] But in Acts (where Luke's sources are no longer available for comparison), it is commonly held, the evangelist employed the freedom and literary conventions of Hellenistic literature. This argument is based on the assumption that while the words of Jesus were authoritative and had to be transmitted with care, no such authority adhered to the tradition incorporated in Acts.[20]

This argument must be challenged. Even in the Gospel, Luke controls his sources; his sources do not control him. He used Mark extensively in composing his Gospel because of the authoritative tradition which Mark incorporated. That it was the tradition which was authoritative for Luke is clear from the fact that he has ordered the material according to his own purpose. In Acts the situation is not different. Here also Luke is dealing with traditional material which he structures in his distinctive way. It is no longer possible to identify his sources. But the authoritative character of the tradition in Acts is clear from Luke's designation of sermonic material preserved by him as ὁ λόγος τοῦ θεοῦ or τοῦ κυρίου.[21]

Luke has incorporated authoritative tradition in the Gospel and in Acts; his material has been kerygmatically structured in order to proclaim Jesus, who is the focus of attention in both parts. The full implication of the fact that Luke-Acts is a single work and that the preface to the Gospel serves to introduce the entire corpus,[22] has not been sufficiently appreciated. The kerygmatic purpose and method which controls the Gospel also controls Acts.

The view of history which controls the presentation of the material in both sections of Luke-Acts is reflected in the attitude Luke takes toward his narrative. The Christian viewpoint that God intervenes in history and leads the messianic community can be clearly discerned throughout the work.[23] The concern to proclaim the gospel governs Acts, as well as the gospel narrative, and the speeches of Acts are the vehicle through which this concern is realized. It is the Jewish tradition of writing history which appears best to account for this approach.[24] Luke was not unaware of the Greek tradition of historical writing and its principles, but in attitude and practice he was more strongly influenced by the Jewish tradition.

The criticism that the brevity of the speeches of Acts underscores the improbability that they are a record of what was actually said on a given occasion contains an element of truth. The speeches in Luke-Acts are not *verbatim* reports of all that was said on any occasion, but purport to be summaries of reliable tradition. After the first important speech in the Gospel (3:7-17) and after the first major address in the Acts (2:14-38), Luke indicates that only a summary of what was actually said has been given (Luke 3:18; Acts 2:40). These statements, occurring after the initial address of the Gospel and of Acts, are programmatic for the other speeches in Luke-Acts; the speeches are summaries of much longer addresses given on various occasions. In the treatment of speech material in the Acts as well as in the Gospel, Luke has been guided by the same principles.

Within the missionary sermons the recurrence of certain themes and motifs is striking, giving the impression of some underlying scheme or formal structure. The great similarity between the different sermons has been cited as evidence that the speeches are stylized compositions. It was Dibelius' opinion that the missionary sermons reflect the preaching with which Luke would be familiar in the ninth decade of the first century.[25] To judge from such sources as I Clement, II Clement, the "Two Ways" discourse of the Didache or Barnabas, this opinion is without foundation. It is necessary rather to turn to I Corinthians 15:3ff., where Paul appeals to the kerygma, for a parallel in content to the early speeches of Acts.[26] Paul insists that he shared the same essential message as the Jerusalem apostles, and he expects the kerygma to be recognized in outline whether in Jerusalem or in Corinth (I Cor. 15:11). This accounts to a large degree for the similarity, and apparent interdependence of thought in the speeches of Acts. Undoubtedly Luke is responsible to a significant degree for the external form and language of the speeches. The fact that they are schematic and brief results in the appearance of a lack of nuances. But the parallel in motif between the missionary sermons of Acts and Paul's schematic recital of the kerygma lends support to the contention that Luke has preserved specimens of early Jerusalem preaching.

A careful analysis, moreover, reveals shades of difference between the speeches of Peter and Paul in Acts which should not be minimized. The archaic Christology of the Petrine speeches has no parallel in the sermons of Paul, nor in his epistles.[27] The expectation that the parousia of Jesus will be conditioned by a national repentence on the part of the Jews appears only in the earliest expressions of Peter (Acts 3:19-21). These characteristics can be ascribed plausibly to a primitive source. On the other hand, the reference to justification by Jesus "from all things, from which you could not be justified by the law of Moses" (Acts 13:38f.), as well as the reference to "the church of God, which he purchased through his own blood" (Acts 20:28), are typical Pauline emphases to which nothing in the first twelve chapters of Acts corresponds. Within the sermons themselves different types of address must be differentiated, if the distinctiveness of the several speeches is to be appreciated.[28]

Luke's preface indicates that in composing his account he had consulted those who from the beginning had been eyewitnesses of the events he reports and ministers of the word (Luke 1:1-4). These were his primary sources for the speech material included in the early chapters of Acts. The integrity of the eyewitnesses is the guarantee of the reliability of the tradition incorporated in the speeches. There is no sound reason for rejecting the speeches as reliable sources for understanding the thinking and expression of the early church.[29]

II.   The Relative Primitiveness of the Tradition

It is not sufficient to form a judgment concerning the essential reliability of traditional elements within the speeches of Acts. It is also necessary to investigate those elements incorporated within a given speech which commend confidence in its primitive character. A basis for confidence in the primitive character of formulations distinctive to Peter's address in Acts 3:12-26 may be found in its Aramaic substructure, in its παῖς Christology and in the tenor of the hope held out for Israel.

A.   *The Question of an Aramaic Sub-structure*

The subject of the early chapters of Acts is the church in Jerusalem. The background of the narrative is clearly Judean. The worship of this earliest Jewish-Christian community was carried on in the vernacular, Aramaic;[30] it is antecedently probable that if written documents or notes emanated from the community, they would be written in Aramaic.[31] The idea that a Semitic source or sources lies behind the early chapters of Acts was suggested by E. Nestle (1896),[32] and was commended as probable by A. Harnack (1908).[33] It was C. C. Torrey, however, who presented most fully evidence for supposing that the early chapters of Acts rest upon an Aramaic foundation.[34] It was his contention that the idiom of the first half of Acts was of such a character that it betrayed dependence upon a single Aramaic document. Primary evidence in support of this theory was a series of passages in which obscure or "impossible" Greek becomes intelligible if translated, word for word, into Aramaic. This evidence was corroborated at a number of lesser points, where the Greek is more intelligible if it be regarded as transliteration-idiom. Torrey expressed his conviction with characteristic vigor:

> It is not enough to speak of frequent Semitisms; the truth is that the language of all these fifteen chapters is translation-Greek through and through, generally preserving even the order of the words. In the remainder of the book, chs. xvi-xxviii, the case is altogether different. Here there is no evidence of an underlying Semitic language. The few apparent Semitisms . . , are chargeable to the κοινή; though their presence may be due in part to the influence of the translation-Greek which Luke had so extensively read and written. In either case they are negligible.[35]

The accuracy of this conviction was challenged by F. C. Burkitt,[36] H. J. Cadbury,[37] and J. de Zwaan,[38] among others. De Zwaan, for example, pointed out that there were far more Semitisms in the latter

half of Acts than Torrey had been willing to recognize,[39] and that
within the first half of Acts there were stretches of strong and weak
passages which had to be evaluated individually.[40] His own conclusion was that the case for an Aramaic substratum was strong for
1:6 – 5:16 and 9:31 – 11:18, but weak or indecisive for the remaining passages in which Torrey had detected the Aramaic document.
In his judgment, the evidence for the existence or unity of a single
Aramaic document was not impressive.

Of those passages in which Torrey detected evidence of mistranslation, Acts 3:16 appeared decisive to de Zwaan. Torrey was able
to account for the awkwardness of the passage by retroversion of the
Greek into Aramaic:

ובהימנתא די שמה להדן די חזין אנתון וידעין תקף שמה והימנתא די בה יהבה

לה חלמות אדא קדם כלכון:

The translator appears to have read in the middle of this sentence
תַּקֵּף שָׁמֵהּ (ἐστερέωσε τὸ ὄνομα αὐτοῦ), while what was intended was
תַּקֵּף שָׁמָה (ὑγιῆ κατέστησεν αὐτόν or ὑγιῆ ἐποίησεν αὐτόν).[41] This
would suit the context, and would run on naturally from what had
preceded it, drawing the subject for ὑγιῆ κατέστησεν from the ὁ θεός
v. 15: "and by faith in His name He has made whole this man whom
you see and know." The solution to the difficulty is attractive, for
the suggested mistake on the part of the translator (whether Luke
or his source) is a very natural one. When he had before him the
same letter which before were correctly read as שָׁמֵהּ (his name),
it did not occur to him to read them as שָׁמָה . The suggested Aramaic
is easy in itself, but admits of a misreading which could account for
the state of the Greek text as it now stands.

A number of Torrey's critics accepted his conjecture as convincing,[42]
while none of them sought to question this particular illustration of
"mistranslation" on linguistic or exegetical grounds. Yet caution should
be exercised before considering Torrey's case as demonstrated. His
retroversion of the Greek into unpointed Aramaic may be accepted as
substantially correct, but his analysis of the proposed mistranslation is
open to challenge. Torrey contends that the translator read in the middle of the sentence תַּקֵּף שָׁמֵהּ , while what was intended was תַּקֵּף שָׁמָה :
in short, the radicals תקף were read as a verb (ἐστερέωσε), when
what was demanded was a noun (ὑγιῆ). The larger context of v. 16,
however, favors the understanding of (the assumed) תקף not as a
noun, but as a verb. Ἐστερέωσν in v. 16 clearly echoes an earlier use
of the verb in v. 7: παραχρῆμα δὲ ἐστερεώθησαν αἱ βάσειν αὐτοῦ καὶ τὰ

σφοδρά. Presumably a form of תקף accounts for the presence of the verb in both verses. While in v. 16 it would be possible to read the radicals as either a noun or a verb., in v. 7 the verbal form is demanded. The probability of mistranslation in v. 16 is accordingly lessened.

To point this out serves to emphasize that in an analysis of the Greek text in the light of a proposed Aramaic sub-stratum all that can be offered is possibility. It is important to recognize that any Greek tradition of the earliest Jerusalem community that has any claims to historicity ultimately must be built on a Semitic foundation: traces of the influence of that foundation may be expected, even in a quite advanced stage of the building. It is probable that an Aramaic source, whether oral or written, accounts generally for the Semitisms which are scattered throughout the third chapter of Acts,[43] and particularly for the awkward construction in Acts 3:16. But critical evaluation of Torrey's presentation indicates that in a discussion of Semitisms no more can be done than to balance possibilities. Proof that in Acts 3 we are in touch with the primitive community must rest on stronger evidence.

B. *The* Παῖς *Christology*

A second factor which may be evaluated is the terminology of the speech. In his review of Torrey's work on the "Aramaic Acts" F. C. Burkitt expressed his judgment that the presence of a παῖς Christology in Acts 3-4 was decisive against the theory of a primitive Semitic source; it is in a Hellenistic context that the term παῖς is significant.[44] In Greek the term παῖς may mean either "servant," "child," or "son," and therefore conveys no offensive meaning; but its Semitic counter-term עבד can only mean "slave." Burkitt assumed that the use of servant motifs to express the passion and character of Jesus was the work of gentile Christians, familiar with the Bible only in Greek, who failed to understand that the term behind παῖς meant "slave." That the primitive church could think of Jesus as God's slave was to Burkitt incredible.[45]

F. J. Foakes-Jackson and K. Lake shared Burkitt's conviction. In a study of possible influence of the suffering Servant of Isaiah upon the passion narrative, they asserted that only in Luke-Acts was the connection of Jesus' ministry with the suffering Servant actually made (cf. Luke 21:37; Acts 8:32). The conclusion to which they felt driven agreed with Burkitt's:

It is tempting to suggest that the interpretation of Isaiah 53 as a prophecy of Jesus was introduced by Hellenistic Christians, for there is no positive evidence of its existence in sources which certainly represent that thought of the first disciples in Jerusalem, but it was clearly part of the teaching of Philip.[46]

To assign the interpretation of Jesus as the suffering Servant to Philip is to predicate an early stage in Greek-speaking Christianity. But, to use Burkitt's phrase, "it is not quite primitive or apostolic." Can this judgment be substantiated?

The term παῖς is used of Jesus four times in Acts, twice in Peter's speech in Solomon's porch (3:13, 26) and twice in the context of prayer (4:27, 30). In each case the term is followed by a pronoun in the genitive case (αὐτοῦ *or* σου) and in each of the instances except one by an appositive, "Jesus." Apart from these passages the concept of παῖς θεοῦ appears in the New Testament only in Matthew 12:18, Luke 1:54, 69, and Acts 4:25. Thus except for the quotation of Isaiah 42:1 in Matthew 12:18 (ἰδοὺ ὁ παῖς μου ὃν ᾑρέτισα), the term is used with the special meaning παῖς θεοῦ only in Luke-Acts.

In the Old Testament the phrase "my servant" occurs often as a description of outstanding men of God. It is used particularly of Moses,[47] but also of the patriarchs, Joshua, Job, David, Daniel, Isaiah, and even Nebuchadnezzar.[48] The term is one of dignity and special honor; its use is restricted to an individual's relationship to Yahweh, not to his fellow-men. The expression is thoroughly Hebraic. Its continued use can be traced back to portions of the liturgy which date to the period of the second Temple.[49]

In the Septuagint עבד was translated primarily by δοῦλος and παῖς, together with the appropriate genitive constructions. Within the canonical books of the LXX the most striking instances of παῖς θεοῦ as a designation of honor occur in the Pentateuch, where with three exceptions it consistently renders the עבד יהוה or the עבדי of divine discourse.

In the period subsequent to 100 B.C. παῖς θεοῦ continues to appear with several shades of meaning, but one is struck with the relative infrequency of this phrase.[50] The collective use of the singular עבד יהוה as a description of Israel, first seen in the latter portions of Isaiah, persists in this period both in Hellenistic and Palestinian Judaism.[51] Παῖς θεοῦ continues to be used in its Old Testament sense as title of honor for outstanding servants of God,[52] and occasionally is extended to the Messiah.[53] In the interpretation of Isaiah's Servant of God in Jewish Hellenistic literature subsequent to

100 B.C. the Servant is consistently called παῖς.[54] This usage prevailed until about the beginning of the second century when Aquila consistently translated עבד by δοῦλος.[55] His example was followed by the later translators, Theodotian and Symmanchus, with the result that παῖς θεοῦ terminology fell into disuse and occurs only rarely in later works.

The material surveyed by Zimmerli and Jeremias indicates that the παῖς terminology is thoroughly Semitic in character and that for the distinctively Lucan instances of παῖς θεοῦ parallels may be cited from near contemporary Jewish sources. Thus Israel is designated God's servant in the Psalms of Solomon (12:7, 'Ισραήλ παῖδα αὐτοῦ; 17:23, 'Ισραήλ παῖδα σου) in a manner analogous to the Lucan expression 'Ισραήλ παιδὸς αὐτοῦ (Luke 1:54), while the designation of David as Δαυείδ παιδὸς αὐτοῦ (Luke 1:69), has its parallel in Jewish prayers of the first century.[56]

The strong presumption that the use of παῖς θεοῦ terminology in early Christian sources is derived from Jewish practice is confirmed by the character of the passages in the New Testament where it occurs. On each occasion when παῖς is used with the meaning of παῖς θεοῦ, the passage has definite Jewish coloring. Since Matt. 12:18 forms part of an actual quotation from Isaiah 42:1, it may be discounted; in Luke the word occurs in the songs of Mary and Zachariah, the Jewish character of which is beyond dispute; in Acts the phrase is found three times in early Christian prayer, and twice in a sermon attributed to Peter, within the framework of what appears to be very early traditional material.

Beyond these eight New Testament occurrences, παῖς is applied to Jesus only rarely in the documents of the late first and second centuries.[57] It occurs primarily in liturgical contexts: the instances in I Clement, the Didache, and the Martyrdom of Polycarp all appear in the context of prayers, while those in the Epistle of Barnabas are quotations. The Epistle of Diognetus stands alone in its use of the term in a non-cultic context.

This restricted use of παῖς θεοῦ tends to confirm that the designation was an early one which was soon abandoned apart from the conservative language of liturgy in which it lay embedded from earliest times. Far from representing the language of Hellenistic Christianity, the abandonment of the description παῖς in the general usage of the church was apparently a result of the decrease of Jewish influence upon Christian thought. Παῖς θεοῦ, apart from its thoroughly Semitic associations, inevitably conveyed the idea of subordination, whether παῖς be understood as "servant" or as "son." In a Greek setting the term appeared disparaging and was replaced by υἱός.[58]

The fact that in Acts reference is never made to Jesus as "the servant," but only as "his servant" or "thy servant," is important. What is emphasized is his special relationship to God. This furnishes an exact parallel to the Old Testament use of the concept עבד יהוה as a designation of honor. Jewish documents from the same general period and later designate the Messiah as God's servant precisely in contexts speaking of his exaltation and glory,[59] as does Acts 3. The unmistakable Semitic coloring of the passages in Acts where the term is used lends support to the suggestion that their origin must be found in the Jerusalem, not in the Hellenistic, community. These passages represent the pronouncements of the primitive Jewish-Christian community. With the rapid growth in the Greek-speaking element of the church παῖς came to be considered inadequate. That Luke has preserved παῖς at all is a testimony to his fidelity to older elements in the tradition, however these elements were known to him. Its dignity in a Jewish context is thoroughly consonant with its application by the primitive church to Jesus. That the origin and home of the designation must be sought in the first Palestinian community is indirectly attested by the disappearance of "Servant of God" as a description of the Messiah in Palestinian Judaism, apparently in reaction to early Christian preaching.[60]

The designation παῖς appeared offensive to the Hellenistic churches because its biblical context was not properly appreciated. By the end of the first century it is found only in the proclamation of an Aramaic-speaking Jewish-Christian sect of Palestine, the Ebionites.[61] The presence of a παῖς Christology in Acts 3 in no way detracts from its purportedly primitive character, but is appropriate to the earliest proclamation of the Jerusalem community.

C. *The Tenor of Israel's Hope*

In evaluating the relative primitiveness of elements within Acts 3:12-26 there should be an appreciation of the tenor of the hope extended for Israel. Following the presentation of the central facts concerning Jesus' death and resurrection there occurs a categorical demand for repentance (3:19-21). The aspect of demand is mitigated by the content of the hope expressed: repentance will occasion the blotting out of sin, the in-breaking of a period of refreshment, and the parousia of the Messiah appointed for Israel. A series of purpose clauses indicate that repentence is the condition of the promised redemption of the coming of the Messiah.[62]

That the repentance of Israel is made in some sense the condition for the sending of the Messiah is of special interest. Reflecting the old biblical pattern of repentance followed by deliverance, the conviction was formed in certain circles during the intertestamental period that the messianic salvation was dependent upon the repentance of the nation.[63] Lack of repentance would delay the coming of the Messiah. By the first century the connection between national repentance and messianic redemption formed part of the popular stock of religious ideas; it was basic to the preaching of John the Baptist that the Messiah cannot come until Israel repents.[64]

Within Pharisaic circles, particularly toward the end of the first century, the relationship of national repentance to the coming messianic deliverance was a matter of debate. The most famous controversy was between the Shammaite, R. Eliezer ben Hyrkanos, and the Hillelite, R. Jehoshua ben Hanaja (c. A.D. 90).[65] R. Eliezer contended that Messiah would not come, and could not come, until Israel repented as a nation. This had not always been his conviction. He had formerly entertained the view that the messianic redemption would dawn wholly apart from repentance. He had based his opinion upon a popular expectation that Messiah would come at the conclusion of Daniel's seventy week-years,[66] which the rabbis calculated should fall on the ninth of Ab, the year 69/70. Instead of the messianic deliverance, on this date Titus burned the Temple![67] The explanation for this reversal in expectation was found in the fact that Israel had not repented. R. Eliezer's reasoning was challenged by R. Jehoshua. On the basis of Isaiah 52:3, Jeremiah 3:4, and Daniel 7:7 he argued that when God's appointed time came the messianic end would arrive, regardless of the repentance of Israel. R. Jehoshua worked with a different set of figures basing his calculations on the sabbatical scheme of seven millennia. He estimated that the Messiah would come in the year A.D. 240,[68] a date sufficiently advanced in the future to allow R. Jehoshua to dispute the reasoning of his colleague with vigor. While the debate is recorded several times in the sources, the briefest account occurs in Tanchuma B to Leviticus.

> R. Eliezer said, If Israel will repent, it will be redeemed. If Israel will not repent, it will not be redeemed, as it is written: *In returning and rest you shall be saved* (Isa. 30:15). R. Jehoshua said: Whether they return or not, as soon as the End is come, so soon

will they be redeemed, as it is written, *I am the Lord. In its time I will hasten it* (Isa. 60:22). R. Eliezer said: God placed over them an evil man like Haman, and he afflicts them, and as a result they will do repentance, as it is written, *For he will come like a rushing stream which the spirit of the Lord drives in that hour,*[69] *and he will come to Zion as Redeemer, even to those in Jacob who turn from transgression* (Isa. 59:19-20).[70]

R. Eliezer is given the final word, for his opinion was unquestionably the more prevalent one. The messianic age is held in abeyance until the people repent.

It is this conviction which lies behind Acts 3:19f., where Peter urges the people to repent "in order that he [the Lord] may send the Messiah appointed for you." The hope that God would inaugurate the Days of the Messiah if only Israel would repent was native to the primitive community, forming part of that eschatological complex which was their religious heritage as Palestinian Jews. It is only in the earliest strata of the tradition that this tenor of hope for Israel, based upon an immediate national repentance, is expressed. The presence of this hope in Acts 3:19-21 confirms the primitiveness of the affirmations found there.

The evidence set forth with respect to an Aramaic sub-structure for Acts 3, its παις Christology and its hope for Israel based upon national repentance, commends confidence in the primitive character of the speech recorded there. The evidence for primitive elements within the speech strengthens confidence in both the primitive character of the tradition embodied and its essential reliability as source material for the thought and practice of the primitive Christian church in Jerusalem.

PART FOUR

ESSAYS IN PHILOSOPHY

AND APOLOGETICS

Robert D. Knudsen

XIV. PROGRESSIVE AND REGRESSIVE TENDENCIES
IN CHRISTIAN APOLOGETICS

The year 1928 marked an important turning point for Christian apologetics. In that year Cornelius Van Til left his pastorate in the Christian Reformed Church of Spring Lake, Michigan, and took the position of Instructor of Apologetics at the Princeton Theological Seminary. The following year the reorganization of that seminary precipitated a break with it on the part of the majority of those who wanted to carry on the witness for the Reformed faith that characterized the Old Princeton. Van Til was one of those who left Princeton to found the Westminster Theological Seminary, Philadelphia. It was then at Westminster, and not at Princeton, that the new method which he was developing began to take root.

In a broad segment of the Christian church apologetics had fallen into almost complete disrepute. That was for the most part the result of the attacks of humanism and of liberal theology. They dismissed apologetics as a case of special pleading, or as the vain attempt to defend an outworn theological position by means of bad arguments. Apologetics was indeed carried on by evangelicals, largely in America and in Britain; but it depended for its insights and its methods almost exclusively on the older apologetic positions, which were widely considered to be outdated.

Even among Reformed thinkers apologetics had received hard blows. The powerful Dutch Reformed tradition had virtually abandoned apologetics under the influence of the penetrating criticism of Abraham Kuyper. To his mind apologetics meant taking a defensive position against the attacks of unbelief. This was too weak, too passive. To support his attitude he could appeal to the history of apologetics itself, which showed the miserable spectacle of the retreat of the defenders of the faith from one rampart to another, including less and less within the radius of that which it was thought necessary or even possible to defend. The defenders of historic Christianity often satisfied themselves with salvaging various fundamentals, which, even though they were certainly basic to the Christian faith, nevertheless did not represent that faith in its fullness and power. The defenders of the faith appeared to be exchanging the grand structure of classical theology for a hovel, from which, after having abandoned the citadel, they might at least carry on guerilla warfare against the interlopers.

That dreary history arose, Van Til thought, not simply because the defenders took a defensive position instead of going over to the attack. It was, first of all, because the defenders of the Christian faith had allowed the attackers to occupy some ground in their own right. To give them some right to territory, to allow that they in their own right could attain to truth, a truth which they could master without any reference to the Christian faith at all, was to allow them within the Christian perimeter, to concede to them an advantage which it was thereafter impossible to stop them from exploiting.

If, on the other hand, the invader could be denied all right to truth, he would be denied a foothold altogether. The entire terrain could be claimed for Christ, and the invader challenged as to his right to be there at all.

Thus Van Til sought to reinstate apologetics, but on a new basis. He admitted the force of Kuyper's criticism of apologetics as it was carried on traditionally. He saw the need for abandoning a passive and defensive attitude and for resuming the offensive. Nevertheless, he recognized that even a good offense demanded that the enemy be denied any foothold behind the defensive lines. Otherwise even the best offense would become stalled because of the confusion the enemy would be sowing in the rear.

*   *   *   *   *

The major trend in modern Christian apologetics had not sought to work on a consistently Christian foundation. It drew from the empiricism which flourished in the soil prepared by modern scientific discovery. Under this influence it was thought impossible to prove Christianity. One could not compel another on rational grounds to accept the Christian faith. Such a proof could be valid only on the foundation of a strict rationalism. That is to say, it would require an argument that proceeded from indubitable premises and drew necessary conclusions on the basis of strict logical deduction. But the idea that any such argument could refer to real states of affairs had long been abandoned. Instead, apologetics declared itself to be satisfied with a lesser goal. It attempted to establish a presumption in favor of the Christian faith, which in the absence of any compelling reason to the contrary, would be enough to establish a practical certainty, i.e., an assurance that was sufficient to act upon. Thus one was supposed to be able to establish a practical certainty which, if acted upon, would not prove contrary to what would be expected of a rational man, i.e., a man of sound judgment in practical affairs.

If it was impossible to set forth the reasonableness of every doctrine of Christianity with the same force, it was at least possible to establish enough to make the acceptance of the rest that much easier.

An illustration of this kind of reasoning is the famed argument for life after death presented by Bishop Butler. In his argument Butler capitalized on the faith in the regularity of nature which had been cultivated by the success of the classical physics. Although it is impossible to construe nature according to an airtight rationalistic scheme, he thought, its regularity is such that we daily exercise a practical faith in it. We assume that in its constitution and course it will continue the same, unless there is a compelling and sufficient reason to think otherwise. We observe life in man with all its vicissitudes; nevertheless, we also observe that none of these is sufficient to destroy the continuity of his life. The question arises whether the discontinuity experienced in death is of such a nature as to break off the continuity we have observed in life. Since reason does not demand it and since we have never experienced this discontinuity, there is no compelling reason to think that it would. Unless death is of a quite different order, we may rationally assume that it will not totally obliterate personal identity. Since there is no sufficient reason to think otherwise, it is rational to place one's practical faith on the probability that there is a life after death.

There are many basic similarities in the argument of William Paley, who is famous for his arguments from design. He also seeks to establish a presumption for the Christian faith and leans heavily on the idea of sufficient reason. If one walks along and his foot strikes a stone, he says, there is no sufficient reason to suppose that it has not lain there from eternity; but if one strikes against a watch, which shows marks of design, the situation is different. There is sufficient reason to think that a watch has not lain inert from eternity but that it is the product of design. If our experience is that things evidencing design are the work of a designer, then by analogy we can argue that the universe, which also shows the marks of design, is the work of a great designer, who has fashioned everything for the benefit of the sensible creation.

Further, he argued for the specific truths of the Christian faith on the basis that there is no sufficient reason to reject the force of the testimony of the original witnesses, a testimony that was able to stand up against persecution. A presumption for Christianity is established which, in the absence of sufficient reason to the contrary, is able to commend itself to the faith of rational man.

*   *   *   *   *

Between Bishop Butler and William Paley came the acute Scotsman David Hume. He brought to bear on Butler's arguments the type of criticism that is current even today in naturalistic circles. The argument of Butler had sought to appeal to experience to establish the probability of things that lay beyond the scope of experience. Hume answered that the only basis for throwing over a bridge between what was within experience to what was beyond experience was by means of the cause-effect relationship. But this relationship had meaning only within the bounds of experience itself. It could not serve to build a bridge over to that which was beyond experience. Butler had opted for an empirical method. Let him then remain with it! Furthermore, Butler had appealed to what was beyond our experience to serve as an explanation of what was within experience. But if one has to cut off the process of explanation somewhere by an arbitrary act, why begin it at all? Could one not just as well assume that the universe is its own explanation as to seek grounds of explanation beyond it?

Just as significant, or more significant, than any rational argument that he set forth was the fundamental shift that took place in Hume's thinking, towards a functional, psychological basis of understanding. He sought to understand the unity of the world and of the self in terms of the tendency of the mind to think in terms of a continuum, filling in the gaps where necessary. Thus, if Butler appealed to the classical physics with its idea of inertia—that there is established a presumption in favor of the Christian faith which in the absence of a sufficient reason to the contrary can merit the practical faith of the rational man—Hume transferred this notion of inertia to the inner life. The ideas of the unity of the world and the self, and also the notions of miracle and the supernatural, are ascribable to the tendency of the mind to proceed beyond what is available to experience. Miracle stories are understandable as the fabrication of the untutored, primitive mind, to which the stories of the miraculous and the wonderful are agreeable.

Reformed apologetics acknowledges that there is an element of validity in Hume's criticism of the traditional apologetical stance. The latter had come to accept much of the same trust in nature and in reason which animated the major thinkers of the time. That attitude was fundamentally deistic. Reason and nature were accorded an independency from God. He created them indeed, as a master watchmaker fashions a wonderful precision watch. But God was thought to have the position of one who could be established by reason instead of being the one without whom reason would lose its foundation and meaning. In the history of deism this independent reason first became the arbiter and later even the substitute for God and for his revelation. Even evangelical thought, which differed from deism by retaining the idea of revelation, nevertheless allowed reason an independent status, only insisting that it be supported and supplemented by faith. Even among the evangelicals the idea took hold that the life of reason was possible to everyone who exercised sound judgment. God would not ask more. More than what was expected of a man of sound judgment, who was capable of regulating his own affairs, would not be required by God. God was thought to be universally available to man by way of his rational powers. Then it was necessary to supplement this natural awareness with truths which were specific to Christianity and which were necessary to salvation. These could be supported by the arguments from miracle and from prophecy.

The result was that a large segment of human life was disengaged from direct contact with the self-revealing God. Man was surrounded in great measure with an impersonal universe in which he would not be confronted with the demands of the Christian faith. The result of this deistic influence upon evangelicalism was to make it vulnerable to the attacks of more radical deists, who sought to depend solely upon reason and to jettison faith. It also laid it bare to the attacks of Hume. The latter simply carried the empirical position, placed in the setting of a neutral reason, to its consistent expression. If one started within experience, an experience which to all intents and purposes was declared to be neutral, was there indeed any sufficient reason to look to a ground of explanation beyond experience—particularly so, if all such attempts were easily explainable in terms of the tendencies to excess of the undisciplined mind? Thus the experience of the man of sound judgment was declared to be sufficient to itself, without the need of anything from outside to interrupt its serene course.

Van Til recognized the validity within limits of Hume's criticism. If one assumes the position of neutrality, there is no reason he can subsequently bring to bear that will be sufficient to deflect him from his path. The law of parsimony will demand that he seek to explain his experience in the simplest available terms, those which are closest to him, which are within his experience itself. And were he to attempt to rise to an explanation which is beyond his experience, the greatest explanation he could attain would still be a finite one. According to the law of parsimony, one cannot reason to a cause which is greater than what is adequate to explain its effect. Since the effect is obviously finite and imperfect, the only god to whom one can reason will himself have to be finite and imperfect.

* * * * *

Recognizing that the method of Hume undermined not only the traditional arguments for Christianity but also the foundations of the unity of the world and the self, the idealists looked for a more adequate approach. Relief was sought in a transcendental direction. This meant a more radical departure. The mind was to be guided back to its own most ultimate presuppositions.

This approach was supposed to be concrete, in the sense that from the outset all the factors involved were to be taken into consideration. In its activity the mind is supposed to be reflecting back on what it is, not only as a goal to be attained but also in its own deepest impulse.

The apologist who sought to capitalize on the idealistic legacy of Kant and Hegel, as they were interpreted and modified by Thomas Hill Green, was the Englishman, James Orr. Orr's method allowed him to begin with a confession of the Christian faith and to insist that it was the full Christian faith, not some preliminary religion of nature, that he was defending. It is, Orr claimed, the Christian faith that offers the presuppositions (postulates) which present us with the possibility of understanding our experience. The Christian faith thus becomes for James Orr the transcendental ground of our experience, that which provides it with its foundation and legitimation.

Orr maintained that without these presuppositions experience would degenerate into chaos.[1] There would no longer be any way to establish the ground of the possibility of experience. The only foundation for the order and the uniformity of nature is not something derived from our experience itself but is the absolute system within the mind of God. To strip away this presupposition and to seek within experience itself for a foundation is to fall into chaos. Similarly, the presupposition for the interpretation of history is the person of Jesus Christ. If one does not presuppose him as the source of meaning, the interpretation of history proceeds by an inner necessity of its own down the road to irrationalism.

Presuppositional apologetics has capitalized upon elements of the method which emerged from the transcendental idealistic movement as were used by James Orr.[2] It has adopted a concrete approach, taking into consideration from the outset the full commitment of the Christian thinker. It has more or less taken over the transcendental method, seeking to establish it more purely. It has also benefited from the dialectical thrust of the argument. Only on the basis of a correct starting point is it possible to provide a transcendental foundation for the possibility of experience. Starting from a false point leads thought inexorably to turn into its opposite and to destroy itself.

Indeed, James Orr's position meant a definite advance along several fronts. He helped to break the hold that the Newtonian world machine idea and the classical physical notion of inertia had obtained on Christian apologetics. No longer was it thought that a presumption could be established for the Christian faith which in the absence of a compelling reason to the contrary would be sufficient to warrant the practical faith of the rational man. Instead, the Christian position became the ground of the very possibility of experience. The world of nature was not thought of so much as an independent world-order from which it could be reasoned to the Christian faith but a world-order whose very foundation was now to be reflected upon and established.

Nevertheless idealistic and rationalistic elements in Orr's position intruded upon and affected his argument. The truths of the unity, simplicity, etc., of God are regarded to be taught by the Hebrew-Christian tradition; nevertheless, they are the truths after which human reason has ever been seeking without ever finally attaining. Throughout Orr emphasizes the affinity between the divine rational spirit and the human rational spirit. This affinity makes it possible to understand and to appreciate the necessity of the incarnation. Orr retains the notion, that once having understood such central ideas, and thus having gained a foothold in the supernatural, one can that much more easily proceed further and accept additional teachings of Christianity. Orr's idealistic faith in the power of the idea of human reason leads him to views that are reminiscent of deism. Christianity becomes too much a republication of what is essentially open to

universal human reason, the reflection on the human level of the
universal divine reason.

*   *   *   *   *

Orr's apologetics stressed to advantage the importance of presuppositions and of one's starting point. This attitude is reflected
even more in the position of Van Til. The latter does not wish to
allow for any starting point that does not take into account from
the outset man's concrete situation as it is revealed in the Scriptures.
That is to say, any starting point will have to take into account that
man is the creature of God, surrounded on all sides by the revelation
of God, a revelation that addresses him and that confronts him at
all times with the responsibility to serve God with his whole heart;
that man has been corrupted in his entire being by the fall into sin,
so that he is of himself unable, apart from the principle of regeneration, to come to a true interpretation and expression of this revelation of God; and that in Christ is God's final revelation, the hub
of interpretation both of the inner meaning of the creation and also
of the redemption that God has provided for the salvation of lost
mankind.

Thus in his important pamphlet, "Why I Believe in God," Van Til
does not consider his early Christian training and his Christian
commitment to be accidental matters, in essence irrelevant to his
intellectual stance; instead, these represent the framework within
which thought and experience have their true foundation and apart
from which they fall away into meaninglessness.

This has then been paramount in establishing Van Til's polemical,
apologetical stance. If one fails to assume a starting point that presupposes the Christian faith, he has no foundation for making intelligible judgments at all. Unbelieving man must be challenged with
this claim. And over against his claims must be set the claim of
Jesus Christ, which alone is adequate to make experience meaningful.

Thus it was Van Til who conceived of a progressive apologetics,
which sought to entrench itself solidly behind the strong walls of
historic Christianity, using the weapons forged by the richest stream
of theological thought, and challenging the opponent, not only to
wrest the initiative away from him but even to deny him a solid
position from which to launch an attack at all. Paradoxically this
apologetical method built upon the foundation which was laid by
Kuyper himself; it sought to avoid that which in Kuyper's eyes stig-
matized all previous apologetical method.

Van Til's apologetics pointed in two directions at once. It tried to show that it is only on the foundation of Christian presuppositions that meaningful discourse is possible. It also tried to show that the failure on the part of non-Christian thinking to attain the true starting point of thought means that it is impaled on the horns of a dilemma. Its attempt to interpret everything according to a criterion acceptable to the autonomous man means that it is driven inexorably to the opposite, namely, to an irrationalism in which meaningful discourse has become impossible. No matter what the difficulties may be, considered in detail, there is the possibility of a meaningful approach to thought and to life only when one is entrenched solidly behind the walls of a full-orbed expression of the Christian theistic position.

The method is, then, not to reason to the full theistic position from a standpoint outside of it, but to stand within the Christian theistic position itself. To fail to stand within this position, and to recognize that God's being is that of the Creator and that man's is that of the creature, is perforce to take a principle of unity that embraces both God and man and that thereby excludes the Creator-creature relationship. Van Til is ready, for the sake of argument, to take the position of the opponent, the one who has rejected the Creator-creature distinction and is therefore bound to set up his own standard as to the unity and the diversity which is in the cosmos. Every possible starting point the autonomous man can assume is not embracive enough, not inclusive enough to interpret all of the facts. One is always confronted with facts that at least possibly will not fit into his scheme of interpretation. His interpretation of the universe along lines that he himself thinks in terms of his self-sufficient reason (his abstract rationalism) strikes up against the irreducible brute facts which he must fail to incorporate in his system (his irrationalism). That one starts out with an autonomous rationality means inevitably that he will land up with an irrationalism. This should be pointed out concerning every possible non-theistic starting point (of which there is really basically only one) in order that the autonomous man may be shown the inherent hopelessness of his position and be challenged to accept the Christian theistic world view, only in terms of which is there the possibility of predicaton.

*   *   *   *   *

The forces at work in Reformed thought have produced a number of apologists who may be called "presuppositionalist" and who in some measure at least have sought to erect an apologetics on a different foundation from that of the classical evangelical position. Van Til, of course, belongs to this number; but so do Gordon H. Clark and Edward John Carnell. All of these are opposed by a number of thinkers who have never felt that the older apologetics has been severely challenged or by men who are fully aware of the method of the new apologetics but have chosen consciously to oppose it.

Prominent among the presuppositionalists has been Gordon H. Clark of Butler University. Clark has maintained that it is impossible to reach a complete, rational foundation for one's world view. A world view must be opted, by the Christian and by the non-Christian alike. The set of presuppositions must be chosen which is able to introduce the maximum amount of coherence into one's position. Clark has consistently argued that it is the central axioms which can be derived from the Christian faith that can bring the maximum amount of consistency into the interpretation of one's experience. Although for the finite mind this consistency cannot be perfect, nevertheless the difference is so great that the choice for the Christian faith is clearly preferable. Thus Clark's apologetical method has entailed showing the internal inconsistencies of the alternatives to the Christian faith and commending Christianity as the option that is most able to produce rational interpretation.

Insofar as Clark maintains that a coherent explanation of experience depends upon the choice of a set of axioms, he can be called a "presuppositionalist." The criterion of adequacy, that of logical consistency, gives Clark's position a rationalistic cast.[3]

In his writings Clark extols reason far more than the majority of secular philosophers do. There is an acid rebuttal of anyone who would ascribe to the idea of truth anything but an analytical sense. According to Clark, truth can be expressed only in propositions. It is only propositions that can be true or false. Furthermore, true propositions are regarded to be true unqualifiedly. Any deviation from this point of view, he thinks, must be unmasked as at best an incipient irrationalism.

As to its method, Carnell's early book, *An Introduction to Christian Apologetics*, follows Clark's position closely. In his early apologetical stance Carnell seemed to be clearly a disciple of Gordon Clark. Later, however, a clear difference emerged between them. The rift can be accounted for in part by a decided shift in emphasis on Clark's part. It also involves, however, a change in Carnell's position. In his later writings he gives a much broader interpretation of the basis of his apologetical method.

Clark has now taken the position that the predicates "true" and "knowledge" can be ascribed only to what is contained in the Scriptures of the Old and New Testaments, as the infallible word of God, and what may be deduced therefrom by good and necessary inference. Whatever is derived from other sources—e.g., from experience—may indeed be helpful and convenient; but it cannot lay claim to being truth and knowledge.

Thus Clark now chooses as his central axiom the statement, "The Bible is the Word of God." Having opted thereby what is to be the source of true statements, he then proceeds to deduce by strict logical inference the truths, the knowledge which can be derived from this axiom system.

This development in the statement of Clark's position is discussed at some length by Dr. Ronald Nash in the volume, *The Philosophy of Gordon H. Clark*.[4] To Nash's mind the new statement involves a major shift, an unfortunate departure, from Clark's earlier viewpoint. Nash leaves the impression that he wants to follow the lead of Carnell. He rejects Clark's new position and stresses the criterion of systematic consistency.

It must be questioned, however, how much Clark's present statement is a real departure from his earlier view. Was it included by implication, or at least as one of the possible consequences, of his earlier viewpoint? Does the present statement simply involve the development in a particular direction of the tendencies within his thought?

If Clark always insisted that one must decide for a system of axioms, and if these axioms were propositions which were unqualifiedly true, the question would naturally arise as to source of these preferred statements. Clark always discovered the source of these fundamental axioms in the Christian faith. Their origin is in the intellect of the sovereign God, who knows all things and is therefore able to know all things correctly. It would follow that it is only by divine revelation that these propositions would be available. Since the Scriptures are the revelation of God, the repository of the divine truths, they easily become the exclusive source for what, in Clark's eyes, has the only claim to being truth and knowledge. So it becomes understandable that he accepts as his central axiom, "The Bible is the Word of God." By this means he establishes the truth and knowledge status of all the statements in the Scriptures. These then serve as subsidiary axioms, universal propositions from which one can deduce additional knowledge.

Clark's position is that of a metaphysical theism in which truth and knowledge are restricted to theoretically founded statements. The source of knowledge is the complete theoretical intuition in the divine mind and whatever portion of that knowledge God has chosen to reveal. Knowledge is possible only because of God's theoretical intuition and only because he has revealed part of that truth in an infallible book.

Carnell, as we have observed, learned much from Clark. In his early thought he was presuppositional and rationalistic. Yet, it appears to me that even in his early thought he did not stress as much as Clark did the metaphysical founding of the principle of formal consistency. Carnell insisted that knowledge depended upon choosing fundamental axioms; but his emphasis lay on testing these axioms by applying the principle of logical consistency. The test of an option is its capability of introducing a superior measure of consistency. The rational man, Carnell said, would accept the system that is attended by the fewest difficulties.

Although he was a pupil of Clark and was long regarded to be an advocate of a Christian rationalism, Carnell's works after his *Apologetics* demand a broader basis of interpretation. Carnell's later development took him well out of the sphere of Gordon Clark, and even requires a re-interpretation of the *Apologetics* itself.

As we have remarked, Carnell did not stress as did Clark the founding of the principle of formal consistency in a metaphysic. He does not escape the problem of content, however. He only approaches it in a different way. The problem appears in his search for a point of contact in "culture" for the Christian faith. His thought then moves in various directions, along functional lines, as he thinks he can find such a point of contact first in one and then in another place.

This insight, it seems to me, is the only means of conceiving as a unity the methodology of his diverse writings. In his early *Apologetics* he seeks his point of contact in the human rational faculty; in *A Philosophy of the Christian Religion* he appeals to values; in *Christian Commitment* it is the judicial sentiment which he exploits; and in his later *The Kingdom of Love and the Pride of Life* he seeks to make contact with the unspoiled consciousness of the happy child.[5] In each case he supposes that he has discovered a fulcrum about which an argument for Christianity can turn. If one can bring the unbeliever to recognize the deeper implications of what he himself is saying, he can lead him gradually into an acceptance of the Christian position.

It is probably Ronald Nash who stands closest to Carnell's early position. He shows, on the one hand, a disinclination to go along with Clark in the outworking of his metaphysical grounding of the principle of logical consistency. On the other hand, there is no indication that Nash is committed to Carnell's later attempt to throw a bridge over between Christianity and culture, by discovering various points of contact between them. Nash appears to want to settle for the law of contradiction, without giving any essential place to a metaphysical foundation for it. In this respect he appears to stand close to the early position of Carnell.

The above positions all claim in some fashion to be presuppositionalist; yet, they all suffer from the disability of not challenging fundamentally enough the neutrality of thought. Clark's position reserves the predicates "knowledge" and "truth" for what is in the Scriptures and to what may be deduced from them. In contrast, what we learn from experience can have only a certain usefulness. Thus he is content to accept an operational interpretation of scientific concepts. Scientific theories are useful in controlling nature; but they have no claim to truth. Thus it is impossible that science should ever be able to challenge the truth content of the Scriptures. Yet, the position on the foundation of which Clark makes this claim also involves that the truth of Scripture does not possess any intrinsic relevancy to scientific investigation. It simply towers over it, as truth towering over that which is useful but not truth. In its own domain, so long as it is content to remain with its claim to operational significance, science goes its own way.

The identification of knowledge with what is absolutely adequate theoretically, and thus with what emanates by revelation from the divine archetypal intellect, paired with the assertion that the content of the Scriptures, as the revelation of God, has exclusive claim to the status of truth, brings with it some interesting consequences. The exalted status of adequately grounded theoretical knowledge is thus accorded to the request of Paul concerning the cloak he left at Troas, while the intimate awareness which exists between husband and wife is denied the status of knowledge altogether, because it is not revealed in Scripture. To be more exact, it might be said to be knowledge that there is a relationship between husband and wife which is called "knowing"; because the Scriptures teach that there is. But on Clark's testimony it is impossible for one to say that he "knows" that such a one is his wife.

The method of the later Carnell is one that expressly seeks a common ground between the Christian and the non-Christian positions. His method is to seek a common ground between the believer and the unbeliever. The kingdom of love, which is the point of contact he seeks in his book, *The Kingdom of Love and the Pride of Life,* is a purely natural love and not an evangelical one. It is the kingdom which is intuited by one who is acting as a happy child would act, according to the dictates of the heart, one who has not yet been duped into the self-assertiveness of the will to power. Carnell's method is to establish a common ground in what "happy children" or "all good men" intuitively feel, and then seek to throw a bridge over to what is specifically Christian, "for the kingdom of heaven is the eternal phase of the kingdom of love."[6] The clash, or at least the uneasy juxtaposition of these two elements (generally religious and specifically Christian) is all too apparent. That is evident, for example, in Carnell's discussion of death. The heart, we are informed, acquaints us with the proper etiquette for attending a funeral. "Since the bereaved have united their hearts with the departed, they cannot believe that death has spoken the last word. They know that if the dead do not count, then the living do not count, for the living and the dead form one unbroken fellowship. Thus, a good person will do his best to assure the bereaved that death has not dissolved the kingdom of love, and that in the kingdom of heaven there will be a renewal of lost fellowship. This means that whenever a person communicates assurances of hope to the bereaved, he is really saying that the soul is immortal and that God will overrule the verdict of death."[7] From such a sentiment, which Carnell appears to ascribe to everyone who intuits like a child, the transition to the more specifically Christian idea of a double resurrection, both of the just and the unjust, appears to be possible only by a sleight of hand.[8]

Methodologically, Carnell announces that his approach is unified. His method is to erect a bridge, by whatever means, between Christianity and culture. However, the term "culture" is used in a popular but very undefined sense to include whatever falls within the human realm, outside of the gospel. Thus a bridge is to be thrown between the human and the divine, between the temporal and the eternal. This clearly does not provide a basis for avoiding the danger of method dispersing in all kinds of directions. Appeal is made at one time to the law of contradiction (the analytical function), at another time to the judicial sentiment (an analogy within the juridical sphere), at another time to the law of love (considered as the sentiment of the healthy child, thus possibly as a sense of harmonious life). What then is to tie these together? Does not the idea of truth dissipate in all directions? Further, if the conception of truth is not controlled from the outset by the Christian commitment, will not the transition from any supposed point of contact in "culture" to the specifics of the Christian faith always take place by an illegitimate infusion of the new wine of Christian meaning into the old skins of unbelieving thought? At least in the above volume the transition appears to be a violent one.

Another apologist who lays claim to being a presuppositionalist and who has been attracting attention recently is Dr. Francis Shaeffer of L'Abri, Switzerland. He has become especially popular for his critique of culture from a Christian point of view. He has been particularly concerned to trace in modern thought and culture a trend towards irrationalism and despair, which is the result of the failure to start with the supposition of the Christian faith.

In his method Schaeffer lays special stress, like Clark and Carnell, on the law of contradiction, especially on the law of excluded middle. One of his most frequent complaints is that thinkers have laid aside the analytical distinction between truth and falsehood. Instead of holding that there is an either-or, they assert that there is a both-and. Thus instead of analytical distinction there is a fateful synthetic attitude, which blurs boundaries. There is a point, he maintains, in the history of thought, somewhere in the period between Kant and Hegel, that the line was crossed irremediably from an analytic to a synthetic point of view. This line he calls the "line of despair."

There is, it must be admitted, a real element of truth in Schaffer's contention that something happened about this time to the idea of truth. There came into being a dialectical logic, which sanctioned the antinomy. This logic is certainly present in Hegel. Further, even though it is difficult to see why Schaeffer is so nonchalant about setting Kierkegaard on one line with Hegel, when the former set his either-or sharply over against Hegel's both-and; nevertheless, a deeper acquaintance with Kierkegaard reveals that he, too, in his idea of truth had little respect for the ordinary canons of logic and that for him existential truth is paradoxical. From these nineteenth-century thinkers it is not difficult to trace a line of irrationalism down into the present and to illustrate this irrationalism in all kinds of movements within contemporary culture.

One thing among others that Schaeffer leaves unexplained, however, is why the apostate philosophy was that much better before it learned to employ dialectical logic. Is a philosophy per se better which is willing to employ simple analytical distinctions, distinguishing, for example, formally between truth and untruth. The answer might lie, as far as Schaeffer is concerned, within his method itself. His critique of the loss of the will to distinguish is propaedeutic. To one to whom the very distinction between truth and falsehood has become blurred, one cannot even speak intelligibly of the gospel. Thus there is the necessity of re-establishing the possibility of communication before one actually proceeds to present the gospel or an apologetic in the narrower sense of the term.

Schaeffer does not ask, however, whether the same apostate motives that are at work in philosophies where there is a rejection of the law of excluded middle and an adoption of a dialectical method are also at work in philosophies where there is a clear distinction between what is true and what is false. He simply tries to reinstate the making of distinctions. Among many who call themselves "presuppositional-ists," it is the custom to defend the law of contradiction on the grounds that it is the only possible foundation for intelligible discourse what-soever, even of the discourse that might go into its own denials. Pos-sibly Schaeffer would be content with such a defense of the law of contradiction and its companion, the law of excluded middle. At least, I have not seen him discuss the question whether there are inherent limits to logic. Even if we grant, however, that all intelligible discourse involves making distinctions, it does not follow that the ana-lytical function is its own foundation, or that it is without limits, or even that all of the law-structures in the creation must be approach-able simply by way of analytical distinction.

*   *   *   *   *

A full discussion of progressive and regressive tendencies in Christian apologetics would have to deal also with those positions which do not see any inherent difficulties with the classical apologeti-cal approaches. A notable case is the view being set forth by John Warwick Montgomery, which he admits is an attempt to revive the type of method advocated by Bishop Butler. Such a discussion is beyond the scope of what can be included here. We must be satisfied with bringing out some of the tendencies of those systems which call themselves "presuppositional," both those which are consistently so and those which allow some element of neutrality in their method.

It is characteristic of Van Til that he has sought to be consistently presuppostional, and his criticism of other positions always centers in the fact that in some way they have fallen short and have introduced an element of neutrality and of autonomy. They have fallen prey to a regressive tendency in apologetical method. Van Til, on the contrary, wants to be truly progressive.

Van Til has asserted again and again, therefore, that one cannot prove Christianity directly. That is an impossible undertaking, because it is impossible to assume a stance outside of Christianity in a meaningful way from which such a proof could proceed. Thus, as we have said, Van Til must entrench himself within the walls of the Christian faith, and he must argue from the impossibility of the contrary. This method seeks to establish an indirect proof of the faith. An outstanding characteristic of Van Til's method is that it is concrete—that it takes into consideration in an intimate way from the outset the full involvement of the committed Christian believer, with his entire background and training. Moreover, it takes into consideration that this believer is one who is responding to God in his revelation, through which the believer knows himself to have been created by God, to have fallen into sin, and to be redeemed in Christ. We have observed that this concreteness is characteristic of a transcendental approach. It involves that there is in all one's activities a reflection back on oneself in the fullness of his selfhood. In this sense, a carefully guarded one, the method might also be called "existential." In this spirit Van Til has continually stressed that man must be seen as a covenant being, one who is continually responding at the very center of his existence, where all his activities come to a focus, to the self-revelation of God through Christ.

With this method we are in fundamental and hearty agreement. Carrying on in the transcendental line, while purifying it of elements foreign to a truly Christian approach, belongs today, we think, to a progressive apologetical stance. It is in this spirit of fundamental agreement and in the same spirit of desiring to further discussion in the interests of stimulating a more progressive attitude in apologetics that we are constrained to pose certain questions concerning this very important movement.

*   *   *   *   *

How do certain elements of Van Til's thought square with his often-asserted stress on the central focusing of man in all of his functions in a unity on God in his self-revelation in Christ?

Van Til maintains that there are only two basic starting points, the believing one and the unbelieving one. The believer will recog-

nize that he is a creature of God and that God is his Creator. In everything he will recognize that he is dependent upon God. The unbeliever will set himself up in the place of God, denying in effect
the Creator-creature distinction. Christian thought is consistent only
when it takes the Creator-creature distinction fully into consideration.
It is important to note the exact meaning that attaches to the recognition of creatureliness. It means, indeed, that the creature recognizes
himself to be dependent altogether on God, who is sufficient to
himself—"self-contained," as Van Til would say. This self-sufficiency
involves also that God knows all things, because all things are comprised in his creative will. The recognition of creatureliness involves
for Van Till, therefore, the recognition that there is a prior and completely adequate theoretical knowledge of a creative character (analysis) in God, both of himself and of his creation, and that all human
activity in knowing must be viewed on the background of this original
knowing, all limited comprehension on the background of the complete comprehension in the divine mind. Thus the creature must think
analogically, thinking the thoughts of God after him.

The denial of creatureliness in this respect Van Til associates with
a claim to have complete comprehension on the human side. That
cannot mean simply that the unbeliever asserts that he has complete
comprehension of everything. That is nowadays generally denied,
and Van Til is aware that most thinkers reject the notion that it is
possible for man to have complete knowledge. In Van Til's thought
the term "comprehensive knowledge" has in this connection a technical meaning. It is any claim to knowledge which does not acknowledge that there is a prior (archetypal) theoretical comprehension on
the part of God and which does not acknowledge that the human mind
is dependent in its own interpretation, as it tries to fit together the
web of its experience, upon that prior interpretation. Thus, whether
the unbeliever claims to know all things or not, he in effect asserts that
he knows all things if he sets up his own judgment as the standard.
Even if he does nothing else, he makes in effect the universal negative
judgment that there is no archetypal intellect to whose thoughts he
must submit.

It is indeed of the utmost importance to claim, as Van Til does,
that there is an analogical relationship between man and God, and
between God's activity and man's activity, in the sense that they
never should be thought to be over against each other. Man's
thought and activity must always be related to God's. Man lives
coram deo. As Van Til himself puts it, man must be aware that he

is living in a totally personal environment and that in all parts of his self and his activity he is responsible and responding to God in his self-disclosure. Precisely how should that analogical relationship between God and man be conceived, however? At what point does man's life come to a focus in its relationship to God? Van Til would undoubtedly reply, as he has done many times, that the focal point is at the very heart of man's existence, as Kuyper put it, where the rays of his life come together.

There is, however, an element in Van Til's approach that leads us to broach questions, and to compare his position with that of the philosophy he himself has ardently recommended for many years, the philosophy of the cosmonomic idea of Vollenhoven and Dooyeweerd.

For Van Til the model for the divine intellect seems to be the analytical judgment. Van Til describes God's knowledge as analytical. That is to say, whatever content is comprised in it is there from the very outset. God is completely open to himself. There is nothing new for God either in himself or in his creation. On the contrary, man's knowledge is synthetic, in the sense that there must always be the weaving of new experiences into the fabric of what is already known. Thus Van Til can say that the synthetic activity of the human mind is possible on the background of the prior analysis in the divine mind.

Such a view brings up immediately the question of the foundation of theoretical thought. Van Til does indeed claim that human theoretical thought is in need of a foundation. This foundation is discovered, however, not in something beyond theoretical thought but in the archetypal theoretical intuition of the divine intellect. For this reason it cannot be said that Van Til dismisses per se the ideal of comprehensive theoretical knowledge. In order to know anything, it is necessary to know everything theoretically—i.e., at least on one level. It is not necessary on the human level to know everything in order to know anything truly, because there is already comprehensive knowledge on the divine level, and God can convey truth to us. To infer that one can have comprehensive knowledge on the human level is, as we have seen, to deny in effect the Creator-creature relationship. To retain the Creator-creature distinction one must accept the limitedness of his own theoretical knowledge and confess his dependence on the prior analysis in the mind of God.

The place that Van Til gives to the theoretical-logical is being emphasized by his current criticism of the distinction between the pre-theoretical and the theoretical. He is asserting that if there is to be intelligibility all discourse must be at least incipiently theoretical. This position, it would appear, makes theoretical thought the locus of intelligibility, the ground of meaning. However such a position might possibly clash with other thoughts in Van Til's philosophy, it certainly dovetails with the status he gives to theoretical analysis in the archetypal intellect.

Our discussion has brought into focus a disagreement between Van Til's position and that of the cosmonomic idea philosophy which demands careful scrutiny. One of the beginning insights of the philosophy of Vollenhoven and Dooyeweerd was that the logical (analytical)[9] is an aspect of the cosmos, dependent for its meaning upon a created structure of reality which is itself not analytical in character. Thus in his early writing, *Logos en ratio*, Vollenhoven struck out against the logos doctrine, which had had such a history in both Christian and non-Christian thought. Logical distinction was itself possible because of the divinely created order in which the logical aspect was embedded. Furthermore, even though the making of a logical judgment was an act which was logically qualified, it could not be thought that man's act-life as such was so qualified. The logical was only one aspect among many of man's total act. Thus analytical distinction takes place in every human act; but man's act life as such cannot be properly conceived as itself being logically qualified. This insight was to have considerable implications for the entire scheme of concept-formation as it was developed in this philosophy.

Thus, for the cosmonomic idea philosophy, meaning and intelligibility do not have their foundation even in the logical—much less in the theoretical-logical, which is a deepening of the logical (analytical) distinguishing which accompanies all our activities.

Thus, too, as one is brought to reflect upon the unity of his selfhood, in the concentrating of his entire life on God in Christ, he cannot think of this concentrating as having a theoretical-logical focus.

For Van Til also the focus of man's life in its wholeness should be deeper than the theoretical-logical. Van Til has constantly asserted that no function of man (his intellect, his will, or his emotions) should have the primacy. He has battled against the prevalent notion of the primacy of the intellect. Nevertheless, it must be asked whether Van Til's metaphysical notion of the archetypal intellect does not clash with the more central notion that man in the center of his being is constantly in the act of responding to God in his self-revelation in Christ. A clearer resolution of this problem is a pressing need.

* * * * *

Without entering into a full discussion, we shall simply sketch at this point a number of the issues that arise if one holds that the concentration point of intelligibility and truth lies in theoretical thought, e.g., in a divine archetypal intellect. These points will be phrased largely in question form, to stimulate the discussion that must arise concerning these crucial problem areas.

1. A particular aspect of Van Til's presentation bears mention first, which concerns his appeal to the analytical judgment. The analytical judgment is one in which there is nothing in the predicate which is not contained already in the subject. In the synthetic judgment, on the contrary, the predicate adds something that is not contained in the subject. It appears that Van Til's approach, even if inadvertently, draws heavily on this distinction. It plays a role in describing the difference between divine archetypal thought (analytical) and human ectypal thought (synthetical). Even if one should grant that it was never the intention to say that the divine intellect is an analytical judgment (which, we admit, would have a strange sound), and if one should grant the possibility that the analytical judgment provides only a philosophical expression for the divine creative sovereignty; nevertheless, the use of this model influences the discussion in an interesting fashion.

Prominent in the definition of the analytical judgment is the question of logical extension. What is included in the subject? Is anything included in the predicate that is not already in the subject? Characteristic of the synthetic judgment is that something new is added to the subject. There is the need of synthesizing the new with what is present already. The question then arises, whether the prominence given to the idea of logical extension will lead to certain emphases, e.g., upon prediction, to the exclusion of others.

No one who truly confesses the Christian doctrines of God's sovereignty and creation will admit that anything falls outside the scope of God's sovereign disposition. He will not admit that there is any counter-force to God, something that is past, present, or future which falls outside his knowledge and his plan. Putting this confession in the context of the pattern of the analytic judgment, however, may well account for peculiarities in the discussion. If on the philosophical level the problem is understood as to whether there is or there is not anything new, as to whether there are any new facts to be incorporated in one's system, and if the crux is discovered in relating one's own finite situation, in which there are new facts, to God, for whom there are no new facts; then the question may have been put in such a way as to eliminate important perspectives. It keeps the discussion on the concrete (plastic) level of individual things (one speaks of "facts" and "events," etc.). It may well obscure the structural question of the law-order of the creation, for this law-order is one which is an overarching framework which makes "facts" and "events," etc., possible. Further, if what the cosmonomic idea philosophy says is true, this framework cannot be described in logical terms; for logic is but one aspect among others of the order, and each one of the meaning aspects of the order is transcendental in character and is not of the nature of a logical category.

2. Our discussion leads us then naturally into another question, whether if we take the theoretical-logical as the concentration point we can do justice to the problem of the formation of theoretical concepts. Taking such a position would appear to entail that the order of the cosmos is itself understood ultimately in terms of theoretical-logical distinctions. Is this the case?

Characteristic of the approach of the cosmonomic idea philosophy is the idea that one cannot understand the basic structure of things in terms of more general and more specific concepts (genera and species). Taking the idea that meaning must be understood in theoretical-logical terms must hide from view the transcendental character of the meaning of the various sides of reality, must eliminate the possibility of understanding the structures of individual things (which do not subject themselves to being understood in terms of genus and species, whole and part), and must obscure the transcendental direction to the point where the rays of life come together, a "point" which is not one aspect or part of the cosmos in distinction from any other part, but that in which all of the rays of the cosmos find their focus or concentration.

To our mind, it also cuts one off from exploring a fruitful avenue to understanding the meaning of the central biblical commandment of love. The latter may not be understood as a particular virtue among others. It is that in which all of the powers of man, in all of their fullness, are oriented to God, responding to him in his self-disclosure in his revelation.

3. The question of concept-formation leads us directly into yet another. If the ground of intelligibility and meaning is found in the

theoretical-logical, are we not faced with a problem? If we admit then that something is not theoretical-logical, we say in effect that it falls outside of the locus of meaning. In that case we must account for the respect in which this non-theoretical element falls short. One of the most common ways of accounting for this, of course, has been by distinguishing between the theoretical-logical and sensation. We have encountered a position, that of Gordon Clark, in which the theoretical-logical is said to coincide with knowledge, but is then distinguished and set over against the terrain of what has operational usefulness.

One can identify this respect in which something falls outside of the locus of meaning, it would seem, only by setting it up *over against* the source of meaning. This is, however, to give up the possibility philosophically of accounting for the coherence and unity of the cosmos. We can render such an account only if we discover a totality of meaning in which all the rays of the cosmos have their focus. It is possible only if the ultimate perspective of thought is seen in a religious concentration on a unity which transcends all of the diversity of the cosmos and thus transcends the possibility of setting up one thing over against another.

Is it not better to lay aside the notion that the locus of meaning resides in the theoretical-logical, and to see the theoretical-logical as a human activity which is taken up in the law-order of God's creation, an activity which must depend upon this law-order for its possibility and whose final service must be a constant transcendental reflection back on the point transcending itself out of which it lives and in terms of which it has its impulse and direction?

4. If the above question is to be answered in the affirmative, and if theoretical-logical thought is to be considered as being transcendental, are we not required to enter into a critique of thought as such, to lay bare its ultimate driving motives and to see that it becomes aware of its ultimately transcendental character? Indeed, in the present stage of discussion in Reformed circles, this is a question that cannot be ignored and is one that is of the utmost concern for a progressive apologetical stance.

If one considers the source of meaning to be in the theoretical-logical, and if he sanctions this idea by seeing the fullness of theoretical knowledge in the divine archetypal intellect, is he not restricted to setting finite theoretical apprehension on the background of ultimate theoretical apprehension? This indeed might be classed as an attempt to found finite understanding transcendentally in the complete theoretical intuition of the divine intellect; nevertheless, it would appear to exclude the very possibility of entering into a critical, transcendental discussion of the roots of theoretical thinking per se.

In the interests of the conceptual clarification of the problems confronting Reformed thinking today, it is of real concern that questions such as the above be faced. They have been set forth here in the interests of furthering the discussion of that progressive apologetics that Van Til has introduced into the Reformed arsenal.

Response by C. Van Til

Dear Dr. Knudsen:

Your survey of the development of apologetics is very interesting. Quite rightly you assert that on my view man is "a covenant being, one who is continually responding, where all his activities come to a focus, in the self-revelation of God through Christ." You say that my line of thinking is truly progressive. You wish now, for yourself, to carry on "in the transcendental line while purifying it of elements foreign to a truly Christian approach."

You are very gentle in pointing out the foreign elements found in my approach. You do it indirectly by asking some questions. These questions spring, basically, from your adherence to the philosophy of the cosmonomic idea of Herman Dooyeweerd. You ask first: "How do certain elements of Van Til's thought square with his often-asserted stress on the central focussing of man in all of his functions in a unity on God in his self-revelation in Christ?"

What then are the elements in my thought which would, if not exscinded, undermine the proper place of Christ in my total point of view. The answer is basically: "For Van Til the model for the divine intellect seems to be the analytical judgment. Van Til describes God's knowledge as analytical." For Van Til "the synthetic activity of the human mind is possible on the prior analysis in the divine mind."

"Such a view," you add, "brings up immediately the question of the foundation of theoretical thought." "Van Til does indeed claim that human theoretical thought is in need of a foundation. This foundation is discovered, however, not in something beyond theoretical thought but in the archetypal theoretical intuition of the divine intellect." You ask whether this commitment to the "metaphysical notion of the archetypal intellect" does not clash with my "more central notion that man in the center of his being is constantly in the act of responding to God in his self-revelation in Christ."

You draw the following very serious negative consequences from "the metaphysical notion of the archetypal intellect" which you think I entertain:

1. I cannot do justice to the creatureliness of man.

2. Such being the case, I can have no proper notion of man's knowledge as analogical.

3. I mistakenly reject the distinction "between the pre-theoretical and the theoretical."

4. I cannot escape describing the "overarching framework which makes 'facts' and 'events' possible" "in logical terms."

5. I cannot "do justice to the problem of the formation of theoretical concepts."

6. By my adherence to the notion of the archetypal intellect I am cut off from a fruitful understanding of "the meaning of the central biblical commandment of love."

7. As a consequence of my idlea that the "ground of intelligibility is found in the theoretical-logical," I cannot account for "the coherence and unity of the cosmos." Instead of the "locus of meaning" residing "in the theoretical-logical," you propose that the "theoretical-logical" be seen as "a human activity which is taken up in the law-order of God's creation, an activity which must depend on this law-order for its possibility. . . ." This has been the common position of the philosophy of the cosmonomic idea. Unless such a position is adhered to, we cannot enter "into a critical, transcendental discussion of the roots of theoretical thinking *per se*."

The sum of these problems is that on my view I am unable to hold to a sound theology and have no proper basis for a sound Christian apologetic. I may still *believe* today what I *believed* in my childhood, but I cannot now give a critical account of my belief, nor can I challenge the world of unbelief to forsake its ways. The philosophy of the cosmonomic idea is alone able to do what I am unable to do.

* * * * *

What is my reaction to all this? It is simply and basically that I have *never* held to the idea that "the locus of meaning resides in the theoretical-logical." I have on the contrary *always* opposed this notion in terms of what I learned from the Scriptures. For me "the analytical judgment" is an invention of apostate thought.

As you know, I have constantly maintained that there are basically only two philosophies of life. One of these views is that which is based on the triune God of Scripture as the final reference point for all predication. This is my position. The other is that which assumes that man, fallen and apostate man, is the final reference point in predication. This is the position which I oppose.

On my position the facts of the universe are what they are ultimately because of their place in the all-comprehensive plan of God. On the other position the facts of the universe are, ultimately, purely contingent. My position is that man should by the logical gifts he has from his Creator discover the "law-structures" of the universe. Man's interpretation of the universe (his scientific, philosophic, and theological efforts) must be a covenantally conscious "re-interpretation" on a created level of God's "interpretation" (revelation) given him centrally in Jesus Christ. Man's God-given task is to discover about all creation—all that God has ordained to be within the scope of his creaturely abilities. He does so from the perspective of that creatureliness and in terms of the central revelation of salvation in Jesus Christ. On the other hand, I clearly oppose the idea that man *is not* a creature and that he *is not* a covenant-breaker. Covenant-breaking man assumes that if he is to have unity in his experience, he must himself be the source of that unity. Accordingly he assumes that his logical efforts *need not be*, indeed *cannot be*, what the Bible plainly says they are: created by God to be used in his service. It is a necessary part of his apostate picture of himself and the world that he talks of "being in general" and "knowledge in general." There is not, nor can there be, on the position of unregenerate man, a distinction either between the "being" of God and the "being" of man or between the "knowledge" of God and the "knowledge" of man. The apostate man must absolutize both his "being" and his "knowledge." He cannot be created and his logical abilities must reign supreme.

If, therefore, I really made the "analytical judgment" the model for my view of the divine mind I would be thinking along the lines of unbelief. I would be giving evidence of the fact that the grace of God had not touched my heart, that I was still a covenant-breaker and not a covenant-keeper.

*   *   *   *   *

Why then did I ever speak of God's knowledge as *analytical*? I shall try to explain this briefly by giving a short survey of my approach to apostate man, as Christian to non-Christian.

I approach apostate men because I am impelled by the love of Christ to tell them that unless they repent and accept as true what God in Christ tells them about themselves and their environment, they will abide under the wrath of God and all their works will come to confusion.

But who is this God? As sinners we can learn about God only from Christ speaking to us in the Scriptures. Looking into these Scriptures we find that God is independent of his creation. God is, as I said on a previous occasion, "in no sense correlative to or dependent upon anything beside his own being. . . . God is absolute. He is sufficient to himself. . . . God's being with its attributes is self-contained."[1] "God's knowledge is what it is because his being is what it is." To speak of God's knowledge as "analytical" is to emphasize "that which needs most emphasis, namely, that God does not need to look beyond himself for additions to his knowledge." God "does not depend in his being, knowledge or will upon the being, knowledge or will of his own creatures. God is absolute. He is autonomous."[2]

In all this, it is "the triune personal God of Scripture that is in view. God exists in himself as a triune, self-consciously active being." This is the "ontological trinity" as taught in Scripture. "The God of Christianity alone is self-contained and self-sufficient. He remains so even when he stands in relation to the world as its Creator and sustainer." God "has self-contained being" and knowledge while man has "created and derivative knowledge."[3]

It appears "that in the Christian doctrine of the self-contained ontological trinity we have the foundation of a Christian theory of being, of knowledge and of action. Christians are interested in showing those who believe in *no* God or in *a* God, a 'beyond,' *some* 'ultimate' or 'absolute,' that it is *this* God in whom they must believe lest all meaning should disappear from human words. Christians are interested in showing to those who hold that "God *possibly* or *probably* exists . . . that the words 'possibility' and 'probability' have no meaning unless the God of Christianity actually exists. It is their conviction that the actuality of the existence of this God is the presupposition of all possible predication."[4] For us "everything else depends for its meaning on this sort of God."[5]

Christians learn about God and his relationship to created reality from Scripture. The Reformed confessions seek to discover "the system of doctrine" found in Scripture. By "system of doctrine" Reformed theologians do not mean that they *deduce* a series of doctrines or concepts from one master concept. Every bit of man's knowledge of God or of the universe of God is "derivative and re-interpretive" of God's revelation (natural and special). It is in this sense "analogical."[6] No one has an exhaustive knowledge of God as revealed in the world. The Parmenidean idea that man has or can have such knowledge of God presupposes that man is autonomous. The Kantian notion that man can have no knowledge of the triune God also presupposes that man is autonomous. Both Parmenides and Kant assume that the autonomous man must use *the* law of contradiction in order to determine what is possible or impossible in the realm of being. But for the Christian the "law of contradiction" has no such ultimacy. "A law of contradiction that is found to be operative in the created world in the sense that man's intellectual operations require its recognition, but that rests on God's nature, is something quite different from a law of contradiction that operates independently of God."[7] In the former case the intelligibility of facts rests "ultimately upon God's internal coherence." In the latter case this intelligibility rests ultimately on man as he operates in pure contingency. If man is to be intelligible to himself he must regard himself as operating as a covenant-reactor to the covenantal requirements and promises of his Creator-Redeemer.

As a covenant being man must seek to implicate himself into the revelation of God. If he is to see the facts of his environment for what they are, he must see them as being nothing more or less than bearers of the covenant requirements and promises of God. We may therefore say that man's proper method of obtaining knowledge is that of "implication into God's revelation."[8] In presenting the "system of truth" of Scripture we use, therefore, the transcendental method. Kant spoke of the conditions which make human experience intelligible. For him these presuppositions rested on the notion of self-sufficiency. For us the condition which makes human experience intelligible is the Word of the self-attesting triune God speaking through Christ in the Scriptures. A truly transcendent God and a truly transcendental method go hand in hand.

Our basic approach then is to accept on authority what Christ says in Scripture. Our basic presupposition is based on our belief that in Scripture God speaks to us. We cannot comprehend, i.e., exhaustively understand, what God says to us about anything. Our knowledge, i.e., our conceptual formations and judgments, are always limiting concepts. Whereas Kant's limiting concepts pointed to the void, ours point to the depth of the wisdom of God in whom no darkness dwells. They do not point to *an* origin, whether or not this origin be called

"God" (as Dooyeweerd maintains!). Concept formation itself must presuppose the Christian world-order if it is to make any intelligible contact with the world at all.

A few words on the philosophy of the cosmonomic idea must conclude my response, for you have talked of its truly progressive character. To be sure, I have already commented considerably in my remarks to Prof. Dooyeweerd, but I would like to add a few additional words here.

From the very beginning of this philosophical movement I have been both interested and appreciative of its efforts. I was especially delighted with Vollenhoven's work on the necessity of a Christian methodology. His work supported basic elements in my own developing thought, especially my idea that a biblical, covenantal framwork of thought includes a Christian view of the place and function of logic. In Eden the sin of Adam, inspired by Satan, presupposes and implies (a) human autonomy, (b) factual contingency, and (c) the sovereignty of man's logical function. In Christianity, the righteousness of Christ, inspired by the Holy Spirit, presupposes and implies (a) human dependence on the being, will, and revelation of God, (b) divine all-embracive providence, and (c) the created character of the ₁ogical function. It is only they who have been renewed unto knowledge by the grace of God into a covenant-keeping attitude of heart who have learned to use logic as a *means* by which the many-faceted aspects of the created universe as a revelation of the triune God might be displayed. In this early work of Vollenhoven I saw a truly Christ-oriented and therefore truly biblical life and world view. In terms of such a Christian perspective I felt a Christian apologetic could be constructed which avoided the pitfalls of traditional Roman Catholic and Arminian apologetics. For years I made use of materials supplied so abundantly by the new "Calvinistic" philosophy. Prof. Dooyeweerd labored hard to show from a comprehensive survey of ancient and modern immanentist philosophy that on its view of human autonomy, of pure abstract logic and of abstract contingency, all things end in confusion. The only escape from this "confusion" is to presuppose the truth of "the story" of Scripture centering in Christ.

In the course of time, however, I began to see certain foreign elements in Dooyeweerd's thinking. For instance, near the beginning of his monumental work, *De Wijsbegeerte der Wetsidee*, Dooyeweerd speaks of H. G. Stoker's difficulty with the very title of the work itself. Stoker maintained that Christians should rather speak of "the philosophy of the creation idea," not of "the philosophy of the idea of law." Calling on Dooyeweerd in his study one day, I told him that his defense of his title against Stoker's objections was not altogether satisfying to me. Should not a Christian point out that the Christian view of law is itself based on the prior idea of divine creation and all-comprehensive providence? Is not the law of the Creator-Redeemer God the only law that any man meets anywhere in the universe? Is it not the only "law idea" which is intelligible? Aren't you seeking by your Christian philosophy to serve the dissemination of the gospel of salvation for the *whole* man? The natural man, who worships the creature rather than the Creator, may well believe in "law" as a formal principle or as constitutive of the universe (Spinoza) while not believing in "law" as a result of the creative, controlling activity of the God of Scripture. You, as a Christian philosopher, are concerned to show men that adherence to any "law idea" except that of their Creator-Redeemer leads to the destruction of all predication. You tell us that only in Christ can we find the meaning-totality of the cosmos. Believing in him by virtue of their regeneration, the redeemed of God confess the absolute sovereignty of the Creator over all his creation. They bow low before the law of the Creator as a universal, uncrossable border between the being of God and the meaning of his creation.[9] In view of this, which in many places you both admit and defend, how can you say that the idea of creation must *not* be brought into the picture at the outset of your presentation of the idea of law? In your reply to Stoker you contend that in our discussion of the preliminary questions of philosophy, we must present our "ground-idea of philosophy" as "the obvious pre-condition *of every philosophical system*." For you the introduction of the idea of creation is a *specialized form* of this ground-idea. This specialized form of the ground-idea of law must not come into the picture till a later point: "De preciseering dezer grondidee komt eerst daarna aan de orde."[10]

As I look back now, over these many years which have elapsed, to that conversation, which I have reported here from memory, I realize that I should have pressed my point even more than I did. *How could I present the Christian position as the necessary presupposition of the possibility of intelligible predication if I first allow that I and all men can speak intelligibly of a "law" which is not from the outset the law of the Creator-Redeemer of men?*

When I wrote my syllabus, *Christianity in Conflict*, I expressed my difficulty with Dooyeweerd's views in this matter for the first time in writing. He has presented to me his reaction to these difficulties in this volume and I again have responded to his construction in a negative way. The basic point of the matter, as I see it, is that whereas I attempt to show the non-Christian that *nothing*, no fact or law, can be seen as it truly is except in the light of the revelation of God in Christ through Scripture, Dooyeweerd attempts to speak intelligently with unbelievers about laws and states of affairs which are intelligible up to a point prior to the introduction of a Christian scheme of things. This difference between us is basic.

In his *New Critique* Prof. Dooyeweerd directs all his attention as he says, to a "sharpening of the method of transcendental criticism." Whereas he had formerly started "from above," he now wishes to start from below. "But in this line of thought, we had to start from a supposition about the character of philosophy which is not at all universally accepted in philosophical circles." By sharpening his transcendental method Dooyeweerd hopes to show that his method does not, from the outset, presuppose the Christian position but that it examines the "theoretical attitude of thought as such."[11] Dooyeweerd thinks that he has escaped the charge that he has prematurely brought in matters pertaining to the Christian faith. To bring Christian principles into the discussion with unbelievers at the outset is, for Dooyeweerd, uncritical. It is to confuse *transcendent* with *transcendental* criticism. It is thus that Dooyeweerd is true to his formal view of the idea of law, his view that it is possible to talk of "law itself" without reference to creation. I do not think that such an approach is truly progressive at all, Dr. Knudsen, much less as progressive as you seem to think. Nevertheless I hope that this further clarification of my position as over against that of the philosophy of the cosmonomic idea will serve in the interest of further discussion of the matter.

—C.V.T.

J. P. A. Mekkes

XV. KNOWING

I

When the Bible-believing intellectual takes the term "knowing" on his lips, he really ought to go in only one direction. Whether he will actually do this, however, is questionable. For, in opposition to this apparently obvious remark, it is easy to place another, namely, that clearly the Christian most often does not really move in a direction different from other men, doing what according to his Christian confession he ought to do.

But it is not enough to make such points. For, apart from the decisive question where the Christian ought to discover the guide to what he is supposed to do, he already stands in the unfolding of his life within a field of force. This field of force is not, for any of us, by nature, the field of Truth. On the contrary! We find ourselves placed within the field of force of human history. What forces are at work there? We do not hesitate to employ, in place of the energetic analogy "force" (*kracht*), the word "power" (*macht*). Its sense is more embracive, including force within itself, but qualifying it, however; giving it a direction and using it.

We know how the apostle Paul speaks about the "powers," and in this personification calls them to account. This is the case even though he recognizes that he himself, together with those to whom he is speaking in his epistles, is also threatened by them. "Power" points beyond itself to responsible and purposeful action.

In the field of force of human history, where we find ourselves placed, willingly or unwillingly, consciously or unconsciously, as we take up our life's task, the "powers" rule over us from the very outset. It is lamentable that the contemporary, humanistically distorted Christian quickly de-personifies what Paul personified hoping secretly to relieve himself of his responsibility for them.

But is it at all possible for one to be responsible for what threatens him? Is this not to confuse things? Yet, the apostle hurls forth his challenge. Consider, for example, Colossians 2. He issues his challenge in the name of his Lord, together with his Lord, united with his Lord. The decisive challenge of the great Conqueror flashes to the disciple: go over to the attack and pursue the enemy. Be on the alert!

May we in this connection speak of a specific task for the believing "intellectual"? The context in which this word occurs encourages us to answer in the affirmative. Who are the intellectuals in the eyes of the Western world? That world wants to think of them as those in general who bear the primary responsibility in science itself or in the functions for which scientific training is a requirement, even though, in the last analysis, science itself is "used." As such this using and being is itself certainly *not* of a scientific character.

It is remarkable that the world of contemporary "powers" does not speak about the intellectuals and their science being used, except perhaps on the occasions when science itself becomes aware of this situation and then subsequently attempts impotently to speak of its own freedom and responsibility. In a position of power, yet threatened by power! Nevertheless the powers that exercise the use are themselves inescapably dependent upon the science which is used. We have to be alert to the fact that, should we desire in this connection to speak of a dialectic of powers, we should already be at the point of transcending the limits of philosophical thought.

II

We have spoken about powers within the human history. Everything having to do with man presents itself within this *history*, which technically takes up nature within itself. However, not *all* of this comes within the field of investigation of the science of history. Meanwhile, man is *interested in* his science of history. Why is that? It is because, in its description of "eventuation," it introduces us to the world of powers which have called the eventuation into being and have guided it in the direction which now also appears to be indicated to us.

That is to say, "appears to be" indicated, because it is indeed the case that we begin by "taking over" what occurs as it has presented itself to us in its direction and its content; but from that point on our own responsibility comes into play and standards inevitably present themselves other than the "eventuation" that the science of history at the beginning investigates.

Taking stock also of its results, it becomes immediately clear to us that it could *not* have taken upon itself its task *apart* from the historical *involvement* of its practitioners in *what* is being investigated and described by them, thus apart from what they also, as concrete, living men, bring to it as an *a priori* judgment.

If we put the question, why is it that not only the specialists in the science of history but also all those who are involved in any special science whatever come to their field of investigation with *a priori* judgments, then our attention is again drawn to the very human history which engages us and which transcends by far the field of investigation of the historian. It, by the way, goes far beyond every special field of knowledge, *every* special sphere of life. It embraces all of them, taking them all up into itself, including nature as the substrate of human life and as the first object of man's cultural activity.

Immediately one is faced at this point with a great danger. The "scientific world" itself discovers that it is in the grasp of that strong *power* which, *in the course of history*, from the very outset of Western thought, has increasingly gotten a hold on it and which is therefore no longer recognized by it—the power of the *a priori* of the scientific *concept*.

We have expressed ourselves in this fashion purposely. We could have done it otherwise, for example, by speaking about the power of a self-sufficient scientific activity, the power of the *a priori* of logical neutrality, of theoretical analysis and synthesis. We did not do this, because we all know too well how much we ourselves are in the grip of the powers of Western human history, which are on the way to becoming powers of universal human history. Against the neutrality of science, against human pride and self-sufficiency, against making theoretical activity independent, we have, as ones who could call themselves Christians, our "historical" objections. Have we probed deeply enough into the center of the sick organism that causes us such spiritual trouble? How much have we taken over from father Parmenides and his sophisticated posterity the veneration of the "concept," and have carried it to even greater heights!

The concept delimits. This is, so to speak, what makes it a "concept." But from what does it set off, and how far can it extend the limitation while it yet answers to its true meaning? What has been its life story within the process of the embracing and developing history of mankind? Or, does it as a matter of fact stand above this process?

A modern reader who has been humanistically formed will be unable from the very outset to understand our way of formulating the problem. That history extends farther than one's own epoch and that the latter cannot be evaluated apart from its influence is also taken for granted by him. But if we ascribe to the history of mankind a position such as there is in mind here, then, for him, its highest status can only be that of a *common denominator* under which it is supposed that all aspects of life should ultimately be theoretically construed, and the professional historian comes to occupy the most privileged position among all the other practitioners of special sciences. The concept that is formed by our humanist concerning this matter, fitted out with consciously provided safeguards against the threat of limitation, brings into being an ultimate answer to the *meaning* of human existence. Those within his own circles who oppose him call him, according to their own way of looking at things, a historicist. Even though it be from a standpoint differing from theirs, we also must call him one.

At this point we do not want to become involved with the positivistically and pragmatistically oriented positions in science, which, even taking into consideration all of the criticism that they lodge against historicism, themselves make their own fundamental contribution to it, and which, in any case, without a dialectical counterpart, could never have laid claim to having an integral world and life view. From whatever concept he proceeds in order to attain insight into the meaning (or meaninglessness) of human history, one cannot avoid the intramural conflict *concerning* the formation of concepts. The equal right and unright of all conceivable common denominators keeps blocking the way. The denominators as such are not brought into being by a "free" science; they are born out of the conflict of the *powers* that drive it forward. The field of battle of these powers is the *living* history of *living* humanity.

III

"Science" is being driven forward at a frantic pace. Some of its practitioners will be ready to concede this and will even warn against the danger of falling prey to it. With this, however, the point in question is by no means answered. The real question is how something like this has become possible. In order to obtain an answer to that question we have to direct our attention to the legitimate place of science as well as to what Western man has thought about it and has made it into. Or, in order to return to our major point, what opinion has he formed about the status and the applicability of his concept formation?

A consideration of the development of thought in the history of Western man gives as an answer, that Western man has expected *everything* from it. His concept formation was supposed to give him "knowledge" as insight into the *being* of the reality which surrounded him. To this end he was supposed to concentrate all of his powers of thought in order, by means of it, to incorporate gradually his own developing individual insight within the totality of knowledge, out of which his own activity of knowing had sprung and towards which it moved, a knowing that in its own fashion "is" and at the same time in its activity of making judgments conditions all "being." An appeal to a divinity was necessary to complete the arch that by means of a knowing, which had its root in thought, appeared to be constructed around both knowing and being.

It was the power of apostasy of a heathendom that was coming to self-awareness that led Western man along this path. The Christians who had been educated in the Hellenistic environment, who because of this forming did not know how to distinguish sharply between the created function of thought and the power that seeks to put its stamp on our "knowing," contributed in a dim awareness of what they were doing to the attempt to close up the horizon of pagan thought along scriptural lines. Neither on the part of the ancients nor on the part of these Christians, however, was it a question of a conscious rebellion against the power of him who rides in triumph over all of the powers.

This defiance became apparent only in the course of the development of humanism. Now it was no longer implicit but explicit that the possibility of *knowing* was bound up with human *thought*. With this not only the identity of the keystone but all of the enveloping arch came into the picture. Was it indeed possible to close it off? And did the Christian in any fashion have something to contribute to it?

It was customary for Christians to think *along with* what pretended to be the *wisdom* of the world, only declaring *out of bounds* that which they thought was unable to be rhymed with thought about the revelation of the Scriptures. The power of the Conqueror, which again in the Reformation raised the standard of the cross alone, pointed out another way; but alas it was only a short while until the compass of the "intellectuals" of the Reformation began to point again to thought. Their debate with humanistic theological thought remained indecisive, and science from henceforth sought even more than ever to go its own way. Along this way it encountered, in the meanwhile, the problem of its own intrinsic limitations.

It does not avail us to make any more than a practical criticism of our Christian forebears, and then we do it only with reservations.

They, too, in many respects were grasped by the powers of their historical era, which envelop again and again all living men without exception. Only a gift from above can bring new light. But we may indeed ask what they ought to have done in the face of the situation confronting them. They should indeed have proceeded to think along with their contemporaries, but *in* this thinking to have taken position against the assumptions from which such thought issued. Even though no one had listened to them, they could have stood at the crossroads, in the crises into which humanism (which from that time definitely had the dominant position) itself acknowledged that it had landed, in order to point out the only direction which would lead them out of the crisis.

Hindsight now tells us that humanism never would have listened and over against the Christian witness would have presented every one of its crisis positions as a new triumph of thought over the Christian faith. Under the given circumstances, however, it was just that much easier to the degree that those on the side of the confessing church let go the reins, indeed, even more than this, attempted to advance their own "theology" with the aid of the humanistic discoveries. This could only increase the confusion and could only give new impetus to the "power of apostasy."

As in ancient philosophy, again and again the silent conviction about the irrepressible power of the unchartable life-process of nature had placed limits on the rational power of form, so in modern reflection on the self and on things the attempt to attain universal domination by way of thought struck up against the irrational element which in the depth of this reflection represented the humanistic idea of autonomy, the element that humanism could not abandon so long as, allowing for all dialectical variation, it still wanted to remain humanism. But—rational or irrational, ancient or modern—it was only by means of systematized and more and more efficient concept-formation that Western man thought that he was able to get into focus for himself the rational approach to his lived reality.

IV

For Western man thus knowing was identified with *knowing in concepts*, made possible and limited by "concepts," that is thoughtful, thoughtfully enveloped and protected, in a thinking that strives after his consummation, appearing in the "idea." The ancients had given it the title "theoria," the moderns sometimes that of "intellectual contemplation"; now they speak of "operational verification," and the existentialists of "Andenken." Finally theologians crown it by their so-called "kerygma."

What can one expect of "conceptual understanding"? What may it mean for *knowing*?

Within the general Western tradition what is called "knowing" can only be constructed out of a progressive forming of logical concepts which have been molded in a process of thinking, as these in an ascending order take their place along the way of a fulfillment of thought which is thus identical with the fulfillment of knowing. With this, two questions which we have already touched upon present themselves: Where does the way *come from*? Where does it *lead*?

It is these mutually presupposing questions (which have been at times, but at other times, not taken into consideration, brought to critical expression and then apparently completely suppressed, but always in a constant mutual tension) which set the Western development in motion and which have kept it going. The tension itself had the character of a fundamental *dynamis*, a moving force at the foundations of human existence, which elevated the "powers," including the power of thought, to the throne and which cast them down again, and which held the spirits in motion until the nihilistic revolutionary tendencies of our time.

As one takes into view philosophically this boundary and origin movement, it appears to be recognizable by a peculiar basic pattern, which, as such, could be domiciled only because of the unfolding process it was undergoing. Not taking account of the "powers" that were driving him, Western man thought he could comprise the trajectory he had to make under what someone has strikingly called the arch of "intelligibility." This arch presupposed the ability in principle to close off the horizon of thought to which we have just referred. Meanwhile, on closer inspection, this arch appeared to be suspended between two abstractions, which were misunderstood as to their nature, and which, as such, could maintain nothing more than an abstract mutual relationship. The fundamental pattern was the duality of "the subject of thought" and "that which was known," subjected, as this pattern furthermore remained, to a necessity that kept cropping up along the way of changing its name.

This necessity presented itself under the influence of the powers of which we have spoken. We shall not speak of it any more in detail, except to call attention to the fact that the term "subject of thought" inescapably anticipates the course of our argument. If one should think that he could sufficiently understand "subjectivity" as correlative over against "objectivity," then he would not only have misunderstood our intention but it would be clear from his misconception that he had already become established in one of the forms of the dualistic pattern that must come under criticism. On our part we understand by "subject" a "being subject to." Can this mean being subjected to what ought to be called "objective"?

The reaction against such an insight from the side of Kant and from the idealistic and phenomenological schools could have only a temporary and relative character; it ran along to emerge currently in Heidegger's philosophical dilemma between the turning course of time and *An-denken*, while positivism on its part dodged this fundamental problem by restricting what, from ancient times, had stood over against *noesis*.

The critical element which, in reality, has come to view in this *verschwiegene Philosophie*, which gradually insinuated itself into the special sciences and practical action, forces us, however, to "isolate" the particular cell upon which our investigation of the scientific "organism" has to concentrate itself. We do not allow ourselves thereby to be led by considerations derived from such positions as positivism, no matter how much, for example, the so-called "instrumental test of truth" has an analogy that may not be ignored with what we have in mind.

From this "test" it appears, namely, that fundamentally the "concept" does not rule but is ruled. If we cannot agree with what positivism and pragmatism understand by "instrumental," we must, nevertheless, say to which horizon it has pointed us. It was always a matter of a criterion of "verification." What had to be verified in terms of its utility was the "knowing" that was arrived at along a positivistic path, which was *not* considered to be adequate until the result was attained in this fashion. Knowing is not adequately verified along the way of "concept" formation. More is necessary.

Where does this "more" lead to for positivism? To this question it is not possible to give an answer that goes farther than that which had already been given; but the path goes *by way of* "objectivity." Just as, on the other side, Heidegger's way over "subjectivity" cannot be pointed out beyond the conscious foundation of *being*, after which there is only the *Absprung*. The pillars upon which the "arch of intelligibility" rested slide in both directions in the quicksand of Western philosophical contemplation which has abandoned itself to the trustworthiness of understanding and concept. And the cause of this is that the opinion has taken hold, under the influence of the powers, that it is possible along the way of thought to bring knowing to its consummation.

V

The initial phase of Western rational reflection consolidated in the duality "noetical-ontical," in which the latter was supposed to establish "objectivity," the law of knowledge for the former, which, in contrast, was held to be subjective and individual with the remote verification test of the infinite divine spirit (*intellectus agens*) that required thought to come to its fulfillment.

The difficulty with respect to this spirit is that it, too, if one is going to treat it, first must *be*. Unwittingly Aristotle brought to the sharpest expression the antinomy which resides here by giving to this spirit *within* the totality of what was in essence "divine" being an exclusive, supreme position, where it was safe from being influenced by the transitoriness of the rest of being—indeed, more, where it emerged as the itself unmoved mover of the incalculable movement. In addition, however, this spirit *knows* the *totality of being* in the divine *intellectual contemplation of itself* and so, it is identical with this totality of being. The principle of transitoriness is not able to be reconciled with it as pure form and consequently cannot be included, yet, as we saw, cannot be excluded by it. It is clear that in this conception of the *intellectus archetypus* we have only to do with a hypostatization of *creaturely* thought in its active function, thus with a *concept* that man has formed of it that has been exalted to the position of the ultimate *former* of all concepts, which can be formed by humankind only in connection with it. Human (philosophical) *thought* has struck here upon its creaturely boundaries and can no longer extricate itself from being enveloped by an ultimate, i.e., speculative, "concept" of a consummated actuality of thought.

It is *this* concept, which has again and again been generated, which has kept the initiative in hand for the progressive generation of all further concepts. It was from the beginning the concept at the most ultimate boundaries of the possibility of thought and remained this as the embracing (further, the ratiocinated) substance of Descartes and Spinoza, the idea of God in Kant which embraces and sifts out morality and theoretical knowing, the "Idea" of post-Kantian philosophy; it remained this in Husserl's "ego-ontologism" and Heidegger's history of Being, and finally in the "belief," that in neo-positivism has been elevated to a "faith," with respect to the exclusive reliability of methodical creative thinking. Under the guidance of the powers we have come to the end of the boundary possibilities. The newly arising interest in the questions of hermeneutics, in whatever form, now that *doxa* (opinion) threatens to get the upper hand over *episteme* (theoretically responsible knowledge), is one indication among others of this.

That Western man will not be brought to capitulation by way of an attack through concepts is apparent. The decision must be reached between the powers, which envelop all concept-formation together with all other activity. Has it not become time for the Christian to give another orientation to his desire for knowing? To whom shall we go?

Not to a *deus ex machina!*

The *deus ex machina* which has threatened the Christian faith from ancient times was, for the most part, by way of Aristotle and neo-Platonism, the scholastic doctrine of the ideas in the divine "Logos," which were supposed to be "thought" after by man in his concept-formation. With this procedure of thought, which immediately lands us in the middle of the aforementioned antinomies of a conceptual thinking which is at once incorporated *in* being and at the same time sets itself above it, it was thought that "by accepting a supernatural gift of grace to his intellect" it was possible to ascribe to the believer in contrast to the unbeliever the possibility of *knowing* the *truth*. It is clear that the concept "Logos" in the fashion previously described is simply a hypostatization of created *human* thought and, consistent with itself, must set us on the track of the identification of *thinking* and *knowing*. Then, in addition, again following out the logic of the position, "thought" is once more viewed as *theoretical* thought on the way towards its consummation. The norming of thought can take place, therefore, only by way of a theo-*logical* supervision out of the revelation of the Scriptures, in order in this fashion to challenge thought which is not subjected to this supervision. Here, in the final analysis, in spite of everything, *thought* still established the norm for thought, and indeed with the aid of an "object" (the contents of the Scriptures which are to be "known" by way of thought) as intermediary, that *as* "object" takes the place which for Aristotle and his followers the norm-establishing rational Being occupied.

The carnage which this uncritically accepted legacy of scholasticism wreaked after the Reformation within Reformational circles, for example, in particular also in the Netherlands after the passing away of the revival of the late nineteenth century, and in connection with which God was thought analogous to man, calls us to reflection, now especially since the "power" of practicalistic pragmatism thinks that it has here an easy prey. Our question is not, What does Jerusalem have to do with Athens?, but whether the *ancilla fidei vitaeque*, theoretical thought in whatever degree or form, has the right of presenting itself as the entrance-way into the personal *knowledge* of the truth.

With an eye to the space available, we are of the opinion that we should bring our confrontation with Western wisdom to a close and should seek to gain some further perspective.

*   *   *   *   *

There is only one word to say about the meaning and the direction of our knowing on the earth, in which thought has to seek out its most humble place. At the decisive moment in the history of the creation the Master, in the midst of his disciples, offered a prayer to the One who had sent him in order to do his will. "This is life eternal, that they might *know* thee the only true God, and Jesus Christ, whom thou hast sent."

If ever faith is called to a responsible choice of position, indeed to the challenging of the dominant powers, then it is at this watershed, of all life and reflection, the watershed of truth and falsehood, the point at which the *idol* of the West calls us to go along creaturely ways which, if they are not mapped out in time, will only prove to emerge in its sanctuary.

At the outset of the gospel story about Jesus' entering upon his ministry, we read that the multitude was astonished at his teaching, because "he taught as one having authority and not as the scribes." That instruction had nothing to do with subsequently *contrived* spheres of "supernature"; it had to do with the service of God *in* the things of terrestrial life, in every thing and for always. Standing at the exit of this life the High Priest of the creation proclaims the word of life about our knowing, about that knowing that *has its initiation* at the very moment that we become conscious and that has to take a particular *direction*. It is *we* who have gone astray in it; yet he sets it right through *his* life, acting, dying. And thereby he speaks and instructs concerning *our* activity as his followers. *This* is the exclusive meaning of creation and the life of man. Whoever thinks that it is otherwise has been deceived by the powers of the history of mankind which is fallen and which seeks to be sufficient to itself.

In our practice we spontaneously go wrong. Therefore we need this instruction. He teaches us, in our activity, in opposition to our apostasy, to discern *properly*. He instructs by means of all the fortunate and the unfortunate experiences of life, activity, and suffering, through the experiences of human history, and he does not thereby speak ultimately to the function of our analysis, which we, together with the intuition comprised in it, are accustomed to call "thought." Our thought is indeed present, in various degrees of overtness, in all of our acts, yet always present therein in a servant (distinguishing) role. If we, who are taught in the Western school, proceed to speak of this distinguishing as "thought," then we are used to attaching something to it as an "object." It is not inadmissible, so far as we are conscious of what we are doing, unless we, as always too eager theoreticians, have engaged ourselves silently in an easy-going abstraction of a *function of our activity, an abstraction which is not present in* that activity itself. I do not experience explicitly the analytical function of my loving, with an "object" included in it to boot, so long as it truly *concerns* loving. This entire act is a conscious *unity*, from beginning to end, in which nevertheless pre-eminently knowing must reach its high point. To this *knowing* our function of distinguishing ("thought") makes an implicit contribution by way of founding it; yet, in this connection can the term "concept" bring any clarification in any fashion into the situation for me? I become acquainted with loving by way of *loving* the one who is loved, just as I become acquainted with right by doing right (or by being subjected to it) in situations where justice is at stake, with nature in its operation and necessary forming, etc. This holds for all of our life, for all of our knowing of this life, that is, of the creation.

For this reason knowing occupies a central position within the *history* of created and called mankind, and the sense it must have can be told us only by the gospel! From it we understand that it has to do with the consummation of all things, a fulfillment that the apostle sets forth for the believer tellingly in Philippians 3:10-11.

The Christian *understands* the gospel and the letters of the apostles; through that he "understands" even the Old Testament, which sometimes appears to be so far removed.

Does he understand *by way of* concept-formation? A concept-formation which, as far as human capabilities extend, in its searching holds its own fulfillment in view?

In his understanding there indeed occurs a formation of concepts. The nobility of love is its awareness, and one cannot speak responsibly of an unconscious faith. We meet God in his self-disclosure, his *revelation* in the creation which is supported and embraced by the

Word—*consciously*, even if we deny him. The encounter and the understanding do *not* occur, however, by why of what Western man after his own fashion has come to call a "concept." In knowing—of God and the neighbor—there are, if one pleases (see above), "objects" involved of the most diverse kinds, *among* which are analytical ("thought") objects. They are all *sub*jected to the subjectivity of concrete experiencing (*belevingssubjectiviteit*), even as this itself is "subjected" to *him who knows*.

VI

If we who are Western Christian "intellectuals" wish to reflect systematically about these things which in their depth transcend our understanding—what we have been doing for centuries—then we must first of all pay close attention to the fact that we are walking *in* the passageway of Western human history. There the dominant force, as we saw, has been from the very beginning another motive than that of the Word (the Power) of God. And this motive confronts us in a peculiar way as soon as we put our hand to the legitimate creaturely task of doing science. It is the motive of the dominancy of concepts, with its insoluble problem of the "arch" that can never be completed. Under its historical suggestiveness we are in danger of forgetting not only that thought is only *one of the* (always menial) *functions*, but most of all that our *act* of *theoretical thinking*, which is among many acts, is carried on just as much as any other in a *living* way. There is one characteristic difference. In the act of *thought* it is not, for example, loving, believing, politicking, etc., that take us in their grasp but the *logical* differentiations which are involved in these experiences. The latter can only be wrested out of the living differentiations of our activities, ultimately to receive its systematic treatment in theoretical thinking by means of the formation of synthetic concepts.

Our non-theoretical "understanding" already takes its practical direction and thereby gives a particular cachet to differentiation, before this is taken up for systematic analysis in the yet to be consummated theoretical act of thought. In the *theoretical concept* which arises out of this are incorporated two kinds of choices of direction, namely, that which arises out of practical activity, followed by that of the equally living theoretical *act* of thought, in which the consequences of the first choice make their contribution in what is now theoretical analytical distinguishing. In both instances the question is whether the activity (act) has become directed to the Truth or to "this world." In both cases the conflict of the decisive choice of direction manifests itself by means of the evangelical or the worldly faith.

The temptation which, out of the Western *cultus* of reason and science, invades the *creaturely* sphere of operation of science is, as we saw, that of the identification of knowing and the consummation of thought. The cultic result for life is the deflection of human knowing from the direction intended by Christ to that which the powers have in mind to pursue with the aid of the Western theoretical pattern. In our days, it would appear, the theological alliance makes even more than ever a deplorable contribution in the service of the powers.

VII

Does our warning mean a deprecation of doing science? By no means! How would it be possible to deprecate the creation as such in its development? It is a matter of the two decisive questions, whence and whither. Do we set out upon the way of knowing from our subjectivity of thought which forms concepts, in the expectation of traveling, if need be supernaturally enlightened and informed, the path of truth? Or is the scientific concept for us once and for all wrapped up in the concrete, living *understanding* of God's history with his humanity in every terrain of life, by which theoretical thought fulfills its doubly *limited* calling, which is pointed out to it by the Creator and is recognizable in faith? Then this limitation, which is to be held fast in faith, holds for philosophy, theology, and all the special sciences alike. In its proper place theoretical thought can never be more than an "aid" to knowing, no matter to what accomplishments for good or for bad it helps man in his power formation.

Knowing itself is illimitable when it is seen in the perspective of him who in his election has known his creation, it in us and us in it.

Only here *lies* the *meaning* of the history of creation: I know whence I have come and whither I am going. . . .

(*Translated by Robert D. Knudsen*)

Response by C. Van Til

Dear Dr. Mekkes:

When your book *Sheppingsopenbaring en Wijsbegeerte* (1961), appeared, it served as a renewed inspiration to me to go on trying to understand the details of modern existentialism. One of my great faults has been to deal with very general and basic thrusts of a move-

ment without giving adequate attention to details. It is a weariness of
the flesh to follow the endless windings of the Heidegger of *Sein und
Zeit* and then of the "later" Heidegger, etc. Yet we must do so if
we are to make the Christian approach to "thinking" intelligible to
men of different philosophical stripe.

Your exposition with respect to *concepts* has helped me understand
more accurately what Dr. Dooyeweerd was getting at in his dealing
with the subject. You will notice that I have dealt with this in my
responses to both Prof. Dooyeweerd and Dr. Knudsen, so I shall
not attempt to discuss it again here.

It may be apropos to say something about "Father Parmenides,"
for it is his "logicism" which we must distinguish clearly from a
Christian notion of rationality. "Father Parmenides" was not, as are
modern humanists, in full self-consciousness, setting up himself as
autonomous and insisting that nothing can exist except what "logical"
"consistent" thinking says can exist. But surely, not only apostate
thinking but also "Christian" thinking has wrought much havoc by
assuming such to be the case! The only escape apostate thinkers
have from the clutches of pure, abstract determinism is pure Chance.
Aristotle attempted a sort of compromise between these two with his
"analogy of being." The Medievals attempted to "Christianize"
Aristotle's "way out." Only further confusion resulted.

But with the Reformers, notably with Calvin, the biblical vision
began to appear. The Christian receives his notion of "coherence"
and of "rationality" from the Bible and in doing so places the "ideal
of conceptualization" in biblical perspective. The God of the Bible
is not Laplace's Great Mathematician or a Supernatural Computer.
The unity of creation is the organic unity of the plan of God. Our
logic touches the "faith" of the world because of the plan of God
back of both. When we talk of the "rationality" of God we do so
after the manner of men, i.e., in view of his plan of creation this is
the way he must appear to us if he is to reveal himself, and if we are to
know him. This is the thrust of Calvin's distinction between knowing
God in his revelation and knowing God in himself. The former is
actual for man, the latter is not even possible. *Omnia abeunt in
mysterium!* We must, as Calvin says, not engage in idle speculation.

How thankful I am to you all who have, in the steps of Calvin and
Kuyper and Bavinck, helped us forward toward thinking biblically.
Your work has, Dr. Mekkes, in this special sense, I repeat, been
of inestimable value to me.

—C.V.T.

Gilbert B. Weaver

XVI. MAN: ANALOGUE OF GOD

Whenever men differ on a given subject, the cause of the disagreement may usually be traced to two factors, the essential and the semantic. The differences between Gordon H. Clark and Cornelius Van Til in theology, philosophy, and apologetics appear to be unexceptional in this regard. In the view of this writer both factors are involved in the present dispute, and it is the purpose of this study to point out at least one verbal problem.

Clark's Charge

When Cornelius Van Til describes man's knowledge as being in an analogical relationship to the knowledge of God, Gordon Clark charges him with skepticism. In a 1957 *Bibliotheca Sacra* article Clark aired his side of an ecclesiastical controversy with Van Til and others. In it Clark alleged that Van Til's theory of the relation of divine knowledge and human knowledge is the same as that of Thomas Aquinas, who also has a theory of analogy. "This theory," writes Clark, ". . . whether found in Thomas Aquinas, Emil Brunner, or professed conservatives, is *unrelieved skepticism* and is incompatible with the acceptance of divine revelation of truth [italics mine]."[1] Noting that Van Til signed a statement that man's knowledge must be "analogical" to the knowledge God possesses, Clark states, "If God has the truth and if man has only an analogy, it follows that he does not have the truth. An analogy of the truth is not the truth; and even if man's knowledge is not called an analogy of the truth but an analogical truth, the situation is no better. An analogical truth, except it contain a univocal point of coincident meaning, simply is not the truth at all."[2]

Aquinas' Doctrine of Analogy

Are Cornelius Van Til's doctrine of analogy and Thomas Aquinas' doctrine of analogy the same essential position? This is the question Gordon Clark would answer in the affirmative. To evaluate Clark's accusation, we may survey the two doctrines of analogy as to their nature and the foundational presuppositions upon which they rest.

The presuppositions of the Thomistic view begin with the belief that human reason is at least *semi-autonomous.* Many things about the world and about God may be known without reference to revelation. For example, Aristotle, "The Philosopher," came to a knowledge of the "Unmoved Mover" without any appeal to a revelation from God. Reason operating on sense experience can thus go far in producing a system of truth, although it cannot complete that system. Aquinas does believe that revelation is necessary to complete it because of inherent limitations of reason. Hence the existence of God can be proven but not, e.g., his triunity. Reason must be adjudged only semi-autonomous.

A second presupposition is clearly related to the first: for Aquinas, as for Aristotle, all knowledge begins in sense experience. "Our knowledge," he writes, "taking its start from things, proceeds in this order. First, it begins in sense; second, it is completed in the intellect."[3] Stated another way, "There is nothing in the intellect which was not first in the senses."[4] Such an epistemology may be designated as a *semi-empiricism.* All concepts, even those used by revelation, are ultimately produced by the reason operating on sense experience.

The third presupposition is also adopted in agreement with Greek philosophy. *Being* exists proportionately, or analogically, on a scale, ranging from pure being at the top to non-being at the bottom. Vernon J. Bourke summarizes this doctrine of the *analogy of being* thus:

> In some sense, all beings, from the highest to the lowest, are alike in the fact that they are. However, beings differ in their essences and as individuals. Since every finite being is the actualization of some essence, we may think of what is common in all beings as the real relation between essence and existence. These relations vary, because many different essences exist, but they are not entirely dissimilar. A dog's existence fits a dog's essence; a man's existence fits a human essence. Being, then, is analogical; it represents a widely varying plurality of ratios (of essence to existence) which are in turn related to each other in some understandable proportion. God is the limit case; his essence is related to his existence by way of identity. This is being at its fullest.[5]

A scale of being is indicated in the above quote by such expressions as "highest" and "lowest" beings, a "widely varying plurality of ratios," and in speaking of God as the "limit case." The scale displays various proportions or ratios of essence to existence, existence being the constant factor common to all beings, while essence differs from existence more and more widely the further down the scale a being finds its place. The limit case opposite God is non-being, at which point existence and essence are infinitely diverse. It follows that all beings on the scale below God to some extent participate in non-being. Hence, this theory of a scale of being might be characterized as a *semi-creationism*, as all finite things, though created by God, are always in danger of "slipping off" the bottom of the scale into non-being. Thus Maritain, a Neo-thomist, suggests that since man is down the scale from God, evil tends him toward nothingness. In Maritain's own words, when an act of man is evil it is "wounded or corroded by nothingness."[6]

Because the relationship of essence and existence is analogical on a great scale of being, all predications about existing things must also be analogical. Hence, for Aquinas, analogy is also a matter of the predication of names or words to subjects. When the same predicate is applied to two or more different subjects, it is not done in exactly the same sense or univocally unless the subjects are on the same level, i.e., their ratios of essence to existence are the same. Thus the word "wise" cannot be predicated univocally of God and man, because, in Aquinas' words

> . . . When the word "wise" is predicated of man, we mean some perfection distinct from this essence of man, and from his act of being, and from all such items. However, when we predicate this name of God, our purpose is not to signify something distinct from his essence, or power, or act of being. Thus, when this name "wise" is predicated of man, in some fashion it circumscribes and includes in its intelligibility the thing that is signified. This is not so when it is predicated of God; instead, it leaves the reality that is signified as not comprehended and as exceeding the meaning of this name. It is consequently obvious that the name "wise" is not predicated of God and of man according to the same intelligibility (ratio). The same explanation applies to other names. Hence, no name is univocally predicated of God and creatures.[7]

But, Aquinas holds, the words are not used in a wholly ambiguous or equivocal sense either. Otherwise, God would be unknowable, a conclusion Aquinas rejects by appeal to both Scripture and Aristotle. Since God is deemed knowable, Aquinas asserts that predication must be by *analogy*, a way of predication "midway between pure equivocation and simple univocity."[8]

Van Til's Doctrine of Analogy

Before making comparisons, it remains to sketch what Cornelius Van Til means when he uses the term analogy.

Van Til's only presupposition is the existence of the God who has revealed himself to man in Scripture. When thus accepted, Scripture gives two crucial doctrines which undergird Van Til's teaching about analogy. These are the doctrines of creation and revelation. The doctrine of creation includes that God has created the universe in general, and man in particular, who is unique among creatures because he is made in God's image. God is revealed in that as God's image-bearer man reflects in his finite way something of the nature of God to himself. Then with his God-given intellect man can perceive the meaning that God has placed in all created reality around him. In this way he receives that message of God's glory which creation declares. So prepared by "general" revelation, he is able to receive "special" word revelation and identify its source as the God of "general" revelation in whom he lives and moves and has his being.[9]

Man, then, is not in any sense autonomous. In all his being and in all his knowledge, Van Til sees man as dependent upon God who made him. Stating this fact another way, there are two levels of being and knowledge, independent (uncreated) and dependent (created). As man is dependent in his being upon his Creator, he is also dependent in his knowledge upon the one who has placed his meaning in all of created reality, including in man himself, God who has given from the beginning a supplementary word-revelation so that man may interpret the general revelation aright.

Since man is dependent upon God in his knowledge, it follows that the Christian must be committed to a two-level theory of knowledge:

> Christians believe in two levels of existence, the level of God's existence as self-contained and the level of man's existence as derived from the level of God's existence. For this reason, Christians must also believe in two levels of knowledge, the level of God's knowledge which is absolutely comprehensive and self-contained, and the level of man's knowledge which is not comprehensive but is derivative and reinterpretive.[10]

This distinction raises the fundamental question of how the two levels of being and knowledge are related. The answer to this Van Til calls *analogy*. As man is God's created image-bearer, he is the finite *analogue* of his Creator in his being, because he is *like* God in some sense. As a personal, self-conscious, intellectual being, he is also the finite analogue of his Creator in the realm of knowledge. Seeing that according to the doctrines of creation and revelation God has previously placed all meaning into reality, Van Til puts it this way:

Christian-theism says that there are two levels of thought, the absolute and the derivative. Christian theism says that there are two levels of interpreters, God who interprets absolutely and man who must be the re-interpreter of God's interpretation. Christian-theism says that *human thought is therefore analogical of God's thought* [italics mine].[11]

Thus for Van Til, to state that man's knowledge is analogical to God's knowledge is simply to say that man's mind operates in an *image-relationship* to God's, since all that the human mind ever learns is the finite reflection of some part of God's prior infinite knowledge. The term "image" is the divinely chosen metaphor drawn from the relation between an object and its reflection in a mirror or pool of water. Van Til's discussion of the concept of God is illustrative of this image relationship:

> . . . We should be careful when we say that God is the being than whom none higher can be thought. If we take the highest being of which we can think, in the sense of *have a concept of*, and attribute to it actual existence, we do not have the biblical notion of God. God is not the reality that corresponds to the highest concept that man, considered as an independent being, can think. Man cannot think an absolute self-contained being; that is, he cannot have a concept of it in the ordinary sense of the term. God is infinitely higher than the highest being of which man can form a concept.
>
> It is true that we can think of a higher being than we can conceive or make a concept of. And we may use the word "concept" of God in this broader and looser fashion. In fact, it is in this broader and looser fashion that we *must* speak when we speak of our concept of God. By it we simply mean that notion or idea which we have, by an analogical process of reasoning, sought to fashion for ourselves, of the being of God. When we speak of our concept or notion of God, we should be fully aware that by that concept we have an analogical reproduction of the notion that God has of himself. Our notions or concepts are finite replicas of God's notions [italics his].[12]

The "image-reflection" motif is referred to in the above quotation by the expressions, "finite replica" and "analogical reproduction of the notion that God has. . . ."

Having gone this far, Van Til does not attempt to tell *how* this image or analogical relationship of God's mind and man's mind operates. As Bernard Ramm observes,

> Van Til does not spend any effort struggling with epistemological theories as realism, neo-realism, critical realism, psychological idealism, etc., but simply says that "if theism is true, our knowl-

edge of the sense world is true because our knowledge of the sense world depends upon God's knowledge of the sense world."[13]

At this point Van Til's use of the term *univocal* may be considered. Besides the doctrines of creation and revelation Scripture gives us its teaching about man's fall into sin. But even sinners still bear the image of God, though marred, and still are able to reason because of God's common grace which permits them to use their faculties while they live in this world. In spite of his using this as it were "borrowed capital," the sinner considers himself autonomous. He refuses to worship the Creator with his mind and, instead, worships the creature. This attempt on the part of rebellious man to erect on his own independence a structure of knowledge Van Til calls "univocal" reasoning. Whereas the Christian-theist makes the crucial distinction in being and knowledge, the non-Christian rejects it.

> In opposition to [Christian-theism], non-Christian thought holds in effect that the distinction between absolute and derivative thought must be wiped out. To be sure, God's thoughts may be more comprehensive than ours but it is not self-complete without ours. This means that as all being was thought of as equally ultimate, so now all thought is thought of as equally ultimate. There is only one level of interpreters; if God comes into the picture at all, it is as a collaborator with man. We do not think God's thoughts after him, but together with God we think out thoughts that have never been thought either by God or by man. Non-Christian philosophies hold that human thought is univocal instead of analogical.[14]

Comparison of Aquinas and Van Til on "Analogy"

The above sketches of Thomas Aquinas' doctrine of analogy and Cornelius Van Til's doctrine of analogy reveal that they are widely divergent. This difference is seen first of all in their respective presuppositions.

(1) Aquinas presupposes a partial autonomy of human reason, that man may know some things about himself and the world whether God exists or not. Van Til in presupposing only the God who has revealed himself in Scripture considers man to be completely dependent in his knowledge on divine revelation both general and special.

(2) Aquinas believes that all knowledge begins in sense experience, functioning quite apart from revelation. Van Til holds to the validity of human sense experience but only because by revelation man is known to be God's image-bearer, the finite reinterpreter of the facts of the created sense world. Even sense-knowledge, therefore, functions in the context of revelation for Van Til.

(3) Aquinas presupposes that being exists as a scale so that all creatures below God are involved to some extent in non-being as well as being. But for Van Til, there exist only two levels of being, the uncreated and the created, and on this created level the existence of an ant or a flea is as much genuine existence as that of man. Van Til considers such a polarization between being and non-being an inevitable conclusion of non-Christian thought.

In their views of the nature of analogy, Aquinas and Van Til also diverge. The basic difference is that for Aquinas analogy purports to be a middle way between univocal and equivocal predication of names or words to subjects. This is not the case for Van Til. For him analogy applies not to terms, but to the overall process of human thought: man is God's created analogue in both his being and his knowledge. Man can know because as the image of God, he is ordained to mirror in a finite way God's infinite knowledge of all things.

In conclusion, it must be adjudged that Aquinas and Van Til have quite distinct concepts in mind when they use the word "analogy." Clark is guilty of the fallacy of equivocation in charging Van Til with the skepticism which is entailed by the Thomistic doctrine of analogy. On the other hand, it might be well if Van Til were to modify his terminology so as to eliminate the possibility of confusion. Instead of speaking of man's knowledge as being related by analogy to God's, it might be said that man's knowledge bears an *image-relationship* to God's knowledge, or that man's knowledge is *reflective* of that of God.

C. Gregg Singer

XVII. A PHILOSOPHY OF HISTORY

If Cornelius Van Til has given to the church a truly monumental apologetics, no less forcefully has he spoken in behalf of the faith once delivered to the saints in those areas of human thought and action which must be brought into captivity to the Word of God if the church of the twentieth century is to have a fully developed biblical world and life view. In providing the church with such a biblical frame of reference Van Til has centered his attention upon those issues which are of critical importance in the conflict with the various forms of unbelief which are rampant in our day.

In spite of the magnificent sweep of his thought and amazing keenness of his insights, he has somehow failed to pay the same attention to the problem of the meaning of history which he has given to the other problem areas of human thought. This is not to say that he has been unaware of the attacks on the historic faith in the area of the proper interpretation of history in that he has neglected the biblical view of history. But it is to say that his application of Reformed doctrine to the problem of the meaning of history has not been his center of interest. Hence references to such a Reformed approach are more scattered throughout his writing than one might expect. Nevertheless, his insights are to be found in nearly all of his writings even though there is no one book or monograph which is directly or exclusively devoted to the relationship between historic orthodoxy and the meaning of human history. Perhaps his most concentrated treatment is to be found in his *Christ and the Jews.*

The basic approach to the meaning of history is to be found in his *Christianity in Conflict* (part III) which he prepared in 1963 as a syllabus for his graduate courses in apologetics at Westminster Seminary. This volume is indispensable, not only for the understanding of his view of history but for his whole approach to both theology and philosophy as well. In personal correspondence with this writer, Van Til went so far as to say that he could well be described as an Augustinian in his interpretation of history, and there can be little doubt that the later Augustine does indeed furnish for him the necessary frame of reference which he claims as the background for his own approach to the biblical view of history.

Although in his discussions on the problems involved in the theistic interpretation of history Van Til includes most, if not all, of the issues which are generally included within the scope of the usual work on the philosophy of history, it is quite doubtful that Van Til should be classifiied as a philosopher of history. It is quite certain that he does not offer a philosophy of history in the usual sense of the word, for his approach differs sharply with such thinkers as Vico, Voltaire, Condorcet, Hegel, Marx, Spengler, Toynbee, and contemporary writers on this subject. His whole approach to biblical apologetics makes it impossible for him to find any common ground with the traditional philosophical approaches or with the contemporary neo-orthodox understanding of human destiny. He is quite critical of those philosophers who, like Hegel and Marx, look upon history as a kind of self-sustaining process, having no reference to any agency or force outside of itself and its own laws. He rightly contends that any form of Kantian thought must ultimately plunge the historian into the vortex of the surging seas of irrationalism, and he reserves some of his most devastating criticism for the position assumed by R. G. Collingwood. He rightly sees that when Collingwood holds that man's thought of reality must be absolutely his own, the facts of history disappear into the subject that interprets them and man becomes his own ultimate interpreter.[1] At the same time Van Til concedes that this view which Collingwood has adopted marks an important milestone in the further development of the Kantian approach to the meaning of history, because he has freed history from the many lingering restraints imposed by the biblical view. In so doing Collingwood has actually destroyed the possibility of finding any meaning in history, for he has made the interpretation of all historical data completely subject to the interpretation imposed on that data by the historian using it. Freedom from the biblical view of history has done nothing more than to subject the study of it to the slavery of the totally subjective interpretation of the historian.

Van Til rightly sees that Collingwood, because of his inconsistency, reveals the ultimate irrationality involved in this approach. He assumes the autonomy of man and in so doing arrives at the logically irrational conclusions which must follow any application of the Kantian principles. In Van Til's treatment of both Dilthey and Collingwood, he makes it abundantly evident that philosophy is totally unable to achieve a meaningful answer to the questions of the meaning of the historical process.

In this connection he stresses the inability of philosophy to answer any of the questions dealing with the great problem of the goal of history. He quotes with approval Augustine's famous rejection of the philosophical approach to the basic problems of human existence. With Augustine he insists that the philosophers have "utterly failed in searching out the succession of more lengthened ages and in finding any goal of that course, down which as a river, the human race is sailing, and the transitions then are of each to its appropriate end."[2] He also concurs with Augustine's insistence that we should not consult the philosophers concerning the succession of the ages since they, knowing God through those things which are made, glorified him not as God. In this manner Van Til rejects every attempt to formulate an explanation of human history derived from a philosophical methodology. In this sense there can be for Van Til no philosophy of history but only a theology of history. He consistently holds to this position in all of his writings. No philosophy, whether it be humanistic or naturalistic in its presuppositions, can offer any true interpretation of history, for history cannot supply the key to its own meaning, and the human mind cannot impose its subjective interpretation upon objective factual data. History is neither self-originating nor self-sustaining and time cannot exist in and of itself.

For the answers to all the questions which must inevitably arise as we survey the human past and present, Van Til turns to theology and even more specifically does he look to Calvinism as that one theology which provides the necessary ingredients for a world and life view capable of supplying answers to the most profound questions of human existence.

Thus the biblical doctrine of creation assumes a role of major importance in his interpretation of history. This could not be otherwise, for his system of apologetics in general rests upon this same presupposition. He quite properly suggests that any philosophy which denies this doctrine must ultimately lead to irrational positions. He thus maintains that history can be explained only in terms of that ultimate meaning which is integrally related to God's act of creation. Initially God gave to both the physical world and to man their meaning and purpose at creation. The subsequent history of man on the earth derives its meaning from this original act of creation.

But for Van Til the doctrine of creation does not stand in isolation from the doctrine of God revealed in the Scriptures. The God of creation is a sovereign being who governs his creation and who entered into a covenantal relationship with man whom he made in his own image. Thus man who bears the divine image and who enjoys this covenantal relationship with the sovereign God was endowed with the ability to discover both the meaning which God has conferred on human life and his own purpose on earth within the will of God.

Standing at the apex of creation, man, the image of God, was by virtue of this fact capable of knowing him and doing his will. At the same time man lives in a world which he can know and which was made known by him. But this knowledge which man has of God, of himself, and of the world is "analogical." Van Til stands with Augustine and Calvin in his emphasis that man can only know himself by that same act by which he knows the living God. Without this original knowledge of God man can neither know himself aright nor interpret correctly his own historical experience.

Man is, therefore, a steward of God, a vice-regent under him in his intellectual life and as such he is fully responsible for not only discovering his purpose for human life through revelation, but the meaning and purpose of the world in which he lives. This is the very essence of that covenantal relationship which man has with God through creation. Man is under a mandate to investigate the meaning of both nature and history.

Equally important in Van Til's view of history is the doctrine of original sin and the fall of man. The acceptance of this biblical doctrine as integral to the proper understanding of history immediately separates Van Til from most of the contemporary philosophers of history. Even those interpreters of the human past who seem to take the doctrine of sin seriously such as Reinhold Niebuhr or Eric Rust do so only in terms of their neo-orthodoxy, which does scant justice to the biblical doctrine of the fall at best. For Toynbee on the one hand and the Marxists on the other, there is no possibility of such an event in history and it plays no relevant part in their thinking.

Man as a steward is not only fully responsible for his understanding of and use of the world in which he lives, but he is also equally responsible for his understanding of his own role in that world. Van Til observes that the fall of man in no way destroyed or lessened the covenantal responsibility which man owes to his sovereign Creator even though it rendered him incapable of fulfilling the conditions of his stewardship. Van Til gives, I believe, a well-balanced and biblical emphasis to the noetic as well as to the moral effects of the fall. By grace the elect are regenerated through faith in Jesus Christ and they are thus to a degree enabled to resume their role as stewards in a manner acceptable to God.

The very great emphasis which Van Til consistently places on the biblical doctrines of creation and the covenant requires that he accord a similar importance to the doctrine of revelation and to the doctrine concerning the Scriptures as these are set forth in Augustine and Calvin. The doctrine of revelation in its scriptural setting assumes a major role in Van Til's apologetics and it is, therefore, equally important in his interpretation of history.[3]

The whole doctrine of the covenant presupposes that God has revealed himself to man with sufficient clarity for man to know his position within this relationship. If there were no such revelation man could know nothing of his origin or destiny and thus the history of the race would be meaningless to him. It would remain a closed book. An essential part of the mandate placed upon man at creation is "thinking God's thoughts after him," for if man could not perform this function he could not rationally do his will. For fallen man a special or biblical revelation is necessary. Without the searchlight of Scripture, history must forever remain a closed book and an impenetrable mystery to the unregenerate human mind.[4]

Equally important for Van Til's conception of history is the doctrine of the sovereignty of God. Indeed, this doctrine rightly underscores his whole approach to both revelation and creation. It is the sovereign God who makes history meaningful and reveals its meaning to man. Without such a sovereign God in control, the historical process must be subject to either chance or fate and thus irrational and without meaning. For Van Til chapter three of the Westminster Confession of Faith is not only essential for a sound biblical theology, but it is equally essential for a sound apologetics. The sovereign God of creation did not abandon his creation to the whims of chance nor the dictates of fate, but continues to exercise over it his power for his own glory and purposes. Although all of human history in general and the actions of men in particular are guided and controlled by God, he is in no sense the author of human sin. For this reason all of human history is meaningful and reveals his purposes. No portion of it is devoid of the divine imprint.

In this theological approach to history Van Til rightly places a great emphasis upon the Reformed doctrine of common grace. Indeed, it is one of the basic motifs in all his efforts. Common grace for Van Til is the sovereign power of God manifestly at work in the whole stream of human events and not merely in those particular events which seem to have a special bearing on the life and work of the church on earth. The unbelieving world with its kingdoms and empires, its hopes and its schemes of conquest and utopias, is subject to the common grace of God, even though its leaders are sublimely unconscious that they are fulfilling the will of a sovereign God. The whole of the intellectual economic and social life of man as well as his political developments is subject to the will of God and realizes his purposes for unbelievers. Yet the reality of common grace in world history and human affairs makes life livable for both the elect and the unregenerate on this earth and at the same time makes it possible for the church to fulfill its divine mission in the proclamation of the gospel. Common grace surrounds the ungodly with the restraining force of God's sovereignty so that even in their sinful condition and blind hatred of the truth they fulfill God's plan for the world. If common grace does not bring the sinner to repentance, neither does it allow him to make a hell out of this world. But it would be a mistake to think that for Van Til common grace is merely a restraining force on evil; it is at the same time, in his thinking, a fulfilling of the will of God in history. It makes human history dynamic rather than static and undergirds the whole of the historical process from creation to the second coming of Jesus Christ with a sense of direction. Unbelievers, to varying degrees, are conscious of the fact that history must have a goal, and they have substituted their humanly contrived utopias for the biblical goal.

In his theistic approach to the meaning of history Van Til pays as much attention to special or redeeming grace and special revelation as he gives to the doctrines of common grace and general revelation. He strongly insists that history is not only the result of the operations of God's common grace in human affairs, but it is at the same time a revelation of God himself. However, unregenerate sinners cannot possibly comprehend the meaning of this revelation. In their failure to understand the meaning and purpose of history they neither honor nor serve God as he requires of them through their covenantal relationship with man given through Adam. Sinful humanity constantly claims for itself and its own glorification the accomplishments and achievements which are the direct results of the influence of the grace of God in the flow of historical events. Indeed, the unbeliever is as unaware of the benevolent and beneficial results of the operation of common grace in human life in general as he is of the necessity of special grace in redemption. The modern mind simply refuses to acknowledge that the amazing technological and scientific developments of the twentieth century are in any way the gift of God. The essence of his blindness lies in his often repeated insistence that such accomplishments are the result of human ingenuity. The sinner cannot and does not become aware of the influences of common grace in his own life and in history until he sees himself as a sinner and in desperate need of God's redeeming grace. The revelation of God in natural history must remain a closed book to the unbeliever until he reads it correctly through the Scriptures. Only when the sinner receives the new birth does he come to understand the meaning of nature and history.

Van Til would agree with Augustine that the birth of Jesus Christ is the pivotal point in the whole flow of history, and he would strongly insist with the apostle Paul that the coming of Christ is literally the fulness of time and that the whole of ancient history looked forward to this event, even as the whole of history since that time looks back to and derives its meaning from this great event. Not only was Christ the *Redeemer* made manifest in history in the flesh, but also Christ was the *Lord* of history. Van Til insists that Christ is now the Lord of history, and he would strongly dissent from the various forms of dispensationalism which seek to postpone this lordship until the millennial kingdom is established. He would strongly argue that dispensationalism makes a theistic view of history virtually impossible.[5] Christ as Lord is now in sovereign control of his church even though his lordship is denied by the unbelieving world. The events of history obey his royal commands today as the winds and waves became still at his command two thousand years ago.

Because the covenant of grace lies at the very heart of the flow of historical events, the church, as the community of the elect, plays an important role in Van Til's interpretation of the human drama. In a very real sense all events are in some way related to the church. To be sure, we do not always understand this relationship, nor do we even see how some events can possibly be connected with the life of the church in the world. But the connection of the events of ancient history is not always too clear. Yet Christians earnestly believe that the whole sweep of ancient history was a preparation for the coming of Christ into the world. Thus the incarnation is readily seen as the fulness of time in the biblical chronology, the high watermark of ancient history. But of equal importance is the fact that in the same manner the myriad events which have taken place since the birth of Christ have a direct bearing upon God's protecting and guiding care for his church in the world today. If certain great movements like the Renaissance and Reformation easily lend themselves to such an interpretation, we must also be as ready to believe that such movements as the American and French Revolutions, the emergence of Communist Russia, and World Wars I and II are also intimately related to the life of the church. All events have their origin in the will of God as his will is realized through his creatures. They thus relate to the church in history.

It is through such a doctrine and through it alone that the problem of evil can be explained in meaningful terms. The tragedies of history, the destructive wars which have continually threatened the very existence of culture and civilization, the frightening dictatorships, past and present, which have arisen to haunt both the church and society at large, all have reference in some way to the church in history, for its temporal judgment and its correction as well as its edification and even its vindication. These forces of evil do not operate apart from and without reference to the will of God, for God throughout history makes the wrath of sinful men to praise him. Men thus serve the living God even in their ignorance and frantic rebellion against him.

The second coming is the final vindication of Jesus Christ in history and at the same time it is the final revelation of that meaning which the sovereign God has assigned to human existence on this earth. Van Til follows Augustine in asserting the majestic and climactic importance of this doctrine for a proper understanding of the historical process.

It is quite obvious from the foregoing analysis of Van Til's dependence upon historic Calvinism as his frame of reference in his approach to the meaning of history that he differs sharply from most modern philosophers of history. It could not be otherwise. Contemporary philosophers of history, for the most part, rely on Marxist presuppositions or are strongly influenced by existentialism. Even those interpretations of history which claim a biblical foundation and sanction are tinted with large doses of neo-orthodoxy and an existentialist atmosphere. Between Van Til and Reinhold Niebuhr, Eric Rust, and Langemead Casserley there is a gulf so wide that there is no possibility of any agreement between them. These philosophers of history, although claiming a biblical sanction for their positions, actually accept the evolutionary hypothesis and the neo-orthodox assumptions of modern theology. Thus the true meaning of history must ever elude them in their scholarly efforts to find in the stream of events a meaningful coherence acceptable to their modern mind.[6] Van Til rightly sees that ultimately all of these various attempts to explain history in terms which are less than biblical must end in utter failure, declaring that history is essentially irrational. Many historians today are verging on such conclusions and more than one historian is asking himself the question: Why teach a subject that contains neither meaning nor purpose?

Reformed theology alone provides the alternative to this dreary conclusion, and Van Til loyally adheres to it in his concept of history. On this basis in his various references to the problem of history throughout his writings, he seeks to provide answers to some of the most basic and persistent questions which confront not only the professional historians but all those who seek in history the answers to many of the greatest issues of human life. His devotion to the Scriptures and Reformed theology also means that Van Til rejects all philosophical attempts to interpret history. He rightly sees that rationalism and contemporary irrationalism both have their roots in the humanism of the Renaissance and came to fruition in the naturalism of the Enlightenment and the Kantian reaction to these developments. He would agree that in the irrationalism of contemporary thought the rationalism of the Renaissance has reached its tragic conclusion.

Rejecting every effort to interpret history in terms of any of these movements, Van Til brings to bear upon the great problems of history his solid foundation in the Reformed theology. Particularly does he seek to provide an insight into the relationship which must exist between historical facts, and he rightly sees that history is a process. But at the same time he would forcefully deny that in calling history a process, there is involved any concession to either Hegel or Marx. For Van Til the historical process is not external, and neither is it governed by a dialectical unfolding of mind or matter. The kind of process which Van Til finds in history cannot possibly be fitted into either one of the schemes of determinism. For Van Til the process of history which relates fact to fact and which is the essence of the causal relationship between facts is to be found in the sovereign control which God exercises over history, so that there is an intimate relationship in the flow of events. The historian may, therefore, speak of causes and effects. He may seek the causes of great movements in history with the assurance that history does not consist of myriad atomic facts and events taking place with no relationship of any kind existing between them except that they are arranged in a temporal sequence. In the same manner he may properly speak of the effects of these movements and developments. The historian who believes in the biblical view of history proceeds on the assumption that God so rules in the minds and hearts of men that in their political, economic, and social decisions and acts they create a meaningful pattern of events and that this pattern derives its meaning and purpose from the fact that ultimately the sovereign God establishes the cause and effect relationship between them.

These causal forces in history do not emanate in a deterministic fashion from event to event or from movement to movement, but rather does God work in the hearts and minds of men in such a manner that they act and react according to his sovereign will.

It is this biblical concept which guarantees the rationality of the historical process. In this Van Til is by no means using rationality as it has been used by the rationalists in philosophy, but rather does he mean that history contains a knowability and purpose because God governs all the actions of men. It is this divine superintendence which makes history rationally comprehensible. Van Til rightly sees that the Hegelian, Marxists, and all other evolutionary concepts of history ultimately declare that history is without purpose and meaning. Apart from this Reformed approach to its meaning, the historian is doomed to failure in his search for truth, and he is logically driven to the conclusion that the historical process is without pattern or goal. The doctrine of "progress" becomes increasingly difficult to maintain in the light of twentieth century realities of war and despotism. If there is no meaning or goal observable within history, the doctrine of progress itself becomes meaningless.

Van Til has much to offer in the solution of this perplexing problem concerning the possibility of progress. The idea itself was almost unknown in Greek historiography, and it only became prominent in Augustine's *De Civitate Dei*, which became the model for Medieval and Reformation historians in their discussions of this issue. With the coming of the Enlightenment and the French Revolution, the doctrine of progress was widely accepted, not only by historians and philosophers, but it became part and parcel of the political thought of the day. Indeed, this concept played a major role in the life of the era. There can be no moral progress in the deepest sense of the word. However, for society as a whole, there is a point of progress. But in this sense it is progress toward the goal of all history, the second coming of Jesus Christ and the last judgment. History is not a static process and does not stand still. It is constantly moving forward toward this final culmination. It is a progress toward a final end which a sovereign God has decreed for men and the world as a result of judgment upon sin. But there is in the second coming of Christ his final vindication and triumph. At that time this world system will give way to the new heaven and the new earth, and Christ will reign forever and forever.

This is the ultimate destiny of human history and Van Til would echo the thought of Augustine when he wrote: "Omnia revocanda ad gloriam Dei est" ("All things must be referred to the glory of God"); and he would also find himself in hearty support and agreement with Augustine when he wrote: "Grace and election are the mystery and essence of history." This is where the Christian must find his ultimate answer as he seeks to find the meaning and purpose of human history.

Rousas John Rushdoony

XVIII. THE ONE AND MANY PROBLEM—
THE CONTRIBUTION OF VAN TIL

A basic problem of philosophy has been the question of the one and the many. Does ultimacy belong to the oneness, to the unity of things, or is it in the particularity of things, in their individuality, that ultimacy is to be sought? The question of the one and the many is more than a philosophical problem: it is a question which is basic to every area of life. It makes a vast difference in society if we hold that the basic structure of man's life is to be sought in the state as the unity or oneness of man and society. Thus, in ancient Mesopotamia, the cosmos itself was seen as a state, and this divine state required the subservience of all individuals to the higher authority and being of the cosmos-state. In such a society, the individual is a man only to the extent in which he is a functioning part of the cosmos-state.[1]

On the other hand, in Greek society, the particularity of things came to triumph over the oneness of being. Early in Greek thought, Heraclitus of Ephesus (c. 500 B.C.) had held that "all things are one." Of Hesiod, Heraclitus said, "Hesiod is the teacher of very many, he who did not understand day and night: for they are one."[2] But if night and day are one, then particularity has no meaning, and there is, indeed, no meaning possible. The mystic most openly expresses this oneness of being, in Western thought, for what it is: beyond meaning and therefore beyond expression. Meaning involves differentiation, delineation, and particularity, among other things; without these, there is no meaning. If day and night are one, if good and evil are one, and if life and death are one, then there is no meaning. The end result of a philosophy of the one as against the many is the abdication of philosophy and meaning. History then ceases also to have meaning; it becomes an endless and eternal cycle. Thus Parmenides of Elia (c. 475 B.C.) declared, "It is all the same to me from what point I begin, for I shall return to this same point." For Parmenides, the basic fact was the one, "that it is, and it is not possible for it NOT TO BE," whereas of "the other," of any particularity, he said, "IT is bound NOT TO BE."[3] Again, Diogenes of Apollonia (5th century

B.C.) held that, "It seems to me, to sum up the whole matter, that all existing things are created by the alteration of the same thing, and are the same thing."[4] Such a philosophy led steadily to the exaltation of the state as the immanent one, as the great and inescapable unity of man and of being. Warner Fite in particular stressed the responsibility of Plato for fathering the tyrants of Greece.[5] The responsibility, however, was far wider. Aristotle, after all, defined man as a political animal, i.e., as one whose true being was to be found in the state, and virtually all Greek philosophy to Plato's time had prepared the way for the absolutism of the immanent one, the state.

There was, of course, a reaction against all this, a bitter rebellion against the tyranny of the one in favor of the reality and freedom of the many, the particulars. The Cynics were a dramatic aspect of this revolt. By denying all universals in favor of the purely particular meaning, they logically renounced all social controls, conventions, and moral standards. They went dirty, unshaven, and unkempt. They mocked the idea of moral law and insisted that man, as another animal, should avoid pretensions and copulate openly like the dogs. (It was from this their name Cynic, cognate with canine, was derived, from *kyos, kynos,* dog.) The Cynics sought to "recoin legal (i.e., conventional) currency" or values; Nietzsche followed the Cynics in seeking the "transvaluation of values," in trying to place man beyond good and evil.[6] The resulting anarchy, however, was as destructive of meaning as the earlier answer. If night and day, and good and evil, are one, then all meaning disappears down the maw of the one. But if every particular, every individual, is his own law and meaning, his own universal, then again there is no meaning. Communication is nullified, since every particular or individual is an autonomous universe. There is no universal, because everything, every last particular thing, is its own universal.

Thus, to affirm the one means that a social order falls into the abyss of meaninglessness, and to affirm the many means the same collapse into the anarchy of meaninglessness. It is not surprising that philosophy as a formal discipline has become gun-shy with respect to the problem of the one and the many and has abandoned any formal or direct consideration of it in recent years. The problem, however, will not disappear. Every social order embodies an answer or a philosophical solution to the question of the one and the many, as does every area of life. Which is more basic, more real, or prior, man or the state? In marriage, is the union more important than the man and the woman, or does the will of the individual prevail over the marital union and contract? Is the church the reality, or is it the reborn individual who is the more important entity? The areas of application can be multiplied at length. Suffice it to say, that while philosophy may shrink at answering the question, after centuries of sorry solutions, every society is an attempted answer to the problem of the one and the many. Moreover, the open confrontation with the problem in the writings of Cornelius Van Til marks his philosophy as most relevant today to the problems of man and society. In an age of consistent avoidance of issues, Van Til's thought is marked by a rigorous and systematic confrontation. In this confrontation, Van Til follows in the school of Kuyper, Bavinck, Vollenhoven, Dooyeweerd, and Stoker.

The word *systematic* in a sense opens up the offense of Van Til's philosophy. Modern philosophy has found systematics to be a deadend for its presuppositions. *First,* to pursue the problem of the one logically in terms of the ultimacy of the one leads to *monism,* a course taken by much Eastern philosophy. The end result has been disillusion; the one has been affirmed, but the triumph of the one has been the triumph of meaninglessness. As a result, Buddhism and other philosophies proclaimed the ultimacy of nothingness. But if the many be affirmed, the end result of such a philosophy is to proceed from *dualism* to total *atomism* and anarchy; again this course has been taken in Eastern thought. To be systematic in terms of either position is to pursue an already proven and established road. This scarcely commends itself to philosophers; why pursue assured defeat?

Second, as a result, Western philosophy has sought to avoid the open confrontation which is apparent in Eastern thought. Its answer has been *dialectical,* and the dialectical answers given have been analyzed by Herman Dooyeweerd as well as Van Til. This entire school of thought has extensively explored the problems of modern philosophy, and, in the analysis, these problems have greatly influenced one another also. Van Til is often at pains to make known his indebtedness to others. The form-matter, nature-grace, and naturefreedom dialectics of Western thought have sought to avoid the logical conclusion of the one and the many problem. By affirming both in dialectical tension, but without affirming dualism, and by seeking to avoid also a commitment to monism, dialectical philosophy has sought to retain both social order and the particular individual, both the unity and the particularity of being. But systematics governs even when it is denied. The attempts of Greek philosophy to avoid this Scylla and Charybdis failed, and with it came the collapse of Greek civilization. The same nemesis pursued Rome, and medieval dialectical as well, and is today leading to the breakdown of modern philosophy. The fact that philosophy today has abdicated its responsibility does not alter the social consequences: the world is torn between growing totalitarianism and growing anarchy as dialecticism breaks down and the one and the many pursue their independent and hostile directions.

The details of this problem, briefly chronicled here, have been extensively reported and analyzed. Dialecticism in particular has received major attention.

To understand Van Til's position with respect to the one and the many, it is important to realize that, in his systematically and rigorously biblical philosophy, there is *first*, a clear-cut distinction between created being and the uncreated being of God. Creationism is fundamental to Van Til's philosophy. In ancient Egyptian thought, the king or pharaoh was the umbilical cord uniting human society with the gods. This cord, however, was not one destined for severing. Rather, a return to the womb of being meant the deification of the human, and the goal of society was to follow the umbilical cord back into the womb of being. In Van Til's philosophy, because of the Creator-creature distinction, there is both true transcendence and true immanence.

This means, *second*, that for Van Til ultimacy belongs, not to the created order, but to God, to the ontological trinity. Van Til, in commenting on modern dialecticism, observes, "All non-biblical thought is dialectical. Dialectical thought expresses itself in the form of a religious dualism. There are assumed to be two ultimate principles, the one of temporal plurality and with it of evil, and the other of eternal being which is a form and is good."[7] Monism and dualism represent the collapse of a dialectic. But, whether in a dialectical philosophy, or in monism and dualism, the ultimate principle is a part of the one continuous chain of being. Van Til, after Scripture, ascribes ultimacy only to the sovereign God, to the ontological trinity. Concerning God's transcendence and immanence, Van Til writes,

> It is not a sufficient description of Christian theism when we say that as Christians we believe in both the transcendence and the immanence of God while pantheistic systems believe only in the immanence of God and deistic systems only in the transcendence of God. The transcendence we believe in is not the transcendence of deism and the immanence we believe in is not the immanence

of pantheism. In the case of deism transcendence virtually means separation while in the case of pantheism immanence virtually means identification. And if we add separation to identification we do not have theism as a result. As we mean a certain kind of God when as theists we speak of God, so also we mean a certain kind of transcendence and a certain kind of immanence when we use these terms. The Christian doctrine of God implies a definite conception of the relation of God to the created universe. So also the Christian doctrine of God implies a definite conception of everything in the created universe.[8]

Because Van Til's position is creationist, he can make this sharp biblical distinction and therefore ascribe ultimacy to God without thereby attributing it to man.

This means, *third,* that Van Til, ascribing all ultimacy to the triune God, must therefore seek the answer to the one and the many problem in God. In one of his earliest publications (a syllabus of 1935), he made this very point and made it emphatically:

In the first place we are conscious of having as our foundation the *metaphysical* presupposition of Christianity as it is expressed in the creation doctrine. This means that in God as an absolutely self-conscious being, in God as an absolute personality, who exists as the triune God, we have the solution of the one and many problem. The persons of the trinity are mutually exhaustive. This means that there is no remnant of unconsciousness of potentiality in the being of God. Thus there cannot be anything unknown to God that springs from his own nature. Then too there was nothing existing beyond this God before the creation of the universe. *Hence the time-space world cannot be a source of independent particularity.* The space-time universe cannot even be a universe of exclusive particularity. It is brought forth by the creative act of God, and this means in accordance with the plan of the universal God. Hence there must be in this world universals as well as particulars. *Moreover they can never exist in independence of one another.* They must be equally ultimate which means in this case that they are both derivative. Now if this is the case, God cannot be confronted by an absolute particularity that springs from the space-time universe any more than he can be confronted by an absolute particularity that should spring from a potential aspect of his own being. Hence in God the one and the many are equally ultimate which in this case means *absolutely* ultimate.[9]

As Van Til makes clear, the metaphysical implications of the creation doctrine are that the ultimacy of the one and the many is to be found only and exclusively in God, and that therefore the one and the many can never exist independently of one another or in essential conflict with one another, in that both are derivative. The one and the many are thus not essentially alien things which imply a dualism and can be held together only in dialectical tension lest the one reduce the other to nothing and itself to meaninglessness. The one and the many are absolutely under God and therefore totally subject to God and his law. They are absolutely subject to his creative purpose and a part of his sovereign decree.

It follows, *fourth,* that, since the answer to the one and the many problem is found in God, Van Til points out that the doctrine of the ontological trinity brings to an end the necessity for any tension between the two. It is not the one nor the many which is ultimate, but it is rather the equal ultimacy of the one and the many because of the ultimacy of the triune God.

As Van Til states, philosophers, seeking a "unified outlook for human experience," have been faced with the problem that "the universe is composed of many things. Man's problem is to find unity in the midst of the plurality of things," and to do this without denying either their plurality or their unity in plurality[10] "In answering this question of the one and many we find it necessary to distinguish between the eternal one and many and the temporal one and many. Non-Christian philosophers on the other hand find it unnecessary to make this distinction." Van Til then continues, in a passage which summarizes his position,

> Using the language of the one and many question we contend that in God the one and the many are equally ultimate. Unity in God is no more fundamental than diversity, and diversity in God is no more fundamental than unity. The persons of the Trinity are mutually exhaustive of one another. The Son and the Spirit are ontologically on a par with the Father. It is a well-known fact that all heresies in the history of the church have in some form or other taught subordinationism. Similarly, we believe, all "heresies" in apologetic methodology spring from some form of subordinationism.

> It may be profitable at this juncture to introduce the notion of a *concrete universal.* In seeking for an answer to the one and many question, philosophers have admittedly experienced great difficulty. The *many* must be brought into contact with one another. But how do we know that they can be brought into contact with one another? How do we know that the many do not simply exist as unrelated particulars? The answer given is that in such a case we should know nothing of them; they would be abstracted from the body of knowledge that we have; they would be *abstract* particulars. On the other hand, how is it possible that we should obtain a unity that does not destroy the particulars? We seem

to get our unity by generalizing, by abstracting from the particulars in order to include them into larger unities. If we keep up this process of generalization till we exclude all particulars, granted they can all be excluded, have we then not stripped these particulars of their particularity? Have we then obtained anything but an *abstract* universal?

As Christians we hold that there is no answer to these problems from a non-Christian point of view. We shall argue this point later; for the nonce we introduce this matter in order to set forth the meaning of the notion of the concrete universal. The notion of the concrete universal has been offered by idealist philosophy in order to escape the *reductio ad absurdum* of the abstract particular and the abstract universal. It is only in the Christian doctrine of the triune God, as we are bound to believe, that we really have a *concrete universal*. In God's being there are no particulars not related to the universal and there is nothing universal that is not fully expressed in the particulars.[11]

The doctrine of the ontological trinity, of the triune God, is thus the answer. In the trinity both particularity and unity are equally ultimate. Every orthodox formulation and expression of the doctrine of God, as hammered out in theological controversy and in the recognized councils and creeds of the early church, stresses the unity of the godhead without any surrender of the particularity or individuality of the three persons, and without any subordinationism.[12]

Van Til, having begun with the doctrine of creation, now returns to it to emphasize that the temporal one and many is created by God. Moreover, "Creation, on Christian principles, must always mean fiat creation."[13] This means, *fifth,* that the entire created one and many is entirely under God and his law. Turning again to Van Til's summary statement of his position, we see that,

If the creation doctrine is thus taken seriously, it follows that the various aspects of created reality must sustain such relations to one another as have been ordained between them by the Creator, as superiors, inferiors or equals. All aspects being equally created, no one aspect of reality may be regarded as more ultimate than another. Thus the created *one and many* may in this respect be said to be *equal* to one another; they are equally derived and equally dependent upon God who sustains them both. The particulars or facts of the universe do and must act in accord with universals or laws. Thus there is order in the created universe. On the other hand, the laws may not and can never reduce the particulars to abstract particulars or reduce their individuality in any manner. The laws are but generalizations of God's method of working with the particulars. God may at any time take one *fact* and set it into a new relation to created law. That is, there is no inherent reason in the facts or laws themselves why this should not be done. It is this sort of conception of the relation of facts and laws, of the temporal one and many, imbedded as it is in that idea of God in which we profess to believe, that we need in order to make room for miracles. And miracles are at the heart of the Christian position.

Thus there is a basic equality between the created one and the created many, or between the various aspects of reality. On the other hand, there is a relation of subordination between them as ordained by God. The "mechanical" laws are lower than the "teleological" laws. Of course, both the "mechanical" and the "teleological" laws are teleological in the sense that both obey God's will. So also the facts of the physical aspect of the universe are lower than the facts of the will and intellect of man. It is this subordination of one fact and law to other facts and laws that is spoken of in Scripture as man's government over nature. According to Scripture man was set as king over nature. He was to subdue it. Yet he was to subdue it for God. He was priest under God as well as king under God. In order to subdue it under God man had to interpret it; he was therefore prophet as well as priest and king under God.[14]

This means, *sixth,* that a world totally under God, a world in which the created one and many is absolutely determined and governed by the eternal one and many, is a world with purpose and meaning. History is rescued from meaninglessness. Instead of being a collection of brute facts without meaning, of abstract particulars and abstract universals, history has purpose and direction. As Van Til has shown,

> The philosophy of history inquires into the meaning of history. To use a phrase of Kierkegaard, we ask how the Moment *is to have significance.* Our claim as believers is that the Moment cannot intelligently be shown to have any significance except upon the presupposition of the biblical doctrine of the ontological trinity. In the ontological trinity there is complete harmony between an equally ultimate one and many. The persons of the trinity are mutually exhaustive of one another and of God's nature. It is the absolute equality in point of ultimacy that requires all the emphasis we can give it. Involved in this absolute equality is complete interdependence; God is our concrete universal.[15]

The solution to the problem of a philosophy of history is found thus in the biblical doctrine of the trinity, the eternal one and many. "The God that the philosophers of the ages have been looking for, the 'Unknown God,' is known to us by grace. It has been the quest of the ages to find an interpretative concept such as has been given us by grace."[16]

Where philosophy seeks to find the meaning of history within history, the consequence is a denial of history. The futility of finding a meaning in a world of brute factuality, a world of autonomous and unrelated facts and of abstract universals, leads to a denial of history, implicitly or explicitly. This denial of history is far gone in Eastern philosophies; it is in rapid progress in Western thought. An American historian opened a new class with the words, "There is no such thing as history, but it is my responsibility to teach it." Not only historians but philosophers of science are increasingly sceptical of meaning.[17] The flight from meaning is a result of the collapse of philosophy.

As against this, Van Til states that "The ontological trinity will be our interpretative concept everywhere. God is our concrete universal; in him thought and being are coterminous, in him the problem of knowledge is solved." It is this which separates a truly Christian philosophy from all else. "If we begin thus with the ontological trinity as our concrete universal, we frankly differ from every school of philosophy and from every school of science not merely in our conclusions, but in our starting-point and in our method as well."[18] At a time when ostensibly Christian philosophies have been more than ever compromised by alien presuppositions, the radically and systematically Christian presuppositionalism of Cornelius Van Til places him in a position of particular relevance. The system Van Til derives from his reliance on the infallible Word of the triune God is not the "systematic consistency" of autonomous man's rationality.[19] Rather, it is that which is derived from the infallible Word of the triune God, the "self-authenticating Christ." "In Christ alone human experience becomes intelligible."[20] When men depart from the eternal one and many, they drift into dialectical thought. "As the chief interpretative category of dialecticism, the individual takes the place of the ontological trinity in orthodox theology; in it being is exhausted in relation and relation is exclusively internal."[21] But the meaning of history lies beyond history in the eternal one and many. It cannot be found in history, nor can it be located in a Jesus who is separated "from the all-inclusive providence of God."[22]

The answer, as Van Til makes abundantly clear, is there. Men have avoided the answer to the problem of the one and the many because they reject the God who is the answer.

In terms of philosophy, the answer is particularly Van Til's. At this point, some hold that the Amsterdam school has failed to meet the challenge of the critical problem of the one and the many because of its lack of adherence to its own presuppositionalism. Instead of accepting the doctrine of creation, the Amsterdam school has dealt very loosely with it. At this point, the very great work of Herman Dooyeweerd is under fire, because of his inadequate concepts of creation and infallibility.[23] It is of interest to note that Van Til has not been so criticized at either point.

The critical problem of a society caught in the continuing tensions of alternating anarchy and totalitarianism, between anarchic individualism and anarchic collectivism, plagues man's history more than ever today. In the face of this problem, much of philosophy has abandoned the battlefield for the academic sterilities of logical analysis. If there is to be any kind of Christian reconstruction, then, in every area of thought, the philosophy of Cornelius Van Til is of critical and central importance.

Response by C. Van Til

Dear Mr. Rushdoony:

Here I have been trying to say over and over again that I'm only interested in stating and defending what Scripture teaches and from reading your first pages you make me out to be a philosopher. Well, I guess I am one of sorts, but you put everything into a better perspective by pointing out that even in my philosophizing on the One-Many problem I am trying to bring out that only the biblical answer to this problem is the true answer. Or, better, you point out that there is no intelligible speech about the unity and diversity of things unless the question itself is placed in a Christian framework.

Your continued interest in all my works is always encouraging.

—C.V.T.

Gordon R. Lewis

XIX. VAN TIL AND CARNELL — PART I

Two of the most influential recent writers in apologetics are Cornelius Van Til and the late Edward John Carnell (1919–1967). Although both are orthodox, Reformed theologians, they pose an embattled contrast on apologetic method.

Van Til charges that Carnell's method of defending the Christian faith actually "requires the destruction of Christianity."[1] Carnell invites the uncommitted to test Christianity's truth-claims before giving themselves to Christ. That invitation, Van Til thinks, encourages human independence of God. It allegedly gives people a temporary impression of their own autonomy. Although Carnell intends to defend orthodox doctrines of God's sovereignty, his method makes man to stand in judgment upon God. Thus it leads to "the rejection of the whole body of his Christian beliefs."[2]

Carnell has not made charges against Van Til's apologetic in his books, but from Carnell's perspective Van Til's method is appropriate for theology, not apologetics. Van Til's declared purpose is to challenge non-Christian thinking and living by presenting Christ to men without compromise. Two steps are involved: (1) he sets forth the gospel of grace in the terms of theology and philosophy; (2) he *presents* this gospel to the natural man in order that he might be saved.[3] From beginning to end Van Til's method assumes Christianity's truth; it does not defend it. As Carnell sees it, "Statement and defense . . . are not the same thing. Statement draws on theology; defense draws on apologetics."[4] Has Van Til a defense of the faith? If not, he has advertised a defense of the faith, but left the faith defenseless!

Such serious charges are by no means merely academic. Generations of students are being trained to feel these deep differences. At stake is the shape of their ministries to outsiders and the potential disruption of churches, denominations, and schools. To help stimulate the long, hard thinking these divisive issues necessitate, this brief essay is penned.

An analysis of Van Til's charges against Carnell's methodology may remove unnecessary suspicion and promote increased understanding of similarities and differences. The comparison and contrast is focused upon three aspects of apologetic method: (1) the logical starting point, (2) points of contact with non-Christians, and (3) the criterion of truth.

I. The Logical Starting Point

Van Til takes his underlying methodological procedure from idealists such as Hegel, Bradley, and Bosanquet. They "think, and we believe think correctly, that every appeal made to bare fact is unintelligible. Every fact must stand in relation to other facts or it means nothing to anyone."[5] The system Van Til brings to factual data involves two presuppositions, one epistemological and the other metaphysical. The epistemological presupposition asserts the infallible truth of the Bible as God's Word written. Metaphysically he assumes the existence of the triune God disclosed in Scripture. Combining them, "A truly Protestant apologetic must . . . make its beginning from the presupposition that the triune God, Father, Son and Holy Spirit, speaks to him with absolute authority in Scripture."[6]

In contrast, Van Til thinks that Carnell starts, not with God but autonomous man. That charge is the major premise of Van Til's criticisms in *The Case for Calvinism* of Carnell's method.

> His method is to start with man as autonomous. Starting from man as autonomous, Carnell worked up a modern form of natural theology under the guise of common grace. . . . Similarly, we now note, starting with the idea of human autonomy Carnell again caters to the idea that God is identical with the projected ideals of the "good man."[7]

Is Van Til's judgment on Carnell's system justified? If not, his arguments against Carnell lose their major premise.

Carnell agrees that no such thing as brute facts can impress a *tabula rasa* mind and yield the ultimate nature of reality as a whole. As vigorously as Van Til, Carnell attacks the empiricist's starting point—nature. Two extensive chapters of *An Introduction to Christian Apologetics* (VII and VIII) criticize natural theology, empirical proofs for God, and the Thomist's analogy of being. Two subsequent chapters defend at length the starting point—God.[8] The content of Carnell's logical starting point is identical to Van Til's, the triune God of the Bible.[9] Epistemologically Carnell assumes the Bible as "the infallibly inspired word of God."[10] Revelation "without God's authority behind it is useless."[11] Although Carnell thought the orthodox label in theology was broad enough to include men who did not hold to complete inerrancy, one of his last contributions to *Christianity Today* revealed his personal commitment to a Warfieldian stance.[12] For his emphasis upon the metaphysical assumption of the trinity providing the perfect pattern for the solution to the problem of the one and many in the universe, Carnell expresses his indebtedness to Van Til.[13]

Both Van Til and Carnell agree on the content of the Christian apologist's logical starting point. Unitedly they deny the wisdom of starting with empirical evidence, rational principles, or human witness to an experience of God. Together they insist that orthodox Christianity will be defended only by starting with the proposition that the triune God of the Bible exists and his written Word is true. How, then, can Van Til persistently allege that Carnell starts with autonomous man?

On the surface it seems that Van Til has intentionally ignored Carnell's assertions identical to his own. But his charges may be partly a result of the difference in Carnell's *manner* of starting with the God of the Bible. Carnell asserts the God of the Bible as a "hypothesis," whereas for Van Til it is a "presupposition." Carnell's hypothesis is a tentative conclusion to be accepted only after confirmation by the criterion of systematic consistencey. Is Van Til's presupposition assumed true independent of all considerations of consistency and evidence? It often sounds as though Van Til voluntarily presupposes the truth of Christian claims in a vacuum. In talking with flesh and bones human beings, however, Van Til places himself in the position of his opponent, assuming the correctness of his argument to show that on such assumptions the facts are not facts nor the laws laws. Then Van Til asks the non-Christian to place himself upon the Christian position for argument's sake to show that only upon this basis do facts and laws appear intelligible.[14] Is that so different from Carnell's invitation to the unbeliever to consider the logical starting point a hypothesis that makes sense of life in terms of intelligent coherence? Van Til's criteria of intelligibility are to be discussed subsequently. For now we can conclude that the difference between Carnell and Van Til can hardly be the verbal difference between a presupposition assumed for the purposes of argument and a hypothesis assumed for purposes of argument.

Part of the reason for Van Til's charge may stem from a failure to give due importance to Carnell's distinction between the logical starting point and the synoptic starting point. The synoptic starting point answers the question, "How do you prove the logical starting point?" Its worth is determined by "its ability to make good the case for the logical starting point."[15] Having proposed that the God of the Bible exists, Carnell devotes considerable time to the basis on which Christians and non-Christians may even argue about their different logical starting points. What Carnell designates common ground in other contexts, he calls "the synoptic starting point" in some portions of *An Introduction to Christian Apologetics*. To this we turn our attention in order to answer the question of whether Carnell's view of common ground with non-Christians can justify Van Til's charges of starting with autonomous man. At this point, however, it is necessary to conclude that Van Til's charges are unjustified in relation to Carnell's logical starting point. On that issue Van Til and Carnell are in agreement. Both begin ultimately with the triune God of the Bible.

II. Points of Contact with Non-Christians

Both Van Til and Carnell also find numerous points of contact with unbelievers. Carnell thinks that all men created in the image of God have certain innate principles of truth, goodness, and beauty. These inner principles differentiate man from the brutes, making possible significant speech, assertion, moral judgment, and aesthetic judgment.[16] Common grace enables even the non-Christian to be accountable for the work of the law written on his heart (Rom. 2:14-15). Total depravity does not annihilate these God-given principles. They are not human inventions held menacingly over God by autonomous men. They do not make men autonomous; they make men responsible. Fallen men are responsible to live according to truth and morality.[17] Invariably men suppress this truth, but they are inexcusable for doing so.[18] The presence of principles of logic, ethics, and aesthetics does not displace the need for special revelation. Instead, it vividly shows how far short men come of God's glory and how desperately they need a special revelation of divine grace.

Far from teaching the autonomy of the human intellect, Carnell explicitly teaches its incompetence. "The reason of man, in addition to being partially corrupted because of sin, is incompetent to work out a complete view of God and man. . . . reason is incompetent to complete a philosophy of life without special revelation from God."[19] As a result of the incompetence of human reason in developing a world view, no common ground exists with unbelievers metaphysically. "Neutrality in metaphysics is impossible. One either believes

God is the Author and Judge of the universe, or he does not; there
is no *tertium quid*." Carnell adds, "So penetrating is the metaphysical level of meaning that it succeeds in reflecting back upon the lower
levels also."[20]

Likewise Van Til denies any common ground on the metaphysical
level. The natural man begins with himself as autonomous, not God.
So Van Til "applies atomic power and flame-throwers to the very
presupposition of the natural man's ideas with repect to himself."[21]
The Christian sees everything from the perspective of the presupposition of the God of the Bible.

> There is no single territory or dimension in which believers and
> non-believers have all things in common. . . . even the descrip-
> tion of facts in the lowest dimension presupposes a system of
> metaphysics and epistemology. So there can be no territory of
> cooperation.[22]

Apart from special revelation in the Bible, as Carnell held, the reason of natural man is incompetent to formulate a true metaphyisics.

Does Van Til rule out any points of contact? Not at all; he admits
several that are quite similar to Carnell's. Van Til's absolute contrast holds only "in principle."[23] The non-Christian does have the
same formal laws of logic as the Christian. Van Til says,

> I do *not* maintain that Christians operate according to new laws
> of thought any more than that they have new eyes or noses. . . .
> The non-Christian uses the gifts of logical reasoning in order to
> keep down the truth in unrighteousness. . . . The question is
> not that of the law of contradiction as a formal principle.[24]

So Christians may use the language of non-Christian philosophers.[25]
Van Til warns that the similarity of wording does not mean identity
of meaning. However, in other contexts he admits that the believer
may share not only the language, but also "much truth."

> The world may discover much truth without owning Christ as
> Truth. Christ upholds even those who ignore, deny, and oppose
> him. A little child may slap his father in the face, but it can do
> so only because the father holds it on his knee. So modern
> science, modern philosophy, and modern theology may discover
> much truth.[26]

Although there is nothing in common ultimately, the Christian and
non-Christian have "all things in common" proximately.[27]

Van Til's points of contact include not only the same laws of logic
and the realm of facts proximately, but also, relatively speaking,
"much good."[28] Van Til finds in man principles of truth and good-

ness similar to Carnell's. He also has Carnell's knowledge of the self and of God. All men owe their life and breath to God. To have self-consciousnessness "presupposes God-consciousness."[29] This knowledge of God was undimmed before the fall. Since the fall it is still inescapable. "It is indelibly involved in his awareness of anything whatsoever."[30] But fallen man suppresses his God-consciousness by seeking to interpret himself and his environment apart from God. Psychologically we have in common this experience of holding the truth in unrighteousness. Morally and spiritually we are all covenant-breakers, guilty of not loving God and neighbor. So all are responsible. "Deep down in his mind every man knows that he is the creature of God and responsible to God. Every man, at bottom, knows that he is a covenant-breaker. But every man acts and talks as though this were not so."[31]

It seems that Van Til admits points of contact in the human consciousness very similar to Carnell's logically, factually, psychologically, morally, and spiritually. Of course Van Til distinguishes the total difference of the ultimate starting point from the points of contact in the proximate level. Similarly, Carnell distinguishes the unique logical starting point of Christians from common ground in the synoptic starting point. Carnell's method does not differ with Van Til's when Van Til says,

> If, then, the human consciousness must, in the nature of the case, always be the proximate starting point, it remains true that God is always the most basic and therefore the ultimate or final reference point in human interpretation.[32]

Van Til's constant charges against Carnell's methodology cannot fairly be directed against his points of contact. Quite clearly these can be held by Van Til and Carnell without making man autonomous.

III. The Criterion of Truth

The precise point of Van Til's criticism is that Carnell *utilizes* these points of contact in his apologetic. According to Van Til, non-Christians always use the formal law of non-contradiction to defend their own autonomy. The non-Christian's reason is like a saw used, if used at all, to rebel against the triune God of the Bible.[33] An unbeliever is not even in a position to test the truth of revelation-claims. He will "certainly find the Christian religion incredible because impossible and the evidence for it . . . inadequate."[34] The unregenerate will always use the elements of truth they possess to support their own human ends rather than God's glory.

When man became a sinner he made of himself instead of God the ultimate or final reference point. And it is precisely this presupposition, as it controls without exception all forms of non-Christian philosophy, that must be brought into question.[35]

In charging Carnell with reinforcing the autonomy of the non-Christian, Van Til again chooses to ignore Carnell's logical starting point. Carnell's hypothesis of the triune God of the Bible challenges human autonomy as much as Van Til's starting point. But Carnell faces the very real possibility that a person can surrender his autonomy not only to God, but also to the devil. Men also surrender their autonomy to the unitarian God of the Koran, or to the flesh and bones God of the Mormon's *Doctrines and Covenants*, or to the impersonal Principles of *Science and Health with Key to the Scriptures*. Although fallen men cannot construct their own ultimate system, Carnell thinks they can discern between bonafide and counterfeit books in human language claiming to speak for God. "The intellect of man is darkened, but it is not extinguished. If this were not so, the mind of man would be quite incompetent to distinguish the voice of God from the voice of the devil."[36]

Were not people in Old Testament times by certain criteria capable of distinguishing true prophets from false prophets? Could not the people of New Testament times employ criteria to distinguish authentic apostles from pseudo apostles? It is all well and good to say that their messages were self-authenticating after the messengers had adequate credentials. Mormons claim the witness of the Holy Spirit to authenticate their sacred writings. The claim that Scripture is self-authenticating does not make it so for any particular individual who does not accredit its writers as spokesmen for God. Its credentials need to be checked. If the claims of Scripture for itself cannot be checked by principles of truth, goodness, and fact, then by what?

Van Til does not completely escape the need to check the Bible's credentials. He expects the natural man to use his reason sufficiently to see the need for his metaphysical starting point. "As a rational creature he can understand that one must either accept the whole of a system of truth or reject the whole of it."[37] He expects the natural man to conclude that "it will be imposible to find meaning in anything."[38] By what capacity does the non-Christian entertain "meaning"? How can he be expected to see this if not by the use of his formal principle of contradiction and coherence with all the proximate truth he does possess? In some way Van Til needs to spell out *how* it can be made evident to the natural man that Christianity alone gives meaning to life. Until he does, a crucial gap in his methodology leaves the apologist without explicit help in understanding what sort of meaning can be evident to non-Christians.

Even in saying that the Christian system can be made evident to the unbeliever Van Til has made man "autonomous." James Daane saw this in reviewing *The Case for Calvinism*.

> Van Til himeself, however, does not escape what he calls the "autonomous man"! His purpose, he writes, is "to bring the challenge of the Gospel of Christ to modern man," because Christianity is modern man's only hope. "However," he adds, "this cannot be shown to be true unless it can be made evident that Christianity not only has its own methodology but also that only its methodology gives meaning to human life." In making this "evident" Van Til himself appeals to something in man to which the truth of Christianity will hopefully appear "evident." And with this Van Til's "autonomous man" has returned.[39]

Surely Van Til has not made man autonomous; he has only made him responsible. Similarly, Carnell has not made man autonomous, but responsible.

Exactly what is Carnell's test of religious truth-claims? He cannot accept sacred writings on the basis of instinct, custom, tradition, feeling, sense perception, intuition, or pragmatism. These criteria endorse contradictory revelations and so must be submitted to a more basic test. Carnell's criterion of systematic consistency is twofold, requiring that a proposed truth be non-contradictory and fit the facts of internal and external experience. Only then can it be held to correspond to the mind of the God who does not deny himself and freely orders everything that actually is.

Van Til has much against Carnell's use of the law of non-contradiction. Both the neo-orthodox writer Hordern and the liberal writer De Wolf

> use the laws of logic in order by them to exclude the claims of the God and the Christ of Scripture. . . . The fourth book of Aristotle's *Metaphysics* is for them more authoritative than is the Bible. For this reason they have argued that God cannot exist in trinitarian fashion.[40]

With the help of fallacious guilt by association Van Til concludes that Carnell must make the rational man stand above revelation in autonomous freedom.[41] As Carnell employs the law of non-contradiction, however, man does not stand above the trinity metaphysically, nor the Scriptures epistemologically. Man stands under a number of conflicting revelation claims and must decide whether to commit himself to any as true. The law of non-contradiction enables a man to distinguish bonafide revelation from counterfeits. Van Til refuses to acknowledge this major objective in Carnell's writings or to face this issue in his own method.

It can be illustrated from the realm of medicine that Carnell's test of truth need not make the natural man more ultimate than Scripture. The physician who diagnoses the case and writes the prescription is the final authority in a case of illness. Both Carnell and Van Til agree on that. Van Til implies that one should accredit the physician even though he contradicts himself and does not take into account all the observable symptoms. For Van Til the physician's claims to be a physician are self-authenticating, regardless of logic or fact. Carnell, on the other hand, thinks a layman can and must intelligently decide between the list of alleged physicians and quacks. Only when the physician's credentials are authentic will Carnell submit to his pre-scriptions and surgery. When the doctor's authenticity is substantiated by sufficient evidence the final authority is the doctor, not the layman. Carnell explains his use of the moral test:

> Since it is necessary that we first be assured that it is God, not the devil, that we are doing business with, we must apply the rule of the good to find God. But once the heart is satisfied that God is worthy of receiving loving trust, the abstract good is then set aside and the will of God becomes the standard of goodness.[42]

Van Til may deny that men will ever give up testing God's Word to accept its authority. Surely several people checked Paul's credentials as an apostle before yielding to his authority as an apostle. Can we accept everyone's claims to speak for God as self-authenticating?

On the surface Van Til rejects the criterion of non-contradiction. He thinks he has found contradictions in the teachings of the Bible.[43] But his examples illustrate complex causes, apparent contradictions only, or incomplete comprehension. They are not actual logical contradictions affirming and denying the same thing at the same time and in the same respect. Clearly Van Til would not accept actual contradictions like the statements: "All men are sinners," and "Some men are not sinners." Not even in the name of self-attesting biblical authority could two such statements be true. One or the other, or both, would be false.

Van Til himself everywhere assumes the validity of the Aristotelian formulation of the law of contradiction. He constantly berates Thomists, Arminians, and many of his Reformed brethren for their inconsistencies. Indeed, the primary purpose of his apologetic has been to set forth a method of defending Christianity which is consistent with his theology.[44] His Reformed theology is notorious for its rigorous consistency. So it is difficult to take seriously Van Til's charge that appeals to consistency necessarily exalt reason above the Deity. If in fact Carnell's explicit methodological consistency destroys the Christian message, does not Van Til's implicit, practicing consistency destroy the Christian message?

Carnell's criterion of truth requires that an alleged revelation be not only logically consistent, but also factually adequate. The Creator orders everything in the universe according to a good and wise plan. The discrete facts of the material universe are related to each other, not by demonstrable necessity, but by God's free purpose. No axiomatic deductions about what is the case can be accepted without evidence. Only facts indicate what God actually chose to do. When we have properly construed the meaning of facts we have discovered the purposes of God. The hypothesis that consistently accounts for the greatest number of facts with the fewest difficulties is true.

Both Van Til and Carnell agree on the impossibility of reasoning on the basis of brute facts. However, both see the importance of one's interpretation fitting the factual data. Van Til writes, "The real question is, therefore, into whose schematism the facts will fit. As between Christianity and its opponents the question is whether our *claim* that *Christianity is the only schematism into which the facts will fit is true or not.*"[45] This statement of Van Til may have been a source of Carnell's emphasis showing that a consistent hypothesis fits the facts. It may even be the source of Carnell's terminology. Apparently it is possible for Van Til to regard his presupposition a *claim* whose concurrence with the facts is not only assumed, but displayed to the natural man without making him autonomous.

Van Til asks whether Carnell's method changed from an earlier emphasis on logic and fact to a later stress upon the heart and personal relationships. Carnell's method did not change; he simply applied it to different points of contact. He explains,

> I have consistently tried to build on some useful point of contact between the gospel and culture. In *An Introduction to Christian Apologetics* the appeal was to the law of contradiction; in *A Philosophy of the Christian Religion* it was to values; and in *Christian Commitment* it was to the judicial sentiment. In this book [*The Kingdom of Love and the Pride of Life*] I am appealing to the law of love.[46]

Carnell's earlier work anticipated the consistent explanation of both inner and outer experience, but it supported the congruence of the Christian hypothesis primarily with objective evidence. By these means he explains how an apologist can show the non-Christian in terms of his points of contact that Christianity gives meaning to all of life.

IV. Summation and Conclusion

Several things have become evident through this analysis of Van Til's charges against Carnell's method. First, Van Til conveniently ignores the fact that Carnell's logical starting point is identical in content with his own. Consequently, he falsely charges Carnell with starting with autonomous man.

Second, Van Til's criticism fails to note Carnell's agreement that on the metaphysical level there is no common ground with non-Christian systems, but that on the proximate level there is much truth in common. If Van Til's admissions of points of contact such as the law of contradiction, facts, and relative goodness do not make man "autonomous," Carnell's acknowledgment of these "synoptic starting points" does not make man "autonomous."

Third, Van Til's criticism of testing revelation-claims by systematic consistency assumes that the Bible is self-authenticating, a claim which begs the apologetic question. That question asks which among the contradictory alleged revelations, if any, is God's Word. Carnell safeguards his means of examining the credentials of these revelation-claims from becoming more authoritative than well-attested revelation. Van Til's constant charges that he thereby makes man autonomous overlook these explanations, and the similarity of his own attempt to make the Bible's revelation-claims the only source of meaning in the world. Interestingly enough, Van Til claims to have given "full recognition" to the relative good in those who are evil in principle.[47] But it is difficult to see how he can think he has done this when his admissions of so much common ground are not to be utilized for any apologetic purpose.

If my analysis has any truth at all, Van Til seriously misinterprets his former student. Followers of Van Til should take the "flame-thrower" to Van Til's criticism of Carnell and read him for themselves. Only then can they responsibly judge whether he makes man autonomous, considers the natural man able to work up a natural theology under the guise of common grace,[48] caters to the idea that God is identical with the projected ideals of the "good man,"[49] raises "man to the position of virtual creator of God,"[50] and sets the autonomous man, the rational man, or the moral man above the Scriptures.[51] If these accusations are unwarranted, Van Til's basic case against Carnell is an instance of tragic misunderstanding.

The two men have a similar ultimate starting point. The two men agree on much truth in common on the proximate level of human consciousness. The two men agree that only on the basis of their ultimate starting point can men find meaning in all of life. Carnell simply spells out the basis on which he can talk about the ultimate meaning to a non-Christian and expect him to be responsible for a decision concerning special revelation of the triune God in the Scriptures. Before fellowships are broken over the differences between these men, their similarities ought to be sounded out loud and clear.

How can Van Til find such a similar method so "destructive of Christianity"? First, he has succumbed to the common occupational hazard of majoring on differences to the neglect of similarities. Second, some of Carnell's statements taken out of his thought-context sound as though he makes man autonomous. Third, Van Til's preoccupation with his system causes him to fall into the fallacy of guilt by association. Carnell's criterion of systematic consistency is similar to the criterion not only of Hordern and De Wolf, but also of Edgar S. Brightman and the Boston personalists. That is enough for Van Til to write,

> Surely, we tend at once to say, Carnell must have known that in using the method borrowed from Brightman he was taking into his hands a dangerous tool to use in the defense, and particularly in a philosophical defense, of Christianity such as his work on *Apologetics* announces itself as being. Does not every method grow out of a system? Is not every system the fruit of its method?[52]

In these inferences Van Til fails to take into account that Carnell's logical starting point is as different from that of the Boston personalists as heaven is different from earth.

One could as effectively but fallaciously argue that Van Til's method is suspect because drawn from the idealists, Hegel, Bradley, and Bosanquet. Surely in adopting their method of demanding a total system to give meaning to disparate facts Van Til must have known that "he was taking into his hands a dangerous tool in the defense of Christianity." These idealists denied the orthodox doctrine of the trinity, the uniqueness of Christ's incarnation, and the literal truth of Scripture in general. "Does not every method grow out of a system? Is not every system the fruit of its method?" Ignore Van

Til's ultimate starting point as he ignored Carnell's, and he is equally guilty of borrowing a method from non-orthodox writers. But enough of this. Of course the fallacy of guilt by association proves nothing against Van Til. Neither does it prove anything against Carnell. Because a method is used by non-orthodox philosophers it does not necessarily lead to the destruction of Christianity.

Van Til must be commended for promoting the authority of Scripture for theological purposes. Granted that apologetics can show how Christianity makes life meaningful by some such test as systematic consistency, one then must spell out implications of God's authoritative word in theological and philosophical language. Today theologians need Van Til's note of authority as never before. For Van Til's contributions to the theological method I am personally grateful. But I must conclude that he has failed both to face the apologetic question and to provide an adequate answer to it. Unfortunately, in the name of defending the faith he has left the faith defenseless.

Response by C. Van Til

Dear Dr. Lewis:

Your carefully articulated essay on the differences between the apologetic methodology of the late Edward J. Carnell and that which I have advocated deserves a full answer. I shall do my best to clarify the situation to some extent in my limited space.

You assert: "If my analysis has any truth at all, Van Till seriously misinterprets his former student." In view of your serious analysis it is proper that I ask myself whether I have done Dr. Carnell such grievous injustice as you suggest. The issue certainly is not merely academic.

May I tell you that Carnell was a student of mine for four years and that he was a friend as well? His Master's examination was a brilliant one and there was in it every indication that we were in agreement regarding apologetic methodology.

When I picked up my copy of his prize book, *An Introduction to Apologetics*, I read in it: "The Word of God is self-authenticating. It bears its own testimony to truth; it seals its own validity. If the Word required something more certain than itself to give it validity, it would no longer be God's Word. If God, by definition, is that than which no greater may be conceived, then his Word is that than which no truer may be conceived."[1]

Well, why then do men not believe on the self-authenticating Word of God? Surely all "men have the *rationes* by which they know that God exists. But, being in defection by their sins, what they see is vitiated. Thus, they are not able to see and appreciate that one of the peculiar characteristics of this God is that he is the Creator of the world and the Saviour of men. God, therefore, gives men up, for they 'exchanged the truth about God for a lie and served the creature rather than the Creator, who is blessed forever! Amen' (Rom. 1:25)." Here Carnell adds the word of Calvin, to the effect that, "notwithstanding the clear representations by God in the mirror of his works, both of himself and of his everlasting dominion, such is our stupidity, that, always inattentive to these obvious testimonies, we derive no advantage from them."[2]

In line with this general notion of the Scriptures as the self-authenticating Word of God and of the clarity of God's revelation in his works, Carnell has this to say of those who do not accept it as such: "Observe, that a fundamental presupposition of the higher critic is that the Bible is just another piece of human writing, a book to which the scientific method may safely be applied, not realizing that the Bible's message stands pitted in judgment against that very method itself. It does not occur to the higher critic that he has started off with his philosophy of life in a way that makes the consistency of redemptively conceived Christianity impossible."[3]

Then he goes on to show that the non-Christian, because he does not begin with the self-attesting Christ, has no intelligible foundation for human predication: "Technically speaking, whenever a man talks and expects something to be meant by it, he is resorting to a prerogative which belongs to a Christian alone."[4]

Carnell quotes from Colossians: "In Christ all things hold together." Christ is the *I am*. Possession of the knowledge of Christ, thus, is possession of the highest form of reality. For this reason, the Christian admonishes men that there is a difference in value between the two levels of being. Being contingent upon God's will, it is this will, and not an antecedent system of logic, which gives meaning to the movement of the space-time world. The many are theologically related to each other according as God has decreed the end (*telos*) of things."[5]

Thus it appears that according to Carnell, it is the theology of the self-authenticating God of Scripture that alone enables man to put logic and fact together in a proper relationship to one another. Here, then, was my young, formerly confused, fundamentalist student broadening out so as to see that only in terms of the fully biblical Reformed philosophy of history is there a metaphysics, an epistemology, and an ethics that is intelligible.

In my little book, *The Case for Calvinism*, I therefore thought it was sufficient to make one general statement on Carnell's faithfulness to the historic Christian faith: "When he says that the 'Word of God is self-authenticating' he does not refer with the New Reformation theology to some word hidden behind the words of Scripture. Carnell believes in the direct revelation of God in history and in the Bible as the direct revelation of God. No further evidence need be given of this fact. [Carl F. H.] Henry is also right when he says that Carnell seeks to tell the Christian story as that which alone gives meaning to life."[6]

Again, "Of course Carnell believes in total depravity. He believes in the whole story of Christianity as told in Scripture. For him there is a genuine transition from wrath to grace in history."[7] And, "Carnell is no Arminian."[8] I am at one with Dr. Carnell when he says, "When God says something, it is true, for God cannot lie; and when man reposes in God's Word, he has faith. If he fails to rest in it as truth, we call him an infidel, i.e., he is not one of the faithful. The power by which the heart is enabled to see that the Word of God is true is the Holy Spirit. The Word of God is thus self-authenticating."[9]

The Rational Man

My disappointment with Carnell's book on apologetics sprang from his presenting the idea of the God of the Bible—the God who controls all things, who cannot lie and who, therefore, appeals to nothing beyond himself in order to establish the truth of what he says—*as a hypothesis which may or may not be true.*

Carnell presents to us two mutually exclusive views of God. First, there is the biblical God who is the source of all space-time possibility and actuality, the God whom Carnell, as a simple believing Christian, worshiped and served to the day of his death. Second, is the god of apostate man, produced by his sinful imagination, a god surrounded by abstract possibility. The first God is, as Carnell said, standing shoulder to shoulder with Calvin and Paul, the God whose face is inescapably present to every living man. As image bearers of God, all men know God (Rom. 1:19). No matter how desperately apostate man seeks to escape from the face of God, he cannot do so. Every fact in the universe, whether within man's own intellectual and moral constitution, or around him on every hand, has, as it were, God's signature on it in plain view. The world is God's estate. This Carnell believed, professed, and gloried in.

No doubt, from his deep desire to win over the cultured despisers of this truth, he tried to do so by starting with them in their interpretation of the universe. Can they not be really open-minded and consider this Christian—this conservative—point of view as a hypothesis that may possibly do better justice to the universally agreed upon requirements of logic and factuality?

As I read certain sections of his *Apologetics* I can hear Carnell saying to E. Brightman, his professor at Boston, "Look here, I as a conservative ardently defend *a* system of authority, but I agree with you that it is up to us as free human personalities to choose between authorities by means of a criterion that, in the nature of the case, must be within ourselves. Plato was surely right when he said that the only place to begin any investigation of our experience is our own drifting raft of experience itself. Descartes and Kant stood firmly on Plato's shoulders and now you have worked out their implied notion of personality in detail. You have spoken of a formal and a material aspect of it, attempting to avoid the 'definition-mongers' such as Spinoza on the one hand and the modern 'flux' theologians on the other. You have, therefore a 'rational basis' for science and also adequate room for personal faith. There is a primacy of the spiritual over the material. With Buber you speak of the I-thou dimension as taking precedence over the I-it dimension.

"But now look, I think my conservative position does *even better justice* to both logic and fact than does yours. 'The Christian believes that a judgment is true when it corresponds to the mind of God, since God is the author of all facts and their meaning.' You might think that when I say this I am, like a fundamentalist, swinging my Bible over my head saying, 'The Bible says so and therefore it is true.' Certainly not! 'The test to which he [the Christian] proposes to subject his propositions, to know when he does correspond to God's mind, is, as Professor Brightman phrases it, "systematic consistency." '[10] 'Truth, therefore, is correspondence with the mind of God. The test for truth is systematic consistency, for God is consistent and the world that he teleologically orders gives system to this consistency. As we unite validity with experience, we have a perfect test for truth.'[11] 'The Christian, by systematic consistency, will be privileged to speak not only of the other side of the moon and of an absolute good, but also of creation, the flood, angels, heaven and hell.' "[12]

As a *conservative* Carnell is now willing, despite all he has said indicating the contrary, to submit the absolute authority of the living Redeemer-God of the Bible to an examination administered by Mr. Natural Man, who no longer thinks of himself as a creature of God, who has never sinned against the grace and love of God, and who is now, supposedly, a fairly innocent seeker for truth in a universe so "open" "that there may be many other gods who have as much right to be candidates for the throne of the universe as does the God of the Bible."[13] What sort of "system of authority" is this where the Creator must pass a test set by his creature who has worked out a system of logic by which he, all on his own, decides what can and what cannot exist, who assumes that any and all facts are thoroughly explicable whether or not God exists, for the existence of God is irrelevant to our understanding of any fact? Carnell seems to answer in this fashion: "Without reason to canvass the evidence of a given authority, how can one segregate the right authority from the wrong one? Shall we count the number of words used, to distinguish between the worth of the Vedas, the Shastras, the writings of Confucius, the Koran, the Book of Mormon, the works of Mary Baker Eddy, the Scriptures, and the *ex cathedra* pronouncements of the popes?"[14] "Any theology which rejects Aristotle's fourth book of the *Metaphysics* is big with the elements of its own destruction."[15] "If Paul were teaching that the crucified Christ were objectively foolish, in the sense that he cannot be rationally categorized, then he would have pointed to the insane and the demented as incarnations of truth."[16] Clearly Carnell believed in a system of authority which was stamped with "Man's Seal of Approval"! For Carnell, as for St. Thomas of the past, faith must have a rational foundation. Both men find a common aid, although in different ways, in Aristotle.

Dr. Lewis, it should be clear by now that my criticism of Dr. Carnell was but an extension and "updating" of my continual criticism of the Aquinas-Butler form of Christian apologetics which I began in the late 1920's. The fatal mistake of this methodology has always been that it expresses, at the very beginning, *areas of ultimate agreement* with the systems of unbelievers. Butler told the deists that he was in accord with them on the interpretation of the "course and constitution of nature." He only wanted them to go on with their method and *add* belief in God the Son to their belief in God the Father.

Now Carnell attempted to say the same thing to the personalists. They must simply see that the *conservative* notion of personalism is even better than theirs. Carnell knew well enough that the starting-point of the self-attesting Christ in Scripture brings with it the pre-requisite of regeneration, the effort of basic exegesis, and a theology closely akin to that of the Reformers. He also knew that the starting-point of personalism transforms the kingdom of Christ into the king-dom of man, and conceives of Christ as the inherent, universal salvation of mankind. Carnell could only establish a common ground with personalism by ignoring the falseness of the Christ of personalism.

Although I have, in my response to Dr. Pinnock, attempted to clarify my criticism of the Butler-Aquinas method, I would like to make a couple of additional observations on this method of a more theological nature.

Any form of a Butler method is both unbiblical and futile.

It is unbiblical because it denies the clarity of God's revelation in man and in his surroundings. The evidence for God's existence is crystal clear, but because of his sinful blindness man does not see it. To ask *whether* God exists and *whether* God realizes his plan for the world through his works of creation and providence, is, in effect, to deny the perspicuity of revelation.

Basic to this approach is the conviction that man is intelligible to himself and can intelligibly ask questions about himself and his world even though God does not exist. But if this were so, wherein would the need of God or of revelation and salvation consist? To tell man that his *mind* does not need to be saved, is to tell him that he does not need to be saved at all.

The Christian should, rather, show that *unless* what God through Christ in Scriptures says is true, man's whole effort at asking and answering questions ceases to have significance, and, worse than that, he himself remains under the wrath of the Lamb. Human predication is reduced to prattle unless it is based upon the truth of what God says in his Word. Idealism, as I have observed in the past, correctly main-tained that bare facts are in themselves unintelligible.[17] But "bare facts" are the only facts which the natural man, including the Idealists themselves, have. Only Christianity brings fact and reason into mean-ingful relation, not through some kind of pan-logism of Parmenides, but in the organic plan of God. Reason is not the autonomous arbiter of truth, but the servant of the heart, believing or not. Despite what may be appearances to the contrary, as I have said before, "No Chris-tian apologetic can be based on the destruction of rationality itself."[18]

The Bible shows us the proper place of reasoning, whether philosophical or theological. "Out of the heart are the issues of life!" Reasoning is an activity of a religiously oriented heart, whether undertaken as a covenant-keeper or as a covenant-breaker.

The gospel of the self-authenticating God speaking through Christ in Scriptures offers man salvation, not only for his life, but for his science and philosophy and theology as well. The would-be self-authenticating man must be challenged to repent and return to God. The natural man whose wisdom has, in the course of history, shown itself to be foolishness, must be taken out of his hall of mirrors, out of Topsy-Turvy Land into the open sunlight. He will then see for the first time that it is not Chance but God's providence that constitutes man's principle of individuation and that it is not some abstract principle of rationality or logic but God's plan which constitutes his proper principle or unity.

We therefore must follow the example of Paul, who lays down the gauntlet with, "Where is the wise man, where is the scribe? Where is the debater of this age? Has not God made foolish the wisdom of the world? For since in the wisdom of God, the world through its wisdom did not come to know God, God was well pleased through the foolishness of the message preached to save those who believe" (I Cor. 1:20, 21, NASB). As made in the image of God, and therefore "knowing God" (Rom. 1:19), men can intellectually understand the contrast between a view of human predication based on man having sprung from Chance and one based on man as God's image. They can intellectually understand the difference between the God of Scripture who is the source of all possibility and who controls whatsoever comes to pass in history and a god who is catapulted out of the void by the logic of man who has himself come from the void. Preaching to men who are, according to Scripture, spiritually dead, is not in vain. God can and does give men light and life and a new heart in the presence of his Word. The same is true of reasoning with them, when that reasoning receives its primary orientation from the Word of God.

Dr. Lewis, you have said: "Van Til's criticism of testing revelation-claims by systematic consistency assumes that the Bible is self-authenticating, a claim which begs the apologetics question. That question asks which among the contradictory alleged revelations, if any, is God's Word." Perhaps you will now see that to face such a problem, in a manner such as you suggest, would be, already, to give the wrong answer. Such a question, as well as any man-made method devised to answer it, would be blasphemous. I remind you of Carnell's own words which I quoted earlier, "If the Word required something more certain than itself to give it validity, it would no longer be *God's* Word."[19]

I wish Carnell had held on to this position, but his book on apologetics exhibits this inconsistency throughout. The fact that all other religions fail Carnell's test (at least he hoped they did) and that Christianity passed it *magna cum laude* is not to the point. The point is that the man who is a creature of God and who has sinned against God is accorded the prerogative of setting the examination which the Creator and Redeemor must pass before he may become what he is.

I hope I have made somewhat more clear to you, Dr. Lewis, why I think I have not seriously misinterpreted my brother in Christ. I have said again, as I have tried to say before, that Dr. Carnell believed in the gospel in the way I believe in it. Secondly, I have said more plainly than before, I hope, that he and I were in basic disagreement on the question of methodology in apologetics. He was sure, as he told me during a whole day we spent together discussing these matters, that since I did not do justice to Aristotle's fourth book of the *Metaphysics*, my faith must be a blind faith. He was sure I could make no intelligible contact with the unbeliever. Everything he wrote in his first book on apologetics, and in all those to follow, he wrote with full consciousness of the differences which arose between us during his days at Boston.

I must leave this discussion now. I hope, above all things, that you now see that the differences between me and the late Dr. Carnell were not imaginary or even semantic, but differences which we *both* saw.

—C.V.T.

Charles M. Horne

XX. VAN TIL AND CARNELL — PART II

The theme of this essay is a critique of the presuppositionalism of Carnell in the light of Van Til's approach. But before we proceed to the main task we must briefly define presuppositionalism as employed in this discussion. As a philosophical method presuppositionalism refers to three distinct claims with regard to the validity of basic assumptions.[1] (Incidentally, it should be clearly understood that all reasoning must begin with certain basic assumptions.) These three as outlined by Hackett are as follows: (1) metaphysical, (2) analytical, and (3) categorical.[2]

The first adopts as its starting point the fact of God's existence and the revelation which he has given of himself in Scripture. This is accepted as a basic assumption beyond either the need or possibility of rational proof. The second adopts the same starting point but then proceeds to seek verification of the same by means of the test of systematic consistency. Finally, the third view adopts as its starting point no world view even hypothetically but simply an epistemology. These three views are represented respectively by Van Til, Carnell, and Hackett.[3] Ultimately these three positions are reducible to two alternatives: either we assume that God is the origin of all predication or we assume that man is.

Another way of stating the issue is simply to address oneself to the question of *ultimate* authority—Who is ultimately determinative of what I am to believe? This was the basic area of debate between classic liberalism and fundamentalism. It still persists as the central point of debate between naturalism and supernaturalism. "The Bible and human experience were plainly and simply set over against one another."[4]

Edward J. Carnell

Man Intellectually Ultimate

Let us then first endeavor to analyze Carnell's principle of authority. What is his *basic* presupposition? As we attempt to discover his starting point we are likely to be confused. In his first book on apologetics he asserts that "for the Christian, God is truth because he is the Author of all facts and all meaning."[5] Therefore, "Truth for the Christian . . . is defined as *correspondence with the mind of God*."[6] This is fine but as Van Til states, "it soon appears that Carnell does not take with utter seriousness the idea of God's revelation through Christ in Scripture as the ultimate standard of truth."[7] For Carnell further writes, "We need a test for truth to aid us in determining when our thoughts are the same as God's thoughts."[8] What is this test? It is the one taken from Ernest Brightman, the Boston personalist. This test is that of "systematic consistency."[9] Now "by *consistency* we mean obedience to the law of contradiction."[10] The validity of this law must be presupposed in everything that man says.[11] But consistency as such is not enough as a test for truth, for there is material as well as formal truth. "The latter, however, is concerned not only with formal validity but with the relation between terms and the real course of history."[12] Thus we need "*systematic* consistency."

> Systematic consistency is the combination of formal and material truth. It is a *consistency* because it is based upon a rigid application of the law of contradiction, and it is a *systematic* consistency because the data which are formed into this consistent system are taken from the totality of our experience, within and without. Validity without real facts is, in Kant's terms, empty (save in mathematics and logic), and the the facts of experience without the formal direction of the law of contradiction are blind. If we reject the law of contradiction, we have nothing to talk about because nothing means anything if the canon be not true, and if we reject the facts of experience, we have nothing in history to talk about because there is no reality beyond us as a point of reference to give content to our words.[13]

Carnell then states that "the Bible, since it contains a system of meaning which is systematically consistent, is a reflection of the mind of Christ."[14] One of the problems with this apologetic approach revolves around the concept of "systematic" as defined by Carnell. The apostle Paul states that the natural man does not only not welcome the things of the Spirit of God, but indeed that he *cannot* because such are only spiritually adjudged (I Cor. 2:14). The *experienced data* (within and without) will never be adequate enough, prior to the sovereign work of the Spirit in regeneration, to convince the natural man of the superiority of Christianity over others.

Again, Carnell distinguishes between what he terms a logical and synoptic point. He writes,

A man's attitude toward what he considers to be the highest logical ultimate in reality determines the validity of his synoptic-point, his method, and his conclusion. The Christian . . . has chosen as his logical starting point the existence of the God who has revealed himself in Scripture.[15]

But he also states,

All logical ultimates must be tested, however, and the only way to do this is to work out *a still more primitive starting procedure* [italics mine]. The synoptic starting point is the servant of the logical starting point. It is the answer to the question, How do you prove the logical starting point?[16]

According to Carnell, the *logical* starting point is the assumption of the God who has revealed himself in Scripture. This is a metaphysical presupposition. But he then states that this presupposition determines the validity of the *synoptic* starting point. Now this logical presupposition of the existence of the God who has revealed himself in Scripture, which alone gives validity to the synoptic starting point must be tested in turn by the synoptic starting point, which is a still more primitive starting point. That which had been the servant now becomes the master!

It appears as though Carnell were indeed reasoning in circles. But then that sort of reasoning is the very thing which Hackett accuses the *analytical* presuppositionalists of doing. He states,

It may be both interesting and comforting to hold at the same time both that we must assume God's existence in order to arrive at it, and that we can show that only God's existence postulates an adequate explanation of reality—it may, I say, be interesting and comforting, but it is not rational![17]

At this point Van Til correctly observes,

It appears then that Carnell has two absolute starting-points. On the one hand is Christ and the Bible. On the other hand it is the idea of systematic consistency which is built upon human experience as ultimate. Brightman's principle of systematic consistency derives from Kant's philosophy! For Brightman, as for Kant, man is autonomous. Man is the ultimate criterion of truth.

Seeking to combine the Christian and the non-Christian absolutes Carnell comes to the conclusion that the Bible and its teachings must be used as an hypothesis which is to be tested by the laws of logic and by the facts which have been already interpreted by man apart from and prior to Scripture. . . .

Carnell does not begin with the fact of God and his revelation in

Scripture as the final criterion of truth. He first seeks to establish the possibility of God's existence and of his revelation by an appeal to human experience.[18]

Man Morally Ultimate

As we probe still further into the thought of Carnell we discover that not only has he made man intellectually ultimate by requiring him to test the truth claims of God, but he has also made him equally morally ultimate. In a more recent work, *Christian Commitment: An Apologetic* (1957), Carnell makes his appeal to what may be called the "moral man."

Van Til gives the following evaluation of this work,

> Just as in his work on *Apologetics,* he compromises the idea of the Bible as the court of final appeal for Christian believers by appealing to the criterion of systematic consistency taken from a representative of Boston Personalism, so in his latter work he again compromises the idea of Scripture, this time by appealing to the idea of the would-be autonomous moral man. In both cases, Carnell fails to discern the anti-Christian nature of the standard of truth that he employs. Carnell fails to see that the idea of morality and experience to which he makes his appeal is in reality identical with the moral man of Kant's practical philosophy. And this moral man is the same man as the rational man of his earlier works. For both the rational man and the moral man are the would-be autonomous man of Kant. Of course Carnell seeks not merely to save but even to advocate the Christian position in both cases. But in both cases he compromises his own faith by making it palatable to the natural man.[19]

In his work entitled *A Philosophy of the Christian Religion*, Carnell once again states that "the foundation of all meaning is the law of contradiction."[20] For him this law is an absolute. "The only demonstration of any absolute is this: Without the presupposition of its existence nothing else has meaning—not even the denial of the absolute."[21] At this point Van Til asks this very relevant question, "Why did not Carnell as a Christian tell us that without the God who speaks in Christ through the Bible as the absolute nothing has meaning?"[22] Do not the very laws of logic appealed to so frequently by Carnell have their origin in God? Could it be that he does not tell us this because of a desire to show the scholarly despisers of Christianity that the truly rational man, using the standards of the great philosophers, can pass the test of coherence?

Again in this work on the philosophy of Christianity, Carnell speaks much of the heart as a test of truth. In discussing man's supposed choice between humanism and Christianity he states:

In deciding between these *two options* [italics mine], the heart has no other recourse than to carefully evaluate what it is left with if it chooses one over against the other. Which leaves the whole individual with the least cause for regret.[23]

In evaluating these two "options" the whole man ("heart") must be satisfied. Humanism accepts the second table of the law and is good as far as it goes. It rightly subordinates love-for-a-thing to love-for-a-person, but Christianity is even higher than humanism. In it the idea of love comes to highest expression.

Whether or not God exists is a matter that each person must settle in his own heart. But as a problem of thought one cannot deny that the love which an omnipotent being offers is theoretically preferable to the love man offers; for it is united with a personality freed from all whimsicality on the one hand, and a will which enjoys complete power over the prevailing conditions on the other.[24]

Thus Christianity is presented as "the most acceptable hypothesis that man can employ for his interpretation of the facts of experience."[25] Now if it be admitted that "as a problem of thought" the above cited conclusion is correct—and it would seem that even on this level it could be challenged—yet, when we come down to interpreting the facts of experience the problem of the theodicy, so forcibly expressed by Camus and others, might make such an argument something less than convincing!

Yet Carnell continues with these bold words,

Christ made no attempt either to alter or to improve upon our native faith that love constitutes the finest expression of freedom. He simply proceeded from this intuition and gave cosmic significance to the relation of love. While rejecting the humanistic ideal as incomplete, therefore, he nevertheless *built* upon its insights rather than derogating it as untruth.[26]

From these statements it would seem that Carnell has fallen into the danger of denying the true supremacy of Christ by attempting to make him acceptable to man. Just as the "rational man" devises a test of his own and will believe in only such a God as meets this test, so "moral man," using his own conception of love as a test, will accept no other Christ than that one who passes this test. It comes as no surprise therefore that Reinhold Niebuhr considers Carnell's criticism of his theology insignificant. Carnell's final standard of truth is no different from his own. Niebuhr writes:

I do not know whether Professor Carnell would regard his criticism of my thought as substantive, but I do not, because he agrees with me up to the point of verifying the Christian faith in the experience of redemption.[27]

Cornelius Van Til

When we turn our attention to Van Til's position we note the following statements:

A consistently Christian method of apologetic argument, in agreement with its own basic conception of the starting point [that of the ontological trinity] must be by presupposition. . . . The Reformed apologist will frankly admit that his own methodology presupposes the truth of Christian theism.[28]

Again,

The true method for any Protestant with respect to the Scriptures (Christianity) and with respect to the existence of God (theism) must be the indirect method of reasoning by presupposition.[29]

Finally,

It is the actual existence of the God of Christian theism and the infallible authority of the Scripture which speaks to sinners of this God that must be taken as the presupposition of the intelligibility of any fact in the world.[30]

Man Intellectually Blind

Van Til maintains in accordance with his acceptance of Reformed theology that as a result of the fall "the set of the whole human personality has changed."[31] The natural man's intellect may be compared to a buzz-saw sharpened and set to cut but at the wrong angle. The boards will not fit the originally intended design of the architect. "So also whenever the teachings of Christianity are presented to the natural man they will be cut according to the set of sinful human personality."[32] The set of man's mind must be corrected by the sovereign and supernatural action of God's Spirit in regeneration. Regeneration is unto ($εἰς$) knowledge, righteousness and holiness (Col. 3:10). Until this has occurred all evidence will be interpreted within a false framework. All so-called "proofs" will be explained away. It is the error of both Roman Catholic and Arminian apologetics that it seeks a point of contact with the unbeliever in a "common area" of knowledge. Van Til criticizes Hodge for dropping from a true Reformed theology to an Arminian apologetics.

The main difficulty with the position of Hodge on this matter of the point of contact, then, is that it does not clearly distinguish between the original and the fallen nature of man. Basically, of course, it is Hodge's intention to appeal to the original nature of man as it came forth from the hands of its Creator. But he frequently argues as though that original nature can still be found as active in the "common consciousness" of man.

. . . .

It is quite in accord with the genius of Hodge's theology to appeal to the "old man" in the sinner [the present remnants of the perfect man] and altogether out of accord with his theology to appeal to the "new man" in the sinner [the present sinful nature of man] as though he would form a basically proper judgment on any question. Yet Hodge has failed to distinguish clearly between these two. Accordingly he also speaks about "reason" as something that seems to operate rightly wherever it is found. *But the "reason" of sinful men will invariably act wrongly. Particularly is this true when they are confronted with the specific contents of Scripture. The natural man will invariably employ the tool of his reason to reduce these contents to a naturalistic level* [italics mine]. . . .

They want to suppress the truth in unrighteousness. They will employ their reason for that purpose. And they are not formally illogical if, granted the assumption of man's ultimacy, they reject the teachings of Christianity.[33]

Rushdoony, an able interpreter of Van Til, rightly states, "The Christian thinker, laboring as he often must on alien ground, has too often embraced as his own a non-Christian principle which he believed would be fruitful in terms of Christian thought."[34] Thus early Christian apologists embraced Platonism; the Scholastics, Aristotelianism; the man of the Enlightenment, Rationalism; and the man of the nineteenth and twentieth centuries, Kantianism and existentialism. The results of such unions have "consistently been semi-alien seed which is in rebellion against its parentage and defiles it more thoroughly than its enemies can."[35]

Either God or man is ultimate in any system; they cannot both be! "Whenever Christian philosophy has had any other starting point than the self-contained God, it has led, despite its protestations, to a man-controlled God."[36] The issue raised in the garden is still with us. Will man be God? Shall he determine for himself what is false and true, what is evil and good? The answer of fallen man is ever the same; man will not be bound to a point of reference beyond himself. "This is the original sin of man, the lust to be as God, and this is the constant drive of his being from which even the redeemed are not free."[37] Man views himself not as a dependent creature but as a god, an autonomous being. Traces of this rebellion are to be found even in the most devout souls.

Only a Christian-theistic philosophy or an epistemologically self-conscious and consistent Calvinism can offer an effective challenge to the non-Christian philosophies of our time. Such a biblical approach will lay bare the failure of all ostensibly Christian thought which attempts to win Christian fruit from alien soil.

Crucial in this discussion is one's view on epistemology. We must ask, Is it possible to consider *how* we know without having presupposed something about *what* we know? The answer would seem to be no. We presuppose something metaphysical by virtue of the very fact that we ask the question "How." For example, Descartes, while purporting to approach the problem of knowledge as though he were without any presuppositions, definitely began with the presupposition of the autonomous human reason. "While the rationalism of Descartes is now out of date, his emphasis on autonomous man is not."[38] Philosophers of many schools still define and identify man in terms of himself, without reference to any outside fact or being. Autonomous man has become the basic source of definition and identification and both God and the world are relative to man.

Through the fall man has become totally depraved. The principle of evil inher 1 by our fall in Adam (Rom. 5:12ff.) has pervaded every aspect of our being—intellect, emotions, and will. The mind has been darkened by sin so that there can be no understanding of the truth of God (I Cor. 2:14). The emotions have become base, sensual, inordinate (Prov. 2:14). The will has been brought into bondage to Satan and sin (Rom. 6:17, 20; 8:7-8). Summing it up, man is spiritually dead (Eph. 2:1, 5; Col. 2:13; Rom. 5:15). Man's circle of reasoning has therefore become utterly vain! Because of this the natural man looks upon the orthodox Christian's circle of reasoning as utterly absurd (I Cor. 2:14). The believer is looked upon as prejudiced and ignorant in that he has already assumed by faith in God all that supposedly needs proof. But has not Paul stated clearly that the wisdom of God is totally ridiculous to the unregenerate mind? The tragedy of the situation is that the unbelieving mind being darkened by sin cannot see that on the basis of his own autonomous nature he has in fact assumed far more than the Christian. He has established his reason as the unprejudiced and valid interpreter of God and the world.

God Sovereignly Ultimate

In this connection we should note the words of Herman Dooyeweerd,

> No philosophical thought is possible without a transcendent starting-point. We contended that even the philosopher who believes that he can find such a point in theoretical thought itself despite all his protestations to the contrary, must exceed the limits of theoretical thought in order to discover its true Archimedian point.

> This apriori transcends the immanent limits of philosophic thought.

> .   .   .   .

> Thus the dogma concerning the autonomy of theoretical thought can never account for the fundamentally different conceptions of it. Thereby it loses its right to serve as an unproblematic starting-point of philosophy.

> It appears again and again that this dogma impedes a mutual understanding among philosophic schools that prove to be fundamentally opposed in their true (though hidden) starting-point. This is a second ground for doubting its character as a purely theoretical axiom.

> For if all philosophical currents that *claim* to choose their standpoint in theoretical thought alone, actually had no deeper presuppositions, it would be possible to convince an opponent of his error in a purely theoretical way.

> But, as a matter of fact, a Thomist has never succeeded by purely theoretical arguments in convincing a Kantian or a positivist of the tenability of a theoretical metaphysics. Conversely, the Kantian epistemology has not succeeded in winning over a single believing Thomist to critical idealism.[39]

The fallacy of giving logical (and experiential) priority to epistemology arises out of the fact that one's view of the knowledge of knowledge itself is necessarily conditioned by his understanding of that which constitutes ultimate reality—how I view *what* man is. And, this "super-theoretical" idea will determine in large measure how I answer the epistemological question. Every philosophical argument is prejudiced by a religious bias—either Christian or non-Christian. "The choice we have made . . . is based upon the fact that we have first been chosen of God, while the choice of our opponents . . . is made entirely by themselves."[40] It is by the work of the Holy Spirit through the Word that we are made Christians. Van Til writes,

> It is therefore the Holy Spirit bearing witness by and with the
> Word in our hearts that alone effects the required Copernican
> revolution and makes us both Christians and theists. . . . And
> it is only when the Holy Spirit gives a man a new heart that he
> will accept the evidence of Scripture about itself and about nature
> for what it really is. The Holy Spirit's regenerating power enables
> man to place all things in true perspective.[41]

Thus Van Til maintains that the Bible is *self-authenticating* and
that therefore it does not need evidences, reason, or apologetics to
make it true. Natural men must be forthrightly confronted with the
absolutely authoritative pronouncements of their sovereign Creator,
as recorded in the Bible. God's Word brings with it through the inner
witness of the Spirit its own best self-attestation, shattering every
claim of man to ultimacy—a claim first made by Eve in the garden.

> The ground of faith emphatically is not our ability to demonstrate
> all the teaching of the Bible to be self consistent and true. This
> is just saying that rational demonstration is not the ground of
> faith. . . .
>
> The nature of faith is acceptance on the basis of testimony, and
> the ground of faith is therefore testimony or evidence. . . . This
> means simply that the basis of faith in the Bible is the witness
> the Bible itself bears to the fact that it is God's Word. . . .
>
> This might seem to be arguing in a circle. . . . We should be
> little disturbed by this type of criticism. It contains an inherent
> fallacy. It is fully admitted that normally it would be absurd
> and a miscarriage of justice for a judge to accept the testimony
> of accused rather than the verdict required by all the relevant
> evidence. But the two cases are not analogous. There is one
> sphere where self-testimony must be accepted as absolute and
> final. This is the sphere of our relation to God. God alone is
> adequate witness to himself.[42]

In conclusion the implications of the presuppositionalism of Carnell and Van Til for apologetic methodology may be summarized as
follows (for a more complete picture, categorical presuppositionalism
has also been included):

A SUMMARIZING OVERVIEW OF CONTEMPORARY APOLOGETICS TYPES

TYPE	RATIONALISTIC		REVELATIONAL
Theologically	Arminian	Moderate Calvinism	Consistent Calvinism
Philosophically	Categorical Presuppositionalism	Analytical Presuppositionalism	Metaphysical Presuppositionalism
	—Assumes no system or world view.	—Assumes the Christian world view hypothetically.	—Accepts unquestioningly the Christian world view.
	—begins only with an epistemology.	—Subjects it to an epistemological verification.	—Rejects all efforts at verification.
Apologetically	Starting Point—Man's Reason.	Starting Point—Ultimately man's reason.	Starting Point—God's revelation.
		—Logical—God.	
		—Synoptic—Man's reason.	
	Common Ground— Epistemological	Common Ground— Epistemological	Common Ground— Metaphysical
Exponents	S. C. Hackett F. J. Sheen	E. J. Carnell B. Ramm G. Clark J. O. Buswell	C. Van Til G. C. Berkouwer H. Dooyeweerd J. M. Spier R. J. Rushdoony

John Warwick Montgomery

XXI. ONCE UPON AN A PRIORI . . .

Van Til's Apologetic Epistemology
in the Light of Three Fables

Much learned controversy has accompanied Cornelius Van Til's apologetic endeavors throughout his long and productive career. The *rabies theologorum* has raged between Van Til and others naming the name of Calvin as to whose apologetic methodology is *truly* Reformed, and large portions of Van Til's writings attempt to distinguish his "genuinely Protestant" approach from what he regards as weakened and compromising variants of Reformed theology ("evangelicalism" or "Arminianism"—a general category in which the fundamentalist *Schwärmer* finds himself in the same bed with Angelican lay apologist C. S. Lewis and Lutheran dogmatician Francis Pieper).

Though by no means a stranger to controversy myself, I do not wish to increase the height of what sometimes appears already to be a dangerously top-heavy pile of refutations and counter-refutations. At the same time, I am too concerned about the plight of the non-Christian in the contemporary world of growing secularity to by-pass the question of apologetic method so ably raised by Van Til. Perhaps a way to discuss the latter without contributing directly to the deadly in-fighting among apologists for historic Christian verities is to proceed in a parabolic manner. Let it be noted, however, that the use of parables here is strictly literary; it must not be construed as a presuppositional, prior commitment to parabolic technique as biblically revealed!

The Universe of Tlön

All is yellow to the jaundiced eye. As he speaks of the facts the sinner reports them to himself and others as yellow every one. There are no exceptions to this. And it is the facts as reported to himself, that is as distorted by his own subjective condition, which he assumes to be the facts as they really are.[1]

What then more particularly do I mean by saying that episte-

mologically the believer and the non-believer have nothing in
common? I mean that every sinner looks through colored glasses.
And these colored glasses are cemented to his face. He assumes
that self-consciousness is intelligible without God-consciousness.
He assumes that consciousness of facts is intelligible without
consciousness of God.[2]

Shall we in the interest of a point of contact admit that man can
interpret anything correctly if he virtually leaves God out of the
picture? Shall we who wish to prove that nothing can be explained without God, first admit that some things at least can
be explained without him? On the contrary we shall show that all
explanations without God are futile.[3]

Thus Van Til's analysis of the human condition; and thus his
apologetic program—with its powerful appeal to Christian believers
who "know" in their heart of hearts that Christianity is true, that the
Bible is God's Word, and that by the work of the Holy Spirit *their*
colored glasses have been de-cemented from their faces (or at least
rendered sufficiently transparent for them to know the Truth), while
non-Christians remain imprisoned in a jaundiced view of total reality.
But now (in a disquietingly unbelieving manner—which is both legitimate and necessary in apologetic discussion, since apologetics by
definition always directs itself to *unbelievers*), let us consider a
reversal of Van Til's approach. Let us contemplate the hypothetical
situation in which the Christian is treated as an unbeliever in an
exactly parallel fashion by the onslaught of an antithetical ideology
(antichristic, but claiming to be christic, as all such viewpoints do).

The blind Argentinian bibliophile and litterateur Jorge Luis Borges
sets out just this situation in his profound short story, "Tlön, Uqbar,
Orbis Tertius." A secret society of hermetic, cabalistic, and rosi-
crucian bent conceives of the idea of producing a total philosophy
of life in the form of a detailed and full description of the world as
it "really" is. The society's work in creating the new world comes
to the attention of an ascetic and nihilistic American millionaire:

At that time the twenty volumes of the *Encyclopaedia Britannica*
were circulating in the United States; Buckley suggested that a
methodical encyclopedia of the imaginary planet be written. He
was to leave them his mountains of gold, his navigable rivers, his
pasture lands roamed by cattle and buffalo, his Negroes, his
brothels and his dollars, on one condition: "The work will make
no pact with the impostor Jesus Christ." Buckley did not believe
in God, but he wanted to demonstrate to this nonexistent God
that mortal man was capable of conceiving a world.[4]

Subsequently, the *First Encyclopaedia of Tlön* was allowed to reach the public. It employed the strategy of "exhibiting a world which is not too incompatible with the real world"—and thus served to prepare the way for a future *Second Encyclopaedia*, written in one of the languages of the imaginary world and so fully and effectively reinterpreting the traditional picture of the universe that "the world will be Tlön."[5] The success of the total plan was assured by the response to the *First Encyclopaedia* in our own time:

> Manuals, anthologies, summaries, literal versions, authorized re-editions and pirated editions of the Greatest Work of Man flooded and still flood the earth. Almost immediately, reality yielded on more than one account. The truth is that it longed to yield. Ten years ago any symmetry with a semblance of order—dialectical materialism, anti-Semitism, Nazism—was sufficient to entrance the minds of men. How could one do other than submit to Tlön, to the minute and vast evidence of an orderly planet?[6]

Borges' point is simply that men have a weakness for "orderly" views of the universe and have been quite willing, again and again, to commit themselves to horrifying philosophies of life for the sake of ordering their experience. Now Van Til would readily agree with this—and would go even farther than Borges: the non-Christian inevitably creates Tlöns because of his jaundiced, sin-impregnated condition. The "facts" of the world, though contrary to such myth-making, are powerless to stop it, since the unbeliever will twist them as he will, in the interests of his unbelief.

But consider: *if* "there are no exceptions" to the jaundiced vision of the sinner, and sin is a universal condition to which both non-Christian and Christian are subject (as all holding to Rom. 3:23 must admit), then *how* is Tlön to be distinguished from reality? Which is the devil's city and which the *civitas Dei*? From Van Til's viewpoint, the internal consistency of the world-picture cannot serve as a naked test, for Tlön will be regarded as consistent by the sinners who propose it, and even where the scriptural world-view is concerned "neither by logical reasoning nor by intuition can man do more than take to himself the revelation of God on the authority of God."[7] Moreover, as Van Til never tires of reiterating, the facts of the world will not help to separate the true world-picture from the false, since they are not "brute" or "neutral": the non-Christian will invariably pervert them in his unbelieving direction.

The conclusion is inescapable: if everyone without exception has colored glasses cemented to his face, no one can criticize another person's spectacles, or indeed the "spectacle" of another world-view. Suddenly Tlön and the New Jerusalem become interchangeable, along with an infinite number of other resting places, e.g. (to repeat Borges' appalling series): "dialectical materialism, anti-Semitism, Nazism."

"Ah, but sovereign grace, the revelation of God in Holy Scripture and the work of the Holy Spirit preserve us from these horrifying options, as well as from Tlön itself," comes the reply. Which brings us to our next parable.

Worlds in Collision

If at this point our opponents smile and intimate that Christianity is, therefore, according to our own notion of it, simply a matter of irrational choice, we need not worry too greatly. For . . . it follows that our opponents as well as ourselves have chosen a position. We have chosen to follow full-fledged Christianity at all costs, while they have chosen to follow the "scientific method" at all costs.

Yet there is even so a difference between the two choices that are made. The choice we have made, we claim, is based upon the fact that we have first been chosen of God, while the choice our opponents have made, they claim, is made entirely by themselves.

Still further we have become aware of the fact that we are chosen of God only after accepting the truth of Christianity from the Bible. Thus the Bible appears at the outset to us as the absolute authority by which we seek to interpret life.[8]

The first point about a truly Protestant or Reformed doctrine of Scripture is that it must be taken exclusively from Scripture. It is, says Bavinck, exclusively from the Scriptures that we learn about Christ and his work of redemption for man. From the Scriptures alone do we learn about God's work of redemption for man. On its authority as the Word of God do we know the whole "system" of Christian truth. Therefore, also, on its authority alone do we believe what the Scripture says about itself.[9]

Van Til's conception of the noetic effects of sin has just been viewed in the light (or better, darkness) of Tlön; now we shall see how his effort through sovereign election, bibliology, and pneumatology to preserve his Reformed position from solipsistic collapse fares in contact with the Shadoks and the Gibis.

We refer to two engaging peoples conceived by Jacques Rouxel and drawn in the form of animated cartoons by J. F. Borredon for French national television (the ORTF).[10] The essence of the story is as follows: Once a very long time ago, the expanse of the heavens exhibited the earth in the center, and two worlds on either side of it. To the left was the planet Shadok, inhabited by Shadoks, and to the right, the planet Gibi, populated by Gibis. The planet Shadok had the unpleasant habit of changing its form without warning, which caused Shadoks to fall off; and the planet Gibi was long, thin, and virtually two-dimensional—much like a knife blade—and by pivoting as a teeter-totter does, it dumped many of its inhabitants whenever they collected at either end of it. Because of the undesirable condition of their home planets, both Shadoks and Gibis conceived the plan of moving to the earth. However, being totally opposed in appearance, temperament, and goals, they constituted an irrevocable threat to each other—and the story of their humorous efforts to beat each other in the conquest and colonization of earth serves as the theme of this delightful television serial.

Like *Alice in Wonderland*, the story of the Shadoks and the Gibis operates on two levels: a simple child's plane of external action and a more profound, philosophically relevant, adult level. Let us pursue the latter in connection with our discussion of Van Til's apologetic presuppositionalism. Suppose that, consistent with their total mutual opposition of life styles, the Shadoks and the Gibis enter into apologetic argument (we could hardly call it dialogue!) in an effort to convince each other of the truth of their respective views. The two positions are logically incompatible, needless to say, so both of them cannot be true (though they can both be false—a possibility not seriously entertained by either protagonist, however!). Each position position is formally similar to the other and thoroughly presuppositionalist (since a Shadok always starts from his world-perspective and a Gibi from his). Shadoks have their doctrine of election (Election-Sh), their inerrant Scripture (Bible-Sh), and their self-attesting inward experience of salvation produced by the immanent work of their God (Holy Spirit-Sh); Gibis affirm their opposing religious tenets on the basis of similar claims (Election-G, Bible-G, and Holy Spirit-G).

Both Shadoks and Gibis appeal, when pressed, to the facts of their world as supporting their religious claims in general and their revelation claims in particular; but neither is willing to make such facts a final test of truth. "For," they are frequently heard to say in religious discussions, "a fact cannot be brute or neutral; my evidence—or anyone else's, for that matter—cannot attain the status of 'fact' at all until one commits himself unreservedly to the true God." The "true

God" refers, of course to God-Sh or God-G, depending on who is stating his case at the moment.

Sometimes the arguments reach a very high level of apologetic sophistication, as in the following instance:

> *Shadok*: You will never discover the truth, for instead of subordinating yourself to revelational truth (Bible-Sh), you sinfully insist on maintaining the autonomy of your fallen intellect.
>
> *Gibi*: Quite the contrary! [He repeats exactly the same assertion, substituting (Bible-G) for (Bible-Sh).] And *I* say what I have just said *not* on the basis of my sinful ego, but because I have been elected by God (Election-G).
>
> *Shadok*: Wrong again! [He repeats precisely the same claim, with the simple substitution of (Election-Sh) for (Election-G).] Moreover, the sovereign election of which I am the unworthy recipient has been sealed by the very work of God the Holy Spirit (Holy Spirit-Sh). And all of this is clearly taught in the self-validating Scripture of our people (Bible-Sh), which, I should not have to reiterate, derives from the true God (God-Sh), not from sinful, allegedly autonomous man.
>
> *Gibi*: How you invert everything. [He laboriously repeats the preceding argument, carefully employing (Holy Spirit-G), (Bible-G), and (God-G).]
>
> *Shadok*: Absurd! The inevitable result of your colored glasses!
>
> *Gibi*: It is *you* who have the glasses cemented to your face. Mine have been made transparent through sovereign grace (Election-G), as proclaimed by God's Word (Bible-G).
>
> *Shadok*: Your religion is but the inevitable by-product of sin—a tragic effort at self-justification through idolatry. Let us see what God (God-Sh) *really* says in his Word (Bible-Sh).
>
> *Gibi*: I will not listen to your alleged "facts." Unless you start with the truth, you have no business interpreting facts at all. Let me help you by interpreting the facts *revelationally* (Bible-G).
>
> *Shadok*: Of course you will not listen to the proper interpretation of facts. Blinded by your sin, you catch each fact as you would a ball—and then you throw it into a bottomless pit![11]
>
> *Gibi*: That's what *you* do with what *I* say—a clear proof of your hopeless, pseudo-autonomous condition. May the sovereign God (God-G) help you!
>
> *Shadok*: May the true God (God-Sh) help *you*!!

The hopelessness of this encounter should be painfully evident. Neither viewpoint can prevail, since *by definition* all appeal to neutral ✓ evidence is eliminated. Even if it is admitted that facts can be known

— Neither view can prevail since all appeal to neutral evidence is eliminated.

by the opposition, this admission is rendered totally valueless because correct *interpretation* of facts, as bearing on the ultimate truth of the religious claims in question, rests only with the one who has seen the *total* picture truly—by revelation (Bible-Sh? Bible-G?).

That this impasse is not simply a humorous *affaire Shadok-Gibi* stands forth in all its stark horror whenever a Christian presuppositionalism confronts a non-Christian presuppositionalism. Such was the case at the 1969 Wheaton College Philosophy Conference, where the final session was devoted to a paper on "Hegel, Marcuse, and the New Left."[12] The essayist, Bernard Zylstra of the Institute for Christian Studies in Toronto, had obtained his doctorate at the Free University of Amsterdam and represented the Dooyeweerdian variety of presuppositional Calvinism, which, like Van Til's apologetic, rejects all "pretended autonomy of philosophical thought"—including the neutral investigation of factual evidence for religious truth-claims—and maintains that the "biblical basic motive is the only possible starting-point" of right thinking.[13]

Now it just so happens that Marcuse, in dependence on Hegel, is equally opposed to factual "neutralism"—but on the ground that all right thinking must begin from dialectic presuppositions ("philosophy originates in dialectic; its universe of discourse responds to the facts of an antagonistic reality"[14]) and must involve passionately subjective commitment to the radical and revolutionary alteration of a non-ideal, repressive status quo ("inasmuch as the struggle for truth 'saves' reality from destruction, truth commits and engages human existence"[15]). To allow objective, factual verification to serve as a court of appeal is "to be satisfied with the facts, to renounce any transgression beyond them, and to bow to the given state of affairs"; it is thus to abrogate the revolutionary frame of reference essential to all genuine truth-seeking.[16]

How does our Dooyeweerdian critic handle such a viewpoint? By showing (1) that factual evidence is necessarily employed by everyone, Hegelian, Christian, or what have you, to evaluate alternative reality-claims in all areas of life? (2) that the facts do *not* support a dialectic-revolutionary *Weltanschauung*? and (3) that there *is* compelling factual support for the Christian affirmation that "God was in Christ, reconciling the world unto himself"? Not at all. Listen to what Zylstra does say:

> The scientist and the philosopher—Marcuse asserts—cannot deal with any supposedly neutral fact "outside" of the human "mind" unless he views it in its meaningful context. I agree with Marcuse

up to this point, though the ultimate context from which "facts" derive their meaning-coherence will be radically different for him than it is for me. Marcuse is a Marxian humanist; I am a Christian.[17]

Thus the irresistible force meets the immovable object; the Shadok confronts the Gibi. Without prior commitment to the *truly* "meaningful context" of fact, facts are not compelling. But which "context" —the Christian or the Marcusean? By definition, this fundamental question can hardly be answered by an appeal to factual evidence— or the argument comes full circle! Claims by one side or the other to the possession of a higher level of internal consistency (with accompanying efforts to demonstrate inconsistency in the opponent's views) will hardly fill the bill either, for neither side allows a "neutral" standard of consistency to be imposed on his position from without—and, even if he did, he would be faced with the disquieting existence of numerous fully consistent, but wholly psychopathic world-pictures (as created, for example, by paranoids and other suffers from autistic derangements who build comprehensive world-views without reference to the facts of the world). And should Christian or Marcusean appeal in the most general sense (as is often done in tight argumentative situations) to his particular "context of interpretation" as "offering the fullest and best picture of universal reality" (the phraseology of course varies stylistically from apologist to apologist), circularity is by no means transcended, for if one does not mean by this that one's view can be judged by the (neutral) facts of "universal reality" in the public marketplace of ideas, one is simply reaffirming the way the universe looks *after* faith commitment to the metaphysic in question.

Van Til rejects the fact-orientated alternative, thereby eliminating in principle the possibility of his opponents' marshalling evidence against Christian claims. But the victory is entirely pyrrhic, for by accepting aprioristic circularity, he at the same time eliminates all possibility of offering a positive demonstration of the truth of the Christian view. Even Van Til's trenchant decimations of non-Christian positions are rendered ineffective by his ultimate presuppositionalism, since, like Marcuse, all the non-Christians whom Van Til chooses to criticize could employ his own two-edged sword against him, crying (in good Shadok-Gibi fashion): "Such criticisms are irrelevant, for right reason—true interpretation of fact and genuine application of the standards of consistency—begins with commitment to *my* presuppositional starting point!" And even if it were possible in some fashion to destroy all existent alternative world-views but that of orthodox Christianity, the end result would still not be the necessary truth of Christianity; for in a contingent universe, there are an *infinite* number of possible philosophical positions, and even the fallaciousness of infinity-minus-one positions would not establish the validity of the one that remained (unless we were to introduce the gratuitous assumption that at least one *had* to be right!).

When world views collide, an appeal to common facts is the only preservative against philosophical solipsism and religious anarchy. Perhaps such results would be tolerable if the conflicts were restricted to Shadoks and Gibis, but when the issue concerns the truth of God in Christ versus soul-destroying options such as Hegelianism, Marxism, and Marcuse's philosophy of total societal upheaval, the stakes are simply too high to operate presuppositionally. Non-Christian positions must be destroyed factually and the Christian religion established factually. Any lesser procedure is the abrogation of apologetic responsibility to a fallen world.

An Ancient Apologetic Parable

Whence arise the presuppositional difficulties underscored by the fable of Tlön and the story of the Shadoks and the Gibis? Still another parabolic narrative offers an answer, for it accurately describes the character of the apologetic situation—a situation which is fundamentally misconceived by the aprioristic apologist. Early in the ninth century, a Syrian theologian and bishop of Harran in Mesopotamia, Theodore Abu Qurra, wrote a treatise on God and the true religion.[18] In it is contained a parabolic treatment of the situation faced by the Christian apologist, and the parable warrants the closest attention.

A great king [God] had a son [mankind] who had grown up out of contact with his father. While journeying in a distant province the son fell seriously ill. The doctor accompanying him [reason] was incapable of treating the disease, but the king, learning of his son's plight, sent instructions [the gospel] for the healing of the boy. However, the king's numerous enemies also discovered what had happened, and they likewise sent remedies—purporting to come from the king—which were actually poisonous [non-Christian religious and philosophical options]. The son's solution to this dilemma was to evaluate the remedies by three tests: first, what each remedy revealed about his father (comparison being made with the likeness to the father possessed by the son himself); second, how accurately each remedy pictured the nature of the disease; and thirdly, how sound the various curative methods appeared to be. With the help of the doctor, the son finally made his decision in terms of the remedy that best satisfied all three tests.

Now one may well smile at the naïveté of a test such as the first (sad to say, the son might easily evaluate the competing pictures of his father on the basis of his own sinful condition, rather than on the basis of the paternal imprint—the image of God—in his own person); but the general outlines of the parable are a most accurate representation of the character of the apologetic task. Abu Qurra, having had contact with Muslim proselytizing, saw clearly what the presuppositional apologist so often forgets: that the religious situation is *pluralistic*. Fallen man is not confronted with but one alleged message from the Father; he hears a cacophony of conflicting religious claims. What is he to do?

He cannot very well try all the various remedies in an arbitrary fashion, for all except the true remedy are poisonous in varying degrees, and his constitution could not possibly tolerate the infinite number of experiential trials necessary. (How true this is is illustrated by accounts such as appear in *The God that Failed*, depicting the traumatic effect of a Marxist commitment on those, e.g., Arthur Koestler, who finally extricate themselves from it.) But the apologetic presuppositionalist, as we have seen, cuts off all opportunity to determine the truth-value of competing religious remedies prior to the acceptance of one of them as a first principle of all meaningful thinking.

Thus the non-Christian is not left "without excuse" in the face of gospel proclamation: he can legitimately "excuse" himself from commitment to Christ on the ground—actually provided for him by the Christian apriorist!—that since no facts can be properly evaluated as evidence for a position without prior acceptance of that position, Christianity can have no more claim to his life than the infinite number of competing views that demand faith in *them* as the necessary condition for discovering "the truth." Theologically, one enters the cloud-cuckoo land of fideism, which borders the philosophical realm of solipsism—where an infinite number of doors open out on Tlön, Gibi, and Shadok.

But what apologetic alternative is available? That of the apostles and of the Lord himself, who continually employ the de facto, *historisch* character of revelatory events (how attractively Van Til stresses such objectivity over against Barthian dialectic evasions of it!) as offering "many infallible proofs" of the truth resident in the gospel. Our apologetic should be modeled on the Christ who offered objective evidence of his power to forgive sins by healing the paralytic and who convinced unbelieving Thomas that he was God and Lord by the undeniable presence of his resurrected body.[19]

With the apostle Paul we must become all things to all men—operate on the non-Christian's territory even as our Lord was willing to incarnate himself in our alien world—and declare to the Agrippas of our day: "The king knoweth these things, before whom also I speak freely: for I am persuaded that none of these things are hidden from him; for this thing was not done in a corner."[20] The evidence of Christianity's truth has never been closeted in a presuppositional corner; it has always been in the public domain, capable of examination by all. As such, it must be brought to bear apologetically on the unbeliever, so that he will indeed stand naked, without excuse, under the sheer pressure of incarnational fact.

What does this kind of apologetic entail? First, a recognition that everyone—non-Christian as well as Christian—employs and must employ inductive procedures to distinguish fact from fiction.[21] Second, the realization that both those out of relation with God and those in proper relation to him can compare alternative interpretations of fact and determine on the basis of the facts themselves which interpretation best fits reality. (It is noteworthy that Adam after the Fall, when he heard the Lord's voice calling to him, was still able to interpret properly both the origin of the voice and its meaning; the Fall did not render Adam incapable of comprehending a word from God. Had it done so, subsequent divine revelation would have been impossible in principle—and the heretical view of Matthew Flacius would have been vindicated: sin would actually have altered human nature and made man something other than man!)

Third, one must see that acceptance of the heuristic assumptions of inductive method does not commit one to a scientistic metaphysic or denigrate God's revelation. What it does do is to open up the possibility of distinguishing true revelation from false—the New Jerusalem from Tlön and the king's remedy from the poisonous drugs of his adversaries.[22]

Fourth, when the non-Christian rejects the factual case for Christianity, he must not be allowed to justify himself by his alien starting-point; rather, he must be led to see that in all spheres other than that of Christian claims he regularly accedes to comparable evidence—and *has* to do so to retain meaningful knowledge of the past and operating existence in the present. Thus the non-Christian is driven to recognize the volitional nature of his rejection of Christ and his consequent moral responsibility for such unfaith. Apologetics fulfils its function only when it brings the unbeliever to the "offense of the cross," i.e., to the cross as evidentially compelling—able to be resisted only by a deliberate act of egocentric will.

Finally, apologetics must never be confused with systematic theology—and this is doubtless one of the chief roots of the misconception we have been discussing. Dogmatics is a field of endeavor directed to Christian believers and thus properly begins with God's inerrant revelation of himself in Holy Scripture. But apologetics is directed to *unbelievers*—to those who by definition do not accept God's Word as divine utterance. Here the focus must be on *their* needs, and the starting-point has to be the common rationality (the inductive and deductive procedures) which all men share. If we insist that non-Christians begin in our sphere of Christian commitment, we ask for the impossible and vitiate all opportunity of reaching them. Indeed, we devalue the very coinage of divine sovereignty that we are endeavoring to hold high, for we give the unbeliever the impression that our gospel is as aprioristically, fideistically irrational as the presuppositional claims of its competitors.

Could it ironically be that the wonderfully successful efforts of Calvin in the realm of dogmatics have sometimes led his followers to create the hydra of a "dogmatic" apologetic—an apologetic modeled on a deductive systematic theology? Whether this is an accurate judgment or not, there is no doubt that such apologetes as Van Til treat the non-Christian very much as if he were a Christian. Strange to say, this was also Barth's method—though for very different reasons. In his treatment of Anselm, Barth describes his own approach when he says:

> Perhaps Anselm did not know any other way of speaking of the Christian *Credo* except by addressing the sinner as one who had not sinned, the non-Christian as a Christian, the unbeliever as believer, on the basis of the great "as if" which is really not an "as if" at all, but which at all times has been the final and decisive means whereby the believer could speak to the unbeliever.[23]

How very odd that Van Til, who, perhaps more than any other critic of Barth, has seen his universalistic tendency, was not thereby reminded that the apologetic approach to the unbeliever must be radically different from the systematic theologizing carried on by the believer. The non-Christian must not be presented with an a priori dogmatic; he must be offered the factually compelling evidence for the Christian truth-claim.

We call upon Van Til to carry further both his laudable stress on the objective character of divine revelation and his penetrating critique of Barthian dialectics: we call on him to see the genuine need of the non-Christian and declare to him concerning the incarnation of God in Christ: "This thing was not done in a corner"!

Response by C. Van Til

Dear Dr. Montgomery:

You bring some imaginary constructions into your article. This is delightful. These are calculated to make the unwary reader think that there is a great gulf fixed between us. Yet if one of your neo-orthodox Lutheran friends and one of my neo-orthodox Reformed friends should meet they would point out to each other the obvious fact that theologically our differences are not too basic. They would regard your article and my response to it as another bit of in-fighting between hopelessly orthodox Christians. Here is a young man still believing in the God, the Christ, and the Bible of Luther attacking an old man who believes in the God, the Christ, and the Bible of Calvin. But what difference does it make whether one believes in the God of Luther or in the God of Calvin? Surely if Van Til and Montgomery would only read Kant they would realize that, in the nature of the case, no man *can* have any knowledge of a God such as that in which either Luther or Calvin believed. If these men would only read post-Kantian theology, especially that of Karl Barth, they would realize that the story of man's creation, his fall into sin, and his redemption from sin through Christ the Son of God and Son of man, as Luther and Calvin believed it, *cannot* be true!

Kant has shown us the significance of the principle of true *inwardness*. Socrates believed in this principle and therefore told Euthyphro that he, Socrates, for all his ignorance, must know what the essence of holiness is, regardless of what gods or men say about it. Following in the footsteps of Socrates, Kant has shown us that on the principle of free human personality we cannot know anything about an "absolute God" and that therefore such an unknowable God cannot be manifest in nature and in history.

Carrying through the principle of *inwardness* of Socrates and of Kant a man like Robert Collingwood, for instance, has shown that when Jesus of Nazareth says that he is one with the Father and that he has come into the world to save men from their sins in the way that Luther and Calvin believed he did, we cannot take this at face value. If a historian took the statements of Jesus about himself at face value, he would disqualify himself as a historian. A true conception of man's inward self-sufficiency implies an inward teleology of history. Thus for the self-respecting historian "the facts of history are present facts. The historical past is the world of ideas which the present evidence creates in the present. In historical inference we do not move from our present world to a past world; the movement in experience is always a movement within a present world of ideas. The paradoxical result is that the historical past is not past at all; it is present. It is not a past surviving into the present; it must *be* the present. But it is not the present as such, the merely contemporary. It is present; because all experience whatever is present; but not merely present."[1]

How wonderfully men like Karl Barth and Rudolph Bultmann have learned and applied this Socratic-Kantian principle of *inwardness* to the biblical story. Thus, for instance, Barth has, he says, *actualized* the incarnation. All the externalism and dualism which such men as Luther and Calvin foisted upon the Christian story has been cut off as so much proud flesh. Moreover, what is true with respect to Christ is also true with respect to the Bible. The theology of Luther and Calvin was hidebound to the old-pre-Kantian metaphysics and therefore to the old-pre-Kantian epistemology. That makes it unbelievable. The old theology was, being hide-bound to the *alte Metaphysik*, not only intellectually unbelievable but also morally and spiritually offensive. The old theology spoke of some men as being arbitrarily elected by "God" to eternal life and of other men as being arbitrarily reprobated without any reference to what they did on earth, whether good or evil. Now that we have the principle of *inwardness*, we truly understand the Bible story for what it is in its inward teleology. We now for the first time understand that it is God's nature to come down into, and be wholly immersed in, time and then, on his return journey, to take all men up into his very aseity. All men are now reprobate in Christ; all men are under the wrath of God. But God's wrath upon man is not his last word. His final word to man is that they have from all "eternity" been in Christ; they could not and would not be men unless they were fellow-men with Jesus.

How thrilling, too, is the realization that this modern *Umdentung* of theology is in accord with the principles of all the major schools of modern philosophy. Where do you find any existing or recent school of philosophy that is not based upon the principle of self-sufficient inwardness of Kant? Do you know any school of modern philosophy that allows for the possibility of the truth of the Christian story as Luther and Calvin believed in it? I know not one.

The moral of what I have said so far, Dr. Montgomery, is that the difference of method of apologetics between you and me will appear to modern theologians like the oppositions between the Liliputian rope-dancers of Dean Swift. Man-mountain was greatly diverted by these rope-dancers. They "performed upon a slender white thread, extended about two feet, and twelve inches from the ground." "These diversions are often attended with fatal accidents, whereof great numbers are on record."

Of course, I must make a qualification here. In the eyes of modern, post-Kantian theologians and philosophers an argument between us appears to them not merely as being superb folly caused by invincible ignorance but also as stubborn opposition to the advancement in intellectual and moral enlightenment of the human race.

Now both of us believe with Luther and Calvin that there is no other name given under heaven by which men must be saved than the name of Jesus. Both of us believe with Luther and Calvin that all men are creatures made in the image of God, and that because of their sin against the law of love of God they are subject to the wrath of God. Both of us believe, together with Luther and Calvin, that Christ Jesus, the Son of God and Son of man, came to die on the cross to bear the penalty due to us for our sin. Both of us believe that as we died to sin with Christ in his death so we rose with him from the tomb for our justification. Both of us believe that though the natural man receives not the things of God because they are Spirit-discerned, we have the testimony of the Spirit witnessing to our hearts that we are the children of God and joint-heirs with Christ of eternal life.

Our common concern is, therefore, to tell this story to men who as creatures made in the image of God thus know God (*gnontes ton theon*) but who, because of their fall into sin, seek to repress the truth about themselves and the world. The most effective means ever invented by men to date by which to make themselves believe that they are not creatures of God and are not sinners against God is the modern process philosophy and theology of which I have just spoken. It is therefore our task as Christian apologists to seek to persuade men that the Christian story as told anew and afresh by Luther and Calvin in their day is true and must be accepted by men as true today if they would escape the wrath of God to come.

Neither you nor I have accepted the Christian story as being what Luther and Calvin believed it to be by starting from the principle of human autonomy, and the idea of pure universal cosmic contingency implied in it, as our absolute standard of truth. Those who have, as you and I have, accepted the theology of Luther and Calvin have accepted it because with them we have learned to regard the self-attesting Christ speaking in Scripture as our absolute standard of truth. Accepting Christ as the Way, the Truth, and the Life implies swearing off allegiance to ourselves, to man as autonomous and as ethically capable of doing what pleases God. Accepting Christ means accepting him as the one from whom, through whom, and to whom are all things. Behold all things are become new!

Now I want to turn to a second point. I have said that modern neo-orthodox theologians will dismiss the difference between Luther and Calvin as unimportant. From their point of view they are right. *But can we between us agree as to what this difference really is?* I mean what the difference is between them in theology is so far as it impinges on apologetic methodology?

Perhaps we are not in full agreement as to the basic principles of Luther and of Calvin. You had no room in your article to say much about the difference between Luther and Calvin. I therefore turned to some of your main works.

I shall call to mind first what you say about Calvin. "Of course Calvin was right when he asserted that 'God is the sovereign Lord of history.' "[2] This accords with what you say in the article of this volume when you speak of "the wonderfully successful efforts of Calvin in the realm of dogmatics." You seem to be mainly concerned lest some of Calvin's followers like myself "create the hydra of a 'dogmatic apologetic'—an apologetic modeled on a deductive systematic theology."

Well, how did it come about that Calvinists tended toward the construction of such a bad theology? You remind us of the fact that Calvinists used to repeat the expression, *finitum non est capax infiniti.* This was, you assert, a purely philosophical, not a biblically, based maxim. Calvinists quoted this maxim against Lutheranism. To hold to this maxim is to set an absolute contrast between God and man, in particular between the eternity of God and the temporality of man.

Holding to this maxim Calvinists cannot see the facts of history for what they are. Because of their philosophical dualism Calvinists cannot see that God is clearly present in history. Accordingly they have no eye for the genuine objectivity found in historical fact. Calvinists cannot challenge those who deny that objective truth is found in the facts of history. There is nothing that they can set over against modern subjectivist theories of reality and knowledge. Still further, the rejection of the traditional orthodox doctrine of the "plenary inspiration of Scripture finds its historic origin in this Calvinist notion of *finitum non est capax infiniti*."

It was to be expected that with this maxim Calvinism would be swept along with the current of modern subjectivist theology. "From Plato's separation of the world of ideas from the world of things and the soul from the body, to the medieval 'realists' with their split between universals and particulars, through the Reformation Calvinist's conviction that *finitum non est capax infiniti*, to the modern idealism of Kant and Hegel, we see the same conviction in various semantic garbs. It is this absolute separation of eternity and time that lies at the basis of the contemporary theological split between *Geschichte* and *Historie*, as I have indicated elsewhere; and it is most definitely the same aprioristic dualism that motivates much of contemporary theology in its refusal to allow the Eternal to express himself in absolutely veracious biblical propositions."[3]

When Søren Kierkegaard asserts that "truth is subjectivity" he is merely carrying forth to its logical conclusion the Platonic-Calvinistic idea that history contains no objective truth. One need not be surprised then that Calvinistic presuppositionalism fails to give an effective answer and antidote to modern subjectivism.[4]

When the Calvinists want, none-the-less, to speak of "objective" truth they have to appeal to "the inward work of the Holy Spirit." Thus their grandiose presuppositionalist seemingly deductive systems reduce to *Schwärmerei*. "The Spirit serves as a *deus ex machina* to resist the overwhelming pull toward solipsism. But Scripture cautions us to 'test the spirits.' How? Not by internal consistency (the devil is an exceedingly coherent logician, as are all great liars), but by an empirical comparison of doctrine with the objective, historically given Scriptures. Thus we are brought back again to the absolute necessity of an objective historiography, for without it we can establish no scriptural testing-stone."[5]

What then is to be done? It is certain that a fresh start must be made. This fresh start must be in line with Luther's theology.

Luther's theology as over against Calvinism, you say, allows for God's genuine presence in the facts of history.

Making a fresh start on the basis of Luther's theology you are in the happy position of being able to use the traditional Butler type of argument. In terms of it you then find the need for the "objective historiography" satisfied.

Finally, in order to bring this Butler type of evidential argument up to date you call in the forces of modern analytical philosophy. Butler shows us that by the use of ordinary historical methodology we may hold that Christianity is very *probably* true. In possession of this probability assurance of the truth of Christianity as taught in Scripture you turn to the analytical philosopher. You request him kindly to apply his criterion of verifiability to the truth-claims made in Scripture. You think you can even borrow his principle and use it yourself. Watch how it works: "We say that a sentence is factually significant to any given person, if, and only if, he knows how to verify the proposition which it purports to express—that is, if he knows what observations would lead him, under certain conditions, to accept the proposition as being true, or reject it as being false."[6]

Allow me now first to take up your analysis of the supposedly speculative, deductive, aprioristic system of Calvinism and then turn to your Luther-Butler-analytic method of apologetic.

In the first place I think your analysis of the maxim *finitum non est capax infiniti* is historically inaccurate and at the same time does injustice to what has, since the time of Calvin, been the basically biblical approach of Calvinism.

I use Herman Bavinck's *Gereformeerde Dogmatiek* as my source of information. I take it that you are relying a good bit on Francis Pieper's *Christian Dogmatics.*

The maxim *finitum non est capax infiniti* was used by Reformed theologians, says Bavinck, in order to urge their Lutheran brethren to remain fully true to the statement of the Chalcedon Creed with respect to the relation of the divine and the human natures of Christ.

Both Lutheran and Reformed theologians accepted the Chalcedon position on Christ as based upon Scripture teaching. Both parties agreed that the Eutychians were wrong in intermingling, as were the Nestorians wrong in separating, the two natures of Christ.

Back of the common acceptance of the Chalcedon Creed was the common acceptance of the fact of man's creation in the image of God, and that he therefore unavoidably knows God. Man is not, as the Greeks taught, participant in the being of God. Both parties also believed that man, made in the image of God, had broken the law of God and was therefore subject to the wrath of God. Both parties agreed that Jesus Christ, the Son of God, became truly man and on the cross paid the penalty for man's sin and rose from the dead for his justification.

In short both parties were devoted to the Bible as the sole source of the revelation of the grace of God through Christ to sinners.

Both parties were equally zealous to protect this Christian story from being buried by Greek types of speculation. On the basis of Greek philosophy there can be no creation, no fall, and no redemption from sin as the Reformers thought of these. There could be no such mediator between God the Creator and man the creature as the Bible presents. According to the Greeks all reality is at bottom one, all temporal plurality has somehow oozed out of this one and is somehow returning to this one. Plato's "dualism" presupposes a basic monism that excludes the creator-creature distinction (cf. my response to Dr. Dooyeweerd). The ever-besetting temptation of the church has always been to allow the monism of human speculation to destroy the Christian story. It was to warn their Lutheran brethren *against* monistic speculation that Reformed theologians applied the phrase *finitum non est capax infiniti* even to the human nature of Christ. Christ's human nature must be truly human, or else there would be probably no true substitution through his suffering for the sin of other men.

Dr. Francis Pieper, like yourself, takes the maxim to be a speculative one. He is quite right in saying that anyone holding such a *speculative maxim* would have to deny the incarnation itself. But he is, I believe, mistaken in thinking that Calvinism holds such a speculative maxim and therefore "inevitably denies the incarnaton, and Christ's vicarious atonement, and so destroys the foundation of Christian faith."[7]

If you really believe that Calvinists base their thinking on such a *speculative* principle, then you might well have said what Pieper says. That would have saved you the trouble of setting my supposed Christian apriorism over against some form of non-Christian apriorism, each trying to shout louder than the other that his brand of apriorism is right and the other's brand of apriorism is wrong without ever appealing to facts. There would then be only one, namely a non-Christian apriorism, and its boast about itself would then be a shout by a non-entity in the vacuum of pure contingency.

But, after all, you are not (as I am not!) interested in *apriori* deductive systems. I have argued on a number of occasions against various people to the effect that the biblical "system of truth" is based upon the exegesis of the authoritatively given truth content of Scripture. When exegesis seems to lead into so-called "antinomies" such as the relation of the all-controlling sovereignty of God to the freedom or responsibility of man, I simply admit that I cannot logically penetrate the situation. The Bible teaches God's sovereign electing grace. It also teaches the universal offer of the gospel. I cannot logically comprehend the relation between these two, but this fact does not lead me to a denial of either one of them. The "system" of Scripture which I develop takes both elements as "limiting concepts" of one another. Some Calvinists have virtually denied the universal offer of the gospel in the interest of maintaining the biblical teaching with respect to electing grace. I have argued against them that such a position is unbiblical and therefore not true. Arminians deny the biblical teaching of God's sovereign grace in the interest of maintaining the universal offer of the gospel. I have argued against them that such a position is unbiblical and therefore untrue.

Both the extreme Calvinist and the Arminian are unwilling, at the most critical juncture, to submit their logical thinking based on the idea of human autonomy, to the obedience of Christ. Neither of them seems to realize that they are virtually employing the methodology of a man like Parmenides, who, in order to relate temporal facts to one another, destroyed their reality.

Again, both the extreme Calvinist and the Arminian fail to see that when they employ a legislative view of human logic such as that of Parmenides, they are bound, willy nilly, also to employ the notion of pure contingency as correlative to their logic. Extreme Calvinists think they can show that the teachings of the Bible can be related to one another in a logically penetrable system. When they construct their logical system they virtually destroy the significance of historical factuality and with it the significance of the Christian story. Arminians think they can show that the teachings of the Bible can be related to one another in the way inductivist philosophers like John Locke and others relate the facts that spring from the womb of chance to one another. When these men construct their inductive systems, believing that all facts "speak for themselves," they build an island of ice floating on a bottomless, shoreless cauldron of chance.

In order to have their non-Christian friends meet their God and

the Christ of the Bible my Arminian friends, following Butler, insist
that the meeting take place on this island. Jesus, too, goes afloat on
this island. On deck he meets the other tourists of the island, among
them one representative of each of the post-Kantian "schools" of
science, of philosophy, and of theology. The representative of the
analytical school of philosophy always walks arm in arm with the
representative of the God-is-dead school of theology.

There is harmony everywhere on this island. Everybody agrees
that the everlasting arms of pure contingency are underneath. Everybody is present at the evening service of religion. Says the "Calvinist" song-leader for the evening: "Tonight we praise the God of
Anaximander; the name we give him is *Apeiron*. Tomorrow night
we worship the God of Socrates; the God of pure *Inwardness* we call
him. Next Friday evening we shall worship the God of Jesus, whom
we are glad to welcome in our midst. Jesus himself will lead the
singing of his favorite hymn: 'Oh Immanuel, Immanuel, how blest
thy Vision Glorious.' Special thanks for arranging our evening services are due to our friends here—I forget their names—great positivist-
analyst philosophers. By means of their verification principle they
make certain that the gods we worship are indeterminate. How else
could we all serve the same God? How else could we all have true
togetherness? How else could we with Plato say that the *Good* is
above all and in us all. How else could we rejoice in the fact that
Good is inherently diffuse. How else could we apply the maxim of
our friend Jesus that the Father's love is *unconditional*? How mar-
velous it is that the greatest recent theologian has drilled into all of
us, all men everywhere, the fact that unconditional grace is the one
all-uniting attribute of God! And now it is time for the evening song
to be sung."

After the Monday evening song service was over the song-leader,
Martin Marty, asked Martin Luther why he had not joined in the
songs of praise to the unknowable God and to the principle of contingency upholding all things.

"Well, Mr. Marty, you must remember that I nailed ninety-five
theses to the door of a famous church in Wittenberg. You know that
I wrote a book on the *Bondage of the Will* against the Dutchman
Erasmus. As you know, Erasmus defended the idea of the 'free will'
of man both metaphysically and ethically. He believed in pure cosmic
contingency and defended it by means of a Parmenidean type of logic.
There must be pure contingency, he argued, or else all the warnings and
promises of Scripture would be appealing to man as a puppet.

"Have you a moment to listen to a few passages from my answer to Erasmus? I challenged Erasmus to *define* free will in terms of his principle of pure contingency. He never even tried it. He knew well enough that if he were to *define* free will on his view of things he would destroy it.

"Well then, I didn't pretend to be able to see through the relation of the sovereignty of God and the will of man. But Scripture teaches both and that is enough for me. As I said before: 'This, therefore, is also essentially necessary and wholesome for Christians to know: *that God foreknows nothing by contingency, but that he foresees, purposes, and does all things according to his immutable, eternal, and infallible will.* By this thunderbolt, "free will" is thrown prostrate and utterly dashed to pieces. Those, therefore, who would assert "free will," must either deny this thunderbolt, or pretend not to see it, or push it from them.'[8]

"Before you say anything, Mr. Marty, let me go on: 'From which it follows unalterably, that all things which we do, although they may appear to us to be done mutably and contingently, and even may be done thus contingently by us, are yet, in reality, done necessarily and immutably, with respect to the will of God.'[9] 'This asserted truth, therefore, stands and remains invincible—that all things take place according to the immutable will of God! Which they call the necessity of consequence. Nor is there any obscurity or ambiguity. In Isaiah he saith, "My counsel shall stand, and my will shall be done" (Isa. XLVI. 10).'[10]

"You see, Mr. Marty, I derived my entire position from Scripture. I told 'Madame Reason,' as I called her, how 'absurdly she tacks her conclusions, based on pure speculation, to the Scriptures.'[11] Scripture 'describes man corrupt and captive.'[12] 'It is, therefore, a settled determination with me, not to argue upon the authority of any teacher whatsoever, but upon that of Scripture alone.'[13] I don't even listen to 'Madame Reason' when she wants to apologize for Scripture teaching. Madame Reason softens the biblical teaching on the electing grace of God. I do no such thing for 'if God be thus robbed of his power and wisdom to elect, what will there be remaining but that idol Fortune, under the name of which all things take place at random! Nay, we shall at length come to this: that men may be saved and damned without God's knowing anything at all about it; as not having determined by certain election who should be saved and who should be damned; but having set before all men in general his hardening goodness and long-suffering, and his mercy showing correction and punishment, and left them to choose for themselves whether they would be saved or damned; while he, in the meantime, should be gone, as Homer says, to an Ethiopian feast!' "[14]

"Well, I see," said Mr. Marty, "you are quite right, Dr. Luther. I am still in name a Lutheran, but my God is not your God, my man is not your man, and my Christ is not your Christ. I can see very well that from your purely *apriori*, deductive, authoritarian, absolutistic, deterministic, and rationalistic point of view, you cannot agree with me on anything. I admit too that I presuppose my view of man as free or autonomous, and I interpret every fact in the universe in terms of a purely contingent principle of individuation as correlative to a purely abstract legislative principle of continuity. You are right in saying that on our view God would know nothing about a process of universal electing grace going on in this world. All of this goes on in terms of the overflowing goodness of the principle of chance. We assume that our island floats on an underlying gulf stream of utter goodness.

"I like you, Dr. Luther. After all, I am named after you. I shall let you in on something. All of us put on a bold front. We know that our island consists of a block of frozen chance and that it is on the way to the equator. But when our chins begin to sag we call upon our theologians of hope to cheer us up. They tell us we'll cross the equator without our island thawing out. But then that means we're on the way to the South Pole, where all of us would be frozen into one block unless we should, by accident, break loose from the all-enveloping ice-sheet found there and return toward the equator, hoping to cross it on our way to the North Pole, and so on *usque ad infinitum*. This is, I agree with you, the only alternative to your view of the triune God of Scripture and his creative-redemptive work in the world. But everybody agrees today in saying first that nobody knows what is back of, underneath us and before us; second, that your position is wrong and that therefore ours must be right.

But tell me, Dr. Luther, now that we are frank with one another, tell me, what do you think of the position of our fellow-Lutheran, Dr. Montgomery? I think he is really on your side. He even holds a view of Scripture that is, it seems to me, virtually identical with yours. Yet he also seems to be on my side. I heard him sing lustily, *Ein Feste Burcht ist unser Gott*, yet joins us in a method of inductivism that presupposes a purely contingent universe. What do you think?"

"Well, Mr. Marty, as you say, you and I stand on opposite ground.

You construct a God out of the only materials you have in order to attack my God. Your God resembles the little girl that must sit on her daddy's lap in order to be able to slap her daddy in the face. Your God presupposes not merely the existence but the all-controlling activity in history of my God in order to act at all.

"Well, then, as to our common friend Montgomery? I not only think, but I am certain he is on my side. I heard him singing *Ein Feste Burcht* too. However, he seems to think that he can at the same time also be on your side. He does not seem to realize that his inductive method, as he uses it in common with the non-Christian analytic-positivists, implies, as it is implied by, a metaphysics of pure chance. I hope he won't continue to try straddling the fence. Don't you think I may, as an old man, call upon him to forsake a position in which men may be saved or damned 'without God's knowing anything at all about it'? As it is he looks like one of the Liliputian rope-dancers, divided into two parts, each part rushing into the other seeking to destroy it."

Our conversations on the imaginary island inhabited by the leaders of the church come to a close. Luther keeps hoping he will get a chance to speak to Dr. Montgomery again. I hope so too. Thank you, Dr. Montgomery, for your very readable essay.

—C.V.T.

W. Stanford Reid

XXII. SUBJECTIVITY OR OBJECTIVITY
IN HISTORICAL UNDERSTANDING?

Many universities today, in seeking to break up their liberal arts faculties into smaller units, face a serious difficulty with the history departments. Is history a humanity or a social science? Is it a subjective or an objective discipline? If historians, themselves, have not succeeded in coming to agreement on this, how can they expect a harassed dean to solve the problem? Ever since the days of Herodotus the question of subjectivity' and objectivity has posed serious problems for historical thought. Does the historian simply record what has happened without his own subjective views entering into the matter, or are all his interpretations inevitably colored by the whole series of prior assumptions that makes up the historian himself? This is the question.

In this debate Christian historians inevitably find themselves involved. Some are clearly presuppositional in their approach. They believe that only if a historian is Christian can he properly understand history, for only the Christian knows the ultimate meaning of history. The empiricists, on the other hand, reject this idea and maintain that the historian, whether Christian or not, can see history more or less as it was and can account empirically for the events that took place. The problem is: which is correct?

That this is important to the Christian should be obvious since all Christians will admit that their faith is based on certain happenings in history, notably Christ's birth, life, death, and resurrection. Furthermore, during the past two centuries most of the attacks upon Christianity have come in the historical field. If the Christian's historical claims can be proven untenable, his faith will also have to go. Consequently, this is a question that must be seriously considered for both evangelistic and apologetic reasons. If the Christian's approach to history is purely subjective, can he have any assurance of faith at all? If it is purely objective, can he prove conclusively that the claims of Christ to be the divine Redeemer are historically viable? Here is the crux of the whole matter.

I. The Clark-Montgomery Debate

A good example of the conflicts that arise even between Christians on this matter appears in the differing views held by Gordon H. Clark of Butler University, a philosopher and a Calvinist, and John Warwick Montgomery of Trinity Evangelical Divinity School, a historian and a Lutheran. In a *festschrift* published in 1968 in in honor of Dr. Clark, Montgomery wrote a critique of the former's philosophy of history, bringing out clearly the antithesis between these two schools of thought. A glance at this debate will make clear the differences, for while Clark and other "presuppositionalists" such as Van Til may not agree on all points, they seem to hold similar positions in this aspect of their understanding of history.

In his evaluation of Clark's view, Montgomery always insists that he and Clark see eye to eye on their basic Christian beliefs. They both accept the Bible as the infallible Word of God, and they both believe that man's only way of reconciliation to God is through faith in Jesus Christ as divine Savior. They stand together, therefore, in the evangelical tradition of Christianity. Consequently they also join in denying the right of secularists and of neo-orthodox thinkers to be regarded as truly Christian, although Montgomery does at times seem to lean towards the views of Paul Tillich. As Christians then they agree on the fundamentals![1]

Montgomery, however, is no Calvinist. He admits that God is over all history, but he is rather indefinite on that subject and accuses Clark, because of his insistence on the divine sovereignty, of making God the author of sin. He also declares that Clark's whole view of history is vitiated by the fact that he starts outside history with God's eternal decree, instead of inside history at the cross of Calvary, i.e., with the empirical facts of history.[2] This leads him to deny Clark's contention that, since every historian's philosophy of history is part of his over-all philosophy, when the historian selects facts as evidence he does so on the basis of his philosophy's evaluation of those facts, thus making an objective interpretation impossible. Furthermore, he disputes Clark's insistence that the Christian philosophical position proves itself to be the only valid one, by virtue of the fact that it alone is self-consistent, and consequently the only one that gives an ultimately true understanding of the meaning of history.[3]

Montgomery counters Clark's views by insisting that facts, not presuppositions, determine one's interpretation of history. If the hypothesis formed by the historian does not fit the facts, then it must be replaced by a better formulation. Without this one falls into a position of complete relativism with regard to history: whatever one *believes* took place, actually took place! This, Montgomery insists, surrenders the whole Christian position.[4] To counteract such a solipsist view, he says, one must hold to the empirical method, which is the same for all whatever their presuppositions. It requires only a few methodological assumptions that are quite self-evident.[5] That one should need the enlightenment of the Holy Spirit to understand Christianity and its historical implications, he tosses out as mere fideism.[6] "Proceeding on the basis of empirical method as applied to history, one can inductively validate the Christian revelation-claim and the biblical view of total history."[7] Christianity can thus be proven objectively by the historical method alone.

He then presents a concrete statement of his method of argument, as he has also set it forth in some of his other writings such as *The Shape of the Past*:

1. By the historical method the Gospels have been proven to be trustworthy sources for the life of Christ.

2. In these documents Christ claims to be God and rests his claims on his future resurrection from the dead.

3. In the Gospels his resurrection is described in such detail that it can be validated empirically.

4. The resurrection cannot be discounted *a priori*, for miracles are impossible only if so defined.

5. If Christ is God he spoke the truth concerning the Old Testament and the soon-to-be-written New Testament (John 14:26f.; 16:12ff.; cf. Acts 1:21ff.; I Cor. 14:37; II Pet. 3:15).

6. "It follows then from the preceding that all biblical assertions bearing on philosophy of history are to be regarded as revealed truth, and that all human attempts at historical interpretation are to be judged for truth value on the basis of harmony with scriptural revelation."

7. He makes light of the criticism that the empirical method's results are only probable, maintaining that this is the case with all human knowledge. The Gospels are sufficiently probable to bring us to faith in Christ. Thus one can use the empirical method to support belief in "a qualitatively unique, inerrantly truthful revelation."[8] Such is the argument of the historical objectivist who trusts in an empirical methodology.

II. How Objective Can One Be?

As one studies Montgomery's views on history, one soon discovers that he has not set forth systematically a general metaphysical statement of his own position. Nor has he attempted to give what one might call an ontology of history, i.e., an exposition of his view of the nature of history. His great interest centers on the epistemology of history, i.e., how one can know and verify historical events. For this reason, in order to understand Montgomery's attack upon Clark and all other "presuppositionalists," one must first analyze his epistemology, and then seek to deduce from it his ontology of history.

In the opening pages of his *The Shape of the Past* Montgomery gives his view of the nature of historical investigation and exposition. He points out that chronicle merely records events has they happened and nothing more. True historical writing, on the other hand, goes far deeper, for while not attempting to force the sequence of events into some pre-arranged philosophical scheme, it nevertheless seeks to explain "why" the happenings took place. In such explanation, he maintains, despite his strictures on Clark, an element of religious decision is involved, from which one cannot escape.[9] He then defines historical study as

An inquiry focusing on past human experience, both individual and societal, with a view towards the production of significant and comprehensive narratives embracing men's actions and reactions in respect to the whole range of natural, rational and spiritual powers.[10]

This definition is apparently valid for all, no matter what religious decision one has made, even if it be in favor of materialism.

In looking somewhat more closely at Montgomery's view of how one can know and interpret history, one finds that he rejects three out of four possible approaches: common sense, intuition, and authority, although in discarding the last he makes no distinction between human and divine authority. The only method left, according to his way of thinking, is the empirical or scientific one. His reason for rejecting the common sense approach is that it is uncritical. The intuitional method can deal only with self-evident truths, i.e., "if A then A," which reveal no factual evidence. The authoritarian approach, even if claiming divine sanction, still must be tested from outside with other measuring techniques before its claim to authority can be accepted. Divine authority apparently cannot be self-authenticating, but must be tried before the bar of man's empirical reason.[11] Consequently the scientific method alone remains viable.

One must then ask, why does he place such great faith in the scientific method? The first reason is that of all techniques for discovering truth it requires the fewest presuppositions. Yet it is right at this point that Montgomery seems to involve himself in multifarious self-contradictions. For instance, he insists that to determine the nature of natural laws, one should evaluate "without *a priori*" the evidence for each event "no matter how unique it is."[12] Natural laws are thus formulated on the basis of bare facts. At the same time, he does admit that some presuppositions insinuate themselves no matter what one does, but "one should *assume* as little as possible and attempt to *discover* as much as possible."[13] "All assumptions should be kept to a minimum, and be as self-evident and beyond dispute, as possible."[14] In this he apparently takes it for granted that even in basic assumptions what is self-evident to the Christian must be self-evident to the unbeliever, despite their radically different presuppositions.

Yet despite his professed anti-presuppositional stance he does have to admit that presuppositions do control the historian's thinking beyond his methodology. Following E. J. Carnell he sets forth three assumptions of all scientists: a law to be meaningful must be true; the universe must be regular, a premise requiring a world-view that allows for this; and the scientist must be honest.[15] He also admits that scientific historians make assumptions concerning human nature, the significance of events, and the actual meaning of the past.[16] Accepting the dicta of two such diverse writers as Giambattista Vico and Raymond Aron he concedes that these all depend upon our metaphysical beliefs or our personal *Weltanschauung*.[17] In other words, despite his disclaimers, he is acknowledging that empiricism rests upon pre-scientific or naive views concerning reality that have come to the historian either by intuition or by authority whether human or divine.

When one also considers his critiques of other historians, one soon discovers that he takes for granted that their different starting points lead them to different conclusions. Thus he tacitly admits that no matter how "empirical" one attempts to be, one consciously or unconsciously assumes a whole metaphysical system.[18] Presuppositions are inescapable.

To this criticism, Montgomery would probably object that non-Christians are deflected from the truth because of their presuppositions, but that the Christian alone is truly objective and inductive.[19]

If he holds to this consistently, he is right back in a "presuppositional" position similar to that of Clark. This indeed appears to be the case in his acceptance of Carnell's dictum that:

> Fair rules in the contest of hypothesis-making ought to dictate that the winner be he who can produce the best set of assumptions to account for the totality of reality.[20]

Assumptions accounting for total reality are, however, much more than merely an acceptance of the scientific method. They involve a whole world-and-life view. Here is Montgomery's basic confusion, for while ostensibly denying the propriety of having presuppositions he, himself, has assumed the validity of the Christian *Weltanschauung.*

Turning from Montgomery's views on presuppositions, one must also consider his view of the scientific method. He believes that it enables one to determine what authority to accept and "what common sense beliefs and *presuppositions* to hold."[21] (Apparently the scientific method could even destroy the presuppositions upon which Montgomery bases his scientific method.) The scientist accomplishes his work by four steps: a) investigation of the universe by observation; b) verification of these by others; c) drawing generalizations and constructing hypotheses; d) the "verification of these hypotheses by others, etc., etc."[22] Although this is a very general and not entirely clear description of the scientific method, he applies it to history, declaring that it is the only way one may come to know the truth without having to refer to anything beyond the method, and that it alone provides public evidence that compels assent.[23] In his debate with Professor Stroll of the University of British Columbia, he presented what he believed to be the empirical evidence for Christianity, but we have no evidence that he convinced Stroll at Vancouver any more than he did Professor Altizer at Chicago or Bishop Pike at Hamilton, Ontario. The fact is, Montgomery's view of the nature and efficacy of the scientific method is wrong.[24]

The trouble with Montgomery's view of the scientific method is threefold. It is not, and cannot be, the same as that of the chemist, physicist, or biologist. For one thing the natural scientists can repeat any number of experiments under controlled conditions. This the historian cannot do. Furthermore, the historian's evidence is much more fragmentary than is that of the chemist or physicist. He cannot enter into the mind of historical characters to discover their motives. He must to a certain extent accept their statements of their motives on *their authority.* His evidence consists in nothing more than the effects left by historical events in time. Therefore, the historian can never be as empirical as is the physical or natural scientist. But even if he were, he would still have to face the fact that the premises or presuppositions of the physical scientist also enter into his method and conclusion. Not Clark, but Max Planck, the physicist, is the authority for saying this.[25] It is because of these deficiencies of both the scientific method and of those who use it that scientific conclusions are, as Montgomery repeatedly states, never more than probable. The degree of probability of their validity depends entirely on the strength of the existing evidence, the probability of new evidence arising, and the integrity of the scientist.[26]

Montgomery defends the "probability" argument vigorously against those who criticize him. In complete accord with Carnell, C. H. Pinnock, and Paul Tillich he declares that probabilism is the usual way of making decisions in life and that "we have no right to demand . . . a certainty transcending the probabilities of historical evidence."[27] In "every theory involving statements of fact, *proof* is impossible, for new information may always turn up to disprove previous findings." Therefore, since this is true in the non-religious it must also be true in the religious sphere. All intelligent decisions between religious alternatives "must rest squarely upon *probability*." One must always ask: "What is the probable validity of the present evidence?"[28] Thus probability is "the criterion of truth for the historian."[29]

While one must admit, with Montgomery, that probability is undoubtedly the basis upon which many decisions are made in this life, one must also ask: is that an adequate basis upon which to settle one's eternal destiny? Further, if the assurance of the truth of Christianity rests upon scientific probability only, largely resulting from the lack of negative evidenc, how can Montgomery be as dogmatic as he is on the subject of the inerrancy of the original manuscripts of the Bible, which neither he nor anyone else for two thousand years has seen, and on the subject of the resurrection of Christ from the dead? Although the probability of the appearance of evidence contrary to the faith in the resurrection is "almost too small to be entertained," it is still there.[30] And after all, one's view of what is probable largely depends upon one's presuppositions. This Montgomery has admitted when he has stated that men will accept any wild idea rather than believe in Christ's resurrection. Exactly so! A probable proof *proves* nothing, for what one believes to be probable is to a great extent determined by one's assumptions.

This brings us to Montgomery's historical method of proving the truth of Christianity under "the most rigorous investigation of science." In his criticism of Clark he presented his historico-apologetic method. Central to his argument is the claim that since he has proven (probably) scientifically that Christ has risen from the dead according to his own prophecy, Christ must be God. Therefore, everything he says must be true, thus guaranteeing the validity of the biblical view of history.[31] This should convince, indeed it should compel, the assent of all reasonable men. By what is really a positivistic method, he would bring religious conviction to unbelievers.

This would be very good if it worked. The Christian historians would then be able to convince all sound thinkers of the truth of Christianity, so that a revival would take place as the result of a historical argument of high probability. Montgomery maintains that the reliability of the New Testament documents can be proven by the use of the historical method which is the same for the Christian, the atheist, or the Tibetan monk.[32] Yet while he insists that Christ's resurrection can be proven scientifically as fully as Columbus' discovery of America, he also admits that many men will not accept it or its implications. Why? Because 1) they are not willing to do Christ's will (John 7:17), and 2) they are more interested in the present, than they are in the future life.[33] But is not this an admission that the scientific method cannot bring Christian conviction without Christian assumptions? And how does one come to Christian assumptions? By the scientific method, or by the regenerating work of the Holy Spirit?

It is at this point that one comes to the unbiblical positivism of Montgomery's whole argument. He makes the acceptance of the gospel purely a matter of intellect and empirical reasoning. He never refers to the effect of sin upon the whole man, nor does he recognize that Christian faith comes only with a radical change of the individual "from above." Hardly ever does he mention the regenerating work of the Holy Spirit, and when Clark holds that it is the inner testimony of the Holy Spirit that gives certainty he dismisses the idea as "fideism," whatever he means by that term. Even more clearly does he show his lack of consideration for the work of the Holy Spirit when treating of the apostolic church. He maintains that it was *Christ's resurrection* that emboldened the discouraged and frightened apostles, thus enabling them to go forth to convert the world. Never once does he mention Pentecost, despite all that both Christ and Peter had to say on this subject (John 14:25; Acts 1 and 2). Moreover, he completely ignores the statements of Paul, in I Corinthians 1 and

2, concerning the need for the regenerating activity of the Holy Spirit before men will accept Christ as the risen living Redeemer.[34]

The question then is: is Montgomery's rejection of presuppositional history correct? Is his professed historical epistemology consistently Christian? The answer to both questions would seem to be, no. He has to admit, despite all his deprecation of presuppositions, that no historian can or does carry on his work without presupposing a view of the whole of reality. His so-called objective, scientific methodology brings him only probability, largely determined by his own presuppositions. And finally his rational-positivistic approach completely ignores, if it does not specifically deny, the necessity of the regenerating work of the Holy Spirit in order that men have truly Christian presuppositions and so reach valid Christian conclusions. One cannot but feel that his rational-positivism largely stems from the fact that he wishes to avoid dependence upon the work of the Holy Spirit in speaking to a rationalistic world, a position that is supported neither by the Gospels nor by the rest of the New Testament. His historical epistemology, therefore, seems to be contrary to a truly Christian approach.

III. What Is History?

When we turn from Montgomery's epistemology to his views of the nature or ontology of history, as mentioned above, we do not have much on which to go. So far his plan to write a multivolume study of history has resulted in only one volume which deals largely with the historical method and the means of knowing history. No doubt in subsequent volumes he will describe the essential nature of history in all its ramifications, but so far all one can find out directly is very little. In *The Shape of the Past* he indicates in summary form the direction of his thinking, but even his "metaphysical principles" always end up in the field of epistemology.[35] Briefly, he holds that the historical process is meaningful since the world is created by God; the center of history is "the act of God in Jesus Christ," which provides the criterion for all other historical events; and that final judgment on the historical process rests in the hands of God. He also insists that although human nature is constant it is fallen. From these he deduces other epistemological principles. He does not in any sense, however, offer a systematic ontology of history. That he praises Voeglin's *Order and History* highly, while admitting that the latter does not "use the Scriptural revelation as the source of his philosophy of history" but only for illustrative purposes, makes one wonder if he believes that one may deduce the true nature of history from historical phenomena, rather than deriving it from the Scriptures, which he accepts as the inerrant Word of God.[36]

One thing to which Montgomery gives little attention is the sovereignty of God over history. To be sure, in one footnote he speaks of the Christian having to believe that, *in at least a spiritual sense,* energy is supplied to the human situation by the regenerating work of the Holy Spirit.[37] But the idea certainly holds no central position in his thinking. In another place he indicates that he takes the neo-orthodox statements concerning God's sovereignty over history seriously, but objects to their stress on the idea of *heilsgeschichte,* which places it outside of "ordinary" history.[38] When one remembers, however, his criticism of Clark's view and his insistence that the latter made God the author of sin by his stress on God's sovereignty, one cannot but feel that the idea finds little favor in his historico-ontological system.

This interpretation of Montgomery's position receives support from his frequent discussions of the question of miracle. In these he indicates that he follows the argument of C. S. Lewis. Quite rightly he rejects modern presuppositions that rule out the possibility of miracle. He does not counter this anti-miraculous faith, however, by pointing out that in a universe ruled over by a sovereign God, miracle, i.e., divine direct intervention, as a vehicle of revelation is not only possible, but, to use his own terms, highly probable. This would, of course, make miracle supra-rational, or even irrational, as far as man is concerned, an approach that seems to make Montgomery's soul curl with displeasure. He apparently feels that one must rationally prove that a miracle has taken place miraculously![39]

In order to verify a miraculous event he, first of all, denies the absoluteness of natural law in the belief that Newton's and Hume's view of law closed the universe, and so excluded the possibility of miracle—a very doubtful, even improbable, point of view. He then casts his vote in favor of what he claims is Einstein's position, that this is an open universe in which anything can happen. Natural law is simply a description of what men have observed taking place.[40] Quoting Compton, Berndtson, Heisenberg, and Carnell, he accepts the principle of indeterminacy in physics as correct. Consequently nothing is to prevent a miracle from taking place, for its miraculous character derives not from the fact that it happens by direct divine action without means, contrary to means, or above means, but from its uniqueness.[41] Apparently miracle is a unique event to which natural law must be made to conform.[42] Therefore, since every historical event is in some respects unique, every historical event is presumably a miracle and by the same token no event is a miracle. The only escape from this dilemma is for Montgomery to posit that there are different degrees of "uniqueness," a contradiction in terms which at one point he seems prepared to accept.[43]

By virtue of his definition, Montgomery believes that one may investigate miracles empirically. He does not explain, however, how one knows that any event is unique in history until the end of history. On the basis of probability the event may be repeated, which would presumably destroy its miraculous character. What, for instance, of Christ's many miracles of healing? Their repetition, according to Montgomery's definition, surely destroyed their miraculous character. Furthermore, without a clear-cut doctrine of God's sovereignty or divine providence, how does he know that a *probably* unique event is not just a matter of chance? Here he falls into the relativism he so much dislikes. Quoting Ethelbert Stauffer of Erlangen, he claims that for the historian nothing is impossible; a view also held by the atheistic existentialist philosopher, Jean Paul Sartre![44] By his definition Montgomery denatures completely the biblical concept of miracle.

In the light of what Montgomery says about miracles, what then does he consider the importance of such events? To him, as to other Christians, the resurrection of Jesus Christ is the supreme miracle. His reason for believing this is that, since religious experience is found only in the empirical realm, it must come either by divine written revelation or the entrance of a divine messenger. The writings would have to be internally consistent, which he appears to deny when he deals with Clark's ideas, and would have to fit the facts of experience, presumably of both believer and unbeliever alike. The messenger would have to prove himself by performing deeds "unable or highly unlikely to be performed by mere human beings," which might also support the claims of Lourdes, Fatima, and Ste. Anne de Beaupré (cf. Exod. 7:11). Bringing book and individual together, he insists that Christ's resurrection, as recorded in the New Testament, therefore proves that Christ is God.[45] But on his own terms does it? First of all, Christ's resurrection is simply part of natural law and cannot be shown to be unique until history ends.[46] Secondly, in a completely open universe, where anything can happen except that which contravenes the law of non-contradiction, which Montgomery apparently accepts as more than merely descriptive, the resurrection may have been simply the result of chance, signifying nothing.[47] Since the proof of biblical inspiration is Christ's resurrection, and the evidence in turn for the resurrection is the New Testament, such circular reasoning is empirically indefensible. On his own grounds, therefore, he has no argument in favor of Christianity. Furthermore, he has virtually destroyed any possibility of history having any meaning at all, for miracles can reveal nothing but their own uniqueness, and even that is never more than probable.

It may perhaps be contended, in reply, that Montgomery's view of the redemptive action of God in history indicates his view of the nature of history. To God history is simultaneous, the eternal present, and in the sacrificial death of Christ his love goes out "to all men of all ages." This means the coherence of all ages, past, present, and future, for in them redemption is actual. Montgomery then points out the meaning of this by referring to Charles Williams' poem, *Taliessen through Logres*, in which Virgil is saved from damnation "by the redemptive love of Christians" who through the ages have been upheld and helped by his poetry. From this he goes on to set forth the idea that a principle of universal substitution and exchange "forces the Christian historian to save from oblivion and misjudgment those who could historically not save themselves." The universal perspective of God's grace prevents the Christian historian from labelling certain nations as inferior, and incites him, on the basis of John 3:16, to rescue from oblivion those neglected or misunderstood historical figures, thus giving them historical immortality.[48] Here one is left in some uncertainty as to whether Virgil's salvation is to eternal *life* or just to undying historical fame. Montgomery's views of both miracle and redemption in history leave one in a state of doubt, to say the least.

The fact is that Montgomery, convinced beyond all probability that Christ is his Savior and Lord, is trying to prove absolutely from objectively and empirically known history that Jesus Christ is Savior and Lord for all who will come to him *in faith*. This he cannot do, for no one comes to Christ except he is drawn by the Father through the Spirit and the Word (John 3:3, 5; 6:63-65). Montgomery, in fact, really acknowledges this when he asserts that the only way in which man can come to a knowledge of God's will concerning history is by receiving knowledge from God himself, from outside history.[49] That knowledge is, however, not merely in Montgomery's terms of empirical fact for the mind, but divine interpretation for the whole man, applied by the Holy Spirit so that man comes to the place of the apostle Thomas when he cried out: "My Lord and my God!"

IV. What Price Presuppositions?

In concluding this essay it would seem only right to set forth positively a brief statement of the "presuppositional" approach to history. Although philosophers and historians may disagree on details, the following statement seeks to give some idea of the "presuppositional" point of view.

To begin with, the Christian is not one who has been merely intellectually convinced of certain propositions concerning a historical personage known as Jesus Christ. To use Christ's own words, he has been "born again" by the regenerating action of the Holy Spirit (John 3:3, 5). He is, therefore, a new person in Jesus Christ, whom he now acknowledges as his Savior and Lord. He now sees all things as in a new dimension (II Cor. 5:17)—not because of some historical argument, but by the inner testimony of the Spirit. He recognizes the Scriptures of the Old and New Testaments for what they are, the Word of God, and in their light he interprets the whole of the world and its history.

This means that he approaches all things in creation with presuppositions different from those he held before his conversion, and from which, as a Christian, he cannot possibly escape. As Paul tells us in Colossians 1:15ff., for instance, Christ is the Lord of history, for he is the Creator, sustainer, and ruler over all things. Therefore, he can sovereignly and directly intervene in creation and history by performing miracles which may take place without, contrary to, or above, secondary causes as we know them. Furthermore, he is the redeemer of history, having miraculously entered it to live, die, and rise again that man and his history might be saved from disintegration. It is with the presuppositions that the Christian, if he be truly a Christian, must approach history.[50] In this way he sees history as it truly is, for to see it *sub specie aeternitatis* is to see it objectively.

That the non-Christian also approaches history with his presuppositions, Montgomery acknowledges. But the unbeliever's assumptions ultimately involve some element of chance or irrationality, whether one speaks of the views of a Dilthey, a Becker, a Toynbee, or a Croce.[51] This means that to the non-Christian no interpretation is ultimately valid. Since history has no ultimate meaning he can have no certainty that there is any real connection between any two events. Thus whether idealist or positivists, non-Christians have to admit that if there is no meaning to history, ultimately there is no knowledge of history. The idealist is reduced to examining his own ideas of what has taken place, and the positivist or empiricist to examining a collection of random, atomistic, disparate facts. Any one interpretation could be as true or as false as any other.

Yet while this is the theoretical situation, even the most irrationalistic historians still claim that they can and do know something of history. They lecture on it and write about it as though it possesses a certain coherence that enables them to interpret it, and even to make the universal negative statement that the historian cannot really know history.[52] Despite Montgomery's disparagement of self-consistency as a criterion of truth, self-consistency does seem to have something to be said for it. Those who contradict their own presuppositions by their practice can hardly be regarded as holding a valid philosophical position.

The biblical view, on the other hand, that God in Jesus Christ is sovereign over history provides the Christian with the basis for a consistent view of history. History began with the plan of God, which includes all events, thus guaranteeing coherence. The Christian can, therefore, speak of such things as cause and effect, retribution, salvation, and the like, in history.[53] He can take it for granted that he is able to know something of history, although he will never attain to an exhaustive comprehension, nor will he have the capacity to link most events directly to God's sovereign plan. But he has the confidence that he does know truly up to a point. The unbeliever, however, despite Montgomery's objections to Clark's doctrine of common grace, can only claim to know something of history when he forsakes his assumption of ultimate chance and meaninglessness to accept the premise of history's ultimate coherence and meaningfulness. When he does so he is unconsciously moving on to the fountain of the Christian, who alone presupposes coherence by virtue of the sovereignty of God.[54]

It is Christian assumptions that make the scientific historical method possible. As Montgomery himself admits, the God-centeredness of the Reformation over against the man-centeredness of the Renaissance made for a radical difference between the two ideas of history. While the latter viewed the temporal decisions of man and the vagaries of *Fortuna* the ultimate forces of history, the former stressed the coherence of the purpose and plan of God. Because of this historical consistency, the Christian believes that he can discover the facts and their relationships by means of an empirical methodology, the use of analogy, and other techniques. In this way, although he must admit that even here his biases and his blind spots undoubtedly cause him to misinterpret and misunderstand, he comes to a relatively or probably true understanding of what has happened.

In a good many cases of historical interpretation Christian and non-Christian may appear to agree in their understandings of limited areas of history, e.g., the causes of the Industrial Revolution, the results of World War I, and similar historical matters. But in the long run they do not, because they fail to see eye to eye on the ultimate meaning of any event. The non-Christian inevitably goes back to some concept of chance, while the Christian sees history as the working out of God's eternal purpose in Jesus Christ. The non-Christian commences without God, and unless the Spirit touches his heart in the process of his work, the non-Christian will end without God. The Christian, on the other hand, begins with God and so cannot but end with him.

Therefore, despite Montgomery's very sound arguments in favor of the resurrection of Christ and its implications, they of themselves cannot possibly bring conviction to the unbeliever. As Montgomery himself states, non-Christians will look for the most ridiculous interpretations rather than accept the biblical claim that Christ rose from the dead. Although they may admit the evidence for the empty tomb, they prefer to believe that Christ's resurrection was nothing more than a chance happening, rather than that it proves his deity. As both Christ and the apostles insisted, only by the action of the Holy Spirit does man find the ultimate assurance that Christ indeed did rise, and so believes in him as his Redeemer. This conviction is something that goes far beyond mere empirical probability enabling the Christian to say with Paul, "I know whom I have believed, and am persuaded. . . ."

Yet while disagreeing with Montgomery in his anti-presuppositional position, we believe that his stress upon the empirical study and investigation of history is of great importance. Philosophers often enjoy spinning their theories and making wide sweeping generalization without being bound to specific facts. This may be part of their vocation, but when Christian historians follow the same practice, it cannot but lead to trouble. The danger is that they will formulate hypotheses or models which they believe accord with their Christian philosophical assumption, and then attempt to force all the facts into this procrustean bed. Furthermore, when they find other Christian historians who do not follow the same practice, or who are not prepared to accept their application of their basic assumptions to some specific series of events, they reject them either as "humanists" or as having no "Christian philosophy of history." Their own interpretations, on the other hand, are often highly speculative in that they are attempting to interpret individual events or trends on the basis of the general statements of Scripture, or of deductions made from Scripture. The Christian, therefore, because of his presuppositions must use the empirical method if he would understand what has happened in history. For his emphasis, therefore, we must be thankful to Montgomery.

To summarize the argument, we would say that Montgomery's empirical position is essentially that of the positivistic school. He ignores completely the effect of sin on man, believing that the Christian can convince the unbeliever of the truth of the gospel by a historical argument. In so doing he rejects, at least implicitly, the need for the regenerating work of the Holy Spirit. Assuming a common human consciousness in both Christian and non-Christian alike, he holds that by the use of the empirical method alone, with only a few methodological assumptions, any man can reach a true interpretation of history, including a correct understanding of the Christian gospel. And Montgomery claims all this despite his constant revelation that he, himself, begins his thinking with all kinds of Christian presuppositions.

The so-called presuppositionalists cannot accept this self-styled empirical position. They take the influence of sin seriously, holding that it has corrupted and biased man to the point that he would quickly bring about his own self-destruction were it not for the benevolent intervention of God. By it he restrains man's sinfulness in order to manifest his glory in his gifts to men, and also for the sake of his elect, that they may be preserved in this world, and that by the regenerating action of his Spirit they may come to know his saving grace in Jesus Christ and serve him in this life. Because of this divine action even the unbeliever is enabled to understand and interpret historical events, more or less correctly, in their immediate contexts. Only when a person has experienced the restorative effect of special grace, however, can he see history truly *sub specie eternitatis*, for only then does he begin with presuppositions that make a comprehensive knowledge of history possible: the sovereignty of the triune God over all things in creation, providence, and redemption.

Clark H. Pinnock

XXIII. THE PHILOSOPHY OF CHRISTIAN EVIDENCES

Exposition

Cornelius Van Til has introduced a heavy dose of metaphysical presuppositionalism into Christian apologetics. Characteristic of this philosophical standpoint is the refusal to allow empirical verification procedures any place in establishing the validity of the starting-point adopted. The absolute principle must be presupposed. Van Til makes no attempt to conceal his methodology. Indeed he sees it as the peculiar genius of his system. "The Reformed apologist will frankly admit that his own methodology presupposes the truth of Christian theism."[1] Elsewhere he writes, "The Reformed apologist assumes that nothing can be known by man about himself or the universe unless God exists and Christianity is true."[2] He candidly admits to circular reasoning. Unless we have an absolute God interpreting reality for us, there can be no true interpretation at all.[3] Indeed, this constitutes the one proof of God. For unless the sovereign God stands behind reality, human experience operates in a void, and reality is unintelligible. The truth of Christianity is thus the axiom on which all rationality depends, rather than the conclusion of a process of argumentation. For there can be no epistemology common to all men. Unless we start with this God, we will never get to him. It is not only useless, but wrong, to appeal to theistic arguments or historical vindications in defense of the Christian faith. "It is impossible and useless to seek to defend Christianity as an historical religion by a discussion of facts only."[4] Facts without God would be brute facts, and bear no intelligible relation to one another. The approach of Bishop Butler (and incidentally Warfield, Greene, and Hamilton) adulterates the faith beyond recognition.[5] For God alone is the starting point of all intelligible thinking.[6] Neutral facts do not exist. Facts are what they are only by virtue of the place they have in the plan of God. Van Til even prefers Hume's scepticism to Butler's probabilities, and an existential historiography in which facts and interpretations are inextricably blended to an empirically objective approach to historical revelation. He believes he can begin with God and Christianity without first consulting objective reality.

For to know any fact truly, man must first presuppose the existence of the Christian God. No God, no knowledge. Van Til stands opposed to any simple appeal to fact.[7] Such would be an "Arminian apologetic."[8] Although the majority Christian view over the centuries has been that Christian theism could be securely grounded by means of rational arguments and empirical demonstrations, Van Til refuses to have anything to do with it. In that they have discredited such an attempt, even Kant and Hume deserve our thanks. Antony Flew may want to examine the case for theism, but Van Til will have nothing to do with it on these terms.[9] From the start Flew must recognize all his logic is vain unless he bows to the Christian revelation. Van Til has come to see that in the last analysis men see what they see by the light of God, and that, paradoxically, even the reason they employ is God's gift to them. His is the light in which alone we see light.

Criticism

1. By inviting us to presuppose the metaphysical ultimate, Van Til has created a neat theoretical package which promises to reduce the labor expended in the defense of Christianity. But as soon as the Scripture is allowed to speak, we perceive that the Christian faith is not an abstract metaphysical system supported by presuppositionalism, but a belief grounded in nonrecurrent historical events seen to be revelatory on the basis of which limited statements are made about the ultimate nature and structure of reality. It is ironical that the criticism against a man who makes so much of an inerrant Bible has to be that he has disregarded its contents in his epistemology. For there is no possible way to deny that Scripture presents the revelation of God occurring in the cosmic and historical stuff of the universe, general and special revelation, and that this divine self-disclosure is objectively valid to all men (Rom. 1:19f.; Acts 17:31). The criticism is not that Van Til denies this state of affairs. God forbid! But that in his philosophy of evidences he disregards and restricts its force. If we may speak of a biblical epistemology of religious knowledge, and we may do so only with great caution, it leans toward a correspondence view of truth, namely, that there exists a form of correspondence between belief and facts, against Van Til's idealist coherence theory that things are true if they hang together in a system. Undoubtedly there is a great deal more to Christian apologetics than merely adducing empirical proofs for this or that aspect in the gospel, but to release an invective against those who

attempt to do this is biblically illegitimate. The God of Scripture has stooped to reveal himself in the empirical world of factuality, and invited sinners to find him there. To refuse empirical investigation of the data in question is to nullify that revelation (at least in its epistemological implications for verification in apologetics) and transmute a historical *apocalypse* into a gnostic *apocryphon.* Van Til frequently complains about the dialectical wedge inserted by neo-orthodoxy between the Jesus of history and the Christ of faith. Yet he himself has made the objective data of divine revelation *inaccessible* to the non-Christian and created a dialectic of his own. Curiously, Holy Scripture, the contents of which Van Til claims to presuppose, compels us to dismantle his system and seek a better way. Our presupposition of Christianity does not give validity and reality to God's revelation in nature and history. It is God's revelation that gives validity and content to our commitment. Scripture encourages us to start from particulars, not universals. The particular disclosure in the cosmic order is that which gives rise to faith in the Creator, and the particular disclosure in history is that which gives rise to faith in the Redeemer. The apostles presented the objective fact of the resurrection as decisive validation of the claims of Christ and the truth of the gospel (Rom. 1:4; Acts 2:22-24). Van Til has committed a peculiarly Calvinistic sin (though Calvin was not guilty of it) in that he works from a logical construction to Christ and the gospel rather than starting with actual revelation. As a result he has cut off all hope of interchange with non-Christian thinkers, a fact of which he seems to be proud, and, worse still, has denied the open-to-investigation form of the gospel. In so doing he comes perilously close to a Barthian philosophy of apologetics, namely, "belief cannot argue with unbelief, it can only preach to it." Let us not confuse the Christian faith with Islam and its grand presupposition of a self-contained God and an inerrant Scripture. The uniqueness of Christianity is the entry of God the Son into time-space history (I John 1:1-3). The fact of Christ is something men must have pointed out to them. If they equivocate, and they surely will, we shall simply continue to point, for it is before him they must bow. It is all very well to presuppose something if we have reason to know the presupposition is justified. Christianity does not begin with the axiom that God exists and the Bible is true, to which all the other Christian beliefs are deductively appended. Barth made his mistake by sleeping with Kant, as it were, while Van Til makes his by becoming wedded to the Dutch metaphysical voluntarists. It may be that one can show how Butler and his kind can present only a probable argument (because synthetic and empirical). However, a probable argument is better than an improbable one. Such is Van Til's own case when he demands the non-Christian make a total and ungrounded commitment to the absolute God of Scripture. Van Til is right to contend that the world is dependable and intelligible because God is its Creator. His existence is basic to the entire rational structure of reality. However, it is the *fact* of his existence, not the awareness or conscious *recognition* of it by man, that makes this so. This insight is one of the sharp pieces of Christian evidence that we ought to employ, but not to the exclusion of all the rest. From our experience of life-in-the-world, rational, cosmical, and historical, we come, under the operations of the Holy Spirit, to the conclusion that God exists and the gospel is true. In the biblical philosophy of evidences, we are not asked to assume the theistic clue to ultimate reality in order to arrive at it. Rather we are challenged to see that reality and revelation being what they are establish the validity of the Christian faith.

2. Philosophically speaking, Van Til is a kind of transcendental idealist for whom the existence of his God is a necessary condition for the possession of any knowledge. Because he transcends the world, nothing in the world of factuality is capable of revealing him of itself. All discussion is meaningless unless at the outset all parties submit to his metaphysical-theological starting-point. Man is thus stripped of sound intelligence, for both ethical and philosophical reasons, and thinks in so complete a vacuum that discussion becomes impossible. Only bottomless scepticism remains for him who refuses to presuppose Christian theism. Rationality is possible only for a Christian. Presumably only he can understand the assertion that apart from God rationality is irrational. Men must *decide* to become Christians and not think about it first. The basis of the choice cannot be known until after the axiom has been espoused. Thus the decision is voluntaristic, an existential leap of faith. Van Til's well-known antipathy to neo-orthodoxy notwithstanding, the resemblance to Barth's unverifiable *kerygma* and Ott's denial of *bruta facta* is unmistakable.[10] He cannot escape the charge of fideism, the view that truth in religion is ultimately based on faith rather than on reasoning or evidence. Van Til did not come to this position out of sympathy for the brooding Dane as Barth did, but by being convinced by Herman Dooyeweerd's transcendental critique of philosophic thought.[11] For Dooyeweerd, the starting-point of philosophy, the Archimedian point, lies deep in

a religious decision. It sees beyond science and precedes all scientific activity. Its starting-point is thus existential. It is one thing for Van Til to contend that secular philosophy, beginning with itself in isolation from divine revelation, cannot attain unto ultimate truth. It is quite another matter to conclude from this that a man cannot even attain knowledge of revelation itself apart from an epistemological miracle. We agree that reality would be unintelligible if God did not exist. However, it is the *fact* of his existence, and not assent to it, which provides valid common ground. Men all live in a single universe. They inhabit the world of created factuality. All facts are God's facts, and therefore coherent and intelligible facts. For Van Til, it seems, presuppositions are real, and facts are not. The presentation of historical evidences for the truth of the gospel, for example, is not a denial that all facts are God's facts, but a special demonstration it is so (Acts 17:31). General and special revelation pinpoint the creative and redemptive activity of God for all to behold. There is no implicit denial in this presentation of Christian evidences of the spiritual inability of man to receive Christ apart from the operations of the Holy Spirit (I Cor. 2:14). We present the data whether men will hear or whether they will forbear. Just as the Spirit can create comprehension in the reading of Scripture, so the Spirit can create comprehension in the reading of Christian evidences. Faith is created by the Holy Spirit acting upon good and sufficient evidences.

Another unfortunate aspect of Van Til's philosophy of apologetics is its tragic irrelevance in the light of the current analytic philosophy.[12] Just at the time when philosophers are asking for verification in support of metaphysical ultimates, Van Til comes forward with his denial of brute facts altogether and the possibility of rational exchange. In turning away from biblical realism in favor of metaphysical presuppositionalism, Van Til has closed the door on what could prove to be the most fruitful dialogue between philosophy and theology in decades. Instead he calls for philosophical segregation. Basically the analytic philosophers are asking for some evidence within the cosmic or historical order that could count for the veracity of the Christian faith. Apart from the residual positivism hovering over the request, the challenge is perfectly reasonable and indeed congenial to the biblical claims. Verification is precisely what God in his self-disclosure has provided. If the request were biblically invalid, we could understand Van Til's recoil from it. But it is not. Basically they are asking, "Why believe?," and we should tell them!

The gospel appears foolish to the natural man. It demolishes his humanistic hopes and dreams, and offends his supposed autonomy. It does not, however, as Van Til implies, dismiss his questions without a hearing and discredit all the knowledge he ever had.

A man like Russell might, in answer to Van Til, prefer to conclude that the universe just is, that's all, and refuse to mar his integrity by presupposing one of the metaphysical ultimates that was handy. For believing in the God of Scripture just because this belief would exorcise the demons of irrationality and absurdity from the universe is dishonest. Scripture has no such pessimistic attitude to a positive apologetic. The revelation of God is objectively valid, accessible to all men, intelligible in and of itself. If men are unwilling to conclude that the evidence points to the truth of the gospel, this is because of a volitional unwillingness to believe and not because of the absence of common ground or the invalidity of the evidence. We begin by pointing men to Christ, and end by seeing that God was throughout the whole process the basis of our vision.[13]

Conclusion

Cornelius Van Til has contributed to a virile twentieth century apologetic by his insistence that the Christian claim, *if true*, is more coherent than any other world-view. Unfortunately, a curious epistemology derived from a modern Calvinistic school of philosophy in Holland has led him to align his orthodox theology with a form of irrational fideism. Van Til believes modern thinkers have passed him by for the most part because he is faithful to the genuine offense of the gospel. This is not altogether true. For he has imported into that gospel an epistemology alien to our faith which requires decision before reflection. A non-Christian can reject this demand without ever considering the actual Christian message. A philosophy of Christian evidences which employs theistic argument and historical evidence is needed, lest the gospel be discredited as a grand and unwarranted assumption. Warfield opposed Kuyper on this score, as we must likewise oppose Van Til. Let not our orthodoxy be crippled by fideism. Faith rests upon an attested and authenticated revelation. The task of apologetics is to ground the truth claim of the gospel. Van Til in his courageous and erudite defense of the faith compels his readers to clarify their understanding. But it may be that the inductive method applied to the cosmic and historical stuff of revelation would yield an even stronger foundation for the orthodox faith we all want to preserve.

Response by C. Van Til

Dear Dr. Pinnock:

I greatly appreciate your frankness in expressing your opposition to my views. You are quite right in saying of me, "he believes he can begin with God and Christianity without first consulting objective reality." This is the heart of the matter. If I were to attempt to know what "objective reality" was, apart from the all-embracive message of God as Christ speaking in Scripture, I would deny, it seems to me, all that it means to be a "Christian"! I would not pick up a lantern to help me find the sun, to see whether it exists. The whole notion of "light" is based upon our intimate acquaintance with the sun, day after day. Organically speaking, if the sun did not exist I could not be alive to look for it (given God's world as it is). Just so I use reason (induction, deduction, forms of implication): in full recognition that I discover truth by means of them because each individually, and all collectively, operate in *God's* world and therefore as part of the realization of his plan. To attempt to understand such abilities of man in using reason apart from what God has revealed about his plan would be, for the Christian, "unscientific."

I agree with you that Scripture should speak for itself. In fact, I want it to tell us what God is, what the world is, and what we as men are, not *after* but *before* we start speaking of metaphysics, epistemology, and ethics. To think that I conceive of the "Christian faith" as an "abstract metaphysical system supported by presuppositionalism" is to misunderstand completely the whole thrust of Reformed thinking. I observe, rather, that as Christians we must look at the world as Christ himself looked at it and, in so far as any man does not, he views it falsely. Consequently the attempt to find God in the world without looking through the eyes of Christ is fruitless, not because the world does not reveal God (it continually shouts of the existence of God to men), but because men need new eyes!

When I beseech men to forsake their unbelief and accept the Christ of Scripture as God over all and therefore as their Savior, I ask them to forsake the obviously sinking raft of experience as it is assumed to be by would-be autonomous man. David Hume has shown, I think, that Bishop Butler's argument to the effect that Christianity is more probably true than other views is based on a view of the world in which Chance is ultimate. Clearly any view of probability which is based on the ultimacy of Chance cannot possibly contact reality in any way, for it can say nothing about the probability of any *particular* event, for all events proceed equally from the belly of Chance. Therefore a "probable" argument for any particular event is of no more value than an improbable one, for both arguments are meaningless in terms of that one "event." A probable argument is not better than an improbable one if the very idea of probability is without meaning.

Only on the biblical basis which says that man is made in the image of God and that the world in all its facts manifests the presence of God are science and philosophy intelligible. You say that "Van Til is right to contend that the world is dependable and intelligible because God is its Creator." I take it you understand me to mean the triune God of the Bible. But then you continue, "His existence is basic to the entire rational structure of reality. However, it is the *fact* of his existence, not the awareness of conscious *recognition* of it by man, that makes this so." Well and good, but it is this "awareness and conscious recognition" that apologetics is all about! We as Christians are seeking to have men recognize not only the existence of God but, as you so rightly insist, what he has done and is doing in the world. Those whom you are seeking to win to salvation in Christ have *all the facts in common* with you. It is the same God and the same world created and redeemed by Christ which confronts both you and them. If men do not accept what God says about himself and about the world, they will remain under the wrath of God. In presenting *what* God says to them you are calling them to repentance. This is certainly true, is it not? God in Christ says it is true. Paul said, "Therefore, my beloved brethren, be ye steadfast and unmoveable, always abounding in the work of the Lord, forasmuch as ye know that your labor is not in vain in the Lord." To talk about the existence of God, the *fact* of God's existence, without bringing in the whole of what God in Christ through the Holy Spirit has done and is doing for men, and to claim that this barren *fact* is the common ground between believers and unbelievers, is not only an abstraction, but complete distortion. To tell someone *that* God exists means nothing unless you tell him who God is and what he does.

But I must leave this discussion now, although I have appreciated having the opportunity again of clarifying my opposition to the Butler-Arminian form of apologetics. Your essay, of course, contains many more points I might wish to discuss, but I think many of them have been answered in the essay by Prof. Stoker. In addition, I hope "My Credo" corrected what I believe to be several total misunderstandings on your part of my position.

—C.V.T.

Arthur F. Holmes

XXIV. LANGUAGE, LOGIC, AND FAITH

Immanuel Kant, it has been said, is the kind of thinker with whom we may agree or disagree but whom it is impossible to ignore. He forces us to face issues and, in formulating our own conclusions, to address what he himself has done. The same may be said by the evangelical of Cornelius Van Til. He too is the kind of thinker with whom we may agree or disagree, but whom we can ill afford to ignore, for he forces us to face issues involved in the project of Christian philosophy, issues that must be confronted if we are to think in a manner that is true to the Christian revelation.

Cornelius Van Til writes as an apologist. His style is polemic, and his concern is with topics directly tangental to theological matters. This is his interest and his calling, and for the seminary professor it is very appropriate. But the college or university professor seeking to inject Christian perspectives into the philosophical rather than the theological dialog, or working with matters that are not as closely related to theology (whether the theory of perception, aesthetics, or modal logic), is accustomed to a style that is more analytic than polemic and a role that is more constructively philosophical than apologetic or theological.

These considerations have shaped this essay. My conscience has been sensitized by men like Van Til, yet my calling has been more philosophical than apologetic or theological. My concern is not so much the defense of the faith against the destructive inroads of non-Christian philosophy, as it is to explore constructive contributions that may be made both by philosophic inquiry to Christian thought and by Christian perspectives to legitimate philosophic thought. This essay therefore explores some aspects of a Christian theory of knowledge in relation to contemporary philosophy. They are aspects which Van Til has stressed, and it will soon be plain that I agree with him in repudiating the so-called autonomy of human reason, and the existence of bare facts, and the idea of a religiously neutral "natural theology." Whether or not he would go along with my understanding of these themes or my elaboration of their epistemological significance he alone can determine, for I want to develop them with reference to comparable themes in contemporary thought: informal logic and the nature of a system, subjectivity and objectivity, and the problem of meaning in religious language. My hope is twofold: to draw him out, not so much in criticism as in clarification of the constructive intent of his thought, and to bring to bear what he has stressed on the present epistemological scene.

I.   Human Knowledge and the Doctrine of Creation

A Christian theory of knowledge must reckon first with the creatureliness of man. On the one hand God fully knows himself and his creation, and his perfect knowledge is both the source and the norm of truth for men. On the other hand, God's knowledge is neither fully nor directly open to human inspection, so that our knowledge neither exhausts the range of information known to God nor fully comprehends the meaning of any one thing. We "know in part" and "see through a glass darkly." Creation, in other words, is an asymmetrical relationship: God's knowledge is complete and self-contained independently of man, but finite man is epistemologically as well as metaphysically and morally dependent on God.

Van Til accordingly speaks of both continuity and discontinuity. The autonomy and self-sufficiency of thought is true of God alone; it is a sinful delusion in men. Man in sin, asserting his own autonomy and without God's self-revelation, has fragmented knowledge; its larger meaning is lost, and its final word is of mystery, not God.

Christian philosophy begins with the confession of our creatureliness, not the assertion of autonomy. This is both desirable for theological reasons and in measure true of the history of Christian philosophy as well. A distinct change occurred in Western thought when the Christian revelation was brought to bear. The Greek philosophers, inquiring into the basis for the unity in plurality that is evident in nature, developed their doctrine of changeless forms and tried to relate the forms to changing particulars, either by some process of participation, or by incorporating forms into the very composition of changing things, or else by necessary emanations that made all of nature less than good. Christian thinkers quickly saw inadequacies here and recognized that the biblical doctrine of God and creation is the needed clue. The history of patristic and medieval philosophy tells of their attempts to bring this doctrine to bear on the theory of universals by relating the Logos of God to the intelligible order of nature. How successful any of them were, or how legitimate their form of the undertaking, is another matter; perhaps it is to their credit that in the end concern for the sovereignty of God in creation and for created individuality among men led Bonaventure and Scotus to change drastically the Greek conception and led William of Ockham to abandon it altogether. In some regards Ockham dodged the metaphysical issue, but the important thing is that for him the doctrine of creation prevailed.

What transpired in metaphysics was not as carefully applied to epistemology. But the consequences of applying the fundamental biblical theme of God and creation to the theory of knowledge must be explored, and in my opinion contemporary philosophy is ripe for just such an attempt. In the first place, the rationalistic optimism of Greek and Enlightenment thinkers is largely passé. The assumption is suspect that human reason can, by the force of its own conclusive logic, master all that is real, and pure empiricism is being soundly criticized in both European phenomenology and Anglo-American analysis. That the real is the rational, in any rationalist sense of "rational," is by no means clear; and the philosophical foundations of formal logic with its necessary truths are no longer firmly entrenched.

This is not to say that contemporary thought is irrationalistic. On the contrary, the concern is to replace reductionists views of reason, modelled on mathematics and early modern science, with a fuller understanding of the richness and diversity of logical thought. An approach to epistemology that is more descriptive than prescriptive has emerged in phenomenology and analysis and the philosophy of science. Logic can be quite "informal," and philosophers no longer strain to force personal knowledge or moral knowledge or theological language into empiricist or formalist molds. They are more content to look at them as they are, to map out the logical relations they actually exhibit, and to understand their meaning in their own terms. The logic of Christian thought may then be seen on its own terms, namely in terms provided by the doctrine of God and creation.

In the second place, the present challenge to classical epistemologies stems in part from a rejection of the neutrality postulate and the intrusion into the theory of knowledge of the role of the knower as subject. We hear in philosophy today that all observation is theory-laden, that *aprioris* are unavoidable, that subjectivity affects scientific thought, that value judgments are inseparable from factual statements, and that personal perspectives shape our metaphysical systems.

This is not to say that contemporary thought is subjectivistic, for objective considerations continue to count, and the public character of our objects is a basic datum in the sociology of knowledge. Rather the knower is recognized as the interpreter who seeks meaning, and whose outlook as subject-to-object may well help reveal the meaning an object has in reality. Knowing, in other words, involves the knower's perspective, and this is something a Christian theory of knowledge clearly affirms.

My point is this: contemporary philosophy is ripe in at least two regards for a Christian theory of knowledge that begins with the creatureliness of men. (1) It is ripe for what by deductivist and inductivist standards is a rather informal logic. (2) It is ripe for what by the standards of objective neutrality is an appeal to subjectivity. Informal logic is not now presumed to be illogical, and subjectivity is not now equated with subjectivism. We shall look at each of these considerations in turn.

II.   The Idea of a Logical System

Van Til regards both induction and deduction as inadequate for a Christian theory of knowledge, because they both assume the autonomy of human thought and its ability to penetrate the truth alone. The criticism has point if such logics try to exhaust the meaning of things and to systematize the truth with finality and as a whole.

Is this induction's intent? For Aristotle, induction tried to grasp the immediate causes of natural processes rather than to build a system as such. The metaphysical system required something further than induction, further arguments and assumptions which may or may not be mistaken but are not themselves inductive. For Francis Bacon, induction only explores natural processes and leaves their larger meaning and purpose to theology. The relation he sees between philosophy and theology may be inadequate and his view of science oversimplified, but these are not results of induction as such. For some later logicians, for whom inductive methods secure predictions and so define our concepts operationally, induction makes no claim at all to know the real. Its claims are not that ambitious. In fact, pure induction may be just a straw man, for philosophers of science now maintain that scientific inquiry is not entirely empirical, that models and constructs are plainly at work both in the past history of science and today.[1]

Now if the intent of induction is not to explore the kind of world-viewish meaning with which Christians are concerned, and if pure induction does not exist, then a Christian theory of knowledge can agree with contemporary thought that something more is needed.

If criticism is needed, it is needed more for the philosophy of logic, more for the justification the methods receive, than for the methods themselves. In this area, a Christian epistemology has something constructive to say, for, as Michael Foster points out in regard to early modern science, if nature is contingent on God rather than self-sufficient then it does not exist of itself and does not of itself have to be the way it is.[2] Men are forced to ask what in fact it is like, and to use empirical tools in their inquiry. Since belief in an intelligent deity leads us to expect an intelligible creation, the doctrine of creation encourages inductive methods to operate as far as they are able.

With regards to deduction criticism is more apt, because deduction does try to build a system around the most ultimate premises available. But if God knows all things as a whole directly rather than inferentially, then discontinuity exists between the structure of God's knowledge on the one hand and that of deductive inference on the other. Even theology does not deduce one final and exhaustive system from Scripture, for revelation is not exhaustive but is adapted to our limited understanding, and systematic theology is a further human attempt to organize the truth of revelation as best we can. Deduction is a human logic and is limited in its usefulness. Contemporary philosophers realize it too: deduction is not the natural logic of ordinary discourse. The logic of ordinary thought is more informal, and our systems are non-deductive.[3] Deduction is often artificial, a man-made logic.

This does not mean either in contemporary logic or in Christian thought that truth is self-contradictory. God's thought, being complete and self-contained, is ultimately unified in itself; man too cannot settle for self-contradiction, even though his knowledge is incomplete. We try to unify our thought, and to express that unity systematically. But if the system is not necessarily deductive then our presuppositions are not necessarily premises from which one and only one system may be derived. What role then do they play?

One thing is clear: correct presuppositions reveal the meaning of facts. The question is, how? How shall we describe their natural logic? Elsewhere I suggest a symphonic model for systematic thought, in which a common theme, played with different variations, gives intelligible unity to the entire piece.[4] The man who knows the theme finds meaning in each movement and discerns a common purpose in what might otherwise seem bare facts or bewildering techniques. The symphonic model is suggested by philosophic systems that are categorial rather than deductive. Descartes and Spinoza exemplify the deductive system. An example of the categorial is Whitehead. He selects from experience concepts he finds especially revealing and uses them as interpretative principles of the utmost generality; they become *categories* of thought which help us conceptualize the world not as a collection of fragmented facts but as a coherent whole.

One does not have to accept Whitehead's own categories to appreciate his point. Everett Hall and others have discussed at length the nature of categorial systems, suggesting that categories give philosophic expression to an integrating world-perspective and that the worked-out system applies these categories (and thereby the world-perspective) to all life and experience.[5] The truth of a system is accordingly seen both in its rational coherence and in the adequacy and scope of its handling of experience. The categories fit.

There is merit to this approach. The categories that are selected represent a more fundamental world-perspective (one's basic presuppositions) and this perspective is logically related to facts via the explanatory power of its categories. Explanatory power may be exhibited in various ways: in deductive form it shows how statements about particular things may be inferred from general principles; in symphonic form its categories reveal analogies between different things and so coordinate our understanding of the whole. But distinctively Christian presuppositions are not drawn from common dimensions of all human experience, nor are such categories as creation and law and grace. They are drawn rather from biblical revelation, and the Bible presents them as somehow given in the covenantal activity of God in history. In other words, the logic of Christian presuppositions is a logic of unique events that give meaning to life as a whole. It is not inductive, for induction deals in generalization, not in the unique; nor is it deductive, for deduction begins with universally extended terms. What is this logic then?

Contemporary philosophers say that categories serve as coordinating analogies, and Van Til speaks of an analogical system himself. He rightly distinguishes his use of analogy from that of the Scholastics and that of Bishop Butler. The difference, I suggest, is twofold. First, analogy is properly a vehicle of understanding and not of proof. It is a means whereby human knowledge approximates the unity of the whole, rather than a ladder whereby we ascend some hierarchy of being and prove what God is like. Analogy aids conceptualization, not demonstration. Second, in biblical thought, understanding is drawn not from the transcendental attributes of being in general, possessed analogically by Creator and all grades of creatures alike, but from the covenantal acts and relationships of God in history. He is the God of Abraham, Isaac, and Jacob, who brought his people out of Egypt, gave them his law, and spoke to them through his prophets. He is the Father of our Lord Jesus Christ who became incarnate for our redemption. God and creation are understood through revelatory events which still stand as symbols of the faith and the basis for Christian understanding.

Historical events carry meaning because they are not isolated facts. The law given at Sinai, for example, is a historical fact, yet its meaning is understandable because it was not an isolated occurrence but a crucial part of God's covenantal dealings with his people. It is a meaning-bearing event by virtue of its context in history, and to it all Jewish and Christian thought looks back. The resultant conception of divine law becomes a key category in Christian ethical theory, one that helps us see our multitudinous desires and obligations from the perspective of God and creation. The incarnation of God in Christ is a further example. His birth, his earthly life, his death and resurrection are a historical fact, whose meaning men grasped because it was no isolated event but the fulfilment of a historical process. He came "according to the Scriptures" and "for our salvation." The incarnation becomes a key symbol of the faith because in context its meaning extends beyond its time to all of history before and after, and to all of Christian thought.

But the meaning of the law and the meaning of the incarnation are alike lost on those who fail to see them from the perspective of God and creation. Apart from this presupposition, it makes no sense to talk either of God's purposive activity in history or of the ultimate meaning of particular events. Events look like bare facts, not acts of God at all. Presuppositions make all the difference. So it is with understanding other things in nature and in life: their full meaning also is lost apart from God, for it is around presuppositions, which help us keep things in context, that a logical system holds coherently together.

What sort of logic is this? Not necessarily deduction, we have suggested, and not induction either. Elsewhere I labelled it "adduction," for we understand most fully and systematize what we know by means of the presuppositions we ourselves "adduce."[6] In this regard the knower as subject contributes kinowledge, as well as the object known.

III.   The Role of Subjectivity

Presuppositions vary. They are world-viewish beliefs not universal and logically necessary first truths, and so they vary with the beliefs of individuals. The individual is a subject; being who he is and believing what he does his subject-role affects his knowledge. The problem is to acknowledge this without relapsing into subjectivism, for subjectivism and objectivism are equally incompatible with the Christian doctrine of creation.

Again we may learn from the medievals. The strength of those who held to a realistic theory of universals lay in their recognition that meaning and ordered unity are intrinsic in God's creation. By contrast the weakness of the nominalists lay in their neglect of this, for from the perspective of God and creation there are no bare facts devoid of relation to other bare facts or to the purposes of God. Things are as they are by and for the Logos of creation. On the other hand the weakness of the realists lay in assuming that the God-given meaning of things is objectively accessible to every rational mind by virtue of our human potentiality, and that the subject-role of the individual knower makes no difference to his understanding. By contrast the strength of Ockham lay in his separating the content of faith from the logical necessities of objective reason. Faith is the willing act of the knower as a subject, not a purely objective consent to the philosophical dictates of logic. By the same token, the strength of the Enlightenment rationalists and of some later idealists lay in affirming that meaning and intelligibility are somehow inherent in nature, while the strength of the existentialist lay in reaffirming the subject-role in life and thought. The weakness of the one, the objectivist, is in assuming that anybody can read the meaning off the facts; the weakness of the other, the subjectivist, is in the claim that facts are not meaning-bearers at all, that life is meaningless apart from what meaning a man creates. Both are wrong. On the one hand, the full meaning of creation is not obvious to all, for discontinuity exists between God's knowledge and man's. On the other hand, creation is no collocation of unrelated facts, for there is objective meaning in life because there is objective truth in life's Creator.

Subjectivity and objectivity have too often been taken as disjuncts, and knowledge has too often been relegated to the latter alone. So it was at least in Greek and Enlightenment thought. This is a mistake. Subject and object are not disjuncts but complementary poles, both essential to the whole. Subjectivity is the subject-pole and objectivity the object-pole. Both poles appear in knowing, both the preconditions of knowing in the subject and the reality of objective meaning to be known. We must preserve both sides of the polarity if we are to avoid objectivism on the one hand, whether rationalist or empirical, and the subjectivism of some existentialists on the other.

For a Christian theory of knowledge, the objective meaning of things lies in their covenantal context in the creation of God. The subjective preconditions of understanding this meaning are met by the man who thinks and lives in that same context as a creature of God, the man who makes the doctrine of creation *his own* and internalizes it as the presupposition of his thought and *raison d'être* of his life. For him, philosophical thought becomes a confession of faith.

This may be seen in the informal logic that is natural to religious discourse, to which contemporary philosophy has given renewed attention.[7] Consider as statement (A), "I believe in God the Father Almighty, maker of heaven and earth." Its meaning embraces both object and subject poles: the objective fact of God and creation, and a confession of faith by the subject. I affirm the fact and I make it "my own." But the objective pole is itself complex: it contains (1) an empirical ingredient—"heaven and earth," as well as (2) an explanatory ingredient—"God the creator." To these two we add (3) a confessional ingredient—"I believe." These three ingredients are the presupposition, the context which gives meaning to the statements which follow in the creed about the historical Jesus Christ.

Consider also statement (B): "He was raised for our justification." It is (1) empirical, in that it refers to a historical event; (2) explanatory, it indicates the divine purpose in the event; (3) confessional, it expresses the faith of those who make this doctrine their own.

Recent religious language philosophy has been divided for and against the empirical verifiability of religious statements. The mistake of the verificationist is now evident: he confines meaning to (1), and since the relation of (1) to (2) is neither inductive nor deductive he makes no sense of the explanation given in (2). The idea of God as creator and the doctrine of justification alike lose their meaning: heaven and earth and the resurrection account seem like bare facts which in themselves carry no meaning for men. Either they and all life are meaningless and the God-concept traditionally associated with them is dead, or else God appears in (1) and (3) apart from (2). That is to say for existential theology the bare resurrection story (see statement B) confronts us existentially and triggers faith, and (statement A) the bare fact of our being-in-the-world kindles concern about the ground of our being. This "faith" is an existential response, purely subjective, that leaps from (1) to (3) without the help of (2). It takes the cognitive act (2) to unite the poles.

Some conservative thinkers too have concentrated on (1) empirical meaning as if a factual apologetic that establishes "empirical truth" will, without further ado, logically establish (2) and (3) as well. But (2) does not follow either inductively or deductively from (1), nor does (3). We must concentrate also on (2) and how it is actually brought to light by (1). In the case of statement B about the resurrection, (2) arises from a larger view of sacred history which in turn presupposes the doctrine of God and creation. To hold this presupposition is to realize that because the historical event (1) has God-given meaning in itself (2), it has meaning for me too (3). To grasp the "for-me-ness" of God's activity in his creation [(3) in statement A] is the subjective precondition of understanding how a historical event (B1) can have the meaning (B2) it does.

This interplay of subject and object is natural to the logic of Christian discourse. The presupposition of God and creation (A) is "adduced" in explaining the resurrection (B2): meaning is brought from a more ultimate level of thought (A2) and faith (A3) in making sense of specifics (B1). So it is with other things in life. How does the Christian look at (C) death and human suffering? According to Paul's logic in I Corinthians 15, death and suffering are not bare facts that leave us without hope. Their significance is seen in the light of a more ultimate beliefe (B) in the resurrection of Christ: in adducing this belief (B) we illuminate the meaning of death (C) for men. Our most ultimate presupposition (A) about God and creation uncovers the meaning of history and the Christ (B), and this in turn illuminates (C) the stark facts we face.

The role of subjectivity in thought does not keep one from discussing truth, for subjectivity is not subjectivism, but its polar relation to objectivity keeps it in touch with objective considerations as well. The empirical ingredient (1) of meaning in statement (B) is somewhat open to historical investigation, and is not unevidenced. The interpretive ingredient (B2) is part of a larger theological scheme, whose systematic coherence attests its veracity as well. But neither the historical evidence for (B1) nor the coherence of (B2) is sufficient to conclude the case: history's case is incomplete, and no theological system exhausts the truth. Faith terminates not on evidence or argument, whatever role these play, but on God himself. The knowledge a man possesses is never self-sufficient.

But if objective considerations do not settle the matter, can the subjective help? Van Til emphasizes the witness of the Holy Spirit, whereby the knower as subject finds "for-himself" that which is true indeed.

This is doubtless the key but the logic is peculiar, for the move from "true-for-me" (3) to "true-for-all" (2) is formally invalid. The response, I think, is that a man is not brought to personal faith (3) independently of the other ingredients of meaning, as if faith is triggered in the subject in some mysterious isolation from objective history or thought. God's gift of faith itself stretches across the subject-object poles: faith comes by hearing the word of God and by learning about certain events and the meaning they disclose (B2) which the apostles and prophets proclaim (B3). The pieces fit coherently together with the right presuppositions (A) and we "get the point." Knowing the truth is in the final analysis a disclosure situation in which the light breaks, it all makes sense, and we confess how clearly and persuasively the truth communicates to us.

If this informal logic is natural to religious thought, then it is a mistake to impose on Christianity some other form of thought, or to require a case for Christianity that is either more or less complete than this suggests. This conclusion is one, it seems, which the contemporary philosophical dialogue should be ready to hear.

Response by C. Van Til

Dear Dr. Holmes:

You disarm me at the outset of your article by your extreme courtesy. I wish you had struck me in the solar plexus in the way Dr. Pinnock did! As it is I shall try to reply to your article *suaviter in modo*.

In order to have a broader perspective on your totality view of life I have read (a) your book *Christian Philosophy in the Twentieth Century*, 1969; (b) your article "Philosophy and Religious Belief" in *Pacific Philosophy Forum*, May 1967; (c) your article on "The Transcendental Method of Herman Dooyeweerd" in *The Gordon Review*, Winter, 1963–1964; (d) your article on "Ordinary Language Analysis and Theological Method" in *The Bulletin of the Evangelical Theological Society*, Summer, 1968; and (e) your article, "The Philosophical Methodology of Gordon Clark" in *The Philosophy of Gordon H. Clark*, 1968.

You are concerned to develop a Christian philosophy, and your special interest is that of methodology. Accordingly, you have dealt especially with the methodology of Dooyeweerd and Clark, two out-standing Christian philosophers in our time.

Of course, you fully realize that "each method reflects a philosophical viewpoint, a larger epistemology and even metaphysical presuppositions."[1]

Now as a Christian apologist I need the help of Christian philosophers. But because Christian philosophers, even Reformed Christian philosophers, differ pretty radically among one another I have to evaluate them myself. I do this by asking which of them is most faithful to the self-attesting Christ of Scripture.

I have written elsewhere of Clark and of Dooyeweerd. Allow me now to have a brief dialogue with you.

You want to draw me out in the "clarification of the constructive intent" of my thought. Well I have tried to bring out the constructive intent of my thought more clearly than before in some of my responses in this *Festschrift*.

I am not certain just how far you will walk with me on the path on which I have gone, but let us see. I am certain, of course, that you will join me in starting with the self-authenticating Christ of the Scriptures.

You agree that to start one's interpretation of human experience from the basis of the autonomy of man leads to futility. We want to make our every thought captive to the obedience of the Christ of Scripture. "In the beginning was the Word, and the Word was with God, and was God." As the *Word* Christ has pre-interpreted all things for us. Our interpretation of anything in any field is a receptively reconstructive reinterpretation of the original creatively-constructive interpretation of him who is truly God and truly man.

This faith-commitment to the self-authenticating Christ of Scripture unites us in a common task. This task consists of bringing the knowledge of the Christ to all men everywhere. All men are covenantally related to the triune God of Scripture. In the fall of Adam all men have become covenant-breakers. Our task is to plead with them to accept the offer of salvation through Christ, the second Adam. When we have dialogue with non-Christian philosophers we point out to them that their labor will be futile and they will abide under the wrath of the Lamb unless they presuppose the truth of what the Christ of Scripture has said about them and about all the universe of God. We are bound as Christian thinkers, whether theologians, philosophers, or scientists, to call men back to the recognition of the state of affairs as it really is, i.e., as we have learned about it from Christ.

Of course, no Christian thinker claims that he has fully and in-fallibly reinterpreted the words and works of Christ. Every true Christian realizes and confesses that he has taken only the first step on the pathway of sanctification and that even this first step has been taken by the help of the regenerating power of the Holy Spirit. Even so, the recognition of much failure and sin does not take away the fact that Christ has wrought a finished redemption in history and that those who accept this redemption do so by virtue of the life and light which the Spirit of Christ has given them.

But stop a minute! While we were walking along together with Tertullian, the later Augustine, and John Calvin, you waved at Justin Martyr and Clement of Alexandria to join us. "Come along, boys. We know that the 'idea of redemptive fulfillment lies at the root' of your 'maligned doctrine of logos.'[2] What you 'glimpsed' in your day 'was that Christianity teaches a unity of truth accessible to man in the image of God, and that Divine providence restricts the noetic effects of sin so that some truth is to be found even in pagan minds.'[3] When you hear some of our company talk about the 'total corruption of reasoning' do not let this frighten you. 'Common grace yields common ground for philosophical intercourse between Chris-tian and non-Christian thinkers.'[4] Again, if you hear some of us speak in particularist fashion do not be alarmed: 'If God is uniquely incarnate in Christ then grace and truth have dawned for all men everywhere and at every time. If Christ is God then the creative Logos has broken into human history and brought order to all life and thought.'[5]

"Still further, if we speak too absolutistically to suit your ears, we only mean to offer the Christ-event as a 'hypothesis about the mean-ing of life. . . .'[6] 'Theology and Scripture give explanations of a metaphysical sort and their truth value is to be judged accordingly— not by direct empirical confirmation or by inference from self-evident axioms, but by the adequacy and coherence with which they "fit" the facts.' "[7]

At this point I pull you aside for a "small conference." "Really, Arthur, I don't see how you can ask Justin and Clement to come with us. Do you really think they will join us in asking the Greeks to accept the truth of what we, following Paul, must ask them to accept? I would surely like to have them come with us to the work of challenging the Greeks to forsake their view of human autonomy, their Parmenidean principle of continuity, and their Heraclitean prin-ciple of discontinuity. But I thought it was their very purpose to make a synthesis of Christian truth and the truth of Greek philosophy by means of the Logos doctrine. Listen to Justin on this point. 'In saying that the Word, who is the first offspring of God, was born for us without sexual union, as Jesus Christ our Teacher, and that he was crucified and died and, after rising again, ascended into heaven, we introduce nothing new beyond (what you say of) those whom you call sons of Zeus.'[8]

"It was by means of his Logos doctrine, wasn't it, Arthur, that Justin effected a union between Greek philosophy and Christianity? The Logos doctrine of his time was, says B. B. Warfield, 'in its very essence cosmological in intention: its reason for existence was to render it possible to conceive the divine works of creation and government consistently with the divine transcendence: it was therefore bound up necessarily with the course of temporal development and involved in a process in God. The Logos was in principle God conceived in relation to things of time and space: God, therefore, not as absolute, but as relative. In its very essence, therefore, the Logos conception likewise involved the strongest subordinationism. Its very reason for existence was to provide a divine being who does the will of God in the regions of time and space, into which it were inconceivable that the Invisible God should be able to intrude in his own person. The Logos was therefore necessarily conceived as reduced divinity—divinity, so to speak, at the periphery rather than at the center of its conception. This means, further, that the Logos was inevitably conceived as a protrusion of God, or to speak more explicitly, under the category of emanation. The affinity of the Logos speculation with the emanation theories of the Gnostics is, therefore, close.'[9]

"Now I don't suppose for a moment, Arthur, that your Logos doctrine is the same as that of Justin. But can you dispute the historical correctness of Warfield's analysis? I wish you would give Justin a nudge and suggest that he leave us at the next exit. He is a true Christian but I don't think he got along with the other members of our Reformation crowd.

"As for Clement the idea of the Logos serves him as a connecting link between the highest and the lowest aspects of metaphysical gradationalism. For Clement God is the ineffable One, wholly unknown, and man is free in the sense that he determines his own ultimate destiny. According to Clement the Logos connects his unknown God and his unknown man.

"Wouldn't you agree, Arthur, that with their view of man as

virtually autonomous, with their Greek view of the principle of continuity and of the principle of discontinuity, Justin and Clement could not possibly join us in bringing the gospel of the creation, fall, and redemption through Christ to the Greeks?

"But it is up to you. Let's go on to the next town. You recognize those four famous adjectives on the old entrance gate, don't you? It must be Chalcedon. The church fathers knew that if salvation through Christ is to be brought to men then the divine and the human natures of Christ must not be intermingled. But that is just what the Eutychians wanted to do. As followers of the Greek philosophers they did not make the Creator-creature distinction basic in their thinking. They therefore thought that if there is to be salvation for man through Christ then he must synthesize the being of God and man. They too, like Justin and Clement, tried to combine loyalty to the self-attesting Christ of Scripture with loyalty to the principles of Greek philosophy. But the church thought otherwise. The Fathers of Chalcedon said there can be no salvation through the death and resurrection of Christ the God-man, no finished salvation, if God is himself subject to an intermingling process with man. Now, I know you believe what the church believes, Arthur. But I could not help but overhear a conversation you had with John Warwick Montgomery when we stopped for lunch at Nicea. In his conversation J.W. seemed to take for granted that you were with him in his desire to have something *objective* to offer the unbeliever by means of a God whose being changes with the passing of time. I heard him quite distinctly warn you against any form of cooperation in evangelism with Calvinists. Calvinists, he said, start their thinking with a philosophical maxim to the effect that eternity and time stand dualistically over against one another. How then can they do justice to the incarnation? How can they show to the unbeliever that God is really present in history? How can they be scientific and offer Christianity as the best hypothesis for the explanation of the facts of our experience?

"These Calvinists, he said, use a disjunctive approach. They hold to an 'unmitigated pessimism about the history of philosophy and an overwhelmingly negative attitude toward secular thought. They have difficulty justifying constructive dialogue with non-Christian thinkers.'

"I must admit that J.W. was really clever when he talked with you. He quoted from your writings to prove, as he thought, that you are basically in agreement with him against the Calvinists. He quoted from your article on Clark. He also quoted from your article on

Dooyeweerd as follows: 'Dooyeweerd may be correct in taking the sovereignty of God as the ground-motive of Christian thought. But God's supra-temporality does not follow from this—only his supra-finiteness, which is biblically expressed in other ways. The Scriptures preserve the sovereignty of the eternal not by his supra-temporality but by his work of creation, by his constant providence, by his historical revelation and incarnation, by his redemptive acts, by the presence of the church in society and by the eschatological hope. The Church Fathers used the Logos concept for much the same purpose.'[10]

"At this point I heard John Warwick remind you of your own suggestion as to the nature of eternity: 'Eternity, I suggest, is free not from temporal experience *per se* but from its limitations, not from duration but from finite duration, not from unified successive experiences but from finiteness of memory and anticipation, not from the pursuit of purpose but from frustrated purpose.'[11]

"I must admit, Arthur, that your conversation with J.W. worried me just a little. You do not really agree with him that God must be temporal in order to become incarnate and in order to be objectively present to man, do you? The great 'advantage' you would then have over against those who stand on the Chalcedon Creed is that you could join the non-Christian inductivist philosophers in their quest for a truth. I know that you do not want to follow the method of these inductivists any more than you want to follow the method of the deductivists. You want neither induction nor deduction. You want *adduction*. 'Categories are adduced, not empirically derived. Metaphysical positions are chosen, not proven.'[12] We need, you say, to do philosophy 'on the symphonic model, explicating a world-view by developing a categorical scheme and so adducing meaning to all realms of experience. . . .' " But here our play-dialogue must come to an end and I must put a serious question to you.

Is it really by a Logos doctrine similar to that of Justin and Clement and by your notion of the inherent temporality of God that you hope to be able to do justice to "a unique historical event like the Incarnation"?[13] I find it hard to believe my eyes? If this is indeed the case then you will have nothing better to present to men than an unfinished symphony. You will have no Christ who has given a final interpretation of his own finished work in Scripture. In a note on your "Dooyeweerd" article you say you are "indebted to Brightman, *Person and Reality*, to Wm. Temple, *Nature, Man and God*, and F. R. Tennant, *Philosophical Theology*." I am just a little afraid that indeed you are! You will, I think, eventually realize that if you follow Brightman you cannot stop short of his finite god, that if you follow Temple you cannot stop short of his rejection of "propositional revelation" and his acceptance of modern non-evangelical dimensionalism, and that if you follow Tennant you are lost in a flux philosophy.

But let us go on together. If you will seek to build a Christian philosophy that avoids the pitfalls into which we as Calvinists have fallen, by seeking to be more true to the self-authenticating Christ of Scripture than we have been, we shall, after much stammering, follow you. I am sure that this is precisely what you are aiming to do. Thank you for your gracious contribution.

Frederic R. Howe

XXV. KERYGMA AND APOLOGIA

I. Introduction

Careful students of the entire realm of Christian apologetics, regardless of perspective and background, have been challenged and strengthened by the writings of Cornelius Van Til. The present essay is an attempt to practice the same consistency of logic which Van Til follows, granting a starting-point on the ground of specific definition of terms. However, this essay will also raise a possible question concerning the meeting of the unbeliever and the believer in Van Til's interesting and analytical writing concerning the interviews between "Mr. White, Mr. Black, and Mr. Grey."[1]

II. Biblical Terms

Any constructive thinking about the realm of apologetics must sink taproots down to biblical bed rock. Three New Testament terms state the interrelationship of the work of defending the faith with the basic mission and message of Christianity. These terms are *kerygma, ecclesia,* and *apologia. Kerygma* is the word which means "proclamation, message, preaching," i.e., "the *substance* as distinct from the act. . . ."[2] This word comes close to the heart of the Christian task of witness. Its use in the New Testament points to the message of the gospel. In Titus 1:3, the *kerygma* is viewed primarily as to its source. The message here is seen as originating with God himself, who gives this as a sacred trust to his proclaimers, or heralds. The method used in setting forth the *kerygma* is found in I Corinthians 2:4, where the enablement of the Holy Spirit is stressed. The content of this proclamation is centered in the person of Jesus Christ, according to the declaration of I Corinthians 15:1-18. The use of the word *kerygma* in verse 14 is closely linked to the content of the gospel. The major purpose for this proclamation is found in the use which a sovereign God makes of the *kerygma*. It is used as a tool by which God saves those who believe, both Jews and Gentiles (I Cor. 1:21; Acts 10:44-48). Of course, the dynamic function of the truth of God's massive work of election comes into focus here as well.

As a result of the preaching of the *kerygma,* the *ecclesia* came into being. This *ecclesia,* or *church,* in the New Testament sense, is the Christian community, the resultant factor when a people is called together around a central core of truth and a central person, the Lord Jesus Christ. When early attacks came against the teaching and preaching of this group and its leaders, defense was made. It is vital to notice that defense, or *apologia,* was made in absolute dependence upon God, even as the preaching was. The word *apologia* simply means *defense.* Its technical usage was limited to a speech of defense, or reply to some specific charge, and it appears in Acts 22:1 in this sense.[3] The elements involved in this activity are all seen in this case. Accusation had been levelled against the apostle, and careful answer, defense, or *apologia* needed to be made. The attitude in giving this defense is certainly one of dignity, yet not condescension. The work of making defense is also pinpointed in Acts 26:1, where the English phrase "made his defense" translates the Greek verb *apologeomai.* The action in this case includes a deliberate "sorting" out and "classifying" of the charges brought against Paul, and a steadfast answer to them. The words, "I cheerfully make my defense," in Acts 24:10 add the clear implication concerning Paul's attitude in giving these various speeches answering charges brought against him and his teaching. No drudgery or weary recitation of cold facts is implied in this verse. The apostle gave meaningful and coherent response. He manifested in all these actions a calm and deliberate dependence upon God to control the circumstances surrounding the defense. The whole point here is that he did speak, he did give a statement, an *apologia.* In so doing, he laid down an example for future generations of believers to make defense in like manner to charges brought against the teachings of the entire biblical system.

In summary, the close relationship of *apologia* as a biblical key word to *kerygma* and *ecclesia* may be seen in this manner:

The Apostolic PREACHING	The Christian COMMUNITY	The Christian DEFENSE
Kerygma	*Ecclesia*	*Apologia*
The preaching or SUMMONS of the herald	Resulted in a PEOPLE SUMMONED or called in congregation	This PEOPLE received attacks against their teaching, and gave DEFENSE.

III.   The Distinction Between Witness and Defense

A clear distinction between biblical *witness* and biblical *defense* must be made and maintained. While the two activities can be seen at times in the New Testament in close proximity, nevertheless they appear to be essentially different.

Let us consider first the matter of bearing or giving witness. All Christians generally are called upon to bear effective witness to the lordship of Jesus Christ and his redemptive grace. The content of this witness ultimately centers in the *kerygma*, and witness is given to the purpose of Jesus Christ as reflected in the truths of the *kerygma*. The sphere of this biblical witness is universal, according to Acts 1:8. The activity of witnessing through life and word is to function any place and any time. The basic reason for this activity is found in obedience to Christ himself, who set forth principles of making disciples in Matthew 28:18-20. Christians find that the method or framework of giving this witness is strictly to be found in the strength of the risen Christ. The real heart of witness is this: the confrontation of an individual with the central issue of the person and work of Jesus Christ. When this biblical activity is functioning at this level of Spirit-directed, Christ-centered witness, definite results can be expected. These results are certain because they are given by God. Acts 16:14 reflects upon the results of a biblical witness with these words: "And a certain woman named Lydia, a seller of purple, of the city of Thyatira, one that worshipped God, heard us: whose heart the Lord opened to give heed unto the things which were spoken by Paul." This was a consistent biblical witness, and the sovereign God was pleased to draw to himself this one who heard the witness.

We must now contrast this with the work of biblical apology or defense. Any given individual Christian who comes under specific attack is expected to give defense (I Pet. 3:15). This will not be as widespread as the activity implied in witnessing. Furthermore, the content of this defense centers finally in the whole biblical system, teaching, or *didache*. The gospel is an integral part of this system, but defense activity might well be found going on with reference to parts of the system that might seem quite remote from the gospel. Biblical apology is definitely limited to response to stated attacks or objections. Too many Christians have overlooked this very simple contrast. Witnessing is *not* argumentative in its basic thrust. We have *not* given full biblical witness until all the facts of the gospel are clearly set forth. When true witnessing is done, there is a real confrontation set up, whereby Jesus Christ confronts the individual who is receiving the witness. By direct contrast, when someone who has already heard this witness, or when someone who is working within an entirely different world-view, brings reasoned objection or attack to the system of truth upon which the gospel is built, then an entirely different operation is set in motion. Defense here functions primarily as clarification of the issues and confirmation of the truth. A wider sphere of issues is dealt with here than those surrounding the person and work of Jesus Christ. To be sure, ultimately all of these issues merge into the biblical theistic system.

Another contrast is observed when we consider the results that we expect when we witness, and when we defend, on the other hand, the Christian position. The result of a clear defense will be perhaps a correction of some possible misunderstanding on the part of the objector. This can be called clarification. Also, there will be a vindication of the truth in this matter of giving defense. But as far as any lasting result which would match that found in the realm of giving a biblical witness, Scripture apparently is silent. The Scriptures declare that the Holy Spirit bears witness primarily to the person of Jesus Christ (John 16:8-15). The Holy Spirit will function in a different manner when true biblical apology is given. He will give wisdom and boldness in the words used in the defense, and he will vindicate the truth. He might be pleased, possibly, to use a situation wherein defense is given to arouse the seeker to pursue further the study of the *kerygma* and the claims of Christ. Again, it must be seen that the Holy Spirit bears witness to Christ, along a specific pattern of biblical confrontation. He does *not* bear witness to our defensive construction or argumentation. There could be no clearer illustration of this that the words of Acts 5:29-33. The apostolic *kerygma* had been given earlier by Peter. It was clearly known. Further apostolic *defense* is then given to the objectors, the officials of Judaism at that time. Of course, in this case, the witness and defense were closely intertwined. In response to the defense, instead of willing change and acquiescence, the religious leaders were "cut to the heart, and were minded to slay them" (Acts 4:33). The point obviously made is that the Holy Spirit assures different kinds of results for different kinds of activity. If the sheer brilliance of logical argumentation had been sufficient, something must have gone wrong somewhere with this violent response to the defense offered.

Christians will do well to ponder the distinction between witness and defense. It can be summarized in this manner:

	BIBLICAL WITNESS	BIBLICAL APOLOGY
Source	ALL Christians	ANY GIVEN CHRISTIAN, ONLY WHEN specific objection is raised
Content	Primarily the gospel (*kerygma*)	Primarily, the WHOLE BIBLICAL TRINITARIAN SYSTEM, INCLUDING THE GOSPEL AND THE TEACHING (*didache*)
Sphere	Universal: Acts 1:8; any place and any time	Limited: only in the sphere of answer to attack (I Pet. 3:15)
Reason	Obedience to the command of Christ (Matthew 28:18ff.)	For the defense of the system, by following the Scriptures (I Pet. 3:15)
Method	In the strength of the risen Christ	In the strength of the risen Christ
Operation	CONFRONTATION	CLARIFICATION
Expected Results	Believing response, in keeping with the Spirit's work (Acts 16:14; John 16:8-15)	Vindication; possible correction of some misunderstanding

IV. An Illustration of Defense

When objection is levelled at concepts and central teachings within Scripture, the believer then offers apology or defense, based upon apologetics, or a study of methods and issues. For a specific example, Scripture indicates that Jesus was born of the Virgin Mary. Critical scholarship denies this facet of the biblical trinitarian system. The Christian theologian, James Gresham Machen, upon studying the objections brought to this part of the system, offered defense in the book, *The Virgin Birth of Christ*. Here he clarified the biblical view, and through careful examination of the charges of unbelief demonstrated the integrity of the system at this point. This activity brought a clarification of the issues. One of the by-products of such a defensive study as this can be the strengthening of the believer. What about those who bring the objections? As far as we can tell, many scholars who brought objection to this particular doctrine were at least given a logical answer in this work by Machen. The limits of apology are reached when such an answer is given. The conversion of the objector to theological orthodoxy is *not* included within the limits of the activity of defense. As far as is known, no scholar who brought reasoned objection to the truth of the virgin birth of Jesus was won to a saving knowledge of Christ in direct confrontation with the intensive study of the arguments of Machen's book. This is the whole point of the distinction made here. This is *not* the expected result of *defense*. It might be possible that a sovereign God would be pleased to lead a seeker from the ground of the activity of defense to the ground of the activity of witness. We would not limit our sovereign God at this point!

The right understanding of this simple contrast between witness and defense could save much agony of soul on the part of the Christian who gives witness and who might be called upon to give defense also. Some well-meaning Christians go forth to do battle with the host of false world views arrayed against Christian trinitarianism, intent upon securing the result of the conversion of these objectors to Christian truth. When by argumentation, the holder of the false world view is not won, and even worse, does not seem at all impressed by the argumentation, the Christian begins to think that the case is lost. He possibly becomes very haughty toward the one who objects, or else very self-defensive, and inwardly disturbed. The ringing words of the apostle Paul, when he triumphantly declared, "I cheerfully give my defense," will help stabilize the eager defender of the faith.

V. Analysis of Van Til's Concept of Witnessing

With the previous concepts in mind, it is now necessary to study the interesting analysis which Van Til presents concerning the meeting of the believer and the unbeliever. His readers remember this effective and helpful analogy in chapter ten of the latest edition of *The Defense of the Faith*, sections III through VI. In the illustration or story used to present varying positions, Van Til likens the holder of the Reformed faith to a person known as Mr. White. He likens the evangelical to Mr. Grey, and the non-Christian to Mr. Black. He strives here for a consistent *witness*. Naturally, the reader is aware of the limitations of such a method. Van Til certainly is using this within proper bounds, and wants to set the pace for consistency.

It appears that even in his discussion there is some need to press even further the biblical distinction between witness and defense. Specifically, it would appear that even "Mr. White" is not consistent with the biblical terms and issues involved in *witness*, on the one hand, and *defense* on the other. This possible realm of inconsistency in the argument of Van Til can be seen when these quotations are read carefully (page citations follow each quotation):

. . . Christians holding to a Reformed faith should also hold to *a specifically Reformed method* when they are engaged in the defense of the faith (233).

His method of defending his faith had forced him to admit that Mr. Black was basically right (236).

It must always be remembered that the first requirement for effective witnessing is that the position to which witness is given be intelligible (237).

In the second place, Mr. White now saw clearly that a false type of reasoning for the truth of God's existence and for the truth of Christianity involves a false kind of witnessing for the existence of God and for the truth of Christianity (256).

From now on Mr. White decided that, much as he enjoyed the company of Mr. Grey and much as he trusted his evident sincerity and basic devotion to the truth of God, yet he must go his own way in apologetics as he had, since the Reformation, gone his own way in theology (257).

Certainly all readers grant to Van Til the right to construct this highly entertaining and readable analysis. However, it would appear that much of the ground of the discussion involves essential elements *within* trinitarianism, such as *doctrines*. For example, the discussion hinges often on doctrines such as the substitutionary atonement, or a consideration of the arguments for the existence of God. Much of what Van Til writes here is excellent, and reveals the inconsistency of "Mr. Grey." However, the question of just what kind of activity Mr. White is engaged in comes into focus. If Mr. White is giving *defense*, then Mr. Black presumably already should have been given a clear and totally biblical statement of the *kerygma*. He then has brought objections to the system upon which the *kerygma* is built. Then, Mr. White should bring Spirit-directed defense. But, judging from the way in which the two areas are dealt with here, Van Til does not make this distinction. At times it appears that Mr. White is strictly *witnessing* along the lines of the *kerygma*. At other times it appears that Mr. White is strictly *defending*, along the lines of the *didache*. To be sure, no one would press down upon this distinction to the point of ridiculous compartmentalization. Nonetheless, there would appear to be some lack of consistent application of the separate and distinct role of *defense* in keeping with the New Testament terms in Van Til's otherwise incisive appeal for consistency.

This apparent lack of consistent distinction between witness and defense is seen in the last quotation cited above. The activity of

Mr. White and Mr. Grey is summarized by the use of the term "apologetics." Yet this same activity is viewed by Van Til, according to the other citations, as "witnessing." It seems possible that there could be a further clarification and strengthening of Van Til's system right at this point if the distinction between these two realms is made.

The present writer is keenly aware of the need for balance, and grants much of the validity of Van Til's reasoned attack against the inconsistency of "Mr. Grey." It is in the spirit of concerned inquiry at this point that the question is raised concerning a possible confusion of the role of witnessing and the role of defending in Van Til's system. The ultimate question will certainly be this: is the system of defense biblical? If so, then the system of witness also must be biblical, and the role of each of these vital operations will be seen more clearly.

Response by C. Van Til

Dear Dr. Howe:

You are certainly right in saying that I did not, in the discussion among Mr. White, Mr. Grey, and Mr. Black, make any sharp distinction between witnessing to and defending the Christian faith. I am not convinced by the evidence from Scripture which you cite that any sharp distinction between them is required or even justified. My defense of the truth of Christianity is, as I think of it, always, at the same time, a witness to Christ as the Way, the Truth, and the Life. We do not really witness to Christ adequately unless we set forth the significance of his person and work *for all men and for the whole of their culture.* But if we witness to him thus then men are bound to respond to him either in belief or disbelief. If they respond in disbelief they will do so by setting forth as truth some "system of reality" that is based on the presupposition of man as autonomous. I must then plead with them to accept Christ as their Savior from the sin of autonomy, and therewith, at the same time, to discover that they have been given, in Christ, the only foundation for intelligent predication.

—C.V.T.

NOTES AND REFERENCES

The following is a key used throughout the notes of this volume to the works of Cornelius Van Til. Fuller bibliographical data to these works will be found in the "Writings of Cornelus Van Til" found at the end of this book. The key is in alphabetical order.

A, *Apologetics*
CB, *Christianity and Barthianism*
CC, *Christianity in Conflict*
CTEv, *Christian Theistic Evidences*
CFC, *The Case for Calvinism*
CG, *Common Grace*
CI, *Christianity and Idealism*
CJ, *Christ and the Jews*
CTK, *A Christian Theory of Knowledge*
C1967, *The Confession of 1967: Its Theological Background and Ecumenical Significance*
DF, *The Defense of the Faith*
HKBBO, "Has Karl Barth Become Orthodox"
IST, *Introduction to Systematic Theology*
MA, *Metaphysics of Apologetics*
NE, *The New Evangelicalism*
NM, *The New Modernism*
PDS, *The Protestant Doctrine of Scripture*
PR, *Psychology of Religion*
SCE, *A Survey of Christian Epistemology*
SG, *The Sovereignty of Grace*
TJD, *The Theology of James Daane*

PART ONE

MY CREDO

1. A chapter by this title is found in G. C. Berkhouwer's *Het Probleem der Schriftkritiek* (Kampen: J. H. Kok, 1938).
2. G. C. Berkouwer, *op. cit.*, p. 33.
3. B. B. Warfield, *Studies in Tertullian and Augustine* (New York: Oxford, 1930), p. 107.
4. *Early Latin Theology*, trans. and ed. by S. L. Greenslade, "The Library of Christian Classics," Vol. V, gen. eds., J. Baillie, J. T. McNeill, H. P. Van Dusen (Philadelphia: Westminster Press, 1956), p. 36. Tertullian, *Prescription Against Heretics*, VII.
5. *Ibid.*, p. 40.

6. *Ibid.*, p. 41.
7. *Ibid.*, p. 43.
8. B. B. Warfield, *op. cit.*, pp. 19-20.
9. B. B. Warfield, *Calvin and Augustine*, ed. Samuel G. Craig (Philadelphia: Presbyterian and Reformed Publishing Co., 1956), pp. 190-191.
10. *Ibid.*, p. 195.
11. *Ibid.*, p. 198.
12. *Ibid.*, p. 251.
13. Stuart Cornelius Hackett, *The Resurrection of Theism* (Chicago: Moody Press, 1957), pp. 174-175.

PART TWO

LETTERS FROM THREE CONTINENTS

I. *Hendrik G. Stoker*

1. I do not intend to make references to publications in this personal letter. My exposition of your theory is restricted to your generally known views. A list of your publications will be published in the *Festschrift* and of my publications I will mention but a few. [A complete list of my publications is given in my *Oorsprongen Rigting*, II (Kaapstad: Tafelberg Uitgewers), henceforth *O en R*, of which I will send you a copy as soon as it appears].

2. I prefer Berkouwer's expression "man created *as* the image of God" to the common usage "man created *in* the image of God."

3. Compare Heidegger's: "Was z. B. Schwimmen heiszt, lernen wir nie durch eine Abhandlung über das Schwimmen. Was Schwimmen heiszt, sagt uns der Sprung in den Strom."

4. For instance, the fear expressed by a frightened person is perceived as such. Even a small child perceives the fear of his frightened mother. For instance, emotions shine through their bodily expressions. Unfortunately I cannot elaborate this point here.

5. When, for instance, trying to move a heavy body, I experience *its* resistance. Cf. my article in *Philosophia Reformata*, "Iets oor kousaliteit en kousaliteitskennis," (II/2 and III/I), henceforth *Phil. Ref.*

6. Sometimes called "sensus divinitatis," "fides qua," "pisteutic function," "aptitude, propensity, ability, capability to beware of God's revelation of himself" and so forth.

7. Theories that somehow or other start with sensations, contending that thought gives meaning to and brings order into sensation and that knowledge is the result of the work of thought, view the problem of knowledge upside down. Man *knowingly* perceives "things" as they are ordered. Even a homing bee perceives its hive in the perspective of its environment.

8. Religion in a specific sense (the worship of God in church, at family devotions or in private) should be distinguished from religion in a comprehensive sense (as the service of God in everything man does).

9. The revelation of God in his Word *as well as* in nature is *supernatural* in

the sense that it is God that reveals himself; *both* are at the same time "*natural*" in the sense that they are *pro forma humana*, God's Word-revelation being heard and handed down in the Holy Writ and his revelation in creation (or "nature") being "seen."

10. Faith comes first. Doubt plays a subordinate role. Doubt presupposes a contact with the knowable, but arises on account of lack of meeting it. (Cf. my *Beginsels en Metodes in die Wetenskap*, tweede druk, Johannesburg: Boekhandel De Jong, 1969, henceforth *B en M*.)

11. Accordingly a geologist, for instance, knowingly *perceives* more in ore than a non-geologist does.

12. Cf. note 6. The absolutization of, for instance, matter by a materialist is possible only on account of his religious "nature" (i.e., of essentially having "religious faith" or a "sense of deity") and of God's revelation in creation ("nature").

13. Cf. *B en M*.

14. The term "things" is taken in a wide sense; it includes, for instance, events and processes as well.

15. Compare, for instance, the knowledge that a farmer, an economist, a geologist, an artist, a surveyor, a prospector, and so forth, have of the same landscape.

16. "Paradox" is a term that belongs to rationalism and irrationalism. Christians should recognize only "hyperdoxes." A hyperdox is truth that surpasses human understanding (for instance, that of the trinity of God or of the two "natures" of Christ or of the connection of God's sovereign will and human responsibility).

17. Many theories (for instance, idealism, psychologism, radical behaviorism, and materialism) reduce the one to the other.

18. Stated in general terms: why should consciousness or awareness of something not be understood as a revelation of this something to man? Current theories stress the *intentional* "nature" of consciousness; but is the intentional "nature" of consciousness primarily not due to that of which man is conscious, in other words, to what is revealed to man by being conscious?

19. For the different types of meanings of "truth" see my *B en M*.

20. Cf. my *B en M*; my article, "Die kosmiese dimensie van gabeurtewisse," in *Phil. Ref.*, 1964; and *O en R*, II.

21. For instance, an evolutionist *perceives* man as a mere animal.

22. "Founding" I call the verification by direct appeal to created reality or to God's Word-revelation. "Proving" I take to be indirect verification, e.g., by logical conclusions, verification of hypotheses, and so forth. Cf. my *B en M* and *O en R*, II.

23. Cf. my *B en M*; and my "Deontology of Scientific Method," *Philosophy and Christianity*, Philosophical Essays dedicated to Professor Dr. Herman Dooyeweerd (Kampen: J. H. Kok, 1965); henceforth *DSM*.

24. This description of sciences includes basic as well as applied sciences.

25. They all fulfil the requirements of scientific enterprise. For instance, the theological methods of exegesis and hermeneutics and the philosophical transcendental, phenomenological, and existential-analytic methods are as scientific as the experimental methods of empirical science. Of course, none of these methods can be applied without the respective presupposi-

tions (Cf. *B en M, DSM*); and a Christian pursuit of science founds the use of all these methods on other presuppositions than a non-Christian pursuit does. To narrow science, however, to mere empirical or even to mere natural science, as currently is done, is, according to my opinion, radically unwarranted and presupposes a thoroughly secularistic view of science.

26. This expression is not meant in a scholastic sense. In this connection I may mention that, according to my opinion, theology should not be "degraded" to a mere particular science (*vakwetenschap*), as the *Wijsbegeerte der Wetsidee* does. Truths concerning, for instance, our triune God certainly do not form a "part" or an "aspect" of our created universe, although they are revealed in the Scriptures.

27. Cf. my *B en M, DSM.*

28. Personally I (as Vollenhoven and Dooyeweerd also do) restrict the meaning of the term "metaphysics" to that of "speculative philosophy." In this sense Calvinist philosophy has no "metaphysics."

29. Cf. my *B en M*; *O en R*, II; my article, "Die eenheid van die wetenschap," in *Phil. Ref.*, 1968; and my article "Die Eenheid van die Wetenskap," *Referate van die Suid-Afrikaanse Akademie vir Wetenskap en Kuns*; Jaarvergadering 1967; henceforth *EW*.

30. See note 29.

31. See note 14.

32. Cf. *Phil Ref*, 1968; *EW*; and *O en R*, II.

33. See note 29.

34. See note 6.

35. The same holds *mutatis mutandis* good for terms used by other Calvinists. In my early writings I called a material thing, a plant, an animal, and a human being "substances." On account of the multivocality of and the unbiblical meanings generally attached to this term, my writings have been greatly misunderstood. Dooyeweerd suggested that I avoid this term. His terms *dingeenheid* and *systase* I considered inappropriate to convey my meaning. To avoid misunderstanding I have substituted a neologism, namely "idiostance," for "substance" in my recent publications (cf. *Phil Ref.*, 1964, and *O en R*, II).

36. *Mutatis mutandis* this is the case with theories of other Calvinists as well. I mention only Dooyeweerd's profound knowledge of Neo-Kantianism (and his preference for a transcendental critique of human thought) and of humanism (and his Christo-centrically founded anthropocentric view of cosmic reality). Personally I am of the opinion that a phanerotic investigation of human thought should precede a transcendental analysis thereof cf. *Phil. Ref.*, 1964, and *O en R*, I and II), and that our created universe has in itself no center, but has its center trans-cosmically in God, of and through and to Whom all things are; furthermore, that Christ is king and man king of our universe but do not constitute a centre thereof.

37. In this connection also may be mentioned your penetrating criticism of Roman Catholicism, Arminianism, Evangelism, and less consistent Calvinism.

38. See note 36.

39. Personally I prefer to avoid the term "phenomenal world."

40. Let us take Freud's view of man as an example. He undoubtedly has discovered significant truths concerning repressions, sub- and unconscious activities, manfestations, and so forth. But what he has seen correctly is veiled by his positivistic, mechanistic, deterministic, and largely sexualistic presuppositions.

41. But we may not forget that Christians also are sinners in our dispensation and often look at facts of created reality (and, in the cases concerned, understand God's Word-revelation) in a veiled fashion, as the differences between Christians clearly testify.

42. Accordingly I prefer V. Hepp's distinction of *theo-centric* and *cosmocentric philosophy* to that of *transcendence-* and *immanence-philosophy* of the *Wijsbegeerte der Wetsidee* (Vollenhoven and Dooyeweerd).

43. A Christian philosophic and a particular scientific theory of knowledge (according to the *P-C* approach) are called to give a systematic account of the fundamental truths of God's Word-revelation that cast their light on our created universe, in other words, to explicitly account for the presuppositions according to which they pursue science. (Cf. *O en R*, II and my article, "Christelikewetenskape—'n noodwendigheid," in *Die Atoomeeu in U Lig* (a centenary publication of the Potchefstroom University for Christian Higher Education, 1969.) We cannot expound but can only mention a number of them here; they are, among others,

 a.i. of, through, and to God all things are;

 a.ii. the necessity of pre-scientific religious faith;

 a.iii. the necessity of the light that God's Word-revelation casts upon the respective fields of scientific research;

 b. the creaturely, derivative, and self-insufficient nature of the created universe (including man);

 c.i. the radical diversity of created reality, having its origin in God's creative will;

 c.ii. the coherence of this radical diversity; a coherence that presupposes and does not level this diversity;

 d. the order of law (including the order of norms) that has its origin in God's legislative will and to which all created reality is subject;

 e. the uniqueness of man, belonging to our universe, created as the image of God, appointed as *mandator Dei* of created reality; entrusted with a divine calling that he has to fulfil to the honor and glory of God; thus being called to realize his freedom in obedience to the love, will, and law of God.

 f.i. the derivative, analogical, non-comprehensive (creaturely limited) nature of human knowledge;

 f.ii. its truth being its answering to the knowable;

 g.i. the abnormality of the universe (including man) on account of the fall of man and the evil in the universe;

 g.ii. common and special grace; the redemptive and re-creative significance of the atonement of Jesus Christ;

 h. the providential guidance of God of all things.

These (and other) presuppositions are of fundamental significance not only for a constructive Christian pursuit of science, but also for its criticism of the fundamental presupposition of non-Christian science ("science" to be taken in a wide sense). The majority of these presuppositions you have elaborated from your *A-P* (or *P-A*) approach.

44. Cf. *B en M*, and *DSM*.

45. On the one hand because of the dualities mentioned in sections G.5.1 and because of the analogous nature of man's knowledge—as we understand it—it is intelligible that the *P-A* (or *A-P*) and the *P-C* approaches differ (i.e., that they intersect one another at right angles). On the other hand, whereas, for instance, absolute idealism does not accept the dualities mentioned and therefore neither the analogous nature of human knowledge, the relevant distinction between the approaches mentioned falls away.

46. See note 32.

47. Cf. *B en M*, and *DSM*.

48. This is clear if we compare your theory of knowledge with, for instance, that of Dooyeweerd or of what I have ventured to give in the first sections of this letter. To this I should add that not only must philosophic and particular scientific theories of knowledge presuppose the truths of your theory of knowledge, but that the latter should also take into account the results of the former. This is the case because, on the one hand, "theory of knowledge" is an interscience and should be pursued as a unity, and on the other hand, because as soon as you specify what you exactly mean by man's knowledge, thought, and perception as well as by method and by science as such, you are confronted by the problems of philosophy-proper and particular science-proper theories of knowledge.

II. *Herman Dooyeweerd*

1. This is part 3, ch. 9 of Vol. II of *CC*.

2. *Ibid.*, p. 47.

3. Herman Dooyeweerd, *A New Critique of Theoretical Thought*, Vol. I (Philadelphia: Presbyterian and Reformed Publishing Co., 1953), pp. 37-38.

4. *CC*/II:3.9, p. 51.

5. *Ibid.*, p. 54.

6. I refer, for instance, to the discovery of the principle of logical economy in theoretical thought, which, by the positivistic thinkers Mach and Avenarius, was reduced to what they called the fundamental bio-physical law of labor saving.

7. *CC*/II:3.9, p. 55.

8. *Ibid.*, pp. 55-56.

9. In *DF*, 1st ed., p. 235, you speak of the "theory of reality" which the Bible contains, and of the definite philosophy of history involved in the biblical conception of eternity (p. 26).

10. *CC*/II:3.9, pp. 56-57.

11. You do not explain how it might be possible to connect my view of the supra-rational character of the central religious ground-motive of the Word-revelation with Kant's doctrine concerning the primacy of practical reason and with his metaphysical ethical idea of the *homo noumenon*. I fear that you have come to this misconception in consequence of the scholastic framework of your Reformed theological thought. You hold to

a Christian theoretical metaphysics which, according to you, is to be derived from the Bible. This metaphysics contains a "two layer theory of being," i.e., first a concept of the triune God in his aseity, and second a concept of created being. Man's creation in the image of God involves, you say, of necessity, a true metaphysical knowledge of God. Sin and redemption are not of a metaphysical but of an ethical character. In consequence you distinguish the merely theoretical knowledge of God from the ethical which combines this rational knowledge with loving. Only the latter is true in a rational ethical sense. In this way the central religious sphere of human existence and knowledge is reduced to the rational ethical aspect of human behavior, which according to both scholasticism and Kantian criticism is controlled by practical reason. Within this framework of thought, attribution of the central place to the *religious* knowledge of God, not conceived of as a theoretical metaphysics, must seem to be tantamount to accepting the primacy of practical reason.

12. In *DF*, 1st ed., p. 58, you emphatically accept this alternative. Christianity is opposed here to "absolute irrationalism" as an "absolute rationalism." The only restriction is that our rational knowledge of God and the universe is "not comprehensive," such as God's self-knowledge and knowledge of the universe. I do not overlook that by "absolute rationalism" you understand the view that every fact has been pre-determined and pre-interpreted by God according to his rational providential plan, so that no single fact comes about by chance. Nor do I overlook that in another context you seek the origin of both rationalism and irrationalism, viewed in their historical forms, in the apostate belief in the autonomy of man over against God. But why do you speak then of the biblical Christian view as an absolute rationalism? Because you identify God's providential plan with absolute rationality. But "absolute rationality" is an obvious metaphysical absolutization, just like Occam's *potentia Dei absoluta*. I shall return to this point in the text.

13. If this identification were correct, an English translation of Dutch conceptual terms would be impossible, since there would be no identity of concepts for lack of identical words.

14. In your *DF*, 1st ed., p. 93, you seem to join in with Hodge, who identifies the heart in its pregnant biblical sense with "that which thinks, feels, wills and acts," i.e., with "the soul, the self." The soul is apparently conceived here in the traditional metaphysical sense as an immaterial substance embracing the feelings, the intellect, and the will. But this traditional view of the human soul is quite different from the radical biblical revelation of the human "heart" as the religious center of the integral whole of man's existence.

15. The explanatory theological addition of the words *ex nihilo* to the word *creatio*, which, since Augustine, has become usual in theological dogmatics, is naturally not to be considered as a conceptual definition. Augustine availed himself of this addition to prevent confusion with the Platonic idea of the divine *demiourgos* and with the neo-Platonic emanation doctrine. For that purpose it has been useful in a degree. But it is well known that the words *ex nihilo* have turned out to be not entirely harmless in Augustine's theological exposition of the doctrine of creation, since they foster

the idea that nothingness would be a second origin of creaturely being bringing about a metaphysical defect in the latter.

16. Calvin, *Institutes*, I:5.9, joined with I:10.2.
17. *DF.*, 1st ed., p. 62.
18. *Ibid.*, p. 26.
19. *Ibid.*, p. 309.
20. *Ibid.*, p. 227.
21. *Ibid.*, p. 309.
22. *Ibid.*, p. 134.
23. *Ibid.*, p. 38.

Response by C. Van Til

1. Herman Dooyeweerd, *A New Critique of Theoretical Thought*, Vol. I (Philadelphia: Presbyterian and Reformed Publishing Co., 1953), p. 34; hereafter *New Critique*.
2. *Ibid.*, p. 37.
3. *Ibid.*, p. 38.
4. *Ibid.*, p. 3.
5. *Ibid.*, p. 34.
6. *Ibid.*
7. *Ibid.*, p. 35.
8. *Ibid.*, pp. 37-38.
9. *Philosophia Reformata*, VI (1941), pp. 1-20; hereafter "Trans. Critiek."
10. *Ibid.*, XXIII (1958), pp. 1-22; 49-84.
11. *Ibid.*, XIII (1948), pp. 26-31; 49-58; hereafter "Thom. Phil."
12. Grand Rapids: Eerdmans (1948); hereafter *Problems*.
13. Philadelphia: Presbyterian and Reformed Publishing Co. (1960); hereafter *Twilight*.
14. *New Critique*, p. 37.
15. *Problems*, p. vii.
16. "Trans. Critiek," p. 5.
17. *Ibid.*, p. 18.
18. *Ibid.*, p. 19.
19. H. Dooyeweerd, "De Vier Religieuze Grondthema's in den Ontwikkelingsgang van het Wijsgeerig Denken van het Avondland," *Philosophia Reformata*, VI (1941), p. 172.
20. "Thom. Phil.," p. 26.
21. *Ibid.*, p. 27.
22. *Ibid.*, p. 29.
23. *Ibid.*, p. 30.
24. *New Critique*, p. 34.
25. *Ibid.*
26. *Twilight*, p. 2.
27. *New Critique*, p. 38.
28. *Problems*, p. 29.
29. *Ibid.*, p. 31.
30. "Trans. Critiek," p. 8.
31. *New Critique*, p. 40.
32. *Twilight*, p. 12.
33. *New Critique*, p. 28.
34. *Ibid.*, p. 45.
35. *Ibid.*, p. 18.
36. *Ibid.*, p. 16.
37. *Ibid.*, p. 22.
38. *Ibid.*, p. 32.
39. *Problems*, p. 54.
40. *Twilight*, pp. 27-28.
41. *Ibid.*, p. 29.
42. *Ibid.*, p. 30.
43. *Ibid.*, p. 32.
44. *Ibid.*, pp. 32-33.
45. *Ibid.*, p. 52.
46. *Ibid.*
47. *Ibid.*, pp. 52-53.
48. *Ibid.*, p. 53.
49. *New Critique*, p. 57.
50. *Ibid.*, pp. 34-35.
51. *Twilight*, p. 53.
52. *Ibid.*, p. 54.
53. *Ibid.*
54. *New Critique*, p. 34.
55. "Trans. Critiek," p. 15.
56. *New Critique*, p. 32.

57. Van Til, *DF*, 1st ed., p. 135. 59. Van Til, *SCE*, p. 1.
58. *Ibid.*, pp. 310-312.

PART THREE

ESSAYS IN THEOLOGY AND THEOLOGICAL METHOD

III. *Philip Edgcumbe Hughes*

1. It is for me a great pleasure to honor Cornelius Van Til with this essay, both as an esteemed friend and also as a steadfast defender of the historic faith. The firmness of his dedication coupled with the profundity of his thought and the humility of his temperament has enabled him to set an example, particularly in the area of apologetics, by which all who are willing to learn cannot fail to benefit.

IV. *J. I. Packer*

1. Some paragraphs in this essay were first printed in *The Churchman* (Spring, 1967), p. 7ff., and are reproduced here by permission.
2. To see Karl Barth's arbitrariness highlighted from various angles, cf. Van Til's *NM* and *CB*; also Colin Brown, *Karl Barth and the Christian Message* (London: Tyndale Press, 1967).
3. Not that there are in fact any substantial problems of harmonizing Scripture for which a plausible solution cannot be, and has not been, suggested. See, e.g., S. Custer, *Does Inspiration Demand Inerrancy?* (Nutley, N. J.: Craig Press, 1968), chapters VIII and IX; T. E. Engelder, *Scripture Cannot Be Broken* (St. Louis: Concordia Publishing House, 1944); J. W. Haley, *Alleged Discrepancies in the Bible* (Andover: Warren F. Draper, 1874).

V. *Jack B. Rogers*

1. Van Til, *DF*, 1st ed., pp. 357-358.
2. *Ibid.*, 3rd ed., pp. 3-4.
3. *Ibid.*, p. 4.
4. *Ibid.*, 1st ed., p. 357.
5. *Ibid.*, 3rd ed., pp. 264-265.
6. *Ibid.*, p. 264. Van Til cites Warfield, "The Real Problem of Inspiration," *The Inspiration and Authority of the Bible*, p. 210.
7. *Ibid.*, pp. 264-265.
8. Van Til, *IST*, 1966 ed., p. 3.
9. Van Til, *DF*, 3rd ed., pp. 260-261.
10. *Ibid.*, p. 265. At the same time Van Til does not conclude with Kuyper that it is useless to reason with the natural man. This is highly significant as we hope later to demonstrate.
11. *Ibid.*, 1st ed., p. 363. 13. *Ibid.*
12. *Ibid.*, p. 383. 14. *Ibid.*, 3rd ed., p. 222.

15. Van Til, "Introduction," *The Inspiration and Authority of the Bible*, by B. B. Warfield, ed. by Samuel G. Craig (Philadelphia: Presbyterian and Reformed Publishing Co., 1948), p. 29; hereafter cited as "Introduction."
16. Van Til, *C1967*, p. 14.
17. Van Til, *DF*, 3rd ed., p. 70.   18. *Ibid.*, p. 82.
19. *Ibid.*, p. 78. Van Til cites from Warfield's *Plan of Salvation* (Grand Rapids: Eerdmans, 1935), p. 111.
20. *Ibid.*, p. 222.
21. *Ibid.*, p. 265.   26. *Ibid.*, 3rd ed., p. 299.
22. *Ibid.*, p. 296.   27. Van Til, "Introduction," p. 22.
23. *Ibid.*, pp. 296-297.   28. *Ibid.*, p. 32.
24. *Ibid.*, p. 297.   29. *Ibid.*, p. 30.
25. *Ibid.*, 1st ed., p. 206. 30. *Ibid.*, p. 31.
31. *Ibid.* On p. 25 Van Til notes: "Both Descartes and Calvin believed in some form of innateness of ideas, yet the former made man and the latter made God the final reference point in human thought."
32. *Ibid.*, p. 33. Van Til contends: "The issue is therefore whether those who were called upon to be prophets or apostles needed the direction and illumination of the Spirit so as to guide them and keep them from error."
33. *Ibid.*, p. 32.
34. *Ibid.*, p. 33.
35. *Ibid.*   39. *Ibid.*, p. 31.
36. *Ibid.*   40. *Ibid.*, p. 37.
37. *Ibid.*   41. *Ibid.*, p. 45.
38. *Ibid.*, p. 22. 42. *Ibid.*
43. *Ibid.*, p. 46. This presumes both that a perfect original text existed (see n. 22) and that an infallible revelation is present in the Bible which we now have. See pp. 46-47.
44. *Ibid.*   46. *Ibid.*, p. 49.
45. *Ibid.*, p. 47. 47. *Ibid.*
48. *Ibid.* Van Til contends that all non-Christian systems of thought have man as the ultimate point of reference.
49. *Ibid.*
50. *Ibid.*, p. 68.
51. B. B. Warfield, *The Westminster Assembly and Its Work* (New York: Oxford University Press, 1931).
52. For an elaboration of this assertion see J. B. Rogers, *Scripture in the Westminster Confession: A Problem of Historical Interpretation for American Presbyterianism* (Grand Rapids: Wm. B. Eerdmans Publishing Co., 1967), pp. 38-40. All references are to the first edition.
53. *Ibid.*, pp. 114-115.
54. *Ibid.*, p. 319, n. 339.   56. Van Til, "Introduction," p. 39.
55. Van Til, *DF*, 1st ed., p. 240.   57. Van Til, *IST*, 1966 ed., p. 3.
58. Rogers, *op. cit.*, p. 323. Because of the general unavailability of the works of the Westminster Divines, all references are to citations in Rogers, *Scripture in the Westminster Confession*. The term "Westminster Divines" in this article always refers to a group of eleven men—seven Englishmen and four Scots—who are shown in the above work to be the principal authors of the Westminster Confession.

59. *Ibid.*
60. *Ibid.*, p. 324.
61. *Ibid.*
62. Van Til, *IST*, 1966 ed., p. 2.
63. *Ibid.*, p. 1.
64. *Ibid.*
70. *Ibid.*, p. 367. Italics are Rutherfords.
71. *Ibid.*
72. *Ibid.*, p. 376.
65. Van Til, *DF*, 3rd ed., p. 81.
66. Van Til, *IST*, 1966 ed., p. 1.
67. *Ibid.*
68. Van Til, *DF*, 3rd ed., p. 8.
69. Rogers, *op. cit.*, pp. 366-367.

73. *Ibid.*
74. This phraseology was suggested in a conversation by my colleague in philosophy, Dr. Thomas M. Gregory.

Response by C. Van Til

1. Benjamin B. Warfield, *The Saviour of the World* (London: Hudder and Stoughton, 1913), p. 105.
2. *Ibid.*, p. 107.
3. *Ibid.*, p. 108.
4. *Ibid.*, p. 109.
5. *Ibid.*, p. 115.
6. *Ibid.*, p. 116.
7. *Ibid.*, p. 117.
8. *Ibid.*
9. *Ibid.*
10. *Ibid.*
11. *Ibid.*
12. *Ibid.*, p. 118.
13. *Ibid.*, p. 119-120.
14. *Ibid.*, p. 120.
15. *Ibid.*, p. 124.
16. *Ibid.*, p. 125.
17. *Ibid.*, p. 127.
18. B. B. Warfield, "Calvin's Doctrine of the Knowledge of God," *Calvin and Calvinism* (London: Oxford University Press, 1931), p. 47.
19. B. B. Warfield, "Faith," *Biblical and Theological Studies* (Philadelphia: Presbyterian and Reformed Publishing Co., 1952), p. 424.

VI. *C. Trimp*

1. Klass Schilder, "Algemeene Genade en Algemeen Oordeel," *De Reformatie* (Nov. 11, 1938), vol. 19, p. 42.
2. G. C. Berkouwer, *De Heilige Schrift*, Vol. II (Kampen: J. H. Kok, 1967), p. 52ff.; cf. C. Van Til, *PDS*, pp. 148, 149.
3. *Ibid.*, p. 49.
4. *Ibid.*, pp. 51, 56.
5. *Ibid.*, p. 52.
6. *Ibid.*, p. 54.
7. *Ibid.*, p. 391.
8. *Ibid.*, pp. 59, 418.
9. C. van der Waal noted the danger in such equalization for the practice of church life when he drew attention to the use which the World Council of Churches makes of the word "witness" in his *Liquidatie der Reformatie* (Enschede: J. Boersma, 1966), pp. 33, 34.
10. R. Schippers, *Getuigen van Jezus Christus in het Nieuwe Testament* (Franeker: T. Wever, 1938).
11. M. Kähler, *Der Sogenannte Historische Jesus und der Geschichtliche*

Christus, 2nd ed., revised by E. Wolf (München: Kaiser Verlag, 1956), pp. 44, 78, 79. First edition published in 1892.

12. In 1938 Berkouwer spoke of the "atheism" of the historical method [*Het Probleem der Schriftkritiek* (Kampen: J. H. Kok, n.d.), p. 64ff.].

13. In the so-called "theological exegesis" of the Barthian school, literary criticism receives complete freedom until it is at last "raised up to" the theological exegesis from out of the authority of Scripture.

14. Berkouwer characterized Kähler's "solution" as the "way of escape of the *kerygma*" to distinguish it from the "way of escape" of "experience" and "paradox" (*Het Probleem der Schriftkritiek*, p. 96ff.). But this distinction must not close our eyes to the typical "moments of experience" of Kähler (M. Kähler, *op. cit.*, pp. 54, 56, 78). In this connection see Kähler's article on "Bible" in *Realencyklopädie für Protestantische Theologie und Kirche*, ed. A. Hauck, 3rd ed., Vol. II (Leipzig: Hindrich'sche Buchhandlung, 1896-1913), pp. 690-691. J. Veenhof's statements concerning the contacts between Kähler and the Netherland's ethical school, which was strongly influenced by Schleiermacher and the so-called *Vermittlungstheologie*, are very interesting [*Revelatie en Inspiratie* (Amsterdam: Buyten & Schipperheyn, 1968), pp. 74-75, 241, 594].

15. Cf. E. Brunner, *Offenbarung und Vernunft* (Zurich: Zwingli Verlag, 1941), p. 117ff.; *Dogmatik*, Vol. I (Zurich: Zwingli Verlag, 1946), pp. 17-45.

16. Cf. Van Til, *NM*, p. 137ff.; Van Til, *HKBBO*, p. 137ff.; K. Runia, *Karl Barth's Doctrine of Holy Scripture* (Grand Rapids: Eerdmans, 1962).

17. Cf. Karl Barth, "Menschenwort und Gotteswort in der Christlichen Predigt, *Zwischen den Zeiten*, III (1925), p. 125ff.; K. Barth, "Das Schriftprinzip der Reformierten Kirche," *Zwischen den Zeiten*, III (1925), pp. 217, 225-226, 237; K. Barth, *Christliche Dogmatik* (München: Kaiser Verlag, 1927), p. 344ff.; *Kirchliche Dogmatik*, Vol. I:2 (Zollikon/Zurich: Evangelischer Verlag, 1938), pp. 513, 516, 546, 563, 588; K. Barth, *Die Schrift und die Kirche* (Zollikon/Zurich: Evangelischer Verlag, 1947), p. 12. See also the quotations from Barth's *Der Römerbrief* as Berkouwer renders them in *Het Probleem der Schriftkritiek*, p. 27ff.

18. K. Barth, "Das Schriftprinzip . . . ," p. 220; *Christliche Dogmatik, p.* 344ff.; *Kirchliche Dogmatik*, I:1/115ff., 120; I:2/8, 113, 512ff., 523, 533ff., 562-563, 566, 588.

19. The so-called double *Welthaftigkeit*. Cf. K. Barth, *KD*, I:1/171ff., I:2/ 244; K. Runia, *op. cit.*, p. 23.

20. K. Barth, *KD*, I:2/553.

21. K. Barth, *Christliche Dogmatik*, pp. 345, 359; *KD*, I:2/563, 588.

22. K. Barth, *KD*, I:2/224, 587.

23. K. Barth, "Das Schriftprinzip . . . ," p. 228.

24. We find a circumspection of the many-faceted word "to raise up" in *KD*, I:1/121.

25. K. Barth, *KD*, I:1/116.

26. *Ibid.*, I:2/512, 554, 557, 562, 568ff., 589, 593, 604ff. especially p. 588.

27. Concerning the likeness of John the Baptist see K. Barth, "Menschenwort und Gotteswort . . . ," p. 130; K. Barth, *Der Christ als Zeuge* (Zollikon: Evangelischer Verlag, 1934), pp. 8, 12; *KD*, III:1/101. Concerning the "to serve" of the Bible see *KD*, III:1/101; IV:1/807. Concerning the dynamic

of the moving of the apostles see *KD*, I:2/752, 806, 912-913, 916; IV: 1/807.

28. K. Barth, *Die Schrift und die Kirche*, p. 5; also *KD*, I:1/119ff.; I:2/11ff. Concerning the "abyss of time" see K. Barth, "Das Schriftprinzip . . . ," p. 228.

29. K. Barth, *Der Christ als Zeuge*, pp. 6, 24; KD, I:2/913, 914; II:2/783.

30. We find a better understanding of the juridical language in Otto Weber, *Grundlagen der Dogmatik*, Vol. I (Neukirchen: Moers, 1959), pp. 205-208. This juridical color of "witness" has been clearly seen by R. Bultmann, *Das Evangelium des Johannes* (Göttingen: Vandenhoeck & Ruprecht, 1964), pp. 30, 31, 103, 104, 197ff., 221. But this insight is continually frustrated by Bultmann's starting points which, for example, keep him from understanding the "beholding" of John 1:14 and the "seeing" of John 3:11 in their evident sense.

31. We consequently take some liberty here with respect to K. Runia's terminology (*op. cit.*, p. 25ff.).

32. Cf. H. Ridderbos, *Heilgeschiedenis en Heilige Schrift van het Nieuwe Testament* (Kampen: J. H. Kok, 1955), p. 119; see also Strathmann in Kittel's *Theologisches Wörterbuch zum Neuen Testament*, Vol. IV, p. 502; cf. R. Schippers, *op. cit.*, pp. 12, 177ff., and C. Van Til, *PDS*, p. 91.

33. K. Runia, *op. cit.*, p. 47; cf. H. Ridderbos, *op. cit.*, p. 123.

34. Cf. K. Barth, *KD*, I:1/114.

35. *Ibid.*, p. 118; I:2/8.

36. Cf. K. Barth, *Christliche Dogmatik*, p. 43; also his "Das Schriftprinzip . . . ," p. 225.

37. K. Barth, *Der Christ als Zeuge*, pp. 13-15.

38. H. Ridderbos, *op. cit.*, pp. 122, 123.

39. In addition to that which was stated in the text, we refer to Hebrews 1:1; 3:7; 10:15; 11:2, 4, 5, 39. The laudable witness of God to the "ancients" is fixed in the Scriptures. In the preaching of the Scriptures, God is speaking as the great Witness, as God has once chosen sides for the righteous. Cf. Schippers, *op. cit.*, p. 77, who in addition refers to Acts 10:43; Romans 3:21; Hebrews 7:8,17. In this connection Luke 24:44ff. should also be noted.

VII. *John A. Witmer*

1. W. H. Griffith Thomas, *Christianity Is Christ* (London: Longmans, Green & Co., 1919), p. v.

2. Bruce Barton, *The Man Nobody Knows* (Indianapolis: The Bobbs-Merrill Co., 1925).

3. Everett F. Harrison, *A Short Life of Christ* (Grand Rapids: Eerdmans, 1968), p. 257.

4. Nels F. S. Ferré, *The Finality of Faith* (New York: Harper & Row, 1963), pp. 48-49.

5. J. A. T. Robinson, *Honest to God* (Philadelphia: The Westminster Press, 1963), p. 65.

6. *Ibid.*, p. 66.

7. *Ibid.*

8. *Ibid.*
9. Donald M. Baillie, *God Was in Christ* (London: Faber and Faber, 1949), p. 118.
10. E. G. Jay, *Son of Man, Son of God* (London: S.P.C.K., 1965), p. 82.
11. Thomas Schultz, "The Doctrine of the Person of Christ with Emphasis upon the Hypostatic Union" (unpublished Th.D. dissertation, Dallas Theological Seminary, 1962), p. 162.
12. Robinson, *op. cit.*, p. 73.
13. *Ibid.*, p. 76.
14. *Ibid.*, p. 77.   15. Jay, *op. cit.*, p. 87.
16. Adolf Harnack, *What Is Christianity?* (New York: G. P. Putnam's Sons, 1902), p. 199.
17. William M. Ramsey, *The Christ of the Earliest Christians* (Richmond: John Knox Press, 1959), pp. 134-135.
18. Rudolf Bultmann, *Jesus and the Word* (New York: Scribner, 1958), p. 9.
19. *Ibid.*
20. Martin Dibelius, *Jesus* (Philadelphia: The Westminster Press, 1949), p. 13.
21. Jay, *op. cit.*, pp. 30-31.
22. Vincent Taylor, *The Person of Christ* (London: Macmillan & Co., 1958), p. 156.
23. J. W. Bowman, *The Intention of Jesus* (Philadelphia: The Westminster Press, 1943), p. 121.
24. Harrison, *op. cit.*, p. 270.
25. Edward W. Bauman, *The Life and Teaching of Jesus* (Philadelphia: The Westminster Press, 1960), pp. 201-202.
26. Harrison, *op. cit.*, p. 271.
27. *Ibid.*, p. 272.
28. Hiram Elfenbein, *Organized Religion* (New York: The Philosophical Library, 1968), p. 234.
29. *Ibid.*
30. *Ibid.*, p. 235.

VIII. *G. C. Berkouwer*

1. A *gravamen* is a written objection submitted to a church body against a clause or statement in a creed, confession, or other doctrinal paper of the church [Ed.].
2. Cf. C. Van Til's "Introduction" to Warfield's *The Inspiration and Authority of Scripture* (Philadelphia: Presbyterian and Reformed Publishing Co., 1955).
3. C. Van Til, *CFC*, p. 116.
4. *Ibid.*, p. 138.
5. C. Van Til, *SG*, p. 52.
6. *Ibid.*, p. 69.
7. See the "Introduction" to Warfield (see n. 2) and, indeed, all his works.
8. C. Van Til, *PDS*, p. 155.
9. *Ibid.*, p. 156.
10. C. Van Til, *CTK*, pp. 52-71.   12. *Ibid.*
11. *Ibid.*, p. 162.   13. *Ibid.*, p. 362.

IX. S. U. Zuidema

1. Self-understanding. Throughout this essay I have translated the German words I have freely used. In doing so I have in several cases used *The New Hermeneutic* by James M. Robinson and John B. Cobb, Jr. (New York: Harper & Row, 1964). This work should be consulted for fuller explanations of the words.
2. Cf. R. Schippers, *De Geschiedenis van Jezus en de Apocalyptick* (Kampen: J. H. Kok, 1964), p. 16.
3. *Ibid.*

X. Paul K. Jewett

1. I understand anti-Semitism to refer to: 1) the view that the Jews are uniquely guilty and cursed of heaven as deicides. We may call this Christian anti-Semitism, or, for those who cannot bear to attach the adjective "Christian" to anything so un-Christian as anti-Semitism, religious, ecclesiastical anti-Semitism; 2) the view that the Jews are a perverse mutation of human stock, a degenerate species of the race (racial anti-Semitism).
2. Edward H. Flannery, *The Anguish of the Jews* (New York: Macmillan, 1965), p. 205.
3. Van Til, *CJ*, p. 17.
4. *Ibid.*, pp. 8-9.
5. *Ibid.*, p. 33.
6. *Ibid.*, p. 36.
7. *Ibid.*, p. 56.
8. *Ibid.*, p. 70.

XI. Richard B. Gaffin, Jr.

1. G. Vos, *The Pauline Eschatology* (Grand Rapids: Eerdmans, 1961), p. vi. This work appeared originally in 1930 and has been reprinted several times without basic alterations.
2. *Ibid.*, p. 149.
3. *Ibid.*, p. 60; cf. G. Vos, *Biblical Theology, Old and New Testaments* (Grand Rapids: Eerdmans, 1959), p. 17: "The Gospel having a precise, doctrinal structure, the doctrinally-gifted Paul was the fit organ for expressing this, because his gifts had been conferred and cultivated in advance with a view to it." (This volume, which first appeared in 1948, is a re-working of class lectures given at Princeton Theological Seminary, prior to the author's retirement in 1932.)
4. *Ibid.*, p. 148.
5. *Ibid.*, p. 60.
6. *Ibid.*, p. 148.
7. *Ibid.*, p. 61.
8. *Ibid.*, p. 149.
9. A. Kuyper, *Encyclopaedie der Heilige Godgeleerdheid*, III (Kampen: J. H. Kok, 1909), pp. 166-180.
10. *Ibid.*, pp. 169f., 401-404.
11. *Ibid.*, p. 167: "Is de Heilige Schrift het principium Theologiae, dan *begint* de Theologia eerst, als de Heilige Schrift er is" (Kuyper's italics).
12. *Ibid.*, p. 176.
13. *Ibid.*, p. 169: "Er is geen Dogmatiek denkbar, tenzij zich vooraf het dogma gevormd hebbe, en het dogma is als zodanig een vrucht van het levensproces *der Kerk*" (Kuyper's italics); cf. p. 395ff.

14. *Ibid.* "In de Heilige Schrift zijn geen dogmata, maar is alleen de stof gegeven, waaruit de Kerk, onder leiding des Heiligen Geestes, de dogmata to construeeren heeft"; p. 404: ". . . en de Schrift ons niet de Dogmata zelve biedt, maar de stof, waaruit de Kerk de Dogmata heeft op te bouwen"; cf. p. 355ff.

15. *Ibid.*, p. 168: "De Openbaring is ons in de Heilige Schrift gegeven, ingewikkeld in de symbolisch-aesthetische kunsttaal van het Oosten. Uit die oostersche wereld wordt nu haar inhoud overgedragen in dat westersch bewustzijn, dat het algemeen menschelijk bewustzijn tot dialectische klaarheid poogt te brengen; en eerst waar deze overgang plaats heeft, ontstaat de Theologie."

16. Just how determinative and clearly defined this pattern of distinctions is for Kuyper's thinking appears from the fact that it furnishes the designations for three of the four major sub-divisions of special encyclopaedia: De Bibliologische, De Ecclesiologische, and De Dogmatologische (which includes dogmatics).

17. Kuyper, *op. cit.*, III/170ff.

18. *Ibid.*, p. 176: "Wel leefde een iegelijk dezer mannen in een religieuze gedachtenwereld, en is deze gedachtenwereld door de Openbaring gebruikt, gebruikt zelfs met die individueele variatiën, die meer dan een hunner daarin aanbracht; maar in de Historia Revelationis doen én deze religieuze gedachtenwereld én deze individueele variatiën slechts dienst als het stramien, waarop de Heilige Geest borduurt; en niet dat stramien, maar het borduursel zelf is hetgeen de revelatie uitmaakt, en waarom het ons te doen moet zijn."

19. Cf. *Biblical Theology*, p. 16: "The didactic, dialectic mentality of Paul. . . ."

20. It is difficult to see how anyone who has read the letters of Paul could ever make such a generalization. Even those who stress the apostle's Jewish, rabbinic background and minimize his contact with Greek culture do not deny that the latter has had some influence on his thinking and the formation of his conceptual apparatus. Besides, the line between "Greek" and "Hebrew" is not a hard and fast one. Cf. W. D. Davies, *Paul and Rabbinic Judaism. Some Rabbinic Elements in Pauline Theology* (New York & Evanston: Harper & Row, 1967), pp. viii ff., 1. Presumably Kuyper's encyclopaedic interest has here obscured for him the witness of the text.

21. Vos's discussion of this and related points is still among the best. See esp. *Biblical Theology*, pp. 14f., 24, 124, 324ff.

22. *Ibid.*, p. 24: "Revelation is so interwoven with redemption that, unless allowed to consider the latter, it would be suspended in the air."

23. It is extremely important to recognize that the basic structure of the New Testament canon is given by this distinction: gospels (attestation)—epistles (interpretation). That this pattern is *intentional* or *constitutive* is confirmed by the shape of Marcion's canon: edited Gospel of Luke—the epistles of Paul with the exception of the Pastorals. [For a brief presentation of the evidence favoring the position that Marcion's canon is molded according to the church's and not vice versa, cf. T. Zahn, *Grundriss der Geschichte des neutestamentlichen Kanons* (Leipzig: A. Deichert, 1904), p. 28f. It may be noted that the recovery of the *Gospel of Truth* in extant form,

which has taken place since the time of Zahn, strengthens his position immeasurably.] As indicated above, the distinction between attestation and interpretation may not be applied in a rigid fashion, as if the gospels contain no interpretation and the epistles no authentication. Such a construction would obviously fail to do justice to the teaching of Jesus. Still, the fundamental perspective from which one must view the New Testament as an organic whole (i.e., as canon) is that Jesus (including his teaching) and the apostles (particularly their letters) are related as "the great fact to be expounded" and "the subsequent interpretation of this fact" (Vos, *Biblical Theology*, p. 324ff.). In this connection, it may be added that one must always appreciate the redemptive-historical remove between the greater part of the teaching of Jesus and that of Paul, as they are separated by the death and resurrection of the former.

24. *Ibid.*, p. 325f.: "Still we know full well that we ourselves live just as much in the New Testament as did Peter and Paul and John." In the same context Vos makes the perceptive and highly suggestive observation that the seeming disproportion in chronological extent of the Old Testament and the New Testament "arises from viewing the new revelation too much by itself, and not sufficiently as *introductory* and *basic* to the large period following" (my italics).

25. The difference in program between Old Testament biblical theology and New Testament biblical theology indicated in this paragraph is already intimated by B. B. Warfield, "The Person of Christ," *Biblical Doctrines* (New York: Oxford University Press, 1929), p. 176: "In its fundamental teaching, the New Testament lends itself, therefore, more readily to what is called dogmatic than to what is called genetic treatment; . . . ." This observation is especially apropos to the writings of Paul.

26. Cf., e.g., Warfield (*ibid.*), who refers to Paul as "the most didactic of the New Testament writers." One may assume that even Kuyper would not take exception to this statement.

27. It is not necessary to read out of the argument developed to this point any unbiblical qualification or relativizing of the perfections of Scripture (necessity, authority, clarity, sufficiency). An analogy from differential calculus may help to make the basic points clear. Redemptive events constitute a function (f), the authentication and interpretation of the New Testament its first derivative (f') and the interpretation of the later church its second derivative (f''). f', to be sure, is of a different order than f'': the former (in its derivative character), infallible verbal revelation (Scripture) which has God as it *auctor primarius*, is the basis (*principium*) of the latter. But both, as derivatives, have a common *interpretative* reference to f. Indeed, it may be said that at its level (characterized by fallibility and tentativeness) f'' "goes beyond" f' in that it draws out the implications of and seeks to make more explicit the structure implicit in the latter. It should also be observed that in the above discussion the redemptive-historical distinction between canonical and non-canonical, between the apostolic and post-apostolic periods is *not* being overlooked or obliterated. Rather, stress has been placed on some of the implications of the fact that in the word "church," the words "apostolic" and "post-apostolic" have their common (redemptive-historical) denominator.

28. It should be observed that in view of this consideration, an "incursion" of biblical theology (concern with revelation *qua* process) into what is usually held to be the domain of systematic theology (concern with revelation *qua* product) is both inevitable and necessary. In need of at least qualification is the attempt customary in the Reformed tradition to distinguish the two disciplines with respect to *method*. Cf. J. Murray, "Systematic Theology. Second Article," *The Westminster Theological Journal*, Vol. 26 (Nov. 1963), p. 33: "The difference is merely one of method. Biblical theology deals with the data of special revelation from the standpoint of its history; systematic theology deals with the same in its totality as a finished product"; Vos, *Biblical Theology*, p. 13: "Biblical Theology deals with revelation as a divine activity, not as the finished product of that activity." However, Murray, toward the end of the article just quoted, makes the following important observation: "But systematic theology will fail of its task to the extent to which it discards its rootage in biblical theology as properly conceived and developed. It might seem that an undue limitation is placed upon systematic theology by requiring that the exegesis with which it is so ultimately concerned should be regulated by the principle of biblical theology. And it might seem contrary to the canon so important to both exegesis and systematics, namely, the analogy of Scripture. These appearances do not correspond to reality. The fact is that only when systematic theology is rooted in biblical theology does it exemplify its true function and achieve its purpose" (p. 45f.).

29. Cf. above, note 25.

30. Cf. M. Kline, "Law Covenant," *The Westminster Theological Journal*, Vol. 27 (Nov. 1964), p. 10: "Surely it does not become systematic theology to unravel what has been synthesized to a degree even in the Scriptures. Systematic theology ought rather to weave together the related strands yet more systematically."

31. Cf. P. Langsfeld, *Adam und Christus (Koinonia—Beiträge zur ökumenischen Spiritualität und Theologie*, 9, ed. by T. Sartory [Essen: Ludgerus-Verlag, 1965]), p. 22: "Die Schrift ist auch Kanon für die Arbeit der Dogmatik (nicht bloss für den Inhalt)."

32. "Niemand hat Paulus je verstanden und der einzige, der ihn verstand, Marcion, hat ihn misverstanden." Whatever else its meaning and validity, Franz Overbeck's cryptic observation reflects the fact that these difficulties have continued down through the centuries. [This statement is reported by Albert Schweitzer, *Die Mystik des Apostels Paulus* (Tübingen: J. C. B. Mohr, 1930), p. 39].

33. Schweitzer's verdict on 19th century "historical-critical" study of Paul has a wider range of application in this respect: "Die paulinische Forschung stellt night eben ein Glanzleistung der Wissenschaft dar. Gelehrsamkeit wurde reichlich aufgewandt; aber es fehlte am Denken und Ueberlegen" [*Geschichte der Paulinischen Forschung* (Tübingen: J. C. B. Mohr, 1911), p. 185]. Mohr, 1911), p. 185].

34. Cf. Warfield, *op. cit.*, p. 175, where he speaks of the conception of Christ's person "which lies on—or, if we prefer to say so, beneath—the pages of the New Testament."

35. Cf. J. Jervell, *Imago Dei. Gen. 1, 26f. im Spätjudentum, in der Gnosis und

in den paulinischen Briefen (Göttingen: Vandenhoeck & Ruprecht, 1960),
p. 171: "Man muss sich ständing vor Augen halten, dass die paulinischen
Briefe Gelegenheits-schriften sind, die oft besondere Probleme der betref-
fenden Gemeinde aufnehmen. Gerade da, wo das Material spärlich fliesst
und wo Paulus keine näheren Definitionen und Erklärungen gibt, liegt oft
das Gewicht seines Kerygmas."

36. Vos, *Pauline Eschatology*, p. 44.

37. *Ibid.*, p. vi.

38. Without approving his conception of Paul's mysticism, well worth repeating
in this connection is the statement of Schweitzer, *Die Mystik des Apostels
Paulus*, p. 140: "Wie sind doch diejeningen im Unrecht, die Paulus nicht
als logischen Denker anerkennen wollen und als höchste Weisheit verkün-
den, dass er kein System habe! Er ist ein logischer Denker, und seine
Mystik ist ein vollendetes System"; cf. E. Käsemann, "Gottesgerechtigkeit
bei Paulus," *Exegetische Versuch und Besinnungen*, II (Göttingen: Vandenhoeck & Ruprecht, 1967), p. 189: "Doch ist die paulinische Theologie
durchreflektiert, und Naivität entspricht ihr am wenigstens."

39. Vos, *Pauline Eschatology*, p. 302.

40. The title, *The Pauline Eschatology*, can be misleading to the reader for
whom "eschatology" is defined by the loci method of dogmatics. He looks
for a specialized study of the "last things" associated with the future
parousia of Christ. Vos, however, intends something more. In the opening chapter he states that "to unfold the Apostle's eschatology means to
set forth his theology as a whole" (p. 11, cf. p. 28); and in this chapter
he is concerned for the most part with uncovering the foundation and
basic structure of Paul's thought in its entirety.

41. H. Ridderbos, *Paulus. Ontwerp van zijn Theologie* (Kampen: J. H. Kok:
1966).

42. Vos, *Pauline Eschatology*, esp. chapter II (pp. 42-61), "The Interaction
between Eschatology and Soteriology."

43. Ridderbos, *Paulus*, pp. 6, 61, 188, 224, 231; cf. pp. 234ff., 242f., and H.
Ridderbos, *When the Time Had Fully Come* (Grand Rapids: Eerdmans,
1957), pp. 47-49.

44. It is pertinent at the close of this section to note something of the negative
response which has been encountered by Professor Ridderbos' recent and
massive study of Paul (cf. above, note 41). Most pronounced disapproval
has been registered by J. Kamphuis. He maintains that there is a *fundamental* objection to the title (*Ontwerp van zijn Theologie*), because it
implies a method whereby the unique apostolic authority of Paul is obscured and he is treated as standing on a par with every theologian and
thinker. ("Op zoek naar het paulinische kernwoord, III," *De Reformatie*,
Vol. 41 (1965-1966), p. 322, note 9: ". . . dat er *fundamenteel* bezwaar
is in te brengen tegen de methode, die zich in deze ondertitel aankondigt,
omdat men nu onder de permanente dreiging verkeert, dat op een ver-
keerd niveau over 'Paulus gehandeld wordt—een niveau, *waarop de apos-
tel met zijn uniek gezag àls apostle principeel in één rij komt te staan met
iedere 'theoloog' en denker.*") In the conception of Paul's "theology" he
can see only a species of "immanentism" with an implicit denial of the
unity and divine origin of Scripture. ("Het is de doolweg van het im-

mantentisme, waarop tenslótte niet meer gewerkt wordt vanuit de geloofs-vooronderstelling, dat de Heilige Schrift in al haar onderdelen één God-delijk auteur heeft.") Essentially the same reaction is expressed somewhat less sharply in the review of P. Y. De Jong. He questions "whether it is really defensible to present Paul as a theologian" and observes that "it seems less than legitimate to label his writings as providing us with a theology" [*Torch and Trumpet*, Vol. 17, no. 5 (May-June 1967), p. 34, col. 1].

These reactions are instructive because they reflect clearly the con-tinuing influence of Kuyper, be it direct or indirect, conscious or un-conscious. It is difficult to see why calling Paul a theologian and speaking of his theology necessarily implies that his writings are not inspired reve-lation. This kind of language is naturally subject to all sorts of misuse. The line between a distortion and a proper understanding of the notion of continuity brought to expression by it is obviously a thin one. It may even be the case that on this score Ridderbos is guilty of deviation. How-ever, the biblical appropriateness, if not the necessity, of thinking of Paul as a theologian, that is, as in a sense standing on a line with later theo-logians and thinkers, has been indicated above. In fact, it is only against the background of this continuity that his significance and uniqueness *qua apostle* can become fully appreciated. Here as elsewhere the distor-tions to which a viewpoint is subject and viewpoint itself will have to be distinguished. Also, it is perhaps not superfluous to state outright what should be obvious: To speak of Paul's theology does not have to mean that he had a fully developed dogmatics or that his writings and preaching provide such. For further discussion of this important book cf. my review, "Paul as Theologian," *The Westminster Theological Journal*, Vol. 30 (May, 1968), pp. 204-232, esp. 222ff.

Response by C. Van Til

1. *Philosophia Reformata*, 1939, p. 193ff.
2. *Ibid.*, pp. 206-207.
3. *Ibid.*, p. 207.
4. *Ibid.*
5. *Ibid.*, pp. 211-212.
6. *Ibid.*, p. 214.
7. *Ibid.*, p. 216.
8. *Ibid.*, p. 217.
9. *Ibid.*, p. 219.
10. *Ibid.*, p. 221.
11. *Ibid.*, p. 223.
12. *Ibid.*, p. 227.
13. A. Kuyper, *Encyclopaedia der Heilige Godgeleerdheid*, Vol. II (Kampen: J. H. Kok, 1908-1909), p. 65.
14. *Ibid.*, pp. 70-71.
15. *Ibid.*, p. 73.
16. *Ibid.*, pp. 73-74.
17. *Ibid.*, p. 75.
18. *Ibid.*, p. 77.
19. *Ibid.*, p. 78.
20. *Ibid.*, p. 80.
21. *Ibid.*, p. 83.
22. *Ibid.*, p. 85.
23. *Ibid.*, p. 86.
24. C. Van Til, *DF*, 1st ed., p. 384ff.
25. C. Van Til, *CG*, p. 34ff.
26. *Ibid.*, p. 37.

27. Kuyper, *op. cit.*, p. 77.
28. *Ibid.*, p. 78.   30. *Ibid.*, p. 97.
29. *Ibid.*, p. 80.   31. *Ibid.*, III, p. 168.

XII. *Herman Ridderbos*

1. I may refer the American reader to *International Reformed Bulletin*, official organ of the International Association for Reformed Faith and Action, 11th year, Nos. 32-33, 1960, pp. 27-92: "An Attempt at the Theological Definition of Inerrancy, Infallibility and Authority."

XIII. *William L. Lane*

1. This essay concerns the character of the tradition embodied in the speeches of Acts. It is offered to Prof. Van Til as an example of the auxiliary task assumed by the Bible scholar who is committed to the presupposition that the Scriptures are the inspired and authoritative Word of God.
1a. This position is widely held: e.g., H. J. Cadbury, "The Speeches in Acts," *The Acts of the Apostles*, Vol. V, "Beginnings of Christianity" (London: Macmillan, 1933), p. 426f. Hereafter simply designated *BC* with volume number. M. Dibelius, *Studies in the Acts of the Apostles* (London: SCM Press, 1956), pp. 3, 70f., 138, *et al.*
2. Note his use of an artistic προοίμιον (Luke 1:1-4) and an imperfect προέθεσις to the second λόγος (Acts 1:1), the division of his work into λόγοι, the threefold dating of his narrative (Luke 3:1-2), etc. See Cadbury, "Commentary on the Preface of Luke," *BC*, II (1922), pp. 489-510.
3. H. J. Cadbury, F. J. Foakes-Jackson, and K. Lake, "The Greek and Jewish Traditions of Writing History," *BC*, II, pp. 13f., 27; Dibelius, *op. cit.*, pp. 138-145, 182.
4. J. T. Townsend, "The Speeches of Acts, *Anglican Theological Review*, Vol. 42 (1960), p. 151.
5. Cadbury, "The Speeches in Acts," p. 406.
6. *Ibid.*, p. 407; Dibelius, *op. cit.*, pp. 147f., 178f.
7. Cadbury, "The Speeches in Acts," pp. 407-410; Townsend, *op. cit.*, pp. 151-153.
8. E.g., Cadbury, "The Greek and Jewish Traditions of Writing History," pp. 7-15; Dibelius, *op. cit.*, pp. 138-142.
9. Thucydides, *Hist.* I. 22. See the discussion of Dibelius, *op. cit.*, pp. 140-142, and the literature cited in his notes; and for a more positive assessment, A. W. Mosley, "Historical Reporting in the Ancient World," *New Testament Studies*, Vol. 12 (1965-1966), pp. 12-14.
10. K. Ziegler, "Polybios," Pauly-Wissowa, *Real-Encyclopaedie der klassischen Altertumswissenschaft* (hereafter abbreviated Pauly *RE*), XXI:2 (1952), col. 1524-1527, esp. the section "Die Behandlung der Reden bei Polybios"; Mosley, *op. cit.*, p. 14f.
11. Polybius, *Hist.* xii.25, τὰ κατ' ἀλήθειαν λεχθέντα; cf. i.14; ii.56; xii.4; xiii.5.
12. This new ideal stems from the influence of Isocrates and his pupils, Ephorus and Theopompus. See A. A. Kalischek, *De Ephoro et Theo-*

pompo Isocratis discipulis (Diss. Münster, 1913).

13. Cf. L. Radermacher, "Dionysius," Pauley *RE*, V (1903-1905), col. 934-971.

14. B. Gärtner, *The Areopagus Speech and Natural Revelation* (Uppsala: Almquist and Wiksells, 1955), pp. 12-18.

15. Cf. Lake and Cadbury in their commentary on the speech of Acts 3: "The construction of almost every sentence in this speech is obscure, and some of it is scarcely translatable, but the general meaning is plain" (*BC*, IV [1933], p. 34f.).

16. Dibelius, *op. cit.*, pp. 138-185.

17. *Ibid.*, p. 181f.

18. *Ibid.*, p. 178; cf. p. 151ff.

19. E.g., F. J. Foakes-Jackson and K. Lake, "The Internal Evidence of Acts," *BC*, II (1922), p. 121.

20. *Ibid.*, p. 121f.; Dibelius, *op. cit.*, pp. 145-158.

21. E.g., Acts 4:29, 31; 6:2; 7:1; 8:14, 25; 11:1; 12:24; 13:5, 7, 44, 46, 48f. *et passim*.

22. See esp. H. J. Cadbury, "The Purpose Expressed in Luke's Preface," *Expositor*, 8th Series, Vol. 21 (1921), pp. 431-441.

23. This fact demonstrates the influence of the Jewish, and specifically the Old Testament, tradition on Luke's writing. See Gärtner, *op. cit.*, pp. 12, 18, 22f., 26; Mosley, *op. cit.*, pp. 22-24.

24. It is the merit of Gärtner, *op. cit.*, pp. 7-37, to have called attention to this fact and to have substantiated it with convincing evidence.

25. Dibelius, *op. cit.*, p. 165.

26. On this passage see B. Gerhardsson, *Memory and Manuscript* (Uppsala: Almquist and Wiksells, 1961), p. 280ff., and esp. pp. 299-306, where he exegetes I Corinthians 15:3ff. in terms of a series of *simanim*: each individual part is a short, heading-like designation for some passage of the tradition about Jesus.

27. E.g. παῖς (on which see below), ἀρχηγὸς καὶ σωτήρ, ἀρχηγὸς τῆς ζωῆς.

28. Bo Reicke, "A Synopsis of Early Christian Preaching," in *The Root of the Vine* (Westminster: Dacre Press, 1953), pp. 132-160.

29. Among those agreeing with this position may be mentioned E. Jacquier, *Les Actes des Apôtres* (Paris: Gabalda, 1926), pp. cclix-cclxxvi; F. F. Bruce, *The Speeches in the Acts of the Apostles* (London: Inter-Varsity Press, 1942); P. Benoit, "Les origines du Symbole des Apôtres dans le Nouveau Testament," *Lumière et Vie*, Vol. 2 (1946), pp. 39-60; Gärtner, *op. cit.*, pp. 7-36.

30. Primary evidence that the Jerusalem Church used Aramaic is found in the ancient liturgical prayer, מרנא תא . That this prayer is not translated, but merely transliterated in a Greek epistle (μαράνα θά, I Cor. 16:22), and that it is preserved in its original form up until the time of the composition of the Didache (10:6), is suggestive of the extraordinarily important role which it must have played in primitive Christian devotion. See K. G. Kuhn, art. μαραναθά *TWNT*, IV (1942), pp. 470-475.

31. Caution must be exercised in any statement about documents emanating from the Aramaic-speaking community. See H. F. D. Sparks, "The Semitisms of the Acts," *Journal of Theological Studies*, n.s. 1 (1950), pp. 23-

26; M. Wilcox, *The Semitisms of Acts* (Oxford: Clarendon Press, 1965).

32. E. Nestle, "Einige Beobachtungen zum Codex Bezae," *Theologische Studien und Kritiken*, Vol. 69 (1896), pp. 102-113.

33. A. Harnack, *Die Apostelgeschichte* (Leipzig: J. Hinrichs, 1908), pp. 184-186.

34. C. C. Torrey, *Composition and Date of Acts* (Cambridge: Harvard University Press, 1916), hereafter abbreviated *CDA*.

35. *Ibid.*, pp. 7-8.

36. F. C. Burkitt, "Professor Torrey on Acts," *Journal of Theological Studies*, Vol. 20 (1919), pp. 320-329; F. C. Burkitt, "Acts 2:47," *Journal of Biblical Studies*, Vol. 37 1918), p. 234.

37. H. J. Cadbury, "Luke—Translator or Author," *American Journal of Theology*, Vol. 24 (1920), pp. 436-485.

38. J. de Zwaan, "The Use of the Greek Language in Acts," *BC*, II (1922), pp. 30-65.

39. *Ibid.*, p. 45f. Cf. Sparks, *op. cit.*, p. 20f.

40. *Ibid.*, pp. 48-53.

41. Torrey, *op. cit.*, pp. 14-16.

42. E.g., de Zwaan, *op. cit.*, p. 50. The only critics of Torrey who have dealt specifically with Acts 3:16 are Cadbury, "Luke—Translator or Author," p. 450, n. 2, and Wilcox, *op. cit.*, pp. 144-146. Both fail to find an adequate basis for accepting Aramaism in the text as it stands.

43. E.g., 3:2, (ἐτίθουν), the impersonal plural [see M. Black, *An Aramaic Approach to the Synoptic Gospels and Acts*[3] (Oxford: Clarendon Press, 1967), pp. 126-128; 3:6 (ὁ δὲ ἔχω, τοῦτο σοι δίδωμι); 3:10 (ἐπεγίνωσκον δὲ αὐτόν, ὅτι οὗτος ἦν κτλ.) *casus pendens* (*ibid.*, pp. 51-55); 3:13, 25, 26 asyndeton (*ibid.*, pp. 55-61); 3:8 (καί...καί...καί...καί...καί) paratactic structure (*ibid.*, pp. 61-69).

44. F. C. Burkitt, "Professor Torrey on Acts," *Journal of Theological Studies*, Vol. 20 (1919), p. 328f.; F. C. Burkitt, *Christian Beginnings* (London: Macmillan, pp. 38-41.

45. In later Christianity, παῖς was fused with the thought of υἱός when applied to Jesus. The Latin Church early rendered παῖς by *filius*. A striking illustration of Burkitt's contention that the [not primitive but later] Church could not think of Jesus as God's slave may be found in the Peshitto of Acts 4:25-30. The translation 'ebed is used in v. 25 when παῖς qualified David, but in vv. 27, 30 when παῖς describes Jesus the term chosen is bar "son."

46. Foakes-Jackson and Lake, *BC*, I (1920), pp. 381-392, esp. 391.

47. E.g., Exodus 14:31; Numbers 12:7f.; Deuteronomy 34:5; Joshua 1:2, 7; II Kings 18:12; I Chronicles 6:49; II Chronicles 24:9; Nehemiah 10:29; Malachi 4:4. Cf. W. Zimmerli, "Der עבד יהוה im AT," *TWNT*, V 1954), p. 662.

48. Cf. Zimmerli, *op. cit.*, pp. 662-664. Sifré Deut. §27, on 3:24 produces a long list of these Old Testament figures described as "servants of God."

49. E.g., *Shemoneh 'Esreh* 15th Beraka (Babylon recession); an old Musaf prayer which is interpolated on the days of the new moon on into the 17th (16th) benediction reads "remember Messiah, the son of David, thy servant. See S. R. Hirsch, *Israels Gebete* (Tübingen: G. B. Tuebner, 1921).

50. Wisd. 2:13; 9:4; 12:7, 20; 19:6; Bar. 1:20; 2:20, 24, 28; 3:36; Ps. Sol. 12:6; 17:21; I Esd. 6:13, 27; 8:82; Philo, *Conf. Ling.* 147 (once); Josephus, *Ant.* X. 215 (once); and in the later Greek translations of the O.T., Isa. 42:1ᴴ v.l.; Jer. 30:10ᴴ; Δαν. 3:95ᴴ; Deut. 34.5 'Αλλ.

51. Zimmerli, *op. cit.*, p. 660; J. Jeremias, art., παῖς, *TWNT*, V (1954), p. 679.

52. Jeremias, *op. cit.*, p. 679f., nn. 183-190.

53. *Ibid.*, p. 680, with references cited there.

54. *Ibid.*, p. 681; also Jeremias' art. 'Αμνος τοῦ θεοῦ, *op. cit.*, pp. 118-121.

55. *Ibid.*, p. 681f.

56. The description of David as Servant of God is to be found solely in prayers, with the exception of the later Old Testament translations. See the passages cited by Jeremias, p. 679, n. 184.

57. I Clem. 59:2, 3, 4; Didache 9:2, 3; Epistle of Barnabas 6:1; 9:2; Martyrdom of Polycarp 14:1, 3; 20:2; Epistle of Diognetus 8:9, 11; 9:1. The meaning of παῖς in these passages is not uniform: in Mart. Polyc. and Ep. Diogn., and probably also in I Clem., the translation must be "child" or "son"; in the Didache and in the Epistle of Barnabas the context demands "servant." In Did. 9:2 the phrase Δαυειδ τοῦ παιδός σου and 'Ιησοῦ τοῦ παιδός σου are closely connected, as in Acts 4:25-30.

58. The difference which the Hellenistic mentality sensed between υἱός and παῖς may be suggested in the fact that the translators of the LXX employed υἱός over 4000 times to render the Hebrew term בנ , but παῖς only twice (Prov. 4:1; 20:7). In a christological context the difference would tend to be more sharply felt.

59. E.g., IV Ezra 7:29, "my servant the Messiah," but thereafter (13:32, 37, 52; 14:9) "my servant"; II Bar. 70:9, "my servant the Messiah"; Targum to the Prophets on Isa. 52:13; 53:12, "my servant the Messiah," עבדי משיחא . In Ezra 7:29 the original reading is preserved by the Ethiopic, while the Latin and Syriac have altered the text to read "my son the Messiah" in keeping with the tendency noted in n. 46 above. So in 14:9 the Arabic and Ethiopic preserve "my Servant" against the rendering "my Son" in the other versions. See further J. Bloch, "Some Christological Interpolations in the Ezra-Apocalypse," *Harvard Theological Review*, Vol. 51 (1958), pp. 89-92. That to Jewish minds there was nothing incredible or derogatory in the identification of the Messiah with the "Slave of Yahweh" is abundantly clear from the Targum to Isaiah, where the Servant of the Lord is explicitly identified with the Messiah in those passages which refer to his exaltation and glory. It is also confirmed by the exegesis of Isaiah in the Midrash and Talmud.

60. Jeremias, *op. cit.*, pp. 680-695.

61. Epiphanius, *Haer.* xxxix.7.3 informs us that the Ebionites ἕνα θεὸν καταγγέλλουσι καὶ τὸν τούτου παῖδα 'Ιησοῦν χριστόν.

62. πρὸς τὸ ἐξαλειφθῆναι. . . ὅπως ἂν ἔλθωσιν . . . καὶ ἀποστείλῃ.

63. E.g., Jubilees 1:15, 22-25; 23:26-31; Test. Dan. 6:4; Assumpt. Mos. 1:18. Cf. I Enoch 1:2-4; Bar. 4:27-30. According to Ps. Sol. 18:4f., God himself must purge Israel through the Messiah. See E. K. Dietrich, *Die Umkehr* (Tübingen: B. G. Tuebner, 1936), pp. 272-274, 418-426.

64. Cf. Dietrich, *op. cit.*, p. 273.

65. On R. Jehoshua see J. Podro, *The Last Pharisee. The Life and Times of*

Rabbi Joshua ben Hananyas (London: Cassell, 1959); on R. Eliezer see
B. Z. Bokzer, *Pharisaic Judaism in Transition. R. Eliezer the Great and
Jewish Reconstruction after the War with Rome* (Philadelphia: Jewish
Publication Society, 1935).

66. Cf. b. Sanh. 97b, where this position is repudiated by R. Nathan.
67. See the early tradition in M. Ta'an. IV. 6.
68. Cf. the tradition attributed to Tanna debe Eliyyahu in Sanh. 97a, b, to-
    gether with the commentary in the Soncino Talmud, *ad loc.*
69. The words "in that hour" are not to be found in M.T.
70. Tanchuma B. בחקתי §5 (ed. Buber, 56a) : . . . אם ישראל עושה תשובה נגאלים

PART FOUR

ESSAYS IN PHILOSOPHY AND APOLOGETICS

XIV. *Robert D. Knudsen*

1. This is the pendant in Orr of the idealistic claim that taking any abstract
   point of view leads thought inevitably into its opposite. To seek the
   ground of meaning is to involve oneself inevitably in meaninglessness.
2. In his syllabus, *Evidences*, Van Til commends James Orr for his transcendental method. He offers some corrective ideas; but in general he
   sides with the elements of the method which we are highlighting.
3. Even though Clark's position may be called "presuppositionalist," it is
   questionable in what sense it is transcendental. Clark does not bring one
   to reflect on what is the fundamental driving motive of his thought.
4. Ronald H. Nash, ed., *The Philosophy of Gordon Clark* (Philadelphia:
   Presbyterian and Reformed Publishing Co., 1968).
5. Edward John Carnell, *The Kingdom of Love and the Pride of Life* (Grand
   Rapids: Eerdmans, 1960), p. 6.
6. *Ibid.*, p. 19.
7. *Ibid.*, p. 21.
8. *Ibid.*, p. 97.
9. We have used the term "analytical" in the sense it has in the expression
   "analytical judgment" and also in the sense pertaining to the analytic
   aspect of logical distinguishing. We use it here in the latter sense.

Response by C. Van Til

1. C. Van Til, *A* (1966 ed.), p. 5.
2. *Ibid.*, pp. 6-7.
3. *Ibid.*, p. 9.
4. *Ibid.*, p. 13.
5. *Ibid.*, p. 14.
6. C. Van Til, *IST*, p. 12.
7. *Ibid.*, p. 37.
8. C. Van Til, *SCE*, p. 6.
9. H. Dooyeweerd, *De Wijsbegeerte der Wetsidee*, Vol. I (Amsterdam,
   1935), p. 64.
10. *Ibid.*, p. 59.

11. H. Dooyeweerd, *A New Critique of Theoretical Thought*, Vol. I (Philadelphia: Presbyterian and Reformed Publishing Co., 1953), pp. 34-35.

XVI. *Gilbert B. Weaver*

1. Gordon H. Clark, "The Bible as Truth," *Biblio-Theca Sacra*, CXIV (April, 1957), p. 166.
2. *Ibid.*, pp. 165-166. See also Gordon H. Clark, "Apologetics," *Contemporary Evangelical Thought*, Carl F. H. Henry, ed. (Great,Neck, N.Y: Channel Press, 1957), pp. 159-161. Note that Clark converts the term "knowledge" of Van Til's statement into "truth" in his criticism of Van Til. Clark takes for granted a virtual identification of knowledge with true propositions, because he denies the possibility of any knowledge in the realm of sense experience. However, Clark and Van Till differ substantially on this point. See Gilbert B. Weaver, "The Concept of Truth in the Apologetic Systems of Gordon Haddon Clark and Cornelius Van Til" (unpublished doctoral dissertation, Grace Theological Seminary, Winona Lake, Indiana, 1967). On Clark's skepticism of sense knowledge, see *The Philosophy of Gordon H. Clark*, Ronald H. Nash, ed. (Philadelphia: Presbyterian and Reformed Publishing Co., 1968), pp. 140-141, 174-175, 413-416.
3. Thomas Aquinas, *Disputed Questions on Truth*, I, II, c. Trans. Mulligan, *et al.*, Vol. I, pp. 48-49, in Vernon J. Bourke (ed.), *The Pocket Aquinas* (New York: Washington Square Press, 1960), p. 12.
4. Aquinas, *Summa Theologica*. I, Q. 84. A. 6, cited by Edward John Carnell, *An Introduction to Christian Apologetics* (Grand Rapids: Eerdmans, 1948), p. 129.
5. Vernon J. Bourke, *op. cit.*, pp. 144-145.
6. Jacques Maritain, *Existence and the Existent*, pp. 96-97, cited by Cornelius Van Til, *Orthodox Protestantism* (address given at Westminster Theological Seminary, Philadelphia, January 5, 1966), p. 18. See this same work by Van Til for a discussion and criticism of the Thomistic use of the Greek-originated "scale of being," pp. 18-26. See also Van Til, *SCE*, pp. 60-64, 117ff.
7. Aquinas, *Summa of Theology*, I, 13, 5, C, reply to Obj. I. Trans. Vernon J. Bourke, *op. cit.*, pp. 163-164. For a discussion of predication by analogy in Aristotle, as well as Van Til's evaluation of Gordon Clark's treatment of the same in the latter's *Thales to Dewey*, see Van Til, *CC/II:I*, pp. 1-22. In this work Van Til relates the Greek-Thomistic concept of analogy to Aristotle's "potentiality-actuality" scheme.
8. *Ibid.*, p. 165. It is not the purpose of this study to refute the Thomistic notion of analogy by showing that it results in skepticism. Such are available: as, e.g., Edward John Carnell, *op. cit.*, pp. 146-151, and Gordon H. Clark, *A Christian View of Men and Things* (Grand Rapids: Eerdmans, 1951), pp. 309-312.
9. See Cornelius Van Til, "Nature and Scripture," *The Infallible Word*, 1st ed. (Philadelphia: *The Presbyterian Guardian*, 1946), p. 255ff. For Van Til's discussion of Clark's position on the relationship of general and special revelation see *PDS*, pp. 62-72.

10. Van Til, *IST*, 1961 ed., p. 12.
11. Van Til, *DF*, 1st ed., p. 64.
12. Van Til, *IST*, 1961 ed., p. 206; see also pp. 69-70.
13. Bernard Ramm, *Types of Apologetic Systems* (Wheaton, Ill.: Van Kampen Press, 1953), p. 192, citing Cornelius Van Til, *Christian Apologetics* (rev. 1939), p. 55. See also Van Til, *DF*, 1st ed., p. 282, and *CFC*, pp. 57-58, 99-100.
14. Van Til, *DF*, 1st ed., pp. 64-65. For a thorough discussion of analogical in contrast to univocal reasoning in Van Til's senses of these terms in connection with the correlative principles of *continuity* and *discontinuity* as these appear in the history of both Christian and non-Christian thought, see *CTK*, pp. 25-40. See also chapter 1 of my dissertation mentioned above in note 2.

XVII. *C. Gregg Singer*

1. Van Til, *CC*, I, p. 10.
2. *Ibid.*, III, p. 143, quoting W. Oates, *Basic Writings of St. Augustine*, Vol. II, p. 666.
3. Since Van Til's theological position is, I am sure, being related elsewhere in the *Festschrift*, I mention only certain doctrines briefly and without development as they apply to this discussion of history.
4. Van Til consistently holds that man must rely on revelation for all of his knowledge of God, before the fall as well as after. All knowledge of God is revelational in character, but the fall made a new form of revelation necessary to meet the needs of man's sinful condition.
5. This is not to say that Van Til agrees with every particular of Augustine's interpretation of biblical eschatology. In general, however, he would accept the amillennial position which most authorities ascribe to the Bishop of Hippo. It is sure that in Van Til's theology there is no room for premillennialism in any of its forms, historical or dispensational. I would identify him as a catastrophic post-millennialist.
6. A similar gulf exists between a Reformed approach to history and an "evangelical" approach such as that of John W. Montgomery, who all too often does not follow a biblical view of history because he rejects the Reformed doctrine of the covenant.

XVIII. *Rousas John Rushdoony*

1. Thorkild Jacobsen, "Mesopotamia," in H. and H. A. Frankfort, John A. Wilson, *Before Philosophy, The Intellectual Adventure of Ancient Man* (Hammondsworth, Middlesex: Penguin Books, 1949, 1951), pp. 137-234.
2. Kathleen Freeman, *Ancilla to the Pre-Socratic Philosophers* (Cambridge: Harvard University Press, 1957), p. 28.
3. *Ibid.*, p. 42.
4. *Ibid.*, p. 87.
5. Warner Fite, *The Platonic Legend* (New York: Charles Scribner's Sons, 1934).
6. Philip Merlan, "Minor Socratics," in Vergilius Ferm, ed., *Encyclopedia of*

Morals (New York: Philosophical Library, 1956), pp. 333-339.

7. Van Til, *CB*, p. 261.
8. Van Til, *DF*, 1st ed., p. 27.   10. Van Til, *DF*, 1st ed., p. 41.
9. Van Til, *PR*, 1961 ed., p. 49ff.   11. *Ibid.*, p. 42ff.
12. See R. J. Rushdoony, *The Foundations of Social Order, Studies in the Creeds and Councils of the Early Church* (Nutley, N. J.: Presbyterian and Reformed Publishing Co., 1968).
13. Van Til, *DF*, 1st ed., p. 43.
14. *Ibid.*, p. 44.
15. Van Til, *CG*, p. 7ff.
16. *Ibid.*, p. 9.
17. Theodore S. Kuhn, *The Structure of Scientific Revolutions* (Chicago: University of Chicago, 1962). For an analysis of this work see R. J. Rushdoony, *The Mythology of Science* (Nutley, N. J.: Craig Press, 1967), pp. 85-93.
18. Van Til, *CG*, p. 64.
19. Van Til, *CFC*, pp. 62-65, 132.   21. Van Til, *NM*, p. 275.
20. *Ibid.*, p. 148.   22. Van Til, *TJD*, p. 31.
23. For an example of the exploitation of Dooyeweerd's position, see Jan Lever, *Creation and Evolution* (Grand Rapids: International Publications, 1958).
24. See Herman Dooyeweerd, *A New Critique of Theoretical Thought*, Vol. I (Philadelphia: Presbyterian and Reformed Publishing Co., 1953); Gordon H. Clark, "Cosmic Time: A Critique of the Concept in Herman Dooyeweerd," *Gordon Review*, Vol. II, no. 3, September, 1956, pp. 94-99.

XIX. *Gordon R. Lewis*

1. Van Til, *CFC*, p. 82.
2. *Ibid.*, p. 85.
3. Van Til, *DF*, 3rd ed., pp. 3, 6.
4. Edward John Carnell, *The Case for Orthodox Theology* (Philadelphia: The Westminster Press, 1959), p. 13.
5. Van Til, *CTEv*, 1961 ed., p. 39.
6. Van Til, *DF*, 3rd ed., p. 179.
7. Van Til, *CFC*, p. 95.
8. Edward John Carnell, *An Introduction to Christian Apologetics* (Grand Rapids: Eerdmans, 1948), pp. 152-187.
9. *Ibid.*, p. 101.
10. *Ibid.*, p. 191.
11. *Ibid.*, p. 101.
12. Edward John Carnell, "Letter to the Editor," *Christianity Today* (October 14, 1966), pp. 21-23.
13. Carnel, *Introduction*, p. 41, n. 23.
14. Van Til, *DF*, 3rd ed., pp. 100-101.
15. Carnell, *Introduction*, pp. 124-125.
16. *Ibid.*, pp. 161-168.   19. *Ibid.*, pp. 156-157.
17. *Ibid.*, p. 170, n. 31.   20. *Ibid.*, p. 215.
18. *Ibid.*, p. 172.   21. Van Til, *DF*, 3rd ed., p. 94.

22. Van Til, *CG*, p. 85.
23. Van Til, *DF*, 3rd ed., p. 50, n. 4.
24. Van Til, *DF*, 1st ed., p. 296.
25. Van Til, *DF*, 3rd ed., pp. 23-24.
26. Van Til, *CFC*, p. 148.
27. Van Til, *DF*, 1st ed., p. 300.
28. Van Til, *PR*, 1961 ed., p. 51.
29. Van Til, *DF*, 3rd ed., p. 90.
30. *Ibid.*, p. 92.
31. *Ibid.*, p. 94.
32. *Ibid.*, p. 77.
33. *Ibid.*, p. 81.
34. *Ibid.*, p. 82.
35. *Ibid.*, p. 77.
36. Carnell, *Introduction*, p. 157, n. 9.
37. Van Til, *DF*, 3rd ed., pp. 149-150.
38. *Ibid.*, p. 150.
39. James Daane, Review of "The Case for Calvinism," *Christianity Today* (September 25, 1964), p. 33.
40. Van Til, *CFC*, p. 80.
41. *Ibid.*
42. Edward John Carnell, *A Philosophy of the Christian Religion* (Grand Rapids: Eerdmans, 1952), p. 315.
43. Van Til, *DF*, 3rd ed., pp. 44-45.
44. Van Til, *DF*, 1st ed., p. vii.
45. Van Til, *CTEv*, 1961 ed., p. 40.
46. Edward John Carnell, *The Kingdom of Love and the Pride of Life* (Grand Rapids: Eerdmans, 1960), p. 6.
47. Van Til, *DF*, 3rd ed., p. 50, n. 4.
48. Van Til, *CFC*, p. 95.
49. *Ibid.*
50. *Ibid.*, p. 99.
51. *Ibid.*, p. 116.
52. *Ibid.*, p. 64.

Response by C. Van Til

1. Edward John Carnell, *An Introduction to Apologetics* (Grand Rapids: Eerdmans, 1st ed., 1948), p. 66.
2. *Ibid.*, p. 72.
3. *Ibid.*, p. 194.
4. *Ibid.*, p. 212.
5. *Ibid.*, p. 40.
6. C. Van Til, *CFC*, p. 65.
7. *Ibid.*, p. 91.
8. *Ibid.*, p. 111.
9. Carnell, *op. cit.*, p. 66.
10. *Ibid.*, p. 56.
11. *Ibid.*, p. 63.
12. *Ibid.*, p. 64.
13. *Ibid.*, p. 71.
14. *Ibid.*, p. 72.
15. *Ibid.*, p. 78.
16. *Ibid.*, p. 85.
17. Cf. C. Van Til, *CI*.
18. C. Van Til, *CTEv*, 1961 ed., p. 50.
19. Carnel, *op. cit.*, p. 66.

XX. *Charles M. Horne*

1. Stuart Cornelius Hackett, *The Resurrection of Theism: Prolegomena to Christian Apology* (Chicago: Moody Press, 1957), p. 154.
2. Ibid.
3. Hackett wrongly classifies Carnell as a metaphysical presuppositionalist. Carnell verified this error in a personal letter to the present writer dated Feb. 5, 1960.

4. Van Til, *NE*, p. 5.
5. Edward J. Carnell, *An Introduction to Christian Apologetics: A Philosophic Defense of the Trinitarian-Theistic Faith*, 4th ed. revised (Grand Rapids: Eerdmans, 1959), p. 46.
6. *Ibid.*, p. 47.
7. Van Til, *NE*, p. 5.
8. Carnell, *An Introduction to Christian Apologetics*, p. 47.
9. *Ibid.*, p. 56.
10. *Ibid.*
11. *Ibid.*, p. 57.
12. *Ibid.*, p. 59.
13. *Ibid.*, pp. 59-60.
14. *Ibid.*, p. 63.
15. *Ibid.*, p. 212.
16. *Ibid.*, p. 124f.
17. Hackett, *op. cit.*, p. 156.
18. Van Til, *NE*, pp. 6-7.
19. *Ibid.*, pp. 7-8.
20. Carnell, *A Philosophy of the Christian Religion* (Grand Rapids: Eerdmans, 1952), p. 184.
21. *Ibid.*, p. 186.
22. Van Til, *NE*, p. 8.
23. Carnell, *op. cit.*, p. 187.
24. *Ibid.*, p. 253.
25. *Ibid.*, p. 270.
26. *Ibid.*, p. 276.
27. "Rheinhold Niebuhr, His Religious, Social, and Political Thought," *The Library of Living Theology*, Vol. II, eds. Charles W. Kegley and Robert W. Bretall (New York: The Macmillan Co., 1961), p. 443.
28. Van Til, *DF*, 1st ed., pp. 116-117.
29. *Ibid.*, pp. 125-126.
30. *Ibid.*, p. 135.
31. *Ibid.*, p. 91.
32. *Ibid.*
33. *Ibid.*
34. Rousas John Rushdoony, *By What Standard? An Analysis of the Philosophy of Cornelius Van Til* (Philadelphia: The Presbyterian and Reformed Publishing Co., 1959), p. 1.
35. *Ibid.*, p. 2.
36. *Ibid.*, p. 4.
37. *Ibid.*, p. 5.
38. *Ibid.*, p. 8.
39. Herman Dooyeweerd, *A New Critique of Theoretical Thought*, Vol. I (Philadelphia: Presbyterian and Reformed Publishing Co., 1953), pp. 22f. 36f.
40. Van Til, *CTEv*, 1947 ed., p. 54.
41. Van Til, "Nature and Scripture," *The Infallible Word*, eds. Stonehouse and Woolley (Grand Rapids: Eerdmans, 1953), pp. 272-273.
42. John Murray, "The Attestation of Scripture," in *ibid.*, p. 7ff.

XXI. *John Warwick Montgomery*

1. Cornelius Van Til, "Introduction" to *The Inspiration and Authority of the Bible by B. B. Warfield* (Philadelphia: Presbyterian and Reformed Publishing Co., 1948), p. 20.
2. Van Til, *CTK*, p. 295.
3. *Ibid.*, p. 294.
4. Jorge Luis Borges, *Labyrinths: Selected Stories & Other Writings*, eds. Donald A. Yates and James E. Irby (New York: New Directions, 1964), p. 15.
5. *Ibid.*, p. 18.

6. *Ibid.*, p. 17.
7. Van Til, *CTK*, p. 37
8. Van Til, *CTEv.*, 1961 ed., p. 53.
9. Van Til, *CTK*, pp. 25-26.
10. The early portions of the Shadok-Gibi saga have recently been made available in book form: J. Rouxel & J. F. Borredon, *Les Shadoks et les Gibis* (Paris: Julliard, 1968).
11. An analogy frequently appealed to by Van Til. Cf. *CTK*, p. 297.
12. November, 7, 1969.
13. Herman Dooyeweerd, *In the Twilight of Western Thought: Studies in the Pretended Autonomy of Philosophical Thought* (Philadelphia: Presbyterian and Reformed Publishing Co., 1960), p. 43.
14. Herbert Marcuse, *One-Dimensional Man: Studies in the Ideology of Advanced Industrial Society* (Boston: Beacon Press, 1964), p. 125.
15. *Ibid.*
16. Herbert Marcuse, *Reason and Revolution: Hegel and the Rise of Social Theory*, 3rd ed. (Boston: Beacon Press, 1960), p. 27.
17. Bernard Zylstra, "Hegel, Marcuse, and the New Left." (mimeographed lecture, Wheaton College Philosophy Conference, Wheaton, Ill., November 7, 1969), p. 6.
18. This work is unfortunately not available in English, but appears in German. See Theodore Abu Qurra, *Traktat. Ueber d. Schöpfer und d. wahre Religion*, tr. and ed. Georg Graf von Hertling ("Beiträge zur Geschichte d. Philosophie d. Mittelalters," XIV/1; Münster i.W.: Aschendorffsche Verlh., 1913).
19. See Montgomery, *Where Is History Going?* (Grand Rapids: Zondervan, 1969), passim; "The Theologian's Craft: A Discussion of Theory Formation and Theory Testing in Theology" *Journal of the American Scientific Affiliation*, XVIII (Sept., 1966), 65-77, 92-95; and "The Place of Reason in Christian Witness," in his forthcoming *Christianity for the Tough-Minded* (Minneapolis: Bethany Fellowship, 1970).
20. Acts 26:26.
21. Cf. Georg Henrik Von Wright, *The Logical Problem of Induction*, 2nd ed. (Oxford: Blackwell, 1957).
22. On the assumptions of scientific method vs. the a prioris of the "Religion of Science," see Montgomery, *The Shape of the Past: An Introduction to Philosophical Historiography* (Ann Arbor, Mich.: Edwards Bros., 1963), p. 264ff.
23. Karl Barth, *Anselm: Fides Quaerens Intellectum*, trans. Ian W. Robertson (Richmond, Va.: John Knox Press, 1961), p. 71.

Response by C. Van Til

1. R. G. Collingwood, *The Idea of History* (New York: Oxford University Press, 1946), p. 154.
2. J. W. Montgomery, *Where Is History Going?* (Grand Rapids: Zondervan, 1969).
3. *Ibid.*, p. 24.
4. *Ibid.*, p. 163.

5. *Ibid.*, p. 178.
6. J. W. Montgomery, *The Shape of the Past* (Ann Arbor: Edwards Bros., 1963), p. 26.
7. Francis Pieper, *Christian Dogmatics*, Vol. I (St. Louis: Concordia Publishing Co., 1950), p. 271.
8. M. Luther, *The Bondage of the Will*, tr. by H. Cole (in 1823), corrected by H. Atherton (Grand Rapids: Eerdmans, 1933), p. 38.
9. *Ibid.*, pp. 39-40.
10. *Ibid.*, p. 42.
11. *Ibid.*, p. 145.
12. *Ibid.*, p. 147.
13. *Ibid.*, p. 210.
14. *Ibid.*, p. 217.

XXII. *W. Stanford Reid*

1. J. W. Montgomery, "Clark's Philosophy of History," *The Philosophy of Gordon H. Clark*, ed. R. H. Nash (Philadelphia: Presbyterian and Reformed Publishing Co., 1968), p. 355ff. (hereafter cited as *Clark*).
2. *Ibid.*, p. 369f. It is interesting that E. J. Carnell in *An Introduction to Christian Apologetics* (Grand Rapids: Eerdmans, 1966, p. 302ff.) does not agree with Montgomery on the idea of God's being accounted the author of sin, although Montgomery seems to approve most highly of Carnell's views.
3. Montgomery, *Clark*, pp. 361ff., 387; cf. also J. W. Montgomery, *The Shape of the Past* (Ann Arbor: Edwards Bros., 1968), p. 287 (hereafter cited as *Shape*). Carnell, *op. cit.*, p. 108ff., accepts systematic coherence as a very important proof of truthfulness.
4. *Ibid.*, p. 372f.
5. *Ibid.*, p. 375f.
6. *Ibid.*, p. 386f.
7. *Ibid.*, p. 388.
8. *Ibid.*, p. 389ff.
9. Montgomery, *Shape*, pp. 3, 12.
10. *Ibid.*, p. 13.
11. *Ibid.*, p. 264ff. Cf. also "The Quest for Absolutes: An Historical Argument," p. 1 (mimeographed paper, hereafter cited as "Quest"). Dr. Montgomery has published his views quite widely and in many different formats: as a book, as articles, or as mimeographed sheets. The present writer has found this rather confusing as the same articles turn up in only slightly different forms with different titles. Because of this, citations herein are to the *first* "authorized version" read, rather than to all the different forms in which it appears.
12. *Ibid.*, p. 292.
13. Montgomery, "Quest," p. 1.
14. Montgomery, *Shape.*, p. 265.
15. *Ibid.*, p. 266; also "Quest," p. 3.
17. *Ibid.*, p. 195; J. W. Montgomery, "Vers une Philosophie Chretiennee d'Historie," *La Revue Reformeé*, no. 71 (1966), p. 11 (hereafter cited as "Philos. Chret.").
18. *Ibid.*, p. 48f. Cf. his "The Christian Church in McNeill's 'Rise of the West,' " *Evangelical Quarterly*, XXVIII (1966), p. 210ff. (hereafter cited as "McNeill"); *Clark*, p. 376; and the comments of W. Johnson in "The Quest for Objectivity," *Journal of the Evangelical Theological Society*, XII (1969), p. 85ff.
19. *Ibid.*, pp. 72, 233, 274, 315f.; "Quest," p. 6f.; J. W. Montgomery, "History

and Christianity," *HIS*, Dec., 1964, p. 2ff. (reprint, hereafter referred to as "Hist."). This is what he claims in his discussion of a Christian philosophy of history ("Philos. Chret.," p. 22f.; "McNeill," p. 214).

20. *Ibid.*, pp. 18f., 240f.; Carnell, *op. cit.*, p. 94.
21. Montgomery, "Quest," p. 2. Italics ours.
22. *Ibid.*, p. 1; *Shape*, p. 258.
23. Montgomery, *Shape*, p. 265; "Quest," p. 2.
24. Montgomery, "Hist.," p. 5ff.; J. W. Montgomery, *The Altizer-Montgomery Dialogue* (Chicago, 1967).
25. M. Planck, *Scientific Autobiography*, p. 80, quoted in *Main Currents of Western Thought*, ed. T. le Van Baumer (New York, 1952), p. 599. Cf. also R. G. Collingwood, *The Idea of History* (New York: Oxford University Press, 1946), p. 249ff.
26. Montgomery, "Hist.," p. 19; *Shape*, p. 266.
27. J. W. Montgomery, "Tillich's Philosophy of History," *The Gordon Review*, X (1967), p. 146; C. H. Pinnock, *Set Forth Your Case* (Nutley, N. J.: Craig Press, 1968), p. 44f.; Carnell, *op. cit.*, p. 113ff.
28. Montgomery, *Shape*, pp. 143, 229, 237. Cf. Van Til's criticism of the probability argument in *DF*, 3rd ed., p. 177ff.
29. *Ibid.*, p. 237.
30. *Ibid.*; "Hist.," p. 19.
31. *Ibid.*, p. 138.
32. Montgomery, "Hist.," p. 10.
33. Montgomery, *Shape*, p. 338, n. 50, 51; cf. p. 274f. Cf. Van Til, *DF*, 3rd ed., pp. 104, 149, 169; Johnson, *op. cit.*, p. 86ff.
34. Montgomery, "McNeill," p. 202f.; "Quest," p. 2; "Hist.," p. 17; Van Til, *DF*, 3rd ed., pp. 104, 168ff.
35. Montgomery, *Shape*, p. 145ff.
36. *Ibid.*, p. 136.
37. *Ibid.*, p. 32, n. 15. He indicates that this idea was given to him by Prof. Gram. It is apparently not essential to his thought.
38. *Ibid.*, p. 119ff.
39. *Ibid.*, pp. 237, 291.
40. Montgomery, "McNeill," p. 212; "Quest," p. 3ff. He holds that to deny miracle one must *assume* the absolute and total uniformity of nature, not as *probable* but as *certain*—a strange demand in view of his own statements.
41. Montgomery, "Quest," p. 5; *Shape*, p. 291; Carnell, *op. cit.*, p. 258ff.
42. Montgomery, "McNeill," p. 213.
43. Montgomery, "Hist." p. 18; "Quest," p. 5; *Shape*, pp. 196f., 291ff.
44. Montgomery, *Shape*, p. 292. Montgomery states that to determine the nature of natural laws one must evaluate evidence for each event "without *a priori* . . . no matter how unique it is," ". . . its very degree [sic] of uniqueness gives strong evidence for the truth of the claim of the one who performed it and/or of the claim of the book in which it is recorded" ("Quest," p. 5). J. P. Sartre, *L'Existentialisme est unhumanisme* (Paris, 1965), *passim*.
45. *Ibid.*, p. 287.
46. *Ibid.*, p. 291; "Hist.," p. 18; cf. Carnell, *op. cit.*, p. 258.

47. *Ibid.*, pp. 11, 212ff.
48. *Ibid.*, p. 147f.
49. Montgomery, "Tillich," p. 148f.; *Shape*, p. 150f.
50. Cf. H. Dooyeweerd, *In the Twilight of Western Thought* (Philadelphia: Presbyterian and Reformed Publishing Co., 1960), chaps. I, II.
51. H. Meyerhoff, *The Philosophy of History in Our Time* (Garden City: Doubleday, 1959), p. 15ff.; W. Dilthey, *Pattern and Meaning in History,* ed. H. P. Rickman (New York, 1961); C. L. Becker, *Everyman His Own Historian* (New York, 1935); A. Toynbee, *An Historian's Approach to Religion* (Oxford, 1956); B. Croce, *History as the Story of Liberty,* S. Sprigge, tr. (New York, 1941).
52. *Ibid.*, p. 15ff.; cf. Toynbee's *Study of History* in 10 vols.
53. Cf. H. Butterfield, *Christianity and History* (London, 1949), *passim.*
54. Van Til, *CG*, p. 50ff.

XXIII. *Clark H. Pinnock*

1. Van Til, *DF*, 1st ed., p. 116f.
2. *Ibid.*, p. 317.
3. Van Til, *IST*, 1952 ed., p. 152.
4. Van Til, *DF*, 1st ed., p. 23.
5. Van Til, *CTEv*, 1961 ed., p. 53.
6. Van Til, *MA*, p. 107.
7. Van Til, *CTEv*, 1961 ed., p. 35.
8. Van Til, *DF*, 1st ed., pp. 156-163.
9. Cf. Anthony Flew, *God and Philosophy* (London: Hutchinson, 1966), p. 9.
10. Heinrich Ott, "The Historical Jesus and the Ontology of History," *The Historical Jesus and the Kerygmatic Christ,* tr. and ed. by Carl E. Braaten and Roy A. Harrisville (Nashville: Abington Press, 1964), p. 166.
11. Cf. esp. H. Dooyeweerd, *A New Critique of Theoretical Thought*, Vol. I, "The Necessary Presuppositions of Philosophy," (Philadelphia: Presbyterian and Reformed Publishing Co., 1953).
12. For the new climate, see James A. Martin, *The New Dialogue Between Philosophy and Theology* (New York: Seabury, 1966).
13. Hackett gives a sharp critique of what he calls voluntaristic rationalism in *The Resurrection of Theism* (Chicago: Moody Press, 1957). John Warwick Montgomery turns his guns on the same phenomenon as it appears in the thought of Gordon H. Clark in his essay, "Clark's Philosophy of History," *The Philosophy of Gordon H. Clark*, ed. by Ronald H. Nash: (Philadelphia: Presbyterian and Reformed Publishing Co., 1968).

XXIV. *Arthur F. Holmes*

1. T. S. Kuhn, *The Structure of Scientific Revolutions* (Chicago: University of Chicago Press, 1962); Norwood Hanson, *Patterns of Discovery* (London: Cambridge University Press, 1958); Mary Hesse, *Models and Analogies in Science* (Notre Dame, Ind.: Notre Dame University Press, 1961); Ian Ramsey, *Models and Mystery* (London: Oxford University Press, 1964); Stephen Toulmin, *Foresight and Understanding* (Bloomington: Indiana University Press, 1961).
2. M. B. Foster, "The Christian Doctrine of Creation and the Rise of Modern Natural Science," *Mind*, XLIII (1934), p. 446ff.; XLIV (1935), p. 439ff.; XLV (1936), p. 1ff.

3. Gilbert Ryle, *Dilemmas* (London: Cambridge University Press, 1954), ch. VIII; Stephen Toulmin, *The Uses of Argument* (London: Cambridge University Press, 1958); John Passmore, *Philosophical Reasoning* (New York: Charles Scribner's Sons, 1961); Henry Johnstone, *Philosophy and Argument* (University Park: Pennsylvania State University Press, 1959).

4. A. F. Holmes, "The Philosophical Methodology of Gordon Clark," ch. VII in *The Philosophy of Gordon H. Clark*, ed. Ronald H. Nash (Philadelphia: Presbyterian and Reformed Publishing Co., 1968).

5. Everett Hall, *Philosophical Systems* (Chicago: University of Chicago Press, 1960); Dorothy Emmet, *The Nature of Metaphysical Thinking* (New York: Macmillan, 1945); Stephen Pepper, *World Hypotheses* (London: Cambridge University Press, 1942).

6. See A. F. Holmes, "Ordinary Language Analysis and Theological Method," *Bulletin of the Evangelical Theological Society*, XI (1968), pp. 131-138. See also A. F. Holmes, *Christian Philosophy in the Twentieth Century* (Nutley, N. J.: Craig Press, 1969), ch. V and VI.

7. I have developed this at greater length in "Philosophy and Religious Belief," *Pacific Philosophy Forum*, V (1967), 4, pp. 3-51. A helpful overview of the religious language discussion may be found in William Hordern, *Speaking of God* (New York: Macmillan, 1964). I am somewhat indebted to Ian Ramsey, *Religious Language* (London: S.C.M. Press, 1957), and to Frank Dilley, *Metaphysics and Religious Language* (New York: Columbia University Press, 1964).

Response by C. Van Til

1. A. F. Holmes, "The Philosophical Methodology of Gordon Clark," *The Philosophy of Gordon H. Clark* (Philadelphia: Presbyterian and Reformed Publishing Co., 1968), p. 202.

2. A. F. Holmes, *Christian Philosophy in the Twentieth Century* (Nutley, N. J.: Craig Press, 1969), p. 36.

3. *Ibid.*, p. 37.

4. *Ibid.*   6. *Ibid.*, p. 118.

5. *Ibid.*, p. 211.   7. *Ibid.*, p. 212.

8. *Early Christian Fathers*, tr. and ed. by Cyril C. Richardson ("The Library of Christian Classics," Vol. I, gen. eds. J. Baillie, J. T. McNeill, H. F. Van Dusen [Philadelphia: Westminster Press, 1953]), p. 255 (*First Apology of Justin*, 21).

9. B. B. Warfield, *Studies in Tertullian and Augustine* (New York: Oxford University Press, 1930), pp. 19-20.

10. A. F. Holmes, "The Transcendental Method of Herman Dooyeweerd," *The Gordon Review* (Winter, 1963-64), p. 70.

11. *Ibid.*

12. A. F. Holmes, "Philosophy and Religious Belief," *Pacific Philosophy Forum*, V (1967), p. 41.

13. A. F. Holmes, *Clark*, p. 226.

XXV. *Frederic R. Howe*

1. Van Til, *DF*, 3rd ed., pp. 225-259.
2. G. Abbott-Smith, *A Manual Greek Lexicon of the New Testament* (New York: Charles Scribner's Sons, n.d.), p. 246.
3. William F. Arndt and F. Wilbur Gingrich, *A Greek-English Lexicon of the New Testament* (Chicago: University of Chicago, 1957), p. 95.

LIST OF CONTRIBUTORS

(in alphabetical order)

G. C. BERKOUWER: professor of dogmatics, Free University of Amsterdam; author, multi-volume "Studies in Dogmatics" and several books on Roman Catholic theology.

HERMAN DOOYEWEERD: emeritus professor of law, Free University of Amsterdam; author, *A New Critique of Theoretical Thought* (1953-58) and *In the Twilight of Western Thought* (1960) and many essays, most appearing in *Philosophia Reformata*, of which he is editor.

RICHARD B. GAFFIN, JR.: assistant professor of New Testament, Westminster Theological Seminary; contributor, *Westminster Theological Journal*; B.A., Calvin College; B.D., Th.M.; Th.D., Westminster Theological Seminary.

E. R. GEEHAN: Dr. Phil. candidate, University of Utrecht, The Netherlands; B.A., University of Illinois; B.D., Westminster Theological Seminary; Drs., University of Utrecht.

ARTHUR F. HOLMES: professor of philosophy, Wheaton College; author, *Christian Philosophy in the Twentieth Century* (1969); frequent contributor to *The Gordon Review, Journal of Philosophy,* and *Journal of Religion*; B.A., M.A., Wheaton College; Ph.D., Northwestern University.

CHARLES M. HORNE: assistant professor of systematic theology, Wheaton Graduate School; author, *Commentary on Thessalonians* (1958); Th.D., Grace Theological Seminary.

FREDERIC R. HOWE: professor of biblical and theological studies, Western Baptist Seminary; contributor to various religious periodicals; B.A., Wheaton College; B.D., Fuller Theological Seminary; Th.M., Dallas Theological Seminary; M.A., University of Portland.

PHILIP EDGECUMBE HUGHES: professor of historical theology, Gordon-Conwell Theological Seminary; author, among other works, *Commentary on Paul's Second Epistle to the Corinthians* (1962), *But for the Grace of God* (1964); editor, *Creative Minds in Contemporary Theology* (1966); B.A., M.A., Cape Town University; Th.D., Australian College of Theology.

PAUL K. JEWETT: professor of systematic theology, Fuller Theological Seminary; author, *Emil Brunner's Concept of Revelation* (1954); *Emil Brunner* (1961); contributor to numerous religious publications; B.A., Wheaton College; Th.B., Th.M., Westminster Theological Seminary; Ph.D., Harvard University.

ROBERT D. KNUDSEN: associate professor of apologetics, Westminster Theological Seminary; managing editor, *Westminster Theological Journal*, and consulting editor, *Journal of the American Scientific Affiliation*; contributor, *Philosophia Reformata*; B.A., University of California; Th.B., Th.M., Westminster Theological Seminary; S.T.M., Union Theological Seminary; Ph.D., Free University of Amsterdam.

WILLIAM L. LANE: professor of New Testament and Judaic studies, Gordon-Conwell Theological Seminary; author (with G. Barker and J. R. Michaels),

The New Testament Speaks (1967); B.A., Wesleyan University; B.D., Gordon Divinity School; Th.M., Westminster Theological Seminary; Ph.D., Harvard University.

GORDON R. LEWIS: professor of systematic theology and Christian philosophy, Conservative Baptist Theological Seminary; author, *Confronting the Cults* (1966) and numerous pamphlets; contributor, *HIS Magazine, Christianity Today, Bibliotheca Sacra*; B.A., Gordon College; Th.M., Faith Theological Seminary; M.A., Syracuse University; Ph.D., Cornell University.

J. P. A. MEKKES: professor of Calvinistic philosophy, University of Leiden, The Netherlands; author, among other works, *Scheppingsopenbaring en Wijsbegeerte* (1961) and *Teken en Motief der Creatuur* (1965); contributor, *Philosophia Reformata*.

JOHN WARWICK MONTGOMERY: professor and chairman, division of church history and history of Christian thought, Trinity Evangelical Divinity School; author, numerous books, including *Crisis in Lutheran Theology* (2 vols., 1967), *Where Is History Going* (1969); A.B., Cornell University, B.L.S., M.A., University of California (Berkeley); B.D., Wittenberg University (Ohio); Ph.D., University of Chicago; docteur dè Universite, University of Strasbourg, France.

J. I. PACKER: warden, Latimer House, Oxford; author, *Fundamentalism and the Word of God* (1958), *Evangelism and the Sovereignty of God* (1961), *God Speaks to Man* (1965); regular contributor to *The Churchman*; member of the Archbishops' Doctrine Commission of the Church of England; B.A., M.A., Ph.D., Oxford University.

CLARK H. PINNOCK: professor of systematic theology, Trinity Evangelical Divinity School; author, *Set Forth Your Case* (1967), *A Defense of Biblical Infallibility* (1966); B.A., University of Toronto; Ph.D., University of Manchester.

W. STANFORD REID: professor and head, department of history, Wellington College, University of Guelph; author, *Problems in Western Intellectual History Since 1500* (1954), *The Protestant Reformation, Revival or Revolution* (1968); contributor, *The Canadian Historical Journal, The Scottish Historical Review, the Evangelical Quarterly*; B.A., M.A., Mc Gill University; Th.B., Th.M., Westminster Theological Seminary; Ph.D., University of Pennsylvania.

HERMAN RIDDERBOS: professor of New Testament, Kampen School of Theology, The Netherlands; co-editor, *Gereformeerd Weekblad*; author, among other works, *Heils-geschiednis en Heilige Schrift van het Nieuwe Testament* (1955), *The Coming of the Kingdom* (1962), and *Paulus: Ontwerp van zijn theologie* (1966, English trans. in preparation).

JACK B. ROGERS: assistant professor of religion and philosophy, Westminster College, New Wilmington, Pa.; author, *Scripture in the Westminster Confession: A Problem of Historical Interpretation for American Presbyterians* (1967); B.A., University of Nebraska; B.D., Pittsburgh-Xenia Theological Seminary; Th.M., Pittsburgh Seminary; Th.D., Free University of Amsterdam (under Berkouwer).

ROUSAS JOHN RUSHDOONY: president, Chalcedon Foundation; author, *By What Standard?* (1959), *Intellectual Schizophrenia* (1961), *The Messianic Character of American Education* (1964), *The Foundations of Social Order* (1968), *Freud* (1966), *This Independent Republic* (1963), *The Nature of the American*

System (1965), *The Mythology of Science* (1968); B.A., M.A., University of California; B.D., Pacific School of Religion.

C. GREGG SINGER: chairman, department of history, Catawba College; author, *A Theological Interpretation of American History* (1964), *Toynbee—A Critical Study, John Calvin: His Roots and Fruits*; contributor, *Christianity Today, Presbyterian Journal*; B.A., Haverford College; M.A., Ph.D., University of Pennsylvania.

HENDRIK G. STOKER: emeritus professor of philosophy, University of Potchefstroom, South Africa; author, over 100 books and essays, mostly in Afrikaans. Works in English appear in *The Critic, The Evangelical Quarterly, Philosophy Today*, as well as the following symposia: *Calvinism and the Current Scientific Outlook* (1947), *Calvin and Ethics* (1959), and *Philosophy and Christianity* (1965).

C. TRIMP: pastor, Groningen, The Netherlands; author (Ph.D. dissertation), *On de oeconomie van het welbehagen. Een analyse van de idee der 'Heilsgeschichte' in de 'Kirchliche Dogmatik' van K. Barth* (1961).

GILBERT B. WEAVER: associate professor of biblical studies, John Brown University; author, "Gordon Clark: Christian Apologist," *The Philosophy of Gordon H. Clark*; contributor, *Grace Journal, Journal of the American Scientific Affiliation*; B.S., John Brown University; Th.M., Dallas Theological Seminary; Th.D., Grace Theological Seminary.

JOHN A. WITMER: assistant professor of systematic theology and librarian, Dallas Theological Seminary; contributor to various religious periodicals and an extractor for *Religious and Theological Abstracts*; B.A., M.A., Wheaton College; Th.M., Th.D., Dallas Theological Seminary; M.S.L.S., East Texas State University.

S. U. ZUIDEMA: professor of philosophy, Free University of Amsterdam; contributor, *Philosophia Reformata* as well as other Dutch journals; author, *Van Bultmann naar Fuchs* (1965); an English trans. of his *Kierkegaard* is available.

WRITINGS OF CORNELIUS VAN TIL

Abbreviations:

B	*The Banner*
CF	*The Calvin Forum*
CT	*Christianity Today*: a Presbyterian Journal, 1930–1938
PG	*The Presbyterian Guardian*
PRP	Presbyterian and Reformed Publishing Co.
PTR	*The Princeton Theological Review*
T&T	*Torch and Trumpet*
WTJ	*The Westminster Theological Journal*

BOOKS

1946   *The New Modernism: An Appraisal of the Theology of Barth and Brunner.* PRP.

1947   *Common Grace*, PRP. (Reprinted from 3 articles in *WTJ*)

1955   *Christianity and Idealism.* PRP. (A reprint of ten articles)
      Christianity and Modern Theology. Author (17 reviews reprinted from *WJT*)
      The Defense of the Faith. PRP.

1959   *The Theology of James Daane.* PRP.

1962   *Christianity and Barthianism.* PRP. (Revised edition in 1965)

1963   *The Defense of the Faith.* Second edition, revised and abridged. PRP.

1964   *The Case for Calvinism.* PRP.

1967   *The Confession of 1967: Its Theological Background and Ecumenical Significance.* PRP.
      The Protestant Doctrine of Scripture. In Defense of the Faith, vol. 1. Den Dulk Christian Foundation. PRP.

1968   *Christ and the Jews.* An International Library of Philosophy and Theology; Biblical and Theological Studies. PRP.

1969   *A Christian Theory of Knowledge.* PRP.
      The Sovereignty of Grace: An Appraisal of G. C. Berkouwer's View of Dordt. PRP.
      A Survey of Christian Epistemology. In Defense of the Faith, vol. 2. Den Dulk Christian Foundation. PRP.

1970   *Christian Ethics.* In Defense of the Faith, vol. 3. PRP.
      The Great Debate Today. PRP.
      The Reformed Pastor and Modern Thought. PRP.

1971   *Psychology of Religion.* In Defense of the Faith, vol. 4. PRP.

1972   *My Credo.* PRP.

1973   *Common Grace* (a collection). PRP.

1974   *Christian Education* (a collection). PRP.
      The New Hermeneutic. PRP.

ARTICLES

1930 "God and the Absolute." *The Evangelical Quarterly* 2:358-388.
"The Story of Westminster Theological Seminary." *B* 65:657f.
1931 "A Christian Theistic Theory of Knowledge." *B* 66:984ff.
"A Christian Theistic Theory of Reality." *B* 66:1032.
"Our Attitude Toward Evolution." *B* 66:1105ff.
1932 "The Cradle and the Grave." *B* 67:1096.
"For What Are We Contending?" *CT* 3, no. 8 (December 1932): 5ff.
"Penitence and Controversy." *B* 67:929.
"Reformed Religion Dynamic." pp. 3-16 (Grand Rapids: American Federation of Reformed Young Men's Societies).
"What Do You Mean?" *B* 67:785f.
1933 "But Ye Are Rich." *B* 68:958.
"A New Princeton Apologetic." *CT* 3 no. 9 (January 1933): 4ff; and 3, no. 10 (February 1933): 5f.
"Psychological Explanations." *B* 68:613ff.
"Who Are You?" *B* 68:320.
1934 "The Christian Experience of Life." *B* 69:320f.
"E. Stanley Jones." *B* 69:72f.
"Recent Events in the Presbyterian Church." *B* 69:582f.
1936 "A Crushing Experience." *B* 71:1062f.
"What Shall We Feed Our Children?" a plea for Christian education. *PG* 3:23f.
1937 "Karl Barth on Scripture." *PG* 3:137f.
"Karl Barth on Creation." *PG* 3:204f.
"Karl Barth and Historic Christianity." *PG* 4:108f.
"Recent American Philosophy." *Philosophia Reformata* 2:1-14.
"Reflections on Dr. A. Kuyper." *B* 72:1187.
"Seeking for Similarities in Theology." *B* 72:75 and 99.
"Seeking for Similarities in Physics." *B* 72:123 and 147.
"Seeking for Similarities in Psychology." *B* 72:171ff.
1938 "Brunner Comes To Princeton." *B* 73:699.
"Changes in Barth's Theology." *PG* 5:221ff.
"The Old Testament Ethical Ideal." *B* 73:507ff.
"Recent Developments at Princeton." *PG* 5:41ff.
"A Strange Debate About Brunner." *PG* 5:106f.
1939 "Arminianisme in de logica." In *De reformatie van het Calvinistisch denken*, edited by C. P. Boodt, pp. 82-119 (s'Gravenhage: Guido de Bres, 1939).
"A Calvin University." *B* 74:1040f.
"Christian Belief." *PG* 6:132-133, 151-152.
"Plato." In *The Proceedings of the Calvinistic Philosophy Club*, edited by T. Hoogstra, pp. 31-44 (Englewood, N.J.).
"The Resurrection as a Part of Christian Truth." *B* 74:339.
"The Theism of A. E. Taylor." *WTJ* 1:89-109.
1940 "Facts." *B* 75:150.
"John Goes to College." *PG* 8:129ff and 8:149ff.
"Princeton's President and Pagan Philosophy." *PG* 7:19ff.

"Reply to Professor J. Vanden Bosch." *B* 75:488.
1941 "Philosophic Foundations." *The Evangelical Quarterly* 13:92-107. [A review of John Thomas, *Philosophic Foundations*]
1942 "Kant or Christ?" *CF* 7:133ff.
1943 "A Substitute for Christianity." *PG* 12:35ff.
1945 – 46 "Common Grace." *WTJ* 8:39-60, 166-200; and 9:47-84.
1946 "Nature and Scripture." In *The Infallible Word: A Symposium*, by the members of the faculty of Westminster Theological Seminary, pp. 255-293 (Philadelphia: Presbyterian Guardian Publishing Corporation, 1946). [Reprinted unchanged, both in second edition, Eerdmans, 1953, and in third edition, PRP, 1967]
1947 "We Are Not Ashamed of Calvinism!" an open letter to the editor of *Time* and *Life* magazines. *PG* 16:245f.
1948 "Calvinism and Art." *PG* 17:272ff.
"Christianity and Crisis Theology." *PG* 17:69f.
"Introduction" to *The Inspiration and Authority of the Bible*, by B. B. Warfield, edited by Samuel G. Craig, pp. 3-68 (Philadelphia: PRP, 1948).
1949 "More New Modernism at Old Princeton." *PG* 18:166f.
"Presuppositionalism; a Reply," in *The Bible Today*, vol. 42:7 (April), pp. 218-228; and completed in vol. 42:9 (June-Sept.), pp. 278-290.
1951 "The Authority of Scripture." *T&T* 1:4:16ff.
"The Believer Meets the Unbeliever." *T&T* 1:2:17ff.
"Defending the Faith." *T&T* 1:1:16ff.
"Needed: A Consistent Witness." *T&T* 1:3:16ff.
"Professor Vollenhoven's Significance for Reformed Apologetics." In *Wetenschappelijke bijdragen*, door leerlingen van Dr. D. H. Th. Vollenhoven, pp. 68-71 (Franeker: T. Wever, 1951).
"Wanted—A Reformed Witness." *PG* 20:125ff.
1952 "Proofs for the Existence of God." *T&T* 2:5:18ff.
"Special and General Revelation." *T&T* 2:2:5-8.
1953 "The Education of Man—A Divinely Ordained Need." In *Fundamentals in Christian Education: Theory and Practice*, edited by Cornelius Jaarsma, pp. 39-59 (Grand Rapids: Eerdmans, 1953).
"Faith and Our Program." *Ibid.*, pp. 121-139.
"The Full-Orbed Life." *Ibid.*, pp. 157-170.
"A More Excellent Ministry"; a sermon at an ordination service. *PG* 22:166ff.
"Religious Philosophy: A Discussion of Richard Kroner's Book, *Culture and Faith*." *CF* 18:126ff.
"Resurrection Witnesses!" *T&T* 3:1:16ff.
1954 "Common Grace and Witness-Bearing." *T&T* 4:1:1-10.
"Dimensionalism or the Word"; comments on the theology of Dr. John A. Mackay. *PG* 23:105ff.
"Has Karl Barth Become Orthodox?" *WTJ* 16:135-181. [Reprinted by PRP, 1954]
1955 "Where Do We Go from Here in Theology?"; article by Nels F. S. Ferré, with responses by Paul Tillich, Cornelius Van Til, and Alden Kelley. *Religion in Life* 25:5-34.

1958   "Evangelical Responsibility." *T&T* 8:3:19f.
1959   "Calvin and Modern Subjectivism." *T&T* 9:4:14ff.
        "Calvin as a Controversialist." *T&T* 9:3:5-9.
        "The Christian Scholar." *WTJ* 21:147-178.
        Funeral Sermon (upon death of John J. de Waard). *PG* 28:214ff.
        "*Umdeutung.*" *PG* 28:51f.
1960   "Experiences in the Orient." *T&T* 10:7:19f.
        "Karl Barth on Chalcedon." *WTJ* 22:147-166. [Reprinted by PRP, 1960]
1961   "Bavinck the Theologian." *WTJ* 24:48-64. [A review of R. H. Bremmer, *Herman Bavinck als dogmaticus*]
1962   "Original Sin, Imputation, and Inability." In *Basic Christian Doctrines*, edited by Carl F. H. Henry, pp. 110-116 (New York: Holt, Rinehart and Winston, 1962).
1964   "Absolute Idealism." In *The Encyclopedia of Christianity* 1:33-34. (Wilmington, The National Foundation for Christian Education, 1964).
        "Analogia entis." *Ibid.* 1:200-201.
        "Barth, Karl." *Ibid.* 1:573-587. [Published separately by PRP in 1962 with the title, *Barth's Christology*, as part of the International Library of Philosophy and Theology; Biblical Studies.]
        "The Later Heidegger and Theology." *WTJ* 26:121-161. [Discussion of James M. Robinson and John B. Cobb, Jr., ed., *The Later Heidegger and Theology*]
1966   "Pierre Teilhard de Chardin." *WTJ* 28:109-144. [Reprinted by PRP, 1966]
1968   "The Holy Roman Empire." *PG* 37:99ff.
        "The Significance of Dort for Today." In *Crisis in the Reformed Churches: Essays in Commemoration of the Great Synod of Dort, 1618–1619*, pp. 150-160. (Grand Rapids: Reformed Fellowship, 1968).
        "Bridgewater Treatises." In *The Encyclopedia of Christianity* 2:178f. (Marshallton, The National Foundation for Christian Education, 1968).
        "Butler, Joseph." *Ibid.* 2:238f.
1969   "Karl Barth—His Message to Us." *B* 104:4f.

REVIEWS

1927   *Religion in the Making* (Alfred North Whitehead). PTR 25:336ff.
1929   *Paedagogische beginselen* and *De nieuwe opvoeding* (H. Bavinck). PTR 27:135f.
1930   *The Doctrine of God* (Albert C. Knudson). *CT* 1, no. 8 (Dec. 1930): 10-13.
1931   Freedom and Restraint (Robert F. Campbell). *CT* 1, no. 11 (March 1931): 14f. [Further discussion in 2, no. 1 (May):12-13]
        The Bondage of the Will (Martin Luther). *CT* 2, no. 7 (Nov. 1931):12f.
        Morals of Tomorrow (Ralph W. Sockman). *CT* 1, no. 11 (March 1931):14f.
        The Christian Life (Joseph Stump) *CT* 1, no. 12 (April 1931):10.
        The Karl Barth Theology, or The New Transcendentalism (Alvin Syl-

vester Zerbe), *CT* 1, no. 10 (Feb. 1931):13f.

1932 *Pathways to the Reality of God* (Rufus M. Jones). *CT* 2, no. 9 (Jan. 1932):16f.

1933 *Is God a Person?* (Edgar Sheffield Brightman). *CT* 3, no. 11 (March 1933):7.

Worship God (James I. Vance). *CT* 3, no. 11 (March 1933):7.

1934 *Christianity: The Paradox of God* (Donald Mackenzie). *CT* 4, no. 10 (Feb. 1934):9ff. [Further discussion in the three following issues]

1935 *The Church of Christ and the Problems of the Day* (Karl Heim). *PG* 1:73.

A Christian Manifesto (Edwin Lewis). *PG* 1:91.

1936 *Methods of Private Religious Living* (Henry Nelson Wieman). *PG* 2:100.

De noodzakelijkeheid eener Christelijke logica (D. H. Th. Vollenhoven). *CF* 1:142f.

Personality and Religion (Edgar Sheffield Brightman). *PG* 2:100.

The Return to Religion (Henry C. Link). *PG* 2:228.

1937 *The Triune God* (C. Norman Bartlett). *PG* 4:209f.

1938 *Christianity in America: A Crisis* (E. G. Homrighousen). *PG* 5:26f.

Der Mensch im Widerspruch (Emil Brunner). *WTJ* 1:43-49.

1939 *Studies in the Philosophy of Religion* (Archibald Allan Bowman). *WTJ* 2:55-62.

1940 *The Philosophy of John Dewey* (Paul Arthur Schilpp, ed.). *WTJ* 3:62-73.

The Philosophy of Physical Science (Arthur Eddington). *WTJ* 3:55-62.

A Sacramental Universe (Archibald Allan Bowman). *WTJ* 2:175-184.

1941 *The Nature and Destiny of Man: A Christian Interpretation*, vol. 1 (Reinhold Niebuhr). *WTJ* 4:51-56.

Philosophic Foundations (John Thomas): see article "Philosophic Foundations."

1942 *The Logic of Belief* (D. Elton Trueblood). *WTJ* 5:88-94.

The Philosophy of Alfred North Whitehead (Paul Arthur Schilpp, ed.). *WTJ* 4:163-171.

1943 *God and Evil* (C. E. M. Joad). *WTJ* 6:114-118.

The Nature and Destiny of Man: A Christian Interpretation, vol. 2 (Reinhold Niebuhr). *WTJ* 5:197-206.

Twentieth Century Philosophy (Dagobert D. Runes, ed.). *WTJ* 6:72-80.

1944 *The Survival of Western Culture* (Ralph Tyler Flewelling). *WTJ* 6:221-227.

1945 *The Christian Answer* (Paul Tillich et al.). *PG* 14:328-329.

The Covenant Idea in New England Theology (Peter Y. De Jong). *WTJ* 8:106-109.

1946 *Die kirchliche Dogmatik*, 2 Band, 2. Halbband, and 3. Band, 1. Teil (Karl Barth). *WTJ* 9:131-138.

Therefore, Stand (Wilbur M. Smith). *WTJ* 8:228-236.

1948 *Algemeene genade en antithese* (I. A. Diepenhorst). *WTJ* 11:97-101.

Christian Apologetics (Alan Richardson). *WTJ* 11:45-53.

Een eeuw van strijd over verbond en doop (E. Smilde). *WTJ* 11:77-80.

An Introduction to Christian Apologetics (Edward John Carnell). *WTJ* 11:45-53.

Karl Barth en de kinderdoop (G. C. Berkouwer). *WTJ* 11:77-80
De theologische cultuurbeschouwing van Abraham Kuyper (S. J. Ridderbos). *WTJ* 11:97-101.

1949 *Geloof en rechtvaardiging* and *Geloof en heiliging* (G. C. Berkouwer). *WTJ* 12:74ff.

1950 *De strijd tegen de analogia entis in de theologie van Karl Barth* (J. J. Louët Feisser). *WTJ* 12:162-166.

1951 *Christianity and Reason: Seven Essays* (Edward D. Myers, ed.). *WTJ* 14:104-107.
Christus in zijn lijden and *Christus in den doorgang van zijn lijden* (K. Schilder). *WTJ* 14:85f.
Geschiedenis der wijsbegeerte (D. H. Th. Vollenhoven). *WTJ* 14:86f.
Heaven: What Is It? (K. Schilder). *WTJ* 13:219f.
A History of Philosophical Systems (Vergilius Ferm, ed.). *WJT* 13:186-189.

1953 *Culture and Faith* (Richard Kroner): see article "Religious Philosophy. . . ."
The Image of God in Man (David S. Cairns). *WTJ* 16:51-54.
The Psychology of Religion (L. W. Grensted). *WTJ* 15:173ff.

1954 *Karl Barth's Church Dogmatics: An Introductory Report on Volumes I:1-III:4* (Otto Webber). *WTJ* 16:237f.

1955 *A New Critique of Theoretical Thought*, vol. 1 (Herman Dooyeweerd). *WTJ* 17:180-183.
De triomf der genade in de theologie van Karl Barth (G. C. Berkouwer). *WTJ* 18:58f.

1956 *Foundations of Christian Knowledge* (Georgia Harkness). *WTJ* 18:176-179.
Reinhold Niebuhr: His Religious, Social, and Political Thought (Charles W. Kegley). *WTJ* 19:57-62.

1957 *The Communication of the Christian Faith* (Hendrik Kraemer). *WTJ* 19:208-212.
The Pattern of Authority (Bernard Ramm). *PG* 26:77f.
Systematic Theology, vol. 2 (Paul Tillich). *WTJ* 20:93-99.

1958 *Church Dogmatics*, vol. 2, part 2 (Karl Barth). *WTJ* 221:75-78.
Faith and Ethics: The Theology of H. Richard Niebuhr (Paul Ramsey, ed.). *WTJ* 21:107-114.

1958 *Die kirchliche Dogmatik*, 4. Band, 3. Teil, 1. Hälfte (Karl Barth). *WTJ* 22:64-69.

1960 *Relativism, Knowledge and Faith* (Gordon D. Kaufman). *WTJ* 23:71-74.

1961 *The Christian Doctrine of History* (John McIntyre). *T&T* 10:10:20ff.
Herman Bavinck als dogmaticus (R. H. Bremmer) see article, "Bavinck the Theologian."

1962 *A Kierkegaard Critique* (Howard A. Johnson, ed.). *WTJ* 25:84-93.
Scheppingsopenbaring en wijsbegeerte (J. P. A. Mekkes). *WTJ* 24:223-227.

1963 *Divine Perfection: Possible Ideas of God* (Frederick Sontag). *WTJ* 25:223-231.

1964 *The Later Heidegger and Theology* (James M. Robinson and John B. Cobb, eds.): see article, "The Later Heidegger and Theology."

1966 *De leer van God bij Augustinus* (A. D. R. Polman). *WTJ* 29:94-102.
1968 *Reformed Dogmatics* (Herman Hoeksema). *WTJ* 31:83-94.
   Science and Faith (Eric C. Rust). *Calvin Theological Journal* 3:86-91.
1969 *How Can a Jew Speak of Faith Today?* (Eugene B. Borowitz). *WTJ* 32:116-119.
1970 *The Scientific Enterprise and Christian Faith* (Malcolm A. Jeeves). *WTJ* 32:236-240.

SYLLABI
(Partial List)

(These syllabi were prepared for class purposes only and are not to be regarded as published books.)
1933 *Metaphysics of Apologetics*
1935 *Christian Apologetics* (1939, 1950, 1953)
   Evidences
   Psychology of Religion (revised 1971)
   Theology of Crisis
1937 *Systematics: Introduction* (1940)
1939 *The Ten Commandments*
1940 *Christian Ethics*
1941 *Christianity and Psychology*
1947 *Christian-theistic Ethics* (1952; revised 1961)
   Christian-theistic Evidences
   An Introduction to Theology. 2 volumes.
1949 *An Introduction to Systematic Theology.* (revised 1952; 1955; 1966)
1954 *A Christian Theory of Knowledge*
1958 *The Triumph of Grace: The Heidelberg Catechism, vol. 1*
1960 *The New Evangelicalism*
1962 *Christianity in Conflict.* 3 volumes.

PAMPHLETS

1951 *The Intellectual Challenge of the Gospel.* Tyndale Press.
1952 *Particularism and Common Grace.* Grotenhuis.
1953 *A Letter on Common Grace.* Grotenhuis.
1954 *The Dilemma of Education.* National Union of Christian Schools.
   Common Grace and Witness Bearing, PRP.
1964 *Karl Barth and Evangelicalism.* PRP.
1966 *Is God Dead?* PRP.